Snorri Sturluson and Reykholt

Snorri Sturluson and Reykholt

The Author and Magnate, his Life, Works and Environment at Reykholt in Iceland

Edited by Guðrún Sveinbjarnardóttir and Helgi Þorláksson

Museum Tusculanum Press

in collaboration with

The Institute of History, University of Iceland, and Snorrastofa at Reykholt

Snorri Sturluson and Reykholt: The Author and Magnate,
his Life, Works and Environment at Reykholt in Iceland

Guðrún Sveinbjarnardóttir and Helgi Þorláksson (eds)
© 2018 Museum Tusculanum Press and the authors
Layout and composition: Janus Bahs Jacquet and Erling Lynder
Cover design: Erling Lynder
Printed in Denmark by Narayana Press
ISBN 978 87 635 4612 6

Cover illustration: King Hákon Hákonarson of Norway (d. 1263) and
Earl Skúli Bárðarson. From Flateyjarbók, 14th century.
The Árni Magnússon Institute for Icelandic Studies, Reykjavík.

This book is published with financial support from
The Institute of History, University of Iceland
Snorrastofa at Reykholt
The Research Council of Norway

Photos of material from codices (folios, illustrations) are kindly provided
by The Árni Magnússon Institute for Icelandic Studies, Reykjavík.
Photos on pp. 16, 19, 122, 236, 401, 415 of Reykholt and the
Borgarfjörður area are provided by Snorrastofa at Reykholt.

Museum Tusculanum Press
Dantes Plads 1
DK-1556 Copenhagen V
www.mtp.dk

Contents

Preface 7

Forms of Names and their Spelling. 9

List of Illustrations 10

General Map of the Borgarfjǫrðr area 12–13

Sturlungar Family, Genealogical Table 15

Introduction
Guðrún Sveinbjarnardóttir and Helgi Þorláksson 17

Snorri Sturluson the Aristocrat Becomes *lendr maðr*
Helgi Þorláksson 33

Snorri Sturluson, the Politician, and his Foreign Relations.
The Norwegian, Orcadian and Götlandish Connections
Helgi Þorláksson 79

Reykholt as a Centre of Power
Viðar Pálsson, Helgi Þorláksson and Sverrir Jakobsson 109

The Palaeoecology and Cultural Landscapes
Associated with Reykholt
Egill Erlendsson, Kevin J. Edwards, Kim Vickers,
Guðrún Sveinbjarnardóttir and Guðrún Gísladóttir. 161

Natural Resources – Access and Exploitation
Benedikt Eyþórsson, Egill Erlendsson, Guðrún Gísladóttir
and Guðrún Sveinbjarnardóttir. 205

The Buildings at Reykholt
Guðrún Sveinbjarnardóttir and Guðrún Harðardóttir. 237

The Deed of the Church of Reykholt
Guðvarður Már Gunnlaugsson 279

Snorri Sturluson and the Best of Both Worlds
Gísli Sigurðsson 291

Oral Rhetoric and Literary Rhetoric
Mats Malm 319

The Learned Sturlungar and the Emergence of Icelandic Literate
Culture
Karl G. Johansson 333

The Social Conditions for Literary Practice in Snorri's Lifetime
Torfi H. Tulinius 389

Reykholt and its Literary Environment in the First Half of the
Thirteenth Century
Else Mundal 409

The Literary Legacy of Snorri Sturluson
Guðrún Nordal and Jon Gunnar Jørgensen 441

List of Contributors 470

Indexes 473

Preface

Snorri Sturluson lived at Reykholt from early in the thirteenth century until 1241, when he was killed by the henchmen of his former son-in-law. He was, until recent times, the best known Icelander abroad, certainly among scholars. This is scarcely surprising given that, as well as having been a magnate, he was also the author of the much admired and important *Snorra-Edda* and most, if not all of the famous *Heimskringla*, a history of Norwegian kings. He was an excellent historian and a knowledgeable scholar, and his works are invaluable sources for the history of Norway and the Vikings, Nordic mythology and skaldic poetry. Snorri had ties to the Norwegian court and stood close to Earl Skúli, a pretender to the Norwegian throne. He was also one of the leading aristocrats of the Norwegian realm and his imposing residence at Reykholt was a reflection of a man of his standing. His life was turbulent and his death dramatic, although paradoxically he was among the most peaceful chieftains in the Iceland of his time and held the office of lawspeaker at the general assembly, the *Alþingi*.

Even before Snorri settled at Reykholt, the site was attractive to Icelanders. It became rather more attractive during his time when it acquired a well furnished church, new abodes built in a relatively new Scandinavian style, a sturdy fortress and of course Snorri's pool (*Snorralaug*) which is still to be seen there along with its adjacent subterranean passageway. This was an appropriate venue for the excellent feasts Snorri hosted. Of the many people who lived in or visited Reykholt were Snorri's family and relatives, clerics, scholars, retainers, life-guards, workers, guests and passers-by, which made it a lively place. Many must have enjoyed Snorri's wealth and hospitality.

In recent years Reykholt has become a centre for medieval studies research and an important destination for tourists. Among its attractions are a new church and the cultural and medieval centre Snorrastofa, which offers visitors an exhibition based on recent archaeological excavations. It has also given rise to a scholarly initiative known as the Reykholt Project. This book makes some of the more important results of the project available to the public. We hope it will also bring to life Snorri Sturluson and the medieval site of Reykholt for its readers.

Thanks are due to our collaborators in publishing this book, Else Mundal, professor emerita, and Bergur Þorgeirsson, the director of Snorrastofa, as well as all those who have contributed to the book. We would like to extend further thanks to the anonymous peer-reviewers and to all our fellow participants in the project. Finally our thanks go to the Institute of History, University of Iceland, Snorrastofa at Reykholt and its employees, and Museum Tusculanum Press.

Guðrún Sveinbjarnardóttir and Helgi Þorláksson

Forms of Names and their Spelling

For spelling, the series *Íslenzk fornrit* is followed

Personal names:

For personal names we use for instance Óláfr for modern Ólafur, Sighvatr for modern Sighvatur, Þorbjǫrn for Þorbjörn, Þórr for Þór.

We never drop accent marks or suffixes, like Olaf for Óláfr. We never anglicize, like Harold for Haraldr.

Place names:

For place names we spell Borgarfjǫrðr for modern Borgarfjörður, Norðrá for Norðurá, Áss for Ás, fors for foss, dalr for dalur, lækr for lækur and so on. Also Álptanes for modern Álftanes and Bœr for Bær.

Some medieval forms for places are different from the modern ones. We always keep the old forms on the maps but the following are too archaic for us to use in our texts:

Hávafell for Háafell

Hvanneyrr for Hvanneyri (and other corresponding, ending with –eyrr)

Rauðavatn for Reyðarvatn

Reykjaholt for Reykholt

Reykjadalr nyrðri for modern Reykholtsdalur, we use Reykholtsdalr

Reykjadalr syðri for modern Lundarreykjadalur, we use Lundarreykjadalr

Skarðsheiðr for Skarðsheiði (and other corresponding, ending with –heiði)

Skálaholt for Skálholt

Stafaholt for Stafholt

Other forms of place names worth mentioning

Kjarardalr, Kjarará, we use these forms, not Kjarradalr, Kjarrá

For Bergen in Norway we prefer Bjǫrgvin to Bjǫrgyn

Sturlunga saga

For the *Sturlunga saga* we follow the edition of 1946 and its orthography but also use the 1988 edition for variants.

List of Illustrations

General map of the Borgarfjǫrðr area   12–13
Sturlungar family, genealogical table   15
Aerial view of Reykholt, looking north-east.
   Photo   16
The hot spring Skrifla at Reykholt. Photo   19
King Hákon *gamli* Hákonarson and
   Earl Skúli Bárðarson. From
   Flateyjarbók, GKS 1005 fol   35
A bell fragment. Drawing   69
Earls of Orkney. Genealogical table   85
Northern Scotland and Western Norway.
   Map   86
Western Götland, Jutland and Norway. Map   93
The family of Earl Hákon *galinn*.
   Genealogical table   94
The family of Kristín Nikulásdóttir.
   Genealogical table   95
Aerial view of Reykholt and its
   environment; looking east. Photo   122
The route between Reykholt and Elliðavatn.
   Map   129
The people of Reykholt. Genealogical table   131
Major farms and chieftains in Borgarfjǫrðr.
   Map   145
The Borgarfjǫrðr area, locations of sites
   studied for palaeoecology. Map   162
Sites sampled for research. Table   163
View from Skáneyjarbunga showing the
   Reykholt lowlands. Photo   171
Pollen percentage diagram   173
View from Skáneyjarbunga showing location
   of Hólakot and Breiðavatn. Photo   176
Pollen percentage diagram from Breiðavatn   177
Selected soil property proxies from Hólakot   178
A: View of Reykholtssel and the REY2 sample
   site.
B: Location of REY2 sample site.
C: Macro-remains of birch. Photo   179
Pollen percentage diagram from
   Reykholtssel   180
Selected soil property proxies from
   Reykholtssel   182
Three soil profiles. Photo   189
The medieval cultural landscape in
   Reykholtsdalr. Map   192
Reykholt and the farms belonging to
   the church, or under its care. Map   210

The shielings of Reykholt. Map   211
Site plan of Norðtungusel   212
A view of Norðtungusel. Photo   213
Radiocarbon dates from the shieling sites.
   Table   215
Site plan of Reykholtssel   216
A view of Reykholtssel. Photo   217
Site plan of Faxadalr   218
A view of the Faxadalr site. Photo   219
The farm sites Kot and Hamraendar in
   Geitland. Photo   221
Aerial view of Reykholt looking
   north-west. Photo   236
A site plan of Reykholt showing the
   excavation area   239
The school building with the farm in the
   background. Photo   241
Aerial view of the farm site. at Reykholt in
   1958/59. Photo   242
Plan of the Phase 1 remains with
   interpretation   245
Plan of the Phase 2 remains   249
Snorralaug before restauration in 1959.
   Photo   250
The subterranean passageway under
   excavation in 1941. Photo   251
Building complex 10/11 under excavation.
   Photo   254
The circular staircase. Photo   255
Reconstruction of the Phase 2 buildings
   at Reykholt. Drawing   257
Boundary wall and conduit. Photo   260
The church during Phase 2ii   263
Auðunarstofa at Hólar. Photo   268
Reykjaholtsmáldagi, f. 1r. Photo   280
Reykjaholtsmáldagi, f. 1v. Photo   281
AM 237a fol., f. 2r. Photo   283
The letter ‹o› with an accent in
   AM 237 a fol. Photo   286
The letter ‹y› with a tick in AM 237 a fol.
   Photo   286
The letter ‹y› with a dot in
   Reykjaholtsmáldagi   286
Askr Yggdrasils (the ash of Yggdrasill),
   Edda oblonga, AM 738 4to   302
Sagas of Icelanders and the earliest
   dates of their manuscripts. Table   308

A folio from a fragment of the oldest
    manuscript of *Egils saga
    Skalla-Grímssonar*. AM 162 A þeta.
    Photo   309
The wolf Fenrisúlfr. Edda oblonga,
    AM 738 4to. Photo   325
Monasteries in medieval Iceland, the
    bishops' seats and places of learning.
    Map   339
The Viðey island. Photo   357
The pool and passageway at Reykholt.
    Photo   401

Stafholt. Photo   415
The family of Helga Sturludóttir and
    her son Egill. Genealogical table   429
A glass goblet of French origin. Drawing   433
A folio from *Snorra-Edda* in Uppsala,
    Sweden, (Uppsala-Edda), DG 11 48   443
The family of Helga Sturludóttir and
    her son Egill. Genealogical table   458
A folio from *Heimskringla* in Kringla.
    Lbs. fragm 82   461

Kolbeinsstaðir

Hítardalr

Langavatnsdalr

Fagraskógr

Selalón

Hraun
Svarfhóll

Hítará

Grísatunga
Þinghó...

Hítarnes

Hraundalr

Munaðarnes

Álptártunga

Svignaskarð

Langá

Stafaholt

M ý r a r

Hvítá

Eskiholt
Þingnes

Álptá

Ferjubakki
Hvítárvelli

Langárfors

Gufuskálar
Hestr

Ánabrekka

Borg

Hvanneyrr

Álptanes

Borgarfjǫrðr

Hafnarfjall

Skarðsheiðr

Narfastaðir

Svínadalr

Melar

Saurbœr

Akrafjall

Akranes

Hvalfjǫrðr

0   10   20

km

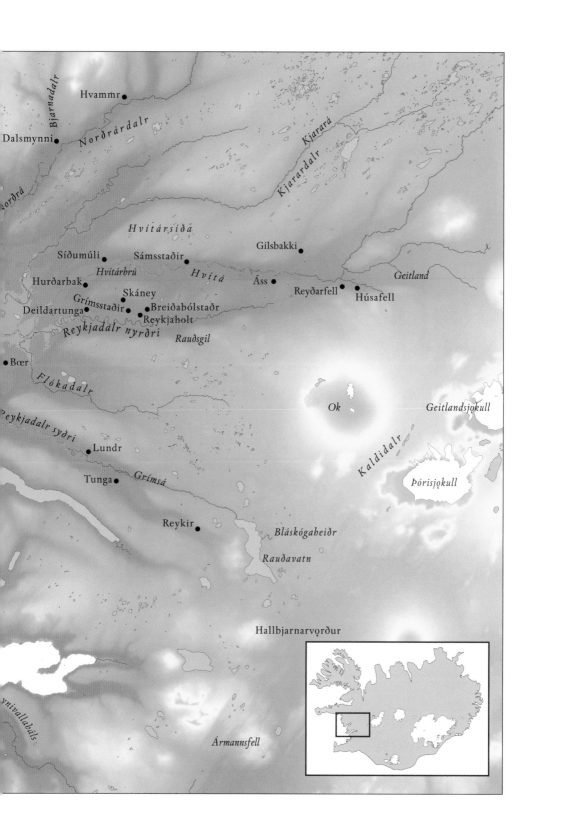

pp. 12–13
General map of the
Borgarfjǫrðr area.

Opposite page
Sturlungar family,
genealogical table.

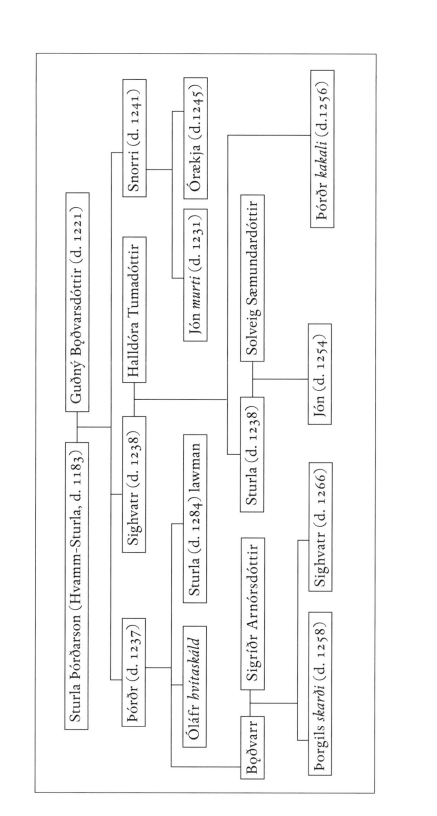

Aerial view of Reykholt, looking north-east. The new church with the spire and the medieval centre Snorrastofa to the left of it, are in the centre, with the old church to the right of it and the old school farthest to the right. The large white building in the background is the hotel. The excavation area is between the old school and the old church. Photo: Guðlaugur Óskarsson, September 2016.

¶ GUÐRÚN SVEINBJARNARDÓTTIR
AND HELGI ÞORLÁKSSON

Introduction

EYKHOLT IN BORGARFJǪRÐR IS PROBABLY BEST KNOWN FOR
its thirteenth-century occupant, the author and chieftain Snorri
Sturluson (d. 1241). He and the place in which he chose to
live together form the focus of this book. It was an important site as the
seat of chieftains, *goðar*, who were also priests, before his arrival there
in the early thirteenth century. The priests have in recent times been
called *kirkjugoðar* (chieftain-priests) in Icelandic. Around the middle of
the twelfth century the majority of chieftains in Iceland may have been
ordained.[1] The church at Reykholt was a major church and an institution
of a certain type, called *staðr* (estate church) in Icelandic. A *staðr* was a
kind of a trust, a self-owning institution. The oldest and most important
ones were established around 1100 and in the first decades of the twelfth
century and are reminiscent of the minsters in England.[2] The high status
of Reykholt may, indeed, have been the reason why Snorri was keen
to acquire it and make his home there in the centre of his domain. He
administered the *staðr* at Reykholt, as well as the *staðr* at the neighbouring
farm Stafholt. The best known *staðr* in Iceland was Oddi in the South,
the farm where Snorri was brought up.

Interest in Reykholt, both within Iceland and abroad, goes back a
long time. Snorri is famous for his works *Heimskringla* and *Edda*, and
these and his fame have attracted travellers to the site. It was included
in the itinerary of almost all the foreign expeditions that visited Iceland

1   Orri Vésteinsson 2000, 187–188.
2   For a description of *staðir* (plural) see pp. 114–116 in this book.

in the eighteenth and nineteenth centuries and produced journals of their trips.[3] The main emphasis of most of these expeditions was directed towards exploring the natural environment of Iceland. From the information provided in the accounts it can be inferred that the reason for including Reykholt seems mainly to have been knowledge about Snorri Sturluson and his works, as well as an interest in the hot springs of the area.

The only remains visible at the site during these eighteenth- and nineteenth-century visits that could possibly be linked to Snorri's time there was the stone-built round pool, Snorralaug. It is fed with hot water from a hot spring located about a hundred metres away through stone-built conduits (fig. 1). According to thirteenth- and fourteenth-century redactions of *Landnámabók* (The Book of Settlements) there was a natural pool at Reykholt before the site was settled, but it is not known when it took the form it has today. The earliest known description of it being round with benches and flags in the floor dates to 1724.[4] In a near-contemporary saga in the compilation *Sturlunga saga*, Snorri is described as sitting in a pool, discussing politics with his men.[5] It is tempting to conclude that this indicates that the pool had benches at that time just as it does today. Some of the eighteenth- and nineteenth-century visitors tried to imagine that they saw remains of the fort mentioned in *Sturlunga saga*, which they were no doubt familiar with, on the farm mound, but these could just as well have been the remains of some other structures.

Before systematic archaeological investigations under the auspices of The National Museum of Iceland began at the farm site in 1987, some discoveries of structural remains had already been made as a result of building activities there. The earliest of these was in 1934 when the subterranean passageway leading from Snorralaug to the farm was discovered during the erection of a sports hall to the east of the school building that had recently been constructed. The excavations which began in the late 1980s were initiated by several events. Preparations had begun for the commemoration in 1991 of the 750th anniversary of the death of Snorri Sturluson. The local parish had also decided to build a new church, and the establishment of the cultural and medieval centre

3   See a summary of these in Guðrún Sveinbjarnardóttir 2012, 130–143.
4   Páll Vídalín 1854, 42–43.
5   *Sturlunga saga* I, 319–320.

Figure 1. The hot spring Skrifla at Reykholt is now covered. It provides water for Snorri's pool (Snorra-laug). In Snorri's time, like today, geothermal water was of importance for the inhabitants. The face on the stone sitting on the cover of the hot spring is that of Snorri as expressed by the artist Páll Guðmunds-son. Photo: Guðlaugur Óskarsson.

Snorrastofa had been approved. Snorrastofa was established in 1995. The excavation ground to a halt after two seasons because of a lack of funding, but it was resumed in 1998 with renewed vigour. The high school which had been in operation at Reykholt since about 1930 had been closed down the year before and the Ministry of Education was keen to do something for this historic site. Among the building foundations exposed during the excavations at the farm and church sites were those of the medieval buildings which may have been in use during Snorri's time.

Following on from the new excavations, a meeting was held at Reyk-holt in 1998, initiated by the National Museum and attended by Icelandic and Scandinavian scholars. The purpose of the meeting was to discuss setting up an international and multidisciplinary project with Snorri Sturluson, his period, and the history of Reykholt from its earliest days up to Snorri's time as its primary focus. This idea was inspired by the pan-Scandinavian excavations in Þjórsárdalr in southern Iceland in 1939.[6] The main aim of the project was to establish a new and fresh perspective on Snorri Sturluson and his period by combining research in the humanities, social sciences and natural sciences. The meeting was followed by a workshop held at Reykholt in 1999 which resulted in the launching of the Reykholt Project. This is described in more detail below in the section entitled "The Reykholt Project: Aims, Organization, Execution".

The present book draws the project to a close. Its contents and organization follow the aims of the project and give a picture of Reykholt from different angles during Snorri Sturluson's time there in the first half of the thirteenth century. One of the topics highlighted in the aims of the project is the process of centralization of power, something that characterizes Snorri's rule, and is discussed in the article "Reykholt as a Centre of Power". Snorri made Reykholt a centre of power in his large domain, which stretched over the whole area from the south-west (the Reykjanes peninsula) to the north-west of Iceland (Húnaþing), where he ruled single-handedly, ensuring peace in the area (at least as far as we know). This was the situation in 1218 when he went to Norway and was given the status of a *lendr maðr* (in modern Norwegian, *lendman*, something similar to a count or a baron). In the article "Snorri Sturluson, the Aristocrat, Becomes *lendr maðr*" a serious attempt is made to define Snorri as an aristocrat. Indications of this are his aristocratic upbringing at Oddi in Rangárvellir, his move to Reykholt and his chieftaincy there, along with his great advancement at the Norwegian court between 1218 and 1220. He prepared to turn Reykholt into the base of the Norwegian king's main representative in Iceland by erecting appropriately impressive dwelling houses and a church, as well as a fortification wall, a subterranean passageway and conduits feeding hot water and steam/hot air into the pool and buildings respectively. This topic is covered in the article "The Buildings at Reykholt" where the buildings exposed during excavations and described in written sources are discussed. They consist of a number of fairly small, specialized buildings, as opposed to the longhouses that characterize the earlier period, and the church is larger than other known

6   Steenberger 1943.

private churches in Iceland at the time. Snorri's status depended very much on political developments in Norway and he most probably kept an eye on the often rather tense relations between the Norwegian regents and the earls of Orkney. This is all discussed in the article "Snorri Sturluson, the Politician, and his Foreign Relations". Things did not go all his way, however, and he was killed at Reykholt in 1241.

The suitability of Reykholt as a chieftain's farm is discussed in the articles "The Palaeoecology and Cultural Landscapes Associated with Reykholt" and "Natural Resources – Access and Exploitation". The land around the farm is not particularly fertile and there was a lack of pasture. The latter was sought in shieling and other resource areas located some distance away from the home farm itself. There is evidence of the land being heavily exploited during Snorri's time, with woodland disappearing and erosion setting in. The importance of the extra resources for the creation of Reykholt as a centre of power is demonstrated.

Snorri Sturluson is not first and foremost remembered as a politician and chieftain, but mainly as an author. This topic is covered in the second half of the book. In "Snorri Sturluson and the Best of Both Worlds" the author stresses the education Snorri received in the secular spheres. The combination of both worlds, the oral and the written, is thought to suggest a personal vision and an authorial awareness of a kind we identify with writers of fiction in later centuries. The next contribution, "Oral Rhetoric and Literary Rhetoric", deals with the interrelation between Latin learning and vernacular cultures, and especially the concept of *kenning* and how it is explained in *Snorra-Edda*. It is followed by "The Learned Sturlungar and the Emergence of Icelandic Literate Culture", which discusses how European learning played a part in the transformation of local traditions in Iceland, implemented through the collaboration of church and elite, the teachings of Benedictines and later Augustinians, and the impact this had on the learned members of Snorri's family, the Sturlungar. In "The Social Conditions for the Literary Practice in Snorri's Lifetime", the author borrows concepts from Pierre Bourdieu to explain the possible social conditions for how *Egils saga Skalla-Grímssonar* came into being in Snorri's milieu. Next, "Reykholt and its Literary Environment in the First Half of the Thirteenth Century" deals with Reykholt as a literary centre and with what became of Snorri's library and his literary legacy. The final contribution, "The Literary Legacy of Snorri Sturluson", discusses

Snorri's Norwegian audience, king and court. It is suggested that the hidden agenda behind Snorri's literary output was to improve relations with the Norwegian aristocracy and royalty and to reflect distinct courtly values. Similar ambitions are found to apply to Snorri's colleague Styrmir and two of Snorri's learned nephews, and to the reception of the works of all four in the fourteenth century.

Other topics covered by members of the Reykholt Project, on which articles have been published elsewhere, include an attempt to establish why Snorri chose Reykholt as his centre of power,[7] a retrospective look at what farming at Reykholt may have been like in the thirteenth century,[8] and a general study of *staðir* (of which Reykholt was one of the earliest), their origins and what may have influenced their establishment.[9] There have also been articles on Reykholt as a centre of learning,[10] and on manuscripts and their production.[11] Remains of white and brown calf skin, the types that were used for producing books in the medieval period, were found in medieval layers at the farm site,[12] but these were too insubstantial to draw any firm conclusions. In the deed (charter) of the Reykholt church, Snorri and his daughter Ingibjǫrg, together with three others, are reported to have donated forty calf skins to the church.[13] Other indications of a writing culture are a polished stone of porphyry which may have been used for smoothing wax on writing tablets, a stone which may have served for scraping hair off animal skin and a number of styluses (implements used for writing on wax tablets) found at the church site.[14] One of the buildings at the farm site had hot air or steam channelled into it, but the purpose of this building is uncertain. It might have been a bathhouse or a building used in connection with brewing,[15] but it is also possible that it was used for processing hide for parchment.

The role and nature of the shieling areas belonging to Reykholt has

---

7   Helgi Þorláksson 2017; also pp. 137–138 in this book.

8   Benedikt Eyþórsson 2008.

9   Helgi Þorláksson (ed.) 2005. A comparison is made with other major churches which were not *staðir* and combined they are called *church centres*.

10   See articles in Mundal (ed.) 2006.

11   See articles in Helgi Þorláksson and Þóra Björk Sigurðardóttir (eds) 2012.

12   Guðrún Sveinbjarnardóttir 2012, 266.

13   *Reykjaholtsmáldagi,* 14–15.

14   Guðrún Sveinbjarnardóttir 2016, 115, 110, 113.

15   For a discussion see pp. 260–261 in this book.

also been discussed in more detail elsewhere.[16] Investigations in two of the areas show that there was human activity in both of them from the late tenth or early eleventh century, which coincides with the present dating of the earliest occupation at Reykholt. In the earliest preserved deed of the church, thought to date to the mid-twelfth century, a third area, Geitland, is listed among resource areas the Reykholt church was entitled to use.[17] In this area there is evidence of human activity from as early as the ninth century. The sites in Geitland seem to have been abandoned at about the same time as Reykholt was first occupied. The nature of the ruins suggests that these were farm sites rather than shielings. Whether there is any connection between their abandonment and the settlement at Reykholt is uncertain. The reliability of sources connecting Geitland with Reykholt, especially *Landnámabók*, has been questioned and explained as an attempt to strengthen Reykholt's position as a centre of power through an increase in the property of the church.[18]

Other topics where more research is needed include farming at Reykholt in the medieval period. Scientific study has proved unable to establish either the size and productivity of infields or the extent of cereal growing, for which there is both some archaeological and some environmental evidence. Preservation of animal bone at the site was on the whole poor and the number that could be identified was small, producing only a partial picture of the number and types of animals kept. In addition to cattle and sheep, there is some evidence of pigs (in the thirteenth century) and goats (in the twelfth or thirteenth century). Saltwater fish bones and a seal bone suggest contact with the sea.[19] More information is needed to put the farming practices of the period into context, to see whether there was perhaps more variety during Snorri's time than both earlier and later, reflecting the status of the site as that of a chieftaincy. Was he able to support his household solely on what was produced at Reykholt, including in its wider resource areas, or did he have to rely on produce from other holdings belonging to Reykholt or to himself personally? The deed of the Reykholt church shows the types of domestic animals the *staðr* was supposed to own. These included cows, ewes and horses,

16   Guðrún Sveinbjarnardóttir *et al.* 2011.
17   On the deed of the church see pp. 279–289 in this book. The utilization rights are called *ítǫk* (sing. *ítak*) and are not property rights.
18   Helgi Þorláksson 2012.
19   McGovern 2012.

but pigs and goats are not mentioned. The bones found from goats and pigs suggest that Snorri, beside running the *staðr*, had his own domestic animals at the farm. Such an arrangement is known for chieftains keeping *staðir*. An example from around the middle of the thirteenth century is a keeper of a *staðr* who had dozens of his own pigs and geese. He also had at least four oxen called *arðryxn,* suggesting that they were yoked for dragging an instrument called an *arðr* (similar to a plough but simpler).[20] Pigs, goats and geese were popular among magnates in medieval Iceland and we can suppose that Snorri also kept geese for himself even though no such bones were found in the excavation. Barley grains and pollen were found at and in the neighbourhood of Reykholt, all from Snorri's time or earlier. The deed says, "*Sáld* shall be sown." *Sáld* is a measure of seed, probably barley, equivalent to approximately a hundred kilograms. The crops from this amount of seed have been estimated to be sixfold and they were to go to the *staðr*.[21] The *goði* and priest Páll Sǫlvason, who served Reykholt in the twelfth century, kept at least three oxen which were probably used for the *arðr*.[22] The place name Svínatóft (which means a ruined pigsty) exists at Reykholt and may very well be medieval. It has been suggested that pigs were fed with scraps from the field and leftovers, and were kept in the field when it lay fallow.[23] Cereal would have been used for eating and for brewing. Pigs were kept for their meat as were goats, although the latter were probably kept mainly for their milk and the cheese made from it. It is of interest that the practice of growing cereals seems to have been common at places with the component *reyk* in their names,[24] a component indicative of steam and geothermal heat. Perhaps the heat was used for brewing or drying the cereal or both.

Fishbones found at Reykholt indicate that fish was consumed. During Lent fish was the staple food, probably together with eggs (geese, hens?), cheese and whale meat.[25] Dried halibut (*rafabelti* (*rafr*), *riklingr*) was a favourite dish in Snorri's time reserved for the well-to-do.[26] Halibut was

20 *Sturlunga saga* II, 95.
21 Björn Magnússon Ólsen 1910, 86–87, 156, 159, 162.
22 *Sturlunga saga* I, 114.
23 Björn Magnússon Ólsen 1910, 87 (fn.), 96 (fn.), 112, 140. Pigs were not kept in Iceland between the Middle Ages and modern times.
24 Examples besides Reykholt are Reykjanes by Djúp, Reykhólar, Reykir in Mosfellssveit and Reykjavík (Akurey, Effersey).
25 On whale meat allowed as food on fast days see *Grágás* (1992), 34. Dairy products were allowed on fast days, including hen's eggs.
26 *Sturlunga saga* I, 379–380.

called *heilagfiski*, the holy fish. During the summer, salmon must have been common, and the *staðr* had important fishing rights where trout was most likely of most importance.[27]

Snorri's farming at Reykholt can be called "chieftain farming". The main purpose was diversity in food and it demanded a greater workforce than the average farmer could afford. He probably also had his own farms elsewhere in Borgarfjǫrðr, such as at Svignaskarð and Deildartunga.[28] These could have supported his own household at Reykholt with their domestic animals and products. He had a major farm at Bessastaðir which he could visit in a boat from another *staðr* in the Borgarfjǫrðr area, Stafholt, which he also administered. In 1247, loads of malt, no doubt produced at Bessastaðir, were transported to Reykholt.[29]

Between 1220 and 1230 Snorri was at the peak of his power and influence. He was the leading Icelandic representative of the regents in Norway, enjoyed great respect, and adopted a lifestyle found among the nobles in Scandinavia. His dignified surroundings have been uncovered by the archaeological excavations at Reykholt. Snorri made Reykholt a place of distinction in the Norse world.

The Reykholt Project: Aims, Organization, Execution

A meeting preceding the launching of the project was held in 1998 to which the National Museum invited, for consultation on future research work at Reykholt, historians and archaeologists from Norway (Reidar Bertelsen, University of Tromsø, Knut Helle and Ingvild Øye, University of Bergen) and from Denmark (Steffen Stummann Hansen, University of Copenhagen). Also present were, from the National Museum, Þór Magnússon (director), Hjörleifur Stefánsson (section head), Guðrún Sveinbjarnardóttir (director of excavations at Reykholt), Guðmundur H. Jónsson (archaeologist), Helgi Þorláksson from the University of Iceland and member of the board of the Museum, Bergur Þorgeirsson, director of Snorrastofa, Bjarni Guðmundsson, chairman of the board of Snorrastofa and the Reverend Geir Waage from Reykholt. The following

27 Helgi Þorláksson 1989.
28 *Sturlunga saga* I, 314–315; 358–360.
29 *Sturlunga saga* II, 84.

year a workshop was held to discuss the ideas put forward, attended by around forty scholars from different disciplines and of different nationalities.[30] The workshop resulted in the launching of the Reykholt Project with a steering committee made up of representatives from the National Museum, the University of Iceland and Snorrastofa.[31] The project was set up with three main components:

Archaeological investigations	Cultural landscape and environment	Reykholt as a centre
Directed by Guðrún Sveinbjarnardóttir	Directed by Guðrún Gísladóttir	Directed by Bergur Þorgeirsson
Sub-components	*Sub-components*	*Sub-components*
a. Farm mound	a. Vegetation	a. Church centre, directed by Helgi Þorláksson
b. Church site, co-directed by Oscar Aldred	b. Cultural landscape	b. Centre of power, directed by Helgi Þorláksson
c. Shielings		c. Centre of textual culture, directed by Karl G. Johansson

The general aims of the project were set out as follows:
- To provide a better understanding of the process of centralization of power during the Commonwealth period in Iceland (930–1262), the creation of political and ecclesiastical centres and how this relates to land-use, settlement development and the creation of literature. Reykholt in the time of Snorri Sturluson (1206–1241) was at the core of the investigation. Comparisons were sought in Scandinavia and in Western Europe.

30 Guðrún Sveinbjarnardóttir 2000 (ed.).
31 The steering committee, comprised of Bergur Þorgeirsson, Guðrún Gísladóttir, Guðrún Sveinbjarnardóttir, Haukur Jóhannesson, Helgi Þorláksson, Margrét Hallgrímsdóttir and Svavar Sigmundsson, convened periodically between 2000 and 2005, and initiated an exhibition at the National Museum in 2005 on the Reykholt Project.

- To combine research in the humanities, social sciences and natural sciences.
- a) to bring together Icelandic scholars from different disciplines in the hope that it would maximize results within each discipline; b) to encourage international cooperation with scholars of various disciplines in order to stimulate Icelandic research and vice versa; c) to encourage young Icelanders and non-Icelanders to do research leading to BA/BS, MA/MS and PhD degrees.
- To publish the main results in an interdisciplinary fashion.

Archaeological investigations

a. **Farm site.** The excavation took place from 1987 to 1989 and 1998 to 2003, funded by a special grant from the Icelandic government to the National Museum. Articles have been published and a book with the final results.[32]

b. **Church site**. The excavation took place from 2002 to 2007. It was one of the projects funded by the Millennium Fund (*Kristnihátíðarsjóður*) between 2002 and 2006. The last year of excavation was funded by a grant from the Icelandic Government. Grants were also received from the Icelandic Archaeology Fund (*Fornleifasjóður,* now *Fornminjasjóður*). Some articles and a book have been published on all the results.[33]

c. **Shielings.** This component was introduced in 2003/2004. Trial trenches were dug in 2005, 2007, 2009 and 2010 at several sites thought to have served as shielings or summer farms for Reykholt in the medieval period. These investigations were part of "The Reykholt Shieling Project", supported by, among others, large grants from the Icelandic Centre for Research (*Rannís*, grant no. 080655021) and *Kultur - og kirkjedepartementet* in Norway. Several articles have already been published on the results of these investigations.[34]

32   See for example Guðrún Sveinbjarnardóttir 2005; 2010; 2012a.
33   See for example Guðrún Sveinbjarnardóttir 2009; 2012b; 2016.
34   E.g. Guðrún Sveinbjarnardóttir 2008; Guðrún Sveinbjarnardóttir *et al.* 2011; Vickers and Guðrún Sveinbjarnardóttir 2013.

Cultural landscape and environment

a. **Vegetation.** The time-span is from before *landnám* (the settlement of Iceland *c.* 870) to modern times with the aim of investigating ecological changes resulting from *landnám* and its development into modern times. The vegetation in the vicinity of Reykholt and in the shieling areas belonging to Reykholt was investigated. The environmental research was part of the "Landscapes circum landnám" project, supported by the Leverhulme Trust in Britain,[35] and of "The Reykholt Shieling Project", which was supported by, among others, large grants from the Icelandic Centre for Research (*Rannís*, grant no. 080655021), *Kultur- og kirkjedepartementet* in Norway, and the University of Iceland Research fund (*Rannsóknarsjóður* Háskóla Íslands). Several articles have been published[34, 36] or are in preparation.

b. **Cultural landscape.** The natural environment in the region around Reykholt varied and offered different opportunities for land use. Linked to the hierarchical structure of the society since the *landnám*, land use and management has transformed the landscape in various ways. Here an attempt was made to explain the processes and reasons for the landscape change from before *landnám* to the present. The idea was that the cultural landscape is formed from a natural landscape by a cultural group. Culture is the agent, the natural area is the medium, and the cultural landscape is the result. These investigations were funded by "The Reykholt Shieling Project", supported by, among others, large grants from the Icelandic Centre for Research (*Rannís*, grant no. 080655021), *Kultur- og kirkjedepartementet* in Norway, and The University of Iceland Research fund (*Rannsóknarsjóður* Háskóla Íslands). Several articles have been published[34, 36] or are in preparation.

Reykholt as a centre

a. **Church centre.** Reykholt was one of the main *staðir* of Iceland in the ecclesiastical sense of the word (ecclesiastical institutions, some of which were quite rich). The purpose of the oldest and largest *staðir*

---

35 Edwards *et al.* 2004.

36 E.g. Guðrún Sveinbjarnardóttir *et al.* 2007; Egill Erlendsson *et al.* 2012; Gathorn-Hardy *et al.* 2009; Guðrún Gísladóttir *et al.* 2011; Guðrún Sveinbjarnardóttir 2012a.

was investigated. The history of the *staðir* was studied and comparisons made with similar establishments abroad. An international workshop on church centres was held at Reykholt in 2002, supported by a grant from the Icelandic Millennium Fund (*Kristnihátíðarsjóður*). Ten papers delivered at the workshop were published in a book.[37] Grants were received from The University of Iceland Research Fund (*Rannsóknarsjóður* Háskóla Íslands) and the Rannís Icelandic Research Fund (*Rannsóknarnámssjóður Rannís*, grant no. 080655021) to study the way the *staðr* at Reykholt was run. The principal results have been published in a book.[38]

b. **Centre of power.** The concentration of secular power in Iceland in the twelfth and thirteenth centuries is noteworthy. Why did it happen? Snorri Sturluson aimed to form a principality or *héraðsríki* (literally "district-state"), as scholars like to call it, and wanted to have widespread influence. One of the research questions has been whether Snorri was interested in obtaining Reykholt on account of its location, the income generated from the place, or whether the symbolic significance of the *staðr* was more important. Did the *staðir* offer respect which secured political following? The importance of social honour to Snorri Sturluson was discussed.[39]

c. **Centre of textual culture.** Snorri Sturluson is a famous author and the Reykholt Project has given specialists in textual or literary culture (*bókmenning*) of the medieval period an opportunity to meet and discuss his works in light of his life and place of residence, his subjects, historical circumstances, his literary world and foreign parallels. The aim was to locate Icelandic textual culture (texts, writing, book-making) within a wider context, e.g. in the light of literacy, literary composition, social roles and European connections.

Between 2002 and 2006, five conferences were held at Snorrastofa in Reykholt as part of the Reykholt Project, supported by grants from the Scandinavian research fund NordForsk (previously NorFa). The conferences mainly addressed the third component of the Reykholt Project under the auspices of the "Reykholt og den europeiske skriftkulturen"

---

37 Helgi Þorláksson 2005 (ed.).
38 Benedikt Eyþórsson 2008.
39 This was the topic of a session at Þriðja íslenska söguþingið in 2006, in Benedikt Eyþórsson and Hrafnkell Lárusson (eds) 2007.

(Reykholt and the European literary culture) network. Four books have been published which include a selection of the papers given at these conferences.[40]

40   Mundal (ed.) 2006; Johansson (ed.) 2007; Jørgensen (ed.) 2009; Helgi Þorláksson and Þóra Björk Sigurðardóttir (eds) 2012.

Bibliography

Benedikt Eyþórsson 2008. *Búskapur og rekstur staðar í Reykholti 1200–1900*. Reykjavík: Sagnfræðistofnun Háskóla Íslands.

Benedikt Eyþórsson and Hrafnkell Lárusson (eds) 2007. "Valdamiðstöðvar á miðöldum". In *Þriðja íslenska söguþingið, 18.–21. maí 2006. Ráðstefnurit*. Reykjavík: Aðstandendur Þriðja íslenska söguþingsins, 189–253.

Björn Magnússon Ólsen 1910. "Um kornirkju á Íslandi að fornu". *Búnaðarrit* 24 (1910), 81–167.

Egill Erlendsson, Kim Vickers, Freddy G. Gathorne-Hardy, Joanna Bending, Björg Gunnarsdóttir, Guðrún Gísladóttir and Kevin J. Edwards 2012. "Late-Holocene Environmental History of the Reykholt Area, Borgarfjörður, Western Iceland". In Helgi Þorláksson and Þóra Björg Sigurðardóttir (eds), *From Nature to Script. Reykholt, Environment, Centre and Manuscript Making*. Snorrastofa, vol. VII. Reykholt: Snorrastofa, 17–47.

Gathorn-Hardy, Freddy G., Egill Erlendsson, Peter G. Langdon and Kevin J. Edwards 2009. "Lake Sediment Evidence for Climate Change and Landscape Erosion in Western Iceland". *Journal of Paleolimnology* 42, 413–426.

Guðrún Gísladóttir, Egill Erlendsson and Rattan Lal 2011. "Soil Evidence for Historical Human Induced Land Degradation in West Iceland". *Applied Geochemistry* 26, S28–S31.

Guðrún Sveinbjarnardóttir 2000 (ed.), *Reykholt in Borgarfjörður. An Interdisciplinary Research Project. Workshop held 20–21 August 1999*. The National Museum of Iceland – Division of Monuments and Sites. Research Reports 2000.

Guðrún Sveinbjarnardóttir 2005. "The Use of Geothermal Resources at Reykholt in Borgarfjörður in the Medieval Period. Some Preliminary Results". In Andreas Mortensen and Símun V. Arge (eds), *Viking and Norse North Atlantic. Select Papers from the Proceedings of the Fourteenth Viking Congress, Tórshavn, 19–30 July 2001*. Annales Societatis Scientiarum Færoensis. Supplementum XLIV. Tórshavn, 208–216.

Guðrún Sveinbjarnardóttir 2008. "Shielings in Iceland Revisited. A New Project". In Caroline Paulsen and Helgi D. Michelsen (eds), *Símunarbók. Heiðursrit til Símun V. Arge á 60 ára degnum 5. september 2008*. Tórshavn: Fróðskapur, Faroe University Press, 222–231.

Guðrún Sveinbjarnardóttir 2009. "Kirkjur Reykholts – byggingasaga". In Guðmundur Ólafsson and Steinunn Kristjánsdóttir (eds), *Endurfundir. Fornleifarannsóknir styrktar af Kristnihátíðarsjóði 2001–2005*. Reykjavík: Þjóðminjasafn Íslands, 58–69.

Guðrún Sveinbjarnardóttir 2010. "The Making of a Centre. The Case of Reykholt, Iceland". In John Sheehan and Donnchadh Ó Corráin (eds), *The Viking Age: Ireland and the West. Proceedings of the XVth Viking Congress, Cork, 2005*. Dublin: Four Courts Press, 483–493.

Guðrún Sveinbjarnardóttir 2012a. *Reykholt. Archaeological Investigations at a High Status Farm in Western Iceland*. Publications of the National Museum of Iceland 29. Reykjavík: Snorrastofa and The National Museum of Iceland.

Guðrún Sveinbjarnardóttir 2012b. "The Reykholt Churches. The Archaeological Evidence in a North Atlantic Context". In Helgi Þorláksson and Þóra Björk Sigurðardóttir (eds), *From Nature to Script. Reykholt, Environment, Centre and Manuscript Making*. Snorrastofa, vol. VII. Reykholt: Snorrastofa, 141–163.

Guðrún Sveinbjarnardóttir 2016. *Reykholt. The*

Church Excavations. Publications of the National Museum of Iceland 41. Reykjavík: The National Museum of Iceland, in collaboration with Snorrastofa and University of Iceland Press.

Guðrún Sveinbjarnardóttir, Egill Erlendsson, Kim Vickers, Tom H. McGovern, Karen B. Milek, Kevin J. Edwards, Ian A. Simpson and Gordon Cook 2007. "The Paleoecology of a High Status Icelandic Farm". *Environmental Archaeology* 12 (2), 187–206.

Guðrún Sveinbjarnardóttir, Kristoffer Dahle, Egill Erlendsson, Guðrún Gísladóttir and Kim Vickers 2011. "The Reykholt Shieling Project. Some Preliminary Results". In Svavar Sigmundsson (ed.), *Viking Settlement and Viking Society. Papers from the Proceedings of the XVIth Viking Congress, Reykjavík and Reykholt, 16–23 August 2009.* Reykjavík: Hið íslenzka fornleifafélag and University of Iceland Press, 162–175.

Guðrún Sveinbjarnardóttir and Bergur Þorgeirsson (eds) 2017. *The Buildings of Medieval Reykholt. The Wider Context.* Snorrastofa, vol. IX. Reykjavík: Snorrastofa and University of Iceland Press.

Helgi Þorláksson 1989. "Mannvirkið í Reyðarvatnsósi". *Árbók Hins íslenzka fornleifafélags 1988,* 5–27.

Helgi Þorláksson 2005 (ed.). *Church Centres. Church Centres in Iceland from the 11th to the 13th Century and their Parallels in other Countries.* Snorrastofa, vol II. Reykholt: Snorrastofa.

Helgi Þorláksson 2012. "Reykholt vokser fram som maktsenter". In Helgi Þorláksson and Þóra Björk Sigurðardóttir (eds), *From Nature to Script. Reykholt, Environment, Centre and Manuscript Making.* Snorrastofa, vol. VII. Reykholt: Snorrastofa, 79–116.

Helgi Þorláksson 2017. "Reykholt as a residence of Snorri the *lendr maðr*". In Guðrún

Sveinbjarnardóttir and Bergur Þorgeirsson (eds), *The Buildings of Medieval Reykholt. The Wider Context.* Snorrastofa, vol. IX. Reykjavík: Snorrastofa and University of Iceland Press, 159–181.

Helgi Þorláksson and Þóra Björk Sigurðardóttir (eds) 2012. *From Nature to Script. Reykholt, Environment, Centre and Manuscript Making.* Snorrastofa, vol. VII. Reykholt: Snorrastofa.

Johansson, Karl G. (ed.) 2007. *Den norröna renässansen. Reykholt, Norden och Europa 1150–1300.* Snorrastofa, vol. IV. Reykholt: Snorrastofa.

Jørgensen, Jon Gunnar (ed.) 2009. *Snorres Edda i europeisk og islandsk kultur.* Snorrastofa, vol. V. Reykholt: Snorrastofa.

McGovern, Tom 2012. "Animal bone". In Guðrún Sveinbjarnardóttir, *Reykholt. Archaeological Investigations at a High Status Farm in Western Iceland.* Reykjavík: Snorrastofa and the National Museum of Iceland, 257–259.

Mundal, Else (ed.) 2006. *Reykholt som makt- og lærdomssenter i den islandske og nordiske kontekst.* Snorrastofa, vol. III. Reykholt: Snorrastofa.

Orri Vésteinsson 2000. *The Christianization of Iceland. Priests, Power and Social Change 1000–1300.* Oxford: Oxford University Press.

Páll Vídalín 1854. *Skýringar yfir fornyrði lögbókar þeirrar er Jónsbók kallast.* Reykjavík: Hið íslenzka bókmenntafélag.

Steenberger, Mårten 1943. *Forntida gårdar.* Copenhagen: Ejnar Munksgaard.

Sturlunga saga I–II. Eds Jón Jóhannesson, Magnús Finnbogason and Kristján Eldjárn. Reykjavík: Sturlunguútgáfan, 1946.

Vickers, Kim and Guðrún Sveinbjarnardóttir 2013. "Insect Invaders, Seasonality and Transhumant Pastoralism in the Icelandic Shieling Economy". *Environmental Archaeology* 18, 165–177.

¶ HELGI ÞORLÁKSSON

Snorri Sturluson the Aristocrat Becomes *lendr maðr*

A Grandson of a Common Farmer Becomes a Leader of the Nobility

SOME OF THE PARTICIPANTS IN THE REYKHOLT PROJECT, the present author included, have suggested that Snorri Sturluson and his lifestyle and surroundings at Reykholt were "aristocratic". But what do we mean by this? How was it "aristocratic" and why? One point of view is that Snorri was aristocratic because he was brought up by the aristocratic family at Oddi, the Oddaverjar. His foster-father, Jón Loftsson at Oddi, was the alleged grandson of King Magnús *berfœttr* (Bareleg) of Norway, who died in 1103. In 1164, when he was crowned as king, Magnús Erlingsson accepted Jón as his relative.[1] Another suggestion is that Snorri became aristocratic because he was a courtier to the Norwegian king. We can ask how he qualified for this role.

Snorri left Iceland for Norway for the first time in 1218. The regents in Norway, King Hákon *gamli* [the Old] and Earl Skúli, made him *skutilsveinn,* a leader among the courtiers (equivalent to a knight), either in the winter of 1218/19 or 1219/20.[2] By 1220 he had already been further

---

1   *Heimskringla* III, 395. Jón's parents were Þóra, daughter of King Magnús, and Loftr (also spelled Loptr), son of Sæmundr at Oddi.

2   In modern Norwegian Hákon and Skúli are called Håkon Håkonsson, or Håkon IV, and Skule.

elevated to the position of *lendr maðr*,[3] which was similar to that of a count or a baron. As far as we know Snorri was the only Icelander to be given that position. There were only about fifteen *lendir menn* (plural) in Norway at any one time in the thirteenth century and usually they were of the most noble families in the country.[4] The only rank bestowed upon anyone in the country which was higher than *lendr maðr* was that of earl. Why was Snorri found fit for such an honour? A man whose father was just a petty chieftain and grandfather only a common farmer before he was elevated to the status of *goði*.[5]

The Old Norse word for the court was *hirð*, meaning both the royal retinue or the king's liegemen as a group and also the royal household. Our main sources for the *hirð* are *Konungsskuggsjá* (The King's Mirror) probably composed in the 1250s, and the *hirðlǫg*, or stipulations for the *hirð*, preserved in *Hirðskrá*, probably dating mainly from around 1275, but with some older parts. Even though ideally the prerequisites for joining the *hirð* were factors like coming from a good family, and possessing considerable means, prowess, courage and courteous manners, *Konungs-skuggsjá* suggests that men who were not of distinguished parentage and had limited means could join the *hirð* and become common courtiers.[6] But Snorri's case, a son of a petty chieftain in Iceland becoming leader of the *hirð*, a *skutilsveinn* and even a *lendr maðr* in Norway, is surprising and calls for some explanation. It is strange that scholars have not attached much significance to this great advancement nor paid much attention to what it implied for Snorri to become a *lendr maðr* and how this affected his life.

It has been argued that during the fierce competition in Iceland be-tween the most powerful *goðar* in the first half of the thirteenth century, at least four of them tried to improve their position in Icelandic politics by becoming the Norwegian king's leading man in Iceland.[7] Snorri apparently was the first to do this and what is interesting (and which has been rather neglected) is how he managed to do so. The others were Sturla

---

3   *Sturlunga saga* I, 271–272, 277.

4   Helle 1974, 74–75.

5   *Goði* (plural *goðar*) was a chieftain, a man of power, one of 39 entitled to have a seat at the middle bench of the law court of the general assembly (*Alþingi*) and to nominate judges. There were no direct equivalents for *goðar* in Norway.

6   *Konungs skuggsiá*, 40 (lines 10 and on, 36), 43 (lines 34 and on).

7   For instance, Helgi Þorláksson 1988, "Var Sturla Þórðarson þjóðfrelsishetja?"; Sverrir Jakobsson 2013, lviii.

Figure 1. King Hákon *gamli* Hákonarson and Earl Skúli Bárðarson as a duke-elect. The image is part of the initial letter to *Hákonar saga Hákonarsonar* in Flateyjarbók. The king creates a duke with a sword and a banner (the empty space was presumably meant to show the duke's coat of arms). The circlet the man on the right is wearing around his head is characteristic for dukes. An illumination from the late fourteenth century. Flateyjarbók, GKS 1005 fol. The Árni Magnússon Institute for Icelandic Studies. Photo: Jóhanna Ólafsdóttir.

Sighvatsson, Þórðr *kakali* Sighvatsson[8] and finally Gizurr Þorvaldsson (who became earl for the Norwegian king in Iceland).

Snorri most probably prepared carefully for his advancement. Around 1210 Earl Hákon *galinn* (literally, "frantic") was the "strong man" in Norway, the foremost leader of the ruling elite, the Birkibeinar, their most able marshal and probably almost equal to the king in power and influence.[9] Snorri supported the Birkibeinar in their strife in Norway against the Baglar and composed a poem, now lost, about Earl Hákon, who thanked him and must have learnt something about Snorri. He probably saw in this young and promising chieftain a prospective ally. The earl wrote a letter to Snorri, invited him to Norway and promised to confer on him some important marks of honour ("gera ... miklar sæmðir"). Earlier he had sent very dignified presents to Snorri, suggestive of the position he might expect: armour or a coat of mail, a shield and a sword, all fit for a distinguished courtier. Earl Hákon seems to have held Snorri in high esteem. The promise of such a great honour appealed to Snorri, and Sturla Þórðarson in his *Íslendinga saga* says "mjök var þat í skapi Snorra" which would most naturally be interpreted to mean that he was bent on accepting the invitation, was eager for it.[10] But before Snorri could leave for Norway Earl Hákon died (in January 1214).

By becoming the leading man of the Norwegian regents in Iceland, Snorri probably envisaged that his political position in the country would be enhanced. He would take on a difficult but tempting role as an intermediary between the Norwegian court and the Icelanders. A dispute and clashes between the Oddaverjar family and some Norwegian merchants in Iceland, which had already begun in 1215 and became grave in 1217, was an opportunity for Snorri. Even though he was brought up by the powerful Oddaverjar family he had clearly distanced himself from them. These collisions were taken seriously by Earl Skúli who welcomed Snorri to Norway in 1218 and made him his counsellor in the case.

But the situation would hardly have automatically led to Snorri becoming *skutilsveinn*; he must have had some other merits that helped his advancement. It seems worthwhile to study how a son of a petty

---

8   On his nickname *kakali* see in this book, pp. 149–150.
9   The nickname *galinn* can mean "rash, showing rage and fury", possibly alluding to how war-like and able Hákon was as a military leader.
10   *Íslendinga saga* in *Sturlunga saga* I, 269. It has also been translated, "much to his liking" but the translation above is more plausible.

chieftain in distant Iceland, without king and court, could so quickly be elevated to a nobleman of distinction abroad. Here a study of the terms "aristocrat" and "nobleman" is in order. In modern usage "aristocratic" has several meanings, such as "noble", "courteous" and "of high social rank". It will be suggested here that in order to understand Snorri's position we have to use and understand the word "aristocrat" in the old sense, in the governmental sense, "as containing connotations of leadership and authority, betraying its classical origins when it referred to a system of government".[11] Secondly, aristocracy was different from nobility in that the nobility were a legally defined group, a privileged group, while the aristocracy drew its importance from economic and social weight.[12] The third point is that experienced and respected leaders with authority would acquire a distinct manner and lifestyle. Usually these incorporated norms that were not written down but generally accepted, what has also been called "habitus".[13] It has been suggested that so-called *preudommes*, civilised nobles, became models for aristocrats and nobles in Western Europe in the twelfth century. It was a common type, admired and imitated as will be explained below. This would imply that real aristocrats were "civilized", had adopted dignified manners, were "aristocratic" in that sense. Aristocratic conduct or performance in Western Europe was usually associated with noblemen, courts and courtesy in the second half of the twelfth century. An aristocratic code of behaviour was fashionable and admired.[14] What is of interest here are the men of means and power in political positions who adopted such an aristocratic code of behaviour. We would call them aristocrats.

The question is, was Snorri seen as an aristocrat in this sense when he came to Norway in 1218 and is that the main reason for him being made *skutilsveinn*? It has been suggested that his poetic and literary skills helped him, and also his education. Is that likely? And what merits led to him becoming *lendr maðr* and what did it imply? Finally, did Snorri not have several anti-aristocratic drawbacks?

11   Coss 2003, 7–8.
12   Crouch 2005, 2–3.
13   A concept introduced by Pierre Bourdieu, cf. Crouch 2005.
14   Bouchard 1998, 13, 24.

The *hirð*, the Positions of *skutilsveinn* and *lendr maðr* and their Tasks

Scholars agree that around 1220 there was an increasing interest at the Norwegian court in locating it within a Western European context, in making life at the court not only more polished and diginified but also more expedient in administrative and diplomatic terms, and in establishing contacts with kings and courts abroad.[15]

The socio-juridical concept of "nobility" is not to be found in Old Norse legal terminology. Nevertheless, it has been suggested that a group of those who became liegemen of the king through certain ceremonies called *handganga,* and were thus distinguished from the rest of society, would have constituted a Norwegian nobility in the Middle Ages.[16] The main corporation of men at the *hirð* were the *hirðmenn* proper (courtiers). Below those were two other groupings, the *gestir,* a group of constables with police functions, and the *kertisveinar,* young men of good descent, corresponding to pages at other Western European courts. Neither of these two groups were counted among the *hirðmenn* proper.[17] The earls ranked highest among the liegemen but next to them came the *lendir menn.* They were royal counsellors, were granted a *veizla* (a kind of benefice or fief), probably often royal lands (thus the term *lendir* derived from *land*) and an annual income of fifteen silver marks. They were entitled to a retinue of forty armed men. The nominations for *lendir menn* seem to have circulated among the members of an exclusive group of families, considered to be leading or outstanding. The holders of the highest *hirð*-offices, *kanseler* (*kanslari*, chancellor), *stallari* (king's spokesman) and *merkismaðr* (literally, "standard man", meaning standard bearer) enjoyed the same rights as *lendir menn.*

Next to these in rank came the *skutilsveinar* (plural). Their tasks were to serve the king and escort the noble *lendir menn* and the *stallari* at special occasions and celebrations. The main obligation of a *skutilsveinn* was to appoint guards to be on watch, to organize their shifts, and supervise them. The guards, whose number could be increased at certain times, were the king's men and always included some courtiers. The *skutilsveinar* were also obliged to take care of guards when the king was travelling, either

15   Helle 1974, 104–105.
16   Imsen 2000, 206. Crouch says that seeing nobility as a privileged court aristocracy is a workable definition, even though it is highly exclusive (Crouch 2005, 4).
17   Helle 1974, 201.

by ship or by horse. Our source, the *hirðlǫg* in *Hirðskrá*, comments that the position of *skutilsveinn* would only befit those who were "hœverskir ok kurteisir", in other words those who knew how to behave in the presence of a king or knew the code of right behaviour at the court.[18] The king should consult the *skutilsveinar* on the appoinments of *dróttseti* and *skenkjari* who were recruited from among them and were responsible for provisions of food and drink. *Skutilsveinar* were also eligible for the higher offices.[19] Both *lendir menn* and *skutilsveinar* were called *hirðstjórar*, the leaders of the courtiers.[20] In 1277 when *lendir menn* became barons the *skutisveinar* became *riddarar* (knights) and both were addressed as *herra* (Sir). The common *hirðmenn* (courtiers) were below them in rank.

What did it mean in Norway to become a *lendr maðr* and what was one supposed to do? *Snorra-Edda* shows that Snorri was well aware of his great advancement. There he explains that *lendr maðr* corresponds to baron in England and *greifi* (count) in Saxony.[21] This is not something he invented; in a letter, probably from 1190, the archbishop explains that *lendr maðr* is the equivalent of *greifi*.[22] In *Háttatal* Snorri himself says that he was granted "hátt hersis heiti" ("the high title of a *hersir*") by the king (Ht. 27).[23] In *Egils saga* the title *hersir* is used interchangeably with the title *lendr maðr*.[24]

Snorri's comment on what *lendir menn* do is "Þeir skulu ok vera réttir dómarar ok réttir landvarnarmenn yfir því ríki sem þeim er fengit til stjórnar".[25] In other words, they were judges and defended the *ríki* (fief) the king granted them.

18   *Hirdskråen. Hirdloven til Norges konge*, 100–107, especially 102.

19   Imsen 2000, 207–210. The position of *skutilsveinn* was probably similar in the 1220s and 1260s.

20   On the importance of *lendir menn* and *skutilsveinar* as leaders of the *hirð* and on the names and number of *lendir menn* see *Hákonar saga Hákonarsonar* I, 217, 257–258.

21   *Edda Snorra Sturlusonar*, 200.

22   *DI* I, 291; the text is somewhat distorted, "greina" in the manuscript is corrected to "greiua" in the edition, which would be the same as *greifa* in modern spelling According to the text the position of a *greifi* (a count) was the same as that of *lendr maðr* ("lendz manz rettvr med oss").

23   Ht. means Snorri's *Háttatal* in his *Snorra-Edda* and the numbers refer to individual strophes.

24   *Egils saga Skalla-Grímssonar*, 147, 177, 257; the *hersir* Arninbjǫrn is also called *lendr maðr*.

25   "They are also proper judges and defenders of the fief granted them to govern" (*Edda Snorra Sturlusonar*, 200).

Snorri and the Concept of Being "Aristocratic"

Thus Snorri Sturluson must have been found *hœverskr* (*höfisch*) and *kurteiss* (*curtois*) enough to become a leader among the courtiers in Norway even though he had never been abroad before and thus had not experienced life at a court. At least he was quick to learn and must have been well prepared. Some scholars may, understandably, find this startling for an inhabitant of a remote island. *Landnámabók* (The Book of Settlements) reports some foreigners as saying that the Icelanders were descendants of slaves and ruffians.[26] The Icelanders, coming from the strange and remote island in the far north, were called *Mǫrlandar* in Norway, literally meaning people who eat fat sausages. Some sagas suggest that their only chance of becoming civilized was being accepted at the court. Many of the Icelandic *þættir* (short tales or sagas), for instance in *Morkinskinna*, seem to support such a view. What this suggests is that Snorri must have been deemed very civilized when he came to Norway.

By Icelandic standards, the *stórgoði* Snorri was both powerful and well-off and this as well as his conduct and manners may have helped his advancement at the Norwegian court.[27] Although it is difficult to establish this, there are some indications of his interest in dignified conduct. One of Snorri's retainers around 1216 was a German called Herburt, a specialist in the art of defence with a small shield called a buckler, and probably in fencing as well.[28] Snorri must have appreciated his skills. Together with another man Herburt is called Snorri's *fylgðarmaðr*, or escort. Snorri apparently adopted a courtly manner by engaging retainers; they were supposed to follow him wherever he went.[29] This points to a man, adopting dignified, foreign lifestyles and conduct in order to become "aristocratic".

An indication of Snorri's longing to be accepted by foreign dignitaries are the poems he composed for the Birkibeinar kings in Norway, Sverrir and Ingi, and also Earl Hákon *galinn*. It was probably not Snorri's intention to be accepted only as a court-poet. The promise of the earl to endow

---

26   *Íslendingabók, Landnámabók*, 336 fn. This is in an epilogue most scholars think must be quite old, even belonging to the original redaction.

27   Around 1200 the number of *goðar* had decreased and their power had increased. These *goðar*, including Snorri, are usually called *stórgoðar* which is a modern construction.

28   *Sturlunga saga* I, 267; Brown 2012, 61–63. The word *buckler* was adopted in Old German from French (Bumke 2000, 156).

29   On *fylgðarmenn* generally see Jón Viðar Sigurðsson 1989, especially 122–123.

him with great honour, meaning some social advancement, is probably what counted most.[30] For Snorri in Norway in 1218 an aristocratic code of behaviour counted as a means to an end. Conduct would include a way of speaking and behaving in general, as *Konungsskuggsjá* shows (see below). Certain standards of dress had to be met. It is evident that Snorri the *skutilsveinn* behaved in a way that was accepted at the Norwegian court and this behaviour of his could be labelled "aristocratic".

Here a distinction will be made between the expressions "code of conduct" and "lifestyle". "Code of conduct" will be used for self-conscious, personal behaviour such as speech, hairstyle, choice of dress and weapons and appearance (including ways of sitting, standing, walking), accepted generally by Western European courtiers. The expression "lifestyle" is used for rituals, banquets, gift-giving, housing and so on.

The Concept of "Aristocrats" in Iceland in the Works of Scholars

Within the Reykholt Project the words "aristocrat" and "aristocratic" have been fairly prominent, particularly in articles written by Guðrún Nordal and Karl Gunnar Johansson.[31] Guðrún says that prior to 1218 Snorri was imitating foreign aristocratic models. She points out that in 1217 Snorri arrived at the *Alþingi* (general assembly) at Þingvellir with eighty Norwegians, *Austmenn*, following him, all of whom were carrying shields. This was probably noteworthy because it was exceptional and can hardly have been a part of Snorri's usual behaviour. The *Austmenn* may have been two crews of Norwegian merchant vessels, merchant sailors who had probably spent the winter at different farms in the Borgarfjǫrðr area, Snorri's home district.[32] Snorri and his relatives were popular among

30 The gifts from Earl Hákon *galinn* seem to have been suggestive of the position of *skutilsveinn* for Snorri and he seems to have been prepared for that.

31 Guðrún Nordal 2006; Guðrún Nordal and Jon Gunnar Jørgensen in this book, pp. 447–448, 453–458; see also Karl G. Johansson in this book, pp. 345–348, 365–376; Torfi H. Tulinius in this book, pp. 394–401; Guðrún Sveinbjarnardóttir and Guðrún Harðardóttir in this book, pp. 271–272. Viðar Pálsson also touches upon this in this book, pp. 123–125.

32 This can be compared to Ari Þorgeirsson, who was such an eager supporter of Earl Erlingr and his son King Magnús that the earl rewarded him with a ship, a *knǫrr*. Ari came to Iceland in 1163 and joined his father for the *Alþingi* in 1164 and had almost 30 Norwegians (*Austmenn*) in his following, probably all with shields

Norwegian merchants, but it is far from likely that Snorri took care
of all their upkeep. They were no doubt also equipped with their own
shields. Guðrún also points out that Snorri at this time called his booth
at the *Alþingi* "*Grýla*", a name also given to a part of the Saga of King
Sverrir.[33] She sees this as an indication of Snorri's inclination towards
an aristocratic lifestyle. In 1231 the name of Snorri's booth at the *Alþingi*
was "*Valhǫll*" (Valhalla), which sounds royal and aristocratic enough since
this was the name of Óðinn's palace and he was seen as the god of kings
and "aristocrats".

Generally speaking, Guðrún must be right about Snorri's aristocratic
code of behaviour and lifestyle.[34] She points out that he, like other Icelandic chieftains in the first half of the thirteenth century, held a court
with "entertainers, writers and troubadours". Her earliest example of an
Icelandic chieftain (*goði*) keeping a poet in his service is Hrafn Sveinbjarnarson (d. 1213).[35] She thinks the poem *Noregskonungatal* shows the same
trend; it was composed for Jón Loftsson at Oddi, Snorri's foster-father,
possibly around 1180 and explains his noble descent. In this she sees a
"leaning of the Icelandic ruling families towards aristocratic codes of
behaviour."[36] Karl G. Johansson, active in the Reykholt Project, refers
to Guðrún, but thinks aristocratic culture was adopted in Iceland from
around 1130 through Benedictine monasteries, and is thus connected
with Latin learning. Even though he speaks of aristocrats in Iceland in
the eleventh century, he thinks foreign court culture was first introduced
in Iceland in the second half of the twelfth century.[37] Aristocrats and
aristocratic life is thus of some interest to scholars, not least the idea of
connecting it with Latin learning around 1130 and with sons of chieftains
who studied at monasteries, as well as with foreign court culture.

Today the words "aristocrat" and "aristocratic" are used repeatedly
by scholars for chieftains in medieval Iceland in texts written in English
or the Scandinavian languages. The word "aristocrat" has been used by
scholars in too *wide* a sense (a) for powerful and well-to-do men, generally

---

(cf. "skjaldasumar"). This was no doubt the crew of his vessel (see *Sturlunga saga* I,
118–119, 122).

33 Guðrún Nordal 2006, 77–78.
34 Earlier Einar Ól. Sveinsson pointed out chivalric influence in Snorri's time (see
Einar Ól. Sveinsson 1940, 37–45).
35 Guðrún Nordal 2001, 131, 21–24, 119–120.
36 Guðrún Norda 2006, 79.
37 See his article in this book, pp. 343–347.

speaking;[38] (b) for *goðar* and their descendants, power and "blue blood" being the decisive factors;[39] (c) for the so-called "clerical gentry", i.e. educated and ordained *goðar* from around 1130; and in far too *narrow* a sense (a) for powerful men/*goðar* who had spent time abroad and become courtiers;[40] (b) for the most important *goðar*, the most powerful and well-to-do of the so-called *stórgoðar*, around 1200 and in the thirteenth century.

Peter Foote contends that there was "a social and cultural aristocracy in Iceland", and the so-called *kirkjugoðar* of the twelfth century he dubbed "clerical gentry", with some reservations. They were a special Icelandic feature, being *goðar* (chieftains) and at the same time ordained priests, who combined native culture with clerical studies and even continental literary culture. Karl G. Johansson writes along these lines when discussing Icelandic aristocrats.[41] It is generally accepted that leading men of the Oddi family were typical of this clerical gentry.[42] An example of a priest-*goði* is Páll Sǫlvason (d. 1185), Snorri's predecessor at Reykholt and a candidate for the office of bishop. *Goðar* ordained as priests or deacons were, however, a typical twelfth-century feature, fading away around 1200.

By gathering examples of aristocratic lifestyles and conduct from different sources, it is possible to draw up a fairly good general picture of this for Iceland around 1200.[43] The main purposes of such lifestyles and conduct would have been to distinguish oneself from the commoners and enjoy their admiration at the same time. Around 1200, the so-called *stórgoðar* (literally, "big *goðar*"), about twelve in all, controlled more than one *goðorð* each and usually reigned alone, each in his own domain (*héraðsríki*), among them Snorri.[44] We know that at least some of these

38   For instance Bagge 1991, 125.

39   Jón Viðar Sigurðsson 2010, 29. The right of the 39 *goðar* to sit on the middle bench at the lawcourt could be shared; the *goðar* attended the court in turns.

40   "Iceland had neither an army nor a true aristocracy ..." (Wanner 2008, 54). It has been suggested that the word "aristocrat" should only be attached to Icelanders in royal service, see Sigríður Beck 2011, 22–25.

41   In this book pp. 336–338, 344–347, 382–383.

42   They were educated in clerical Latin learning, and ordained as priests; although admittedly Jón Loftsson and three of his best known sons were only ordained as deacons. In the late twelfth century it was not as common as before for the *goðar* to be priests but they still appreciated being deacons. The reason is not obvious; for possible explanations see Orri Vésteinsson 2000, 193.

43   Helgi Þorláksson 1979a, 53–58; *Biskupa sögur* II, 166, 212; *Sturlunga saga* I, 483; Helgi Þorláksson 1989, 77–79.

44   On *stórgoðar* generally, see Valdamiðstöðvar á miðöldum (listed in the bibliography).

stórgoðar, especially the Oddi people (Oddaverjar), adopted dignified lifestyles and held excellent banquets, and there are many indications of their refined manners. The Haukdælir were not much inferior. Of some of the other *stórgoðar*, on the other hand, we do not know if they practised aristocratic lifestyles in any sense or adopted specific codes of conduct. But Snorri did before 1218 and for him connections with the Norwegian court were important.[45]

From *preudommes* to Courtly Administrators

When scholars mention medieval courtiers, for instance in France or England, the prowess of knights, of fighting horsemen, and "chivalry" get the most attention, whereas able officials, such as the noblemen who were counsellors of kings, are found to be less interesting. Some of the nobles were summoned to the courts of kings to serve them. A nobleman who was engaged by a king or a prince in the second half of the twelfth century as a major functionary, would be used to some aristocratic conduct. This was a noble habitus, based on an uncodified code, as Crouch puts it.[46] Knights, on the other hand, were warriors, often uncouth. However, the gap in this sense between nobility and knighthood became narrower during the second half of the twelfth century.[47] At that time, as Crouch explains, it was found imperative to civilise the knights who stayed at courts. The civilized noblemen became their models and the knights tried to live up to chivalric ideals. The noble habitus became a codified code in the period between 1170 and 1220, Crouch says. In the thirteenth century these two groups merged.

The ideal noblemen are described in some French works of the twelfth century, referred to by Crouch, depicting their conduct, their skills and abilities. Like Bloch before him, Crouch uses the expression *preudomme* for such a man, an expression emerging in written sources around 1100. Such men seem to have been much admired and their characteristics were

On how they should be explained in an international context, see Helgi Þorláksson 2017.

45   For a more detailed general discussion see Helgi Þorláksson 1979a,. On banquets and gifts see Viðar Pálsson 2016; and 2003; Jón Viðar Sigurðsson 2015.

46   Crouch 2005. The word "habitus" is used as explained by Bourdieu. On Bourdieu see also the article by Torfi H. Tulinius in this book, pp. 392, 396–404.

47   Keen 1984, 31.

not only that they were able and courageous warriors, but also men of restraint, prudent and wise. Ideally they were reasonable and could even be modest. Despite that, they were self-confident, upright men who could be outspoken when needed. When summoned to kings and princes they were mindful and just, reticent but resolute at the same time. They were faithful and loyal to the king or prince. This ideal type is reminiscent of the type called *drengr góðr* (brave man of restraint) in Old Norse.[48] The habitus of such a noble *preudomme* became the ideal, the accepted conduct, and Crouch has tried to explain what it implied. This brave, just and unobtrusive man, the *preudomme*, was severe towards haughty men, lenient with the poor. Usually he was affable at the court, decent and modest in his behaviour or *curialius* (courtlike). He was knowledgeable, a man of letters. The aim was to be worthy as an important servant of kings and princes, to enjoy respect as an able functionary and honest administrator and thus also to be rewarded and protected. The concept *preudomme* was well known in France and among the Normans in England.[49] Around 1130 kings and princes would look around for *preudommes* with legal talent who were honest and able administrators.[50]

When the groups of *preudommes* and knights merged, the word used for them was *chevalerie*, not *preudommie* and Crouch explains why. The word *chevalerie* was used in connection with a noble code of conduct. The boorish and unruly knights were civilized, became "chivalrous" but that did not make them *preudommes*.[51] War was still their occupation, not administration. Their behaviour became aristocratic but they were not administrators and therefore not aristocrats in the sense used here.

Crouch admits that clerical influence is to be found in descriptions of *preudommes* and their conduct. No wonder they were expected to be literate, men of letters, interested in books.[52] The same goes for *curiales* as Jaeger explains them. He studied the origins of courtliness, especially in Germany, and draws attention to *curiales*, the educated members of

48 *Drengskapr* is explained by Sigurður Nordal 1942, 186–199. *Þorsteins þáttr stangar-höggs* is to some extent a study in *drengskapr*, how a physically able and courageous man can be yielding and peace-loving without losing face and self-confidence and still be loyal to his boss. In 1221 the *goði* Arnórr Tumason died abroad and his men missed him because they felt he was "inn bezti drengr ok mikill einurðarmaðr" (*Sturlunga saga* I, 287). "Einurðarmaðr" means that he was upright.

49 Crouch 2005, 29–56.

50 Crouch 2005, 41, 43.

51 Crouch 2005, 84–85.

52 Crouch 2005, 85–86.

courts who served kings and secular princes. They were civilized and their ways were polite. Most of them were clerics who received their education within the Church, but they were wordly in their manners and prepared the usually illiterate young nobles for state administration. Some of the *curiales* became statesmen themselves and were models for others in their refined manners.[53]

These educated courtiers were important instructors and statesmen. Additionally, there were the officials, called *ministerials* in German, those who became high officials to kings, bishops and secular princes and were not necessarily of the most noble social origins.[54] Snorri may have heard about such courteous and influential men. Around the middle of the twelfth-century Abbot Nikulás Bergsson wrote about the most courteous men in Saxony whom Norwegians (Northmen) saw as their models. He writes, "Á Saxlandi er þjóð kurteisust og nema þar Norðmenn mart eftir að breyta".[55] This was probably their habitus which was imitated around 1150, but around 1220 a strict code of conduct had been introduced in Norway. Aristocratic codes of conduct were a serious matter for those who aspired to join the Norwegian court. *Konungsskuggsjá* stresses the importance of dignified conduct at the court, and repeatedly uses words like *kurteiss, siðgóðr, siðaðr, siðir, hœverskr, hœverski, ráðvendi*, which all refer to courteous conduct, and also uses *aðferð* and *meðferð* meaning conduct. The narrator (the father) gives a detailed description of a man who wishes to be accepted as a courtier, of his dress, his haircut, the trimming of his beard and how he should make his appearance, how he should walk and move his hands, and what kind of posture he should assume.[56] This applied, he says, when he himself was a young courtier, possibly between 1220 and 1230. *Konungsskuggsjá* says that in the first half of the thirteenth century the members of the Norwegian court trimmed their beards in the German way.[57] For German courtly influence we may also keep in mind the fact that it was a *Suðrmaðr*, a man from Germany, who taught Snorri to fight with a buckler in around 1216.[58]

---

53 Jaeger 1985/1991, refers to the English Thomas Becket as an example, 15–16; see also 12, 261 and generally 3–16, 157, 219–224, 255–272.

54 Bumke 2000, 33–35.

55 "In Saxony the most courteous men are found and the Norwegians try to imitate them in many ways" (Leiðarvísir Nikuláss Bergssonar ábóta á Þverá, 54).

56 *Konungs skuggsiá*, 39–40, 42–44, 46–48.

57 *Konungs skuggsiá*, 46.

58 *Sturlunga saga* I, 267. It has often been suggested that the court of Hákon was under

The experienced warriors, upright and wise men of restraint, were turning more and more into educated administrators. Their habitus was turned into a strict code of conduct.

How Did Snorri see Aristocrats and Aristocratic Conduct and Lifestyle?

Heimskringla by Snorri, or at least the *Óláfs saga helga* (The Saga of St Óláfr; Óláfr in modern Norwegian is Olav), should be a good indicator of how Snorri saw and appreciated certain traits and conduct of courtiers and aristocrats in general and their lifestyles. To Sigurður Nordal, *Heimskringla* clearly showed that Snorri appreciated good banquets and enjoyed discussing them, that he must have been fond of good alchoholic beverages, and indeed that he felt that half the fun was the goblet which had to be worthy of the fine drink.[59] This is borne out by his poem *Háttatal* where Snorri praises the ale, beer and mead and the excellent wine he was offered by King Hákon and Earl Skúli (Ht. 23, 24, 25). He drank from golden bowls and a golden jug (*skál*, *ker*, Ht. 23, 87, 91).[60] He also had a keen eye for generosity, not least golden gifts. Bagge is, however, right when he points out that in *Heimskringla* Snorri "rarely gives elaborate descriptions of dress, buildings, ceremonies and so forth." He goes on to say:

> There is little trace of the courteous ideal that became prominent in feudal Europe from the twelfth century, emphasizing polite manners, courteous behaviour toward women and romantic love ... Snorri is less concerned with pomp, ceremony and lavishness which are often extremely important in European aristocratic literature.[61]

In *Háttatal* Snorri expresses less admiration than might be expected for dignified objects and utensils or furnishing which he must have seen at the

influence from the English court but this has been contradicted, see Wanner 2008, 82–84.

59 Sigurður Nordal 1920, 82–84.
60 *Skál* = bowl, goblet; *ker* = jug, cask, vessel.
61 Bagge 1991, 149, 151.

courts of Hákon and Skúli. The quality and quantity of food and drink were, however, important to Snorri as well as the goblets and probably the ceremonies of filling them and drinking a toast.

Of great importance to Snorri are the aristocrats themselves, their abilities and skills. As Bagge has pointed out, by contrasting Halldórr Snorrason and Úlfr Óspaksson, Snorri explains what traits he found important for courtiers. Of the heroic Halldórr he writes, "Halldórr var maðr fámæltr ok stirðorðr, bermæltr ok stríðlundaðr ok ómjúkr ".[62] This is meant to explain why Halldórr was not a success at the court of King Haraldr harðráði (Hard Ruler) and left for Iceland. He is contrasted with Úlfr Óspaksson, kind and joyful, an extroverted and eloquent person whom the king liked very much and who was a political success. The saga says, "Hann var inn vitrasti maðr, snjallr í máli, skǫrungr mikill, tryggr ok einfaldr".[63] When he died the king said, "Þar liggr sá nú, er dyggvastr var ok dróttinhollastr".[64] The king made him his *stallari* (spokesman) and also a *lendr maðr*, and thus he was well rewarded.[65] This deliberate juxtaposition of Halldórr and Úlfr is not found in *Morkinskinna*, but is Snorri's calculated addition.[66]

Reading about *preudommes* and *anti-preudommes* is just like reading about Halldórr and Úlfr. Both were brave and experienced warriors. Halldórr fits the *anti-preudomme* as explained by Crouch thus, he "could not guard his tongue and said things he had better not have said".[67] On the other hand the affable Úlfr corresponds completely to the ideal *preudomme* Crouch describes.

Snorri also elaborated on the contrast between the brothers and kings Sigurðr Jórsalafari (Jerusalemfarer) and Eysteinn, and added several traits to the description of the latter. Even though he minimises the difference between the two found in *Morkinskinna*, there is hardly any doubt that he favoured King Eysteinn. In *Morkinskinna* Sigurðr is strong and a great warrior; Eysteinn on the other hand is dexterous (hagr). Snorri stresses this second trait and makes Eysteinn supple in sports (skating, skiing).

---

62 "Halldór seldom spoke and was not eloquent, but outspoken, grumpy and unrelenting" (*Heimskringla* III, 120).

63 "He was among the wisest of men, most eloquent, a very upright man, faithful and frank" (*Heimskringla* III, 120).

64 "There lies the one who was most trustworthy and loyal" (*Heimskringla* III, 175).

65 Bagge 1991, 171, 152–153.

66 Andersson 2012, 122–123.

67 Crouch 2005, 51.

He also stresses his intelligence and adds to his abilities saying that he has a much better understanding of law and is a much smoother talker (*sléttorðari*).[68] This last trait was much admired by Snorri, demonstrated by his description of the smooth and convincing talker, the god Óðinn "talaði svá snjallt ok slétt at ǫllum er á heyrðu þótti þat eina satt".[69] Eysteinn had a knowledge of law in common with Snorri. Thus, Eysteinn must have been much more to Snorri's liking, even though he does not belittle physical strength or martial achievements.[70] Sigurðr is reminiscent of able and warlike knights, or even an *anti-preudomme* like Halldórr, while Eysteinn is more of a *preudomme*, a *curialis* type.

It is of some interest to notice that both King Sverrir and his grandson, King Hákon, were of small stature. We have a reason to believe that Snorri was not tall either and rather lightly built and stood closer to Eysteinn in that respect.[71]

It is the political side of aristocratic behaviour that interests Snorri most. His heroes are men who knew the law and historical rights of the subjects, and who explained them eloquently and boldly at assemblies in the presence of the king. Secondly, Snorri seems to be fond of men who are wise, eloquent and bold when addressing dignitaries, and of clever envoys because of their diplomatic skills. In fact, Sighvatr Þórðarson is a member of both groups. Most of these stories seem to be Snorri's own inventions or adaptations and much expanded by him, which indicates a special interest in such men and their political skills.[72]

The more we study *Heimskringla*, the clearer it becomes that Snorri must have been interested in the position of *preudommes* and *curiales* at courts. Úlfr Óspaksson was the ideal for Snorri, a magnificient man, wise, eloquent, a poet, enterprising and upright (*skǫrungr mikill*), and became *stallari*, faithful and resolute. This is reminiscent of the ideal *curialis*, except that Úlfr was not a learned man in the usual sense.

---

68 *Morkinskinna* II, 131–133; *Heimskringla* III, 259–262.

69 "... talked so eloquently and smoothly that all who heard it regarded it as the only truth" (*Heimskringla* I, 17).

70 Andersson 2012, 131–134; Helgi Þorláksson 1979b. Bagge thinks Snorri's ideal is a tall and strong king (see Bagge 1991, 150). This is doubtful since Snorri seems to like men who are agile, supple, smooth and dexterous more than the ones who are just strong. For a more detailed discussion of this see pp. 88–90 in this book.

71 Helgi Þorláksson 1979b.

72 For more detail on this and the political side see pp. 87–88 in this book.

Snorri's Anti-aristocratic Flaws?

Snorri no doubt looked up to ideal courtiers, but what about noble descent and wealth, courage and martial dexterity in his case? Snorri was not a high-born man, even though his father was a *goði*. Snorri's father's line has already been described, but his mother was of quite distinguished descent, although men in her male line must be regarded as no more than petty chieftains. However, Snorri was only third in line of her sons and of limited means when he married in 1202. His wife Herdís was the daughter of Bersi, a wealthy priest of obscure descent, probably of humble stock. This indicates that Snorri was not counted among the most distinguished families. Was not this an impediment to his rise as a royal servant of distinction? The most likely answer is that the Birkibeinar, not least King Sverrir himself, had promoted lowly men, elevated many commoners.[73] The chances of Snorri becoming a common courtier were fair.

However, King Sverrir's policy was far from anti-aristocratic. Some of the families of *lendir menn* supported him, others he tried to reconcile with after he had defeated King Magnús Erlingsson in 1184 and some of his own men he married off to women of the old *lendir menn* families.[74] In the eyes of the Birkibeinar, noble descent was important. When King Sverrir died in 1202, more men of the old families of *lendir menn* were willing to serve the kings.[75] And since there were probably only fifteen or so *lendir menn* during the reign of King Hákon *gamli*, the chances around 1220 for such an advancement were scant. Snorri must have had something extra to compensate for his lack of noble descent. Early in his reign the adversaries of King Sverrir called one of his *lendir menn* "þorparason" (a son of a common farmer), but a source in Latin calls the same man "*vir praeclarus et elegans*" which indicates some important merits (*praeclarus* meaning "famous" or "excellent").[76] Of course Snorri was not a *þorparason* but he was not of old-established high-ranking men on his father's side and therefore would have had to excel in something else to become a *lendr maðr*. His upbringing at Oddi was important so he may have been seen as a man *praeclarus et elegans*. However, such an advancement to *lendr maðr*

73 Bagge 1991, 9, 20, 126.
74 *Sverris saga*, 155.
75 Helle 1974, 74–76.
76 *Sverris saga* 72, 140.

was probably not as straightforward in 1220 as it had been in the early years of Sverrir's reign.

There are scholars who maintain that Snorri was not so warlike, lacked prowess and might even have acted in a cowardly manner at times.[77] His alleged cowardice may have had other causes, such as a hatred of bloodshed, a strong desire to keep the peace, serious reverance for the holy days of the church and so on.[78] Generally speaking his contemporaries do not seem to have found fault with him in this respect.[79] It has also been suggested that he may have followed in the steps of Richard Lionheart and Philip Augustus, who avoided battles; it is claimed that they followed the advice of the most popular military handbook of the time, Vegetius's *Art of War,* to try every expedient before bringing matters to that last extremity of war.[80] Even though a *preudomme* was knowledgeable in the art of war, he was a man of restraint in terms of violence, as explained by Crouch. Snorri owned armour, learned to use a buckler and built a so-called *kastali* (castle) in 1213,[81] and was probably knowledgeable about martial matters. Otherwise he would hardly have been appointed as a *skutilsveinn*.

Crouch mentions six points as qualities that were found desirable in noble conduct: 1. loyalty; 2. forbearance; 3. hardiness; 4. largesse or liberality; 5. the Davidic ethic; and 6. honour.[82] As to the first point, there is no doubt that through his poems Snorri must have convinced the leaders of the Birkibeinar of his support, even loyalty. The second point, forbearance, means self-control, restraint, reticence, patience. For instance, a violent man who captured an enemy would most likely slaughter or mutilate him. A *preudomme* would avoid a heedless and needless violence and consider demanding a ransom for the captured, as Crouch points out. The difference is clear when Snorri is compared with some of his contemporary *goðar*, who mutilated their enemies or had them killed, burnt their houses and had their churches deprived of

---

77 Sigurður Nordal 1920, 50–59; Árni Pálsson 1947, 119–120, 158.

78 In 1236 Snorri withdrew and would not engage in battle because of the impending holidays (either the beginning of Lent or Easter, *Sturlunga saga* I, 390). The Church preached peace during certain periods of the year and Snorri's behaviour would have been found acceptable by prelates and most kings.

79 Wanner 2008, 44–46.

80 Brown 2012, 54–55.

81 *Sturlunga saga* I, 333.

82 Crouch 2005, 56–80.

their belongings. Snorri was neither violent nor cruel and seems to have spared the lives of his enemies and treated them mercifully. As a *goði* he had to be prepared to have men killed. However, the point was restraint, tamed and limited violence that could be justified.

For the third point, hardiness, Crouch has not much to say. "Hardy" did not just mean being physically strong and bold and able as a warrior, it also referred to endurance, to keeping calm at difficult moments, and to rising early and working hard all day long. What Snorri may have lacked in physical strength and abilities to fight he would have compensated for in his efficiency and industriousness and we have reason to believe that he kept a level head at difficult moments. Sigurður Nordal writes that Snorri was fairly civilized and suggests that he was in fact unjust even though it was not evident because he lacked hardness.[83] Here it is suggested that Snorri restrained his violence because he wanted to be civilized.

The fourth point, largesse or Snorri's generosity has been doubted. He has been seen as a greedy and mean man.[84] We can ask (if it is true) whether this was a disadvantage? Evidently not, since we hear of splendid banquets he gave at his home and of precious gifts, and that is what counted.[85] He seems to have met the general demands for a chieftain in banquets and gifts whether he was mean or not.

By the Davidic ethic Crouch means the clerical ethic, securing peace, protecting church buildings and the activities of the clergy. When Bishop Guðmundr Arason was in dire straits in 1209, almost mobbed by several of the Icelandic *stórgoðar*, Snorri invited him to stay with him at Reykholt. The bishop accepted and stayed with Snorri for the best part of a year. This the bishop would not have done had Snorri not somehow been to his liking. In 1234 he considered Snorri to be his friend.[86] When Snorri settled in the Borgarfjǫrðr district in 1202, it did not take him long to become the most powerful *goði* of the area. There is hardly any doubt that the farmers opted for a strong and peaceful leader and the church supported this if this leader would also support and protect the routine operations of the clergy.[87] Snorri mastered his task and became the *stórgoði*

---

83   He writes, "að meir hafi hann brostið til ofbeldisverka harðfengi en ranglæti" (Sigurður Nordal 1942, 343).

84   Sigurður Nordal 1920, 44–50; Árni Pálsson 1947, 146–147, 183.

85   *Sturlunga saga* I, 304 (two eminent banquets), 315, 347, 362.

86   *Sturlunga saga* I, 371.

87   Helgi Þorláksson 2010, 68–71.

of the area, without any incidents as far as we know. All was quiet and peaceful and the church in Borgarfjǫrðr must have operated in a most satisfying way for the clergy. Unlike the *goði* Þorvaldr Vatnsfirðingr, Snorri would not attack his adversaries during Lent or Easter.[88]

The last point of honour, enjoing social respect, was important to Snorri and here he enhanced his reputation just before he left Iceland. *Íslendinga saga* says his social honour (*virðing*) increased considerably just before 1218.[89]

Groups of Aristocrats in Iceland

We can now turn back to the question of how to understand and use the concept "aristocratic" in twelfth- and thirteenth-century history in Iceland. It is suggested here that a possible way of explaining twelfth-century and early thirteenth-century aristocrats in Iceland is to divide them into two groups. On the one hand is the clerical gentry and on the other those who were aspiring for some advancement at courts abroad and for whom the Latin word *curalitas* would apply, i.e. *courtliness* or *cortoisie*.[90] In the first group were those *goðar* who were ordained as deacons or priests, but did not (as far as we know) become courtiers or seek any advancement at foreign courts. These *goðar* were able clerics at major churches which they kept well, men like Jón Loftsson and two of his sons (Sæmundr and Ormr), and also Páll Sǫlvason at Reykholt and Þorvaldr Gizurarson and many more from the times of Ari *fróði* (the Learned) onwards.[91] In the other were *goðar* like Loftr Pálsson, Hrafn Sveinbjarnarson, Snorri Sturluson, Árni *óreiða* Magnússon and Gizurr Þorvaldsson. They were of *goðar* families, brought up to become administrators and men of power.[92] They were not ordained or only had the lower orders of ordination, but

---

88   *Sturlunga saga* I, 390. Scholars have had difficulties in believing that Snorri told the truth when he said he would not fight in 1236 because of the coming holidays and find it most probable that he flinched but they are not justified in this. Here Snorri paid heed to the teachings of the Church.

89   *Sturlunga saga* I, 269.

90   On these words see Crouch 2005, 8, 16, 24.

91   On these ordained chieftains, their numbers, social position and more see Orri Vésteinsson 2000, 182–194.

92   Loftr was a son of Bishop Páll who earlier had functioned as a *goði*, a position taken over by Loftr. His alleged dexterity, learning and wisdom has already been mentioned. Árni *óreiða* (literally, "chaos") was of the family of *allsherjargoðar*, who had

adopted the conduct of *curiales* and prepared for becoming accepted by foreign dignitaries. The days of the first group were doomed when in 1190 the archbishop stipulated that *goðar* could no longer take holy orders, at least not the higher ones, and subdeacons, deacons and priests could not bring cases to courts.[93] Finally, it dawned on the *goðar* that they had to take the policy of the Church seriously, and could not function as ordained clerics and secular chieftains simultaneously. This fact must have shaped the second group.

A man of the first group was Gizurr Hallsson (d. 1206), a *goði* and deacon, the father of Þorvaldr and grandfather of Earl Gizurr Þorvaldsson. Since Gizurr Hallsson became *stallari* at a Norwegian court he may, however, be seen as belonging to both groups. Another was Páll, son of Jón Loftsson. He seemed not to know which path to follow, the clerical or the courtly-secular. He was deacon and married and was said to be *courtois*. Then he travelled abroad and stayed with the Earl of Orkney, who kept him in high esteem, according to *Páls saga byskups* (The Saga of Bishop Páll). Afterwards Páll studied in England and when back home he excelled in "the courtoisie of his learning". He became a *goði*, was a great administrator, his saga says, and it describes him as if he were a typical *preudomme*. Páll was consecrated bishop in 1195.[94]

The decisive factor for the second group, Snorri, Loftr, Hrafn, Árni *óreiða* and Gizurr Þorvaldsson, are the Western European codes of conduct and lifestyles for aristocrats of the late twelfth century, which they tried to match and live up to. The first group, the clerical gentry (*kirkjugoðar*), must have been aristocratic in their own way around 1130 and later, and they had their own habitus, both secular and clerical. However, as far as we know, they did not have any specific code of conduct, no prescriptions for their conduct, only general norms. They are mostly left out of this discussion because Snorri did not belong to their group. Even though Snorri's group had a foreign code of conduct to follow and foreign models for their lifestyles, it must have been markedly influenced by the first group.

the dignified role of "presidents" at the *Alþingi*. Árni himself held this occupation of *allsherjargoði* for some time.

93   For more details see below.

94   *Páls saga byskups*, 297–299. The *goði* Þorvarðr Þorgeirsson was a courtier in Norway and ended his days as a monk (d. 1207), but we know too little to put him into a group here. There are, however, indications, he is the first *goði* we hear of having *fylgðarmenn* (a retine).

Then there were those who belonged to neither group. We are in the fortunate situation of having the full (or the so-called separate) saga of the *goði* Hrafn Sveinbjarnarson preserved. It explains the courtliness of Hrafn and draws a picture of his adversary as a distinct opposite. His adversary was the *goði* Þorvaldr Vatnsfirðingr, brought up in a violent milieu where there was not much restraint on killing and maiming, if the saga speaks true. Þorvaldr is shown as deceitful and is compared to a wolf. He attacked Hrafn during Lent, set his buildings on fire, had Hrafn killed in 1213 and his close relative mutilated, and deprived the church at Hrafn's homeplace Eyrr (Eyri) of its belongings. Þorvaldr acted in opposition to foreign codes of conduct for nobles, behaved like an unruly knight and was uncivilized in that respect. His behaviour was not aristocratic in the sense described and he could not be accepted as an aristocrat in Snorri's group as explained above. The picture of him is most likely very biased in the saga and on the other hand Hrafn is depicted in an idealized way as civilized, a man of restraint, placable, reasonable, humble, helping the inferior and so on.[95] The contrast is very interesting and explains what courtly men were like, and how they were expected to behave. Þorvaldr was not *kirkjugoði* and neither was he courtly. According to the saga of Hrafn, Þorvaldr did not meet the demands of his times for aristocratic conduct and is therefore not counted here among the aristocrats.[96]

Needless to say, in the first half of the thirteenth century, many *stórgoðar* must have tried to adapt to the new codes of courtly conduct and follow new lifestyles even though they did not aspire to becoming common courtiers or administrative *curiales*. However, the transformation obviously took some time and the new way of courtly behaviour among the magnates was probably only fully introduced after 1262. Despite their more civilized habits, the prowess of knights was always admired and when they were defending their rights or honour they were supposed to show some rage and fury. This often manifested itself as unrestrained violence against commoners.[97] Rage and fury (*ofsi*), were seen as praiseworthy for promising young chieftains in thirteenth-century Iceland

---

95   On the adversaries Hrafn and Þorvaldr, see *Hrafns saga hin séstaka*.
96   In accordance with an arbitration after the killing of Hrafn, Þorvaldr had to stay abroad for some years and was in Rome for some time. He later became Snorri's son in law and may have tried to improve his conduct after spending time abroad.
97   Kaeuper 1999, 84–86, 144, 185–190.

prior to 1262.[98] It has been suggested that this may have been due to influence from abroad.[99]

Nordic Aristocratic Traits

If the Norwegian court adopted chivalrous or courteous ways during the early years of King Hákon *gamli*, as is often pointed out, what was the situation like before? In Norway there were old, noble families, probably with their own aristocratic values, and kings and courtiers who had travelled widely abroad and most certainly knew aristocratic ways of life. One example is Earl Rǫgnvaldr Kali (d. 1158) of Orkney, who was Norwegian in origin. There is a strophe by him where he explains what he could accomplish. This he prided himself on, but most of it was probably appropriate for aristocrats in general, as we will see below. According to the strophe, an aristocrat like him knew how to read books, construe verses and understand runes. He was also accomplished in sports like chess, skiing, shooting and sailing (rowing). Still another art he mastered was carpentry (and/or the work of blacksmiths) and finally he mentions playing a harp.[100]

Snorri must have been able to read and probably also to write since he functioned as lawspeaker at the *Alþingi*. He most certainly knew how to construe verses and probably knew runes. Of his knowledge of sports we do not hear much. A certain Tafl-Bergr was staying with him in 1222, probably clever at *tafl* (*tafl* usually means chess, here possibly *hnefatafl* or some other kind of a board game), and Snorri prided himself in his poem *Háttatal* of sailing skills and sailing experience and says he is widely known for this (Ht. 27, 28). And he apparently admired King Eysteinn for being clever at skiing and skating.

The *goði* Hrafn Sveinbjarnarson was an accomplished man, his saga tells us. Hrafn seems to have adopted aristocratic codes of conduct and the arts which explains, according to his saga, why he was held in high

---

98 *Sturlunga saga* I, 311, 411; II, 86. The word *ákafi* is also used (I, 271).
99 Einar Ól. Sveinsson 1940, 27, 63–64, 79; Einar Ól. Sveinsson 1934, xxix.
100 Brown 2012, 30. The strophe goes like this: "Tafl emk ǫrr at efla/íþróttir kannk níu/ týnik trauðla rúnum/tíð er mér bók ok smíðir./Skríða kannk á skíðum/skýtk ok ræ'k svát nýtir/hvárt tveggja kannk hyggja/harpslǫtt ok bragþǫttu" (*Orkneyinga saga*, 130).

esteem among dignitaries abroad. He was a master craftsman in wood and iron as well as a poet, the saga says that "He was the greatest of physicians and a man of fine learning even though he only took the lowest of holy orders." The saga goes on to say:

> ... lǫgspakr maðr ok vel máli farinn, minnigr, at ǫllu fróðr. ... syndr vel ok við allt fimr, þat er hann hafðisk at, bogmaðr mikill ok skaut manna bezt handskoti. Hrafn fór ungr brott af landi ok fekk góða virðing í ǫðrum lǫndum af hǫfðingjum sem vitni bar um þær gǫrsimar, er Bjarni biskup sendi honum ...[101]

Bjarni was of noble breed in Orkney and bishop there after 1188.

The terms that were applied to Earl Rǫgnvaldr, Hrafn and King Eysteinn were *mjúkleikr* and *fimi*, meaning that they were all physically supple and swift and agile. We are not told that they were physically strong, heavy or warlike. Skiing, skating and swimming were their sports and when they were shooting their physical strength was not their merit, rather they were good marksmen.[102] We can conclude that courtiers to the Norwegian kings did not necessarily have to be warlike, physically strong, tall and heavy.

Even though the saga of Hrafn may exaggerate his merits, it is worthwhile studying what accomplishments it identifies as appropriate for aristocrats. The following, said about Hrafn, applies to Snorri: "He was knowledgeable about law and spoke eloquently ... and was learned in all things". Knowledge of law and eloquence also distinguished King Eysteinn. And all four mastered oral arts in one way or another.

Somewhat unexpectedly both Earl Rǫgnvaldr Kali and the narrator of *Hrafns saga* mention carpentry or the art of blacksmiths as fit for them and therefore aristocrats; King Eysteinn was called *hagr* (dexterous) and Sturla Þórðarson says in his *Íslendinga saga* that Snorri was "hagr á allt þat, er hann tók höndum til" ("skilled with his hands"), perhaps including

---

101 *Hrafns saga Sveinbjarnarsonar*, 2. "... knowledgeable about law and spoke eloquently, had an excellent memory and was learned in all things [*at ǫllu fróðr*] ... He was a good swimmer, agile [*fimr*] in all that he did. He was a great archer and among the best at throwing. He travelled abroad as a young man and gained respect from dignitaries in other countries. To prove this were precious things [*gǫrsimar, gersemar*] which Bishop Bjarni ... sent to him" (translation based on Brown 2012, 30).

102 Eysteinn prided himself of this, Rǫgnvaldr says "skýtr svá at nýtir" and Hrafn was good at "handskot".

carpentry.[103] We have reason to think that this was seen as an important trait for aristocrats, since Snorri himself says about St Óláfr, "hagr ok sjónhannarr um smíðir allar".[104] Something similar is told of Páll Jónsson from Oddi, who later became bishop, "hagr at hvívetna því er hann gerði, bæði at riti ok at öðru".[105] Páll spent time in Orkney and gained respect from the earl, his saga tells us.[106] His son Loftr was also in Orkney and met Bishop Bjarni and later stayed with King Ingi of Norway and Earl Hákon *galinn* and accepted precious gifts from the latter. We are told that the greatest merits of Loftr were *hagleikr* (dexterity), *lærdómr* (learning) and *vitrleiki* (wisdom).[107]

King Eysteinn, Earl Rǫgnvaldr and Hrafn were intelligent men, dexterous, supple and eloquent and the legal knowledge of Eysteinn and Hrafn was noteworthy. We may call them, and Bishop Páll and his son Loftr, Nordic aristocrats but in fact they seem much akin to the foreign courtiers we mentioned above, men whose merits did not lie mainly in physical strength or fighting skills. They were depicted as being close to an international ideal of a nobleman which became more important during the twelfth century.

Old Lore

Earl Rǫgnvaldr seems to have been quite versatile. With the Icelander Hallr, he composed a poem called *Háttalykill* on ancient kings (including Danish ones) in about 1142. To a certain extent Snorri imitated them in his *Háttatal*. By around 1185 the Icelanders had become well known in Denmark and Norway for their knowledge of the Nordic kings of former times and their history.[108]

When Snorri lived at Oddi as a young man he must have known the poem *Noregskonungatal*, mentioned above, composed to honour his foster-father, Jón Loftsson, whose grandfather was the Norwegian king,

---

103 *Sturlunga saga* I, 269.
104 "dexterous and had a keen eye for all kinds of 'smíðir'" (*Heimskringla* II, 4). Carpentry, ironworking?
105 "dexterous in all that he was doing, equally so in writing and in other activities" (*Páls saga byskups*, 297).
106 *Páls saga byskups*, 297–298.
107 *Páls saga byskups*, 315–316, 324.
108 On this see Bjarni Guðnason 1982, v–xviii; Theodoricus Monachus, 1.

Magnús *berfœttr*. In the poem, Jón's ancestry is traced back to ancient kings and the poem gives some information on the lives of each of them. The knowledgeable Sæmundr *fróði* of Oddi was Jón's other grandfather, and many scholars have pointed out that the Oddaverjar must have preserved tales of the royal lines of Denmark and Norway and a vast collection of old poems, precious sources for the history of ancient kings. Such knowledge obviously aroused great interest at the Danish and Norwegian courts. It appealed to Nordic aristocrats, the men of noble breed who aspired to become accepted by the highest ranking in society

A man like Snorri with a vast knowledge of old lore, history, gene-alogy, mythology and a knowledge of kings of former times would have aroused interest at the courts and would have been welcomed and well rewarded. However, he would have been looked upon as an entertainer and would not necessarily have been accepted as a courtier unless he was proficient in other matters and followed a code of conduct found fit for courtiers.

Education and Prerequisites for the Leaders of the Court

What about Snorri's education? As some scholars have pointed out, there are reasons to believe that his knowledge of Latin learning was at least limited.[109] His *Edda* does not indicate that he went in for hard Latin or religious studies.[110] Was not that a serious drawback for an aristocrat aspiring to become a royal servant and even a counsellor to the king? And how could Snorri function as a lawspeaker without a firm grasp of Latin? The answer is simply that he could hire priests or other well-educated clergy to explain Latin texts to him. By way of comparison German nobles did not usually understand Latin and had to have letters in that language translated.[111] This is not to say that Snorri's knowledge of Latin might not have been considerable but we do not know. It has been suggested that Snorri received the education of a layman.[112] Why did

109 Helgi Þorláksson 2014, 357–362.
110 Faulkes 1993; Wanner 2008, 51, 66–68.
111 For corresponding cases, help from experts for kings and nobles with limited or no knowledge of Latin see Bumke 2000, 426–436.
112 Turville-Petre 1967/1953, 121; Gísli Sigurðsson 2013, 201–202, 206–207, 212.

not he acquire a thorough Latin learning and what does "the education of a layman" mean?

Archbishop Eiríkr sent a letter to Iceland in 1190, when Snorri was about twelve, which stipulated two things. First, subdeacons and men with higher orders could not act as plaintiffs, they could not bring their own cases to court. Secondly, *goðar* could no longer be ordained.[113] In his early twenties, Snorri functioned as a representative for Sæmundr, the eldest son of Jón Loftsson, in a political dispute and brought a case to a court.[114] He therefore could hardly have had orders higher than those of acolyte, one of the inferior ones. Snorri's role as a plaintiff thus seems to be the reason why he did not take any higher orders, if he took any at all. He might, despite that, have known some Latin. In the 1190s the Oddaverjar, however, probably decided that Snorri should prepare for some political content to his studies, engage in legal matters and not take the higher orders. Latin learning was, therefore, not to be his main concern among the arts, but rather law, lore and poetry. Political disputes and manoeuvres and legal cases were to be his line. Before we turn to the law we will consider the old lore and poetry.

As a receptive pupil at Oddi, Snorri laid the foundations for his work on poetry and kings, *Snorra-Edda* and *Óláfs saga helga*. Such a scholarly approach could be seen as influenced by the renaissance of the twelfth century.[115] More typical of such an influence may be the interest in the old gods, such as those of Greece and Rome, while the Nordic ones were of interest too. We are told that Earl Skúli once asked Snorri to compose a verse about a certain courtier and compare him with Óðinn, which Snorri did, of course.[116] Snorri is seen by Skúli as both a poet and a scholar, knowledgeable about the old gods. Snorri not only presented old metres in a systematic way in his *Háttatal* and *Skáldskaparmál*, he also presented the mythology in a systematic way in his *Gylfaginning*. Moreover, he connected old Greek and Nordic lore by tracing the origins of the god Óðinn back to Asia Minor, thus tracing old royal lines back to Troy. Such a connection was seen as vital for noble families in Western Europe, and the Nordic ones could not be inferior.

---

113 *DI* I, 291; the letter refers especially to *kennimenn*. The wording is "að vígja eigi þá menn er goðorð hafa".
114 *Sturlunga saga* I, 237–238.
115 Mundal 2007; Lindkvist 2007.
116 *Hákonar saga Hákonarsonar* II, 42–43.

Would Snorri, as a chieftain, have been welcomed at the Norwegian court and been offered the position of a courtier if he had not also excelled as a poet and a scholar with a vast knowledge of old poetry? Snorri's poetic skills drew the attention of Hákon *galinn* and could have given admission to his court. However, it is difficult to see why poetic skills and a knowledge of old poetry could have been a prerequisite for becoming a common courtier any more than a knowledge of mythology, old lore or history. Most powerful chieftains from Iceland who visited Norway in Snorri's time became courtiers, Kolbeinn *ungi* (the Young) being an exception. Snorri therefore naturally became a courtier and his poetic skills and vast knowledge of old poetry was probably not a prerequisite.

In Snorri's case his political position in Iceland and his support of the Birkibeinar were no doubt of more importance for him being accepted as a courtier, and a dignified manner must have helped. But the main questions here are what secured his acceptance as a *skutilsveinn* and *lendr maðr*. Of the skills mentioned above, what would have helped a *skutilsveinn* most were his abilities as a foreman or supervisor or administrator. At the court, Snorri was in charge of a group of men and he was used to giving orders. Icelandic chieftains had some basic knowledge of mustering a force. In around 1216 Snorri did this against his enemies at the *Alþingi* and was criticized by his brother for his method. Later Snorri's former son-in-law, Árni *óreiða* Magnússon, a good friend of King Hákon, helped Snorri at the *Alþingi* and mustered a force in a Norwegian fashion, but did not do it skilfully because of inexperience.[117] This shows that experienced chieftains in Iceland had to understand strategy, and how to plan an army's movements and positions. The *skutilsveinn* was also obliged to take care of guards when the king was travelling, either by ship or by horse. We have no reason to doubt Snorri's horsemanship and he prides himself on his sailing skills and experience in *Háttatal*.

Many Icelandic poets and scholars, even a few who were also *goðar*, stayed at the court, but did not experience such an advancement as Snorri did. What is more, Snorri's nephew Sturla Sighvatsson was close to King Hákon and went on his errand to Iceland, but did not enjoy such a promotion. Besides Snorri only his son, Jón *murtr* (Small Trout), and Gizurr Þorvaldsson, later earl, were promoted to become *skutilsveinar*.[118]

---

117 *Sturlunga saga* I, 267, 375.
118 Jón Jóhannesson 1958/1948, 210–211.

This was most probably a political decision in both cases, but all three probably had to merit it. Of Jón's character we know next to nothing, but Gizurr was both able and aristocratic and important to the king. He had much experience of strategic matters and in one instance we hear of him sailing, or directing the course of an oceangoing vessel to Iceland.[119] The tasks of the *lendir menn* were similar, they defended the *ríki* (fief) the king granted and were also judges. For this they had to have some understanding of law and legal matters.

Snorri the Lawman

Snorri became a lawman (called a "lawspeaker" in Iceland), and is therefore likely to have studied law. His first term as a lawman started in 1215 and ended in 1218. In this period he was successful in his political dispute with the Oddaverjar family and enjoyed the support of Norwegian merchants. The saga says that it was during this period that his social respect increased most.[120] The office of lawman must have helped in this respect.

While there was no law school as such in Iceland, the Oddi people must have found a teacher for Snorri in legal matters. Prior to 1181 the lawspeakers seldom or never were men of great political importance.[121] In that year the leader of the Haukdælir family, Gizurr Hallsson, was, however, given the position and after that this obviously became a post of considerable significance for the Haukdælir and Sturlungar families. One reason may have been that this post, the only official position in Iceland, gave opportunities to take the initiative in legal matters. However, that was nothing new because powerful chieftains could use lawspeakers as straw men to gain such ends. There was probably another reason for the increased importance of this post. In the twelfth century, jurisprudence was gaining in importance abroad because it was useful for kings, secular princes and prelates in power struggles. Canon law was studied as well as the code of Justinian (d. 530), and new law schools were founded, for instance in Oxford around 1180.[122] The learned Gizurr Hallsson

---

119 "hafði hann mjök leiðsögn í hafinu" (*Sturlunga saga* I, 524).
120 *Sturlunga saga* I, 269.
121 Helgi Þorláksson 2014, 362–367.
122 On the importance of jurisprudence at this time see for instance Cruz and Gerberding 2004, 321–323, 356–357, 360–361.

was widely travelled, had been to Bari and Rome and became *stallari* in Norway, apparently in the early 1150s when negotiations for a new archdiocese in Norway were taking place.[123] The importance of Roman law was increasing, a new understanding of legal issues was being introduced and new legal approaches and men with knowledge in this field became important. It has been argued that Roman law influenced legislation in Iceland prior to 1200.[124] Snorri functioned as lawspeaker from 1215 to 1218, until just before he left Iceland for Norway. There are good reasons to believe that he was acquainted with canon law, which was important at the time of Gregorianism and the *libertas ecclesiae* movement. In 1213 it was announced that the Fourth Lateran Council would convene in Rome in 1215. When some of its resolutions were being introduced in Iceland, the bishops had to cooperate with Snorri the lawspeaker.[125] Snorri's predecessors as lawspeakers, including Gizurr Hallsson (lawspeaker from 1181 to 1202), were educated clerics. But Snorri, no less than Gizurr, was an important politician, which probably counted for more when indigenous laws and canon law were to be merged, as in matters of fasting, and more lenient stipulations for blood affinities in matrimony which were introduced in accordance with the Lateran deliberations. Snorri took care of these legal changes in 1217.

If one person in Iceland was more of an aristocratic model for Snorri than anyone else, it would have been Gizurr Hallsson. From what we can conclude, Gizurr Hallsson was a *curialis* type as Jaeger explains it, learned, polished, politically skilled, very knowledgeable about law, and able as an administrator. That is probably what Snorri aspired to become, a man seen as able to become a close counsellor of kings.[126]

There is little doubt that Snorri had some knowledge of Roman laws

123 *Sturlunga saga* I, 60; Hungrvaka, 35.
124 Sveinbjörn Rafnsson 1977, 720–732; also 1990, 131–148. On critical views of this see Gunnar Karlsson 2004, 34–39.
125 Torfi H. Tulinius 1996.
126 Moore has suggested that clerical skills and clerical culture became fundamental for increasing secular power in Europe in the eleventh and twelfth centuries. He refers to disinherited men who became clerics and emphasizes their role in the formation of state bureaucracies (Moore 2004, 89–92). Bagge criticizes this and does not find anything to support the idea that a class of professional bureaucrats, who depended solely on the king for advancement, existed in Scandinavia. He writes, "On the contrary, some of the best educated royal servants belonged to the top aristocracy" (Bagge 2004, 157–159; also Sverrir Jakobsson 2009, 153–155. Gizurr Hallsson seems to fit in very well with Bagge's description and it is suggested here that Snorri did as well.

and how they could affect Nordic ones. In 1218 this was probably found crucial in Norway and it is interesting to see how Snorri established contact with the lawman Dagfinnr *bóndi* (Farmer), a leading Birkibeinn, and his family in Norway.[127] In 1219 he also visited lawman Áskell (Eskil) in Väster-Götland (Western Götland in modern Sweden). These men probably had plenty to discuss. Those who know the saga of King Hákon *gamli* are well aware of the high regard in which important lawmen were held in Norway around 1220.[128] Back home, Snorri became lawspeaker again, which indicates that this job was vital to him.

There were other ways of establishing contacts in Norway besides sending poetry. Birkibeinar probably needed men who were experienced administrators, knew law, understood government and were experienced speakers at assemblies. Literacy could probably also be very helpful. The prospects were probably not so bleak for Snorri once he had received the presents from Earl Hákon. He then added the office of lawspeaker to his list of promotions. Increasing royal power needed men of this kind and lawman Dagfinnr *bóndi* is a good example.

In summary, we can say that Snorri aspired to become a man of the king of Norway and prepared carefully for that as an aristocrat, poet and a man of law, lore and literature. He had probably made a name for himself in certain circles in Norway as a shrewd political leader, knowledgeable about the past, about poetry and oral traditions, and with a good grasp of legal matters, even Roman and canon law. He was not of the noblest of families in Iceland, but his social and political standing in the country, his administrative skills, learning and conduct helped.

A Courtier and *lendr maðr*

In the spring of 1220 Snorri wanted to take leave from Norway and go home. He was in Bjǫrgvin (Bergen) when the regents prepared a military expedition to Iceland with a host of vessels to retaliate for the alleged injustice of the Oddi people towards Norwegian merchants. Snorri got involved, tried to dissuade the earl from the plan and suggested that instead he himself might intervene in Iceland, sort matters out and

127 *Bóndi* could be used as an honorary title for a yeoman or a squire.
128 *Hákonar saga Hákonarsonar* I, 261–265.

establish peace. Again we become aware of his policy of avoiding physical clashes. The earl agreed and after consultation with him, the young king called off the expedition.[129] The king then made Snorri *lendr maðr* and Snorri received fifteen splendid gifts from the earl. They included a ship on which he left for Iceland.

Hákonar saga Hákonarsonar says: "Var þá í fyrsta sinni rætt um þat af jarli at Snorri skyldi koma landinu undir konung".[130] According to this, Skúli already planned a Norwegian rule in Iceland and Snorri would have been a prospective earl. However, it turned out to be difficult to translate this dignity of *lendr maðr* into Icelandic reality when Snorri returned to Iceland. His return caused a commotion among the Oddi people, probably because of Snorri's title and gifts, and they expected him to turn against them and fight for Norwegian interests. One wonders if the lower title of *skutilsveinn* would not have stirred up less of a commotion.

As mentioned, the *lendir menn* were judges and defended the *ríki* the king granted. Scholars have generally had problems with this and do not find it conceivable that Snorri was granted a fief in Norway. A sixteenth-century annal reports that Snorri "kom fyrstur manna eignum undir konung hér á landi sem var Bessastaðir og Eyvindarstaðir".[131] Could he have given these landholdings in Iceland to the king and then received them back as a fief? Jón Jóhannesson doubted this and said it was possible that Snorri received such a fief in Norway, not in Iceland.[132] We should not be in much doubt since Snorri himself explains the situation in his *Háttatal*: "Vandbaugs veitti sendir/vígrakkr, – en gjöf þakkak/skjaldbrags skylja mildum,/skipreiðu mér – heiða./Fann næst fylkir unna/föl dýr at gjöf stýri/stálhreins. Styrjar deilis/stórlæti sá ek mæta" (Ht. 28).[133] This is in the part of *Háttatal* on King Hákon for whom Snorri uses the words

129 There are different accounts in *Sturlunga saga* and *Hákonar saga* concerning the role of the king in this.

130 "At that occasion for the first time the earl advised that Snorri should arrange for the land to be subjected to the king" (*Hákonar saga Hákonarsonar*, I, 230). *Sturlunga saga* does not state this as explicitly, only mentions "hlýðni við Noregshöfðingja", i.e. "submissiveness towards the regents in Norway" (*Sturlunga saga* I, 278).

131 "... was the first to subjugate some landholdings in the country to the king, i.e. Bessastaðir and Eyvindarstaðir" (*Oddaannálar* og *Oddaverjaannáll*, 146).

132 Jón Jóhannesson 1958/1948, 210–211.

133 Should be read as, Vígrakkr vandbaugs sendir [warrior] veitti mér skipreiðu en þakkak skjaldbraks mildum skylja [the king] heiða gjöf. Fylkir [the king] fann næst unna dýr [ships] föl at gjöf stýri stálhreins. Ek sá mæta stórlæti styrjar deilis.
"The war-bold warrior gave me a ship-levy estate and I thank the prince, generous with battle, for the fine gift. The ruler next found available as a gift ships for the

for kings *fylkir* and *skyli*. Here he says that he was granted a *skipreiða* by the king, and calls it a gift. Further he says that the king (*fylkir*) provided ships for him and again he calls this a gift. Each area called *skipreiða* had to provide one or two ships for *leiðangr*, i.e. for a military expedition to defend the country.[134] During times of peace each *skipreiða* had to contribute a fee to the king.[135] The *skipreiða* Snorri mentions was probably his *veizla* or benefice as a *lendr maðr* and he was expected to receive fifteen marks in silver annually from it as his remuneration.[136] Snorri's *skipreiða* must have been in the west. Firðafylki (Fjordane) had fifteen *skipreiður* and was supposed to provide twenty vessels. Some of the *skipreiður* there therefore had to provide more than one vessel, as Snorri's area was obliged to do, and as is mentioned in the strophe.[137] It has been suggested that Snorri's later title, *fólgsnarjarl* (given to him in 1239), was derived from the name of the island Fólgsn or Fosen.[138] It is, however, difficult to see that Fosen (Storfosna) in Mæri (Nordmøre) in Skúli's area was Snorri's *skipreiða* in 1220. If it was not a *skipreiða*, it could have been granted as a *lén* or benefice (a manor or manors), but then Snorri would not have called it *skipreiða*.

Lendir menn were usually wealthy men of noble origin; and since they were allowed to have their own retinue of armed men, people would respect them, if only for that. During social unrest and uprisings the *lendir menn* were active; rioting groups like Slittungar and Ribbungar often saw *lendir menn* as their most important targets. The *lendir menn* were always expected to defend their king. Snorri was not a great warrior; on

---

steersman [the poet]. I saw the splendid munificence of the king" (transl. Faulkes, *Snorri Sturluson, Edda*, 184).

134 Wanner thinks the king gave the ships personally to Snorri which then would be inconsistent with what Sturla says, that the earl gave a ship to Snorri, not the king (Wanner 2008, 109,110). However, if Snorri is saying that the ships the king gave were a part of the *skipreiða* there is no inconsistency.

135 See for instance *Hákonar saga Hákonarsonar* I, 231; each *skipreiða* at that time (in 1220) contributed to both the earl (1/3) and the king (2/3).

136 *Hirdskråen. Hirdloven til Norges konge*, 86.

137 The numbers are based on *Norges historie* (Cappelens) 15, see no. 47. Leidangen, skipreidene (map). Sunnmæri and Hǫrðaland are out of the question, see the map in *Norges historie*.

138 Hallan thinks Snorri kept Fosen as his benefice or fief (Hallan 1972, 165–166, 169–171). *Hákonar saga* only says that Hákon made Snorri a *lendr maðr*; *Sturlunga saga*, on the other hand, says that both the king and the earl did. Formally it was a task of the king but the earl no doubt gave his consent. *Fólgsnarjarl* is usually taken to mean "a secret earl", i.e. the nomination was kept secret until the time was right to announce it.

the other hand, as mentioned above, he may have been knowledgeable about the art of war.

We see that some of the *lendir menn* provided new warships for the king, as in 1219 Jón *stál* (Steel) did, possibly for the Iceland expedition, Ívar *nef* (Nose) did against the Ribbungar in 1221 and in around 1253 Gunnarr *konungsfrændi* (the king's relative) did.[139] Was Snorri also expected to provide some armament or victuals? One possible answer is *vaðmál* (homespun), and especially the better types for sails and covers of ships (*tjǫld*). The *lendr maðr* had to see to it that sails for the warships of the navy (*leiðangr*) were in order or else to provide for what was needed.[140] At that time Icelandic *vaðmál* was in demand in Norway, as evidenced by the amount confiscated by the Oddi people at the Eyrar harbour in 1218; they are reported to have seized no less than twelve tons of *vaðmál*, belonging to some Norwegian merchants there.[141]

Snorri says that the *lendr maðr* was supposed to function as a judge in his fief. Further the *lendr maðr* was expected to function as a policeman or constable in cases of manslaughter, wounding, fighting of groups of five or more and thefts. He had to take violators into custody and protect ordinary people from thieves and robbers.[142] Snorri was used to such tasks as a *stórgoði* in Iceland.

As a counsellor to the king, Snorri the *lendr maðr* must often have been in the presence of the king in 1220 before he left for Iceland. Under such circumstances he could make use of his vast knowledge of history, lore and mythology. It is a tempting thought that the regents in Norway charged Snorri with the task of writing about Norwegian history and lore.

Before Snorri left Norway for Iceland he made a deal with the earl to send his son as a hostage or as a surety for carrying out what he had promised, which was to make the Icelanders submissive towards the regents in Norway. His son, Jón *murtr,* left Iceland for Norway in 1221 and stayed with the earl. He came back in 1224. Snorri had secured peace for the Norwegian merchants and the Norwegian regents seem to have found this satisfying.[143]

139 *Hákonar saga Hákonarsonar* I, 227, 243, 250–251; II, 130, 163.
140 Bøe 1965, 501.
141 *Hákonar saga Hákonarsonar* I, 214; *Islandske Annaler*, 125.
142 Helle 1974, 188–189.
143 *Sturlunga saga* I, 278, 286, 304

Back Home, Snorri the Magnate

Snorri returned from Norway a different man in the social sense. Most important for our context is that *lendir menn* were as aristocratic as could be expected for the king's men. They behaved accordingly as is indicated by *Morkinskinna* which says about a certain lady, a "dýrlig kona" ("a glorious woman") who arrived in Bjǫrgvin in a ship that she "fór svá vegliga sem lendir menn" ("travelled in a stately manner like *lendir menn*").[144] This means that from now on Snorri was expected to adopt the most aristocratic conduct and dignified lifestyle.

How did Snorri act as a *lendr maðr* and how did this affect his lifestyle and code of conduct? Already by 1222 he had taken over as lawspeaker and kept that post for nine years or even longer. In 1224 he took a second wife, Hallveig Ormsdóttir, a wealthy woman of noble descent (the Oddi family), after which he had more property at his disposal than any other man in the country, according to the saga.[145] Hallveig descended from King Magnús *berfœttr* and it has been suggested that by this connection Snorri became more eligible or better qualified to be earl.[146] Between around 1221 and 1225 Snorri lived at Stafholt. Some think this was because of extensive building activities that Snorri started at Reykholt.[147] These activities cannot be dated precisely. Archaeological investigations at Reykholt have, however, shown that individual houses were built, probably in Snorri's time, replacing the earlier dwelling which was a longhouse of a type commonly found in Iceland from the time of its earliest settlement.[148] The building of separate houses was a fairly new trend in Sweden and Norway at that time, and Snorri had ample opportunity to study this style while staying in these countries. *Sturlunga saga* mentions a *stofa* which Snorri had built in 1233 of timber which was brought from Skagafjǫrðr. It was most probably imported from Norway. It has been suggested that the *stofa* was based on the model of buildings like the Raulandsstova in Norway.[149] A *loft* is mentioned at Reykholt in 1236 and 1241. It has been argued that this was a special two-storey building made of timber in a

---

144 *Morkinskinna* II, 223.
145 *Sturlunga saga* I, 304.
146 Torfi H. Tulinius 2000. 54–55, 60. Close in-laws of the king were eligible as earls.
147 Óskar Guðmundsson 2009, 237–240.
148 Guðrún Sveinbjarnardóttir 2012, 262–264; see also Guðrún Sveinbjarnardóttir and Guðrún Harðardóttir, pp. 253–261 in this book.
149 Arnheiður Sigurðardóttir 1966, 56–57; Guðrún Harðardóttir 2006, 49–52; see also Guðrún Sveinbjarnardóttir and Guðrún Harðardóttir, pp. 243, 256 in this book.

Figure 2. The church at Reykholt seems to have been rather well furnished in Snorri's time. The deed of the church shows that Snorri donated a shrine with relics and in 1224 or somewhat later he and his wife donated two or more *klukkur* (sing. *klukka*), which were probably bells of some considerable size. On the same occasion the church was furnished with six *sǫngmeyjar* (lit. "song maidens"), probably rather small bells, and in addition first class vestments and tvo enamelled crosses and an image (*skript*). A bell fragment, dated to the early twelfth century, was found at the church site. It may have been a *sǫngmær* (plur. *sǫngmeyjar*) which bright sound will have been heard when the priest walked into the chancel together with his assistant. Drawing: Stefán Ólafsson.

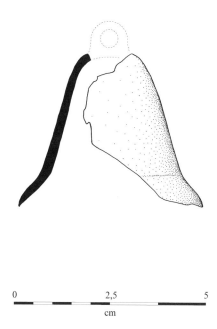

```
0                        2,5                        5
                          cm
```

Norwegian style.[150] Snorri had a warm pool and seems to have made use of steam, for heating or other purposes.[151] All around the buildings at Reykholt he had a sturdy fortress erected ("virki øruggt"). The walls of the fortress must have been at least two metres high and therefore quite imposing.[152] It is not obvious that such walls were of much use in terms of defence. On the other hand, such structures must have been found imposing, prestigious, even admirable. Snorri's surroundings were most probably very dignified.[153]

The fine banquets Snorri gave were mentioned above. Of special interest are *jóladrykkir* he gave in the winter of 1226/27 "eftir norrænum sið", i.e. Christmas drinks (meaning feasting) in a Norwegian style. Among his many guests was the courtier Bárðr *ungi* (the Young) the brother of Dagr, who was a son-in-law of the powerful lawman, Dagfinnr *bóndi*. More Norwegian courtiers were staying with Snorri, like the *kertisveinar*

150 Guðrún Harðardóttir 2006, 54–56; see also Guðrún Sveinbjarnardóttir and Guðrún Harðardóttir, pp. 255, 257, 267–272 in this book.
151 Guðrún Sveinbjarnardóttir 2012, 79–82, 91–93.
152 *Sturlunga saga* II, 155 (a group assaulting Reykholt had to lift one of its members up on the top of the wall in order to make it possible for him to surmount it).
153 On all this see further pp. 237–278 in this book.

Hákon Bótólfsson *galinn* and Sigurðr *vegglágr* (literally, "low as a wall"), who stayed with him in 1239.[154] Several of the Norwegian merchants were courtiers. One of them was Eyvindr (Øyvind) Eyvindsson *brattr* (literally, "steep") who is mentioned in Iceland several times during the period 1229 to 1254, and presented as a good friend of the Sturlungar.[155] Another was Óláfr Ragnfríðarson from Stein (Steinn), mentioned in Iceland in 1234 and 1239, later to become the king's *stallari* and royal envoy to Iceland. Even though it is not stated, Snorri must have met both of them. The Norwegian Sǫlmundr was Snorri's brother-in-law.[156]

In Snorri's circle were two *goðar*, Árni Magnússon, who continued to be in Snorri's company even though he divorced his daughter, and Loftr Pálsson, Snorri's friend and protegé. Loftr had accepted gifts from Earl Hákon *galinn*, apparently during a stay in Norway 1209/10 and stayed with King Hákon in Norway from 1221 to 1223. And when Árni stayed with King Hákon in 1221 we learn that the king was his great friend. It has been pointed out that Loftr and Árni were probably courtiers, even though it is not stated.[157] At least they must have been well acquainted with an aristocratic code of conduct.

As was mentioned, Guðrún Nordal suggests that Snorri had a court at Reykholt; she has especially court poets in mind. Other *stórgoðar* in Iceland at that time had such courts with poets, connoisseurs in some fields, bodyguards and so on. It has been pointed out that *stórgoðar* had priests in their following who acted as counsellors for them.[158] In Snorri's case this must have been Styrmir *fróði*.

Life at Snorri's "court" may have been lively and entertaining. We have mentioned a certain Tafl-Bergr who stayed with Snorri in 1222, and there was another Bergr serving Snorri in 1222, called Dansa-Bergr who must have been knowledgeable about or fond of dancing.[159] However, as *Heimskringla* shows, Snorri had a sense of dignity, and the orderly and proper. His position was dignified and respectable because he was the representative for St Peter at Reykholt and St Nicholas at Stafholt. It

---

154 On *kertisveinar* at the Norwegian court see above. Instead of *vegglágr* the form *veglágr* is a possibility, meaning of low advancement or honour.

155 *Sturlunga saga* II, 122.

156 On some noble Orcadians in Borgarfjǫrðr in the 1230s see pp. 81–82, 100–102 in this book.

157 Jón Jóhannesson 1958/1948, 215–216.

158 Orri Vésteinsson 2000, 217–219.

159 Brown 2012, points this out; see also Wanner 2008, 89–92.

has often been pointed out that the dedication of Reykholt to Peter and Stafholt to Nicholas was taken seriously by some people, who, because of the dedications, were willing to show the churches and their belongings some reverence.[160] Among the belongings of the church at Reykholt was Pétursskógur (Peter's Forest), and the church at Stafholt for instance owned Nikulásarker, a deep pool in a river, well known as a rich salmon fishing site. Snorri was in charge of everything that belonged to the churches and their patron saints.

Sverrir Jakobsson discusses how Snorri's position as *lendr maðr* may have affected his political position in Iceland. Snorri says, in *Óláfs saga helga* in *Heimskringla*, that in each *fylki* in Norway it was as if the *lendir menn* were the leaders of the farmers.[161] Sverrir asks whether Snorri could stop at ruling anything less in Iceland than an area corresponding to a *fylki* or at least "a territorially demarcated region, probably Borgarfjörðr". Such demarcated territories represented by a *stórgoði* or other leaders were a novelty in Iceland.[162]

One further point is worth considering. Apparently Hrafn Sveinbjarnarson tried to enhance his political situation in Iceland through advancement abroad. Such advancement was not easily transferable to Iceland and when Hrafn died in 1213 he was more like a petty chieftain even though he had made considerable progress in terms of political power. Snorri had a different approach. He became politically big in Iceland before going to Norway, where he also succeeded in becoming politically big. The question is whether his advancement in Iceland helped him in Norway. It most probably did, but it may be said once more, the ultimate goal for Snorri must have been to use the Norwegian connection to gain even more power in Iceland.

Around 1230 Snorri was at the peak of his power and influence. His political position appeared to be secure and his Norwegian connection must have been a great help. However, his ties with the Norwegian regents had some drawbacks which became evident in the 1230s, when there was political strife and clashes between King Hákon and Skúli who lost. Snorri was on the latter's side but these events will not be discussed any further here.[163]

---

160 Helgi Þorláksson 2005, 140–145.
161 *Heimskringla* II, 58.
162 Sverrir Jakobsson 2012, 114 and further 115–117.
163 On the lasting bonds between Snorri and Skúli see pp. 103–104 in this book.

Conclusion

Around 1200 and early in the thirteenth century there were *goðar* in
Iceland who were adopting aristocratic conduct and lifestyles, and looking
abroad for models. We would be justified in calling them aristocrats. The
decisive factors are the Western European codes of conduct and lifestyles
for aristocrats of the twelfth century and the Icelandic *stórgoðar* around
1200 are seen in this context. What counted most among foreign aristocrats was usually to be summoned and engaged as a major functionary
of a king. Around 1200 such a functionary would preferably have had
some experience of administration. In the twelfth century there was an
unwritten code for such men, for their habitus, well known to aristocrats
of the time but difficult for scholars to figure out exactly. However, in the
period from 1170 to 1220 this changed completely and written codes of
conduct emerged. Here an attempt has been made to draw up a picture
of some elements of the lifestyles and conduct of those *stórgoðar* in the
first half of the thirteenth century who wanted to be counted among
the noblemen in Norway and be ready to play an important role for the
king in Iceland. The questions of good family, social respect in Iceland,
distinguished matrimony, education and skills have been studied.

Snorri Sturluson probably easily qualified as a common courtier and
it was politically expedient for the Norwegian regents to "stamp" him
as their man and reward him for his support. What is surprising is, first
why Snorri was nominated *skutilsveinn*, a leader within the *hirð*, with
only very limited experience as a courtier. It must also have been seen as
politically expedient, but Snorri had to be able enough to merit it. His task
as a commander was to lead a group of guards, plan their shifts and be in
charge during journeys by sea or land. Snorri was a good foreman, we are
told, an able administrator, with considerable experience as a *stórgoði* in
Iceland. His horsemanship can hardly be doubted and he prided himself
on his sailing skills. He also had some experience of mustering forces.
Soon enough he was nominated a *lendr maðr*, which is also surprising, and
all in less than two years. He had probably done well as a *skutilsveinn* and
was seen as qualifying for this high position. An important factor was
probably his experience as a lawman. However, his opponents in Iceland,
the Oddaverjar, had played into his hands, probably making it politcally
advantageous for the Norwegian regents to make him *skutilsveinn*. Now he
probably understood how to make use of Nordic aristocratic culture in a

systematic way for his own political advancement at the Norwegian court to become *lendr maðr* and thus a counsellor to the king. The ultimate goal of this advancement for Snorri was most probably to enhance his own political position in Iceland, preferably to become earl. It is suggested here that Snorri's political and administrative skills and his experience as lawman were decisive factors when the Norwegian regents made him their leading man in Iceland.

Acknowledgements

Else Mundal read a draft of this article and made some useful comments for which I am most grateful.

Bibliography

Andersson, Theodore M. 2012. *The Partisan Muse in the Early Icelandic Sagas (1200–1250)*. Islandica LV. Ithaca, New York: Cornell University Library.

Arnheiður Sigurðardóttir 1966. *Híbýlahættir á miðöldum* Reykjavík: Bókaútgáfa Menningarsjóðs og Þjóðvinafélagsins.

Árni Pálsson 1947. "Snorri Sturluson og Íslendingasaga". *Á víð og dreif. Ritgerðir*. Reykjavík: Helgafell, 110–190.

Bagge, Sverre 1991. *Society and Politics in Snorri Sturluson's Heimskringla*. Berkeley, Los Angeles, Oxford: University of California Press.

Bagge, Sverre 2004. "The Transformation of Europe: The Role of Scandinavia". In Johann P. Arnason and Björn Wittrock (eds), *Eurasian Transformations, Tenth to Thirteenth Centuries: Crystiallizations, Divergences, Renaissances*. Leiden, Boston: Brill, 131–165.

Biskupa sögur II. Ed. Ásdís Egilsdóttir. Íslenzk fornrit XVI, Reykjavík: Hið íslenzka fornritafélag, 2002.

Bjarni Guðnason 1982. "Formáli". *Dana konunga sǫgur*. Ed. Bjarni Guðnason. Íslenzk fornrit XXXV, Reykjavík: Hið íslenzka fornritafélag,

Bouchard, Constance Brittain, 1998. 'Strong of Body, Brave and Noble'. *Chivalry and Society in Medieval France*. Ithaca and London: Cornell University Press.

Brown, Nancy Marie 2012. *Song of the Vikings. Snorri and the Making of Norse Myths*. New York: Palgrave, Macmillan.

Bumke, Joachim 2000. *Courtly Culture. Literature and Society in the High Middle Ages*. Translated by Thomas Dunlap. Woodstock New York: Overlook. London: Turnaround.

Bøe, Arne 1965. "Lendmann". *Kulturhistorisk leksikon* X, 498–505.

Coss, Peter 2003, *The Origins of the English Gentry*. Cambridge: Cambridge University Press.

Crouch, David 2005. *The Birth of Nobility. Constructing Aristocracy in England and France 900–1300*. Harlow: Pearson/Longman.

Cruz, Jo Ann Hoeppner Moran and Richard Gerberding 2004. *Medieval Worlds: An Introduction to European History 300–1492*. Boston, New York: Houghton Mifflin Company.

DI = *Diplomatarium islandicum, Íslenzkt fornbréfasafn*, I-XVI. Copenhagen, Reykjavík: Hið íslenzka bókmenntafélag, 1857–1972.

Edda Snorra Sturlusonar. Nafnaþulur og Skáldatal. Ed. Guðni Jónsson. Reykjavík: Íslendingasagnaútgáfan, 1949.

Einar Ól. Sveinsson 1934. "Formáli". *Laxdæla saga*. Ed. Einar Ól. Sveinsson. Íslenzk fornrit V. Reykjavík: Hið íslenzka fornritafélag.

Einar Ól. Sveinsson 1940. *Sturlungaöld. Drög um íslenzka menningu á 13. öld*. Reykjavík: Kostnaðarmenn nokkrir Reykvíkingar. [Also an English translation, *The Age of the Sturlungs. Icelandic Civilization in the 13th Century*. Ithaca: Cornell University Press, 1953.]

Faulkes, Anthony 1993. "The Sources of Skáldskaparmál: Snorri's Intellectual Background". In Alois Wolf (ed.), *Snorri Sturluson. Kolloquium anlässlich der 750. Wiederkehr seines Todestages*. ScriptOralia 51. Tübingen: Gunter Narr Verlag, 59–76.

Foote, Peter 1984/1974. "Secular Attitudes in Early Iceland". *Aurvandilstá. Norse Studies*.The Viking Collection 2. Odense: Odense University Press, 1984, 31–46.

Foote, Peter. 1984/1951. "Sturlusaga and its Background". *Aurvandilstá. Norse Studies*. The Viking Collection 2. Odense: Odense University Press, 1984, 9–30.

Gísli Sigurðsson 2013. *Leiftur á horfinni öld. Hvað er merkilegt við íslenskar fornbókmenntir?* Reykjavík: Mál og menning.

Guðrún Harðardóttir 2006. "The Physical Setting of Reykholt According to Sturlunga saga". In Else Mundal (ed.), *Reykholt som makt- og lærdomssenter i den islandske og nordiske kontekst*. Snorrastofa, vol. III. Reykholt: Snorrastofa, 43–64.

Guðrún Nordal 2001. *Tools of Literacy. The Role of Skaldic Verse in Icelandic Textual Culture of the Twelfth and Thirteenth Centuries*. Toronto, Buffalo, London: University of Toronto Press.

Guðrún Nordal 2006. "Snorri and Norway". In Else Mundal (ed.), *Reykholt som makt- og lærdomssenter i den islandske og nordiske kontekst*. Snorrastofa, vol. III. Reykholt: Snorrastofa, 77–84.

Guðrún Sveinbjarnardóttir 2012. *Reykholt. Archaeological Investigations at a High Status Farm in Western Iceland*. Reykjavík: Snorrastofa and The National Museum of Iceland.

Gunnar Karlsson 2004. *Goðamenning. Staða og áhrif goðorðsmanna í þjóðveldi Íslendinga*. Reykjavík: Heimskringla, háskólaforlag Máls og menningar.

Hallan, Nils 1972. "Snorri fólgsnarjarl". *Skírnir* 146, 159–176.

Hákonar saga Hákonarsonar I. Ed. Þorleifur Hauksson, Sverrir Jakobsson and Tor Ulset. Íslenzk fornrit XXXI. Reykjavík: Hið íslenzka fornritafélag, 2013.

Hákonar saga Hákonarsonar II. Ed. Sverrir Jakobsson, Þorleifur Hauksson and Tor Ulset.

Íslenzk fornrit XXXII. Reykjavík: Hið íslenzka fornritafélag, 2013.

Heimskringla I. Ed. Bjarni Aðalbjarnarson. Íslenzk fornrit XXVI. Reykjavík: Hið íslenzka fornritafélag, 1941.

Heimskringla II. Ed. Bjarni Aðalbjarnarson. Íslenzk fornrit XXVII. Reykjavík: Hið íslenzka fornritafélag, 1945.

Heimskringla III. Ed. Bjarni Aðalbjarnarson. Íslenzk fornrit XXVIII. Reykjavík: Hið íslenzka fornritafélag, 1951.

Helgi Þorláksson 1979a. "Snorri Sturluson og Oddaverjar". *Snorri, átta alda minning*. [Eds Gunnar Kalsson and Helgi Þorláksson.] Reykjavík: Sögufélag, 53–88.

Helgi Þorláksson 1979b. "Hvernig var Snorri í sjón?" *Snorri, átta alda minning*. [Eds Gunnar Kalsson and Helgi Þorláksson.] Reykjavík: Sögufélag, 161–181.

Helgi Þorláksson 1988. "Var Sturla Þórðarson þjóðfrelsishetja?". In Guðrún Ása Grímsdóttir and Jónas Kristjánsson (eds), *Sturlustefna. Ráðstefna haldin á sjö alda ártíð Sturlu Þórðarsonar sagnaritara 1984*, vol. 32. Reykjavík: Stofnun Árna Magnússonar á Íslandi, 127–146.

Helgi Þorláksson 1989. *Gamlar götur og goðavald. Um fornar leiðir og völd Oddaverja í Rangárþingi* (Ritsafn Sagnfræðistofnunar 25. Ed. Jón Guðnason). Reykjavík.

Helgi Þorláksson 2005. "Why were the 12th century staðir established?". In Helgi Þorláksson (ed.), *Church Centres. Church Centres in Iceland from the 11th to the 13th Century and their Parallels in other Countries*. Snorrastofa, vol II. Reykholt: Snorrastofa, 127–155.

Helgi Þorláksson 2010. "Milli Skarðs og Feykis. Um valdasamþjöppun í Hegranesþingi í tíð

Ásbirninga og um valdamiðstöðvar þeirra". *Saga* XLVIII (2), 51–93.

Helgi Þorláksson 2012. "Reykholt vokser fram som maktsenter". In Helgi Þorláksson and Þóra Björg Sigurðardóttir (eds), *From Nature to Script. Reykholt, Environment, Centre and Manuscript Making.* Snorrastofa, vol VII. Reykholt: Snorrastofa, 79–116.

Helgi Þorláksson 2014. "Snorri í Odda". *Skírnir* 188, 353–380.

Helgi Þorláksson 2017, "Reykholt as a Residence of Snorri Sturluson the *lendr maðr*". In Guðrún Sveinbjarnardóttir and Bergur Þorgeirsson (eds), *The Buildings of Medieval Reykholt: the Wider Context.* Snorrastofa, vol. IX. Reykjavík: Snorrastofa and University of Iceland Press, 159–181.

Helle, Knut 1974. *Norge blir en stat 1130–1319.* Handbok i Norges historie 3. Bergen: Universitetsforlaget.

Hirdskråen. Hirdloven til Norges konge og hans håndgangne menn. Etter AM 322 fol. Ed. Steinar Imsen. Oslo: Riksarkivet, 2000.

Hrafns saga Sveinbjarnarsonar. Ed. Guðrún P. Helgadóttir. Oxford: Clarendon Press, 1987.

Hrafns saga hin sérstaka. *Sturlunga saga* II. Ed. Örnólfur Thorsson. Reykjavík: Svart á hvítu, 1988.

Hungrvaka, in *Biskupa sögur* II.

Islandske Annaler indtil 1588. Ed. Gustav Storm. Christiania: Grøndahl & Søns Bogtrykkeri, 1888.

Imsen, Steinar 2000, "King Magnus and his Liegemen's 'Hirdskrå': A Portrait of the Norwegian Nobility in the 1270s". In Anne J. Duggan (ed.), *Nobles and Nobility in Medieval Europe. Concepts, Origins, Transformations.* Woodbridge: The Boydell Press, Reprinted as Paperback, 2002, 205–220.

Íslendingabók, Landnámabók. Ed. Jakob Benediktsson. Íslenzk fornrit I. Reykjavík: Hið íslenzka fornritafélag, 1968.

Jaeger, C. Stephen 1985/1991. *The Origins of Courtliness. Civilizing Trends and the Formation of Courtly Ideals 939–1210.* The Middle Ages, a Series ed. Edward Peters. Philadelphia: University of Pensylvania Press.

Jón Jóhannesson 1958/1948. "Hirð Hákonar gamla á Íslandi". *Íslendinga saga.* II. *Fyrirlestrar og ritgerðir um tímabilið 1262–1550.* [Ed. Þórhallur Vilmundarson.] Reykjavík: Almenna bókafélagið 1958, 205–225.

Jón Viðar Sigurðsson 1989. *Frá goðorðum til ríkja. Þróun goðavalds á 12. og 13. öld,* Sagnfræðirannsóknir X, ed. Bergsteinn Jónsson, Reykjavík: Sagnfræðistofnun Háskóla Íslands, Bókaútgáfa Menningarsjóðs.

Jón Viðar Sigurðsson 2010. *Den vennlige vikingen. Vennskapets makt i Norge og på Island 900–1300.* Oslo: Pax forlag A/S.

Jón Viðar Sigurðsson 2015. "The Wedding at Flugumýri in 1253. Icelandic Feasts between the Free State Period and Norwegian Hegemony". In Wojtek Jezierski, Lars Hermanson, Hans Jacob-Orning, and Thomas Småberg (eds), *Ritual, Performatives and Political Order in Northern Europe c. 650–1350.* Turnhout: Brepols.

Kaeuper, Richard W. 1999. *Chivalry and Violence in Medieval Europe.* Oxford: Oxford University Press.

Keen, Maurice 1984. *Chivalry.* Second printing, with corrections. New Haven and London: Yale University Press.

Konungs skuggsiá. Ed. Ludvig Holm-Olsen. Norsk historisk kjeldeskrift-institutt. Norrøne tekster nr. 1. Oslo 1983.

Leiðarvísir Nikuláss Bergssonar ábóta á Þverá.

Skýringar og fræði, [Sturlunga saga]. Ed. Örnólfur Thorsson. Reykjavík: Svart á hvítu, 1988.

Lindkvist, Thomas 2007. "1100-talsrenässans eller den första europeiska revolutionen?" In Karl G. Johansson (ed.), *Den norröna renässansen. Reykholt, Norden och Europa 1150–1300*. Snorrastofa vol. IV. Reykholt: Snorrastofa, 11–24.

Messuskýringar. Liturgisk symbolik frå den norsk-islandske kyrkja i millomalderen. Ed. Oluf Kolsrud. I. Oslo: Norsk historisk kjeldeskrift-institutt, 1952.

Moore, R.I. 2004 "The Transformation of Europe as a Eurasian Phenomenon". In Johann P. Arnason and Björn Wittrock (eds), *Eurasian Transformations, Tenth to Thirteenth Centuries: Crystiallizations, Divergences, Renaissances*. Leiden, Boston: Brill, 77–98.

Morkinskinna I–II. Ed. Ármann Jakobsson and Þórður Ingi Guðjónsson. Íslenzk fornrit XXIII–XXIV. Reykjavík: Hið íslenzka fornritafélag, 2011.

Mundal, Else 2007. "Med kva rett kan vi tale om ein norrøn renessanse?" In Karl G. Johansson (ed.), *Den norröna renässansen. Reykholt, Norden och Europa 1150–1300*. Snorrastofa vol. IV. Reykholt: Snorrastofa, 25–39.

Norges historie. Ed. Knut Mykland. Vol. 15. *Historisk atlas – Oversikter, årstall, tabeller – Hovedregister*. J.W. Cappelens forlag A.S. Oslo, 1980.

Oddaannálar og Oddaverjaannáll. Ed. Eiríkur Þormóðsson and Guðrún Ása Grímsdóttir. Reykjavík: Stofnun Árna Magnússonar á Íslandi, 2003.

Orkneyinga saga. Ed. Finnbogi Guðmundsson. Íslenzk fornrit XXXIV. Reykjavík: Hið íslenzka fornritafélag, 1965.

Orri Vésteinsson 2000. *The Christianization of Ice-*land. *Priests, Power, and Social Change 1000–1300*. Oxford: Oxford University Press.

Óskar Guðmundsson 2009. *Snorri. Ævisaga Snorra Sturlusonar 1179–1241*. Reykjavík: JPV útgáfa.

Páls saga byskups, in *Biskupa sögur* II.

Sigríður Beck 2011. *I kungens frånvaro. Formeringen av en isländsk aristokrati 1271–1387*. Göteborg: Göteborgs universitet.

Sigurður Nordal 1920. *Snorri Sturluson*. Reykjavík: Þór. B. Þorláksson.

Sigurður Nordal 1942. *Íslenzk menning* I. Arfur Íslendinga, Reykjavík: Mál og menning. [Also an English translation, *Icelandic Culture*, Ithaca: Cornell University Press, 1990]

Snorri Sturluson, *Edda. Translated from the Icelandic and Introduced by Anthony Faulkes*. London and Melbourne: Dent: Everyman's Library, 1987.

Sturlunga saga I–II. Eds Jón Jóhannesson, Magnús Finnbogason and Kristján Eldjárn. Reykjavík: Sturlunguútgáfan, 1946.

Sveinbjörn Rafnsson 1977. "Grágás og Digesta Iustiniani". In Einar G. Pétursson and Jónas Kristjánsson (eds), *Sjötíu ritgerðir helgaðar Jakobi Benediktssyni 20. júlí 1977*, vol. 12. Reykjavík: Stofnun Árna Magnússonar á Íslandi, 720–732.

Sveinbjörn Rafnsson 1990. "Forn hrossreiðarlög og heimildir þeirra. Drög til greiningar réttarheimilda Grágásar". *Saga* XXVIII, 131–148.

Sverrir Jakobsson 2009. "The process of state-formation in medieval Iceland". *Viator* 40 (2), 151–170.

Sverrir Jakobsson 2012. "The Territorialization of Power in the Icelandic Commonwealth". In S. Bagge, M.H. Gelting, F. Hervik, The. Lindkvist and B. Poulsen (eds), *Statsutvikling i Skandinavia i middelalderen*. Oslo: Dreyers forlag, 101–118.

Sverrir Jakobsson 2013, "Formáli". *Hákonar saga*

Hákonarsonar I. Eds Þorleifur Hauksson, Sverrir Jakobsson and Tor Ulset. Íslenzk fornrit XXXI. Reykjavík: Hið íslenzka fornritafélag.

Sverris saga. Ed. Þorleifur Hauksson. Íslenzk fornrit XXX. Reykjavík: Hið íslenzka fornritafélag, 2007.

Theodoricus Monachus, *Historia de Antiquitate Regum Norwagiensium. An Account of the Ancient History of the Norwegian Kings*. Ed. D. McDougall and I. McDougall. London: Viking Society for Northern Research, University College, 1998.

Torfi H. Tulinius 1996. "Guðs lög í ævi og verkum Snorra Sturlusonar". *Ný Saga* 8, 31–40.

Torfi H. Tulinius 2000. "Snorri og bræður hans. Framgangur og átök Sturlusona í félagslegu rými þjóðveldisins". *Ný Saga* 12, 49–60.

Turville-Petre, G. O. 1967/1953. *Origins of Icelandic Literature*. Oxford: The Clarendon Press. [Corrected and reprinted 1967.]

Valdamiðstöðvar á miðöldum. A heading for seven articles by six authors on centres of power and chieftains (*goðar, stórgoðar*) in medieval Iceland. In Benedikt Eyþórsson and Hrafnkell Lárusson (eds), *Þriðja íslenska söguþingið 18–21. maí 2006*. Reykjavík 2007, 189–253.

Viðar Pálsson 2003. "Var engi höfðingi slíkr sem Snorri. Auður og virðing í valdabaráttu Snorra Sturlusonar". *Saga* XLI (1), 55–59.

Viðar Pálsson 2016. *Language of Power: Feasting and Gift-Giving in Medieval Iceland and Its Sagas*. *Islandica*. Cornell: Cornell University Library.

Wanner, Kevin J. 2008. *Snorri Sturluson and the Edda. The Conversion of Cultural Capital in Medieval Scandinavia*. Toronto, Buffalo, London: University of Toronto Press.

Þorsteins þáttr stangarhöggs. In *Austfirðinga sögur*. Ed. Jón Jóhannesson. Íslenzk fornrit XI. Reykjavík: Hið íslenzka fornritafélag, 1950.

¶ HELGI ÞORLÁKSSON

Snorri Sturluson, the Politician, and his Foreign Relations

The Norwegian, Orcadian and Götlandish Connections

Introduction

HAT WAS THE POLITICAL PERSUASION OF SNORRI STURLU-son? Was he a royalist or an anti-royalist or even a "democrat" in some sense? Scholars have tried to answer such questions by studying *Heimskringla*, Snorri's much acclaimed work about the Norwegian kings. Another approach would be to study Snorri's foreign relations. Do his close relations with the Birkibeinar in Norway, King Sverrir and his successors, show his political conviction? Does it mean that he opposed the policy of their opponents, the Baglar, and so did not support *libertas ecclesiae*, the endeavour of the Church to gain independence? Or did Snorri have no such political conviction?

The court of King Sverrir in Norway offered opportunities for Icelanders as poets, scholars or saga scribes and courtiers, and there were more opportunities to come at the demise of King Sverrir (d. 1202) when other leaders of the Birkibeinar took over. One of those who seized the opportunity was Snorri, who had great success from 1218 to 1220 at the Norwegian court when he was rewarded for his unfailing support of the Birkibeinar and charged with some serious tasks and became *lendr maðr*.[1]

Back home after 1220, Snorri was supposed to defend the interests of the Norwegian regents, support their men and give advice. He was in a del-

---

1 On *lendr maðr*, a top courtier, see pp. 33–73 in this book.

icate situation because of friction between the leaders of the Birkibeinar themselves, King Hákon *gamli* (the Old) and Earl Skúli.[2] The position of individual *lendir menn* in difficult dealings with the regents must also have been of interest and importance to him. Orcadian-Norwegian relations were complex and difficult to manage. Since Snorri was the number one man of the Norwegian regents in Iceland the affinities between them and their earls of Orkney must have been of great interest to him. Finally, in light of all this he had to consider his own political position in Iceland.

Snorri must have been eager to hear tidings from abroad about the latest political events, not only in Norway but also where Norwegian interests were at stake, whether in parts of Sweden, the Orkney Islands or Caithness, the northernmost part of mainland Scotland. He probably received news mainly via Norwegian and Orcadian merchants, and we also hear of Norwegian courtiers being his guests at Reykholt.

Snorri's foreign relations were important for his life and work. He travelled to Norway in 1218, and in 1219 he spent some time in Gautland (Västergötland (Western Götland) in modern day Sweden) with Lawman Eskil (Áskell) and his wife. It has been suggested that Eskil and Snorri were of the same political conviction or orientation, positively disposed towards the resolutions of yeomen at assemblies and against increased royal power.[3] In Norway Snorri seems to have been close to Lawman Dag-finnr and later one of the latter's associates stayed with Snorri at Reykholt. This begs the question whether there was some political understanding between lawmen who tried to hinder increased royal or central power. This will be discussed below.

Seen in a wider context, around 1200 there was friction in the Nordic countries between, on the one hand the Church leaders who preached *libertas ecclesiae* and their supporters, kings or pretenders, who would defer to the Church and obtain its political support for their own ambitions for increased power. On the other hand, there were their opponents who would not defer to the Church. In Norway the adversaries were King Magnús (d. 1184) and his followers, who were supported by the Church, and against them King Sverrir (d. 1202) and his supporters, the Birkibeinar. In 1196 all the opponents of King Sverrir joined forces and were called the Baglar.

---

2   In modern Norwegian spelling their names are written Håkon Håkonsson, or Håkon IV, and Skule.

3   Magnús Már Lárusson 1967, 31, 33.

The Orkney Islands loomed large in the life of Snorri. He was brought up at Oddi and the aristocratic family there had close contacts with leading men in the islands, namely Bishop Bjarni and the earl himself, Haraldr Maddaðarson.[4] The bishop and the earl were close collaborators. Snorri, on the other hand, when living as a young chieftain at Borg in Borgarfjǫrðr, encountered some Orkney merchants. One of them was Þorkell *rostungr* (the Walrus), who was the nephew of Bishop Bjarni. Snorri and his men fought with the merchants, who escaped and sought shelter in Oddi where they were welcomed.[5] This is how the friction and discord between Snorri and the Oddaverjar (the family at Oddi) began.

How much can we read into this incident? Snorri sided with the Birkibeinar fraction in Norway, who punished Earl Haraldr of Orkney harshly in 1195 for supporting the followers of the King Magnús faction when they rioted in Norway in 1194. This group of men, called the Islanders, joined the Baglar in 1196. In 1202 when King Sverrir died, Earl Haraldr seized the opportunity and had the representative of the Norwegian king in Orkney killed. His hostility towards the Birkibeinar was obvious and he supported their enemies. Does this mean that Snorri opposed the Baglar and the policy they stood for? This will be considered below.[6]

Scholars generally believe that Snorri was the narrator of *Óláfs saga helga in sérstaka* (The Separate Saga of St Óláfr),[7] which later made up the bulk of *Heimskringla*. It is clear that the narrator of the saga was well acquainted with the earlier version of *Orkneyinga saga* which is lost. What is preserved is the revised version with a supplement. Parts of the revised version are taken from *Heimskringla*, and it has been suggested that the revisions were made by Snorri, or someone working for him. Chapters 109 to 112 of *Orkneyinga saga* in the edition of Hið íslenska

4   Einar Ól. Sveinsson 1937, 7–11, 16–39.
5   *Sturlunga saga* I, 240–241.
6   The rioting group against the Birkibeinar in 1194 came from Norway, Orkney and Shetland, were supported by Earl Haraldr and were called the Islanders (*Eyjarskeggjar*). They attracted many new members and support in the Oslo area where they were soon in control. They were defeated by the Birkibeinar close to Bjǫrgvin (Bergen) and one of the leaders of the Islanders, Sigurðr Erlingsson, was later at the forefront of the Baglar group against the Birkibeinar, together with those of the group who escaped with him. The group of Baglar was formed in 1196 under the leadership of Bishop Nikolaus who had supported the Islanders in 1194. On this see *Sverris saga*, 180–194; Helle 1974, 91, 92, 118, 123.
7   Óláfr *helgi*, in modern Norwegian *hellig* Olav.

fornritafélag (ÍF) were added to the saga in the Middle Ages, as was the account of the death of Bishop Adam in 1222.[8] This addition is found only in *Flateyjarbók*. Sigurður Nordal suggested that the sources for these addenda were Andréas Gunnason and Andréas Hrafnsson, who stayed in Snorri's district in Borgarfjǫrðr in 1234/35.[9] This has been accepted by several scholars.[10]

When we realize that one of these two Andréases was a son of the lawman Hrafn (Rafn) in Caithness, it seems evident that he must have been the source for the chapters added to *Orkneyinga saga*. The reason for such a conclusion is that the stories are recounted from the viewpoint of Hrafn, the Caithness lawman who was an enemy of Earl Haraldr Maddaðarson. As mentioned, in the early thirteenth century Snorri supported those who opposed the earl and punished him, the Birkibeinar, and furthermore he attacked the friends of the earl in Iceland. One therefore wonders whether it is coincidence that the two Andréases stayed in Snorri's district. In other words, whether in 1234 Snorri still opposed the cause of Earl Haraldr and his successors. I would like to elaborate on this thought and take into consideration how the political situation had changed in Orkney and Norway in the interim, from around 1206, and how this affected Snorri's political position.

The aim here is to consider Snorri's political views concerning the policies of regents in the Orkney Islands and Norway, and how political affairs in Norway and the islands affected his political life. The main question is whether the lawman Snorri was conservative and against the increased power of both the king and the Church. Did he support power from below, the policy of the leaders of the farmers at assemblies who opposed increased royal power? What were the further implications of his support of the Birkibeinar? Did he necessarily oppose all their foes?

Snorri and the Orcadians *c.* 1202–1206

There were lively connections between Iceland and the Orkney Islands in the period from 1180 to 1240. First of all, *Orkneyinga saga* should be

---

8   Finnbogi Guðmundsson 1965, vi, xxvii, xc, cviii.
9   Finnbogi Guðmundsson 1965, cvi–cviii.
10   Finnbogi Guðmundsson 1965, cvi–cvii; Chesnutt 1981, 47; Helgi Guðmundsson 1997, 278–284.

mentioned. It was composed in the late twelfth century, perhaps as early as 1180 but hardly later than 1190, according to its editor, Finnbogi Guðmundsson.[11] The version in which it has been preserved contains revisions made in the second quarter of the thirteenth century. Whether the saga was composed by an Icelander or an Orcadian is difficult to say. However, it was preserved in Iceland and indicates that Icelanders took some interest in Orkney. It will be argued here that the revised version is Icelandic.

Several Orcadians and Shetlanders were in Iceland during the period from 1180 to 1240. In around 1200, there were four ships from Orkney in Iceland, and one from Shetland.[12] There were Orcadian merchants in Iceland in 1234 who brought some grain, and in 1238 we hear of an Icelander who fled to Orkney and returned in 1239.[13] This means that at least one ship left Iceland for Orkney in 1238 and one ship probably arrived in Iceland in 1239, coming directly from Orkney. Three men from Shetland are mentioned in Iceland around this time. One of them was a courtier to the Norwegian king, and was only temporarily in the country, but the others seem to have lived there permanently.[14]

There are indications of active communications between Iceland and Shetland during this period, evidenced for instance in the form of meal sent as votive gifts for St Þorlákr, if *Þorláks saga* can be trusted.[15] The inhabitants of Shetland were rather few and it is possible that the more numerous and better off Orkney Islanders provided the transport for some of the gifts of the Shetlanders. It is certainly easy to imagine that the saga exaggerates, but it is difficult to say how and the account is hardly sheer fabrication.

It is interesting to see the friendship that existed between men in Iceland and Orkney; there were more affinities than are usually reckoned. The leading family in Iceland, the people of Oddi, were on very friendly terms with influential men in Orkney, Earl Haraldr Maddaðarson and his friend, the poet Bjarni Kolbeinsson, who was a bishop from 1188. The magnate at Oddi, Jón Loftsson (Loptsson), was of high status because King Magnús *berfœttr* (Bareleg) of Norway was his grandfather. At a

---

11   Finnbogi Guðmundsson 1965. On the writing of *Orkneyinga saga* see Jesch 1993, 206.

12   *Biskupa sögur* II, 93, 212; *Biskupa sögur* I, 309–310; *Sturlunga saga* I, 194, 240–241.

13   *Sturlunga saga* I, 439; II, 274–275.

14   *Sturlunga saga* I, 102, 267 (a brewer); II, 128 (a courtier).

15   Þorláks saga A, Jarteinabók II, *Biskupa sögur* II, 99, 234–235.

fairly young age Jón's son Páll stayed in Orkney for a while, probably sometime between 1175 and 1180. Later he became a bishop in Iceland and his saga tells us that Earl Haraldr held him in high esteem.[16] When looking for the most likely author of *Orkneyinga saga*, Páll is a good candidate. He must have been a contemporary of Bishop Bjarni, who has also been suggested as the author; and the saga has even been seen as their joint effort.[17]

In around 1200 the head of the Oddi family, Sæmundr Jónsson, almost became the son-in-law of Earl Haraldr. Messengers travelled between the earl and Sæmundr; the earl wanted Sæmundr to come to Orkney to marry there, while Sæmundr wanted the earl's daughter to be sent to Iceland. As a result nothing came of the match.[18] Bishop Páll had a son, Loftr, who spent some time, probably in 1209/1210, in Orkney with Bishop Bjarni. According to the saga his stay with Bjarni was a success.[19] Another Icelandic chieftain who had spent time in the Orkney Islands, Hrafn Sveinbjarnarson, was also a good friend of Bjarni and received some very precious gifts from him.[20]

It has been pointed out that *Orkneyinga saga* is biased. Its editor, Finnbogi Guðmundsson (and Einar Ól. Sveinsson before him) pointed out that the saga is very much *pro* Earl Hákon Pálsson and *contra* Earl Magnús Erlendsson, the saint (fig.1). In Finnbogi's view, the work looks like a polemical piece, opposing the biased story of St Magnús and championing Hákon.[21] The most likely source for this view would be Earl Haraldr Maddaðarson, who was descended from Earl Hákon. In Haraldr's time there were two opposing lines, his own, the so-called Páll line, and competing with them the so-called Erlendr line or the saintly line of St Magnús, St Rǫgnvaldr and finally Haraldr *ungi* (the Young), who allegedly had a very saintly death in 1198 with mystical lights appearing where his blood was spilt in Caithness and innumerable miracles taking place.[22] However, he was never canonized. *Orkneyinga saga* is told from the point of view of the two friends, Earl Haraldr Maddaðarson and Bishop Bjarni Kolbeinsson.

16 *Biskupa sögur* II, 297.
17 Helgi Guðmundsson 1997, 268.
18 *Sturlunga saga* I, 242.
19 *Biskupa sögur* I, 324.
20 *Hrafns saga Sveinbjarnarsonar,* 2–3.
21 Finnbogi Guðmundsson 1965, xxxix–xl, xcii–xciii.
22 Haki Antonsson 2007, 157–160.

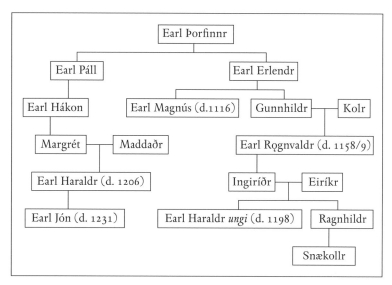

Figure 1. Earls of Orkney, two competing lines, from Páll and Erlendr.
Source: *Orkneyinga saga*: II. Niðjar Þorfinns Sigurðarsonar.

Earl Haraldr Maddaðarson had to serve two feudal lords simultaneously.[23] He owed allegiance to the King of Norway for Orkney, and to
the King of the Scots for Caithness (see map, fig. 2). Both kings were
inclined to recognize the claims of other members of Haraldr's family
and divide the earldoms. In order to survive, Earl Haraldr had to be
resourceful and he was a survivor. Not all his moves were equally clever,
however. He supported the opponents of King Sverrir in Norway in
1194, which proved a costly mistake. He stood close to the opponents
of Sverrir, the Baglar group, and so apparently did his friends, the Oddi
people. Snorri Sturluson, on the other hand, became a keen supporter
of the Sverrir group, the Birkibeinar in Norway, which turned out to be
very beneficial for him. The Birkibeinar found the Oddi family suspect
because of their royal descent[24] and their connections with Earl Haraldr.
This harmed the Oddi people politically, not least around 1220, when

23 Crawford 2010, especially 86–90.
24 See for instance *Sturlunga saga* I, 269–270.

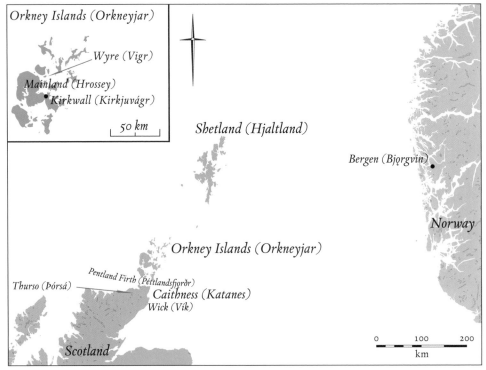

Figure 2. Northern Scotland and Western Norway. Map: Stefán Ólafsson.

Snorri rose to prominence and became one of the leading courtiers in Norway, a *lendr maðr*.[25]

When the nephew of Bishop Bjarni Kolbeinsson, Þorkell *rostungr* came to Iceland between around 1202 and 1206, he stayed initially with Snorri Sturluson, who decided the price of the grain that Þorkell had brought with him. Þorkell took offence, rejected any such arrangement and fled in his vessel, after having killed one of Snorri's men. As mentioned, Þorkell sought refuge at Oddi with Bjarni's friends. Snorri sent three assassins to kill him, but to no avail.[26] These were grave hostilities and we can hardly expect any gifts to have been exchanged between Bjarni and Snorri. On the other hand, Snorri did receive some valuable gifts from the Birkibeinar in Norway.

25   Helgi Þorláksson 1979.
26   *Sturlunga saga* I, 240, 241.

Snorri, Leaders of Yeomen, and *þingvald*

Some scholars think Snorri was shrewd, astute and successful as a politician, and refer to him at the height of his career when he, the *lendr maðr*, functioned simultaneously as *stórgoði* and lawman (called lawspeaker in Iceland).[27] Icelandic scholars, brought up when the Icelanders were fighting for independence, were not so sure about Snorri's political dexterity and some came to the conclusion that he was vacillating, helpless, even a political failure.[28] They referred to Snorri as being accommodating towards the regents of Norway, Earl Skúli and King Hákon. Despite this, he suffered the fate of execution at the instigation of the king in 1241, alone and abandoned in a cellar. Notwithstanding these comments, the narrator of *Heimskringla* was a clever and receptive man with a keen sense of political actors and political positions.

As explained in the introduction of this article, the question of the relationship between Norwegian magnates and the ruling kings is of interest here. Scholars have studied *Heimskringla* from a political point of view and tried to figure out what Snorri's political persuasion and sentiments were. Gudmund Sandvik was of the opinion that he sympathized with leaders of yeomen, supported their views and liberties, which were stated and defended at assemblies through spokesmen such as Járn-Skeggi at Ørje (Yrjar), Ásbjǫrn at Melhus (Meðalhús), Ǫlvir at Egge (Egg) in Trøndelag, Einar *þambarskelfir*[29] and also Lawman Þorgnýr in Sweden.[30] These were leaders who defended traditional rights and customs and expressed their views at assemblies of farmers. This shows, says Sandvik, that kings who tried to introduce novelties were met with resistance. This has been called *þingvald* (literally, "thingpower") policy[31] and Sandvik and others have suggested that Snorri supported it. Sverre Bagge disagrees and says that Snorri was not interested in the "constitutional" or democratic side of affairs. On the other hand, Bagge agrees that the leaders or magnates were not representing the people, even though their power was based in the people; the discussions at assemblies were between the magnates and the kings, and the commoners were usually easily led by

---

27   Foote 2004/1993, 171.

28   Sigurður Nordal 1920, 50–62, 71–76.

29   The meaning of this nickname is not clear. It may refer to someone who makes a bowstring (*þǫmb*) tremble or quiver, i.e. an able archer.

30   Sandvik 1955, 29. On Torgny and the importance of lawmen in Sweden according to *Heimskringla* see *Heimskringla* II, 110–117. Further Lindkvist 2007.

31   The Icelandic term *þingvald* is suggested by the present author.

an influential leader. Bagge, however, thinks that Sandvik emphasizes the disagreement between the king and the leaders too strongly, and rejects his suggestion that the magnates were exclusively popular leaders. He says that Snorri implies that they derived a considerable portion of their power from the king.[32]

Snorri's accounts of these magnates are more detailed than those found in his sources; he seems to have taken pleasure in elaborating on speeches given by them. They have contacts with both sides, the king and the people, and so are in a way between the people and the king. The problem for the magnate was not to be too daring, not to go too far; the fate of Einar *þambarskelfir*, who was killed by a king, was a warning. In Snorri's time royal power had increased and the magnates were becoming royal servants or royal officials. The role of the magnate had to be different. He would probably have become more like a diplomat, a man who explained the opinions of the yeomen or commoners to the king and vice versa. *Heimskringla* is probably the best source on "thingpower", on assemblies restraining the attempts of kings to increase their power. But it does not necessarily mean that Snorri fully supported such views or endorsed them.

Snorri and Kings

Snorri entered freely into the role of courtier to the king of Norway and was willing to accept advancement. He committed himself to the king and was obliged to serve him. But, even though he thus indebted himself, he had hopes of increased power and further promotion, which was probably his aim.[33] Since Snorri did not necessarily support the "thingpower" cause, does this mean that he was a resolute royalist, no matter what?

Theodore M. Andersson criticizes Sverre Bagge for reading *Heimskringla* in isolation as an autonomous work and suggests that it should be seen in its political context as a part of an ongoing political discussion. He refers to *Morkinskinna* and reminds us of the political situation in Iceland in 1220 when the Norwegian regents were threatening to invade Iceland. The reason was serious clashes in Iceland between the Oddaverjar

---

32   Bagge 1991, 108, 123, 125, 129.
33   Gunnar Karlsson 1979, especially 47–50.

and some Norwegian merchants from Bjǫrgvin (Bergen), leading the Oddaverjar to confiscate commodities, and the merchants committing manslaughter in revenge.[34] This political situation in fact gave Snorri a splendid opportunity to play the role of an intermediary. He was in Norway in 1220, was elevated to a *lendr maðr* and tried to settle the case. He was successful in a way; Norwegian merchants could once again operate in Iceland and in peace.

Andersson thinks *Morkinskinna* was composed in this political climate. It suggests, he says, that some kings were good and some were bad. Good kings attended to the welfare of the subjects, but bad kings coveted foreign lands. He thinks Snorri reacts to this in *Heimskringla* which could be read as a systematic censoring of the Icelandic attitudes in *Morkinskinna* that might have offended Norwegian readers.[35] Andersson's views are convincing, but we might still wonder about the speech of Einar *Þveræingr* (from Þverá) in *Heimskringla*. It has been argued that Snorri is the author of this speech.[36] It reads like a speech of the narrator in *Morkinskinna*; some kings are good, others bad since they are aggressive and levy taxes. In his speech, Einar recommends friendly terms with the then ruler, King Óláfr *digri* (the Stout) who died in 1030.[37] These were patriotic sentiments and economic views which Snorri was bound to hear when he tried to calm things down on behalf of the Norwegian merchants. He was probably ready to explain them to the Norwegian regents, and might even have intended the speech to be used for that purpose.

In *Heimskringla* Snorri elaborated on the contrast between the brothers and kings, Sigurðr and Eysteinn, and added several traits to the description of the latter. Even though he minimizes the difference found in *Morkinskinna* between the brothers, there is hardly any doubt that he favours King Eysteinn.[38] He was one of those who took care of welfare and was not aggressive. Earl Skúli, on the other hand, was aggressive when preparing an invasion in Iceland and Snorri could be proud of himself for having prevented it. That probably helped him in securing peace for the Norwegian merchants and he could convincingly say that such a peace would prevent further plans of invasion. The earl had suggested,

34   Further on this see in this book, pp. 36, 64–65.
35   Andersson 1994; Andersson 1999, 929.
36   Sigurður Nordal 1942, 344–345; Jón Jóhannesson 1956, 267–269.
37   The same as Óláfr *helgi*.
38   See in this book, pp. 48–49.

probably prematurely, that Snorri make the Icelanders submit to the king of Norway.

Even though Snorri preferred regents like Eysteinn, that did not stop him supporting Earl Skúli. Why was that? When discussing Snorri's political ideas, it is important to keep in mind that he wanted to benefit politically from his support of the king of Norway and the earl. Bagge wrote, "Thirteenth century politics was personal rather than institutional, it did not consist of struggles over constitutional questions, monarchy versus aristocracy etc., but of conflicts between individuals over personal interests." Further he wrote: "Thus Snorri is not a modern rational choice theorist, but holds a social ideal in which a considerable amount of self-interest and aggressivity, combined with friendship and generosity, leads to social acceptance." However, Snorri does not shun ideology completely. He explains the defeat of King Óláfr *helgi* (the Holy, St Olav, also *digri*, the Stout) in terms of his upholding justice, a point he would not give in on. Around 1230 the idea of *rex iustus* and impersonal justice was gaining ground and found favours with the Norwegian regents. Bagge is probably right when he further writes, "Icelandic magnates [at least some of them, Snorri especially] were willing to accept some kind of subordination to the Norwegian king, in return for gifts and favours."[39] Snorri had Earl Skúli to thank for his advancement at the court and in 1220 received fifteen splendid gifts from the earl, among them an oceangoing vessel.

Birgit Sawyer points out correctly that Snorri is fond of tales about independent magnates criticizing kings. However, notwithstanding Bagge's discussion and criticism of Sandvik, Sawyer concludes that in *Heimskringla* Snorri opposes kings *Dei gratia* and increased royal power, but supports old traditions, just like Earl Skúli.[40]

Peter Foote warned his readers when he wrote that Snorri is "adept at seeing both sides, or more, of a question or conflict. This makes it difficult to define his tendency ..." Did he stand for the independence values of yeomen? Or was he a convinced believer in social hierarchy, as Foote is inclined to believe?[41] Snorri seems to have been rather close to Earl Skúli, who was harsh in his dealings with the *bœndr* (yeomen,

---

39   Bagge 2004, 110–116.
40   Sawyer 2010, especially 50–55.
41   Foote 2004/1993, 173–174.

peasants, commoners) in Trøndelag, followed an aristocratic lifestyle and called himself *dux Dei gratia*.[42]

It is quite probable that in 1220 Snorri already saw himself as a prospective earl of Iceland. There is no reason to doubt that he was willing to become the earl of Skúli, might he have succeeded in becoming the king of Norway. The title of earl was to belong to Gizurr Þorvaldsson, who for a long time acted in the way it is suggested here Snorri might have liked to have done himself. Gizurr explained the policy of the king to the Icelanders and reported their reaction to the king. At long last he was pressed to act and secure an extensive part of Iceland for the king. There is hardly any doubt that Snorri might have done that, provided he had the position of earl. As has been pointed out, earls were quite independent even though they were responsible politically and economically to the king.[43]

Snorri was not necessarily a typical royalist. He would seize the opportunities that existed to improve his political position. The backing of royal power in Norway was obviously something Snorri opted for. This turned out to be dangerous for him but he must have hoped to find ways of solving problems whenever they might occur and preferably of improving his position.[44]

Snorri and the Church

In about 1202 Snorri had placed his political bet on the Birkibeinar. Accordingly he opposed the Baglar and those friendly with them which included the leaders in the Orkney Islands. The Icelanders seem to have been interested in the political situation of the islands, as well as that of the Faroes, and the political affinities of these islands with Norway.[45] Is it possible that Snorri opposed the Orcadian leaders because he disliked the Baglar and their course? A state of contention between Snorri and

42 Helgi Þorláksson 1979.
43 Jón M. Samsonarson 1958.
44 Magnús Fjalldal thinks that Snorri in *Heimskringla* warns the Icelanders against the Norwegian regents and sees the Norwegian kings, as a rule, as tyrants (2013). This is not easily acceptable, for instance because the author does not distinguish well enough between the material handed down to Snorri which he only copied and the material he elaborated on, and where in the text and how he did it.
45 Berman 1985, 113–129.

the Oddaverjar, and his support of Birkibeinar seem to be better reasons. Did Snorri dislike *libertas ecclesiae?* What he did was to support Birkibeinar who disliked *libertas ecclesiae*. However, during the reign of King Hákon Sverrisson (1202–1204) the political climate changed. King Hákon negotiated with the Church and a solution was found, a *modus vivendi*. This meant the *status quo*, which led to peace and dealings between the two sides. They made a final pact in Kvitingsøy in 1208 and the country was divided into two parts with the Baglar ruling in the east. There was peaceful coexistence. Snorri most probably took notice of this as borne out by the fact that he invited Bishop Guðmundr of Hólar to stay with him in 1209. The bishop was an ardent and relentless advocate of *libertas ecclesiae*, would not accept any right of secular chieftains to have clergymen sentenced and as a result, seriously clashed with them. In their eyes Guðmundr was a problem which Snorri tried to solve by inviting him to stay at Reykholt. The bishop accepted the offer and must have found Snorri sincerely friendly towards the Church and its stand. In Norway the situation improved, and the secular regents and the bishops were on good speaking terms. Finally in 1217/18 the Birkibeinar and Baglar joined forces under the leadership of the Birkibeinar regents, King Hákon and Earl Skúli against a common threat. Seen in this light it was not unexpected that when he returned from Norway, Snorri supported the foundation of a monastery in Viðey in 1224. It was of the Augustinian order. Around 1200 the most eager supporters of *libertas ecclesiae* were of the Augustinian order and were seriously opposed by the Birkibeinar. In 1202 it would have been found strange for Snorri to support such a monastery, but not in 1224 because of the changed political climate in Norway.[46]

Snorri in Västergötland

Snorri travelled to Norway in 1218, and in 1219 he was in Gautland or more exactly Western Götland (Västergötland) (see map, fig. 3).[47]

---

46 Helgi Þorláksson 1982; Helgi Þorláksson 2006.
47 Västergötland will be used for Gautland in the following.

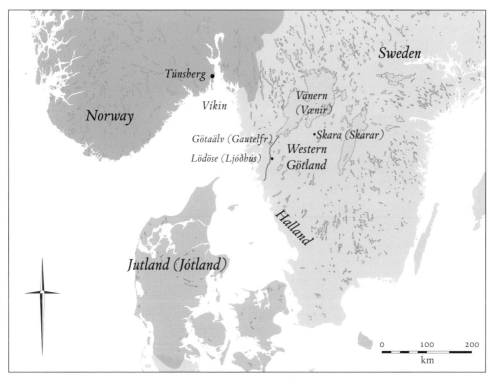

Figure 3. Western Götland, Jutland and Norway. Map: Stefán Ólafsson.

Snorri stayed with Lawman Eskil (Áskell Magnússon) and his wife Kristín, the widow of Earl Hákon *galinn* (literally, "frantic") who had died in 1214 (fig.4).[48] The earl had asked Snorri to compose a poem for her, and she handsomely rewarded him for doing so. Among the gifts he received was "... merki þat, er átt hafði Eiríkr Svíakonungr Knútsson. Þat hafði hann þá er hann felldi Sörkvi [Sørkvi] konung á Gestilsreini."[49] Eiríkr (d. 1216) was Kristín's uncle, and was king of Sweden from 1208 to 1216 (fig. 5). Could there have been a political meaning to her rewarding Snorri with such splendid gifts?

48   See pp. 36, 40–41, 61 in this book.
49   "... the banner, formerly in the possession of the king of Swedes, Eiríkr [Erik] Knútsson. He had it when he defeated King Sørkvir [Sverker] at Gestilsrein" (*Sturlunga saga* I, 269, 271–272). [All translations by the present author, unless otherwise stated.] The 1988 edition of *Sturlunga saga* (I, 257) reads "á Gestilsreyni".

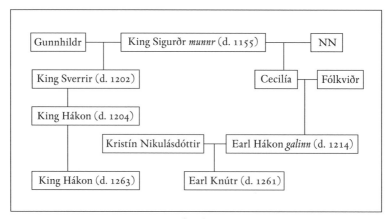

Figure 4. The Family of Earl Hákon *galinn* (Source: *Sverris saga*: III. Niðjar Haralds *gilla*).

Eskil was the lawman of Västergötland and Sturla Þórðarson tells us that he was the nephew of the earl of Västergötland, Birgir (Birger) *brosa* (literally, "smile") who had died in 1202. The earl had been a supporter of King Sverrir of Norway. Later this family and their descendants were called Fólkungar (or in Swedish *folkungaätten*), which was earlier the name for a group of Swedish aristocrats who fought against increasing royal power.[50]

Fólkungar were among the supporters of King Eiríkr in the battle at Gestilsrein (Gestilren) in 1210. The Church sided with the opponent of King Eiríkr, King Sørkvir who franchised the Church in return for its backing. The aim was to increase royal and ecclesiastical power. This policy, favoured by the Pope, the Fólkungar opposed.[51] Sørkvir enjoyed the support of the Danish king, and later the support of the Baglar in Norway, who were also supported by the Danes. The Baglar were the main opponents of the Sverrir group, the Birkibeinar, as already mentioned. King Eiríkr, on the other hand, enjoyed the support of the Birkibeinar, who were not only the followers of King Sverrir but also allies of Earl Birgir. Now, Lawman Eskil was an ally of the Birkibeinar, i. e. Skúli and

---

50   Carlsson and Rosén 1962, 129, cf. 110. On the conservative and aristocratic policy of the Fólkungar see Lönnroth 1944. Further Sandvik 1955, 95–97; Lindkvist 2008; Lindkvist 2013, especially 59–60. How this policy concerned Snorri and his standpoints see Magnús Már Lárusson 1967.
51   Harrison 2001, 106–109.

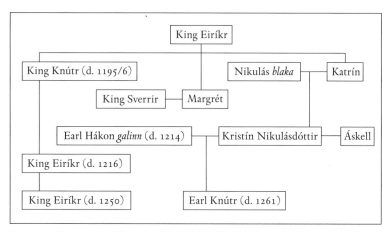

Figure 5. The Family of Kristín Nikulásdóttir.(Source: *Danakonunga sǫgur*, 240).

Hákon, who had, however, made a final peace with the Baglar in 1217, and the division of the country between the two groups came to an end. A position of supporting Birkibeinar and antagonism towards Baglar was not of much political consequence in 1219 when Snorri visited Eskil and Kristín, and there is no reason to see the gifts in that light.

Magnús Már Lárusson has suggested that we should see the gifts in light of Eskil, Snorri and Earl Skúli having a common interest in constitutional or democratic ideologies, that is, in a "thingpower" policy. There are several arguments against such an alleged political persuasion of Skúli and Snorri.

Snorri occupied the office of lawman in Iceland from 1215 to 1218 and Eskil had had a similar position. Snorri probably had much in common with the lawmen Eskil, and Dagfinnr in Norway as far as legislative matters are concerned.[52] Lawmen traditionally represented the rather conservative views of the farming community. Eskil probably opposed increased royal power in Sweden, but Dagfinnr is unlikely to have supported such views against increased royal power in Norway, being one of the king's most trusted men. However, he usually tried to mediate between Hákon and Skúli, and probably accepted Skúli's powerful position to some degree. It was King Sverrir's policy that lawmen should

---

52   See pp. 64, 69 in this book.

succumb to royal power and become judges representing the king.[53] His grandson, King Hákon, took this policy over with the full support of Earl Skúli. Whether such a policy offended Dagfinnr we do not know, but probably not.

In 1218 Earl Skúli already had the idea of becoming king and was supported by the archbishop.[54] We have reason to believe that he did not share the views of the leaders of the farming community as presented in *Heimskringla*. And even though Snorri could appreciate the views of lawmen of ancient times, to prevent royal aggression and secure peace and stability, he supported Skúli. In 1222 Snorri again became lawman in Iceland and built his power on the support of the leading farmers. On the other hand, as a *lendr maðr* he was probably prepared for a king of Norway one day becoming the main source of his own power, a *rex Dei gratia*, whether his name be Hákon or Skúli.

The most likely reason for the great gifts Snorri received from Kristín in Västergötland is that his poem was good, as well as some understanding that he had been a sincere supporter of the Birkibeinar, not least the deceased Earl Hákon *galinn*.[55] Snorri sought the abode of Dame Kristín because he wanted to further establish a name for himself as an accomplished and acclaimed skaldic poet. His trip must also have served his historical interests well and it has been pointed out that the narrator of *Óláfs saga helga* in *Heimskringla* must have visited Skara (Skarar) in Västergötland.[56]

We have reason to believe that Snorri's trip to Västergötland was important in the eyes of Earl Skúli because young Knútr, the son of Earl Hákon and Dame Kristín, was in Kristín's custody. He was a pretender to the Norwegian throne. In 1217 the Norwegian regents (meaning Earl Skúli while Hákon was still a minor) had invited young Knútr to the court. A meeting was arranged between the earl and Lawman Eskil to bring this about. But the latter did not turn up, and did not trust the Birkibeinar. Again in 1224 Knútr was invited to the Norwegian court, this time by King Hákon. Eskil was positive about the invitation, but with

---

53   Helle 1995, 73, 133, 185–186.

54   Helle 1995, 75.

55   Bjarni Einarsson stresses the importance of the poem and suggests it may have been a Minnesang, in the style of troubadours (1987/1969, 100–106); also Guðrún Nordal 2010, 40–42.

56   *Heimskringla* II, 94; Gräslund 1983–1984, 44–46.

some conditions the king could not accept. In 1225 Knútr was invited again. This time Dame Kristín rejected the offer and in the following year, 1226, Kristín arranged for Knútr to become the pretender of the Ribbungar, a group rioting against the Norwegian regents.[57] This was a very delicate matter and Snorri will at least have brought some news about the position and views of Dame Kristín and Lawman Eskil on the matter. Earl Skúli must have found Snorri totally loyal during his Västergötland trip because in 1220 he was charged with a difficult task and elevated to the high position of a *lendr maðr*.

To summarize, the Västergötland trip indicates Snorri's self-interest as a skaldic poet, and his presence there may have been a reminder to Kristín that Snorri had been an ardent supporter of the Birkibeinar and her former husband, Hákon *galinn*. This may explain the choice of gift. However, Snorri was not only a poet from a distant island; he was also a courtier and possibly at this time *skutilsveinn*, a leader of the Norwegian court and a representative of the Norwegian regents.[58] The earl was apparently pleased with Snorri's performance. The lesson to learn from the trip is, therefore, not about Snorri's political persuasion, but rather his faithful service to Skúli.

More Orcadian Affairs

As Skúli's man and a prospective earl in Iceland Snorri must have had a keen interest in Orcadian affairs in the 1220s and once more the relations between the earls of Orkney and the Norwegian regents became Snorri's concern. Two leading Orcadians met in Snorri's home district in 1234 and it is interesting to see this in light of the political development in the islands. Earl Haraldr Maddaðarson had to deal with a competitor, Haraldr Eiríksson, the one who was called Haraldr *ungi* (the Young). He was of the Erlendr line, and was seen as the successor to his grandfather, Earl Rǫgnvaldr Kali (see fig. 1). He was given the title of earl over half of the Orkney Islands by King Magnús Erlingsson, before 1184. But King Sverrir also confirmed Haraldr *ungi's* right to half the earldom of

---

57 *Hákonar saga Hákonarsonar* I, 208, 276, 308–309, 313.
58 Snorri stayed with Skúli in 1218–1219, was in Västergötland in 1219 and back with Skúli in 1219–1220. We do not know exactly when he became *skutilsveinn*.

Orkney.[59] The idea of the Norwegian kings was probably to divide and rule, and hence they were willing to split the Orkney Islands between two earls. The canonization of Rǫgnvaldr in 1192 was without doubt greatly to the advantage of Haraldr *ungi*, but it is possible that Sverrir decided to support Haraldr *ungi* because the old Haraldr, i.e. Haraldr Maddaðarson, rebelled in 1194.[60] Old Haraldr opposed the young pretender in Orkney, and Haraldr *ungi* settled down in Caithness where the Scottish king accepted him as earl of half of the dominion (fig. 2). This was, of course, to the dismay of the old Haraldr, who defeated his namesake near Wick in Caithness in 1198 and had him killed. The King of the Scots reacted, and Hrafn (Rafn) the lawman took his side and became sheriff in Caithness. This probably means that Hrafn supported Haraldr *ungi*. The other Haraldr tried to have Hrafn killed and later, in 1201, he had John, a Scottish bishop of Caithness mutilated.[61] This event led to the lawman Hrafn fleeing to the king of Scots, while Haraldr Maddaðarson confiscated all his belongings. We are informed in the supplement to *Orkneyinga saga*, seen from the point of view of Hrafn the lawman, how the king of the Scots compensated him handsomely for his loss.

In 1195, after the rebellion in 1194, King Sverrir came up with a new idea; he appointed his own sheriff in Orkney to collect fines, administer the crown lands and keep the earl in check. As already mentioned, as soon as Sverrir died in 1202, Haraldr Maddaðarson had this sheriff killed, and was nominally the sole earl both in Caithness and Orkney until he himself died in 1206. Two sons of Haraldr Maddaðarson took over, but had to submit to the Norwegian rulers in 1210 and pay large sums of money, and a sheriff was reinstated in order to counteract the independent tendencies of the earls.

Earl Jón (John), son of Haraldr Maddaðarson, ruled alone after 1214 and sometimes found himself in trouble in Caithness. Around 1220 the Scottish bishop of Caithness, named Adam, was a nuisance to the earl. The bishop doubled some annual levies and was threatened by angry peasants. The earl had little sympathy with the bishop's exaction of increased sums, and ignored his pleas in 1222 to mediate between him and the peasants; the bishop was suffocated in a building which was set on fire by the enraged populace. At the end of *Orkneyinga saga* there is a

---

59 Chesnutt 1981, 38; according to Roger of Howden (a medieval source).
60 Suggested by Chesnutt 1981, 40.
61 Thomson 1987, 10, says 1201.

detailed account of this event, stating that the lawman Hrafn was with the bishop, kept him company and was obviously close to him; again, the episodes are seen from the point of view of the lawman. On the bishop's initiative, the lawman intervened, and tried to settle the case between the peasants and the bishop. At first the peasants accepted; however, hot-heads among them assaulted the bishop, who met his fate in the burning house, after being reviled, stoned and beaten.[62]

In this account, Hrafn the lawman, no less than the bishop, is the focus of attention, and it is natural to conclude that his son Andréas was the source for this supplement to *Orkneyinga saga*. The other Andréas, Andréas Gunnason, who was also present in Borgarfjǫrðr in Snorri's district in 1235, was the great-grandson of Sveinn Ásleifarson. (On the two namesakes see the introduction.) Some detailed information in *Orkneyinga saga* about Sveinn's banqueting hall can be traced to him.[63]

Now we turn to a certain Snækollr Gunnason; *Hákonar saga Hákonarsonar* (The Saga of King Hákon Hákonarson) is the main source about him. Like Haraldr *ungi*, Snækollr was of the Erlendr line, a descendant of Earl Rǫgnvaldr Kali and nephew of Haraldr *ungi* (fig. 1). Snækollr made a plea to Earl Jón to return some of the manors the family of Rǫgnvaldr formerly had in their possession. The earl ran these farms and was evasive. Snækollr was persistent in his demands, and finally the earl grew angry and asked if Snækollr would follow the example of his nephew, Haraldr *ungi*, and claim the Orkney Islands. Because of this obvious animosity, Snækollr left the earl and sought refuge with the king of Norway's sheriff, Hánefr. This sheriff probably had good reason to fear the earl, bearing in mind how Haraldr Maddaðarson had killed the sheriff in 1202. Once when Hánefr, the sheriff, and Snækollr were in Thurso (Þórsá) in Caithness they met with Earl Jón, and killed him as he hid among barrels in a cellar; he also seems to have been burnt.[64] This happened in 1231, and the next year these two protagonists and many other aristocrats in Orkney agreed to leave for Norway to meet King Hákon and ask him to settle the matter. Hánefr and Snækollr were arrested in Bjǫrgvin in 1232, and their henchmen were executed. The Orcadian aristocrats left for

---

62   Chesnutt 1981, 51–52.
63   Sveinn seems to have fascinated people in Iceland, and has been seen by some scholars as a model for Egill Skalla-Grímsson, cf. Bjarni Einarsson 1975, 156–186; Helgi Guðmundsson 1997, 294–295.
64   He was "combustus" according to *The Melrose Chronicle*, see Chesnutt 1981, 53.

Orkney the same year, but strayed off course and never returned to the islands. Hánefr and Snækollr left Bjǫrgvin for Niðaróss (Þrándheimr) in the company of Earl Skúli. Hánefr died in 1233, but Snækollr is reported to have stayed with Earl Skúli for a long time.

This connection between Orkney and Skúli makes the visit of the two Andréases to Snorri's district in 1234 rather interesting. The line which stands out is the illustrious Erlendr line, with St Magnús, St Rǫgnvaldr Kali, Haraldr the Young and finally Snækollr. What their political ideas were is difficult to say; their interest was to rule both in Caithness under the king of the Scots, and in Orkney under the Norwegian king, at least in half of each dominion. However, during the last decade of his rule Haraldr Maddaðarson of the other line, the Páll line, would hear of no such thing; he wanted to rule alone over both Orkney and Caithness. The same goes for Jón, his son, after 1214. The idea of a king's sheriff who was to counteract this in Orkney was obviously annoying for the earls of the Páll line, and explains the bond between Hánefr and Snækollr. The lawman Hrafn opposed the Orcadian earls as the sole earls in Caithness. He must have supported Haraldr *ungi* as earl in Caithness and, since Haraldr was an earl of the king of the Scots, Hrafn naturally became an ally of the king against the Orcadian earls. He was therefore also friendly towards the Scots bishops, who had clashes with the Orcadian earls. And if Andréas Hrafnsson pursued the same policy as his father, he would of course have supported Snækollr and Hánefr against Earl Jón. Killing Earl Jón was not exactly what King Hákon and his men expected from Hánefr, and the king had to mollify the earl's supporters. On the other hand, Skúli took both Hánefr and Snækollr with him north to Niðaróss. In 1232/33 Earl Skúli seems to have been displeased; his relations with King Hákon were delicate and in 1234 they hardly trusted each other anymore.[65] From now on a war between them was imminent. We can ask why Skúli kept Snækollr at his court. The answer is, to have him ready as his representative in the Orkney Islands at the right moment. There never was a right moment, and King Hákon had Skúli killed in 1240.

In 1234 Snorri Sturluson was at the peak of his power and influence. He was not only a *lendr maðr*, one of the top courtiers in Norway, he was also Skúli's close friend. Andréas Hrafnsson would probably have been interested in discussing Orcadian politics with Snorri, and even Snækollr's

65   Helle 1974, 110.

options. We do not know where the other Andréas stood, but he was a member of the elite in Orkney, a great-grandson of Sveinn Ásleifarson and also of Kolbeinn *hrúga* (lit. pile) or Cobbie Roo of Wyre (Vigr). These families used to support Haraldr Maddaðarson, but we do not know what the situation was like for them around 1230. There was a degree of friction between King Hákon and Earl Jón which became very serious in 1224, and the situation afterwards was always tense until Earl Jón died in 1231. It has been suggested and seems plausible that Earl Jón supported Earl Skúli in his power struggle with King Hákon.[66] In other words, around 1230 the family of Haraldr Maddaðarson and their followers supported Skúli as did Snorri Sturluson. And even though Snækollr might have been close to King Hákon, he also became Skúli's man.[67] This means that Andréas Gunnason no less than Andréas Hrafnsson supported Snækollr and sided with Skúli.

A trip to Iceland was probably not only lucrative for those Orcadians who had cereal, meal and malt to sell for *vaðmál* (homespun); it might, no doubt, also be enjoyable to stay with close relatives of the Norwegian kings at Oddi around 1200, or later enjoy the company of the important courtier and narrator Snorri Sturluson. It is quite possible that young Orcadian aristocrats saw it as social or political advancement to stay with the Oddi family or Snorri. The two Andréases should not be seen as professional merchants. They would have enjoyed the company of Skúli´s leading man in Iceland and appreciated his views of the prospects of Snækollr as earl in Orkney. However, the source on their trip to Iceland, *Sturlunga saga,* does not say that the two stayed with Snorri at Reykholt or ever met him. All the same, it can be inferred. There was great discord between Snorri and his son Órækja and sometime during the winter 1234/35 Órækja had some 2100 kilograms of meal belonging to the Andréases confiscated. There can be two reasons for this. Firstly, the harbour was close to the important manor of Stafholt which Órækja wanted his father to hand over to himself, and this is probably where the meal was stored. Secondly, by this Órækja proved that his father could not protect the Andréases. Snorri came to the harbour and must have met the two but otherwise he was staying at Reykholt, about seventeen kilometres away as the crow flies. The two stayed either at Stafholt or

---

66 Wærdahl 2011, 80–81 (following Crawford in her unpublished PhD. thesis).
67 Both Snækollr and the second Andréas were Gunnason, but we do not know if they were brothers.

Reykholt during the winter and if they were staying at Stafholt they must at least have been invited to Reykholt during the Christmas period. Had Snorri refused to see them this most probably would have been mentioned in the *Sturlunga saga* account.[68]

Snorri versus Sturla Sighvatsson and the Question of Earls

In 1235 Sturla Sighvatsson, Snorri's nephew, came back to Iceland from Norway. He had committed himself to winning Iceland for King Hákon and be remunerated in an appropriate way, probably by becoming earl. Their plan was to drive leading Icelanders to Norway. Snorri fled to Norway in 1237 and stayed with his friend Skúli, who was now a duke. In 1238 Sturla was killed and Snorri came back from Norway in 1239. At that time the duke had decided to fight the king for the throne and Snorri was his accomplice in this. The king denied Snorri the right to leave Norway, but Snorri left anyway. Sturla Þórðarson is rather vague about Snorri's part in Skúli's schemes and uses the term *fólgsnarjarl* for Snorri. There is little doubt that Snorri was to become Skúli's earl in Iceland, in the event that the latter became the king of Norway. However, Skúli was defeated by King Hákon who sent a letter to Iceland to his trusted man, Gizurr Þorvaldsson, either to send Snorri to Norway or kill him. Gizurr had Snorri killed in a cellar at Reykholt in 1241.

As the title of earl was intended for Snorri in Iceland, something similar was probably planned by Skúli for Snækollr in the Orkney Islands. Snækollr was one of Skúli's sheriffs in Norway in 1239 and was captured by the king's men. Snorri must have been familiar with Snækollr and well informed about the Orkney Islands. Obviously there was great interest in Iceland in Orcadian affairs. This is borne out by the fact that the Icelandic annals have detailed information about events in the islands prior to 1240.[69] Relations between Norway and the islands could indicate what might happen in relations between Iceland and Norway.

---

68 *Sturlunga saga* I, 387. The harbour Seljaeyri which is mentioned was at the confluence of Hvítá and Norðrá.

69 *Islandske Annaler.*

Conclusion

In about 1202 Snorri Sturluson turned against the Oddaverjar in Iceland as well as the leading men in the Orkney Islands. Snorri supported the Birkibeinar in Norway and their policy, which does not mean that he was a fervent opponent of the Baglar and what they stood for. Snorri admired resolute and eloquent lawmen reminding the kings of the limits of their rights and power as is borne out by *Heimskringla*. However, that would not have been a very successful policy of lawmen or counsellors in Norway in around 1230. As a consequence of the policy of Birkibeinar, royal power was increasing fast and Snorri was a sincere supporter of the Birkibeinar. It is hardly possible to see Snorri and the other lawmen, Hrafn in Caithness and Dagfinnr in Norway, forming a group of men actively supporting the "thingpower" policy of strong lawmen, backed by yeomen at assemblies and checking royal power. On the other hand, Lawman Eskil may have been an active supporter of such sentiments. Earl Skúli was rather aggressive and prepared an invasion of Iceland which Snorri succeeded in preventing. Even though Skúli was aggressive and Snorri probably wrote Einar Þveræingr's speech, he was a good friend of Skúli. Here it is argued for that the connecting theme in Snorri's foreign relations was Earl Skúli and his policy. But there were also personal interests at stake. Snorri most probably hoped to become the leading representative in Iceland of the Norwegian regents. It turned out badly for him that the king and earl in Norway were at loggerheads, and Snorri sided with Skúli who lost. High hopes of becoming earl in Iceland came to nothing.

During his lifetime Snorri was probably very interested in political affairs of the Orkney Islands and especially in the relations between the earls there and the Norwegian regents. The relations between the Fólkungar in Västergötland and the Birkibeinar and Baglar must also have been of great interest to him.

Snorri's political life was about personal interests, gifts and favours, less about political persuasion. During his stay in Norway between 1218 and 1220 he began his friendship with Earl Skúli. Snorri enjoyed his generosity and had him to thank for his advancement. He was faithful to Skúli for the rest of his life; such loyalty meant more to Snorri than different political views. Generally speaking, he probably had a good understanding of political possibilities, as indicated by the way he handled the situation in 1220 when an invasion of Iceland was being prepared.

He probably saw himself more than anything else as a diplomat, an intermediary between the Icelanders and the Norwegian king, a speaker at assemblies explaining the options and a counsellor to regents pointing out some sensible moves.

Acknowledgements

Haki Antonsson read a draft of this article for which I am most grateful.

Bibliography

Andersson, Theodore M. 1994. "The Politics of Snorri Sturluson". *JEGP* 93 (1), 55–78.

Andersson, Theodore M. 1999. "The King of Iceland". *Speculum* 74 (4), 923–934.

Bagge, Sverre 1991. *Society and Politics in Snorri Sturluson's* Heimskringla. Berkeley, Los Angeles, Oxford: University of California Press.

Bagge, Sverre 2004. "Snorri as a Political Historian". In Vassil Giuzelev *et al.* (eds), *Snorri Sturluson and the Roots of Nordic Literature.* Sofia: University of Sofia, 110–116.

Berman, Melissa A. 1985. "The Political Sagas". *Scandinavian Studies* 57 (2), 113–129.

Biskupa sögur I. Eds Sigurgeir Steingrímsson, Ólafur Halldórsson, Peter Foote. Íslenzk fornrit XV. Reykjavík: Hið íslenzka fornritafélag, 2003.

Biskupa sögur II. Ed. Ásdís Egilsdóttir. Íslenzk fornrit XVI. Reykjavík: Hið íslenzka fornritafélag, 2002.

Bjarni Einarsson 1987/1969. "Andvaka". In Sigurgeir Steingrímsson (ed.), *Mælt mál og forn fræði. Safn ritgerða eftir Bjarna Einarsson, gefið út á sjötugsafmæli hans 11. apríl 1987.* Rit 31. Reykjavík: Stofnun Árna Magnússonar, 1987, 100–106.

Bjarni Einarsson 1975. *Litterære forudsætninger for Egils saga.* Rit 8. Reykjavík: Stofnun Árna Magnússonar.

Carlsson, Sten and Jerker Rosén, 1962. *Svensk historia* I. *Tiden före 1718.* Av Jerker Rosén. Tredje upplagan. Stockholm: Svenska bokförlaget.

Chesnutt, Michael 1981. "Haralds saga Maddaðarsonar". In Ursula Dronke *et al.* (eds), *Specvlvm norroenvm. Norse Studies in Memory of Gabriel Turville-Petre.* Odense University Press, 33–55.

Crawford, Barbara 2010. "The Joint Earldoms of Orkney and Caithness". In Steinar Imsen (ed.), *The Norwegian Domination and the Norse World c.* 1100–c. 1400. Norgesveldet, Occasional Papers No. 1. Trondheim Studies in History. Trondheim: Tapir Academic Press, 75–97.

Danakonunga sǫgur. Ed. Bjarni Guðnason. Íslenzk fornrit XXXV. Reykjavík: Hið íslenzka fornritafélag, 1982.

Einar Ól. Sveinsson 1937. *Sagnaritun Oddaverja. Nokkrar athuganir.* In Sigurður Nordal (ed.), Studia islandica. Íslenzk fræði 1. Reykjavík

Finnbogi Guðmundsson 1965. "Formáli". *Orkneyinga saga.* Ed. Finnbogi Guðmundsson Íslenzk fornrit XXXIV. Reykjavík: Hið íslenzka fornritafélag, v–cxli.

Foote, Peter 2004/1993. "Icelandic Historians and the Swedish Image. Comments on Snorri and his precursors". In Alison Finlay *et al.* (eds), *Kreddur. Selected Studies in Early Icelandic Law and Literature.* Reykjavík: Hið íslenska bókmenntafélag, 154–181.

Gräslund, Bo 1983–1984 "Snorre, Ragnvald Ulfsson och Brunnsbo Storäng. Till frågan om ett jarlssäte i Västergötland vid skiftet mellan forntid och medeltid". *Västergötlands fornminnesförenings tidskrift,* 39–50.

Guðrún Nordal 2010. "Trúbadúrinn Snorri Sturluson?" *Margarítur hristar Margréti Eggertsdóttur fimmtugri 25. nóvember 2010.* Reykjavík: Menningar- og minningarsjóður Mette Magnussen, 40–42.

Gunnar Karlsson 1979. "Stjórnmálamaðurinn Snorri". In Gunnar Karlsson and Helgi Þorláksson (eds), *Snorri. Átta alda minning.* Reykjavík: Sögufélag, 23–51.

Haki Antonsson 2007. *St. Magnús of Orkney. A Scandinavian Martyr-Cult in Context.* Leiden: Brill.

Harrison, Dick 2002. *Sveriges historia. Medeltiden.* Stockholm: Liber.

Hákonar saga Hákonarsonar I. Eds Þorleifur Hauksson, Sverrir Jakobsson, Tor Ulset. Íslenzk fornrit XXXI. Reykjavík: Hið íslenzka fornritafélag, 2013.

Heimskringla II. Ed. Bjarni Aðalbjarnason. Íslenzk fornrit XXVIII. Reykjavík: Hið íslenzka fornritafélag, 1945.

Helgi Guðmundsson 1997. *Um haf innan. Vestrænir menn og íslenzk menning á miðöldum.* Reykjavík: Háskólaútgáfan.

Helgi Þorláksson 1979. "Snorri Sturluson og Oddaverjar". In Gunnar Karlsson and Helgi Þorláksson (eds), *Snorri. Átta alda minning.* Reykjavík: Sögufélag, 53–88.

Helgi Þorláksson 1982. "Rómarvald og kirkjugoðar". *Skírnir* 156, 51–67.

Helgi Þorláksson 2006. "Snorri Sturluson, Reykholt og augustinerordenen". In Else Mundal (ed.), *Reykholt som makt- og lærdomssenter i den islandske og nordiske kontekst.* Snorrastofa, vol. III. Reykholt: Snorrastofa, 65–75.

Helle, Knut 1974. *Noreg blir en stat 1130–1319. Handbok i Noregs historie, 3.* Bergen, Oslo, Tromsø: Universitetsforlaget.

Helle, Knut 1995. *Under kirke og kongemakt 1130–1350.* Aschehougs Norges historie 3. Editor-in-chief Knut Helle. Oslo: Aschehoug.

Hrafns saga Sveinbjarnarsonar. Ed. Guðrún P. Helgadóttir. Oxford: Clarendon Press, 1987.

Islandske Annaler indtil 1588 Ed. Gustav Storm. Kristiania 1888.

Jesch, Judith 1993. "England and Orkneyinga Saga". In Colleen Batey, Judith Jesch and Christopher Morris (eds), *The Viking Age in Caithness, Orkney and the North Atlantic. Selected Papers from the Proceedings of the Eleventh Viking Congress, Thurso and Kirkwall, 22 August–1 September 1989.* Edinburgh: Edinburgh University Press, 285–303.

Jón Jóhannesson 1956. *Íslendinga saga I. Þjóðveldisöld.* Reykjavík: Almenna bókafélagið. [In English, *A History of the Old Icelandic Commonwealth: Íslendinga saga.* Winnepeg: University of Manitoba Press, 1974.]

Jón M. Samsonarson 1958. "Var Gissur Þorvaldsson jarl yfir öllu Íslandi"? *Saga* II (4), 326–365.

Lindkvist, Thomas 2007. "The lagmän (Law-speakers) as Regional Elite in Medieval Västergötland". In Tuomas M.S. Lethonen and Élisabeth Mornes (eds), *Les Élites Nordiques et l'Europe Occidentiale (XIIe–XV Siècle):* Actes de la Recontre Franco-nordique organisée à Paris 9–10 juin 2005. Paris, 67–78. [Used here as a manuscript, kindly provided by the author.]

Lindkvist, Thomas 2008. "Ett svenskt bakslag. Om Sverige som korsfararrike i början av 1200-talet". In Auður Magnúsdóttir, Henrik Janson, Karl G. Johansson, Mats Malm and Lena Rogström (eds), *"Vi skal alla vara välkomna!" Nordiska studier tillägnade Kristinn Jóhannesson.* Göteborg, 297–308.

Lindkvist, Thomas 2013. "Västergötland as a Community and the Making of a Provincial Law". In Steinar Imsen (ed.), *Legislation and State Formation. Norway and its Neighbours in the Middle Ages. Norgesveldet, Occasional Papers No. 4.* Rostra Books - Trondheim Studies in History. Trondheim: Akademika Publishing, 55–65.

Lönnroth, Erik 1944. "De äkta Folkungarnas program". *Kungliga humanistiska vetenskaps-samfunnet i Uppsala.* Årsbok.

Magnús Fjalldal 2013. "Beware of Norwegian Kings". *Scandinavian Studies* 85 (4), 455–468.

Magnús Már Lárusson 1967. "Þrístirnið á Norðurlöndum". *Skírnir* 141, 28–33.

Orkneyinga saga. Ed. Finnbogi Guðmundsson. Íslenzk fornrit XXXIV. Reykjavík: Hið íslenzka fornritafélag, 1965.

Sandvik, Gudmund 1955. *Hovding og konge i Heimskringla*. Oslo: Akademisk forlag.

Sawyer, Birgit 2010. "Snorre Sturlason som balanskonstnär". *Collegium medievale* 23, 33–57.

Sigurður Nordal 1920. *Snorri Sturluson*. Reykjavík: Þór. B. Þorláksson.

Thomson, William P.L. 1987. *History of Orkney*. Edinburgh: The Mercat Press.

Sturlunga saga I–II. Eds Jón Jóhannesson, Magnús Finnbogason, Kristján Eldjárn. Reykjavík: Sturlunguútgáfan, 1946.

Sturlunga saga I–II. Ed. Örnólfur Thorsson. Reykjavík: Svart á hvítu, 1988.

Wærdahl, Randi Bjørshol 2011. *The Incorporation and Integration of the King's Tributary Lands into the Norwegian Realm, c. 1195–1397*. Translated by Alan Crozier. The Northern World. Leiden, Boston: Brill.

¶ VIÐAR PÁLSSON, HELGI ÞORLÁKSSON
AND SVERRIR JAKOBSSON

Reykholt as a Centre of Power

1. Reykholt and Centres of Power in Context

VIÐAR PÁLSSON

Introduction: Centres of Power as a Concept

STUDENTS OF EARLY ICELANDIC POLITICAL CULTURE HAVE increasingly adopted the term *valdamiðstöðvar* (centres of power) as a shorthand for seats of power that became more than simply the physical residences of leaders (*höfðingjasetur*) and came to embrace broader functionalities of power, variously combining social, cultural, economic, topographical, and political dimensions.[1] Although the distinction is on the one hand functional, it is, however, also concerned with functional dynamics and gravitational force. Key characteristics might include a large farm (forty or fifty hundreds or more), a church (often but not necessarily a *staðr*),[2] geographical centrality and proximity to main routes, and various attractions such as a pool, facilities for feasts or other large-scale gatherings, and cultural institutions such as a scriptorium and a book production.

The term *valdamiðstöðvar* is abstract and has not been rigidly defined; this, if anything, enhances the term's analytical utility rather than diminishes it. Oddi and Reykholt immediately come to mind as centres

---

1 For an introduction to these concepts, see Helgi Þorláksson 2007a.
2 For a definition see note 13.

of power *par excellence* but if one seeks a rigid definition of the term, there is a risk of ruining the concept's useful abstractness by turning Oddi and Reykholt into Platonic forms and, by extension, lesser candidates into the shadowy reflections of these preeminent centres. Not only would this hinder the fair evaluation of these "lesser candidates" but it might also reduce Oddi and Reykholt to mere products of developmental necessity and play down their dynamic uniqueness. Moreover, centres of power were the products of combinations of factors, many of which drew their force from the inner dynamics of the socio-political culture of a pre-state society and its twelfth- and thirteenth-century transformations, while simultaneously being influenced by historically specific and contingent circumstances. It is thus better to evaluate the concept by approaching it from different angles, thereby acquiring an adequate sense of its basic outlook and nature. The aim is to locate Reykholt in the larger landscape of centres of power in medieval Iceland, considering its conformity as well as its uniqueness. The following survey of the basic forces and factors that produced and shaped centres of power straightforwardly renders the conclusion that centres of power proper are essentially a twelfth- and thirteenth-century phenomenon. But just as their outlook and dynamics heralded novelties, many of their roots ran deep. Reykholt cannot be properly understood without taking into consideration the larger social and political context surrounding it.

Centres of Power and the Social Topography of Ecclesiastical Institutions

The rise of ecclesiastical institutions in early Iceland arguably represents the most powerful means of shaping social topography that was then at the disposal of those devoted to furthering their political prominence. Although the earlier stages of the process are obscure on many points, it is eminently clear that it was largely driven by, and profoundly shaped by, aristocratic initiative and competitive impulses. Among other things, this is witnessed by the uneven development of tithe areas and ministries following the introduction of the tithe towards the end of the eleventh century: this clearly bears the marks of the struggle for social prominence between men of political means and the absence of a systematizing central ecclesiastical authority.[3] In a marginally institutionalized culture of power, where social and political ties were principally structured on the basis of personal relations and networks, the instigation of ecclesiastical institutions established a unique venue for fostering stable points of social gravity.[4]

Smaller churches and chapels appear to have multiplied rapidly in the eleventh century, most probably in close correlation with farm-stead burial sites. Once larger churches appeared, however, whose services extended beyond the immediate farmsteads' households and embraced neighbouring households as well, favourable conditions were reached for reshaping social relations. Churches mobilized bodies, living and dead, along with a sizable proportion of those people's wealth. Church farmers, whose churches enjoyed the services of clerics in times when priests were in short supply and grew in size so they could host several households when most church buildings could barely hold one, thus attained a uniquely advantageous social position. This development gained momentum no later than the early twelfth century and prominent church farmers emerged whose churches commanded a considerable degree of centrality in terms of both religious services and, following the introduction of the tithe, the administration of ecclesiastical finances.[5]

The salvation of souls and religious observance in medieval Christi-anity was a communal enterprise and so by definition a social activity.[6]

---

3   The uneven and unsystematic formation of tithe areas and ministries is discussed in, e.g., Orri Vésteinsson 1998; 2000b, 73–74, 78–79, *passim*; cf. also Hjalti Hugason 2000, 200–212.

4   On the whole, there is every reason to question the centrality assigned to the early bishops by Ari fróði in *Íslendingabók* (*c.*1130) and *Hungrvaka* (*c.*1200), i.e. we may assume that the organizational and administrative authority of bishops was weak up until the later twelfth century, and this effectively made early church organi-zation the project of the secular aristocracy. The issue is important for the early development of seats, and later centres, of power. For divergent views on the extent and strength of early episcopal power, see Jón Jóhannesson 1956, 176–187; Magnús Stefánsson 1975, 69–72; Einar G. Pétursson 1986; Orri Vésteinsson 2000b, 144ff, *passim*; Hjalti Hugason 2000, 247ff; Benedikt Eyþórsson 2005, 29–35.

5   The location of burial sites and the size and location of the earliest churches are discussed in Orri Vésteinsson 2005, cf. 2000b, 45–54; 2000a; Steinunn Kristjáns-dóttir 2003; Vilhjálmur Örn Vilhjálmsson 1996; Hjalti Hugason 2000, 170–174; Guðbjörg Kristjánsdóttir 2000, 175–182. The early scarcity of priests is discussed in Helgi Skúli Kjartansson 2005.

6   This is brilliantly illuminated and contrasted with late medieval and early modern individualization by Bossy 1985.

Amongst other things, it ensured that medieval Christian Icelanders did
not neglect, and went out of their way for if necessary, the baptism of
their young, the last rites of their dying, the proper burial of their dead,
and the sufficiently regular reception of communion by their living,
generally by attending mass. Surrendering the administration of such religious and social necessities to fellow neighbours fundamentally affected
and shaped the bonds of those involved. Those fostering leadership and
influence within society (which generally meant those struggling for
power) therefore actively sought the status of eminent church farmers,
thereby situating themselves at the forefront of social activity. The formation of sophisticated networks of social relations through the emergence
of ecclesiastical bodies was no doubt driven by a host of disparate factors,
both practical and more abstract, but central among them must have
been the endeavours of politically ambitious men to create and ensure
their own social centrality. On the basis of the factors that contributed
to building up centres of power in the twelfth and thirteenth centuries,
prominent and important church farms appear most explicitly as their
sine qua non. Almost every serious candidate that might be considered a
centre of power out of which the most powerful men of the twelfth and
thirteenth centuries operated was, with some variation, either a great
church farm or, effectively, a church centre.[7]

It is equally evident that the achievements of rising twelfth-century
church farmers rested above all on their ability to emerge successfully
from what must essentially have been an adjudicative local process in
determining social and political leadership. For aspiring church farmers
this meant, above all, acquiring communal recognition of their churches
via payments of tithes, and this underpinned their functional hegemony,
religious and social.[8] While it seems easy enough to understand that centres of power generally became intimately connected with such nexuses of
social relations, nevertheless, precisely which factors ensured the success
of one aspiring church farmer over another must have varied from case
to case. Together, these crucial factors might ultimately be brought under
the rubric of charismatic leadership. And once trust was gained and the
balance tilted, the ability to negotiate favourably and persuade politically

7   For a definition of a church centre see note 15.
8   The influence of local political persuasiveness in the early formation of tithe areas is
    addressed by, e.g., Orri Vésteinsson 1998, 154–156, and alluded to in Hjalti Hugason
    2000, 200ff, especially 204, 213.

must have grown correspondingly. Doubtless, socially climbing church farmers must have run their churches impressively and appealingly in outlook and operation.

Centres of Power and Economic Resources

Among the least understood aspects of the culture of power in medieval Iceland are its economic mechanisms and the finances of political relations, an issue, we should note, not of bare economics but, fundamentally, of mentality and culture as well. This all revolves to a great extent (at least in modern scholarship if not always in past reality) around centres of power, church farms in general and *staðir* in particular.

It used to be assumed more readily and generally among scholars than is fashionable today that tithe-collecting church farms, principally *staðir*, were lucrative and important sources of wealth through which political leadership was financed to a decisive degree.[9] By subjecting the medieval Icelandic culture of power and its social institutions, principally church farms, to such a socio-economically oriented explanatory model, the institutions in question were necessarily seen as having originated primarily as tools of economic exploitation, at once aimed against the one while correspondingly securing the privileges of the other (which, from such a theoretical standpoint, is the essence of political assertion). The basic thesis here received its most influential treatment at the hands of the eminent historian Björn Þorsteinsson, who postulated that a powerful aristocracy had sought to ensure its position as a privileged elite by casting itself as *kirkjugoðar* and turning their church farms into ecclesiastical fiefs fit for economic, and thereby social and political, exploitation. Supposedly, then, wealth in the form of tithes and gifts flowed towards greater church farms and filled the pockets of men whose skills, objectives, exemptions from tithe payments, and rental incomes and interests from growing private investments, secured a handsome overall

---

9   Links between tithe-collecting church farms, economic imbalance, and political consolidation fuelling the demise of an original equilibrium had been identified by the 1940s, cf. Sigurður Nordal 1942, 296 (who there coined the term *goðakirkja*). Jón Jóhannesson made the link as well but without emphasizing it to the same degree, cf. 1956, 212, 271, *passim*. Ólafur Lárusson may be considered ahead of Sigurður in making similar connections, though his exposition is somewhat vaguely phrased, cf. Ólafur Lárusson 1944, 38–39 (the relevant article was originally published in 1929).

profit and in so doing laid the foundations for their economic advantages and political leadership.[10]

Aside from the obvious danger of subjecting the exercise of political power in general to such a narrowly defined economic determinism, the thesis of church farms functioning as income-generating institutions yielding private profit on a grand scale has itself been proven to be more easily assumed than convincingly demonstrated.[11] To this end, Gunnar F. Guðmundsson's critical analysis of such presumed personal economic benefits, published in 1997, may have stripped the thesis of whatever credibility it had left.[12] To Gunnar's illuminating calculations of the tithe incomes and tax benefits to be had from endowing ecclesiastical institutions under one's own control, we may add crucially important questions left glaringly unanswered in previous scholarship, in particular that of a Marxist or neo-Marxist nature. Some of these questions relate to the presumed ability of prominent church farmers to run their institutions properly and impressively while at the same time securing a private profit from these same payments on a large enough scale to contribute significantly to the financial basis of their political standing, even to the point of underpinning it. Another and closely related set of questions begs an explanation of how exactly, in the first place, an admittedly leading segment of society would have managed to impose such undisguised taxation on their fellow commoners in as uniform, effortless, and apparently collaborative manner as then would seem to be the case.

Perhaps the most vexatious questions, however, address the twelfth-century practice of transforming a proprietary church farm into a private institutional corporate entity (a kind of trust), i.e. *staðr*, and how this fits a larger interpretive model of an ecclesiastically-funded political

10   Björn contrasted a non-feudal and egalitarian agrarian society with feudal economic relations, the former allegedly representing an indigenous and original state of affairs while the latter a foreign and ecclesiastical (meaning above all episcopal) incentive. The transformation produced an economically violent and politically viable elite, *kirkjugoðar*, and their corresponding *kirkjugoðaveldi*. See primarily Björn Þorsteinsson 1953, 229–292; 1966, 207–24; 1978, 100–112. The context and development of Björn's Marxist interpretation is discussed in Helgi Þorláksson 1988.
11   See, e.g., Lúðvík Ingvarsson 1986, 1, 180–191.
12   Gunnar F. Guðmundsson 1997. The issue also figured large in past debate on the finances of power round the middle of the thirteenth century that was conducted by Gunnar Karlsson and Helgi Þorláksson, cf. Gunnar Karlsson 1972; Helgi Þorláksson 1979a; Gunnar Karlsson 1980; Helgi Þorláksson 1982.

elite.[13] Simply put, financial coercion dressed in religious garments used to be identified as the *staðir*'s true *raison d'être* and proper historical context. It is alarming, therefore, to see how uneasily the *staðir* in general conform to such a grand formula of financial resources and power; for each *staðr* representing a plausible example for private economic advancement, there is a counterexample pointing in the opposite direction. Thus there are *staðir* that appear to have been established at enormous cost yet without obvious financial returns. The establishment in around 1140 of Stafholt in Stafholtstungur for example, one of the most handsomely endowed *staðr* on record, hardly served to increase tithe revenues, given its circumstances. Further examples of proprietary churches turned into *staðir* without apparent hopes of larger tithe areas include Staðarhraun (Staðr undir Hrauni) by Hítardalr, Hítarnes on Mýrar, and Húsafell, later belonging to Hálsasveit.[14]

True, the majority of major churches or church centres were *staðir* and many of them were seats or centres of power. It must be remembered, however, that many particularly prominent and wealthy major churches remained as proprietary churches while still serving as important seats or centres of power. One might mention, for example, Vatnsfjǫrðr by Ísafjarðardjúp, Skarð on Skarðsströnd, Garðar on Akranes, Bœr in Bœjarsveit, Haukadalr in Biskupstungur, and Mǫðruvellir and Hrafnagil in Eyjafjǫrðr.[15] The legal-institutional format may thus have been important

13   *Staðr* (benefice) is a legal concept but not a shorthand for *kirkjustaðr*, "church farm". *Staðr* was a kind of trust, a church institution acting as the sole owner (or its patron saint) of the farmland on which it stood, along with all its rights and revenues. Thus, *staðr* is a parallel to or even a translation of the concept *locus sacer*. The episcopal seats at Skálholt and Hólar, the monasteries, and all churches as owners of the farmland on which they stood were *staðir* (approximately 30–40% of all church farms in Iceland). The dispute over episcopal authority over *staðir* in the later twelfth and thirteenth centuries, the so-called *Staðamál*, were bitter not least because church farmers had traditionally administered *staðir* just as they did other church farms in their possession (*bændakirkjur*), and had probably not foreseen that such an institutional arrangement would divest them of the right to do so. Furthermore, many church farmers endowed their churches with their entire landownings explicitly on the condition that the *staðr* so created should be administered by themselves and their descendants for all time. See principally Magnús Stefánsson 2002.
14   Cf. Helgi Þorláksson 2005a, 15; Benedikt Eyþórsson 2005a, 44; Helgi Þorláksson 2005b, 127. Apparently, *staðir* ceased to be established after 1185, and for those established around or after 1150 there cannot have been any real hope of reshaping the tight pattern of tithe areas by then in place. Of the *staðir* mentioned above, Stafholt is likely the oldest, cf. *DI* 1, 178–180 (Stafholt), 217–218 (Húsafell), 275–276 (Hítarnes), 279 (Staðarhraun).
15   For an overview of major churches and their ecclesiastical status as either pro-

but not decisive. The matter is further complicated when we recall that powerful men sometimes chose to operate from church farms that were neither *staðir* nor particularly wealthy. Guðmundur *dýri* (the Powerful), for example, chose to operate from the relatively meager Bakki in Øxnadalr around 1200, and Sauðafell in Dalir, which became an important centre of power in the thirteenth century, evidently attracted chieftains for reasons other than being a major church.[16]

Major proprietary churches and *staðir* were an exceedingly expensive enterprise. Their establishment probably called for an initial minimum endowment close to twenty or thirty hundreds, which was commonly provided by the church farmer himself. Furthermore, the running of most church farms would have required a steady flow of income from its existing property and/or in the form of gifts and additional endowments supplemental to tithes; otherwise, a church might easily become a financial burden on the shoulders of its farmer or caretaker.[17] Skilful and politically inclined church farmers would, however, acquire priceless valuables from their enterprises other than cash: social, cultural, and symbolic capital in Bourdieuean terms, honour and prestige in medieval terms, power in universal terms.[18]

prietary churches [*bændakirkjur*] or *staðir*, see Magnús Stefánsson 2000, 253–331. Major proprietary churches and their place in the political culture of the thirteenth century is addressed in Jón Viðar Sigurðsson 2005, cf. also 2007. The expression "church centres" has been coined for the most important *staðir* and proprietory churches combined. On their characteristics see Benedikt Eyþórsson 2005b, see e.g. 106, 116.

16   Neither church is included on Jón Viðar Sigurðsson's list of major churches (in Norwegian *storkirker*), which counts 33 churches in total on grounds of their size (>49 hundreds) and number of hired clerics (>3): Jón Viðar Sigurðsson 2005, 159–160. The choices of Bakki and Sauðafell have been discussed in detail by Helgi Þorláksson 1994; 1992.

17   Cf. Gunnar F. Guðmundsson 1997, 62–63.

18   The emphasis here on the political value of ecclesiastical structures as social units rather than their (possible or at least highly variable) economic value is in line with Orri Vésteinsson 2000b, 85–92. Magnús Stefánsson, on the other hand, emphasizes the financial benefits for chieftains overseeing *staðir*, claiming their control to have been a prerequisite for political strength, Magnús Stefánsson 1975, especially 89–91. The issue of economic links, in particular as relating to centres of power, still revolves around two key questions: firstly, whether landowning patterns generally developed from allodial landholding to tenancy over the medieval period and beyond; secondly, what role, if any, the introduction of the tithe played in that assumed process. For a recent introduction to both issues (arguing for a growing number of tenancies), see Sverrir Jakobsson 2005, cf. also Jón Viðar Sigurðsson 1989, 81–107; Orri Vésteinsson 2000b, 85–92.

Centres of Power and Political Consolidation

The emergence of centres of power stands in a dialectical relation with the consolidation of power witnessed principally by the late twelfth and early thirteenth centuries. The process involved not only a geographical expansion of power but also an apparent transformation with regard to its nature: leading chieftains acted increasingly like petty lords within given territories.[19] And even if their political activities required them to be mobile, they nevertheless operated out of relatively few and fixed residences. These became centres of power. Thus Svínafell in Œrœfi, Valþjófsstaðr in Fljótsdalr, and Hof in Vopnafjǫrðr became clear focal points in the East while Oddi became a focal point in Rangárþing, Reykholt in Borgarfjǫrðr, Staðarstaðr (Staðr á Ǫlduhrygg) in Snæfellsnes, Vatnsfjǫrðr in Vestfirðir, Sauðafell in Dalir, and Grund in Eyjafjǫrðr. This process needs to have been neither unilateral nor uniform, however, as evidenced by the Ásbirningar and Haukdælir families: Kolbeinn *ungi* (the Young) operated variously out of Áss, Víðimýri (-mýrr), and Flugumýri (-mýrr) in Skagafjǫrðr while the Haukdælir operated primarily out of Hruni in Hrunamannahreppr, Brœðratunga in Biskupstungur, Reykir in Ǫlfus, and Kallaðarnes in Flói[20]. Residential centres of power thus became fewer as a rule, but there was never just a single one in each area of influence. They now stood rather as focal points for domains that were larger and markedly different in character from what had come before.[21]

Among the factors that raised certain *loci* above others were those concerned with basic practicality and function. Thus, geographical and topographical conditions certainly imposed limits as much as creating opportunities in this respect. By its nature, political leadership depended upon active communication between the chieftain and his followers, both in terms of its proper execution and prerequisite support. This is obvious in such basic matters as those of security and defence: the actual fortresses of political leaders were the followers amongst whom they situated them-

---

19 The topic runs like a thread through the literature on medieval Icelandic political culture; the debate is far-reaching. Key contributions include Jón Jóhannesson 1956, especially 265–338; Björn Sigfússon 1960; Jón Viðar Sigurðsson 1989; 1999, especially 39–83; Gunnar Karlsson 1975, 29–54; 2004; Lúðvík Ingvarsson 1986–1987.

20 Modern Kaldaðarnes.

21 Gunnar Karlsson argues, though, that the consolidation of power began rather later than sometimes thought and that the resulting domains were, if anything, quite loosely attached to fixed seats or centres of power, cf. Gunnar Karlsson 2007a, especially 212–213. See also Sverrir Jakobsson 2002; Helgi Þorláksson 2013.

selves and on whose recruitment they relied. Accessibility was crucial to both parties. Active leadership required, in peace as well as in conflict, proximity to major routes along which people and news travelled. Being at the centre of communications was fundamental.[22] The flexibility of choice of residence was itself largely determined by the extent to which ambitious men were successful in counterbalancing, or perhaps rather complementing, geographical and topographical factors by bending the social grid itself. Church organization has already been noted in this regard. Further arrangements might include securing routes by ferries or bridges and attracting travellers by impressive appearance and hospitality; both of these were lucrative sources of social and political opportunities.[23] It has likewise been suggested that the immunity attached to the sacrality of churches (helgi), and in particular that of staðir, significantly advanced the social and political gravity of their respective farms.[24]

Our knowledge of the early stages of this development is patchy. Recent and important archaeological findings and discussions, not least those about early Icelandic hof sites, has emphasized the variety among what are collectively labelled central places in modern terminology, and shown how different social, political, and cultural ambitions may have separated functional aspects otherwise commonly joined together by the modern mind, which inherently seeks unity. Hof sites, which undoubtedly served as venues for socially significant feasting, thus appear closely connected with local assembly sites vis-à-vis being tied to the foremost

22 On the relations between centres and routes of communication, see (in addition to the above-cited entries on Bakki and Sauðafell) Helgi Þorláksson 1989; 1998.

23 Hrafn Sveinbjarnarson of Eyri (Eyrr) has been interpreted in the context of such ambitions by Helgi Þorláksson 2007a, 193. Revered seats sometimes gave way to new locations in times of political consolidation. Thus Hvammr in Dalir gradually lost its importance while Sauðafell became prominent; in the West Fjords, Vatnsfjǫrðr was preferred to Eyri; in the South, the Haukdælir abandoned Haukadalr as their seat towards the end of the twelfth century; and in the West, Snorri chose Reykholt rather than Borg, to name just a few examples. Apparently, the convenient location of Reykholt did not detract from its appeal to Snorri, cf. Tryggvi Már Ingvarsson 2000.

24 Helgi Þorláksson has argued that the enhancement of immunity for the sake of the security of both travelers and residents was a prime motive for transforming proprietary churches into staðir, thus significantly advancing their social and political status. Typically, he argues, these sites were linked to routes of travel which increased immunity in turn promoted. Prior to Helgi's examination of this matter, Orri Vésteinsson drew a connection between the relocation of churches in the early thirteenth century and the benefits of their immunity. See, Helgi Þorláksson 2005b; Orri Vésteinsson 2000b, 54.

central political residences.[25] In certain cases, *hof*s may even have been deliberately removed from the context of political centrality, as Hofstaðir in Mývatnssveit suggests.[26] But whatever the finer details of the earlier landscape of power were, we should be mindful that centres of power as they came to be in the twelfth and thirteenth centuries were no less the result of conscious decisions than a necessary product of impersonal factors.

This brings us back to the Ásbirningar and Haukdælir. Due to our inclination to view the emergence of centres of power squarely within the context of political consolidation, any divergence from the norm is seen as an anomaly that must be accounted for specifically (usually in the form of explanations of hindrances). But since we allow ourselves to interpret the emergence and characteristics of Reykholt in the context of Snorri's conscious cultural and political agenda, Kolbeinn *ungi* and Gizurr must be granted equal attention as far as the ways in which they chose to present and execute political leadership are concerned. The Haukdælir probably withdrew from Haukadalr in the late twelfth century in order to operate more centrally within Árnesþing, but the fact that neither they nor the Ásbirningar worked from a single principal centre out of their handful of residences may have had as much to do with their deliberate style, strategy, and leadership ideologies as with failed attempts to do so. When Gizurr returned from Norway in 1258 he operated out of Kallaðarnes in the south and Reynistaðr (Staðr í Reyninesi) in the north; the reasons behind these choices are not fully clear, nor is whether Kolbeinn *ungi* could not or would not sit at Reynistaðr previously. However, as Helgi Þorláksson has recently argued, the residential pattern of the Ásbirningar indicates that an axis between the Vatnsskarð pass in the west and the Glóðafeykir mountain in the east had indeed emerged as a political centre proper in Skagafjǫrðr by the end of the twelfth century. He argues that a shift of operation from the Hegranes area (Áss) to the centre of major inland

---

25 For previous debates on this issue, see, e.g., Ólafur Lárusson 1958 (originally published 1952); Jón Hnefill Aðalsteinsson 1985.

26 Not for the first time, Hofstaðir in Mývatnssveit draws much attention. Gavin Lucas suggests that it was deliberately removed from political centrality in order to serve its social function better as a grand feasting hall for the community at large (cf. theories of heterarchy). It is likewise possible, as Lucas remains open to and Orri Vésteinsson argues for, that *hof* establishments such as Hofstaðir were attempts at promoting new centres of power in opposition to existing ones; if so, then Hofstaðir ultimately failed. See, Orri Vésteinsson 2007; Gavin Lucas 2009, cf. also 2007.

routes between Vatnsskarð (Víðimýri) and Glóðafeykir (Flugumýri) should be interpreted as a logical consequence of political consolidation in the area, and thus analogous to, rather than divergent from, the formation of centres of power in Borgarfjǫrðr, Eyjafjǫrðr, and elsewhere.[27]

Centres of Power and Cultural Context

The accelerated, and in most respects novel, textualization of power in the central Middle Ages and thereafter has long been recognized as a fundamental aspect of the transformation and early modernization of European society. In twelfth- and thirteenth-century Iceland as elsewhere, power — its philosophy, legitimacy, and practice — was increasingly negotiated and mediated through text as a medium; this reinforced the practice of literacy and text production and the practice of power in general under a single authority. The Oddaverjar were early pioneers in such a fusion of text-cultural guidance and political leadership, advancing their hegemony by turning Oddi into by far the most sophisticated centre of learning and power in Iceland before and around 1200.[28]

Despite the prominence of literary culture in thirteenth-century Iceland and the rich legacy it left behind, we still know frustratingly little about the details of text production and consumption, such as exactly where given texts were put together, by whom, what their distribution and reception was, or how general the access or exposure of different social groups to individual texts was. It remains beyond doubt, however, that a growing elite of *literati* played an increasingly important political role in this new social environment and that the scriptoria out of which the *literati* worked became focal points of power. There is every reason, therefore, to believe in a firm connection between the culture of the

27 Helgi Þorláksson 2010. It should be mentioned, however, that Snorri in fact resided at Stafholt and not Reykholt for as long as three consecutive winters. Stafholt was well-situated at a crossroads, and close to the harbour of Norðrá, the *sælubú* at Ferjubakki, and the assembly site at Þverá. It is possible, however, that his temporary residence in Stafholt sprung from immediate causes. See Helgi Þorláksson 1979b, especially 143–159; cf. also Orri Vésteinsson 2006.

28 The centrality of textual culture in building political and social identity amongst the Oddaverjar is made clear in Einar Ól. Sveinsson's standard introduction to the subject but has been developed more fully since. Einar Ól. Sveinsson 1937.

written record and the culture of power, and correspondingly between clerics and centres of power.

For one thing, clerics serviced all major church farms: commonly there were three or four hired clerics at the wealthiest and foremost church farms; five was exceptional, and six or seven unique.[29] These church farms must have stood at the forefront of text production and dissemination of all sorts and they thereby added to the political weight of their respective farms. As a result, major church centres were foremost among centres of power. For another thing, instituting this particular field of culture and financing text and manuscript production must likewise have proved a lucrative source of symbolic and cultural capital. Identifying with, and operating within, the culture of records became a source of power *per se*, and converting economic resources into texts and books was an important social marker. As is true of power generally, this was not the business of common men.[30]

Centres of Power and the Construction of Political Space

The wider context of Snorri's Reykholt has now been sketched out as well as the criteria for identifying it as a centre of power, and it was an impressive centre in every respect. It was an important *staðr* with illustrious history, possibly the first to be established following Skál-holt;[31] its continuous occupation and service from the late tenth century onwards by the venerable family of Þórðr Sǫlvason must have generated considerable respect;[32] its standing as a church centre was supported by

---

29 Jón Viðar Sigurðsson (2005) provides tables which give a convenient overview.

30 Thus the employment of *lærdomssenter* in the title of Else Mundal (ed.) 2006.

31 The date of establishment of individual *staðir* is almost without exception circum-stantial, even if they fall within a relatively narrow window of *c.*1100 to *c.*1185. In all likelihood, Magnús Þórðarson made Reykholt a *staðr* before 1118, cf. Magnús Stefánsson 2005, 123–124.

32 Lúðvík Ingvarsson believes that the Reykhyltingagoðorð was initially shared between Þórðr's forefathers, the Geitlendingar, and Tungu-Oddr Ǫnundarson at Breiðabólstaðr. If we take the sources at face value (and this is not straightforward), then the chieftaincy passed to Þórðr's father in 998 and thence into Þórðr's own hands in 1035 and his descendants, down to Magnús Pálsson from whom Snorri received the *staðr* and presumably the chieftaincy along with it. Men in this male line were renowned and respected clerics. This is, of course, the very family that Hvamm-Sturla quarreled with during the infamous Deildartungumál dispute. See

Figure 1. Aerial view of Reykholt and its environment, looking east. To the right the Reykjadalr valley (Reykholtsdalr) and the river Reykjadalsá. In the background the glacier Eiríksjǫkull. Photo: Guðlaugur Óskarsson, September 2016.

its large ministry and annex churches;[33] it boasted four or possibly five hired clerics, among them known literary authorities, who, together with the five clerics attached to Stafholt, made a uniquely impressive cohort of *literati*;[34] its sacral immunity as a *staðr* was specifically noted

further Lúðvík Ingvarsson 1986, 2, 371–398 and for a different understanding, Helgi Þorláksson 2012a, and further pp. 130–133 in this book. On Deildartungumál, see *Sturlunga saga* I, 105–114.

33   On the size of the ministry of Reykholt and its annex churches, see Benedikt Eyþórsson 2005b, especially 111, 113–115.

34   Including Styrmir Kárason *fróði*, at Reykholt. Styrmir was the son of the abbot of the monastery at Þingeyrar and probably grew up there, and the great-grandson of Bishop Ketill Þorsteinsson. Styrmir was twice elected lawspeaker, later became prior in Viðey, was the author of a now lost redaction of *Landnámabók* and a lost saga on King Óláfr *helgi*, possibly wrote on King Sverrir, and more. On Styrmir see pp. 140, 295–299, 368–370, 375–376, 423, 452–453 in this book. See, generally, Benedikt Eyþórsson 2003, 23-24. Gunnar F. Guðmundsson argues that there were two priests and one deacon at Reykholt in the fourteenth century, 2016, 168–169.

by contemporaries;[35] its superb geographical location made it central, visible, and accessible from a large area;[36] and, finally, Snorri's ambition for promoting it as his principal residence and a symbol of his power made it outstanding.

Despite there being few, if any, centres of power that were on a par with Reykholt as far as its dynamic character was concerned, it resembled other centres in other ways. What truly set Reykholt apart as a centre of power at the beginning of the thirteenth century, however, was its adoption into a calculated politico-cultural project run by its new master. As a centre of power and a politico-cultural symbol, Reykholt therefore appears to have been distinctively constructed or established rather than emerging more neutrally as a candidate.[37] It is noteworthy in this respect how insignificant Reykholt's potential as a farm was in comparison with most other centres of power. It was hardly worth more than about thirty hundreds, or forty at best. Fifty or sixty hundreds was common for manors while an average farm was worth twenty hundreds. [38] Furthermore, for the *staðr* to be able to meet its ambitious financial obligations it had to secure considerable income from extra endowments in land and pasture and other rights fit for lease.[39] This leaves one with the impression that Reykholt became established as a major church centre through considerable effort. As such, it was of much value to Snorri.

Rather than drawing money from it, Snorri seems to have poured money into the place from the start. There is every indication that upon arrival, Snorri worked hard and paid considerable sums in order to reconstruct the cultural and political space in Reykholt, not only regarding book production and intellectual leadership but also via a major transformation of the physical appearance of the place. Recent archaeological excavations have unearthed unparalleled material splendour and style which indicate a truly aristocratic setting.[40]

---

35   *Sturlunga saga* II, 171; cf. Helgi Þorláksson 2005b, 140–141.

36   Cf. note 23.

37   Cf. Helgi Þorláksson 2007b, especially 214–217.

38   Benedikt Eyþórsson 2008, 108–114.

39   At the time of Snorri's arrival in 1206, the *staðr* owned Hœgindi, Breiðabólstaðr, and Norðrreykir, plus various rights; cf. Reykholt's inventory: *Reykjaholtsmáldagi*, 14–15. Páll Sǫlvason seems to have been quite aware of such pressure for income, cf. *Sturlunga saga* I, 106.

40   This is described well by Guðrún Sveinbjarnardóttir 2006 and Guðrún Harðardóttir 2006. See most recently and thoroughly Guðrún Sveinbjarnardóttir 2012; 2016. See further, pp. 266–274 in this book.

Snorri's Scandinavian travels must have made a major cultural and political impression on him. Indeed, they come across primarily as an aristocratic schooling of sorts and an attempt to forge elite ties. His identification with the Norwegian aristocracy is likewise unmistakable in the aristocratic setting of Reykholt, his hosting of Norwegians distinguished by fashionable weaponry,[41] his feasting in Norwegian style,[42] and last but not least his claim to authority over the history of kingship and aristocratic culture in Norway.[43] Such ambitions should properly be read against the background of high medieval Europe more widely. As historians have persistently argued in the last twenty or thirty years, high medieval Europe experienced a major societal transformation, characterized as a "revolution" by one, foremost amongst them.[44] These social and economic changes exerted pressure on the aristocracy to differentiate itself more actively and to a greater extent than before; the elevation of an eleventh-century martial *miles* to a twelfth- and thirteenth-century socio-cultural ethos of chivalry (the knight's ennoblement, as it were) is emblematic in that respect. Consequentially, social markers of all sorts were cultivated and advanced, not least in terms of material lifestyle and distinct social preferences. Another product of the age was the peculiar marriage of the fortress and the palace from which the castle was born; despite the castle's practical usefulness in war, its primary function was that of the palace, symbolically and socio-politically organizing space.[45]

Norwegian and Scandinavian aristocrats and kings were not untouched by such developments which they knew from Angevin and other contemporary cultures. On the contrary, they embraced such ideas, claimed their share in them, imitated them, and adopted their style of fashion and social distinction. But since such identification and borrowing was neither automatic nor simple, King Hákon *gamli*'s (the Old's) well-

---

41   *Sturlunga saga* I, 269.

42   *Sturlunga saga* I, 315.

43   On Snorri's interpretation of political culture, see, e.g., Bagge 1991. On Snorri's predilection for Norwegian aristocratic culture, see Guðrún Nordal 2006.

44   Moore 2000. In effect, this signalled the birth of Europe, hence this being her first revolution.

45   An introduction to aristocratic transformations, with a focus on France, is Bouchard 1998, especially 15–21 on castles and their symbolic and social rather than military function. The castle proper was exclusively a high medieval phenomenon, born not during but after the violence of the ninth and tenth centuries. For the German lands, see Bumke 1991, 103–119. For England, see Eales 1990. On fortresses in Iceland, see Guðrún Harðardóttir and Þór Hjaltalín 1998.

known efforts towards this end can only be seen as a proactive cultural programme.[46] Snorri thereby came into direct contact with an aristocratic culture in the making, and it no doubt influenced him.[47]

It is hard to imagine the impression Reykholt made on Snorri's contemporaries once finished, on the common farmer approaching it from a distance, this seat of the king's man with its magnificent facilities and grandeur, its pool, a large church, a mighty fortress, a storehouse of wealth and learning. There must have been more than a whiff of aristocratic cosmopolitanism in the air.

2. Reykholt before Snorri's Time

HELGI ÞORLÁKSSON

Introduction

In this section indications of how Reykholt was built up from scratch as a centre of power (in modern Icelandic *valdamiðstöð*) will be discussed. First a description of centre of power and its characteristics would be appropriate. It is not just any place where a chieftain is living.[48] First, it would preferably be more than twice or even three times as large as the average farm.[49] Secondly, it had to be well located on a main thoroughfare or at a crossroads. And last but not least, it was a place with activities that attracted people. This could include premises that could accomodate many people for gatherings probably similar to the so-called *hof* (often translated as "pagan temples"), a major church, or even a pool. The second and third point concern *centrality* which is best demonstrated by the attendance of people. Attendance could be increased through certain arrangements. A church could be transformed into a *staðr* and

---

46 On King Hákon, Norway, and European aristocratic and courtly cultural connections, see Helle 1968. An old but useful study is Leach 1921; on literary connections, see principally Sif Ríkharðsdóttir 2012; Wanner 2008, 80–87. On Snorri's aristocratic aspirations see in this book pp. 33–73.

47 This is not the same as saying that such changes were transparent or easily navigable, as Wanner's (2008) stimulating interpretation of Snorri's miscalculated skaldic investments argues.

48 *Goðar* were living at the remote Selárdalr and Hraun in Keldudalr in the West but that would not automatically turn these seats of chieftains (in modern Icelandic *höfðingjasetur*) into centres of power.

49 50 to 60 hundreds instead of 20.

some of the early rich *staðir* were seen as sanctuaries or holy places. The church buildings at the rich *staðir* were usually well built and beautifully furnished. Thus the *staðr* would become an attraction. The same would apply to a pool if it was made accessible. Or the chieftain of the place would invite people to some festivities, like games. In order to attract people he might build causeways to make boglands passable, or contribute to a ferry. He would do this to increase his political influence.[50]

In the late twelfth century, before Snorri Sturluson settled there, Reykholt was apparently a distinguished place of power. This was the seat of Páll Sǫlvason (d. 1185) and his son and heir Magnús Pálsson. Both were *goðar* and ordained priests. The great-grandfather of Páll was Þórðr who was the first man we hear of living at Reykholt. He is supposedly the Þórðr Sǫlvason, priest at Reykholt, mentioned in *Bandamanna saga*, the only source of information concerning his priesthood. Working from this and the estimated age of his son, we can infer that Þórðr was probably in his prime between 1040 and 1050, and born between 1000 and 1015.[51] Guðrún Sveinbjarnardóttir concludes that the farm buildings at Reykholt might have been just a little older than the first church building, erected around the year 1000.[52] This would make Þórðr, or his father, the first settler at Reykholt and Þórðr might even have had the first church built. Why did they settle at Reykholt and what was the situation like before they appeared on the scene? It is interesting that Breiðabólstaðr, about a kilometre east of the old pool at Reykholt, is allegedly the first place of settlement in the area. The first settler of the Reykholt valley was, according to *Landnámabók* (The Book of Settlements), either Krǫmu-Oddr[53] or Ǫnundr *breiðskeggr*[54] and the son of Ǫnundr was the chieftain (*goði*) Tungu-Oddr at Breiðabólstaðr, prominent in some of the Icelandic sagas.[55]

---

50   A well known example of a *höfðingjasetur* which a *goði* tried to turn into a centre of power is Eyrr (Eyri) at the time of Hrafn Sveinbjarnarson; we are told that he kept a ferry on Arnarfjǫrðr and another on Breiðafjǫrðr. On the concept of centres of power in Iceland see Helgi Þorláksson 2007a, and at a later stage (mainly the rich *staðir*) see Viðar Pálsson above.

51   Lúðvík Ingvarsson 1986, 2, 388–389.

52   Guðrún Sveinbjarnardóttir 2009, 60. Guðrún Sveinbjarnardóttir et al., 2007, 202. Guðrún Sveinbjarnardóttir 2010, 483–493 (a *bær* (farm) was erected in Reykholt close to the year 1000).

53   *Krǫmu* could refer to *krǫm*, meaning "weakness", "infirmity".

54   *Breiðskeggr* could mean Broadbeard. *Skeggr* could also mean "inhabitant", "resident"; on *breið* as a "grown plain", see below and fn. 105.

55   *Tunga* in the name of Oddr could allude to the area ("tongue") between ther rivers Hvítá and Reykjadalsá.

Generally speaking, historians do not take *Landnámabók* at face value and this invites questions such as whether Breiðabólstaðr was really the original place of settlement in this area and why Reykholt was settled at a later date. Furthermore, why did Reykholt become the residence for the "strong man" or chief of the area? (see the general map on pp. 12–13 in this book).

The church at Reykholt was a *staðr* and among the most important churches in Iceland. Recent excavations have shown that the church building was about twelve metres in length in the thirteenth century, a reasonable size for its time.[56] Communications must have played a part in making Reykholt a centre of ecclesiastical and secular power; it lies at a crossroads, which is important.[57]

Breiðabólstaðr had become the property of the church (the *staðr*) at Reykholt as early as 1204. It also appears that Breiðabólstaðr did not have an annex church or chapel in medieval times and this may also reflect the relatively low status of the farm. A possible reason why Breiðabólstaðr did not function as the residential place of the chieftains and as the site of the important church in the twelfth century is the presence of the hot spring at Reykholt and the pool a little over a hundred metres to the west of it. The eleventh-century building which has been excavated at the church site at Reykholt, and which is interpreted as the earliest church, was located about seventy metres from the pool, which is likely to have been in the same location from the outset. In thirteenth-century narratives it is taken for granted that the pool existed in the tenth century, even though people were not living then at the site.[58] The pool, either natural or man-made at that time, was possibly an attraction for a politically ambitious man. Such pools could be very important when people gathered at some of the most popular sites in the twelfth and thirteenth centuries, like Laugar in Sælingsdalr and Vallalaug in Skagafjǫrðr.[59]

---

56 See pp. 261–266 in this book.

57 Tryggvi Már Ingvarsson 2000. Two important centres of power in the thirteenth century, Sauðafell and Grund, were not *staðir*. Their size and central location was what counted most.

58 *Íslendingabók, Landnámabók*, 192. *Landnámabók* says about Tungu-Oddr, "fór Oddr frá húsi til laugar í Reykjaholt; þar váru sauðahús hans ...", Oddr went from the farmhouse [at Breiðabólstaðr] to the pool in Reykholt; that was the location of the shed for his sheep".

59 Helgi Þorláksson 1998, 51–53; 2010, 57–59; 2015, 53–54.

It has been suggested that ambitious "big-men"[60] were attracted to living at or close to popular pools on main routes and so were taking advantage of the locality for their churches and struggle for power (examples are Bœr, Hruni and Hrafnagil, which were residences of chieftains, all close to pools).[61] Well-to-do farmers without any political ambitions who enjoyed bathing may certainly have preferred places with pools. However, in centres of power pools will usually have been turned into attractions for passers-by and neighbours. A man with political ambitions might have seen an opportunity at Reykholt and made use of the situation by making the pool at the crossroads attractive and by building farm houses and a church close by. The aim would have been to attract as great a number as possible of farmers and peasants of the district, who would have been willing to contribute fiancially or otherwise to the church building. The idea might also have been to attract travellers who would otherwise have passed by.

Breiðabólstaðr

If churches existed in tenth-century Iceland they were probably not so important then, and at that time a chieftain was, it seems, fairly well located at Breiðabólstaðr. Why might Breiðabólstaðr have been chosen as the site for the first settler in the area? The name itself may explain what the settler was after. *Breiða* in compounds like this is usually supposed to mean "broad" but there is a better explanation.

The settlers most probably brought with them young cows or heifers and cows were not able to survive during the winter without some shelter and fodder. Scientists seem to be in agreement that the lowland in Iceland was covered with birchwood around 870. Land for haymaking was probably limited in many low-lying places, and it was not easy to cultivate infields for haymaking. However, farmers in medieval and later times in Iceland not only mowed hay in cultivated, manured infields, for fodder, they also cut sedge in outfields, in wetlands and meadows.

---

60 Used as a concept here, as in *big-men and chiefs*, postulated by Sahlins 1972/1981 and others.

61 Which came first, church or farm buildings, at some of the pools (or close to them) is open for speculation. Helgi Þorláksson 2011, 211. On churches built at some distance from farm houses see, Orri Vésteinsson 2000b, 50–53.

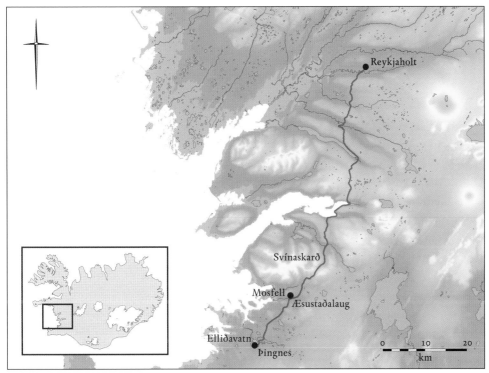

Figure 2. The route between Reykholt (Reykjaholt) and Þingnes at Elliðavatn, via Mosfell. Map: Stefán Ólafsson.

This was often naturally grown sedge which had not been manured at all, in many instances not much inferior to grass or hay as fodder for the animals.

The noun *breið* occurs in Icelandic meaning "plain", often wet, and usually grown with sedge. Just above present-day Breiðabólstaðr there is a pond called Breiðavatn. A possible explanation for the name of the farm is that the area around Breiðavatn is *breiðar*, i.e. flat land, wet and well covered. This area is called Breiðaflói, and *flói* means "wetland", wetter than *mýrr* or *mýri* (mire or bog-land). It is obvious that this area around the lake could have been mowed.[62] During the earliest period of settlement, sites with good *breiðar* were important whereas in the second half of the tenth and in the eleventh century other considerations

62 The plains around the river in the Reykholtsdalr valley (Reykjadalr nyrðri on the maps) were only sparsely wooded and much wetter than they are at present, see in this book pp. 171–172, 175.

were of more interest, such as possibly the church and its connection with the pool at Reykholt. The residence of chieftains in the Reykholt valley was therefore moved from Breiðabólstaðr to a more favourable place.[63]

Demise of the Chieftaincy of the Tungu-Oddr Family

Hœnsa-Þóris saga (Hen-Thorir's Saga) tells us that two of the sons of Tungu-Oddr died abroad, and this could well be true.[64] Another blow to the family was probably the administrative division of the district introduced around 965, according to Ari's *Íslendingabók*. The general opinion among scholars is that this new system was indeed introduced. As a consequence, the Hvítá river marked a new border between two Quarters of Iceland, the southern and western Quarters and this division remained in place for centuries. It was not a natural boundary, as the river ran straight through the middle of the rather densely populated agricultural area of Borgarfjǫrðr and was blessed with several fords, most of them fairly easily passable on horseback. Scholars do, however, tend to take seriously what Ari says about this new demarcation and the events leading up to it.[65] Tungu-Oddr was defeated and obviously this new border blocked him from having formal *thingmenn* (followers) to the north and west of the Hvítá. The spring assembly was moved from Þingnes to a new site, Þinghóll, farther west in Borgarfjǫrðr, while Tungu-Oddr had to attend a different assembly site, far to the south, in Kjalarnesþing (see fig. 2 for Þingnes at Elliðavatn, and a general map in this book 12–13).

This means that the power of Oddr was seriously curtailed. However, by around 1140 this new system had been abandoned, as is indicated by the fact that the assembly site of the area was at that time at Þingey, in the middle of the Borgarfjǫrðr area, close to the Hvítá and Þverá rivers, as well as Stafholt (Stafaholt).[66] This site must have served everyone in the whole area south and west of the Hvítá.

---

63   On Breiðabólstaðr and *breiðar* see Helgi Þorláksson 2011.

64   *Hœnsa-Þóris saga*, 41, 46.

65   For instance the classic treatment by Jón Jóhannesson 1956, 68–70.

66   See Helgi Þorláksson 2012a, 96–98. Þingey was most probably a part of the modern Stafholtsey.

Sturlubók		Hauksbók, Geirmundarþáttr (Melabók)
Úlfr in Geitland		Bjǫrn austræni
Hróaldr		Kjallakr
Hrólfr		Hrólfr at Ballará
Sǫlvi in Geitland		Sǫlvi
Þórðr at Reykholt		Þórðr
Sǫlvi		Sǫlvi
Þórðr the younger [priest]		Þórðr
Magnús		Magnús
Þórðr	Sǫlvi (d. 1129)	Sǫlvi
Helga	Páll (d. 1185)	Páll
Guðný	Magnús (d. 1223)	Magnús
Snorri		

Figure 3: The people of Reykholt
To the left we see how *Sturlubók*, one of the redactions of *Landnámabók*, a work of Snorri's nephew, accounts for the family at Reykholt (Reykhyltingar) and traces them back to Geitland. To the right we see how the other redactions and the *Geirmundarþáttr* account for them, tracing them to Hrólfr at Ballará in the west.

These problems of Tungu-Oddr and his family probably opened up some new possibilities for others. Þórðr Sǫlvason or his father Sǫlvi was allegedly the first master of the house in Reykholt. What more do we know about them, for instance where they came from? In some genealogical lists Þórðr's ancestry is traced back to a family in possession of the important grazing land at Geitland in Borgarfjǫrðr which was later claimed by the church (the *staðr*) at Reykholt, which some believe to be true.[67] The present author, on the other hand, agrees with those who argue that the tracing of the Reykholt people back to people living in Geitland in *Landnámabók* is a fabrication, and that the tracing of them

67 Lúðvík Ingvarsson believes that *Reykhyltingagoðorð* was previously shared by Þórðr's forefathers, Geitlendingar, and Tungu-Oddr at Breiðabólstaðr. If the sources like *Landnámabók* are to be taken at face value here, which is far from obvious, then the chieftaincy passed to Þórðr's father and afterwards to himself. One of Þórðr's descendants was Magnús Pálsson, from whom Snorri received the *staðr* and presumably along with it the chieftaincy. Lúðvík Ingvarsson 1986, 2, 371–398. The *goðorð* of Magnús most probably came from Tungu-Oddr but there is little reason to believe that people in Geitland ever shared the *goðorð* with the Reykholt people.

to the Breiðafjǫrðr area in the west is the more original account and may be authentic.[68] Stories about the people of Geitland and Tungu-Oddr sharing the responsibility for running the *hof* at Hofstaðir (about four kilometres east of Reykholt) are also suspect and invite scepticism and scrutiny. The word *hof* could either refer to a building which could be used for social activities such as feasts, or to a farm where such a special building was found.[69] It has been suggested that the place name element *-staðir* in Hofstaðir is a secondary part of names for landholdings, usually only of average value. It indicates a part of a landed property that was parcelled out for some purpose. The first part of such place names usually indicates its owner or the one who used it.[70] Assuming that this is correct, Hofstaðir may have belonged to Breiðabólstaðr and the *hof* was therefore at Breiðabólstaðr. The word *hof* would then indicate some spacious abode at Breiðabólstaðr, fit for major gatherings.[71] Even though Geitland can be used as summer pastures it has limited possibilities for agriculture at a fairly high altitude above sea level and was usually uninhabited. Thirteenth-century tales about tenth-century farmers of Geitland (almost thirty kilometres away from Reykholt) being responsible for one half of the expenditure of the *hof* is not credible.[72] The point being made here is that connections between the Reykholt people and the Geitland people are dubious. In the thirteenth century, Geitland was important for the *staðr* at Reykholt as a grazing land and for its forest and other resources and this may explain some questionable connections which seem to be fabricated.

Þórðr Sǫlvason, who seems to have been a priest at Reykholt (see above), and his father, probably of a family from the west, were related to, and had family links with, the people of Breiðabólstaðr.[73] When the family of Oddr had been badly hit politically and perhaps mourned the

---

68 *Íslendingabók, Landnámabók*, 78 fn.; argued by Jón Jóhannesson and supported by Jakob Benediktsson.

69 Orri Vésteinsson 2007, 72–75, 89–90.

70 Svavar Sigmundsson 1979, 238–248.

71 Helgi Þorláksson 2012a, 90–94.

72 Signs of habitation in longhouses have been found in Geitland, see Guðmundur Ólafsson 1996. Its date is ninth century and it did not last long, cf. Guðrún Sveinbjarnardóttir *et al.* 2011. More such "pioneer fringe" sites are known in Iceland.

73 This is the line which seems authentic from the well known Kjallakr and his descendants, the chieftain family Kjalleklingar in Dalir. Hrólfr at Ballará, son of Kjallakr, was most likely grandfather of Þórðr who moved to Reykholt. See Helgi Þorláksson 2012a, 96, cf. 87.

loss of young men who would have been the inheritors of the chief-taincy (*goðorð*), the family of Sǫlvi and Þórðr replaced them and seized the opportunity to build a new centre of power, and established their residence close to the pool.[74] They began from scratch, so to speak, and gradually became very successful. We should see the eleventh century as a transitional period for Breiðabólstaðr/Reykholt; after the collapse of the Tungu-Oddr family a new family found its footing and rose to prominence.

How did the Þórðr family manage? It is suggested here that they strove to increase the centrality of Reykholt mainly by building the church and turning it into a *staðr*. Accordingly they would also have tried to benefit politically from the pool and the church.

Centres Created and Abolished

The centrality of places could be increased and there are several examples of this which it would be interesting to compare with Breiðabólstaðr and Reykholt. One such place is Hrísbrú, abolished as a centre of power and replaced with Mosfell, which was close by. Both of them lie about fifty-five kilometres directly south of Reykholt (fig. 2).

The initial Mosfell farm, a power centre of its age, was most probably at present-day Hrísbrú, about five hundred metres west of present-day Mosfell. According to *Egils saga Skalla-Grímssonar* the church at Hrísbrú was dismantled ("ofan tekin") and a new one built at the Mosfell farm, around the middle of the twelfth century.[75] Farm buildings at the new site may have been built somewhat earlier, possibly in the eleventh century since the longhouse at Hrísbrú, which has been excavated, was abandoned at that time.[76] The older farmstead was given the name Hrísbrú.[77] Was this similar to how Reykholt may have developed; a new site became the

---

74 Helgi Þorláksson 2012a, 95–98. It is quite possible that Torfi Valbrandsson, who figures prominently in some of the Sagas of Icelanders and *Landnámabók* , was in charge at Breiðabólstaðr at the end of the tenth century. On him and his relations with Tungu-Oddr see *Íslendingabók, Landnámabók*, 74–75; *Hænsa-Þóris saga,* 4 and fn.; *Harðar saga*, 6 fn., and Helgi Þorláksson 2012a, 96.

75 *Egils saga Skalla-Grímssonar*, 298.

76 Zori 2014, 61–62.

77 *Egils saga Skalla-Grímssonar*, 298 fn. Byock et al., 2005, 198–199. Byock and Zori 2013, 134–137.

main one and the old settlement site acquired a lower status? Here, as in the Reykholtsdalr, this did not signal the permanent abandonment of the original farmstead but allowed for the formation of the new farm, Hrísbrú. The main obvious difference here is that the old Mosfell farm had its name changed to Hrísbrú, whereas the name Breiðabólstaðr in the Reykholtsdalr valley remained in place. However conservative in nature the society may have been during the earliest centuries of settlement, it seems that there was room for some social and political tinkering. Byock suggests[78] that the residence of the local chieftain was moved to Mosfell because Hrísbrú is rather windy. Secondly, it was no longer important to be able to have a view over the harbour in Leiruvágr, which the old site at Hrísbrú provides. Finally, he thinks that considerations of defence were not seen as equally important in the twelfth (or eleventh?) century as they were earlier. Breiðabólstaðr certainly lies higher than Reykholt, more uphill, and questions of defence are worth considering.

To this we can add that there were not only push-effects, there was a pull-effect as well. Not only was present-day Mosfell a less windy place, but it was also considerably closer to a main road through Svínaskarð, leading to the pool at Æsustaðir, almost directly opposite the new site (fig. 2). A pool in this area is mentioned in *Egils saga* and it is generally understood that it refers to a pool at Æsustaðir.[79] After around 965 and prior to around 1140 the road would have been used by the people of the Reykholt area when they were heading towards the spring assembly of the Kjalarnesþing area, as mentioned above. The assembly site was most probably the one that has been excavated at the Þingnes promontory in Lake Elliðavatn.[80] The Borgarfjǫrðr people attending would probably

---

78 Personal communication.

79 The author (or narrator) of *Egils saga* makes Egill Skalla-Grímsson pretend that he was heading towards the *laugar*, and in that case the author must have imagined that Egill travelled along the road leading from Mosfell towards Æsustaðir (*Egils saga Skalla-Grímssonar*, 297). There was a hot spring at Æsustaðir and a good site for a pool ("laugastæði gott") has been pointed out, where the hot water could be mixed with cold water from Reykjaá (Suðurá). Three scholars who investigated the area in the second half of the nineteenth century were on the whole in agreement about this, Magnús Grímsson 1886, 263, 266; Kålund 1877, I, 51; Sigurður Vigfússon 1884–1885, 71. On the old road system see Connors 2014, 207–219 (with maps and photos).

80 Guðmundur Ólafsson 1987, 343–249; 2004. *Kjalnesinga saga* (c. 1310–1320) claims that a *várþing* (the major spring-assembly) was held at the Kjalarnes proper, "south by the sea" (probably Kollafjǫrðr), apparently around 950 (*Kjalnesinga saga*, 8). In the 1720s Árni Magnússon was aware of an alleged assembly site here (1955, 61).

have travelled on from Æsustaðir along the Skammadalr pass rather than taken the road along the banks of the Reykjaá and Kaldakvísl rivers (fig. 2). The comparison suggests interests similar to those suggested for Reykholt, to benefit politically from communications. As in some other places, the pool at Æsustaðir would have made the route popular and this prompted an ambitious farmer at Mosfell (later Hrísbrú) to relocate the farm.

Farms probably seldom grew naturally and automatically into centres of power, even when conditions were quite favourable. It usually took some effort for ambitious "big-men" to turn farms into places of political importance and make them centres of power by increasing their centrality. Some such efforts were failures and one example of an abortive place of this kind is probably Bólstaðr in Álftafjǫrðr, the alleged dwelling-place of the *goði* Arnkell, the protagonist of Snorri the *goði* at Helgafell.[81]

A comparison can also be made here with Hofstaðir in Mývatnssveit, a farm where a great hall was constructed in the late tenth or early eleventh century.[82] This activity has been thought to represent an attempt to create a new power centre in the area.[83] Although the demolition of the hall sometime in the eleventh century probably reflects the failure of this ploy, it may provide an example of an effort made to defy the locally established social structure.

As our examples show, an important part of the story of the centres of power was to increase their centrality by making them more easily accessible and more attractive.

The place names Leiðvöllur and Leiðhamrar occur in Kollafjǫrðr in the nineteenth century. Therefore an assembly site for *a leiðarþing* (the more inferior *leið*-assembly) was possibly at the site by the sea and the names indicate that a *várþing* may have been moved and replaced by a *leiðarþing*. However, *leið* could also refer to a route and a track (see *Harðar saga*, 56–57, 78; xxxii). It has been suggested that the original Kjalarnesþing was held by Kollafjǫrðr on Kjalarnes (thus the name) but soon moved to Þingnes by the lake Elliðavatn, cf. Björn Þorsteinsson and Bergsteinn Jónsson 1991, 31.

81 Helgi Þorláksson 2007b 214–224. Orri Vésteinsson 2007, especially 84–85, has more interesting examples of similar kind. On archaeological excavations at Bólstaðr see Matthías Þórðarson 1932.

82 McGovern *et al.*, 2007; Lucas 2009, 394–408.

83 Orri Vésteinsson 2007, 58–62. For another possible explanation see fn. 26 above.

The Rise of the Descendants of Þórðr
Sǫlvason to Prominence

Magnús, son of Þórðr Sǫlvason (see fig. 3), was probably among the very
first to be named after King Magnús Ólafsson of Norway which is indicative of the political ambition of his father.[84] Magnús is counted among
the dignitaries (*virðingarmenn*) who were ordained as priests during the
time of Bishop Gizurr (d. 1118) and are called *hǫfðingjar* (chieftains).[85]
It is usually taken for granted that Magnús was a *goði*. This indicates that
Þórðr Sǫlvason was also a man of some standing. And Magnús must have
been the one who founded the *staðr* at Reykholt, which existed prior
to 1118.[86] Even though he donated the farmland and its various assets
to the church, he was in charge of the whole landholdings and all the
possessions of the *staðr*. The general understanding among scholars is that
the donors of *staðir* and their descendants reaped some benefits from such
donations. The *staðir* had more income, more clerics and more tasks than
other churches, and people were urged to donate to their saints. In around
1150 the *staðr* at Reykholt (which was dedicated to St Peter), for instance
owned a wood in Sanddalr, later called Pétursskógr (Peter's forest),
and also grazing lands, pasturages, rights to take firewood, rights to cut
turf, land for a shieling, fishing rights, and later rights to driftwood and
beached whales.[87] This had all been amassed by the Reykholt people and
Páll Sǫlvason was probably instrumental in this. A rich man proposed to
his daughter and Páll accepted on certain conditions; it was reckoned that
this rich man gave to Páll and the *staðr* no fewer than thirty hundreds.[88]
An average farm is usually estimated to be have been twenty hundreds.
Páll was the grandson of Magnús Þórðarson and in a charter of 1143 he
is counted among *kynbornir prestar* (noble priests), i.e. ordained priests
who were probably all *goðar*.[89] He inherited a rich matrimony, was well
connected and had Jón Loftsson at Oddi among his friends. Páll was seen
as erudite and is called "lærdómsmaðr mikill ok hinn mesti búþegn"
("a very learned man and an accomplished farmer"). No wonder he is
also called "dýrligr maðr" ("a splendid man"). He was among the three

84 Lúðvík Ingvarsson 1986, 2, 389.
85 Kristni saga. *Biskupa sögur* I, 42–43.
86 Magnús Stefánsson 2005, 123–125.
87 *Reykjaholtsmáldagi*, 15.
88 *Sturlunga saga* I, 106.
89 *DI* I, 186.

episcopal candidates when Þorlákr Þórhallsson (later St. Þorlákr) was elected as bishop in 1174.[90] Páll therefore was a *kirkjugoði*, as they have been called, a part of what Peter Foote called the "clerical gentry". His lifestyle was aristocratic at least. During Páll's time Reykholt became a *staðr* of distinction; in the oldest collection of St Þorlákr's miracles, from around 1200, Reykholt is called, "Í stað þeim, góðum ok dýrligum er í Reykjaholti heitir ..."[91] Obviously some people at least held Reykholt in high esteem and saw it as a sanctuary, a place of immunity even.[92] Probably no one contributed as much to making Reykholt such a splendid place as Páll Sǫlvason.

In the early twelfth century Reykholt must still have been seen as inferior to other residences of chieftains in the Borgarfjǫrðr area, such as Borg and Gilsbakki. However, during the time of Páll it rose to eminence, both as *staðr* and as a residence of a chieftain. Páll as a *kirkjugoði* probably managed to get much out of his position as a secular *goði* to strengthen the position of the *staðr* as a dignified church site, as well as having the *staðr* help him to gain increased political honour and influence. In that respect he also enjoyed the centrality of Reykholt which the other residences, Gilsbakki and Borg, only had to a very limited extent. A glance at a map shows that Reykholt occupied a central place in Snorri's domain (his *héraðsríki*) in Borgarfjǫrðr and even his extended domain from Reykjanes in the South to Húnaþing in the North.

The successor to Páll was his son Magnús, both a *goði* and an ordained priest like his father. He had two sons who also became priests. There was a problem in about 1190 when the archbishop decided that *goðar* could no longer be ordained as priests. As Sverrir Jakobsson points out (see below), the sons of Magnús were thought unfit to wield leadership, possibly because of their plans to enter the priesthood. This gave Snorri Sturluson an opportunity which he seized and he acquired Reykholt for himself. Even though he was not ordained as a priest himself, he was bent on honouring the legacy of Reykholt as a splendid *staðr*.

The question has been asked repeatedly, at many meetings of the Reykholt project, why Snorri chose Reykholt as his centre of power.

90 On Páll's episcopal candidacy and status, see Þorláks saga byskups in elzta and Þorláks saga byskups yngri, *Biskupa sögur* II , 62, 79, 154, 183–184.
91 "At the *staðr* which was both good and splendid and was called Reykjaholt" (Jarteinabók I, *Biskupa sögur* II, 119).
92 Helgi Þorláksson 2005b, 140–147.

This will not be discussed in any detail here.[93] Suffice it to say that neither the quality of the land nor the income from the *staðr* can have been of much significance to Snorri. On the other hand the place was centrally situated and at a crossroads, which was important. It must also have been important that the *staðr* was dignified, probably a place of asylum, and had symbolic value for Snorri because his father had had an unsuccessful dispute with the people at Reykholt. What Snorri did was to continue to increase the centrality of Reykholt and build it up as a centre of power.

3. Regional Power Centres – the Case of Borgarfjǫrðr

SVERRIR JAKOBSSON

Introduction

During the ascendancy of Snorri Sturluson, Reykholt rose to prominence as the most important power centre in the region of Borgarfjǫrðr. This coincided with a local consolidation of power which contributed to the evolution of a proto-state (in Old Norse, *ríki*) in the thirteenth century. Following the era of Snorri, the region became a unit governed by a single ruler, with the king sometimes reserving the right to appoint his representative over the region. The unique status of the region was indicated in 1262 when its representatives submitted to the king of Norway.[94]

Any overview of power centres in the region of Borgarfjǫrðr has to take account of the waxing and waning of different means of asserting local authority. In the Commonwealth period, power was not as a rule territorialized. The authority of a chieftain or a prominent farmer depended upon a personal relationship with his followers, a system of patronage which did not adhere to strict regional lines. Accordingly, there could be any number of people wielding power within any particular region. Most,

---

93 See Helgi Þorláksson 2017.

94 This is indicated in the Króksfjarðarbók version of *Sturlunga saga*, in the narrative about the submission of the western Quarter to the king. There five "leaders" (Old Norse *formenn*) are listed as swearing oaths to the king, each with three farmers. These leaders coincide with the traditional chieftains of the region. Then it is said that "[þ]rír bændr sóru ok fyrir Borgfirðinga" ("three farmers also swore oaths on behalf of the Borgfirðingar"), as if the region no longer belonged to a chieftain. Cf. *Sturlunga saga* II, 281–282.

but not necessarily all, of them would be based locally. This structure was reformed in the thirteenth century, with the rise of a single individual to a position of supreme authority. This period of proto-state government was brief and characterized by conflict, as there were many legitimate contenders for this type of power. Following the killing of Snorri in 1241, the most prominent actors on the political scene in Borgarfjǫrðr were Sturla Þórðarson (1214–1284), Þorgils *skarði* (the Harelip) Bǫðvarsson (1226–1258) and Hrafn Oddsson (1226–1289); the first two had claims to power since they were Snorri's kinsmen, and thus Sturlungar, and Hrafn through his connections with the family of Sturlungar.[95] After the introduction of state power, government of the region became territorialized but the wielders of power owed their position to the king, rather than depending solely on their regional following.

The intention here is to elucidate the role of regional power centres within different types of power structure. Among such power centres were the residences of influential magnates, usually also the sites of a church, which later evolved into centres of a new type of region, the domain (*héraðsríki*). How did these units affect the development and consolidation of territorial power and how were they themselves affected by it? The periods looked at are, first, the period from settlement until around 1150. In this period the traditional structure of local interactions and power relations evolved into the non-territorial system dominant in the twelfth century. Secondly, the period from the middle of the twelfth century to 1262 will be analyzed in view of the development of a proto-state and a system of territorial power. Thirdly, the period of state power and regional government will be analyzed and compared to the earlier periods.

Important Sources

It should be stressed that most of the existing sources pertaining to the earlier periods, even those usually regarded as "contemporaneous", come

---

95 Þorgils *skarði* actually claimed to rule as the king's representative, but it is hardly a coincidence that the king chose a kinsman of Snorri for this task. In 1261, the king selected another member of the Sturlungar family to rule Borgarfjǫrðr, i.e. Hrafn Oddsson, the son-in-law of Sturla Sighvatsson. This would seem to indicate that the king's options in the choice of his officials were as yet somewhat limited.

from the period after 1262 and it can be argued that to some degree
their authors enjoyed the benefit of hindsight and were aware of the
end-result of earlier developments. For the settlement period and the
period before the twelfth century, the single most important source
is *Landnámabók* (The Book of Settlements), of which there exist three
medieval versions. Curiously, all of the authors of these versions had
close ties to the region of Borgarfjǫrðr. The oldest, Sturla Þórðarson,
was a cousin of Snorri Sturluson and had his power base there in the
1250s. His successor, Haukr Erlendsson (*c*.1265–1334), was the brother
of Jón Erlendsson, who resided at the important farm of Ferjubakki.[96]
Haukr also drew on a lost version of *Landnámabók* composed by Styrmir
fróði (the Learned) Kárason (d. 1245), a cleric who lived at Reykholt
and was a close collaborator of Snorri Sturluson. The third surviving
medieval version, *Melabók* (The Book of Melar), is only preserved in
fragments. It is named after an important farm in Borgarfjǫrðr and
was in all probability composed by a scion of that family, either Snorri
Markússon (d. 1313) or his son, Þorsteinn Snorrason (d. 1353), later
abbot at Helgafell.[97]

The main source for the period of power consolidation is *Sturlunga
saga*, which was probably written in the first decade of the fourteenth
century. A possible editor of the whole work is Þórðr Narfason (d. 1308),
who had been an assistant and close collaborator of Sturla Þórðarson,
although other names have been mentioned. Sturla himself contributed
with the history of a large part of the work, covering the period from
1183 to 1264.[98] Other valuable sources cannot be connected to individual
authors and scribes with any kind of certainty. Among family sagas
pertaining to the region which were composed in the thirteenth century
are *Egils saga Skalla-Grímssonar*, *Gunnlaugs saga ormstungu*, *Heiðarvíga saga*
and *Hœnsa-Þóris saga*. Of these the largest in scope is *Egils saga*, which has,
in modern times, often been connected with Snorri Sturluson, although

---

96 Ferjubakki was not among the biggest farmsteads (its value was 40 hundreds in the Old
    Norse system of land evaluation, whereas the important main farms were 60 hundreds).
    It nevertheless had a strategic location, a control of the ferry across the river Hvítá and
    an opportunity to serve travellers.

97 For a recent overview of different versions of *Landnámabók* cf. Gunnar Karlsson
    2007b, 123–134. Cf. also Jón Jóhannesson 1941, especially 55–56.

98 Cf. Gunnar Karlsson 2007b, 194–197, 200–202; Helgi Þorláksson 2012b; Úlfar Bragason
    2010, 52.

no actual evidence of his authorship exists.[99] The family sagas are useful as corollaries to *Landnámabók*, as many of them may have been used as sources by the authors of the existing versions. This is particularly true of the version made by Sturla Þórðarson, which has been shown to have used family sagas as source material on many occasions.[100]

It thus follows that the sources on the earliest period are to some degree unreliable due to their late dating and are best used as an indication of the historical consciousness of later generations. However, the structure of power relations in *Landnámabók* and the family sagas may reflect the author's knowledge of how these things stood in more recent times, before the development of the proto-state of Snorri Sturluson. Due to its relative closeness to the actual events, *Sturlunga saga* is more trustworthy, although it is not without a certain bias or even literary conventions in its depiction of events.[101]

Power Centres before 1150

The region that was governed by Snorri Sturluson in the early thirteenth century did not enjoy a structural coherence right from the settlement, as in Iceland power was generally not territorialized. The region where Snorri's core of supporters was located, the territory generally known as Borgarfjǫrðr in thirteenth-century sources, was in fact divided between the grander units of the southern and western Quarters of Iceland. Thus, Snorri's first regional base at Borg belonged to the western Quarter whereas Reykholt belonged to the southern Quarter.[102] This was hardly important in the twelfth century but may have mattered more earlier, for instance in the case of Tungu-Oddr mentioned before.

The number of settlers in *Landnámabók* only consists of about four hundred farmers, or less than ten per cent of the farmers in the country according to the census of 1096/97.[103] Any site of a farmer mentioned

99   For a more critical view of Snorri's presumed authorship cf. this review: Ármann Jakobsson 2006, 1266–1267.

100 Cf. Jón Jóhannesson 1941, 75–128.

101 Cf. Úlfar Bragason 2005, 433–442. See also Úlfar Bragason 1988.

102 Cf. *Íslendingabók, Landnámabók*, 58–105.

103 *Íslendingabók, Landnámabók*, 23.

in *Landnámabók* can thus be classified as a local centre to a lesser degree, perhaps typically surrounded by ten farms not worthy of mention.[104] And yet, within the elite of farmers residing at such centres there was a more concentrated elite of people with regional influence. Their habitations might properly be regarded as regional centres.

In the *Sturlubók* and *Hauksbók* versions of *Landnámabók* there are lists of "important settlers" in each Quarter of Iceland. They number about eight to eleven in each Quarter. Among settlers in the vicinity of Snorri's later power base are three in the southern Quarter: Kolgrímr *enn gamli* (the Old) at Ferstikla on Hvalfjarðarströnd, Bjǫrn *gullberi* (Gold-bearer) at Gullberastaðir in Lundarreykjadalr and Ǫnundr *breiðskeggr* (Broad-beard?) at Breiðabólstaðr in Reykholtsdalr.[105] In the western Quarter there are also three settlers mentioned in the region of Snorri's later hegemony; Skalla-Grímr (Grímr the Bald) at Borg in Mýrar, Hrosskell at Hallkelsstaðir in Hvítársíða and Sel-Þórir (Seal-Þórir) at Rauðamelr in Hnappadalr.[106] The descendants of two of these settlers are listed among the notables of Iceland in 930, Tungu-Oddr, the son of Ǫnundr, and Egill, the son of Skalla-Grímr.[107]

This rather tidy scheme, possibly a construction of thirteenth-century historiographers, suggests a neat regional division of power, with none of the most powerful magnates living adjacent to a possible rival. It also suggests that power quickly became concentrated in the hands of two major lords, residing on each side of the river Hvítá. One was Egill and although he is the protagonist of *Egils saga Skalla-Grímssonar*, the saga mainly revolves around his adventures abroad and his relationship to Anglo-Saxon and Norwegian kings, rather than local rivalries in Iceland.

On the other side of Hvítá there was Tungu-Oddr, who is one of

---

104 Another, and in my view far less apposite, way to interpret this number would be to claim that only 10% of later farms in Iceland were inhabited during the age of settlement. This, however, does not fit well with archaeological evidence. See especially Orri Vésteinsson and Thomas McGovern 2012, and the following debate. In any case, the evidence of *Landnámabók* in this matter concerns mainly which farms were regarded as important during its time of composition in the twelfth and thirteenth centuries.

105 *Íslendingabók, Landnámabók*, 396–397. Ǫnundr's nickname, *breiðskeggr*, is far from self-explanatory. It could just simply refer to his residence at Breiðabólstaðr and even to *breiðar*, see above (cf. fn. 54). In *Melabók* his father, Krǫmu-Oddr, is regarded as the settler and his settlement reckoned much bigger than that attributed to Ǫnundr in the other versions, cf. *Íslendingabók, Landnámabók*, 74.

106 *Íslendingabók, Landnámabók*, 209–210, 397.

107 *Íslendingabók, Landnámabók*, 396.

the main characters in *Hœnsa-Þóris saga*, but other influential farmers in the region include Arngrímr the chieftain Helgason at Norðtunga in Þverárhlíð, and Þorkell *trefill* (the Fringe) Rauða-Bjarnarson at Svigna-skarð in Norðrárdalr, magnates residing on the other side of Hvítá and thus in the western Quarter. Breiðabólstaðr is evidently the main power centre in Reykholtsdalr and Oddr seems to enjoy some kind of hegemony in the region, as his local adversaries have to seek aid from the distant chieftain Þórðr *gellir* (the Yeller).

This demarcation along the river Hvítá is continued in a similar list of important lords in *Kristni saga*, pertaining to the year 981.[108] One of them is Illugi *rauði* (the Red) at Innri-Hólmr on Akranes and the other Þorsteinn, the son of Egill Skalla-Grímsson. In contrast, *Gunnlaugs saga ormstungu* reckons Illugi *svarti* (the Black) Hallkelsson at Gilsbakki in Hvítársíðu as the second greatest lord in Borgarfjǫrðr in the 980s, a possible consequence of the waning of the power of Tungu-Oddr. Illugi was the grandson of Hrosskell the settler, and in the twelfth century Gilsbakki was the residence of important local magnates. Illugi also figures in *Heiðarvíga saga* where he belongs to a group of local lords which included Þorsteinn Gíslason at Bœr and Kleppjárn at Kleppjárnsreykir. Unfortunately, this tale of intrigues in Borgarfjǫrðr around 1000 has only survived in fragments.[109]

Kristni saga, however, continues with listing important notables, usually rather few and probably the ones who wielded the power of chieftaincies at the parliament, although such a correlation is not referred to in any of the sources. In 1118 there are again five important lords mentioned in the region, the priests Magnús Þórðarson at Reykholt and Símon Jǫrundarson at Bœr, Skúli Egilsson, Halldórr Egilsson at Borg and Styrmir Hreinsson at Gilsbakki.[110] Three of these belonged to the southern Quarter and two to the western Quarter. However, their geographic distribution is less tidy than that depicted in *Landnámabók*, as they are heavily concentrated in the vicinity of Hvítá. No mention is made of lords residing at the more marginal regions of Hvalfjarðarstrǫnd or Hítardalr.

It must be noted that these reconstructions of local authority in

---

108 *Biskupa sögur* I, 5–6.
109 For sagas which take place in the Borgarfjǫrðr region cf. *Egils saga Skalla-Grímssonar*, and *Borgfirðinga sǫgur*, *in toto*.
110 *Biskupa sögur* I, 42–45.

Borgarfjǫrðr belong to the thirteenth and fourteenth centuries in their present form and thus invite both scepticism and scrutiny. At that time power had been territorialized in the proto-state of Snorri and in the royal domains of the sheriffs (in Old Norse, *sýslumenn*), which doubtless influenced depictions of regional authority in earlier sources. Nevertheless, these are the sources available to us and they give an important indication of how the history of power in Borgarfjǫrðr was viewed in the thirteenth and fourteenth centuries. The following are some of its main characteristics.

To begin with, if the residences of the main lords in the region can be defined as regional power centres, it is evident that some places continued to be important from the time of the settlement to 1150. There is a marked continuity concerning which farms could maintain such a status. Chief among such seats of power are Borg, the centre for the descendants of Skalla-Grímr, and Gilsbakki, the centre for the descendants of Hrosskell. Bœr also seems to have been an important local centre, frequently mentioned in the narratives of *Sturlunga saga*, although we lack evidence as to how it passed on from generation to generation. Reykholt, however, does not appear as a seat of a local lord until the early twelfth century. As mentioned above, it was located close to another important farm, Breiðabólstaðr, and some time may have elapsed before it was established as the foremost residence in the vicinity.

Also noteworthy is the emphasis on the essential unity of the Borgarfjǫrðr region, both in *Landnámabók* and the Sagas of the Icelanders.[111] The sources are remarkably consistent in their depiction of political relations and alliances across Hvítá. This unity seems paradoxical in view of the region's division between two Quarters. It may of course be influenced by later developments, in particular the creation of a regional state in the time of Snorri Sturluson. However, the existence of an assembly site on the island Þingey in the river Þverá in around 1140, at the borders of the western and southern Quarters but in the centre of the region of Borgarfjǫrðr, indicates that a unity already existed at that time.

111 Which has often been commented on, see for instance Orri Vésteinsson 2009, 303–306.

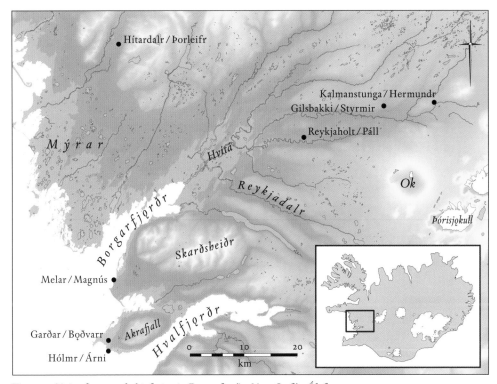

Figure 4. Major farms and chieftains in Borgarfjǫrðr. Map: Stefán Ólafsson.

The Borgarfjǫrðr Region in the
Late Twelfth Century

In the 1160s, the father of Snorri Sturluson, Sturla Þórðarson at Hvammr
(c. 1115–1183), married the mother of Snorri, Guðný Bǫðvarsdóttir (c.
1147–1221). Guðný was the daughter of Bǫðvarr Þórðarson who seems
to have been a powerful magnate in Borgarfjǫrðr, probably residing
at Garðar in Akranes.[112] Bǫðvarr had an inheritance dispute with Páll
Sǫlvason, the priest and chieftain at Reykholt, in which his son-in-law,
Sturla, became embroiled. In *Sturlu saga* there is consequently some
information on local alliances in the region in the 1170s.[113] Bǫðvarr

---

112 This is never made clear in *Sturlu saga*, but his son Þórðr later resided at Garðar, cf.
   Sturlunga saga I, 240, and Bǫðvarr cannot have resided far from Magnús Þorláksson
   at Melar, if they were reckoned as being "from the same county" in inter-regional
   disputes.
113 Cf. *Sturlunga saga* I, 105–114.

was supported by Árni Borgnýjarson at Hólmr in Akranes, while Páll enjoyed the support of Þorleifr *beiskaldi* (the Embittered) (d. 1200) at Hítardalr and Magnús Þorláksson at Melar.[114] Magnús was a kinsman of Páll but he was also invited to support Bǫðvarr as they were "báðir í einni sveit" ("both from the same district").[115] Magnús was married to the grand-daughter of Styrmir Hreinsson at Gilsbakki and may have been a chieftain (fig. 4). Another lord, Hermundr Koðránsson at Kalmanstunga (d. 1197), a direct male descendant of Illugi *svarti* at Gilsbakki, also had an ambiguous position as he was a friend of Bǫðvarr but related to Páll through marriage. Sturla later termed Hermundr and his sons "traitors" due to Páll's trust in them.[116]

The conflict is clearly depicted as regional ("vandræði í heraðinu"), although lords from both sides of the river are involved.[117] Kinsmen from other regions also offered their support, such as Sturla Þórðarson at Hvammr, who supported his father-in-law, and Ari *sterki* (the Strong) Þorgilsson (d. 1188), who was a kinsman of Páll through the marriage of their children. In the end, however, the conflict was settled at the general assembly (*Alþingi*) through the mediation of chieftains from more remote regions.

As far as this episode can be interpreted, local relationships in Borgar-fjǫrðr in the 1170s were multipolar, characterized by shifting alliances between many local notables, none of whom enjoyed any sort of local hegemony. Although Bǫðvarr has the support of most of his neighbours, an important man such as Magnús Þorláksson could opt to support the other side. Páll Sǫlvason was clearly a well-connected man locally; yet he had no way of prevailing over Bǫðvarr without outside assistance.

As a part of the final settlement the youngest son of Sturla, Snorri Sturluson (1178–1241) went to live with Jón Loftsson at Oddi.[118] The protagonists of the dispute died soon after, Sturla in 1183, Páll Sǫlvason in 1185 and Bǫðvarr Þórðarson in 1187. Sturla left three young sons as his main heirs, Þórðr, Sighvatr and Snorri. They would have been at a disadvantage in taking over the mantle of their able and scheming father

114 Þorleifr's nickname, *beiskaldi*, has been translated by the Latin *acerbus* (cf. Cleasby and Vigfússon, 56), suggesting that he was considered somewhat of a nag.
115 *Sturlunga saga* I, 107.
116 *Sturlunga saga* I, 111.
117 *Sturlunga saga* I, 108.
118 *Sturlunga saga* I, 113–114.

at a tender age, yet during the next few decades these brothers, the Sturlungar, went from strength to strength. Not only did Þórðr and Sighvatr become predominant in the Breiðafjǫrðr region, gaining hegemony over all other chieftains; their younger brother Snorri gained a similar position in the Borgarfjǫrðr region, as well as a foothold in the northwest of Iceland.

Several factors might explain the unparallelled success of the Sturlungar. One that should not be neglected is the shrewd manipulations of their mother, Guðný Bǫðvarsdóttir.[119] She formed a romantic and political alliance with the chieftain Ari *sterki*, and succeeded in securing the hand of his daughter, Helga, for her oldest son Þórðr. When Ari died in 1188, Þórðr became his chief heir.[120] Þórðr seems to have had some following in the Borgarfjǫrðr region, among them a man named Hámundr Gilsson in the valley Lundarreykjadalr. Among his allies there was the priest Hǫgni *auðgi* (the Wealthy) who lived at Bœr. Another important ally was his uncle, Þórðr Bǫðvarsson at Garðar (d. 1220).[121]

Another important factor came into play here. In 1190, due to pressure from the archbishop in Trondheim, a distinction was made between secular and ecclesiastical power in Iceland. In order to protect the sanctity of priests from violence it was decided they should no longer participate in secular quarrels. This changed the balance of power within the chieftain class, as the scions of many of these families had become priests. In the Breiðafjǫrðr region, the Sturlungar soon gained a monopoly on secular authority as the families of their main rivals concentrated on ecclesiastical careers.[122]

In the Borgarfjǫrðr region, this shift also had important implications. Among those lords who now found it difficult to fulfil their roles as chieftains was Magnús Pálsson at Reykholt, the son of Páll and a priest like his father. The sons of Hermundr at Kalmanstunga, Ketill and Hreinn, were also ordained and Ketill served for a time as abbot at the monastery at Helgafell. Another family affected by the change was the old line of Mýramenn. At this time the priest, Bersi *auðgi* (the Wealthy) (d. 1202) was residing at Borg. Through the agency of Guðný Bǫðvarsdóttir and Þórðr Sturluson, Snorri was married to Herdís, the daughter of Bersi.[123]

119 Sverrir Jakobsson 2013, 161–175.
120 *Sturlunga saga* I, 231.
121 *Sturlunga saga* I, 232–234.
122 Cf. Sverrir Jakobsson 2009, 151–170.
123 *Sturlunga saga* I, 237.

His foster-father, Jón Loftsson, had also gained a great following in Borgarfjǫrðr, perhaps due to the political impotence of many of the region's chieftain-priests in the 1190s.[124]

After the death of Bersi, Snorri Sturluson moved to Borg and soon became a leading magnate in the region. Among his patrons was his uncle, Þórðr Bǫðvarsson, who wanted to set him up as a counter-balance to the depredations of Snorri's brother, Þórðr Sturluson. Ironically, Snorri then started to harry the followers of Þórðr Bǫðvarsson, no less than his brother had done before him.[125] Yet Þórðr and his sons continued to support Snorri; perhaps having limited options in the matter.

With the descendants of Bǫðvarr Þórðarson in control of both Garðar and Borg, the main counterforce in the region would have been the family of Magnús Pálsson at Reykholt. However, his sons were regarded as unfit to wield leadership (at least according to later reports, possibly relating to their plans to enter the priesthood) and Þórðr Bǫðvarsson greatly desired the church at Reykholt, having some claim to inheriting it.[126] Magnús did not wish to yield to Þórðr so he made a pact instead with his younger kinsman Snorri Sturluson and offered him the site (staðr) of Reykholt instead, on the condition that he "skyldi taka við ... þeim hjónum ok koma sonum þeira til þroska, þess er auðit yrði".[127] Snorri moved to Reykholt around 1206 and "[g]erðist hann þá höfðingi mikill því at eigi skorti fé".[128] From then on, Snorri's hegemony in the region seems to have been assured.

In the following decades, Snorri's lordship in the region was not threatened by internal factors. The most prominent men in the region, such as Þorleifr Þórðarson (d. 1257), the son of Þórðr Bǫðvarsson, were close allies of Snorri. Þorleifr and his two brothers, Bǫðvarr and Markús, resided at the strategically located farms of Garðar, Bœr and Melar, and were dedicated followers of Snorri and his sons. The chieftain at the northern margin of Borgarfjǫrðr, Þorlákr Ketilsson (d. 1240), in Hítardalr, was allied with Þórðr Sturluson, Snorri's brother, and played

---

124 Cf. *Sturlunga saga* I, 237–238.

125 *Sturlunga saga* I, 240.

126 Þórðr Bǫðvarsson was the grandson of Þórðr Magnússon, who had been the uncle of Magnús' father Páll Sǫlvason (fig. 3). Páll Sǫlvason had been illegitimate and his inheritance, along with that of his descendants, could thus be contested at all times.

127 "... kept him and his wife with him and pushed their sons towards such maturity, as would be possible" (*Sturlunga saga* I, 241).

128 "... became a great lord, as he was not short of funds" (*Sturlunga saga* I, 242).

little part in regional affairs. Snorri extended his domain to Húnaþing in northwestern Iceland and nominally also south to the Reykjanes peninsula.

Several other reasons have been suggested for the consolidation of power in Iceland, such as the impact of *staðir* and the attempt to secure peace through a handful of "strong men", possibly inspired by the peace movement of the church.[129]

Power Centres in the Proto-state

Snorri's move to Reykholt marks the rise of this farm as the unchallenged regional centre in Borgarfjǫrðr. In the sources, Snorri's move is explained by the fact that he "felldi mikinn hug til staðarins" but of course the explanation is less straightforward.[130] In the twelfth century, Borg had become something of a backwater and its residents had not been prominent in regional politics. In contrast, the ancestors of Magnús Pálsson had thrived at Reykholt.

A little later, Snorri Sturluson also managed to secure control of Stafholt, by now a *staðr*. Stafholt had been the residence of Eyjólfr Þorgeirsson (d. 1213) in the 1170s and later. Eyjólfr had been a farmer of some note but of less prominence than Páll Sǫlvason or Bǫðvarr Þórðarson. For example, he had attempted to form a third party in the inheritance dispute between Páll and Bǫðvarr, but to no great effect.[131] Following Eyjólfr's death, Snorri seems to have gained possession of Stafholt and used it for some years as an alternate residence to Reykholt.[132]

Following the death of Snorri in 1241, the king claimed Snorri´s possessions as he regarded Snorri as a traitor to the crown. He appointed Snorri's nephew, Þorgils *skarði* Bǫðvarsson, as his representative in Borgarfjǫrðr in 1252. This was a cause of strife as the king's former representative, and another nephew of Snorri, Þórðr *kakali* Sighvatsson (*c.* 1210–1256) had, in turn, appointed Þorleifr Þórðarson as his representative.[133] Yet another nephew of Snorri, Egill Sǫlmundarson

---

129 Helgi Þorláksson 2013
130 "developed a great affection for the place" (*Sturlunga saga* I, 241).
131 *Sturlunga saga* I, 107.
132 See for instance *Sturlunga saga* I, 283, 290, 297, 301–304, 335, 360, 361, 387, 388, 452.
133 *Sturlunga saga* II, 119, 149. The meaning of Þórðr's nickname is disputed. It has

(*c.* 1210/1215–1297), was in control of Reykholt and led the opposition to Þorgils along with Þorleifr. Þorgils' uncle, Óláfr Þórðarson (*c.* 1212–1259), had taken up residence at Stafholt, an indication of the pre-eminence the Sturlungar family still enjoyed in the region.[134] Late in 1253 Þorgils *skarði* was chased away from the region by the lords of Breiðafjǫrðr, Sturla Þórðarson and Hrafn Oddsson.

Egill Sǫlmundarson is of particular interest among the leaders of Borgarfjǫrðr, as he had taken up residence at Reykholt. He was the son of Helga, daughter of Hvamm-Sturla Þórðarson and Guðný Bǫðvarsdóttir, and thus a nephew of Snorri (see p. 429 in this book). He was among the retinue of Snorri when he returned from Norway in 1239, but following the death of Snorri, his parents were led to renounce their claim to Snorri's inheritance by his rival Gizurr Þorvaldsson (1209–1268).[135] By 1243, however, Egill had become a follower of his kinsman, Þórðr *kakali*.[136] In 1248 Þórðr was at Reykholt and that winter there was a wedding at Reykholt between Gyða, Egill's sister, and Nikulás Oddsson, an important follower of Þórðr from the eastern Quarter.[137] The family of Egill and Gyða may have gained possession of Reykholt at that time as part of Egill's service to Þórðr. In 1255, Egill made his peace with Þorgils *skarði*, and was a trusted ally of his kinsman from then on.[138] In 1262 he mediated between Sighvatr Bǫðvarsson (d. 1266), Þorgils' brother, and the slayer of Þorgils, Þorvarðr Þórarinsson (*c.* 1228–1296).[139] Sighvatr is mentioned as one of the leaders in the western Quarter in 1262, but not Egill Sǫlmundarson.[140] Egill appears in *Árna saga biskups*, in relation to events of 1273, when he was forced to divorce his wife as their marriage was deemed to be against the rules of the Church.[141] Egill had been consecrated as a subdeacon, which may have hampered his rise to the position of a lord and certainly

been variously translated as "earthen pot" or "stutterer". *Kakali* (Danish *kakel*) was most probably a porcelain bowl, fastened on an earthen oven (Danish *kakkelovn*) to conduct heat away. It could also be used as a drinking bowl, cf. Helgi Þorláksson 1984.

134 Cf. *Sturlunga saga* II, 120. Óláfr Þórðarson was a committed royalist and may have received Stafholt as a fief from King Hákon, who had a claim to the property of Snorri Sturluson.

135 *Sturlunga saga* I, 444, 455.

136 *Sturlunga saga* II, 36.

137 *Sturlunga saga* II, 84.

138 *Sturlunga saga* II, 171–173, 176, 215.

139 *Sturlunga saga* II, 224.

140 *Sturlunga saga*, II, 281–282.

141 *Biskupa sögur* III, 44–45.

made him subject to the authority of the bishop in an age where magnates could no longer always get their own way.

A few years later, following the development of enmity between Sturla Þórðarson and Hrafn Oddsson, Sturla moved his seat of residence to Svignaskarð in the Borgarfjǫrðr region, most probably for defensive purposes. Sturla expected the newly appointed earl of Iceland, Gizurr Þorvaldsson (1209–1268), to appoint him formally as lord of the Borgarfjǫrðr region. Instead Hrafn Oddsson received the region at the hands of the king in 1261.[142] In 1262, farmers in the region swore allegiance to the king without any chieftain representing them.

Following Iceland's entrance into the Norwegian kingdom, the Quarters were ruled by royally appointed sheriffs. Hrafn Oddsson became the king's representative in the western Quarter but he made Stafholt his place of residence.[143] He was later succeeded by Erlendr Ólafsson (c.1230–1312) who lived at Ferjubakki.[144] Borgarfjǫrðr was thus the seat of powerful men for the first decades of royal rule in Iceland.

4. Reykholt as a Centre of Power. Final Remarks

VIÐAR PÁLSSON, HELGI ÞORLÁKSSON AND SVERRIR JAKOBSSON

In 1118 power was divided between several *goðar* (plual of *goði*) and "strong men" in the Borgarfjǫrðr area and was not formally territorialized. These *goðar* were Skúli Egilsson (the *goðorð* of the men of Lundr or Garðar), Styrmir Hreinsson at Gilsbakki and Halldórr Egilsson at Borg. *Kristni saga* mentions these three among the most powerful men of the country. It also mentions Magnús Þórðarson at Reykholt and Símon Jǫrundarson at Bœr among the chieftains and the most distinguished men who were learned and ordained as priests. Magnús is called *hǫfðingi* and *virðingarmaðr* and was most probably a *goði*. It has also been suggested that Þorvarðr at Stafholt was a *goði*. This is a considerable number, considering that in around 1210 half of the *goðorð* of the men of Lundr came under the control of Snorri Sturluson, who at around that time also controlled the *goðorð* of the men of Reykholt, Borg, Stafholt (if that *goðorð* was connected

142 *Sturlunga saga* I, 527–528; *Sturlunga saga* II, 207–208, 211–212.
143 *Biskupa sögur* III, 28.
144 *Biskupa sögur* III, 205.

with Stafholt at this time) and Gilsbakki. This picture is symptomatic of the consolidation of power that took place in different places in Iceland late in the twelfth century, around 1200 or early in the thirteenth century.

Garðar, Borg and Gilsbakki were of limited centrality and not on main roads, let alone at crossroads. Stafholt and Reykholt were different in that respect and became the residences of Snorri, Stafholt as a kind of a reserve-place or substitute. Like a modern political candidate, Snorri offered his services in Borgarfjǫrðr and was welcomed. A "strong man" who could promise peace seems to have been in demand in many areas around 1200. Such "strong men" tended to create a domain by defining the borders of the area they were ruling and having the regular convention of the spring assemblies abolished. Such domains are called *héraðsríki* and centrally placed in them was the residence of the *stórgoði* or his *valda-miðstöð* (centre of power). Reykholt became such a centre of power for the domain of Snorri, where he would settle disputes. With one powerful man holding the reins of government in his hands, the skirmishes and feuds between individual *goðar* of the area and clashes at spring assemblies were avoided, and peace prevailed within the domains (*héraðsríki*). All the farmers of the area automatically became followers of the *stórgoði*.

Snorri had high ideas and ambitious plans. He was well acquainted with the Birkibeinar group who were in power in Norway and while abroad in 1218/20 enjoyed their hospitality. Back in Iceland with the recently acquired title of *lendr maðr* he had to live accordingly, building a *valdamiðstöð* that would fit his position. He made Reykholt not only a central place of power for his *héraðsríki*, but rather for a huge territory, namely the part of the country reaching from Reykjanes in the South to Húnaþing in the North.

Reykholt was probably the most aristocratic centre of power in Iceland during the time of Snorri, who had a keen eye for the visible and impos-ing. It kept its position as a centre of secular power until at the end of the thirteenth century when the church took it over as the other *staðir*, Oddi included. Under the administration of the church Reykholt lost some of its importance. Magnates moved from *staðir* to other rich farms and the king became the main source for their power and political positions.[145]

---

145 On these changes around 1300 see Helgi Þorláksson 2012.

Bibliography

Ármann Jakobsson 2006. "Torfi H. Tulinius, Skáldið í skriftinni: Snorri Sturluson og Egils saga. (Íslenzk menning) Reykjavík: Hið íslenzka bókmenntafélag, for Reykjavíkur Akademían, 2004. Pp. 292; 7 black-and-white figures and genealogical tables". *Speculum* 81, 1266–1267.

Árni Magnússon 1955. *Chorographica Islandica*. Safn til sögu Íslands og íslenzkra bókmennta. Annar flokkur I, 2. Reykjavík: Hið íslenzka bókmenntafélag.

Bagge, Sverre 1991. *Society and Politics in Snorri Sturluson's* Heimskringla. Berkeley: University of California Press.

Benedikt Eyþórsson 2003. "Í þjónustu Snorra. Staðurinn í Reykholti og klerkar þar í tíð Snorra Sturlusonar." *Sagnir* 23, 20-26.

Benedikt Eyþórsson 2005a. "History of the Icelandic Church 1000-1300. Status of Research." In Helgi Þorláksson (ed.), *Church Centres. Church Centres in Iceland from the 11th to the 13th Century and their Parallels in other Countries*. Snorrastofa, vol. II. Reykholt: Snorrastofa, 19-69.

Benedikt Eyþórsson 2005b. "Reykholt and Church Centres." In Helgi Þorláksson (ed.), *Church Centres. Church Centres in Iceland from the 11th to the 13th Century and their Parallels in other Countries*. Snorrastofa, vol. II. Reykholt: Snorrastofa, 105–116.

Benedikt Eyþórsson 2008. *Búskapur og rekstur staðar í Reykholti 1200–1900*. Reykjavík: Sagnfræðistofnun Háskóla Íslands.

Biskupa sögur I. Eds Sigurgeir Steingrímsson, Ólafur Halldórsson and Peter Foote. Íslenzk fornrit XV. Reykjavík: Hið íslenzka fornritafélag, 2003

Biskupa sögur III. Ed. Guðrún Ása Grímsdóttir.

Íslenzk fornrit XVII. Reykjavík: Hið íslenzka fornritafélag, 1998.

Björn Þorsteinsson 1953. *Íslenzka þjóðveldið*. Reykjavík: Heimskringla.

Björn Þorsteinsson 1966. *Ný Íslandssaga. Þjóðveldisöld*. Reykjavík: Heimskringla.

Björn Þorsteinsson 1978. *Íslensk miðaldasaga*. Reykjavík: Sögufélag.

Björn Þorsteinsson, Bergsteinn Jónsson 1991. *Íslandssaga til okkar daga*. Reykjavík: Sögufélag.

Björn Sigfússon 1960. "Full goðorð og forn og heimildir frá 12. öld." *Saga* III, 48–75.

Borgfirðinga sögur. Eds Sigurður Nordal and Guðni Jónsson. Íslenzk fornrit III. Reykjavík: Hið íslenzka fornritafélag, 1938.

Bossy, John 1985. *Christianity in the West 1400–1700*. Oxford: Oxford University Press.

Bouchard, Constance Brittain 1998. "*Strong of Body, Brave and Noble.*" *Chivalry and Society in Medieval France*. Ithaca: Cornell University Press.

Bumke, Joachim 1991. *Courtly Culture. Literature and Society in the High Middle Ages*. Translated by Thomas Dunlap. Berkeley: University of California Press.

Byock, Jesse, Phillip Walker, Jon Erlandson, Per Holck, Davide Zori, Magnús Guðmundsson and Mark Tveskov 2005. "A Viking-Age Valley in Iceland. The Mosfell Archaeological Project". *Medieval Archaeology* XLIX, 195–218,

Byock, Jesse and Davide Zori 2013. "Viking Archaeology, Sagas, and Interdisciplinary Research in Iceland's Mosfell Valley". *Blackdirt. Annual Review of the Cotsen Institute of Archaeology at UCLA*, 124–141.

Cleasby, Richard and Guðbrandur Vigfússon 1874.

An Icelandic-English Dictionary. Oxford: Claredon Press.

Connors, Colin Giola 2014. "Viking Age Routes". In Davide Zori and Jesse Byock (eds), Viking Archaeology in Iceland. Mosfell Archaeology Project. Turnhout: Brepols, 207–219.

DI = Diplomatarium islandicum. Íslenzkt fornbréfasafn I-XVI, Copenhagen and Reykjavík, 1857–1972.

Eales, Richard 1990. "Royal Power and Castles in Norman England." In Christopher Harper-Bill and Ruth Harvey (eds), Ideals and Practice of Medieval Knighthood 3. Papers from the Fourth Strawberry Hill Conference. Woodbridge: Boydell Press.

Egils saga Skalla-Grímssonar. Ed. Sigurður Nordal. Íslenzk fornrit I. Reykjavík: Hið íslenzka forn-ritafélag, 1933.

Einar G. Pétursson 1986. "Efling kirkjuvalds og ritun Landnámu." Skírnir 160, 193-222.

Einar Ól. Sveinsson 1937. Sagnaritun Oddaverja. Nokkrar athuganir. Studia Islandica 1. Reykjavík: Heimspekideild Háskóla Íslands.

Guðbjörg Kristjánsdóttir 2000. "Fyrstu kirkjur landsins." Kristni á Íslandi 1. Frumkristni og upphaf kirkju. Reykjavík: Alþingi, 175-184.

Guðmundur Ólafsson. 1987. "Þingnes by Elliðavatn: The first Local Assembly in Iceland?" In Charlotte Blindheim and James E. Knirk (eds), Proceedings of the Tenth Viking Congress. Larkollen, Norway, 1985. Universitetets Oldakssamlings Skrifter. Ny rekke. Nr. 9, 343-249.

Guðmundur Ólafsson 1996, Friðlýstar fornleifar í Borgarfjarðarsýslu. Rit Hins íslenska fornleifa-félags og Þjóðminjasafns Íslands 2, Reykjavík.

Guðmundur Ólafsson. 2004. "Þingnes við Elliðavatn og Kjalarnesþing. Rannsóknarsaga 1841–2003". Vinnuskýrslur Þjóðminjasafns 2004/2. Reykjavík: Þjóðminjasafn Íslands.

Guðrún Harðardóttir 2006, "The Physical Setting of Reykholt according to Sturlunga Saga". In Else Mundal (ed.), Reykholt som makt- og lærdomssenter i den islandske og nordiske kontekst. Snorrastofa, vol. III. Reykholt: Snorrastofa, 43–64.

Guðrún Harðardóttir and Þór Hjaltalín 1998. "Varnir heimilis í miðstjórnarlausu samfélagi. Hlutverk virkja og skipulags bæjarhúsa í ljósi Sturlungasögu". In Guðmundur J. Guðmunds-son and Eiríkur K. Björnsson (eds), Íslenska söguþingið 28.-31.maí 1997. Ráðstefnurit 1. Reykjavík: Sagnfræðistofnun Háskóla Íslands and Sagnfræðingafélag Íslands, 95-106.

Guðrún Nordal 2006. "Snorri and Norway". In Else Mundal (ed.), Reykholt som makt- og lærdomssenter i den islandske og nordiske kontekst. Snorrastofa, vol. III. Reykholt: Snorrastofa, 77-84.

Guðrún Sveinbjarnardóttir 2006. "Reykholt, a Centre of Power. The Archaeological Evidence". In Else Mundal (ed.), Reykholt som makt- og lærdomssenter i den islandske og nordiske kontekst. Snorrastofa, vol. III. Reykholt: Snorrastofa, 25-42.

Guðrún Sveinbjarnardóttir 2009. "Kirkjur Reyk-holts – byggingasaga". In Guðmundur Ólafsson and Steinunn Kristjánsdóttir (eds), Endurfundir. Fornleifarannsóknir styrktar af Kristnihátíðarsjóði 2001–2005. Reykjavík: Þjóðminjasafn Íslands, 58–69.

Guðrún Sveinbjarnardóttir 2010. "The Making of a Centre: The Case of Reykholt, Iceland". In John Sheehan and Donnchadh Ó Corráin (eds), The Viking Age: Ireland and the West: Proceedings of the XVth Viking Congress, Cork 2005. Dublin: Four Courts Press, 483–493.

Guðrún Sveinbjarnardóttir 2012. Reykholt.

Archaeological Investigations at a High Status Farm in Western Iceland. Publications of the National Museum of Iceland 29. Reykjavík: Þjóðminjasafn Íslands, Snorrastofa.

Guðrún Sveinbjarnardóttir 2016, *Reykholt. The Church Excavations.* Publications of the National Museum of Iceland 41. Reykjavík: The National Museum of Iceland, in collaboration with Snorrastofa and University of Iceland Press.

Guðrún Sveinbjarnardóttir, Egill Erlendsson, Kim Vickers, Thomas H. McGovern, Karen B. Milek, Kevin J. Edwards, Ian Simpson and Gordon Cook 2007. "The Palaeoecology of a High Status Icelandic Farm". *Environmental Archaeology* 12 (2), 187–206.

Guðrún Sveinbjarnardóttir, Kristoffer Dahle, Egill Erlendsson, Guðrún Gísladóttir and Kim Vickers 2011, "The Reykholt Shieling Project. Some Preliminary Results". In Svavar Sigmundsson (ed.), *Viking Settlements and Viking Society. Papers from the Proceedings of the Sixteenth Viking Congress, Reykjavík and Reykholt 16–23 August 2009.* Reykjavík: Hið íslenzka fornleifafélag and University of Iceland Press, 162–188.

Gunnar F. Guðmundsson 1997. "Guði til þægðar eða höfðingjum í hag? Níu aldir frá lögtöku tíundar á Íslandi". *Ný Saga* 9, 57–64.

Gunnar F. Guðmundsson 2016. "Liturgical Practices at Reykholt in the Middle Ages". In Guðrún Sveinbjarnardóttir, *Reykholt. The Church Excavations.* Publications of the National Museum of Iceland 41. Reykjavík: The National Museum of Iceland, in collaboration with Snorrastofa and University of Iceland Press, 167–174.

Gunnar Karlsson 1972. "Goðar og bændur". *Saga* X, 5–57.

Gunnar Karlsson 1975. "Frá þjóðveldi til konungs-

ríkis". In Sigurður Líndal (ed.), *Saga Íslands* II. Reykjavík: Hið íslenzka bókmenntafélag and Sögufélagið, 1–54.

Gunnar Karlsson 1980. "Völd og auður á 13. öld". *Saga* XVIII, 5–30.

Gunnar Karlsson 2004. *Goðamenning. Staða og áhrif goðorðsmanna í þjóðveldi Íslendinga.* Reykjavík: Heimskringla.

Gunnar Karlsson 2007a. "Valdasamþjöppun þjóðveldisaldar í túlkun fræðimanna". In Benedikt Eyþórsson and Hrafnkell Lárusson (eds), *Þriðja íslenska söguþingið 18.–21.maí 2006. Ráðstefnurit.* Reykjavík: Aðstandendur Þriðja íslenska söguþingsins, 205–213.

Gunnar Karlsson 2007b. *Inngangur að miðöldum. Handbók í íslenskri miðaldasögu* I. Reykjavík: Háskólaútgáfan.

Harðar saga. Eds Þórhallur Vilmundarson and Bjarni Vilhjálmsson. Íslenzk fornrit XIII, Reykjavík: Hið íslenzka fornritafélag, 1991

Helgi Skúli Kjartansson 2005. "Thin on the Ground. Legal Evidence of the Availability of Priests in 12th century Iceland". In Helgi Þorláksson (ed.), *Church Centres. Church Centres in Iceland from the 11th to the 13th Century and their Parallels in other Countries.* Snorrastofa, vol. II. Reykholt: Snorrastofa, 95–102.

Helgi Þorláksson 1979a. "Stórbændur gegn goðum. Hugleiðingar um goðavald, konungsvald og sjálffræðishug bænda um miðbik 13. aldar". In Bergsteinn Jónsson, Einar Laxness and Heimir Þorleifsson (eds), *Söguslóðir. Afmælisrit helgað Ólafi Hanssyni sjötugum 18. september 1979.* Reykjavík: Sögufélag, 227–250.

Helgi Þorláksson 1979b. "Miðstöðvar stærstu byggða. Um forstig þéttbýlismyndunar við Hvítá á hámiðöldum með samanburði við Eyrar, Gásar og erlendar hliðstæður". *Saga* XVII, 125–164.

Helgi Þorláksson 1982. "Stéttir, auður og völd á 12. og 13. öld". *Saga* XX, 63–113.

Helgi Þorláksson 1984. "Mesti örlagavaldur íslenskrar þjóðar". *Pétursskip búið Peter Foote sextugum 26. maí 1984*. Reykjavík: [s. n.], 29–32.

Helgi Þorláksson 1988. "Stéttakúgun eða samfylking bænda? Um söguskoðun Björns Þorsteinssonar". In Gunnar Karlsson, Jón Hnefill Aðalsteinsson and Jónas Gíslason (eds), *Saga og kirkja. Afmælisrit Magnúsar Más Lárussonar gefið út í tilefni af sjötugsafmæli hans 2. september 1987*. Reykjavík: Sögufélag, 183–191.

Helgi Þorláksson 1989. *Gamlar götur og goðavald. Um fornar leiðir og völd Oddaverja í Rangárþingi*. Ritsafn Sagnfræðistofnunar 25. Reykjavík: Sagnfræðistofnun Háskóla Íslands.

Helgi Þorláksson 1991. "Sauðafell: Um leiðir og völd í Dölum við lok þjóðveldis". In Helgi Þorláksson and Gunnar Karlsson (eds), *Yfir Íslandsála. Afmælisrit til heiðurs Magnúsi Stefánssyni sextugum 25. desember 1991*. Reykjavík: Sögufræðslusjóður, 95–109.

Helgi Þorláksson 1994. "Þjóðleið hjá Brekku og Bakka. Um leiðir og völd í Öxnadal við lok þjóðveldis". *Samtíðarsögur 1. Forprent*. Akureyri: Níunda alþjóðlega fornsagnaþingið, 335–349.

Helgi Þorláksson 1998. "Hruni. Um mikilvægi staðarins fyrir samgöngur, völd og kirkjulegt starf á þjóðveldisöld". *Árnesingur* 5, 9–72.

Helgi Þorláksson 2005a. "Inngangur". In Helgi Þorláksson (ed.), *Church Centres. Church Centres in Iceland from the 11th to the 13th Century and their Parallels in other Countries*. Snorrastofa, vol. II. Reykholt: Snorrastofa, 5–16.

Helgi Þorláksson 2005b. "Why were the 12th Century *staðir* Established?". In Helgi Þorláksson (ed.), *Church Centres. Church Centres in Iceland from the 11th to the 13th Century and their Parallels*

in other Countries. Snorrastofa, vol. II. Reykholt: Snorrastofa, 127–155.

Helgi Þorláksson 2007a. "Höfðingjasetur, miðstöðvar og valdamiðstöðvar". Inngangur að málstofunni *Valdamiðstöðvar á miðöldum*. In Benedikt Eyþórsson and Hrafnkell Lárusson (eds), *Þriðja íslenska söguþingið 18.–21. maí 2006. Ráðstefnurit*. Reykjavík: Aðstandendur Þriðja íslenska söguþingsins, 190–197.

Helgi Þorláksson 2007b. "Veraldlegar valdamiðstöðvar, hvernig urðu þær til?". In Benedikt Eyþórsson and Hrafnkell Lárusson (eds), *Þriðja íslenska söguþingið 18.–21. maí 2006. Ráðstefnurit*. Reykjavík: Aðstandendur Þriðja íslenska söguþingsins, 214–224.

Helgi Þorláksson 2010. "Milli Skarðs og Feykis. Um valdasamþjöppun í Hegranesþingi í tíð Ásbirninga og um valdamiðstöðvar þeirra". *Saga* XLVIII (2), 51–93.

Helgi Þorláksson 2011. "A Seat of a Settler? – A Centre of a Magnate: Breiðabólstaður and Reykholt". In Svavar Sigmundsson (ed.), *Viking Settlements and Viking Society. Papers from the Proceedings of the Sixteenth Viking Congress, Reykjavík and Reykholt, 16–23 August 2009*. Reykjavík: Hið íslenzka fornleifafélag and University of Iceland Press, 209–224.

Helgi Þorláksson 2012a. "Reykholt vokser fram som maktsenter". In Helgi Þorláksson and Þóra Björg Sigurðardóttir (eds), *From Nature to Script. Reykholt, Environment, Centre, and Manuscript Making*. Snorrastofa, vol VII. Reykholt: Snorrastofa, 79–116.

Helgi Þorláksson 2012b. "Sturlunga – tilurð og markmið". *Gripla* 23, 53–92.

Helgi Þorláksson 2012c, "Succumbing Secular Chiefs. On Secular Chiefs in Iceland, their Loss of Ground to the Church, *c*. 1270 to 1355 and its Impact". In Steinar Imsen (ed.), *'Ecclesia Nidrosiensis' and 'Noregs veldi'. The Role of the Church in the Making of Norwegian Domination in the Norse World.* 'Norgesveldet', Occasional Papers No. 3. Trondheim: Akademika Publishing, 261–281.

Helgi Þorláksson 2013. "Ódrjúgshálsar og sæbrautir: Um samgöngur og völd við Breiðafjörð á fyrri tíð." *Saga* LI (1), 94–128.

Helgi Þorláksson 2015, "Tunga við leiðamót". *Breiðfirðingur* 63, 48–60.

Helgi Þorláksson 2017. "Reykholt as a Residence of Snorri the *lendr maðr*". In Guðrún Sveinbjarnardóttir and Bergur Þorgeirsson (eds), *The Buildings of Medieval Reykholt. The Wider Context.* Snorrastofa, vol. IX. Reykjavík: Snorrastofa and University of Iceland Press, 159–181.

Helle, Knut 1968. "Anglo-Norwegian Relations in the Reign of Håkon Håkonsson (1217–63)". *Mediaeval Scandinavia* 1, 101–114.

Hjalti Hugason 2000. *Kristni á Íslandi 1. Frumkristni og upphaf kirkju.* Reykjavík: Alþingi.

Hœnsa-Þóris saga. Borgfirðinga sǫgur. Ed. Sigurður Nordal and Guðni Jónsson. Íslenzk fornrit III. Reykjavík: Hið íslenzka fornritafélag, 1938.

Íslendingabók, Landnámabók. Ed. Jakob Benediktsson. Íslenzk fornrit I. Reykjavík: Hið íslenzka fornritafélag, 1968.

Jarteinabók I, Biskupa sögur II. Ed. Ásdís Egilsdóttir. Íslenzk fornrit XVI. Reykjavík: Hið íslenzka fornritafélag, 2002.

Jón Hnefill Aðalsteinsson 1985, "Blót og þing. Trúarlegt og félagslegt hlutverk goða á tíundu öld". *Skírnir* 159, 123–142.

Jón Jóhannesson 1941. *Gerðir Landnámabókar.* Reykjavík: Hið íslenzka bókmenntafélag.

Jón Jóhannesson 1956. *Íslendinga saga 1.*

Þjóðveldisöld. Reykjavík: Almenna bókafélagið. [In English, *A History of the Old Icelandic Commonwealth: Íslendinga saga.* Winnepeg: University of Manitoba Press, 1974.]

Jón Viðar Sigurðsson 1989. *Frá goðorðum til ríkja. Þróun goðavalds á 12. og 13. öld,* Sagnfræðirannsóknir 10. Reykjavík: Bókaútgáfa Menningarsjóðs.

Jón Viðar Sigurðsson 1999. *Chieftains and Power in the Icelandic Commonwealth.* Translated by Jean Lundskær Nielsen. The Viking Collection, Studies in Northern Civilization 12. Odense: Odense University Press.

Jón Viðar Sigurðsson 2005. "Islandske storkirker før 1300". In Helgi Þorláksson (ed.), *Church Centres. Church Centres in Iceland from the 11th to the 13th Century and their Parallels in other Countries.* Snorrastofa, vol. II. Reykholt: Snorrastofa, 157–166.

Jón Viðar Sigurðsson 2007. "Stórkirkjur, sagnaritun og valdamiðstöðvar 1100–1400". In Benedikt Eyþórsson and Hrafnkell Lárusson (eds), *Þriðja íslenska söguþingið 18.–21. maí 2006. Ráðstefnurit.* Reykjavík: Aðstandendur Þriðja íslenska söguþingsins, 225–233.

Kjalnesinga saga. Ed. Jóhannes Halldórsson. Íslenzk fornrit XIV. Reykjavík: Hið íslenzka fornritafélag, 1959.

Kristni saga. Biskupa sögur I. Ed. Sigurgeir Steingrímsson, Ólafur Halldórsson and Peter Foote. Íslenzk fornrit XV (1–2). Reykjavík: Hið íslenzka fornritafélag, 2003.

Kålund, Kristian 1877. *Bidrag til en historisk-topografisk Beskrivelse af Island* I, Copenhagen: Gyldendal.

Lucas, Gavin 2007. "The Viking Settlement at Hofstaðir in Mývatnssveit". In Benedikt Eyþórsson and Hrafnkell Lárusson (eds), *Þriðja* íslenska söguþingið 18.–21. maí 2006. Ráðstefnurit. Reykjavík: Aðstandendur Þriðja íslenska söguþingsins, 198–204.

Lucas, Gavin 2009. *Hofstaðir. Excavations of a Viking Age Feasting Hall in North-Eastern Iceland.* Institute of Archaeology Monograph Series 1. Reykjavík: Fornleifastofnun Íslands.

Lucas, Gavin 2009. "Hofstaðir in the Settlement Period". In Gavin Lucas (ed.), *Hofstaðir Excavations of a Viking Age Feasting Hall in North-Eastern Iceland.* Monograph No. 1. Reykjavík: Institute of Archaeology, 371–408.

Lúðvík Ingvarsson 1986–1987. *Goðorð og goðorðsmenn* 1–3. Egilsstaðir: s.n.

Magnús Grímsson 1886. "Athugasemdir við Egils sögu Skallagrímssonar". *Safn til sögu Íslands og íslenzkra bókmenta* II. Copenhagen, 251–276.

Magnús Stefánsson 1975. "Kirkjuvald eflist". In Sigurður Líndal (ed.), *Saga Íslands* 2. Reykjavík: Hið íslenzka bókmenntafélag og Sögufélagið, 55–144.

Magnús Stefánsson 2000. *Staðir og staðamál. Studier i islandske egenkirkelige og benficialrettslige forhold i middelalderen* 1. Historisk Institutts skriftserie 4. Bergen: Historisk institutt, Universitetet i Bergen.

Magnús Stefánsson 2002. "Um staði og staðamál". *Saga* XL (2), 139–166.

Magnús Stefánsson 2005. "De islandske stadenes egenart". In Helgi Þorláksson (ed.), *Church Centres. Church Centres in Iceland from the 11th to the 13th Century and their Parallels in other Countries.* Snorrastofa, vol. II. Reykholt: Snorrastofa, 117–125.

Matthías Þórðarson 1932, "Bólstaður við Álftafjörð. Skýrsla um rannsókn 1931". *Árbók Hins íslenzka fornleifafélags* 1932, 1–28.

Moore, Robert Ian 2000. *The First European Revolution, c. 970-1215. The Making of Europe.* Oxford: Blackwell Publishing.

Orri Vésteinsson 1998. "Íslenska sóknaskipulagið og samband heimila á miðöldum". In Guðmundur J. Guðmundsson and Eiríkur K. Björnsson (eds), *Íslenska söguþingið 28.-31. maí 1997. Ráðstefnurit* 1. Reykjavík: Sagnfræðistofnun Háskóla Íslands and Sagnfræðingafélag Íslands, 147–166.

Orri Vésteinsson 2000a. *Forn kirkja og grafreitur á Neðra-Ási í Hjaltadal.* FS 109–98174. Reykjavík: Fornleifastofnun Íslands.

Orri Vésteinsson 2000b. *The Christianization of Iceland. Priests, Power, and Social Change 1000–1300.* Oxford: Oxford University Press.

Orri Vésteinsson 2005. "The Formative Phase of the Icelandic Church ca 990–1240 AD". In Helgi Þorláksson (ed.), *Church Centres. Church Centres in Iceland from the 11th to the 13th Century and their Parallels in other Countries.* Snorrastofa, vol. II. Reykholt: Snorrastofa, 71–81.

Orri Vésteinsson 2006. "Central Areas in Iceland". In Jette Arneborg and Bjarne Grønnow (eds), *Dynamics of Northern Societies. Proceedings of the SILA/NABO Conference on Arctic and North Atlantic Archaeology, Copenhagen, May 10th-14th, 2004.* Studies in Archeology and History 10. Copenhagen: National Museum of Denmark, 307–322.

Orri Vésteinsson 2007. "'Hann reisti hof mikið hundrað fóta langt...'. Um uppruna *hof*-örnefna og stjórnmál á Íslandi á 10. öld". *Saga* VL (1), 53–91.

Orri Vésteinsson 2009, "Upphaf goðaveldis á Íslandi". In Guðmundur Jónsson, Helgi Skúli Kjartansson and Vésteinn Ólason (eds), *Heimtur.*

Ritgerðir til heiðurs Gunnari Karlssyni sjötugum. Reykjavík: Mál og menning, 298–311.

Orri Vésteinsson and Thomas McGovern 2012. "The Peopling of Iceland", *Norwegian Archaeological Review* 45 (2), 206–218.

Ólafur Lárusson 1944. "Úr byggðarsögu Íslands". *Byggð og saga.* Reykjavík: Ísafoldarprentsmiðja h.f., 9–58.

Ólafur Lárusson 1958. "Hof og þing". *Lög og saga*, Reykjavík: Hlaðbúð, 91–99.

Reykjaholtsmáldagi. Ed. Guðvarður Már Gunnlaugsson. Reykholt: Reykholtskirkja, Snorrastofa, 2000.

Sahlins, Marshall 1981/1972. *Stone Age Economics.* London: Tavistock Publications.

Sif Ríkharðsdóttir 2012. *Medieval Translations and Cultural Discourse. The Movement of Texts in England, France and Scandinavia.* Cambridge: D.S. Brewer.

Sigurður Nordal 1942. *Íslenzk menning* 1. Reykjavík: Mál og menning.

Sigurður Vigfússon 1884–1885. "Rannsókn í Borgarfirði 1884". *Árbók Hins íslenzka fornleifafélags 1884–1885*, 61–138.

Steinunn Kristjánsdóttir 2003. "Timburkirkja og grafreitur úr frumkristni. Af fornleifauppgreftri á Þórarinsstöðum í Seyðisfirði". *Árbók Hins íslenzka fornleifafélags 2000–2001*, 113–142.

Sturlunga saga I–II. Eds Jón Jóhannesson, Magnús Finnbogason and Kristján Eldjárn. Reykjavík: Sturlunguútgáfan, 1946.

Svavar Sigmundsson 1979. "Íslensku staðanöfnin". *Íslenskt mál og almenn málfræði* I, 238–248.

Sverrir Jakobsson 2002. "Braudel í Breiðafirði? Breiðafjörðurinn og hinn breiðfirski heimur á öld Sturlunga". *Saga* 40 (1), 150–179.

Sverrir Jakobsson 2005. "Frá þrælahaldi til landeigendavalds: Íslenskt miðaldasamfélag, 1100–1400". *Saga* 43 (2), 99–129.

Sverrir Jakobsson 2009. "The Process of State-Formation in Medieval Iceland". *Viator. Journal of Medieval and Renaissance Studies* 40 (2), 151–170.

Sverrir Jakobsson 2013. "Konur og völd í Breiðafirði á miðöldum". *Skírnir* 187, Spring, 161–175.

Tryggvi Már Ingvarsson 2000. "Reykholt í Borgarfirði. Þjóðleiðir um Vesturland á Sturlungaöld". *Sagnir* 21, 28–33.

Úlfar Bragason 1988. *On the Poetics of Sturlunga.* Ann Arbor, MI: University Microfilms, 1988.

Úlfar Bragason 2005. "Sagas of Contemporary History (Sturlunga saga): Text and Research". In Rory McTurk (ed.), *A Companion to Old Norse-Icelandic Literature and Culture.* Oxford: Blackwell, 427–446.

Úlfar Bragason 2010. *Ætt og saga. Um frásagnarfræði Sturlungu eða Íslendinga sögu hinnar miklu.* Reykjavík: Háskólaútgáfan.

Vilhjálmur Örn Vilhjálmsson 1996. "Gård og kirke på Stöng i Þjórsárdalur. Reflektioner på den tidligste kirkeordning og kirkeret på Island". In Jens Flemming Krøger and Helge-Rolf Naley (eds), *Nordsjøen. Handel, religion og politikk.* Stavanger: Karmøyseminaret 1994 og 1995, 118–139.

Wanner, Kevin 2008. *Snorri Sturluson and the Edda. The Conversion of Cultural Capital in Medieval Scandinavia.* Toronto Old Norse and Icelandic Series. Toronto: Toronto University Press.

Zori, Davide 2014. "Interdisciplinary Modelling of Viking Age and Medieval Settlement in the Mosfell Valley". In Davide Zori and Jesse Byock (eds), *Viking Archaeology in Iceland. Mosfell*

Archaeological Project. Cursor 20. Turnhout: Brepols, 55–79.

Þorláks saga byskups in elzta. *Biskupa sögur* II. Ed. Ásdís Egilsdóttir. Íslenzk fornrit XVI. Reykjavík: Hið íslenzka fornritafélag, 2002.

Þorláks saga byskups yngri. *Biskupa sögur* II. Ed. Ásdís Egilsdóttir. Íslenzk fornrit XVI. Reykjavík: Hið íslenzka fornritafélag, 2002.

¶ EGILL ERLENDSSON, KEVIN J. EDWARDS,
KIM VICKERS, GUÐRÚN SVEINBJARNARDÓTTIR
AND GUÐRÚN GÍSLADÓTTIR

The Palaeoecology and Cultural Landscapes Associated with Reykholt

Introduction

CELANDIC ARCHAEOLOGISTS HAVE MADE EXTENSIVE USE of palaeoenvironmental techniques over the past few decades, especially with the aim of explaining how people exploited natural landscapes and how this activity affected environments and resource availability. As a result, a wealth of research findings concerning environmental change has been gathered through archaeological projects such as those at Hofstaðir in Mývatnssveit,[1] the Eyjafjǫll region,[2] and the Mosfell Archaeological Project.[3]

In association with the Reykholt Project, a large body of palaeoenvironmental data has also been accumulated. From environmental contexts, eighteen sample sites in ten different locations have been examined (fig. 1; table 1). The first to take place involved the study of pollen and

---

1   E.g. McGovern *et al.* 2007; Lawson *et al.* 2007; 2009; Lucas 2009.

2   E.g. Buckland and Perry 1989; Buckland *et al.* 1991; Dugmore and Buckland 1991; Vickers *et al.* 2011.

3   Bathurst *et al.* 2010; Zori *et al.* 2013; Egill Erlendsson *et al.* 2014.

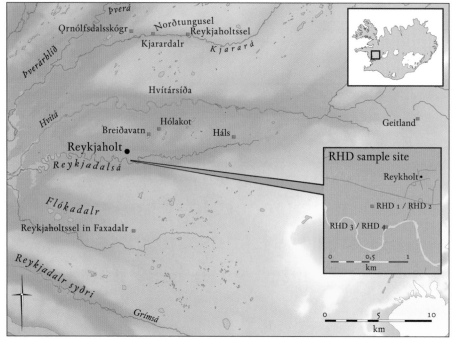

Figure 1. Map of the Borgarfjǫrðr (Borgarfjörður) area showing locations of sites studied for palaeoecology. Map: Stefán Ólafsson.

plant macrofossils at Háls, where excavations revealed a Viking age iron production site.[4] As part of the Landscapes circum-*Landnám* Project,[5] a number of sites were sampled to study the effects of climate and land use on late-Holocene natural environments.[6] Most recently, numerous sites have been sampled within the "Reykholt Shieling Project".[7] Palaeoenvironmental techniques have also featured prominently in the study of cultural contexts within the ruin complexes at Reykholt.[8]

In this chapter we will summarize the environmental conditions in the Reykholtsdalr valley at the time of first settlement (*c.* AD 870), how the cultural landscape became established in its landscape context, and how the natural landscape developed after the initial settlement. For this

---

4   Smith 1995; 2005; Dixon 1997.
5   Edwards *et al.* 2004.
6   Vickers 2006; Bending 2007; Egill Erlendsson 2007; Egill Erlendsson and Edwards 2009, 2010; Egill Erlendsson *et al.* 2012; Gathorne-Hardy *et al.* 2009.
7   Guðrún Sveinbjarnardóttir 2008; Guðrún Sveinbjarnardóttir *et al.* 2011; Vickers and Guðrún Sveinbjarnardóttir 2013.
8   Guðrún Sveinbjarnardóttir *et al.* 2007; Guðrún Sveinbjarnardóttir 2012.

Table 1. Sites sampled for palaeoenvironmental research in Borgarfjǫrðr

Project	Locations	Site codes	Context	Period captured by one detailed dataset, or more	Studied for:
Háls project	Háls	N/A	Peat	Pre-settlement to present	S, P, PM
LCL	Reykholtsdalr	RHD1/2	Peat/soil	~AD 500 to present	S, P, PM
LCL	Reykholtsdalr	RHD3/4	Peat/soil	~2750-230 BC to present	S, PM, C
LCL	Hólakot	BR2	Peat	~2260 BC to present	S, PM, C
Soil project	Hólakot	HOL	Peat	~2650 BC to present	S
LCL	Breiðavatn	BR1	Gyttja	~1000 BC to ~AD 1900	S, P, Ch
Soil project	Breiðavatn	BV	Gyttja	~2260 BC to present	S
Shieling project	Geitland	KOT1	Soil	Pre-settlement to present	S, P
Shieling project	Faxadalr	FAX 1	Soil	Pre-settlement to present	S
Shieling project	Faxadalr	FAX 2	Peat/ cultural	Medieval to present	P
Shieling project	Faxadalr	FAX 3	Peat/ cultural	Medieval to present	C
Shieling project	Ǫrnólfsdalsskógr	ORN1	Peat	~1000 BC to present	S, P, C
Shieling project	Norðtungusel	NOR1	Soil	~2260 BC-present (hiatus?)	S
Shieling project	Norðtungusel	NOR2	Peat	Pre-settlement (~3000 BC?) to present	S, P
Shieling project	Reykholtssel	REY1	Soil	~2100 BC to present	S
Shieling project	Reykholtssel	REY2	Peat	~100 BC to present	S, P, C
Shieling project	Reykholtssel	REY3	Soil/ cultural	Medieval to ~AD 1700	P
Reykholt project	Reykholt midden	Cont. 577	cultural	Medieval	P, PM, C, A

A = Archaeofauna; Ch = Chironomids; C = Coleoptera; PM = Plant macrofossils; P = pollen;
S = Soil properties; LCL = Landscapes circum Landnám project

purpose we have selected three study areas for consideration (fig. 1): the meadows between Reykholt (sample sites RHD1, RHD2, RHD3 and RHD4) and the river Reykjadalsá, the uplands between Reykholtsdalr/Reykjadalr and Hálsasveit (Breiðavatn, Hólakot) and the Reykholtssel/Reykjaholtssel area in Kjarardalr, where a shieling existed in the past. These sites provide information about environmental change over a transect stretching from the agricultural land near the farm to the nearby upland and to the hinterland that provided summer grazing. While data from palynology (pollen analysis) and soil study provide a framework, the associated studies of Coleoptera (beetles) and plant macrofossils also supply valuable information about environmental change.[9]

Background to Land-use History and Post-settlement Landscape Change in Iceland

The most extensive account of the long journey on open boats from Scandinavia or the British Isles and subsequent settlement in Iceland is provided in *Egils saga Skalla-Grímssonar*, which describes the settlement of Skalla-Grímr (Grímr the Bald) at Borg in western Iceland. The saga demonstrates that while traditional livestock (such as cows, sheep and pigs) was initially scarce, Skalla-Grímr and his people relied greatly on natural resources such as fish, birds, eggs and seals. Later, as introduced livestock numbers increased, subsistence farming strategies involved both arable and pastoral agriculture, including grazing in highland pastures.[10] Although the reliability of the saga literature as evidence for past events is often doubtful,[11] *Egils saga* seems to describe the nature and formation of early Icelandic agriculture with reasonable accuracy when compared with environmental and archaeological records. Midden deposits from the age of settlement often contain an abundance of seal bones, eggshells and skeletal remains of marine birds and fish, while from the beginning of the eleventh century such data show an increased emphasis on keeping a range of domesticated animals, of which cattle were the most prominent

---

9   Vickers 2006; Bending 2007; a summary of the plant and Coleopteran macrofossil records is available in Egill Erlendsson *et al.* 2012.

10   *Egils saga Skalla-Grímssonar*, 75–76.

11   Adolf Friðriksson and Orri Vésteinsson 2003.

species.[12] The cultivation of cereals (mainly barley) from the outset is demonstrated by pollen analysis,[13] literary sources,[14] archaeology[15] and the landscape features and soil stratigraphies created by arable agriculture.[16] Archaeology and palynology attest land use in remote areas from the early settlement period, including the exploitation of summer pastures in the form of shieling activity.[17] All this would seem to agree with the saga account of how Skalla-Grímr exploited the resources and landscape within his reach. Overall, the early Icelandic farming structure closely resembles agriculture in western Norway in the late ninth century,[18] and may reflect an attempt to replicate the methods that the settlers knew from their previous homes. The Norse-style farming techniques were imported into a starkly different environment in terms of climate, soil and vegetation, which perhaps contributed to later adjustments to the farming methods, although social factors such as increased tenancy and/ or other changes in land ownership cannot be exempt from this equation. The most notable change is the gradual abandonment of a livestock mix of cattle, pigs, sheep and goats through the medieval period in favour of a simpler and more pragmatic approach, predominantly keeping sheep with some cattle.[19]

The land-use practices introduced to the island in the late-ninth century set in motion or accelerated a dramatic process of landscape change that is still ongoing. Since settlement, the island has lost almost all of its birch (*Betula pubescens*) woodland, which may have covered as much as a quarter of the total land area at the time of settlement. Likewise, continuous vegetation cover has shrunk tremendously over the same period, from between 54 and 65 per cent to about only 25 per cent.[20] Icelandic volcanic soil is sensitive to erosion, and when it became exposed, soil removal was bound to accelerate. Soil erosion has had a marked and extensive impact upon the landscape, leaving some areas depleted of soil and others subject to soil accumulation as a result of mass movement,

12 Dugmore *et al.* 2005; McGovern *et al.* 2006.
13 Þorleifur Einarsson 1962; Margrét Hallsdóttir 1987; Egill Erlendsson 2007; Egill Erlendsson *et al.* 2012; Zori *et al.* 2013.
14 Jónatan Hermannson 1993.
15 Guðrún Sveinbjarnardóttir *et al.* 2007; Zori *et al.* 2013.
16 Garðar Guðmundsson *et al.* 2004.
17 Lucas 2008; Guðrún Sveinbjarnardóttir 1991a; Guðrún Sveinbjarnardóttir *et al.* 2011.
18 E.g. Dugmore *et al.* 2005.
19 Dugmore *et al.* 2005; McGovern *et al.* 2007.
20 Andrés Arnalds 1987; Rannveig Ólafsdóttir *et al.* 2001; Ólafur Arnalds 2008.

water and wind transport. Important sinks of eroded soils are lakes, vegetated soils and wetlands.[21] Healthy soils are basic to the functioning of terrestrial ecosystems. Soil organic matter (OM) and soil organic carbon (C) are among the key components vital to the sustainability of soil fertility and consequently of agricultural productivity. Iceland has lost an estimated 6 to 24 per cent of all the Icelandic pre-settlement soil organic C pool.[22]

Although it is clear that there was a significant loss of woodland and the wider vegetation cover, along with soils, the temporal, spatial and social aspects of these processes are rather more complex.

How was Iceland Settled?

Where did the initial settlers locate their farms, and why? It seems logical that the pioneer settlements were scattered around the coast in order to access marine food resources, which were relied upon while livestock numbers grew.[23] But how did the colonization proceed from there? Geographical considerations form the core of Orri Vésteinsson's modelling of early Icelandic settlement development.[24] He used late- and post-medieval written sources to locate the richest farms, which are typically those associated with medieval parish churches, and then assumed that these would have been the farms of earliest settlement and greatest power. These form a group of farms, large in terms of area, which are typically located near extensive wetlands or floodplains. In an environment where much of the lowland areas were wooded,[25] openings in the woodlands would have been important for the collection of winter fodder, in particular for cattle, which were a prominent component of the early settlement livestock. Wetlands and floodplains are most likely to have supported the high water table needed to maintain habitats suitable for fodder and to keep birch woodland at bay. By seeking out such openings, the early settlers would have avoided the considerable effort of initial woodland

---

21   Ólafur Arnalds *et al.* 2001; Dugmore *et al.* 2005; 2009; Guðrún Gísladóttir *et al.* 2010.
22   Hlynur Óskarsson *et al.* 2004; Guðrún Gísladóttir and Stocking 2005.
23   E.g. Smith 1995, 331.
24   Orri Vésteinsson 1998; Orri Vésteinsson *et al.* 2002.
25   Margrét Hallsdóttir 1987; Egill Erlendsson and Edwards 2010.

clearance.[26] Such clearance would probably have involved the burning of woodland, for which there is only scant evidence.[27]

The erection of farms or farming outposts in areas near or beyond the upper woodland edge also took place very early in the settlement process. Ruins, stranded in eroded areas in Mývatnssveit in the north-east[28] and in Þórsmǫrk in the south,[29] testify to this development. Farm establishments in the more densely wooded areas may, on the other hand, have been delayed until woodland exploitation had reduced the cover and density of woodland, making the underlying fertile volcanic soils accessible for exploitation, and as the growing population made expansion into more marginal or less accessible areas a necessity.[30]

While it is fairly certain that the first settlers gained an advantage from being able to select the most desirable locations and to claim authority over large areas of land, less is known about the way in which the cultural landscape evolved spatially and temporally in the subsequent centuries. Absolute dates for the establishment of individual farms may often be lacking, but the apparent late- and post-medieval hierarchical order of farms offers a means of establishing a plausible retrospective reconstruction of the settlement process. A threefold division of farms into "earliest establishments", second phase "large farms" and, thirdly, numerous simple "planned farms" is becoming a widely accepted and applied model.[31] This model dictates that those who came first were able to claim large areas of land of high quality from which they gave or sold parts to later arrivals, though maintaining the greatest resource base for the parent farm. Subsequently, the remaining inhabitable land was divided into "planned settlements", farming units established in the areas of lowest quality. In this manner, the early settlers perhaps gained political support by establishing farms, variously dependent upon the parent farm, while ensuring that the "dependent" farms would not gain precedence.[32]

26 Orri Vésteinsson 1998.
27 Sigurður Þórarinsson 1944; Margrét Hallsdóttir 1987; Buckland *et al.* 1995; Smith 1995.
28 McGovern *et al.* 2007.
29 Guðrún Sveinbjarnardóttir 1991b.
30 Orri Vésteinsson 1998; McGovern *et al.* 2007.
31 Orri Vésteinsson 1998; Orri Vésteinsson *et al.* 2002; McGovern *et al.* 2007; Guðrún Sveinbjarnardóttir *et al.* 2008; Zori 2014.
32 E.g. Orri Vésteinsson *et al.* 2002.

The Modern Environment of Borgarfjǫrðr

The Borgarfjǫrðr district (fig. 1), between Norðrárdalr and Skarðsheiði (formerly Skarðsheiðr), consists of eight glacially-carved valleys (including Norðrárdalr, through which the Norðrá river runs) with a general east-west alignment. All the valleys have been permanently inhabited for all or most of the historic period, apart from Kjarardalr, where agricultural lowland is limited. A key component of the Borgarfjǫrðr landscape is the Hvítá, a glacial river fed by the Langjǫkull glacier. A great quantity of water flows into the Hvítá from its subsidaries before it reaches the ocean, where the offloading of sediment has produced extensive floodplains.[33]

The soils in the Borgarfjǫrðr lowlands are predominantly histosols or histic andosols, with andosols across slopes.[34] Different gradients in the valleys dictate that they sustain wetlands and lowlands to a varying degree. Much of the lowlands are today given over to hayfields or are drained to provide better pasture. At higher elevations, infertile heathlands commonly lead up to barren, windswept hilltops, although overall land degradation and erosion in Reykholtsdalr and neighbouring areas is minimal compared to many other parts of Iceland. Remnants of natural woodland are found in patches in several locations; the most extensive ones are in Húsafell, Þverárhlíð and in Skorradalr. The Borgarfjǫrðr region is rich in natural resources. It is among the best farming districts in Iceland, owing to fertile lowlands and a favourable climate.[35] Many of the best rivers for salmon fishing are found here, which must have been as much of an attraction in the past as it is today.[36]

Reykholtsdalr is situated centrally in the valley system of Borgarfjǫrðr. It is about twenty kilometres long and is divided into two rural municipalities (*hreppar*), Reykholtsdalshreppr and Hálsaveit. The Reykjadalsá drains the valley and meanders increasingly in its lower reaches until reaching the Hvítá river. The most fertile lands are found along the lower course of the river, but further inland from Reykholt the soils become thinner and the quality of the farmland becomes inferior.[37] The floodplains of the Reykjadalsá are considered to have provided a basis for a prosperous

---

33   Freysteinn Sigurðsson 2004.
34   Ólafur Arnalds and Einar Grétarsson 2001.
35   Freysteinn Sigurðsson 2004.
36   Freysteinn Sigurðsson 2004; see pp. 208, 225, 230 in this book.
37   Guðrún Sveinbjarnardóttir *et al.* 2007.

early settlement at Reykholt, contributing to the chieftain-status of the initial farm.[38]

The nearest weather station to Reykholtsdalr is Síðumúli in Hvítársíða, about three kilometres north of Reykholt. The average annual temperature was 3.8°C for the years 1931 to 1960 and for the same period the average annual precipitation was 720 mm/yr.[39] Another weather station, Stafholtsey, some nine kilometres west of Reykholt, has recorded an annual average temperature of 4.3°C and precipitation of 786 mm/yr for the period 1989 to 2005.[40] Generally speaking, the climate at Reykholt is colder and drier than in southern Iceland but warmer and wetter than in the north of the country.

Palaeoecology from the Landholdings of Reykholt

Climate in Reykholtsdalr over the last 3000 years

Preserved remains of Chironomids (non-biting midges) taken from a core (BR1) from the lake sediments of Breiðavatn (fig. 1 and table 1) were used to reconstruct past summer temperatures.[41] The data show that from around 800 BC to AD 1000, the July temperature remained near 9°C, with only small fluctuations. Following a cool phase around AD 1000, there is a rise of about 0.5°C from around AD 1100 to 1300, which corresponds to the so-called Medieval Warm Period (MWP). Subsequently, around AD 1500, the temperature reconstruction indicates a cooling of about 1°C, taken to represent the Little Ice Age (LIA). This cooling trend extends to the top of the core, with the exception of two adjacent samples dated to around AD 1800 and 1825, which indicate some warming, followed by the coldest point in the core (about 7.2°C) which dates to the latter half of the nineteenth century AD. High levels of sea ice observed in the late nineteenth century,[42] and particularly enhanced environmental instability

38 Orri Vésteinsson 1998.
39 Markús Á. Einarsson 1976.
40 Egill Erlendsson 2007, 161 (citing data from the Icelandic Met Office).
41 Gathorne-Hardy *et al.* 2009 provide a more detailed discussion of the Breiðavatn climate record.
42 Ogilvie and Ingibjörg Jónsdóttir 2000.

recorded in southeast Iceland,[43] are among other climate-driven features of the late nineteenth century.

In broad terms, the results from the Breiðavatn core correlate quite well with other studies from terrestrial and marine stratigraphic records. Many of those indicate a favourable climate during the medieval period and a subsequent cooling from around AD 1250 to 1500,[44] earlier than is depicted in the Breiðavatn data, with further cooling around AD 1500. It nevertheless seems that the climate during the first five or six centuries of settlement was relatively favourable in Reykholtsdalr, and perhaps for Iceland in general, at least in comparison with that during the coldest part of the LIA. Although the onset of the LIA is temporally unclear and it was not a continuously cold episode,[45] its cold spells would probably have had detrimental effects such as shortening the growing season and reducing ecosystem productivity equivalent to about a 180 metre rise in altitude.[46] The cooling would have exerted a greater strain on ecosystems already under pressure because of grazing, particularly in elevated areas where erosion fronts probably moved to lower altitudes.[47] Under such conditions, vegetated areas serve as sinks for the eroded soils and the uppermost sub-surface strata become coarser, less compact, less fertile and increasingly susceptible to hummock (*þúfur*) formation through frost action and erosion.[48] As far as cultivation is concerned, the post-medieval cooling would have significantly undermined its potential by reducing the number of day-degrees attainable over the summer. Cereal cultivation at Reykholt may have ceased, however, before the main cooling set in (see below).

Environmental change in the Reykholtsdalr lowland

Studies on vegetation growth and development in the lowlands have been conducted at two sites in the meadows below Reykholt. Records of plant macrofossils and Coleoptera spanning the period from around 2750 to 230 BC were constructed from samples taken from an exposed section by the Reykjadalsá river (RHD3 and RHD4; figs. 1 and 2; table 1). An

---

43 McKinzey *et al.* 2005.
44 E.g. Jón Eiríksson *et al.* 2006; Sicre *et al.* 2008; Áslaug Geirsdóttir *et al.* 2009; Miller *et al.* 2012.
45 E.g. Ogilvie and Trausti Jónsson 2001.
46 Gathorne-Hardy *et al.* 2009.
47 Dugmore *et al.* 2009.
48 Guðrún Gísladóttir *et al.* 2011.

Figure 2. View from Skáneyjarbunga showing the Reykholt lowlands, and the study sites RHD1/2 and RHD3/4. Photo: Egill Erlendsson.

adjacent site (RHD1 and RHD2; figs. 1 and 2; table 1) was studied mainly for pollen over the period from roughly AD 475 to the present. Together these records allow us to draw inferences about vegetation development during the last quarter of the Holocene, although with a hiatus of around seven hundred years between about 230 BC and AD 475.[49]

The macrofossil records from site RHD4 indicate a wet environment over the period between roughly 2750 BC and 230 BC in which the sedges *Carex rostrata* (bottle sedge) and *Carex nigra* (common sedge) flourished.[50] Seeds of *Menyanthes trifoliata* (bogbean), a species that favours shallow water around lakes or ponds or in wetlands where the ground water table is high, also reflect this.[51] This is also the case with the Coleopteran remains from this site where the presence of taxa that require open water or high levels of moisture and inhabit *Sphagnum* mosses were in evidence.[52] The vegetational landscape in the fields around the Reykjadalsá was probably quite open, as suggested by the limited wood remains in the deposits.

The nearby site RHD1, which covers the period around the time

49 Egill Erlendsson *et al.* 2012.
50 Egill Erlendsson *et al.* 2012.
51 Hörður Kristinsson 1986.
52 Egill Erlendsson *et al.* 2012.

of settlement, also reflects damp pre-settlement conditions. The plant macrofossil assemblage suggests an abundant growth of *C. rostrata* and, to a lesser extent, *C. nigra*. Seeds of *Hippuris vulgaris* (mare's tail), a tall and damp-loving herb, were also recorded immediately below the apparent first settlement (*landnám*) horizon. Closer to the valley slopes, the presence of *Betula* (birch) is demonstrated in the plant macrofossil record, whilst in the Coleopteran record the *Salix* feeder *Dorytomus taeniatus* confirms the presence of *Salix* (willows).[53] The pollen assemblages (fig. 3) preceding the settlement from RHD1 concur with the plant macrofossil records. High percentages of Cyperaceae (sedge family), along with significant values for pollen of other wetland taxa, such as *Filipendula ulmaria* (meadowsweet), *Angelica* (angelicas) and *Caltha palustris* (marsh marigold), signify the damp nature of the floodplain. Pollen of *Betula* (cf. *pubescens*, downy birch) also reach prominent values here, which indicates the growth of woodland in the vicinity of the site prior to settlement.

Overall, the floodplain around Reykholt seems to have been predominantly wetland, dominated by tall sedges and herbs, with drier patches sustaining woody taxa. Open or sparse woodland are terms that have been used for this sort of environment,[54] and inferred to consist of trees or shrubs of lower stature than would have grown on the drier valley slopes which were more favourable for woodland growth. Such woodland is assumed to have been relatively easily cleared to facilitate agriculture.[55]

Land-use change associated with farming activities is reflected across a tephra horizon dated by two Carbon 14 age-estimates (calibrated to AD 770–970 and 780–990 [2 σ]; fig. 3) to around the time of settlement. In Iceland, the archetypical palynological response to settlement is a rapid decline in values for birch pollen,[56] but here the percentage values for *Betula* (cf. *pubescens*) do not indicate a great decline of woodland. This could be an aberration of relative values. A more independent parameter is the calculation of annual deposition of pollen. Using this method, Egill Erlendsson demonstrated a decline in the annual deposition of birch pollen from somewhere between 500 to 1200 pollen per cm^2 yr^{-1} before settlement to consistently below 400 pollen per cm^2 yr^{-1} above the

53   Egill Erlendsson *et al.* 2012.
54   Egill Erlendsson and Edwards 2009.
55   Bending 2007.
56   Margrét Hallsdóttir 1987; Vickers *et al.* 2011.

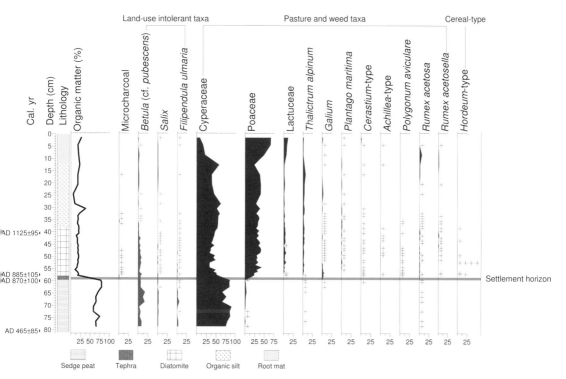

Figure 3. Pollen percentage diagram from RHD1. Selected taxa are displayed. + signifies values below 1% of the ~500 land pollen counted for each level, but for *Hordeum*-type they signify numbers of pollen grains encountered. Diagram: Egill Erlendsson.

settlement horizon.[57] Given the limited support for woodland growth across the damp flat areas of the valley it can be assumed that this decline in woodland is, to some extent at least, attributable to woodland clearance across the more distant valley slopes. Any shrubs or woodland growing locally in the meadows were probably also removed, given the absence of seeds from woody taxa in the plant macrofossil assemblages.[58]

Another prominent feature of the early *landnám* is increased soil drainage. In the pollen record this is shown by the replacement of pollen from wetland taxa by the pollen of herbs that favour dry soil conditions and open environments (e.g. Poaceae (grass family), Lactuceae (a tribe within the daisy family), *Thalictrum alpinum* (alpine meadow-rue), *Ga-*

57   Egill Erlendsson 2007.
58   Egill Erlendsson *et al.* 2012.

lium (bedstraw), *Plantago maritima* (sea plantain)). These dryland taxa commonly serve as apophytes in Icelandic pollen studies (apophytes are native taxa which expand under agricultural activities).[59] The significant drop in organic matter across the *landnám* horizon also shows how the soils change from being highly organic peat (histosol), to diatom-rich soils and then to organic silt, which is perhaps best described as histic andosol and is the predominant modern surface soil in Reykholtsdalr. Such a change in lithology could be the result of two factors: firstly, diminished biomass production resulting from altered species composition or the removal of biomass as part of haymaking; secondly, increased inputs of minerogenic material from soil erosion, which is strongly linked to woodland removal,[60] could have altered the sediment properties.

The reason for converting shrubby or wooded areas to open and better agricultural land near the farms is perhaps displayed in the pollen assemblages. The cultivation of barley was almost certainly a part of the Scandinavian farming package, and this practice is apparent in the RHD1/2 pollen assemblages in the form of *Hordeum*-type pollen and associated weeds (e.g. *Cerastium*-type (e.g. chickweed) and *Polygonum aviculare* (common knotgrass)). These finds compare favourably with historical and archaeological evidence for local arable activity associated with Reykholt.[61]

After the period of rapid vegetation change soon after settlement, the floral community reached a new equilibrium, which is a common trend displayed in Icelandic pollen diagrams over this period.[62] In fact, modern plant composition compares favourably with that established during the first few centuries of occupation. An assessment of modern vegetation composition within a four square metre quadrad between sites RHD1/2 and RHD3/4 revealed that grasses dominate the vegetation, with other prominent taxa being *Taraxacum* spp. (dandelions), *Ranunculus acris* (meadow buttercup), *Cerastium fontanum* (common mouse-ear), *Rumex acetosa* (common sorrel) and *Achillea millefolium* (yarrow).[63] All of these species, or pollen groups to which they belong, either attain increased representation in the pollen assemblages or emerge soon after settlement

59 Margrét Hallsdóttir 1987; Vickers *et al.* 2011.
60 Guðrún Gísladóttir *et al.* 2011; Vickers *et al.* 2011.
61 Egill Erlendsson *et al.* 2012.
62 Margrét Hallsdóttir 1987; Egill Erlendsson and Edwards 2010.
63 Egill Erlendsson 2007.

and most of them are represented throughout the post-settlement era, albeit some only sporadically.

Environmental change in the Reykholtsdalr upland

The pollen data from Breiðavatn (BR1; figs. 1 and 4; table 1) cover the last three thousand years. They indicate a stable pre-settlement environment, where the presence of birch woodland within the lake catchment seems to have been continuous (fig. 5). Annual accumulation (influx) of pollen of *Betula* (cf. *pubescens*) before the settlement measures typically 300 to 600 grains per cm^2 yr^{-1}.[64] Compared to reference data from Finland,[65] this would suggest that open woodland may have persisted throughout the pre-settlement period. *Betula* seeds and wood fragments in pre-settlement deposits at Hólakot also attest to the continuous presence of woodland throughout this period, while the recording of seeds from the light-demanding *Arctostaphylos uva-ursi* (bearberry) indicates that the woodland was open. Like the macrofossil data, the Coleoptera samples reflect a heterogeneous environment with rich vegetation and litter, thought to represent woodland understorey, mixed with taxa that favour dry open areas and wetland.[66] The wetland next to the lake was probably always devoid of tall woody taxa, like birch and willows, given that the prefix *Breið* in the lake's name (Breiðavatn) could indicate an open wetland area. The initial chieftain farm in the valley, Breiðabólstaðr, might also take its name from this landscape element.[67]

Floristic changes around the time of settlement are more subtle in the Breiðavatn record than usually found in pollen assemblages from this period. The lake catchment probably continued to sustain much of the pre-settlement birch woodland, as only a nominal decrease in the abundance of birch pollen is recorded. Apophytic taxa do not increase noticeably at this time other than for a slight rise in values for *Rumex acetosa* and the apparent emergence of *Rumex acetosella* (sheep's sorrel) at around the same period. It is not until between around AD 1150 and 1300 that the woodland becomes adversely affected, for which land-use activity of some sort is probably responsible, given that the chironomid-inferred temperatures from the core indicate that the main LIA cooling took place

64 Egill Erlendsson 2007.
65 Hicks and Sunnari 2005.
66 Egill Erlendsson *et al.* 2012.
67 Helgi Þorláksson 2011.

Figure 4. View from Skáneyjarbunga showing the location of Hólakot and Breiðavatn. The Háls ridge is in the middle distance, separating Hvítársíða and Hálsasveit to the left of the picture and the upper reaches of Reykholtsdalr (Reykjadalr nyrðri) to the right. Photo: Egill Erlendsson.

later at around AD 1500. Many of the typical apophytes in the Icelandic flora, for example Poaceae, *Thalictrum alpinum*, *Plantago maritima* and *Selaginella selaginoides* (lesser clubmoss) had greater opportunities to expand after the retreat of the woodland.

A continued presence of woody taxa in the area after settlement is also shown by the lingering presence of wood fragments in BR2 up to a level dated to AD 1030±130. Although the woodland indicator taxa become less prominent above this level, seeds of *Betula* and wood fragments are present in the peat until around AD 1700; these could be the remains of *Betula nana* (dwarf birch)[68] for which a continued presence is also indicated in the pollen assemblages from the lake core.

The soil proxies at the nearby site Hólakot (HOL; figs. 1, 4 and 6; table 1) follow closely the two-step decline in birch woodland around the lake. Around AD 870 a decline in organic carbon (C), organic matter content (LOI) and soil moisture content (SMC), and an increase in dry bulk density (BD) could indicate both reduced biomass and increased soil instability. Eroded soils from the surrounding hills were deposited in the wetlands close to Hólakot, resulting in a trebling of annual soil mass

68   Egill Erlendsson *et al.* 2012.

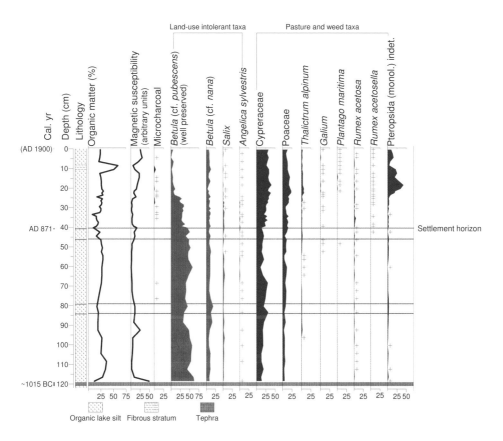

Figure 5. Pollen percentage diagram from Breiðavatn (BR1), showing selected taxa. + signifies values below 1% of the ~300 land pollen counted for each level. The red and grey horizontal lines represent tephra layers in the sequence. Diagram: Egill Erlendsson.

kg/m² accumulation.[69] Reduced organic matter and increased sedimen-tation rates are not evident in the lake deposits, but soil instability is represented in the reworking of tephra, with the re-deposition of the *landnám* tephra[70] producing discernible layers identified by geochemistry.[71]

69   Guðrún Gísladóttir *et al.* 2011.
70   The *landnám* (or Settlement) tephra is typically a two- (sometimes one-) layered tephra stratum derived from Torfajǫkull and Vatnaǫldur (Guðrún Larsen and Jón Eiríksson 2008) dated until recently to AD 871±2 (Karl Grönvold *et al.* 1995), now corrected to 877±1 (Schmid *et al.* 2016).
71   Egill Erlendsson 2007.

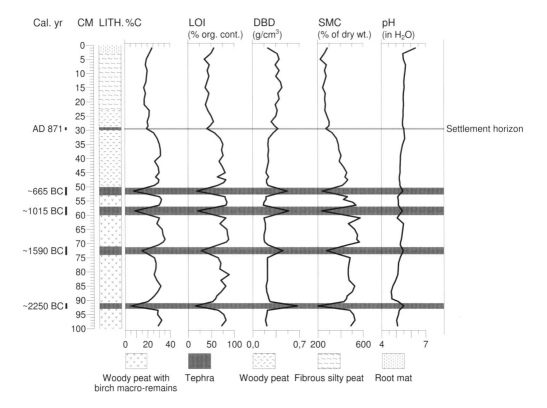

Figure 6. Selected soil property proxies from Hólakot (HOL). The red and grey horizontal lines represent tephra layers in the sequence. Diagram: Egill Erlendsson.

Environmental change in the Kjarardalr hinterland

The part of Kjarardalr that belonged to Reykholt (fig. 1) is now devoid of woodland, which contrasts with the adjacent Ǫrnólfsdalsskógr west of Skjaldmeyjargil, a gulley that acts as the boundary between Reykholt's land and that of the Ǫrnólfsdalr farm. Reykholt operated two shielings in the valley, Norðtungusel and Reykholtssel further up the valley. Historical sources indicate that Norðtungusel is the older of the two,[72] and this is supported by radiocarbon age-estimates from cultural deposits suggesting the earliest activity at the site was in the late tenth or early eleventh century.[73] A date obtained on charred wood from a cultural layer

72   Benedikt Eyþórsson 2008.
73   Guðrún Sveinbjarnardóttir *et al.* 2011. See also p. 214 in this book.

Figure 7. A: View to north across Kjarará showing the locations of Reykholtssel and the REY2 sample site. B: The patch of wetland (centre) at Reykholtssel where the REY2 sample was taken. C: Macro-remains of birch at about 65–80 cm depth from surface. Their age is estimated to between 660 and 0 BC. The scale units are 5 cm. Photos: Guðrún Gísladóttir.

within one of the ruins at Reykholtssel, on the other hand, indicates its earliest formation in the fourteenth century.[74] In the past some of the biggest farms in Borgarfjǫrðr (e.g. Gilsbakki, Síðumúli and Reykholt) enjoyed rights to use areas in the valley for summer pasture or shielings.[75]

The site (REY2) sampled for palaeoecological work at Reykholtssel is situated in a small patch of wetland (about a hectare) some 250 metres east of the shieling ruins (figs. 7A, 7B). A pit was dug near the centre of the bog down to levels where a layer of logs and branches was encountered (fig. 7C). This and other less well-preserved wood fragments and relatively high percentage values for *Betula* pollen (20–60 per cent TLP; fig. 8)

74 Guðrún Sveinbjarnardóttir *et al*. 2011. See also p. 216 in this book.
75 Freysteinn Sigurðsson 2004.

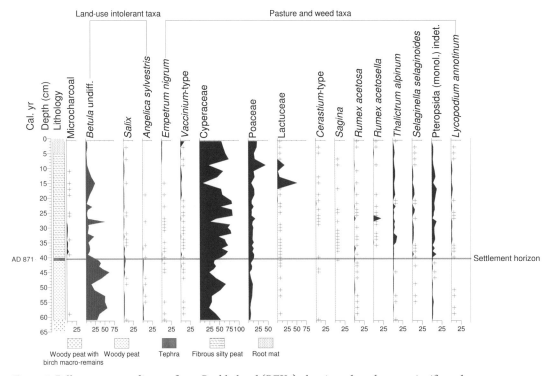

Figure 8. Pollen percentage diagram from Reykholtssel (REY2), showing selected taxa. + signifies values below 1% of the 250–500 land pollen counted for each level. The red horizontal line represents a tephra layer. Diagram: Egill Erlendsson.

demonstrate the growth of birch woodland between about AD 0 and 870. Fluctuations in values for *Betula* pollen conceivably denote fluctuations in climate and mire hydrology over this period.[76]

Even though situated away from the main settlement areas, there is a decline in *Betula* pollen soon after the deposition of the *landnám* tephra (fig. 8). Early settlement woodland decline is the typical cultural impact on vegetation around permanent settlements,[77] while the more remote sites often show a belated woodland retreat.[78] Removal of woodland to allow for arable activity or haymaking is unlikely at Reykholtssel, as the Kjarardalr valley supposedly never sustained a year-round occupation. Lawson and colleagues have argued that for all its importance to the inhabitants, woodland was also an obstacle in some ways, difficult to

76 Egill Erlendsson and Edwards 2009.
77 Margrét Hallsdóttir 1987; Vickers *et al.* 2011.
78 Lawson *et al.* 2007; Gathorne-Hardy *et al.* 2009; Lilja B. Pétursdóttir 2014.

traverse, and its removal undoubtedly improved pastures.[79] Given that shieling activity was the predominant form of land use in Kjarardalr from the twelfth century at the latest, it could be that the valley's woodland was soon cleared after settlement to provide better grazing. Shieling activity here could also have started earlier at Reykholtssel than historical sources and limited archaeological work indicate, but greater certainty as to when this activity began would probably require full-scale excavation of the shieling ruins.

The consequences of decreased woodland cover in Kjarardalr are demonstrated in the lithological proxies (fig. 9) in much the same way as was seen at Hólakot. Lowered values for organic carbon and other organic content above the *landnám* tephra are probably a result of both decreased biomass and increased transport of erosion-derived soil into the bog. Soils on the steep slopes of the valley were probably easily destabilized when no longer protected by woods and shrubs, resulting in their removal to sink areas, such as the bog where they would also affect the mire hydrology (e.g. via SMC).

Following the initial decline in woodland, the palaeoenvironmental data suggest that some degree of stability was reached and this was maintained until around AD 1500. Many of the typical apophytes expand during this period, for example *Thalictrum alpinum*, *Selaginella selaginoides* and Pteropsida (monolete) indet. (fern spores). The fern spores could also be a contaminant derived with eroded soil.[80] From a palynological perspective, the most significant feature in the pollen assemblages over this period is the apparent introduction of *Rumex acetosella* to the local flora. This species can serve as a "footprint" taxon for human occupation in Greenlandic pollen analysis and this may be the case for Iceland as well, as it may have been introduced by early settlers.[81] The renewed environmental stability also applies to remaining stands of birch, which seem to have been able to survive around Reykholtssel beyond AD 1700 or thereabouts.

After around AD 1500, the palaeoenvironmental proxies indicate a new period of environmental decline. Further destabilization of soils is reflected in values for organic carbon and organic matter, which are at their lowest between about AD 1500 and 1700. This process indicates

79   Lawson *et al.* 2009.
80   Gathorne-Hardy *et al.* 2009.
81   Þóra E. Þórhallsdóttir 1996; Edwards *et al.* 2011.

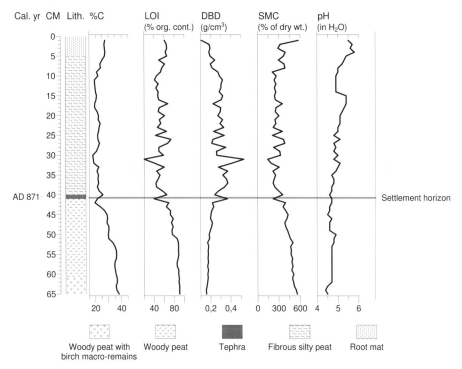

Figure 9. Selected soil property proxies from Reykholtssel (REY2). The red horizontal line represents a tephra layer. Diagram: Egill Erlendsson.

increased and/or extended grazing pressure, which supports the historical and archaeological evidence for the operation of a shieling at this time. The expansion of Lactuceae (dandelions and hawkweeds) over this period may furnish palynological evidence for such inferred land use. Some species within this tribe (e.g. *Taraxacum* spp.) are common in hayfields, gardens and other places with fertilized soils and their increase could be a consequence of increased livestock density associated with the shieling. Another taxon to expand within this period is Poaceae. Grasses are predominantly dry-loving taxa and the rise in pollen representation might indicate diminished moisture levels in the bog's surface strata (which could also be shown by reduced peat moisture (SMC) resulting from increased erosion-derived soil inputs).

By the time that the shieling was abandoned, probably sometime in the latter half of the seventeenth century,[82] its operation had exerted

82 Based on radiocarbon age-estimates (AD 1430–1670; Guðrún Sveinbjarnardóttir

a considerable strain on the local ecology. The final decline of birch woodland or shrubs (fig. 8) occurs near the end of this activity and the uppermost cultural deposits in the ruins are capped by mudslide debris whose extent reaches hundreds of metres beyond the ruins. The mudslide demonstrates slope instability, conceivably resulting from the unsustainable use of land in a marginal environment which was also under pressure from the deteriorating climate of the Little Ice Age.

The pre-settlement terrestrial ecosystem

The period prior to settlement was not ecologically static. Data from the Reykholtsdalr lowlands reveal fluctuations in soil hydrology, probably driven by an unstable climate over the latter half of the Holocene.[83] These changes affected the local biota with periods of expansion in wetland vegetation and declines in dryland taxa, and vice versa. Based on the evidence presented here, it seems fair to assume that conditions for woodland growth deteriorated after around 665 BC. Wood became less prominent in the deposits at Hólakot and the subfossil tree remains at Reykholtssel probably date to around or before this time. In Breiðavatn there is a period after 1000 BC where a decline in the pollen of downy birch occurs and there are expansions in the pollen of the more cold- and moisture-tolerant dwarf birch, alpine meadow-rue and sedges.

Bog woodland is sensitive to fluctuations in hydrology because elevated moisture levels hamper the growth of birch. The apparent reduction in wood content in peats after about AD 665 is perhaps the result of such processes. Closer to *landnám*, a phase called the "dark age cold period" has recently been dated to between AD 550 and 950.[84] Suppressed values for birch pollen within the periods AD 500 to 600 and 800 to 870 reflect poor conditions for both flowering and growth of birch in wetlands. Elevated values for birch pollen between these periods, shown in records from the Reykholtsdalr lowland and Reykholtssel, indicate a warm interval within the cold period.[85] Contraction in woodland and vegetation cover is also supported by soil parameters at Reykholtssel. At a depth of around fifty centimetres (corresponding to about AD 500),

2005) on charred wood just below the mudslide which covered the site, and on palaeoenvironmental variables. See also p. 216 in this book.

83   Margrét Hallsdóttir and Caseldine 2005.

84   Larsen *et al.* 2012.

85   Egill Erlendsson and Edwards 2009.

there is a decline in organic carbon, LOI and SMC, which, added to raised levels for BD, indicate increased erosion in the area. This trend continues until the time of settlement, suggesting that elevated values for birch pollen do not necessarily signify woodland recovery, but rather an ability to produce and eject greater quantities of pollen over a short period.[86] Poorer conditions for woodland growth in the late Holocene could have pushed upper woodland limits to lower altitudes and impeded its growth in unfavourable areas such as in wetlands. However, based on the palaeoenvironmental evidence, the birch woodland remained the dominant vegetation in the Borgarfjǫrðr lowlands, but with less dense or no woodland in the wetland areas.

The historical evidence also attests to the dominance of birch woodland. Some farm names in the valleys may take their names from the prevailing flora at the time of settlement, and presumably within a matter of decades of *landnám*. The names Hrísar (shrubs), Skógar (woods) and perhaps Lundr (patch of woodland) in Lundarreykjadalr (on the maps Reykjadalr syðri) suggest the presence of woodlands (fig. 1). Even though under climatic pressure for several centuries or millennia, the upper limits of woodlands and shrubs probably reached deep into the interior of Borgarfjǫrðr. Several place names and landscape descriptions from the saga literature and historical sources indicate the presence of woodlands in locations between 400 and 600 metres above sea level.[87] It is open to question what sort of vegetation managed to thrive across the woodland floor, but given the copious records of monolete spores from pteridophytes (ferns) in eroded soils,[88] they were probably common in these pre-settlement habitats. Pollen from tall herbs, like angelicas and meadowsweet, are also frequently recorded in pre-settlement contexts along with pollen from grasses and sedges.

The formation of a "human-made" landscape

The most striking aspect of the impact of settlement on vegetation is the widespread retreat of the birch woodland and a concurrent increase in soil erosion right from the start of *landnám*. It is fair to assume that any attempts at arable activity would require clearance of land. Evidence for woodland clearance near Reykholt is unsurprising because, as around

86   Egill Erlendsson and Edwards 2009; Hicks and Sunnari 2005.
87   Egill Erlendsson *et al.* 2012.
88   Gathorne-Hardy *et al.* 2009; Vickers *et al.* 2011.

other large farms, this was a prerequisite for haymaking and cultivation.[89] The extent of woodland retreat in the wider inhabited area was probably great too. Recent considerations about the speed at which Iceland became fully inhabited suggest that this took place within decades from when it started in earnest.[90] If, as the palaeoecological evidence suggests, woodland clearance was effectively a precondition for farming, then the scale of clearance in this densely settled district must have been significant and rapid.

The prompt retreat of woodland in Kjarardalr is perhaps more peculiar given that such remote sites often exhibit later retreats of woodland, as at Breiðavatn where woodland lingered until between AD 1150 and 1300. The decline of woodland in Kjarardalr may be the result of a deliberate, and probably successful, attempt to provide improved, open pasture for summer grazing in remote places. *Landnámabók* describes the woodland and its removal in Kjarardalr: "Fyrir ofan Klif heitir Kjarradalr, því at þar váru hrískjǫrr ok smáskógar milli Kjarrár ‹ok› Þverár, svá at þar mátti eigi byggja. Blund-Ketill var maðr stórauðigr; hann lét ryðja víða í skógum ok byggja".[91] Obviously it cannot be determined whether this description has any foundation, and what the author is saying was "built" could be constructions of any type: farms, cottages or shielings. Yet palaeoecology corroborates what the text says about woodland clearance at the very beginning of settlement, not only at Reykholtssel, but also at Norðtungusel and in Qrnólfsdalsskógr,[92] which can be viewed as a deliberate action taken to improve pasture. The detail about shrubs and small woods is also interesting because of high proportions (around ten per cent) of deformed birch pollen from Qrnólfsdalsskógr, which demonstrates that this woodland consisted to a large extent of a triploid hybrid between *Betula nana* and *Betula pubescens*.[93] The hybrid does not reach the height of downy birch. It is usually heavily branched and crooked and this may have prompted the

---

89   Margrét Hallsdóttir 1987; Zori *et al.* 2013.

90   Orri Vésteinsson and McGovern 2012.

91   "Beyond Klif is called Kjarradalr (shrub-valley), because there used to be shrubs and small woods between Kjarrá ‹and› Þverá, so that farms could not be established. Blund-Ketill was a very rich man; he had woodlands cleared and buildings erected" (Landnámabók, 84).

92   Guðrún Gísladóttir *et al.* 2011; Egill Erlendsson and Guðrún Gísladóttir 2011.

93   Lilja Karlsdóttir *et al.* 2009.

name of the valley and the assertion about the shrubs making the area difficult to traverse and farm.

More activities destructive of woodlands can be cited for Reykholts-dalr. At Háls, some fourteen kilometres east of Reykholt, excavations led by Kevin Smith uncovered large quantities of remains attributable to the production of bog-iron. Perhaps as much as 350 to 600 kilograms of fully processed iron was produced at this site in the tenth century from an estimated 6200 kilograms of bog ore. Smith calculated that the total processing of such a quantity of iron would require some fifty tons of charcoal. The quantity of fuel needed translates to between five and ten hectares of birch woodland, which he considers an underestimation of the total quantity used because more slag heaps may remain unex-cavated. Smith presumed that the cessation of iron-production at Háls by the end of the twelfth century was driven by the over-exploitation of woodlands in the vicinity of the site.[94] It is difficult to ascertain what limits might have been imposed on access to woodland from the site. It also remains unknown if this was an industry operating independently or run from an external farm. What seems certain is that this was a unit specialized in iron production at a commercial rather than a domestic scale – an industry that perhaps required fuel beyond what the local woodland could sustain. What is peculiar is that the expected decline in arboreal taxa seems elusive in the palaeobotanical records. Pollen and macrofossils of birch maintain their representations throughout the period of iron production but decline after land use changed to conventional farming in the beginning of the eleventh century.[95] The reason for this could be that both the pollen and macrofossil analyses are recording vegetation within the bog itself, where conditions for the growth of birch to the stature needed for charcoal production were too poor; the principal use of the mire was probably to provide ore, not to serve as a source of charcoal. This would have changed as domestic cooking and heating required firewood rather than charcoal. Grazing, a characteristic feature of the medieval farm, would also have been detrimental to the growth of any bog shrubs.

94   Smith 1995; 2005.
95   Dixon 1997; Bending 2007.

Early planning and later management of hinterlands?

The apparently different fate of woodlands in Kjarardalr and around Breiðavatn raises the question as to whether the landscape was divided into specific units for different uses soon after settlement. The Breiða-vatn pollen record has been thought to represent late woodland removal because of its distance (about two kilometres) from the main farming complexes (e.g. Breiðabólstaðr),[96] but why would woodlands vanish within about a century of settlement in one "off-site" area (Kjarardalr) but remain for centuries in other parts of the landscape such as around Breiðavatn? Factors such as topography, climate and soils could be cited, but as regards birch woodland, conditions would seem to favour Kjarardalr, which possesses a considerable extent of well-drained soils and is less exposed to the wind. The sites are also similar in altitude. It seems possible that while one area was earmarked for grazing (e.g. shieling activity) with woodlands removed to improve pasture, in other locations woodlands were perhaps managed and maintained for forestry or as sources for fuel.[97]

The modern woodless landscape of the part of Kjarardalr that belonged to Reykholt may also be a reflection of how the proprietors of Reykholt managed their lands. The present birch woodland west of Skjaldmeyjargil is probably the remnant of continuous woodland that reached at least as far as Reykholtssel by the time of settlement and probably further up the valley. The Ǫrnólfsdalr woodland now terminates exactly at the boundary of the land held by Reykholt and this may not be a coincidence. Different farms may have had different priorities and strategies, not only at the beginning of settlement but throughout the historical period. A recent study from Þjórsárdalr has suggested that the form of ownership was a fundamental factor for the fate of the woodlands. Historical sources indicate that over 6000 hectares of birch woodland existed there in AD 1587, which is around half of the land area of the district. By AD 1938, when the remaining woodland was put under conservation, this woodland coverage had shrunk to 388 hectares, a reduction of 94 per cent. What is interesting is that the woodlands that survived were all privately owned or controlled, whereas the woodland that disappeared over this period was under the authority of the bishop's see in Skálholt (formerly Skálaholt).

---

96   E.g. Egill Erlendsson *et al.* 2012; Gathorne-Hardy *et al.* 2009.
97   Cf. Church *et al.* 2007; Lawson *et al.* 2007.

This contrast has been taken to represent different attitutes towards resources.[98] Whether the medieval proprietors of Reykholt were more reckless towards this important resource than many other landholders in Borgarfjǫrðr is uncertain. It is clear that by AD 1300, the pollen data indicate a virtually deforested landscape at all three locations. A probable consequence of using wood unsustainably as an initial and primary fuel source is the apparent change in fuel economy at Reykholt after around AD 1300, when micromorphological evidence indicates that peat and dung had replaced wood as the main source of fuel.[99]

Soil erosion, the lasting consequence of woodland decline

The acceleration of erosion in parallel with reduced arboreal cover shown at Reykholtssel and Hólakot is typical for Iceland and has much to do with how the ecosystem had evolved prior to settlement. Deforestation has an impact through the entire ecosystem. It alters hydrological patterns, reduces biomass production, and exposes soils previously constrained by deep-root systems and sheltered from winds by tree trunks and canopy. Changed vegetation patterns and poor protection for dryland soils are among the consequences of these processes, whereas the more erosion-resistant wetland soils (histosols and andic histosols) continue to occupy large areas especially in the lowlands, even though soil erosion has changed their properties. In Reykholtssel and Hólakot vegetation change and soil exposure during historical times initiated a cycle of erosional-depositional processes that severely depleted the terrestrial ecosystem of the area.

Comparing the environmental impacts of settlement in Iceland and the Faroe Islands shows the significance of the type of ecosystem in place when humans arrive in a "pristine" ecosystem. In the Faroes, the environment was exposed and largely unwooded prior to the Norse colonization. Palynological signals for vegetation change as a consequence of settlement are, as a result, muted and increase in soil erosion nominal. The vegetation simply continued to be low-statured and open and the taxonomic composition adjusted to withstand the exposure in which it developed.[100] A rare Icelandic example of such a scenario comes from the apparently unwooded environs of Ketilsstaðir, south Iceland, where the

98   Friðþór S. Sigurmundsson *et al.* 2014.
99   Guðrún Sveinbjarnardóttir *et al.* 2007.
100 Lawson *et al.* 2008.

Figure 10. Photographs of three soil profiles that show significant change in their sediment characteristics. The brown, erosion-derived soil sediment is of historical age, underlain by black, organic peat with macro-sized wood remains. A: Norðtungusel in Kjarardalr. B: Sturlureykir in Reykholtsdalr. C: RHD1 near Reykholt in Reykholtsdalr. Photos: Guðrún Gísladóttir, Egill Erlendsson, Kevin J. Edwards.

impacts of settlement were minimal and greater changes in the local flora could be linked to tephra deposition than to settlement.[101]

Another feature of the landscape change reported here is the suffocation of wetland areas by re-deposited soil. The lower reaches of the slopes of the valleys around Reykholt now predominantly support grassy meadows growing on top of soil classified as andosol or histic andosol. Before settlement, some of these locations were sloping fens where organic-rich deposits, histosol, accumulated under anaerobic conditions. For site RHD1, the post-settlement soil organic matter measured only a third or so of that measured for prehistoric deposits, signifying the impact of soil deposition on the hydrology of the organic surface soil and attendant decomposition. More sites (fig. 10) show this change from prehistoric dark brown or black, organic peat, to predominantly light brown or yellowish soils that have been transported to the sites by aeolian

101 Egill Erlendsson *et al.* 2009.

or fluvial processes from destabilized higher elevation slopes. The extent of the area of low-lying wetland which became smothered by eroded soil is, however, difficult to quantify.

The drying out of wetlands concomitant with the addition of eroded mineral material has had an effect on lowland vegetation patterns and also on other elements of the biota. Post-settlement beetle assemblages from Iceland commonly indicate a shift from species associated with damp humus and mosses to those that live in drier grassland habitats, a change often observed in samples taken from stratigraphy which indicates an influx of eroded material. While this may in some cases reflect drainage or changes in infield land use, it is clear that widespread drying out of soils following settlement had an impact across many ecosystems in the Icelandic landscape.[102]

The Formation of the Cultural Landscape of Reykholtsdalr

It is uncertain how exactly the farm at Reykholt emerged. Based on radiocarbon dates it seems that it became established around AD 1000, and by around 1200 it had succeeded the adjacent initial chieftain farm of Breiðabólstaðr, on whose land it was built, and added it to its land holdings. A church was probably established at Reykholt in the eleventh century, and the farm's stature, in terms of culture and politics at least, seems to have been progressively enhanced, culminating in the near-continuous "reign" of Snorri Sturluson (1178–1241) there from 1206 to 1241.[103] It must be assumed that the establishment and maintenance of a large medieval power centre required the availability of extensive natural resources. This was not only necessary to provide food for the family and workers of the farm, but also to fund gifts, feasts and to maintain influence, along with the luxurious lifestyle required of a medieval chieftain family.[104]

---

102 E.g. Buckland *et al.* 1991; Vickers *et al.* 2011.
103 Guðrún Sveinbjarnardóttir *et al.* 2007; Guðrún Sveinbjarnardóttir 2012; 2016.
104 Zori *et al.* 2013.

Was Reykholt/Breiðabólstaðr an appealing early settlement location?

The environmental data suggest that for the person who first set foot in Reykholtsdalr there would have been much to admire. Sparsely wooded plains around the river may have provided an ideal initial location for grazing or hay collection. By contrast, the slopes that flank the valley lowland were probably covered with a more continuous and dense birch woodland. The lower-lying area around Breiðavatn was probably quite wet, and wetland vegetation is likely to have dominated the lower, damper parts of the slope fens around the lake, as is indicated by the plant macro-fossils. The location of Breiðabólstaðr (fig. 11), the initial settlement farm in Reykholtsdalr according to *Landnámabók*, as an early settlement site seems logical from a geographical viewpoint. The farm is located close to the primary wetland areas in the valley, the plains beside the river and the mires around the lake. The growth of tall plants, for example meadowsweet, angelicas and some species of sedges would have provided high-yielding biomass. Whether this applies to all parts of the valley is unknown, but wetland areas would have enjoyed a considerably greater coverage than they did later. Wetland vegetation, as indicated around Reykholt, was probably the predominant form of vegetation in the lower parts of the valley, before its later transformation to an area more suitable for extended pastoral with some arable agriculture.

Besides the quality of the land, the farm is also central to what is assumed to have been the initial settlement area of Breiðabólstaðr, which accounts for the whole area between the Reykjadalsá and the Hvítá (fig. 11).[105] It is also near where access to Hálsasveit and the Hvítá is easiest, across the defile where Breiðavatn is located – the best travel route to the valley north of Reykholtsdalr.

Yet whether the Reykholtsdalr area represented a desirable location for early settlement requires comparison with neighbouring areas, and this creates an inevitable problem: comparative palaeoenvironmental data from other areas of Borgarfjǫrðr are unavailable. Based on the modern environment, the extensive wetlands of Reykholtsdalr are at least as prominent as those in the nearby valleys. By assuming that these have been the areas of greatest appeal,[106] Reykholtsdalr would seem to have been as attractive for settlement as any other valley. Measured against

105 Landnámabók, 74.
106 Cf. Orri Vésteinsson 1998.

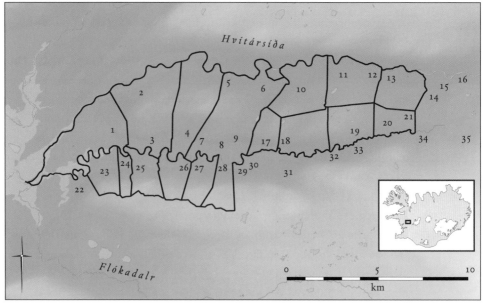

Figure 11. The medieval cultural landscape in Reykholtsdalr (Reykjadalr nyrðri). 1=Deildartunga; 2=Hurðarbak; 3=Sturlureykir; 4=Skáney; 5=Háfr; 6=Norðrreykir; 7=Grímsstaðir; 8=Reykholt (Reykjaholt); 9=Breiðabólstaðir; 10=Signýjarstaðir; 11=Bolastaðir; 12=Refsstaðir; 13=Sigmundarstaðir; 14=Hraunsáss; 15=(Stóri) Áss; 16=Vatnskot; 17=Úlfsstaðir; 18=Hofstaðir; 19=Uppsalir; 20=Kollslœkur; 21=Hálsar; 22=Stórikroppr; 23=Hamrar; 24=Kleppjárnsreykir; 25=Snœldubeinsstaðir; 26=Kjalvararstaðir; 27=Kópa-reykir; 28=Hœgindi; 29= Vilmundarstaðir; 30= Steindórsstaðir; 31=Rauðsgil; 32=Búrfell; 33=Auðsstaðir; 34=Giljar; 35=Augastaðir. Map: Stefán Ólafsson.

the lower reaches of the Borgarfjǫrðr area, Reykholt would not always have compared favourably. The vast wetlands and floodplains around Hvanneyri are, for example, far greater than those in Reykholtsdalr. West of the Hvítá, the important church farm of Stafholt, which became one of the wealthiest farms in Borgarfjǫrðr, is also located amid more extensive wetlands than those found around Reykholt.

First phase settlement

On the basis of the model described above, Breiðabólstaðr would have been the primary settlement farm within the proposed initial settlement (a position later taken over by Reykholt). An argument supporting this, in addition to the environmental and location-based reasoning noted above, is Reykholt's later complex nature. As well as being the possessor of the parish church, a charter from 1204 demonstrates that by that time the Reykholt church had acquired at least three of its neighbouring farms: Hœgindi, Norðrreykir and the early settlement farm of Breiðabólstaðr, and was also looking after Háfr (fig. 11).[107] The same charter shows that in addition to the ownership of neighbouring farms, Reykholt church owned land for shieling activity and woodland exploitation in Kjarardalr, salmon fishing in the adjacent Kjarará, and had grazing rights in Hrútafjarðarheiði, Faxadalr and in Geitland, where it also had access to woodland. The charter also notes fishing rights in the Grímsá and possibly in Reyðarvatn (Rauðavatn on the maps).[108] The ownership of the neighbouring farms ensured that Reykholt possessed the largest area of farmland in Reykholtsdalr. The acquisition of remote farms and other areas of land ensured fishing rights and the important access to summer pastures where shielings could be established.[109] The number of farms owned by Reykholt church continued to grow, and by around the mid-fifteenth century a total of eleven farms belonged to it, providing it with a vastly improved revenue from the rent of land and livestock and an increasingly varied and extensive resource base.[110]

Although the initial site selection for farms was perhaps controlled to some extent by the floral and physical landscapes in place at the time of *landnám*, it must also be considered that none of those inland locations would have had direct access to marine resources. This raises questions about their initial potential for prosperity. Comparison can be made here with the early inland settlement locations in Mývatnssveit, where midden deposits contained extensive remains of marine fauna, demonstrating that direct contact, trade or exchange, existed between coastal and inland locations and probably from the earliest settlement times. Survival in Mývatnssveit was further supplemented by the exploitation of the rich local wildlife (e.g. birds, eggs and freshwater fish).[111] It would thus seem that the coastal contacts and local wildlife were important for the early inland farm sites, especially while the settlement was still in its infancy and livestock limited. In terms of local wildlife, the rivers of the Borgarfjǫrðr

107 *Reykjaholtsmáldagi*, 14–15; Guðrún Sveinbjarnardóttir *et al.* 2008.
108 *Reykjaholtsmáldagi*, 14–15
109 Benedikt Eyþórsson 2008; Guðrún Sveinbjarnardóttir *et al.* 2008.
110 Benedikt Eyþórsson 2008.
111 McGovern *et al.* 2007.

region, as today, would have provided ample salmon and trout fishing.[112]
Even if it seems likely that the subsistence pattern found in Mývatnssveit would have been applicable to other parts of Iceland, this is only
vaguely demonstrated archaeologically in the earliest cultural contexts
from Reykholtsdalr, in the form of single finds of seal bones at Háls and
Reykholt and some fish bones at Reykholt.[113] It should be noted that there
have only been limited analyses of the medieval excavation contexts from
both sites, and they do not represent incontrovertible proof of anything
less in terms of contacts between coastal and inland areas than have been
demonstrated in the north-east of Iceland. The Reykholtsdalr lowlands
were also transformed almost instantly to accommodate agriculture, in-
volving barley cultivation on better-drained sites, as can be inferred from
the palynological and dating evidence from the meadows near Reykholt
(site RHD1).[114] It may also be that the period during which any early
settlement coastal connection was vital was short, and is hence transient
or invisible in the archaeological record. So far cultural contexts of the
early settlement age are absent from Reykholt's archaeological records,
indicating that settlement was only established later, thus post-dating any
possible period of dependence on the local or marine fauna, given the
apparently superior status of the nearby Breiðabólstaðr farm during the
earliest decades of *landnám*.[115] In any case, the overall evidence indicates
that coastal-inland connections were established quickly and that direct
access to the sea was not necessarily a prerequisite for early settlement.

Second phase settlements

Other farms in Reykholtsdalr with annex churches and of substantial
medieval stature were those of Skáney, Sturlureykir and Deildartunga
(fig. 11). They can be categorized as "second phase" large but simple
farms, based on their occupation of high quality land which was perhaps
the most readily accessible land during the settlement period. These
farms are located in the westernmost part of the valley, where damp
lowland is ample compared to the areas east of Reykholt and south of
the Reykjadalsá, and, like Reykholt, enjoy significant exposure to the sun

112 See pp. 225–227 in this book.
113 Guðrún Sveinbjarnardóttir 2012, 259.
114 Egill Erlendsson *et al.* 2012.
115 See pp. 128–130 in this book.

owing to their south-facing aspect.[116] Orri Vésteinsson notes that farms of such substantial stature are commonly found adjacent to the major "first-phase" farms of particular areas and uses examples from the districts Bœjarsveit and Andakíll in Borgarfjǫrðr to support this. In general, they tend to be respectable in size and to have good quality land for haymaking and pasture, but may lack or have limited access to other resources.[117]

Planned settlements

The remaining farms within the initial Breiðabólstaðr settlement, as well as those south of the Reykjadalsá, occupy lands that are more restricted in terms of both area and quality (fig. 11). They have limited lowland, occupy well-drained soils, and large proportions of the land is confined to higher elevations. Those south of the Reykjadalsá enjoy less exposure to the sun because of their northern aspect. Within the settlement model these are categorized as later "planned settlements".[118] These areas probably supported denser and more extensive birch woodland than was found on the wetlands associated with the bigger farms around the time of settlement. It is possible that these locations became farms only after the retreat of woodland following some period of forestry and grazing, or after the considerable time and effort needed for the physical removal of trees and shrubs. Finding direct evidence for the burning of woodland in Reykholtsdalr has proved elusive during the archaeological and environmental investigations there. The sole hint of this activity is perhaps the farm-name Brennistaðir (Brenni = burn) in the neighbouring Flókadalr. The burning of woodlands may have been practised elsewhere, however, as several tenth- and eleventh-century farms, as in Þjórsárdalr in south Iceland, seem to have been built on top of charcoal layers, thought to stem either from the deliberate burning of woodland to facilitate farm construction or accidental fires, perhaps caused by nearby charcoal production.[119]

The way in which the mosaic of unwooded wetlands and dense woodland helped to dictate the development of the cultural landscape is depicted in studies from Mývatnssveit. The settlement pattern there suggests that the more densely wooded parts of the inhabitable land

116 Guðrún Sveinbjarnardóttir *et al.* 2008.
117 Orri Vésteinsson 1998.
118 Guðrún Sveinbjarnardóttir *et al.* 2008.
119 Smith 1995.

(as represented by the well-drained valleys) were settled later than the upper, less densely wooded areas. The upland areas, perhaps close to the upper woodland edge, may have provided more easily traversed land and accessible pasture; these areas are now largely barren.[120] A similar scenario is possible for the Eyjafjǫll district, where environmental evidence from Stóra-Mǫrk does not suggest full-scale human activity until after the deposition of a Katla tephra there in around AD 920.[121] This may even post-date the upland settlement in Þórsmǫrk for which early colonization is noted in *Landnámabók*[122] and for which pagan burials and artefact typology suggest a ninth or tenth century date.[123] There is evidence for extensive charcoal making in the vicinity of Stóra-Mǫrk soon after the deposit of the *landnám* tephra and perhaps this, combined with other forms of woodland utilization, was required in order to make the more densely wooded areas attractive as farm locations.[124] This may also have applied to Reykholtsdalr and to the farms along the Hvítá river. The smaller and less valuable farms that are located between Háls and Reykholt, for instance, occupy well drained but shallow and less fertile soils, and these areas may only have been settled after the woodland had been largely removed and sufficient space had been opened up to facilitate their establishment.

Highland settlements in Borgarfjǫrðr

There are also remains of early upland settlement in Geitland, Borgar-fjǫrðr (fig. 1), which according to *Landnámabók* became inhabited as a second-generation settlement by Úlfr, who was the son of the initial settler of Hvanneyri.[125] There are two known sites in Geitland with numerous ruins, which may be of different ages. Among them are long-houses of the early settlement type.[126] Radiocarbon dates obtained on cultural layers within some of them suggest that these sites were already occupied in the ninth century.[127] The fenced infields indicate a more substantial activity than mere summer farms. Any farm in Geitland must have been abandoned before the end of the twelfth century, when the

120 McGovern *et al.* 2007; Lawson *et al.* 2009.
121 Vickers *et al.* 2011.
122 Landnámabók, 344–346.
123 Guðrún Sveinbjarnardóttir 1983.
124 Vickers *et al.* 2011.
125 Landnámabók, 70–71.
126 Guðmundur Ólafsson 1996.
127 Guðrún Sveinbjarnardóttir *et al.* 2011.

area is listed as a summer pasture belonging to Reykholt church.[128] The Geitland area has probably suffered the same fate as the upland settlements in Mývatnssveit and Þórsmǫrk, which were deserted by the twelfth or thirteenth century.[129]

Acknowledgements

The environmental research in and around Reykholtsdalr has enjoyed financial support from numerous funding bodies: The Leverhulme Trust, UK; Rannís (grants no. 080655021 and 081069); University of Iceland Research Fund; *Det Kongelige Kultur-og kirkedepartementet,* Norway; Snorrastofa Medieval Centre; Targeted Investment in Excellence, Climate, Water and Carbon Project, Carbon Management and Sequestration Centre, The Ohio State University. The Universities of Aberdeen, Iceland and Sheffield are also thanked for their support. Freddy Gathorne-Hardy, Ian Lawson and Mike Church participated in the fieldwork.

128 *Reykjaholtsmáldagi,* 14–15.
129 Guðrún Sveinbjarnardóttir 1983; Dugmore *et al.* 2006; McGovern *et al.* 2007.

Bibliography

Adolf Friðriksson and Orri Vésteinsson 2003. "Creating a Past: A Historiography of the Settlement of Iceland". In James H. Barrett (ed.), *Contact, Continuity, and Collapse: The Norse Colonisation of the North Atlantic*. Turnhout: Brepols Publishers, 139–162.

Andrés Arnalds 1987. "Ecosystem Disturbance in Iceland". *Arctic and Alpine Research* 19, 508–513.

Áslaug Geirsdóttir, Gifford H. Miller, Þorvaldur Þórðarson and Kristín Ólafsdóttir, 2009. "A 2000 Year Record of Climate Variations Reconstructed from Haukadalsvatn, West Iceland". *Journal of Paleolimnology* 41, 95–115.

Bathurst, Rhonda, Davide Zori and Jesse Byock 2010. "Diatoms as Bioindicators of Site Use: Locating Turf Structures from the Viking Age". *Journal of Archaeological Science* 37, 2920–2928.

Bending, Joanna M. 2007. *The Economy of the Norse Settlement of the North Atlantic Islands and its Environmental Impact: An Archaeobotanical Assessment*. Unpublished PhD thesis, University of Sheffield.

Benedikt Eyþórsson 2008. *Búskapur og rekstur staðar í Reykholt 1200–1900*. Reykjavík: Sagnfræðistofnun Háskóla Íslands.

Buckland, Paul C. and Dave W. Perry 1989. "Ectoparasites from Stóraborg, Iceland and their Palaeoecological Significance". *Hikuin* 15, 37–46.

Buckland, Paul C., Andy J. Dugmore, Dave W. Perry, Diane Savory and Guðrún Sveinbjarnardóttir 1991. "Holt in Eyjafjallasveit, Iceland: A Palaeoecological Study of the Impact of *Landnám*". *Acta Archaeologica* 61, 252–271.

Buckland, Paul C., Kevin J. Edwards, Jeff Blackford, Andy J. Dugmore, Jon Sadler and Guðrún Sveinbjarnardóttir 1995. "A Question of *Landnám*: Pollen, Charcoal and Insect Studies on Papey, Eastern Iceland". In Robin A. Butlin and Neil Roberts (eds), *Ecological Relations in Historical Times*. Oxford: Institute of British Geographers, Blackwell, 245–264.

Church, Mike J., Andy J. Dugmore, Kerry-Ann Mairs, Andrew R. Millard, Gordon T. Cook, Guðrún Sveinbjarnardóttir, Philippa A. Ascough and K.H. Roucoux 2007. "Charcoal Production During the Norse and Early Medieval Periods in Eyjafjallahreppur, Southern Iceland". *Radiocarbon* 48, 659–672.

Dixon, Alexander T. 1997. *Landnám and Changing Landuse at Háls, Southwest Iceland: A Palaeoecological Study*. Unpublished MSc. thesis, University of Sheffield.

Dugmore, Andy J. and Paul C. Buckland 1991. "Tephrochronology and Late Holocene Soil Erosion in Iceland". In Judith Maizels and Chris Caseldine (eds), *Environment and Change in Iceland*. Dordrecht: Kluwer, 147–159.

Dugmore, Andy J., Mike J. Church, Paul C. Buckland, Kevin J. Edwards, Ian Lawson, Tom H. McGovern, Eva Panagiotakopulu, Ian A. Simpson, Peter Skidmore and Guðrún Sveinbjarnardóttir 2005. "The Norse *Landnám* on the North Atlantic Islands: An Environmental Impact Assessment". *Polar Record* 41, 21–37.

Dugmore, Andy J., Mike J. Church, Kerry-Ann Mairs, Tom H. McGovern, Anthony J. Newton and Guðrún Sveinbjarnardóttir 2006. "An Over-optimistic Pioneer Fringe? Environmental Perspectives on Medieval Settlement Abandonment in Þórsmörk, South Iceland". In Jette Arneborg and Bjarne Grønnow (eds), *The Dynamics of Northern Societies*. Copenhagen: PNM, Publications from the National Museum, Studies in Archaeology and History, Volume 10, 335–345.

Dugmore, Andy J., Guðrún Gísladóttir, Ian A. Simpson and Antony Newton 2009. "Conceptual Models of 1200 Years of Icelandic Soil Erosion Reconstructed Using Tephrochronology". *Journal of the North Atlantic* 2, 1–18.

Edwards, Kevin J., Paul C. Buckland, Andy J. Dugmore, Tom H. McGovern, Ian A. Simpson and Guðrún Sveinbjarnardóttir 2004. "Landscapes Circum-*Landnám*: Viking Settlement in the North Atlantic and its Human and Ecological Consequences – a Major New Research Programme". In Rupert A. Housley and Geraint Coles (eds), *Atlantic Connections and Adaptations. Symposia of the Association for Environment Archaeology No. 21.* Oxford: Oxbow Books, 260–271.

Edwards, Kevin J., Egill Erlendsson and J. E. Schofield 2011. "Is there a Norse 'footprint' in North Atlantic Pollen Records?" In Svavar Sigmundsson (ed.), *Viking Settlements and Society. Papers from the Proceedings of the Sixteenth Viking Congress, Reykjavík and Reykholt, 16–23 August 2009.* Reykjavík: Hið íslenzka fornleifafélag and University of Iceland Press, 67–84.

Egill Erlendsson 2007. *Environmental Change Around the Time of the Norse Settlement of Iceland.* Unpublished PhD thesis, University of Aberdeen.

Egill Erlendsson and Kevin J. Edwards 2009. "The Timing and Causes of the Final Pre-settlement Expansion of *Betula pubescens* in Iceland". *The Holocene* 19, 1083–1091.

Egill Erlendsson, Kevin J. Edwards and Paul C. Buckland 2009. "Vegetational Response to Human Colonisation of the Coastal and Volcanic Environments of Ketilsstaðir, Southern Iceland". *Quaternary Research* 72, 174–187.

Egill Erlendsson and Kevin J. Edwards 2010.

"Gróðurbreytingar á Íslandi við landnám". *Árbók Hins íslenzka fornleifafélags,* 29–55.

Egill Erlendsson and Guðrún Gísladóttir 2011. "Tímabil og eðli landnýtingar við Norðtungusel í Kjarardal, Borgarfirði, greind með frjókornum, örkolum og gróum taðsveppa". In *Vorráðstefna JFÍ 15 April 2011. Ágrip erinda og veggspjalda.* Reykjavík: Jarðfræðafélag Íslands, 14–15.

Egill Erlendsson, Kim Vickers, Freddy Gathorne-Hardy, Joanna Bending, Björg Gunnarsdóttir, Guðrún Gísladóttir and Kevin J. Edwards 2012. "Late-Holocene Environmental History of the Reykholt Area, Borgarfjörður, Western Iceland". In Helgi Þorláksson and Þóra Björg Sigurðardóttir (eds), *From Nature to Script.* Snorrastofa, vol. VII. Reykholt: Snorrastofa, 17–47.

Egill Erlendsson, Kevin J. Edwards and Guðrún Gísladóttir 2014. "Landscape Change, Land Use and Occupation Patterns Inferred from Two Palaeoenvironmental Datasets from the Mosfell Valley, SW Iceland". In Davide Zori and Jesse Byock (eds), *Viking Archaeology in Iceland. The Mosfell Archaeological Project.* Turnhout: Brepols, 181–192.

Egils saga Skalla-Grímssonar. Ed. Sigurður Nordal. Íslenzk fornrit II. Reykjavík: Hið íslenzka fornritafélag, 1933.

Freysteinn Sigurðsson 2004. *Borgarfjarðarhérað milli Mýra og Hafnarfjalla. Árbók Ferðafélags Íslands 2004.* Reykjavík: Ferðafélag Íslands.

Friðþór S. Sigurmundsson, Guðrún Gísladóttir and Hreinn Óskarsson 2011. "Decline of Birch Woodland Cover in Þjórsárdalur Iceland from 1587 to 1938". *Human Ecology* 42, 577–590.

Garðar Guðmundsson, Mjöll Snæsdóttir, Ian A. Simpson, Margrét Hallsdóttir, Magnús Á. Sigurgeirsson and Kolbeinn Árnason 2004. "Fornir akrar á Íslandi: meintar minjar um kornrækt á fyrri öldum". *Árbók Hins íslenzka fornleifafélags* 2002–2003, 79–106.

Gathorne-Hardy, Freddy G., Egill Erlendsson, Peter G. Langdon and Kevin J. Edwards 2009. "Lake Sediment Evidence for Climate Change and Landscape Erosion in Western Iceland". *Journal of Paleolimnology* 42, 413–426.

Guðmundur Ólafsson 1996. *Friðlýstar fornleifar í Borgarfjarðarsýslu*. Rit Hins íslenzka fornleifafélags og Þjóðminjasafns Íslands 2. Reykjavík: Hið íslenzka fornleifafélag and Þjóðminjasafn Íslands.

Guðrún Gísladóttir and Michael Stocking 2005. "Land Degradation and its Global Environmental Benefits". *Land Degradation Development* 16, 99–112.

Guðrún Gísladóttir, Egill Erlendsson, Rattan Lal and Jerry M. Bigham 2010. "The Effect of Soil Erosion on Soil Organic Carbon and Terrestrial Resources over the Last Millennium in Reykjanes, Southwest Iceland". *Quaternary Research* 73, 20–32.

Guðrún Gísladóttir, Egill Erlendsson and Rattan Lal 2011. "Soil Evidence for Historical Human Induced Land Degradation in West Iceland". *Applied Geochemistry* 26, S28–S31.

Guðrún Larsen and Jón Eiríksson 2008. "Holocene Tephra Archives and Tephrochronology in Iceland – a Brief Overview". *Jökull* 58, 229–250.

Guðrún Sveinbjarnardóttir 1983. "Byggðaleifar á Þórsmörk". *Árbók Hins íslenzka fornleifafélags* 1982, 20–61.

Guðrún Sveinbjarnardóttir 1991a. "Shielings in Iceland: An Archaeological and Historical Survey". *Acta Archaeologica* 61, 73–96.

Guðrún Sveinbjarnardóttir 1991b. "A Study of Farm Abandonment in Two Regions of Iceland".

In Judith K. Maizels and Chris Caseldine (eds), *Environmental Change in Iceland. Past and Present*. Dordrecht: Kluwer, 161–177.

Guðrún Sveinbjarnardóttir 2005. *Reykholtssel í Kjarardal*. Vinnuskýrslur fornleifa 2005:4. Reykjavík: Þjóðminjasafn Íslands.

Guðrún Sveinbjarnardóttir 2008. "Shielings in Iceland Revisited: A New Project". In Caroline Paulsen and Helgi D. Michelsen (eds), *Símunarbók*. Tórshavn: Tórshavn University Press, 222–231.

Guðrún Sveinbjarnardóttir 2012. *Reykholt. Archaeological Investigations at a High Status Farm in Western Iceland*. Publications of the National Museum of Iceland 29. Reykjavík: Þjóðminjasafn Íslands and Snorrastofa.

Guðrún Sveinbjarnardóttir 2016. *Reykholt. The Church Excavations*. Publications of the National Museum of Iceland 41. Reykjavík: The National Museum of Iceland, in collaboration with Snorrastofa at Reykholt and University of Iceland Press.

Guðrún Sveinbjarnardóttir, Egill Erlendsson, Kim Vickers, Tom H. McGovern, Karen Milek, Kevin J. Edwards, Ian A. Simpson, and Gordon Cook 2007. "The Palaeoecology of a High Status Icelandic Farm". *Environmental Archaeology* 12 (2), 187–206.

Guðrún Sveinbjarnardóttir, Ian A. Simpson and Amanda M. Thompson 2008. "Land in Landscapes Circum *Landnám*: An Integrated Study of Settlements in Reykholtsdalur, Iceland". *Journal of the North Atlantic* 1, 1–15.

Guðrún Sveinbjarnardóttir, Kristoffer Dahle, Egill Erlendsson, Guðrún Gísladóttir and Kim Vickers 2011. "The Reykholt Shieling Project: Some Preliminary Results". In Svavar Sigmundsson (ed.), *Viking Settlements and Viking Society*.

Papers from the Proceedings of the Sixteenth Viking Congress. Reykjavík and Reykholt, 16–23 August 2009. Reykjavík: Hið íslenzka fornleifafélag and University of Iceland Press, 162–188.

Helgi Þorláksson 2011. "A Seat of a Settler? – a Centre of a Magnate: Breiðabólstaður and Reykholt". In Svavar Sigmundsson (ed.), *Viking Settlements and Viking Society. Papers from the Proceedings of the Sixteenth Viking Congress. Reykjavík and Reykholt, 16–23 August 2009*. Reykjavík: Hið íslenzka fornleifafélag and University of Iceland Press, 209–224.

Hicks, Sheila and A. Sunnari 2005. "Adding Precision to the Spatial Factor of Vegetation Reconstructed from Pollen Assemblages". *Plant Biosystems* 139, 127–134.

Hlynur Óskarsson, Ólafur Arnalds, Jón Guðmundsson and Grétar Guðbergsson 2004. "Organic Carbon in Icelandic Andosols: Geographical Variation and Impact of Erosion". *Catena* 56, 225–238.

Hörður Kristinsson 1986. *The Flowering Plants and Ferns of Iceland*. Reykjavík: Örn og Örlygur.

Jón Eiríksson, Helga B. Bartels-Jónsdóttir, Alix G. Cage, Esther Ruth Gudmundsdottir, Dorthe Klitgaard-Kristensen, Fabienna Marret, Teresa Rodrigues, Fatima Abrantes, William E.N. Austin, Hui Jiang, Karen-Luise Knudsen and Hans-Petter Sejrup 2006. "Variability of the North Atlantic Current During the Last 2000 Years Based on Shelf Bottom Water and Sea Surface Temperature Along an Open Ocean/ Shallow Marine Transect in Western Europe". *The Holocene* 16 (8), 1017–1029.

Jónatan Hermannsson 1993. *Kornrækt á Íslandi*. Rannsóknastofnun landbúnaðarins, Reykjavík.

Karl Grönvold, Níels Óskarsson, Sigfús J. Johnsen, Henrik B. Clausen, Claus U. Hammer, Gerard

Bond and Edouard Bard 1995. "Ash Layers from Iceland in the Greenland GRIP Ice Core Correlated with Oceanic and Land Sediments". *Earth and Planetary Science Letters* 135, 149–155.

Landnámabók in *Íslendingabók, Landnámabók*. Ed. Jakob Benediktsson. Íslenzk fornrit I. Reykjavík: Hið íslenzka fornritafélag, 1968.

Larsen, Darren J., Gifford H. Miller, Áslaug Geirsdóttir and Sædís Ólafsdóttir 2012. "Non-linear Holocene Climate Evolution in the North Atlantic: A High-resolution, Multi-proxy Record of Glacier Activity and Environmental Change from Hvítárvatn, Central Iceland". *Quaternary Science Reviews* 39, 14–25.

Lawson, Ian T., Freddy J. Gathorne-Hardy, Mike J. Church, Anthony J. Newton, Kevin J. Edwards, Andy J. Dugmore and Árni Einarsson 2007. "Environmental Impacts of the Norse Settlement: Palaeoenvironmental Data from Mývatnssveit, Northern Iceland". *Boreas* 36, 1–19.

Lawson, Ian T., Kevin J. Edwards, Mike J. Church, Anthony J. Newton, Gordon Cook, Freddy J. Gathorne-Hardy and Andy J. Dugmore 2008. "Human Impact on an Island Ecosystem: Pollen Data from Sandoy, Faroe Islands". *Journal of Biogeography* 35, 1130–1152.

Lawson, Ian T., Karen B. Milek, W. Paul Adderley, Andrew F. Casely, Mike J. Church, Luisa Duarte, Andy J. Dugmore, Kevin J. Edwards, Freddy J. Gathorne-Hardy, Garðar Guðmundsson, Stuart Morrison, Anthony J. Newton and Ian A. Simpson 2009. "The Palaeoenvironment of Mývatnssveit During the Viking Age and Early Medieval Period". In Gavin Lucas (ed.), *Hofstaðir: Excavations of a Viking Age Feasting Hall in North-Eastern Iceland*. Reykjavík: Institute of Archaeology, 26–54.

Lilja Karlsdóttir, Margrét Hallsdóttir, Ægir Th.

Thórsson and Kesara Anamthawat-Jónsson 2009. "Evidence of Hybridisation Between *Betula pubescens* and *B. nana* in Iceland During the Early Holocene". *Review of Palaeobotany and Palynology* 156, 350–357.

Lilja B. Pétursdóttir, 2014. *Post-Settlement Landscape Change in the Mosfell Valley, SW Iceland: A Multiple Profile Approach.* MSc thesis, University of Iceland. http://hdl.handle.net/1946/18576

Lucas, Gavin 2008. "Pálstóftir: A Viking Age Shieling in Iceland". *Norwegian Archaeological Review* 41, 85–100.

Lucas, Gavin (ed.) 2009. *Hofstaðir. Excavations of a Viking Age Feasting Hall in North-Eastern Iceland.* Reykjavík: Institute of Archaeology, Monograph No. 1, 26–54.

McGovern, Tom H., Sophia P. Perdikaris, Árni Einarsson and Jane Sidel 2006. "Coastal Connections, Local Fishing, and Sustainable Egg Harvesting: Patterns of Viking Age Inland Wild Resource Use in Mývatn District, Northern Iceland". *Environmental Archaeology* 11, 187–206.

McGovern, Tom H., Orri Vésteinsson, Adolf Fridriksson, Mike Church, Ian Lawson, Ian A. Simpson, Árni Einarsson, Andy Dugmore, Gordon Cook, Sophia Perdikaris, Kevin J. Edwards, Amanda M. Thomson, Paul Adderley, Anthony Newton, Gavin Lucas and Oscar Aldred 2007. "Landscapes of Settlement in Northern Iceland: Historical Ecology of Human Impact and Climate Fluctuation on the Millennial Scale". *American Anthropologist* 109, 27–51.

McKinzey, Krista M., Rannveig Ólafsdóttir and Andy J. Dugmore 2005. "Perception, History, and Science: Coherence or Disparity in the Timing of the Little Ice Age Maximum in Southeast Iceland?" *Polar Record* 41, 319–334.

Margrét Hallsdóttir 1987. *Pollen Analytical Studies of Human Influence on Vegetation in Relation to the Landnám Tephra Layer in Southwest Iceland.* Lund: Lundqua Thesis 18. Lund University.

Margrét Hallsdóttir and Chris Caseldine 2005. "The Holocene Vegetation History of Iceland, State-of-the-Art and Future Research". In Chris Caseldine, Jim Rose, Jórunn Harðardóttir and Óskar Knudsen (eds), *Iceland: Modern Processes and Past Environments.* Amsterdam: Elsevier, 319–334.

Markús Á. Einarsson 1976. *Veðurfar á Íslandi.* Reykjavík: Iðunn.

Miller, Gifford H., Áslaug Geirsdóttir, Yafang Zhong, Darren J. Larsen, Bette L. Otto-Bliesner, Marika M. Holland, David A. Bailey, Kurt A. Refsnider, Scott J. Lehman, John R. Southon, Chance Anderson, Helgi Björnsson and Thor Thordarson 2012. "Abrupt Onset of the Little Ice Age Triggered by Volcanism and Sustained by Sea-Ice/Ocean Feedbacks". *Geophysical Research Letters* 39, L02708, Doi: 10.1029/2011GL050168.

Ogilvie, Astrid E.J. and Ingibjörg Jónsdóttir 2000. "Sea Ice and Icelandic Fisheries in the Eighteenth and Nineteenth Centuries". *Arctic* 53, 383–394.

Ogilivie, Astrid E.J. and Trausti Jónsson 2001. "'Little Ice Age' Research: A Perspective from Iceland". *Climatic Change* 48, 9–52.

Orri Vésteinsson 1998. "Patterns of Settlement in Iceland: A Study in Prehistory". *Saga-Book* 25, 1–29.

Orri Vésteinsson and Tom H. McGovern 2012. "The Peopling of Iceland". *Norwegian Archaeological Review* 45, 206–218.

Orri Vésteinsson, Tom H. McGovern and Christian Keller 2002. "Enduring Impacts: Social and Environmental Aspects of Viking Age Settlement in Iceland and Greenland". *Archaeologia Islandica* 2, 98–136.

Ólafur Arnalds 2008. "Soils of Iceland". *Jökull* 58, 409–442.

Ólafur Arnalds and Einar Grétarsson 2001. *Soil Map of Iceland*. Second edition. Reykjavík: RALA. http://www.rala.is/desert/kort/ice_soilmap_apr02.pdf

Ólafur Arnalds, Elín Fjóla Þórarinsdóttir, Sigmar Metúsalemsson, Ásgeir Jónsson, Einar Grétarsson and Arnór Árnason 2001. *Soil Erosion in Iceland*. Reykjavík: The Soil Conservation Service and the Agricultural Research Institute.

Rannveig Ólafsdóttir, Peter Schlyter and Hörður V. Haraldsson 2001. "Simulating Icelandic Vegetation Cover During the Holocene. Implications for Long-term Degradation". *Geografiska Annaler* 83, 203–215.

Reykjaholtsmáldagi. Ed. Guðvarður M. Gunnlaugsson. Reykholt: Reykholtskirkja and Snorrastofa, 2000.

Schmid, Magdalena M.E., Andrew J. Dugmore, Orri Vésteinsson and Anthony J. Newton 2016. "Tephra Isochrons and Chronologies of Colonisation". *Quaternary Geochronology* 2016, 1–11.

Sicre, Marie-Alexandrine, Jérémy Jacob, Ullah Ezat, Sonia Rousse, Catherine Kissel, Pascal Yiou, Jón Eiríksson, Karen-Luise Knudsen, Eystein Jansen and Jean-Luise Turon 2008. "Decadal Variability of Sea Surface Temperatures off North Iceland Over the Last 2000 Years". *Earth and Planetary Science Letters* 268, 137–142.

Sigurður Þórarinsson 1944. Tefrokronologiska studier på Island. *Geografiska Annaler* 26, 1–217.

Smith, Kevin P. 1995. "*Landnám*: the Settlement of Iceland in Archaeological and Historical Perspective". *World Archaeology* 26, 319–347.

Smith, Kevin P. 2005. "Ore, Fire, Hammer, Sickle: Iron Production in Viking Age and Early Medieval Iceland". In Robert Bork, Scott Montgomery, Carol Neuman de Vegvar, Ellen Shortell and Steven Walton (eds), *Du re Metallica. The Uses of Metal in the Middle Ages*. AVISTA Studies in the History of Medieval Technology, Science and Art, Volume 4, 183–206.

Vickers, Kim 2006. *The Palaeoentomology of the North Atlantic Islands*. Unpublished PhD thesis, University of Sheffield.

Vickers, Kim, Egill Erlendsson, Mike J. Church, Kevin J. Edwards and Joanna Bending 2011. "1000 Years of Environmental Change and Human Impact at Stóra-Mörk, Southern Iceland – a Multiproxy Study of a Dynamic and Vulnerable Landscape". *The Holocene* 21, 979–995.

Vickers, Kim and Guðrún Sveinbjarnardóttir 2013. "Insect Invaders, Seasonality and Transhumant Pastoralism in the Icelandic Shieling Economy". *Environmental Archaeology* 18, 165–177.

Zori, Davide 2014. "Interdisciplinary Modelling of Viking Age and Medieval Settlement in the Mosfell Valley". In Davide Zori and Jesse Byock (eds), *Viking Archaeology in Iceland. Mosfell Archaeological Project*. Turnhout: Brepols, 55–79.

Zori, Davide, Jesse Byock, Egill Erlendsson, Steve Martin, Thomas Wake and Kevin J. Edwards 2013. "Feasting in Viking Age Iceland: Sustaining a Chiefly Political Economy in a Marginal Environment". *Antiquity* 87, 150–155.

Þorleifur Einarsson 1962. "Vitnisburður frjógreiningar um gróður, veðurfar og landnám á Íslandi". *Saga* 24, 442–469.

Þóra E. Þórhallsdóttir 1996. "Áhrif búsetu á landið". In Guðrún Ása Grímsdóttir (ed.), *Um landnám á Íslandi – fjórtán erindi*. Reykjavík: Vísindafélag Íslendinga, 149–170.

¶ BENEDIKT EYÞÓRSSON, EGILL
ERLENDSSON, GUÐRÚN GÍSLADÓTTIR
AND GUÐRÚN SVEINBJARNARDÓTTIR

Natural Resources –
Access and Exploitation

Introduction

N *EGILS SAGA SKALLA-GRÍMSSONAR* THERE IS A FAMOUS account of how Skalla-Grímr (Grímr the Bald), the leading sett-ler in the Borgarfjǫrðr region, organized his farming in the early years of the settlement period. His main farm was at Borg but at selected locations he operated satellite farms, utilizing available natural resources:

> Skalla-Grímr was an industrious man. He always kept many men with him and gathered all the resources that were available for subsistence, since at first they had little in the way of livestock to support such a large number of people. ... Skalla-Grímr was a great shipbuilder and there was no lack of driftwood west of Mýrar. He had a farmstead built on Álptanes and ran another farm there, and had men rowing out from it to catch fish and cull seals and gather eggs, all of which were there in great abundance, and had driftwood taken back to his farm. The area was visited by whales, too, in great numbers, and could be hunted at will at this hunting post ...[1]

---

1 "Skalla-Grímr var iðjumaðr mikill; hann hafði með sér jafnan mart manna, lét sœkja

At a third farm, also by the sea, Skalla-Grímr had crops planted and walruses were hunted from offshore islands. He sent his men upriver to catch salmon and when his livestock grew in numbers he had a farmstead built close to the mountain pastures and "ran a farm there where his sheep were kept. ... In this way, Skalla-Grímr put his livelihood on many footings."[2]

Although this frequently cited passage has to be viewed as representing the ideas that the thirteenth-century author of the saga had of Skalla-Grímr's farming strategy and how a primary settler and a chieftain might have organized his extensive land-claim,[3] it can be argued that the passage is in essence a description of medieval Icelandic farming strategy, even of that of the dispersed North Atlantic region. Behind this tale of a prehistoric pioneer and his extraordinary prowess and industriousness is a reality that the thirteenth-century audience of the saga could easily relate to from their own experience of subsistence farming, including winter grazing, highland pastures in summer time, cereal cultivation, salmon fishing, offshore fisheries, culling of seals, whale hunting, and collection of eggs and driftwood. The passage touches upon most of the main exploitable natural resources available to medieval Icelanders, and although it must be assumed that precious few were in a position to exploit and have access to them all from their farmsteads, it is likely that most tried to incorporate as many of the available natural resources within their own farming strategy as possible to subsidize livestock farming.

Pastoral farming was important in the Norse world. Its success relied on grazing and fodder resources from outfields and hinterlands. The use of outfields was vital, not only for the farming economy, but also as a source for products like fish and other sea animals, wild game and fowl, berries and herbs, as well as products of metal and minerals.[4] For more than two

---

mjǫk fǫng þau, er fyrir váru ok til atvinnu mǫnnum váru, því at þá fyrst hǫfðu þeir fátt kvikfjár, hjá því sem þurfti til fjǫlmennis þess, sem var ... Skalla-Grímr var skipasmiðr mikill, en rekavið skorti eigi vestr fyrir Mýrar; hann lét gera bœ á Álptanesi ok átti þar bú annat, lét þaðan sœkja útróðra ok selveiðar ok eggver, er þá váru gnóg fǫng þau ǫll, svá rekavið at láta at sér flytja. Hválkvámur váru þá ok miklar, ok skjóta mátti sem vildi ..." (*Egils saga Skalla-Grímssonar*, 75) [English translation adapted and amended from Viðar Hreinsson (ed.) 1997, vol. 1].

2   "... ok átti þar bú; lét þar varðveita sauðfé sitt; ... Stóð þá á mǫrgum fótum fjárafli Skalla-Gríms" (*Egils saga Skalla-Grímssonar*, 76).

3   For further discussion of this passage from *Egils saga* and its influence see Orri Vésteinsson *et al.* 2002, 102ff.

4   Øye 2005, 11–12.

decades, zooarchaeological and palaeoecological research has expanded the understanding of medieval Icelandic household subsistence. The results have been summarized by leading scholars in this field as follows:

> The economy of the Viking Age North Atlantic settlers was based around stock raising but yet flexible and supplemented by limited barley growing and often extensive use of wild species. The ultimate source of wealth and power was pasture, and the correlation between cattle, good grazing, and chieftainship is clear both in the historical and archaeological record.[5]

A recent study, based largely on the written sources concerning the operation and management of the Reykholt estate, reaches a similar conclusion.[6]

The earliest record relating to farming at Reykholt is a church charter or deed, the original text of which is now thought to date from about the mid-twelfth century. The charter has six later additions, four of them dating from between AD 1204 and 1247, and two from the latter part of the thirteenth century and around AD 1300.[7] In the oldest part it is stated that the church at Reykholt owned twenty cows, a two-year-old bull and 150 ewes, and a measure of grain to be sown. Raising cattle for dairy produce, supplemented with barley cultivation, was the strategy that was meant to provide for the church and its proprietors. The inventory of livestock is followed by a list of properties and rights in the surrounding land belonging to the church, river fishing, a shieling area, pastures for grazing, woods and cutting of turf or peat:

> Þar liggr til fimm hlutir Grímsár allrar en þrír hverfa undan ... ok ástemma at Rauðavatnsósi. ... Þar hverfr ok til selfor í Kjor með áveiði þeirri er þar fylgir at helmingi ok afréttr á Hrútafjarðarheiði ok ítok þau er hún á í Faxadal ok Geitland með skógi. Skógr í Sanddal niðr frá Slakkagili ... Þar fylgir ok skógr í Þverárhlíð at viða til sels. Torfskurðr í Steinþórsstaðaland.[8]

---

5   McGovern *et al.* 2007, 29.
6   Benedikt Eyþórsson 2008.
7   *Reykjaholtsmáldagi*, 17, 32. See also pp. 279, 288 in this book on the date of the earliest part of the charter.
8   To it [the church at Reykholt] belong five parts of Grímsá, but three are excluded

These properties and rights provided the farmstead of Reykholt with access to better pastures, woodland areas and freshwater fishing in addition to what was already in place. They also resonate well with the passage from *Egils saga*, quoted above, where emphasis is placed on having access to various natural resources and exploiting them for subsistence. A comparison with other medieval church charters in the Borgarfjǫrðr region shows that Reykholt's assets and property rights were more extensive than those of most ordinary churches, but consistent with the properties and rights of the major churches in the region, such as Stafholt, Gilsbakki, Hítardalr and Bœr.[9] Access to summer pastures, shieling areas and salmon fishing in the main rivers was central to these churches, while access to woodland is more evident in the case of Reykholt. This article will examine Reykholt's access to and exploitation of natural resources, both within the boundaries of the estate and outside it, and the extent to which land-use management played a part in the overall farming strategy. Emphasis will be placed on examining the late twelfth and early thirteenth centuries, but evidence from later written sources will also be used, in order to shed light on earlier and less well documented periods and give insight into long-term historical development.

Grazing Resources

Grazing resources in the immediate vicinity of the Reykholt farm were limited, both for summer and winter grazing, and the farm had no direct access to highland pastures. Although the original settlement of

... as well as the dam at Rauðavatnsóss. ... It has the right to use a shieling in Kjǫr with half of the fishing that goes with it, and mountain pasturage on Hrútafjarðar-heiði, and all the property rights which it has in Faxadalr, and Geitland, with woods. Woods in Sanddalr below Slakkagil ... Along with it goes the right to firewood for the shieling from the woods in Þverárhlíð. Turf-cutting in the land of Steinþórsstaðir (*Reykjaholtsmáldagi*, 14–15; normalized, medieval spelling, English translation is amended by the present authors). Rauðavatn here (and called so on the maps) is modern day Reyðarvatn.

9   For the medieval deeds of the major churches in the region see *DI* I, 178–180; *DI* III, 88–89 (Stafholt); *DI* III, 84 (Hítardalr); *DI* II, 358–359 (Gilsbakki); *DI* III, 123–124 (Bœr); *DI* I, 417–418, *DI* II, 403–404 (Garðar). For medieval deeds of other churches in the region see e.g. *DI* I, 217–218 (Húsafell); *DI* I, 264–265 (Saurbœr); *DI* I, 270–272, 418–419 (Melar); *DI* I, 413–416 (Innri-Hólmr); *DI* I, 420–421 (Hvammr); *DI* I, 589–592; *DI* III, 125 (Hvanneyri (-eyrr)); *DI* I, 593–594 (Stóri-Áss); *DI* II, 577–578 (Svignaskarð).

Breiðabólstaðr – on which land Reykholt was later established – had an extensive landholding and was one of the largest settlements in the Reykholtsdalr valley, by around AD 1200 it was divided into four independent farms: Reykholt, Breiðabólstaðr, Grímsstaðir and Norðrreykir, and two more, Háfr and Hœgindi, which were dependent farms of Reykholt.[10] Reykholt, Breiðabólstaðr and Grímsstaðir are clustered together in a relatively small area, surrounded by infields and meadows, while Norðrreykir, Háfr and Hœgindi are somewhat further away (see fig. 1). In a visitation in the year 1639, Bishop Brynjólfur Sveinsson commented on Reykholt's grazing limitations and stressed the importance of access to grazing resources on its properties of Norðrland (a landholding of the then deserted farm Háfr) and Hraunsáss (a farm belonging to the Reykholt church). He wrote that Reykholt could not do without those grazing areas since "hér heima er ekkert land nema tún og engjar".[11] At that time these areas were used for the winter grazing of sheep. In the *Jarðabók* (Land Register) of Árni Magnússon and Páll Vídalín, from the turn of the eighteenth century, it is also stated that Reykholt's access to the summer pastures and shieling areas, belonging to the church, was pivotal for the farming strategy.[12]

For dairy farming at Reykholt, access to good summer pastures and shieling areas was of the utmost importance. The use of shielings is a good example of grazing strategies applied in the infield-outfield system. Shielings form part of a "decentralized farming economy, which involved the summer transhumance of livestock away from the main farm to preserve the homefields for winter fodder".[13] The milking cows and ewes were kept at the shielings and tended to, but as well as dairy production, other exploitation of outfield resources often occurred, such as additional winter fodder collection and charcoal production.[14] The oldest part of the Reykholt church charter contains the earliest reference to a shieling belonging to Reykholt in the valley of Kjarardalr. The acquisition of the

---

10 Orri Vésteinsson 1998, 18–19; Guðrún Sveinbjarnardóttir *et al.* 2008, 1–3.
11 "there was nothing surrounding the homestead but infields and meadows for haymaking". The full text in the visitation is as follows: "þessi tvö kot [Norðrreykir and Hraunsáss] hljóta þar til þéna [as grazing lands for the *staðr*], því hér heima er ekkert land nema tún og engjar sem allir sjá". See ÞÍ. Skjalasafn presta. Reykholt. AA/2; Benedikt Eyþórsson 2008, 98–99.
12 *Jarðabók* IV, 230.
13 Lucas 2008, 85.
14 Øye and Myhre 2002, 369; Lucas 2008, 85; Guðrún Sveinbjarnardóttir 2008, 222.

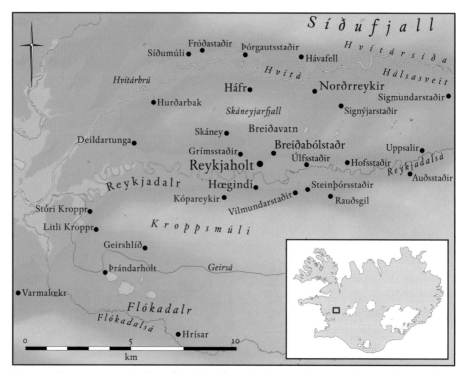

Figure 1. This map shows Reykholt (Reykjaholt) and the farms belonging to the church, or under the care of the church (*staðr*) in the early thirteenth century; these are Breiðabólstaðr, Hœgindi, Háfr and Norðrreykir, called Reykir in the medieval deed of the church. Later Grímsstaðir also became dependent. The modern form for Steinþórsstaðir is Steindórsstaðir. Map: Stefán Ólafsson.

land can be seen as a testament of the importance of this resource to the farm, especially in light of the abovementioned grazing limitations of the homestead.

Kjarardalr lies parallel to Reykholtsdalr, approximately eleven kilometres to the north, running inland from the lowland area of Borgarfjǫrðr and orientated roughly east-west.[15] As well as being referred to as a shieling site belonging to Reykholt in the old Reykholt charter, the valley as a whole is referred to as a shieling area for the farms in the Hvítársíða region and Reykholt in a thirteenth-century saga.[16] Shielings belonging to churches and farms in Hvítársíða are also mentioned in church charters and other documents from the fourteenth to the sixteenth centuries. The

15   Guðrún Sveinbjarnardóttir and Kristoffer Dahle 2008, 4–5.
16   *Heiðarvíga saga*, 284.

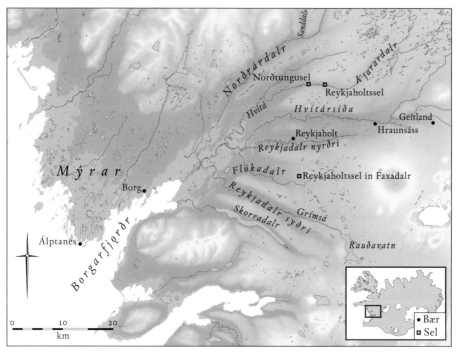

Figure 2. The shielings of Reykholt (Reykjaholt), marked with squares. Map: Stefán Ólafsson.

shieling area belonging to Reykholt was on the north side of the river Kjarará, bounded by two gorges. Two shieling sites are known in the area, one close to the western limit, referred to as the older or the lower shieling in documents from the year 1596, and the other further up the valley, close to the eastern limit. According to written sources from the end of the sixteenth century and onwards, this shieling area was mainly rented out to farmers living in Hvítársíða, although there is evidence that the proprietors of Reykholt used it themselves for some years in the latter part of the sixteenth century. On modern maps the lower shieling site is referred to as Norðtungusel, since in the mid-nineteenth century a farmer at the nearby farm Norðtunga rented the shieling area, built up the site and used it as *beitarhús* (shelter for grazing sheep) for winter grazing. The other shieling further up the valley is referred to as Reyk-holtssel on the same maps and here as Reykjaholtssel (see fig. 2).[17]

17   Benedikt Eyþórsson 2008, 138–143.

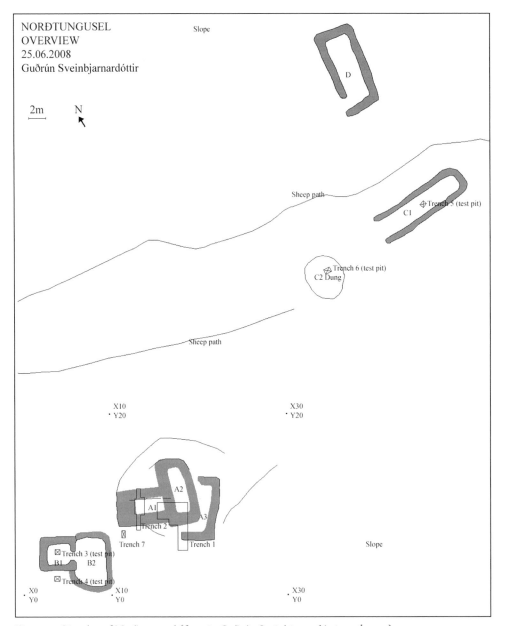

Figure 3a. Site plan of Norðtungusel (fig. 2 in Guðrún Sveinbjarnardóttir *et al*. 2011).

Figure 3b. A view of Norðtungusel, looking west. Photo: Guðrún Gísladóttir.

The site of Norðtungusel lies on a slight platform about 600 metres to the east of the western limit of the shieling area, about 166 metres above sea level. A survey and limited excavation at the site in the summer of 2008 revealed four separate ruins and complexes (see figs. 3 and 3b). The main complex contained the dwelling and probably two other structures, one of which may have been a fold. A ruin and a fold just west of the main complex were believed to be contemporaneous with it and probably housed animals, whereas the two other ruins were interpreted to be of a later date, most probably from the time when the site served as the location for a *beitarhús* in the nineteenth century. Evidence gathered during the excavation indicated that there may have been human activity at the site before the houses were originally built, possibly a clearing of woodland, although the limited size of the excavation trench means that this cannot be proven.[18]

18   Guðrún Sveinbjarnardóttir *et al.* 2011, 166.

Radiocarbon dating of samples taken during the survey and excavation of trial trenches at Norðtungusel indicate that there may have
been human activity at the site from as early as around AD 1000 or
the early eleventh century. This date comes, on the one hand from a
charcoal sample from a midden outside the main building which gave
estimates falling between AD 972 and 1050, on the other from a charcoal
layer some distance below the lowest of three floor layers inside the
building with estimates between AD 1017 and 1155. A sample from that
lowest floor layer, on the other hand, gave estimates falling between
AD 1437 and 1522.[19] A sequence of floor layers is a sign of temporary
occupation which again suggests shieling activity. An indication of iron
ore extraction in the form of a piece of clean iron smelting slag was
discovered in the lowest floor layer. The composition of the slag suggests
that it derives from bog ore and that fuel may have been scarce at the
time it was produced.[20] Whether the iron ore extraction took place at
Norðtungusel or somewhere else is, however, uncertain. The piece of
slag could have been carried to the site from elsewhere. A noteworthy
decline in birch woodland from around AD 1500 is demonstrated in
pollen data from a wetland patch nearby (see below). This can perhaps
be seen as supporting evidence for iron production at Norðtungusel,
given how much fuel this activity required.[21]

Results from the study of pollen, and spores from ferns (*pteridophytes*,
in Icelandic, *byrkningar*) and dung-fungi (associated with grazing animals)
undertaken at the site, demonstrate the presence of grazing animals from
the time of the deposit of the *landnám* tephra around AD 870 to around
AD 1380 when signs of dwindling land-use pressure at Norðtungusel
start to appear. From around AD 1550 elevated levels of microscopic
charcoal particles and no increase in spores from dung-fungi suggest that
woodland use, possibly charcoal production, rather than grazing, was the
main activity in the vicinity. Signs of increased grazing are not clear until
around AD 1880 when spores from dung-fungi become prominent again.[22]

---

19 AAR12756, 12755, 12754 in Table 1.
20 Analysis was carried out by Professor Thilo Rehren at the Institute of Archaeology,
    University College London.
21 See e.g. Smith, 1995.
22 Egill Erlendsson and Guðrún Gísladóttir 2011, 14–15.

Table 1. Radiocarbon dates from the shieling sites.

Lab. no.	Material	Sample no. and context	Age (^{14}Cyr BP; 1 σ)	cal AD2σ
AAR12756	Charcoal (birch)	NOR-08–9	1010±31	972AD (80.2%) 1050AD 1084AD (11.3%) 1125AD 1136AD (3.5%) 1152AD
AAR12755	Charcoal (willow)	NOR-08–8 [17]	969±28	1017AD (95.4%) 1155AD
AAR12754	Charcoal (birch)	NOR-08–6 [14]	399±27	1437AD (79.5%) 1522AD 1576AD (0.9%) 1583AD 1591AD (15.0%) 1622AD
SUERC-30822	Charcoal (birch)	RKHsel-10-1 [2]	550±35	1300AD (42.5%) 1370AD 1380AD (52.9%) 1440AD
AAR12758	Charcoal (birch)	FAX-08-16 [28]	975±32	1014AD (95.4%) 1155AD
SUERC-26682	Charcoal (birch)	HAM-09-04 [8]	1140±35	780AD (95.4%) 990AD
SUERC-26683	Charcoal	HAM-09-14 [7]	1140±35	780AD (95.4%) 990AD
SUERC-26684	Charcoal (birch)	KOT-09-16 [7]	1140±35	780AD (95.4%) 990AD
SUERC-26685	Charcoal (willow)	KOT-09-17 [8]	1085±35	890AD (95.4%) 1020AD
SUERC-27650	Charcoal (birch)	KOT-09-03 [8]	1065±35	890AD (95.4%) 1030AD
SUERC-26681	Charcoal (birch)	HAM-09-01	1110±35	890AD (95.4%) 1020AD
SUERC-27654	Charcoal (willow)	KOT-09-13 [5]	1090±35	890AD (95.4%) 1020AD

These are AMS dates. Calibrations are performed using OxCal v.4.0.5 (Bronk-Ramsay 2007) for the AAR dates, v. 3.10 (Bronk-Ramsay 2005) for the SUERC dates. Laboratory Codes: AAR: Institut for Fysik of Astronomi, Aarhus Universitet, Denmark. SUERC: SUERC Radiocarbon Dating Laboratory.

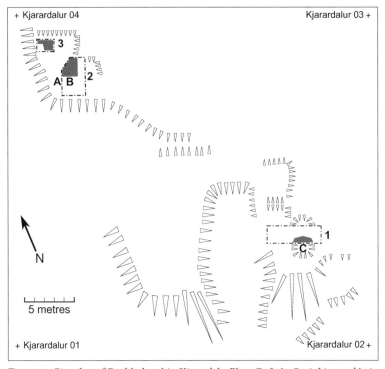

Figure 4a. Site plan of Reykholtssel in Kjarardalr. Plan: Guðrún Sveinbjarnardóttir.

The site of Reykholtssel is placed between 700 and 800 metres west of the eastern boundary of the shieling area, on a platform about 160 metres above sea level. In surveys and limited excavations carried out in the summers of 2004 and 2005, and again in 2010, two areas of structures were identified, with the main complex being located close to a stream (see figs. 4a and 4b). Samples of charred birch obtained in the area of the secondary structure at Reykholtssel gave a date, with calibrated estimates falling between the years AD 1430 and 1670.[23] The samples were taken below a layer of gravel which was evident at other locations at the site. It has been interpreted as a landslide that post-dates the radiocarbon dates. Dates on charred birch from heavily layered cultural deposits within the main complex at Reykholtssel gave calibrated estimates for the earliest formation of these which fall between AD 1300 and 1440.[24]

23 Guðrún Sveinbjarnardóttir 2008, 226.
24 Guðrún Sveinbjarnardóttir *et al.* 2011, 166; SUERC-30822 in Table 1.

Figure 4b. A view of Reykholtssel, looking west. Photo: Guðrún Sveinbjarnardóttir.

These dates indicate that at least the main building complex at this site was first occupied in the fourteenth century and the layered nature of the deposits is again an indication of seasonal occupation, i.e. a shieling.

Soil cores were analysed in the area close to the site of Reykholtssel. The pre-settlement soil was fertile and rich in organic carbon and nitrogen. The soil quality declined soon after settlement and there is evidence suggesting that soil erosion had already begun in the area at that time. Between AD 1400 and 1700 the soil quality declined sharply and in around AD 1500 the ecosystem seems to have collapsed. This is reflected in severely degraded soils, slope instability and soil depletion. There is also a sharp drop in *Betula* (birch) pollen along with microscopic charcoal preserved in peat soil in the tenth to thirteenth centuries, indicating human activity and even charcoal production in the general area during the initial soil degradation period.[25]

25   Guðrún Gísladóttir *et al.* 2010, 56.

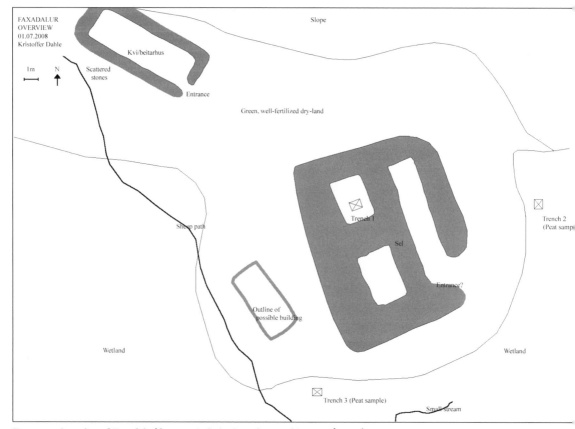

Figure 5a. Site plan of Faxadalr (fig. 3 in Guðrún Sveinbjarnardóttir *et al.* 2011).

In the mid-twelfth-century Reykholt charter it is mentioned that Reykholt has unidentified rights in Faxadalr, a heathland belonging to the farm of Hrísar in the Flókadalr valley. In a mid-fourteenth-century charter it is stated that the right in Faxadalr is two months' access to grazing resources. By the latter half of the fourteenth century Reykholt had acquired half of the land of Hrísar, the other half belonging to the church farm Bœr. Reykholt's access to grazing resources in Faxadalr is repeated in all other late medieval charters. In one of the fifteenth century charters it is also stated that Bœr – a lowland farm like Reykholt with no direct access to mountain pastures – has a shieling in the heath above Hrísar. The earliest written evidence of Reykholt using its grazing resources in Faxadalr as a shieling are from the mid-sixteenth century, and from the seventeenth century to the mid-nineteenth century the shieling

Figure 5b. A view of the Faxadalr site, looking south-south-east. Photo: Guðrún Sveinbjarnardóttir.

site in Faxadalr was the one Reykholt primarily exploited. The shieling in Faxadalr was still being used from Reykholt in the 1840s but it seems that soon after the mid-nineteenth century this ceased.[26]

The site of the shieling in Faxadalr lies in a depression in the heathland with a stream that runs through it. A survey in the summer of 2008 revealed a main complex which on the surface seems to contain three rooms with a separate structure just to the north-east, believed to have been either a fold where the sheep were milked or a *beitarhús* (see fig. 5a).[27] The remains of buildings in Faxadalr were clear on the surface and left little scope for doubt so far as the layout of the site is concerned, which is in keeping with the account that the site was used until the mid-nineteenth century.[28] A trial trench was dug into the northernmost of the two small rooms in the main complex. It revealed a sequence of

26 Benedikt Eyþórsson 2008, 145–147.
27 Guðrún Sveinbjarnardóttir and Kristoffer Dahle 2008, 14–15.
28 Guðrún Sveinbjarnardóttir and Kristoffer Dahle 2008, 16; Guðrún Sveinbjarnardóttir 2008, 228.

five floor layers with windblown material in between.[29] Charred birch was dated from the bottom layer giving calibrated estimates that fall between AD 1014 and 1155.[30] The floor sequence is consistent with the temporary nature of a shieling and the earliest dates show that there was such an occupation at the site long before it is mentioned in the written sources. Whether it was occupied by the people of Reykholt or by a different farm, is not known.

Other summer grazing resources Reykholt had access to in the twelfth and thirteenth centuries were in Hrútafjarðarheiði (-heiðr) and possibly in Geitland, both mentioned in the old Reykholt charter. Geitland is a vegetated lava field, situated between the Geitá and Svartá rivers, in the highland margin, just above the uppermost farms in the district, Húsafell and Kalmanstunga.[31] There are remains of two medieval farms in Geitland (see fig. 6). Each site has two longhouses and a number of smaller ruins which are obviously not all contemporaneous.[32] Following a survey and limited excavations at the sites in the summer of 2009,[33] samples of charred birch from the lower floor layers within the longhouses at both sites were dated, giving calibrated estimates which suggest that the sites were first occupied in the ninth century.[34] Subsequently, samples from the less distinct second floor layers within the same buildings, suggesting a brief second phase of occupation, were also dated, giving calibrated estimates that may indicate somewhat later dates (although the difference is not great).[35] The dates suggest that these sites were not occupied for very long. Whether the second, less substantial phase of occupation indicates that they were used as shielings for a time could not be established. The early abandonment of these sites is supported by the wording in the charter which suggests that the area was not occupied at the time it was written, but rather used solely for its resources. Prior to these new datings, and those for the initial settlement at Reykholt, which are similar to the abandonment date of the sites in Geitland,[36] it had been suggested that the proprietors of Reykholt removed their tenants from Geitland to

29 Guðrún Sveinbjarnardóttir and Kristoffer Dahle 2008, fig. 10.
30 AAR12758 in Table 1.
31 Benedikt Eyþórsson 2008, 100.
32 Guðmundur Ólafsson 1996, 74–81; Guðrún Sveinbjarnardóttir *et al.* 2011.
33 Guðrún Sveinbjarnardóttir and Kristoffer Dahle 2009.
34 SUERC-26682, 26683, 26684, 26685, 27650 in Table 1.
35 SUERC-26681, 27654 in Table 1.
36 Guðrún Sveinbjarnardóttir 2012, 25–26, 48.

Figure 6. The farm-sites Kot and Hamraendar in Geitland are located on the vegetated slopes; looking south-east. Photo: Guðrún Sveinbjarnardóttir.

preserve the woodland and pasture in the area.[37] There is little evidence of any settlement in Geitland after the abandonment of the two sites until much later which makes this suggestion perhaps now seem unlikely. Whether the inhabitants of Geitland abandoned the sites to go and settle at Reykholt or somewhere else we do not know.[38] Geitland is a typical area for an early inland settlement in Iceland where habitation did not last very long.[39] One of the sites in Geitland was allegedly occupied again in the late sixteenth century.[40] By at least the sixteenth century, Geitland was Reykholt's main summer pasture for lambs and castrated rams as well as for most farms in the Reykholtsdalr valley, with each farmer who used

37   Orri Vésteinsson 1996, 35; Orri Vésteinsson 1998, 25.
38   On this issue see Guðrún Sveinbjarnardóttir 2012; Guðrún Sveinbjarnardóttir 2010, 484–485; Helgi Þorláksson 2012.
39   Guðrún Sveinbjarnardóttir 1992.
40   Kristleifur Þorsteinsson 1944, 11.

it needing permission from the proprietors of Reykholt and paying a toll, one lamb from each flock of sheep grazing there.[41]

According to medieval charters Reykholt had rights to highland pastures on Hrútafjarðarheiði, a heathland which lies a considerable distance to the north-west of Reykholt. It is in an area renowned for good highland pastures. There is no direct evidence in the written sources of early modern times of Reykholt exploiting it. In the nineteenth century Reykholt had access to and exploited the heathland surrounding Lake Reyðarvatn as a summer pasture (see fig. 2). Reykholt's proprietor claimed the land in the mid-eighteenth century and after that it was listed as a property of Reykholt and sold as such to the municipality Lundarreykjadalshreppr in the late nineteenth century. There is no evidence of Reykholt using the area for grazing in earlier times and the legal reasons for claiming the land in the eighteenth century seem to have been based on dubious grounds, to say the least.[42]

Winter grazing was in all probability carried out in the vicinity of Reykholt in the twelfth and thirteenth centuries just as it was in later centuries. The dependent farms mentioned in the old Reykholt charter, Háfr and Hœgindi, served as Reykholt's main winter grazing areas in late-medieval and early-modern times. Háfr (or Norðrland as it is referred to in later sources) was situated some distance north of the farm of Reykholt, on the bank of the Hvítá river (see fig. 1). Háfr seems to have been abandoned in the fourteenth century. It is only in the early seventeenth century that any mention is made of Norðrland in the written sources and by that time it formed an integral part of Reykholt as a winter grazing area. Reykholt had a *beitarhús* there that could shelter 180 sheep according to seventeenth-century documents. In more recent sources, Norðrland is described as a good winter grazing area and it was used for that purpose until the early twentieth century, as well as for outfield haymaking.[43] Another grazing area that was a part of the Reykholt landholding, was the land of the dependent farm Hœgindi, situated opposite Reykholt, on the south side of the Reykjadalsá river. The farm is mentioned in twelfth- to fourteenth-century charters, but was deserted between the early fifteenth century and the late seventeenth century. It is recorded that around AD 1600 it served as a winter grazing area for

---

41 Benedikt Eyþórsson 2008, 101–103.
42 Benedikt Eyþórsson 2008, 107–108; see also *Byggðir Borgarfjarðar* III, 399, 403.
43 Benedikt Eyþórsson 2008, 96–98.

Reykholt.[44] Even though these farms were occupied in the twelfth and thirteenth centuries, it must be borne in mind that they were dependent farms of Reykholt and the tenants probably did not have large numbers of livestock. The proprietors of Reykholt could easily have rented out the cottages and used the landholdings as grazing areas for livestock belonging to the church and/or themselves.

Fuel Resources

At the time of settlement in the late ninth century AD, the Reykholtsdalr valley seems to have supported woodlands, consisting primarily of downy birch but also willows and some rowan. During the settlement period the landscape was subject to human impact, signified by a rapid decline in woodland and accelerated soil erosion. The effects of settlement, however, appear in two different ways. In the lowland, in the valley bottom, wood-land almost instantly shrank and is thought to have been replaced by areas of meadowland. Further away from the farms and at a higher altitude the woodland lingered on into medieval times.[45] In the vicinity of Breiðavatn, by the ridge between Reykholt and the Hvítá river to the north, there was a continuous presence of birch woodland from the time of settlement to around AD 1200. In the thirteenth century the woodland declined rapidly and by around AD 1300 it had all but disappeared.[46] Simultaneously the records show a rise in the values for microscopic charcoal, indicating that burning, perhaps associated with charcoal production, was being undertaken closer to the lake than previously.[47] Other research indicates that in the area between the churches of Reykholt and Stóri-Áss, near Lake Breiðavatn, the land was covered with woodland in medieval times and exploited for charcoal making and iron extraction.[48]

Apart from the woodland on its landholding in medieval times, Reykholt had access to several other woodland areas through the church properties, three of which are mentioned in the twelfth-century Reykholt

---

44   Benedikt Eyþórsson 2008, 99–100.
45   Egill Erlendsson 2007, 247, 251.
46   Egill Erlendsson 2007, 259–260; Gathorne-Hardy *et al.* 2009, 421.
47   Egill Erlendsson 2007, 262.
48   Guðrún Sveinbjarnardóttir *et al.* 2009, 3–5; for detailed discussion see Smith 1995; 2005.

charter: woodland in the highland area of Geitland, a forest in Sanddalr which leads off Norðrárdalr, called the Forest of St Peter, and a woodland in Kjarardalr belonging to Reykholt's shieling area (see fig. 2). In the fifteenth century Reykholt acquired the farm of Hraunsáss in Hálsasveit. At Hraunsáss there was extensive woodland, regarded as one of the best woodland areas in the region in the early eighteenth century.[49]

A micromorphological analysis of a medieval midden at Reykholt reveals that there was a mixed fuel economy in those times, with wood and peat both being exploited. In a section dated to after around AD 1300, peat is prevalent, but wood disappears and animal dung becomes a feature of the fuel economy. This has been interpreted as suggesting an emerging shortage of wood for fuel, which could have been offset by the use of animal dung.[50] Peat was widely used as fuel in Iceland, either as a supplementary or as a primary fuel.[51] In the charters for the church at Reykholt, access to peat resources at the neighbouring farm of Steindórsstaðir is mentioned. There are also references to peat-cutting in Reykholt's landholding in early-modern written sources, and remains of old peat mines could still be seen in recent times.[52] There seems to have been a good potential for the use of peat as fuel in Reykholtsdalr, at least around Reykholt and in the lower reaches of the valley where wetland is ample. Measurements of organic content of pre-historic peat are high for Icelandic standards, typically around 60 to 85 per cent where they are not contaminated with tephra.[53] In general, locations away from the main volcanic activity and palagonite-dominated bedrocks are the ones that produced peat (where found) with the highest organic content. This applies, for example, to Borgarfjǫrðr. Prehistoric peat deposits in the lowlands of southern Iceland, by comparison, typically consist of organic content that is only half that in Borgarfjǫrðr, between 30 and 45 per cent.[54]

Hot springs are among natural resources that Reykholt has in greater abundance than most farms, and use was made of the geothermal activity from the earliest times. The warm pool Snorralaug is the best known example of the use of this resource and there was even a twelfth- or

49   Benedikt Eyþórsson 2008, 63–65.
50   Guðrún Sveinbjarnardóttir *et al.* 2007, 198, 200.
51   Orri Vésteinsson and Ian A. Simpson 2004, 184.
52   Benedikt Eyþórsson 2008, 65; The Árni Magnússon Institute for Icelandic Studies – The Place-Name Collection. Reykholtshreppur 3508. Reykholt.
53   Egill Erlendsson 2007, 187, 195.
54   Egill Erlendsson 2007, 89, 92, 135.

thirteenth-century tradition that the pool predated the establishment of the farm at Reykholt.[55] This is supported up to a point by the results of archaeological investigations which date the earliest occupation to around AD 1000 or the early eleventh century, placing it among the second generation of settled farms in the area.[56] The archaeological investigations have also revealed further examples of the exploitation of the geothermal activity at the site. Rescue excavations in the 1960s and 1980s revealed remains of conduits, two of which fed water from the hot spring Skrifla into the warm pool and one which is assumed to have directed steam up towards the farm site. In the most recent excavation remains of a building dated to medieval times was unearthed. Steam or hot air assumed to come from the hot-spring was led through a conduit into the building and used to heat it up to optimal temperature, thus saving valuable alternative fuel resources.[57] It has proved difficult to assign a particular function to the building. Despite this, the building and associated conduit are a unique example of experiments carried out in making use of the geothermal resource at Reykholt in medieval times.

Freshwater and Maritime Resources

The Borgarfjǫrðr region is renowned for its salmon rivers, many of which are now regarded as some of the best in the country. As might be expected, Reykholt had its share in these extensive resources. Reykholt's landholding is situated between the Reykjadalsá and Hvítá rivers, and so Reykholt had the right to exploit both of them. Belonging to Reykholt's shieling area in Kjarardalr was salmon fishing in the Kjarará river, and more than half of the fishing rights in the Grímsá river were the property of the church. Fishing rights in the Kjarará and Grímsá rivers are mentioned in the old Reykholt charter, where there is also a reference to a dam (*ástemma*) on the outlet of Lake Reyðarvatn.[58]

As far as can be deduced from the written sources, the fishing in

55 Landnámabók, 192; for general discussion see Guðrún Sveinbjarnardóttir 2005, 208–209.

56 On the earliest occupation see pp. 237, 246 in this book, and regarding how the pool may have influenced the establishment of the farm see pp. 127–128 in this book.

57 See pp. 258–260 in this book for further discussion of this building.

58 *Reykjaholtsmáldagi*, 14–15.

the Grímsá river was the most extensively exploited resource, at least in early modern times. In seventeenth- to nineteenth-century documents belonging to the church at Reykholt there are many references to fishing nets for catching salmon, and in some instances it is stated that a net is kept at Hestr, a farm by the side of the Grímsá river, which also had fishing rights in the river. In 1729 the fishing season started on June 22 and the days were, according to tradition, divided up between the holders of the fishing rights, with Reykholt fishing the first five days, Hestr farm the next two days and Hvanneyri (-eyrr) farm for a day. This cycle was continued throughout the summer, with the exception of Sundays when there was to be no fishing. In their travel book, written in the mid-eighteenth century, Eggert Ólafsson and Bjarni Pálsson commented on the salmon Reykholt caught in the Grímsá river and said it was believed to be the church's most valuable asset. In those times two men were usually in charge of the fishing, and in an average year they would each catch as many as five or six hundred salmon during the summer season. In the early sixteenth century Reykholt had the river every other week sharing it with the other holders of the fishing rights. Reverend Ólafur Gilsson, proprietor of Reykholt from AD 1518 to 1537, was not satisfied with this division and had it changed so that Reykholt would also have the Monday of the following week, on the basis that Reykholt owned five eighths of the fishing rights and the other rights holders three eighths. He also installed fishing equipment in the Grímsá river called a salmon pocket (*laxapoki*). How it worked is unknown today, and he was apparently the first and only proprietor of Reykholt to use this technique.[59]

Written sources do not reveal much about exploitation of other freshwater fishing areas and the evidence regarding the nature of their exploitation is circumstantial at best. A fourteenth-century charter of Síðumúli, a church farm in Hvítársíða, refers to the church's fishing rights in the Kjarará river. Síðumúli owned a shieling area in Kjarardalr, south of the river opposite Reykholt's shieling area, and the fishing rights were divided equally between the two of them. In a written contract dated to 1722, concerning the rent of Reykholt's shieling area in Kjarardalr, it is

---

59 Benedikt Eyþórsson 2008, 67–69. The Reverend Jón Halldórsson (1665–1736) of Hítardalr says this about the fishing of the Reverend Ólafur Gilsson in his manuscript of *Prestasögur*. The Reverend Jón was born and brought up at Reykholt, son of Halldór Jónsson (1626–1704) of Reykholt whose forefathers had been proprietors of Reykholt since AD 1569.

emphasized that exploitation of the fish in the river is included with the rent of the shieling area. This is repeated in a record from 1596 on the same issue. If this was the general custom for tenants of the shieling area in Kjarardalr, it indicates that the Kjarará river was not Reykholt's primary salmon fishing river, certainly not from the sixteenth century onwards, since the shieling area was rented out to others for most of that period.

The only reference made to the *ástemma* in Reyðarvatnsós in medieval and late-medieval documents is in the mid-twelfth century Reykholt charter.[60] During a survey in the summer of 1988 remains of a stone wall were studied in the outlet of Lake Reyðarvatn. The interpretation of the remains is that the *ástemma* was used as a dam to block water flowing from the lake into the river. Thus fish – in this case arctic charr (*Salvelinus alpinus*) – in the upper part of the river could easily be caught in small pools and pits in the almost dried-up riverbed. This is the only known example of the flow to a whole river being blocked, whereas blocking the flow of one of two branches of a river was a known practice.[61]

Indications in the historical sources of the importance of freshwater fishing at Reykholt are not consistent with the archaeological evidence. In fact, no bones from freshwater fish have been recovered from the midden or other waste disposals excavated and analysed from Reykholt, either from medieval times or early modern times. This might suggest that fresh-water fishing is over-represented in the written sources when compared to the actual exploitation of the resource. It should be noted, however, that conditions for bone preservation at Reykholt were extremely variable, with the main midden deposits being both to a large extent truncated by building works in the early twentieth century and showing acid soils in the low pH range with only sporadic bone preservation. Other deposits were better preserved, for example those around and within the medieval buildings, but overall the taphonomic conditions at Reykholt have been seen as marginal for bone preservation.[62] It should also be pointed out that very little midden material was excavated at the site.

The last part of the old Reykholt charter, dated to around AD 1300, lists some rights that the church had for driftwood collection and ex-ploitation of beached whales in certain coastal areas in the Strandir region

60 Benedikt Eyþórsson 2008, 69–70.
61 Helgi Þorláksson 1989, 5–8, 15–18.
62 Guðrún Sveinbjarnardóttir *et al.* 2007, 201; see also McGovern 2012.

in the north-west of Iceland.[63] According to written sources, the church at Reykholt was rebuilt in the early sixteenth century with driftwood collected in that region.[64] Archaeological investigations at Reykholt revealed four main types of buildings at the old church site, dated to between the eleventh and nineteenth centuries. The investigations also indicated that the Reykholt churches were made more or less exclusively of timber until the sixteenth century.[65] Wood remains from the first three building types were analysed and confirm that driftwood was used in the earliest building phase, dated to the eleventh century, and in the second phase, from the twelfth to fourteenth centuries. The preservation of the wood remains found in the third building type, dated to the fourteenth to sixteenth centuries, was poor and the results were, therefore, not conclusive. They did, however, indicate that driftwood was also used in that building.[66] This is evidence of contact with the coastal region, both prior to the established rights of the church, as well as after it. Other evidence of connections between the farm at Reykholt and the coastal region in the twelfth and thirteenth centuries came from medieval deposits investigated during the archaeological excavation in the form of skeletal remains of fish belonging to the cod family which had been processed, and a single seal bone. All the fish bones found at Reykholt were of marine origin and their presence at this inland site has been thought to support the idea of an extensive exchange of fish and probably other marine products within Iceland from early medieval times.[67] An alternative interpretation is that Reykholt sent some of its workforce to the sea to work on a seasonal basis.

Discussion

Reykholt's main grazing resources lay outside its landholdings and belonged to the church. However, two areas within Reykholt's landholdings, Norðrland and Hœgindi, were used as winter grazing areas for sheep in the seventeenth century and the former until the early twentieth century.

63   *Reykjaholtsmáldagi*, 15.
64   Benedikt Eyþórsson 2008, 60–61.
65   Guðrún Sveinbjarnadóttir 2009, 60, 66–68; 2016.
66   Lísabet Guðmundsdóttir 2008, 30–35.
67   Guðrún Sveinbjarnardóttir *et al.* 2007, 202; McGovern 2012; for further discussion and references on the idea of an early medieval exchange system of marine products see McGovern *et al.* 2007, 42–44.

There were dependent farms in Norðrland and Hœgindi around AD 1200 but they had been deserted by the fourteenth and early fifteenth centuries respectively. It is likely that Reykholt exploited both Norðrland and Hœgindi for grazing after they were deserted and possible that they were exploited as such to some extent as early as the twelfth and thirteenth centuries. Winter grazing became more important when castrated rams became a larger proportion of the livestock in early modern times.

Geitland was Reykholt's main highland pasture for lambs and castrated rams from at least the sixteenth century. Earlier the pasture in the heathland of Hrútafjarðarheiði may have been the main summer pasture. There is evidence of a shieling site in Faxadalr from as early as the eleventh or twelfth century, suggesting that the grazing rights there were exploited for ewes and cows in a shieling rather than for lambs and castrated rams. It is, however, uncertain whether the site was being used by Reykholt at that early date. There is also evidence that Reykholt's shieling area in Kjarardalr was exploited continuously from the eleventh or twelfth century. The archaeological evidence is consistent with the historical record which suggests that Norðtungusel was the earlier site, with Reykholtssel first being used as a shieling in the fourteenth century. The environmental evidence does, however, show that the area around Reykholtssel had been grazed, or otherwise exploited, well before that. According to written sources the whole shieling area in Kjarardalr was mostly rented out to other farmers from the early sixteenth century to the nineteenth century, and Faxadalr was the main shieling area of Reykholt during that period.

Initially Reykholt had access to woodland and brushwood on its own landholding. Wood was Reykholt's primary fuel in the eleventh to thirteenth centuries while peat was also used. Reykholt had access to peat on its own land, as well as at Steindórsstaðir according to the twelfth-century charter. The wood collected for fuel could have come from various sources. The obvious choice would have been the woodlands around Lake Breiðavatn, while the church's woodlands in Geitland and Sanddalr could also have provided firewood. The archaeological evidence for Reykholt using wood as its primary fuel until around AD 1300 coincides with the recorded deforestation in the closest vicinity of Reykholt, and suggests that Reykholt's proprietors took the option of exploiting the woodland around Lake Breiðavatn for firewood collection while the resources lasted. The woodland in Geitland and Sanddalr may either have been deemed to be too far away to be a source of firewood or these woodlands were a source of building timber – a prized asset and a clear sign of quality woodland. It is possible to imagine that the forest in Sanddalr was of such high quality, since it is located a long distance from Reykholt. A donation to the church and its patron saint would probably have been more highly regarded if it was high quality woodland that was being donated rather than average quality woodland. The woodland in Kjarardalr by Norð-tungusel provided the shieling with firewood. It may also have been used for charcoal production and there are indications of iron ore extraction at the site in the fifteenth and sixteenth centuries. In the seventeenth and eighteenth centuries Reykholt's main source of charcoal and firewood was the woodland of Hraunsáss, where there was also access to building timber until the mid-seventeenth century. It is probable that Reykholt exploited the woodland of Hraunsáss from the time it acquired the farm in the fifteenth century. The addition of woodland in Hraunsáss to the church's list of properties is of some interest. By this time historical records become silent on woodland usage in Geitland, Sanddalr and Kjarardalr, perhaps as a consequence of decline of this resource through over-exploitation. Conversely, under the management and exploitation by Reykholt, the woodland in Hraunsáss survived through the Little Ice Age and until the present day. Perhaps this reflects an improved attitude towards this increasingly sparse, yet important resource, bearing in mind also that wood ceased to be Reykholt's primary type of fuel at a similar time, either by choice or necessity.

Freshwater fishing seems to have been an integral part of Reykholt's economy to judge by the documentary sources, something that is not supported by the archaeological evidence. In early modern times the Grímsá river was the most important location for salmon fishing. Salmon fishing in the Kjarará river was not exploited by Reykholt in the seventeenth to nineteenth centuries, but some salmon fishing may have been practised in the river in conjunction with Reykholt using the shieling site in the area in the twelfth to sixteenth centuries. The indications of the *ástemma* in Reyðarvatnsóss only being used in medieval times could suggest that freshwater fishing played a more important role in Reykholt's extensive agricultural strategies during that period than it did later. The written sources indicate that Reykholt had access to numerous and in many cases relatively good freshwater fishing areas, suggesting that they were important in the overall economic strategy.

That this is not supported by the archaeological evidence may perhaps be explained in terms of the preservation and/or the limited extent of excavation of midden material.

Driftwood was used at Reykholt as building timber for the churches from the outset and this provides clear evidence for contact with the coastal region. From around AD 1300 Reykholt had access to its own coastal areas for the collection of driftwood. It is possible that most of the driftwood used at Reykholt from around that time and onwards came from the areas in the Strandir region where Reykholt had the right to collect it, although the evidence for this is in all but one case only circumstantial. Cod and other fish of the cod family, consumption of which is evident in medieval times at Reykholt, also suggest contact with the coastal zone at an early stage.

Through the properties of the church, Reykholt had access to an array of resources outside the farmstead and their exploitation ensured a resilient economy based on a diverse land-resource base. This was vital for the emergence of Reykholt as a centre of power and a prerequisite for the large-scale farming that was practised at Reykholt from medieval times to at least the mid-eighteenth century.

Bibliography

Benedikt Eyþórsson 2008. *Búskapur og rekstur staðar í Reykholti 1200–1900.* Reykjavík: Sagnfræðistofnun Háskóla Íslands.

Byggðir Borgarfjarðar III. Mýrarsýsla og Borgarnes. Ed. Bjarni Guðráðsson and Björk Ingimundardóttir. Borgarnes: Búnarðarfélag Borgarfjarðar, 1993.

DI = *Diplomatarium islandicum, Íslenzkt fornbréfasafn* I-XVI. Copenhagen and Reykjavík, 1857–1972.

Egill Erlendsson 2007. *Environmental Change Around the Time of the Norse Settlement of Iceland.* Unpublished PhD thesis submitted to the College of Physical Sciences of the University of Aberdeen, June 2007.

Egill Erlendsson and Guðrún Gísladóttir 2011. "Tímabil og eðli landnýtingar við Norðtungusel í Kjarardal, Borgarfirði, greind með frjókornum, örkolum og gróum taðsveppa". In *Vorráðstefna JFÍ, 15. apríl 2011. Ágrip erinda og veggspjalda.* Reykjavík: Jarðfræðafélag Íslands, 14 (abstract).

Egils saga Skalla-Grímssonar. Ed. Sigurður Nordal. Íslenzk fornrit II. Reykjavík: Hið íslenzka fornritafélag, 1933.

Gathorne-Hardy, Freddy J., Egill Erlendsson, Peter G. Langdon and Kevin J. Edwards 2009. "Lake Sediment Evidence for Late Holocene Climate Change and Landscape Erosion in Western Iceland". *Journal of Paleolimnology* 42 (3), 413–426.

Guðmundur Ólafsson 1996. *Friðlýstar fornleifar í Borgarfjarðarsýslu.* Rit Hins íslenzka fornleifafélags og Þjóðminjasafns Íslands 2. Reykjavík.

Guðrún Gísladóttir, Egill Erlendsson and Rattan Lal 2010. "The Impact of Shieling Activity on Terrestrial Ecosystem in Kjarardalur, West Iceland". In *The Engineering and Natural Sciences Research Symposium, October 8th–9th 2010.* Reykjavík: School of Engineering and Natural Sciences, 56 (abstract).

Guðrún Sveinbjarnardóttir 1992. *Farm Abandonment in Medieval and Post-Medieval Iceland. An Interdisciplinary Study.* Oxbow Monographs in Archaeology 17. Oxford: Oxbow Books.

Guðrún Sveinbjarnardóttir 2005. "The Use of Geothermal Resources at Reykholt in Borgarfjörður in the Medieval Period". In Andreas Mortensen and Símun V. Arge (eds), *Viking and Norse in the North Atlantic. Select papers from the Proceedings of the XIVth Viking Congress, Tórshavn, 19–30 July 2001.* Annales Societatis Scientarium Færoensis Supplementum XLIV. Tórshavn: The Faroese Academy of Sciences, 208–216.

Guðrún Sveinbjarnardóttir 2008. "Shielings in Iceland Revisited. A new project". In Caroline Paulsen and Helgi D. Michelsen (eds), *Símunarbók. Heiðursrit til Símun V. Arge á 60 ára degnum 5. september 2008.* Tórshavn: Fróðskapur, Faroe University Press, 222–231.

Guðrún Sveinbjarnardóttir 2009. "Kirkjur Reykholts – byggingasaga". In Guðmundur Ólafsson and Steinunn Kristjánsdóttir (eds), *Endurfundir. Fornleifarannsóknir styrktar af Kristnihátíðarsjóði 2001–2005.* Reykjavík: National Museum of Iceland, 58–69.

Guðrún Sveinbjarnardóttir 2010. "The Making of a Centre. The Case of Reykholt, Iceland". In John Sheehan and Donnchadh Ó Corráin (eds), *The Viking Age. Ireland and the West. Proceedings of the XVth Viking Congress, Cork, 2005.* Dublin: Four Courts Press, 483–493.

Guðrún Sveinbjarnardóttir 2012. *Reykholt. Archaeological Investigations at a High Status Farm in Western Iceland.* Publications of the National

Museum of Iceland 29. Reykjavík: Snorrastofa and The National Museum of Iceland.

Guðrún Sveinbjarnardóttir 2016. *Reykholt. The Church Excavations*. Publications of the National Museum of Iceland 41. Reykjavík: The National Museum of Iceland, in collaboration with Snorrastofa and University of Iceland Press.

Guðrún Sveinbjarnardóttir, Egill Erlendsson, Kim Vickers, Tom H. McGovern, Karen B. Milek, Kevin J. Edwards, Ian A. Simpson and Gordon Cook 2007. "The Paleoecology of a High Status Icelandic Farm". *Environmental Archaeology* 12 (2), 187–206.

Guðrún Sveinbjarnardóttir, Ian A. Simpson and Amanda M. Thompson 2008. "Land in Landscapes Circum *Landnám*. An Intergrated Study of Settlements in Reykholtsdalur, Iceland". *Journal of the North Atlantic* 1, 1–15.

Guðrún Sveinbjarnardóttir and Kristoffer Dahle 2008. *The Shielings of Reykholt*. Archaeological Investigations in 2008. Unpublished report.

Guðrún Sveinbjarnardóttir and Kristoffer Dahle 2009. *The Shielings of Reykholt*. Archaeological Investigations in 2009. Unpublished report.

Guðrún Sveinbjarnardóttir, Kristoffer Dahle, Egill Erlendsson, Guðrún Gísladóttir and Kim Vickers 2011. "The Reykholt Shieling Project. Some Preliminary Results". In Svavar Sigmundsson (ed.), *Viking Settlement and Viking Society. Papers from the Proceedings of the XVIth Viking Congress, Reykjavík and Reykholt, 16–23 August 2009*. Reykjavík: Hið íslenzka fornleifafélag and University of Iceland Press, 162–175.

Heiðarvíga saga. In *Borgfirðinga sögur*. Ed. Sigurður Nordal and Guðni Jónsson. Íslenzk fornrit III. Reykjavík: Hið íslenzka fornritafélag, 1938.

Helgi Þorláksson 1989. "Mannvirkið í Reyðar-vatnsósi". *Árbók Hins íslenzka fornleifafélags* 1988, 5–27.

Helgi Þorláksson 2012. "Reykholt vokser fram som maktsenter". In Helgi Þorláksson and Þóra Björg Sigurðardóttir (eds), *From Nature to Script. Reykholt, Environment, Centre and Manuscript Making*. Snorrastofa, vol. VII. Reykholt: Snorrastofa, 79–116.

Hænsa-Þóris saga. In *Borgfirðinga sögur*. Eds Sigurður Nordal and Guðni Jónsson. Íslenzk fornrit III. Reykjavík: Hið íslenzka fornritafélag, 1938.

Jarðabók Árna Magnússonar og Páls Vídalín IV. Borgarfjarðar- og Mýrasýsla. Copenhagen, 1925–1927.

Kristleifur Þorsteinsson 1944. "Geitland". In Þórður Kristleifsson (ed.), *Úr byggðum Borgarfjarðar* I. Reykjavík: Ísafoldarprentsmiðja, 9–22.

Landnámabók in *Íslendingabók, Landnámabók*. Ed. Jakob Benediktsson. Íslensk fornrit I. Reykjavík: Hið íslenska fornritafélag, 1968.

Lísabet Guðmundsdóttir 2008. *Viðargreiningar á fornum við úr kirkjum Reykholts*. Unpublished BA thesis at the University of Iceland, May 2008.

Lucas, Gavin 2008. "Pálstóftir. A Viking Age Shieling in Iceland". *Norwegian Archaeological Review* 41 (1), 85–100.

McGovern, Tom H., Orri Vésteinsson, Adolf Friðriksson, Mike Church, Ian Lawson, Ian A. Simpson, Árni Einarsson, Andy Dugmore, Gordon Cook, Sophia Perdikaris, Kevin J. Edwards, Amanda Thomson, Paul Adderley, Anthony Newton, Gavin Lucas, Ragnar Edvardsson and Oscar Aldred 2007. "Landscapes of Settlement in Northern Iceland. Historical Ecology of Human Impact and Climate Fluctuation on the

Millennial Scale". *American Anthropologist* 109 (1), 27–51.

McGovern, Tom H. 2012. "Animal Bone". In Guðrún Sveinbjarnardóttir, *Reykholt. Archaeological Investigations at a High Status Farm in Western Iceland.* Publications of the National Museum of Iceland 29. Reykjavík: Snorrastofa and The National Museum of Iceland, 257–259.

Orri Vésteinsson 1996. *Menningarminjar í Borgarfirði norðan Skarðsheiðar.* Svæðisskráning. Reykjavík: Fornleifastofnun Íslands.

Orri Vésteinsson 1998. "Patterns of Settlements in Iceland. A Study in Prehistory". *Saga-Book* 25 (1), 1–29.

Orri Vésteinsson, Thomas H. McGovern and Christian Keller 2002. "Enduring Impacts. Social and Environmental Aspects of Viking Age Settlement in Iceland and Greenland". *Archaeologia Islandica* 2, 98–136.

Orri Vésteinsson and Ian A. Simpson 2004. "Fuel Utilisation in Pre-Industrial Iceland. A Micromorphological and Historical Analysis". In Garðar Guðmundsson (ed.), *Current Issues in Nordic Archaeology. Proceedings of the 21st Conference of Nordic Archaeologists, September 6th–9th 2001.* Akureyri and Reykjavík: Society of Icelandic Archaeologists, 181–187.

Reykjaholtsmáldagi. Ed. Guðvarður Már Gunnlaugsson. Reykholt: Reykholtskirkja – Snorrastofa, 2000.

Smith, Kevin P. 1995. "Landnám. The Settlement of Iceland in Archaeological and Historical Perspective". *World Archaeology* 26 (3), 319–347.

Smith, Kevin P. 2005 "Ore, Fire, Hammer, Sickle. Iron Production in Viking Age and Early Medieval Iceland". In R.H. Bjork (ed.), *De Re Metallica. The Use of Metal in the Middle Ages.* AVISTA Studies in the History of Medieval Technology, Science and Art, Vol. 4. Aldershot: Ashgate Publishing Ltd, 183–206.

The Árni Magnússon Institute for Icelandic Studies – The Place-Name Collection. Reykholtshreppur 3508. Reykholt.

Viðar Hreinsson (ed.) 1997. *The Complete Sagas of Icelanders, including 49 Tales.* Reykjavík: L. Eiríksson.

ÞÍ. = *Þjóðskjalasafn Íslands* [National Archives of Iceland]. Skjalasafn presta. Reykholt. AA/2.

Øye, Ingvild 2005. "Introduction". In Ingunn Holm, Sonja Innselet and Ingvild Øye (eds), *Utmark. The Outfield as Industry and Ideology in the Iron Age and the Middle Ages.* University of Bergen Archaeological Series, International 1. Bergen: University of Bergen, 9–20.

Øye, Ingvild and Björn Myhre 2002. *Norges landbrukshistorie* I. *4000 f.Kr.–1350 e.Kr. Jorda blir levevei.* Oslo: Det Norske Samlaget.

Aerial view of Reykholt looking north-west. The excavation area is in the centre of the photograph, between the old church and the old school (the four storey white building with the tower). The pool and passageway are just to the right of the old school, at its east gable. Photo: Guðlaugur Óskarsson, September 2016.

9   GUÐRÚN SVEINBJARNARDÓTTIR AND
GUÐRÚN HARÐARDÓTTIR

The Buildings at Reykholt

Introduction

NTEREST IN REYKHOLT AS AN HISTORICAL SITE IS long-standing and is connected to Snorri Sturluson and his importance in the Icelandic literary tradition and the history of the Commonwealth (930–1262). With a growing antiquarian interest in Europe in the nineteenth century, due to the emergence of romanticism and nationalism, Reykholt became one of the most important places foreign observers visited during their stays in Iceland. Some valuable descriptions and drawings of what they saw are preserved. The preservation of the dry-stone built pool, Snorralaug, created a link with the medieval past of Reykholt and was an apparent relic from it. The near-contemporary *Sturlunga saga* contains some information on the buildings at Reykholt during Snorri's time there. One of the objectives of the excavations carried out at the site around the turn of the twenty-first century, the results of which are discussed in this article, was to attempt to compare the archaeological remains and the written sources. This is the first time such a comparison has been formally attempted for this type of site. The excavation at Reykholt is also the first to produce medieval structural remains at a church and magnate farm site in Iceland. Comparative material is, therefore, obviously very limited.

The site was operated as a farm from its earliest settlement (now dated to around AD 1000 on the basis of archaeological remains) until the twentieth century. This continuous activity has inevitably had a great effect on the physical landscape of the site through the centuries and obscured some of the observations made in past accounts. The disturbances were particularly severe in the period after the introduction of concrete buildings in the twentieth century.

Iceland became a sovereign state in 1918, and in 1930 it celebrated the millennium of the establishment of the *Alþingi*. During these times of optimism, the high school established at Hvítárbakki in 1905 was relocated to Reykholt. The new building can be interpreted as a witness to the optimism and progressive thinking that was evident in Iceland in the early days of sovereignty. The decision to move the school to Reykholt may perhaps be interpreted as a tribute to Snorri, although the rediscovery by Icelanders of the value of hot springs as a natural resource almost certainly played a part, and the location of the building right on top of the farm mound was motivated first and foremost by practical considerations, demonstrating a complete lack of concern for the preservation of archaeological remains. A location down by the river was also considered but was, unfortunately, thought to be too far from the hot spring from which water was taken to heat it.

The year 1929 saw the beginning of the erection of the large school building on the farm midden located just to the south of where the farm buildings stood at that time. The deep foundations of this concrete building wiped out most of the rich midden material that is presumed to have represented the farm waste through the centuries. The north wing of the building was built on top of the then byre, which was rebuilt in concrete together with a barn in the eastern half of the farm site (figs. 1 and 2). The excavation showed that these concrete buildings were placed partly within, but also extending beyond, the wall enclosing the farm buildings on the east side (figs. 3 and 5). Their deep foundations wiped out all structural remains in a large section of the easternmost part of the farm mound.

A house was built for the headmaster just to the west of the excavation area, with service pipes put in trenches cutting across the area which was excavated, disturbing all the upper deposits. A sports hall was built at right angles to the east of the north wing of the school building. It was a wooden building which rested on concrete pillars set into the ground at regular intervals. Some of these pillars penetrated through to the subterranean passageway which runs from the pool Snorralaug to the

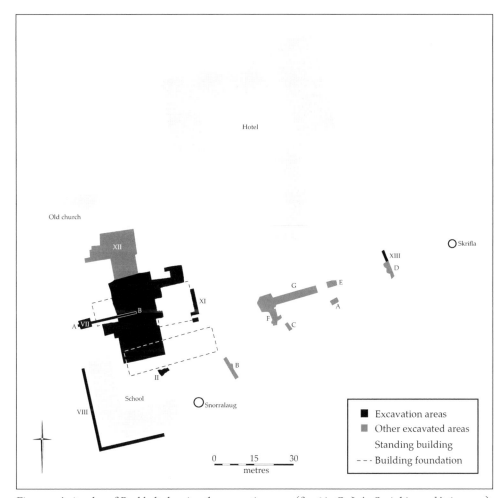

Figure 1. A site plan of Reykholt showing the excavation areas (fig. 6 in Guðrún Sveinbjarnardóttir 2012a).

farm. This passageway and a later wall fragment were the only remains discovered under the sports hall.

Despite the knowledge that the site had been heavily disturbed by modern building activities, archaeological excavations were initiated at the farm site in the late 1980s. One of the reasons for this initiative at that point was to commemorate the 750th anniversary of Snorri's death, and this is further evidence of the persistent interest in Reykholt as an historical site. Funding ran out after two summers, but the investigation was resumed in 1998 and finished with the completion of the investigation of the church site in 2007.[1] Ironically the archaeological remains that came to light in the wake of the laying of the foundations for the school building, namely those of the subterranean passageway leading from Snorralaug to the farm site, may have initiated the interest in carrying out the subsequent archaeological excavations at the site.

Only about a third of the farm mound was excavated. The choice of excavation area was guided by the extent of the farm site and the nature of the deposits that were established before the excavation started, as well as the knowledge of the concrete building foundations described above. The excavation area fell between the foundations of the schoolmaster's house and those of the byre and barn, and covers the middle section of the farm mound (figs. 1 and 3), the total extent of which is estimated to be at least 22 to 23 metres north to south by 45 to 46 metres east to west, covering a total of between 990 and 1058 square metres. The excavation revealed that the main farm complex had stood more or less in the same place until it was moved to a more westerly location in 1833, as described in the written sources. The preservation restraints and the fact that only part of the farm mound was excavated means that it is not possible, on the basis of the building remains, to obtain a complete picture of the layout of the farm buildings at the site at any one time. The interpretations presented in this article should be viewed with that in mind.

The church at Reykholt was located about ten metres north of the farm site from the time it was first established, probably in the eleventh century, until 1886 when it was dismantled and a new timber church built where it still stands a few metres further north, leaving the original site free for investigation (see fig. 1). The area where the older churches stood was used for burials until around 1920. Some of the burials had inevitably encroached upon the building foundations and disturbed them. Some burials ended up inside the buildings, others in the walls, some post-dated the last church in this location, others were contemporary with the church at some stage. In view of the fact that some of the burials in that part of the cemetery are relatively recent, a decision was taken to concentrate on the structural remains and only excavate the burials necessary for that purpose. One building foundation on top of another was unearthed, dated to between the eleventh and nineteenth centuries.

---

1   Guðrún Sveinbjarnardóttir *et al.* 2007; Guðrún Sveinbjarnardóttir 2009; 2012b; 2012a; 2016.

Figure 2. The newly built school building with the last farm in the background.
Photo: Jón Kaldal, Þjms. JK 5–48. Þjms. stands for Þjóðminjasafn Íslands (National Museum of Iceland).

Four different building types were identified, three of which were in use
with some variations for a period of time, representing a total of eight
phases. Only building types 1 and 2, covering three phases which are
dated to between the eleventh and fourteenth centuries on the basis of
stratigraphy, radiocarbon dates and datable artefacts, are relevant to the
time frame covered in this book.

Despite the fact that Snorri Sturluson only lived at Reykholt for
a short period of time in the history of the farm, there is a desire to
link some of the archaeological remains with his years there. This is
encouraged by the descriptions in *Sturlunga saga*. The possibilities for a
comparison of the archaeological and written sources are limited because
only a small portion of the original farm mound could be excavated,
and also because of the nature and state of preservation of the written
sources. Where there are possibilities for a dialogue is between, first,
the information in *Sturlunga saga* and some of the excavated material,

Figure 3. Aerial view of the farm site taken in 1958/9. Photo: Halldór Einarsson.

secondly, the post-1732 appraisal records (*úttektir*) and a part of the excavated *gangabær* (passageway farm), and thirdly, the excavated remains and appraisal records of the post-medieval churches.

The first attempt to give a visual shape to the buildings and other structures at Reykholt based on the accounts in *Sturlunga saga* was made by Sigurður Vigfússon, the curator of the Antiquities Collection of Iceland, after visiting Reykholt in 1884.[2] He pays special attention to the construction of the fortress (*virki*) which, according to *Sturlunga saga*, Snorri had erected around the farm, and its relation to other structures at the site. He also speculates about the construction of the subterranean passageway (*forskáli*) which led from the pool to the farm and what form the cellar (*kjallari*) may have had.

2   Sigurður Vigfússon 1885, 113–124.

In her master's dissertation (published in an extended version in 1966), Arnheiður Sigurðardóttir also tries to interpret the buildings at Reykholt on the basis of the descriptions in *Sturlunga saga*. Of special interest is her suggestion concerning the *stofa*, which (according to *Sturlunga saga*) was built at Reykholt in 1233, for which she finds parallels in Norway, in particular in the thirteenth-century Raulandsstova.[3] In an article published in 2006, Guðrún Harðardóttir discusses all the buildings mentioned in *Sturlunga saga* in the light of Norwegian and Icelandic building traditions, and compares them with the excavated remains at the farm site. She attempts to interpret their construction and use on the basis of the descriptions.[4]

Since this book addresses the time Snorri occupied Reykholt, the focus here will be on the first option mentioned above: the comparison of the information in *Sturlunga saga* and the excavated material, both of the church and the farm buildings. Only Phases 1 and 2 of the excavation, the latter of which coincides with Snorri's occupation, will be discussed. The comparison between the written sources and the archaeological remains will be in the form of a dialogue, since a direct connection between the two types of sources is almost impossible. The limited comparative material available from other archaeological sites in Iceland will be mentioned when relevant.

The Source Material

The stratigraphical phases of the farm and church sites

The remains of the farm mound which were excavated have been divided into six phases, which are dated on the basis of stratigraphy, radiocarbon dates on charred barley, birch and animal bone, datable artefacts and written sources. On that basis, Phase 1 is dated to between around AD 1000 and the twelfth century, Phase 2 to between the twelfth and fourteenth centuries, Phase 3 to the fifteenth/sixteenth centuries, Phase 4 to the sixteenth/seventeenth centuries, Phase 5 to between the seventeenth and nineteenth centuries and Phase 6 to the nineteenth century and later. The

3   Arnheiður Sigurðardóttir 1966, 57.
4   Guðrún Harðardóttir 2006.

remains at the church site have been divided into a total of eight phases, with Phases 1 and 2i coinciding with Phase 1 on the farm site, Phase 2ii with Phase 2 on the farm site, Phases 3i and 3ii with Phase 3 on the farm site, and Phases 4i, 4ii and 4iii with Phases 4 and 5 on the farm site.[5] The discussion below only covers remains belonging to Phases 1 and 2.

The nature of the written sources

The written source material on Reykholt in the middle ages is mainly derived from charters, narratives and appraisal records (*úttektir*). The most important source containing descriptions of the farm buildings at Reykholt is *Sturlunga saga*, generally regarded as a more reliable historical source than the Sagas of Icelanders, which are written two or more centuries after the events they describe are supposed to have happened. This claim about *Sturlunga saga's* reliability as a source has, however, been challenged and it has been suggested that a narrative bias can be detected in the text.[6] Since the houses form part of the background information in the saga, a narrative bias would be unlikely to affect the use being made of the source in this study, and indeed the bulk of *Sturlunga saga*, the so-called *Íslendinga saga*, where the majority of the references to the buildings at Reykholt are to be found, is still regarded as a trustworthy source in this respect.

Charters and early appraisal records are published in the series *Diplomatarium islandicum* (*Íslenzkt fornbréfasafn*), a collection of medieval documents. Charter information on the church reaches back further in time than on the secular buildings at Reykholt. In the earliest entry for the farm buildings, dated to 1503, the main buildings are listed, together with what they are worth, "kirkjan firir u. c. stofan firir x. c. skalenn firir uij c. forstofan oc onden oc elldaskalenn firir iij. c. buret oc skemman firir c. enn oll útihús firir c. oc x. aurar betur baðstofan oc gongin oc þarbohus firir iij. c.".[7] The value of the individual buildings tells us something about how elaborately they are constructed and can be taken as an indication of the amount of usable wood in the buildings.

5   Guðrún Sveinbjarnardóttir 2012a; 2016. The following discussion is based on these works where the remains are also described in more detail.
6   Úlfar Bragason 2005, 441; Gunnar Karlsson 2007, 203–205.
7   "The church 5 hundred, *stofa* 10 hundred, *skáli* 7 hundred, hallway, entrance and kitchen 3 hundred, pantry and storage room 1 hundred, all the outhouses 1 hundred and 10 aurar, work room, passageway and privy 3 hundred" (*DI* VII, 667).

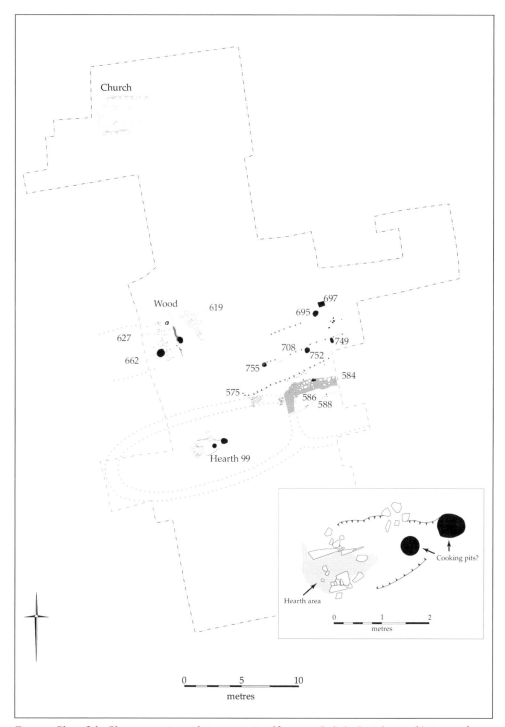

Church

Wood 619

627

662

695

697

749

708 752

755

575 584

586 588

Hearth 99

Cooking pits?

Hearth area

0 1 2
metres

0 5 10
metres

Figure 4. Plan of the Phase 1 remains with interpretation (fig. 12 in Guðrún Sveinbjarnardóttir 2012a).

This interpretation is supported by information in a source where the rebuilding of the church after 1528 is described. The church was made of driftwood from Trékyllisvík in the West, and the value of this rebuilt church was estimated to be forty hundreds[8] in 1537.[9] The archaeological evidence indicates that in the sixteenth century the church was a large wooden building (probably referring to the Phase 3ii church). Before the rebuilding the value of the church was only five hundreds, suggesting that it was in a bad state of repair at that time, containing little in the way of usable wood. In comparison, the value of the *stofa* and *skáli* was ten and seven hundreds respectively. Although this information post-dates the period which is being discussed in this article, it gives some indication of the nature of the sources that tell us something about the quality of the buildings and gives a vivid indication of how impressive the farm buildings must have been at that time.

The archaeological remains belonging to Phase 1

The cultural remains that belong to Phase 1 are fragmentary and do not give a comprehensive picture of the initial occupation phase of the farm site. This phase is dated to around AD 1000 on the basis of radiocarbon dates obtained on charred barley discovered in a hearth. The hearth took the form of an elongated depression, placed directly on top of and partly sunken into the natural subsoil. It was a longhearth (*langeldr*), about 1.5 metres in length, of a type that is common in the early hall buildings in Iceland, with the remains of a stone setting and a stone-lined box (*felu-hola*) about 0.4 metres deep at one end, covered with a fire-cracked flat stone, which contained the charred barley. To the east of the longhearth there were two circular hollows which may have been used as cooking pits. The total length of the elongated depression, including the pits, was around 3.5 metres. Remains of turf walls containing the *landnám* tephra[10] were found close to the hearth but could not be associated with it directly with any certainty. These fragmentary remains are interpreted as those of a turf-built longhouse, about 15 metres long, with a central hearth,

---

8   120 ells of homespun. From the latter half of the fourteenth century it was as a rule the equivalent of one legal cow or six legal ewes. In earlier times it could vary somewhat. It was also used as a measurement in the estimation of land value. An average farmland was valued at 20 hundreds.

9   Benedikt Eyþórsson 2008, 61.

10 Until recently dated to 871±2 (Karl Grönvold *et al.* 1995), now corrected to 877±1 (Schmid *et al.* 2016).

orientated roughly east-west, placed at the southern end of the group of farm buildings belonging to this phase (fig. 3). Fragmentary remains to the east of it have been interpreted as a separate building which was probably attached to it. The arrangement of separate buildings placed in a row seems to be a development post-dating the Viking period hall.[11] The picture which can be gained on the basis of these remains of the layout of the farm site during its earliest period of occupation is of a longhouse orientated approximately north-east to south-west with additional buildings of similar orientation to the east and north of it. No written sources exist for that period.

About 15 metres to the north of the farm site, at the old church site which is located within the present cemetery, a building of a similar date to the longhouse at the farm site was discovered. The dating is based on radiocarbon dates on birchwood found in the earliest floor deposits and on stratigraphy. The building was unusual in that it consisted of a sunken featured building, approximately 4.5 metres by 2.5 metres (or around 11.25 square metres in area internally), sunk by about 1.2 metres into natural subsoil, with the wall foundations inside the cut made of stone and turf. There is some indication, however, that this earliest building extended further to the east where there was a chancel in later structures. This is suggested by the remains of what is interpreted as large post holes in this area which pre-date the Phase 2 churches (see fig. 4). If this interpretation is correct, the building would have been longer than other eleventh-century churches known in Iceland, which range from 2.7 to 5 metres in length.[12] Only disturbed floor material was discovered within the building foundation which, if this was indeed a church, would be most likely to represent a cellar or crypt beneath a wooden floor. Small flat stones at even intervals along the sides are interpreted as post-pads, perhaps for internal panelling or to support a floor. No remains of protective walls of stone and turf were found on the outside of the sunken area. The building is interpreted to have been made of wood, and samples from inside the building were analysed as larch and pine.[13] Larch will almost

---

11   See e.g. some of the sites in Þjórsárdalr (Stenberger 1943, figs. 58, 69) and Aðalstræti in Reykjavík (Roberts *et al.* 2003).

12   For a list of early churches in Iceland and their dimensions see Table 30 in Guðrún Sveinbjarnardóttir 2016.

13   Lísabet Guðmundsdóttir 2008.

certainly have arrived in Iceland as driftwood.[14] This building foundation forms part of the subsequent church buildings at Reykholt and is for that reason, and the lack of a convincing alternative interpretation,[15] assumed to have been used for religious purposes.[16]

The archaeological remains belonging to Phase 2

Building remains belonging to Phase 2, coinciding with Snorri's occupation at Reykholt, were better preserved. The remains include two building foundations, 10/11 and 12, conduits which run between the hot spring and the farm mound, part of the wall which encloses the farm buildings and runs into the old cemetery wall, the subterranean passageway which runs from the Snorralaug into the farm complex which, together with its water-conduits, is also regarded as belonging to this phase, a midden which revealed information about the economy and ecology of the site in the medieval period, a church, and a smithy to the north of it (fig. 5).

The pool and subterranean passageway

A pool at Reykholt is mentioned in *Landnámabók*, where it is not described in any detail, but is said to have been used by the inhabitants of the farm Breiðabólstaðr, which lies about a kilometre to the east of Reykholt and is listed as the earliest farm in the area.[17] It is not known whether it was in the same place as the present pool. The earliest description of the pool in the form it has today, circular in shape, about four metres in diameter, built of stone with a flagged floor and benches (see fig. 6), dates to 1724.[18] The pool is fed with hot water from the hot spring which is located about a hundred metres to the east of it, through a stone-built conduit. It has not undergone any archaeological investigation and is only dated through its apparent association with the subterranean passageway, part of which was excavated and dated to Phase 2. It is potentially the only structure at the site which can be directly connected to Snorri Sturluson, as indicated

---

14 Ólafur Eggertsson 1993.
15 The sunken nature of the building makes it similar to a pit house, but these always had fireplaces and post- and pin-holes (see Milek 2012) none of which is present in the Reykholt structure.
16 Guðrún Sveinbjarnardóttir 2016.
17 *Íslendingabók, Landnámabók*, 192–193.
18 Páll Vídalín 1854, 42–43.

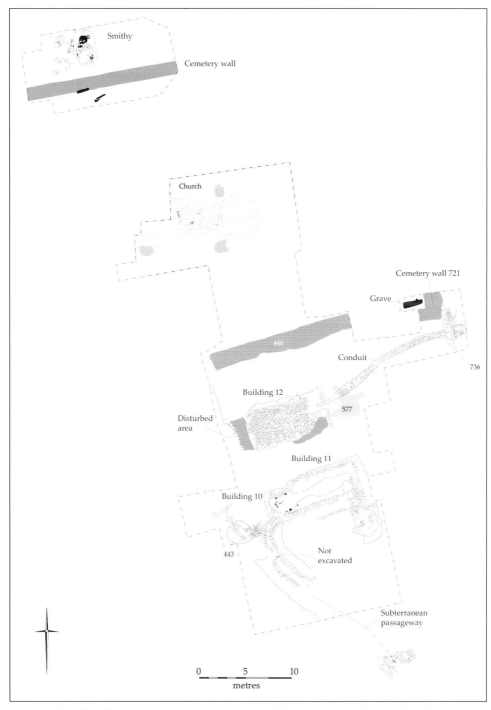

Figure 5. Plan of the Phase 2 remains at Reykholt, with the Phase 2ii church which may have been built during Snorri's time (fig. 15 in Guðrún Sveinbjarnardóttir 2012a).

Figure 6. Snorralaug before its restoration in 1959 with the subterranean passage-way in the background which was first restored in 1941. Photo: Þjms. Gísli Gestsson.

by the description of the pool in *Sturlunga saga*: "Þat var eitt kveld, er Snorri sat í laugu, at talat var um höfðingja".[19]

The subterranean passageway leading from the pool into the farm mound is about 36 metres long and runs uphill to the corner of one of the southernmost buildings at the farm site, Building 10. It was made in such a way that a trench about 2.5 metres wide was dug down to a depth of around 0.6 metres. In the middle of this trench a narrower trench was dug into which the dry-stone built walls of the passageway were inserted, creating a passage which was a maximum of about 0.8 metres wide. The walls were preserved up to a maximum height of about 1.4 metres and the floor was made up of dense tuff (fig. 7). The passageway was almost

19   "It was one evening, when Snorri sat in the pool, that chieftains were discussed" (*Sturlunga saga* I, 319).

certainly roofed, with the frame resting on the stone walls or just outside them, on top of the upper step of the trench. The only possible remains of a roof discovered during the excavation are some turf remains in the fill, but these could also come from elsewhere.

Figure 7. The subterranean passageway under excavation in 1941. Photo: Bjarni Árnason.

The dating of the Phase 2 remains places them in the time Snorri Sturluson lived at Reykholt, a period which is described in *Sturlunga saga*. It is this phase that gives the best opportunity for a comparison with the written sources, mostly *Íslendinga saga*.[20] Snorri is said to have had a secure fort ("virki øruggt") erected around his farm. It had two entrances, one from the north via the cemetery, the other from the south by the pool, and the wall was so high that a ladder had to be used to mount it.[21] Access from the south is said to be via a *forskáli* leading from the pool.[22] This is generally assumed to refer to the subterranean passageway which was excavated and is described above. It is not clear from the description whether the fort was made of timber, or stone and turf. Timber-built fortifications are known in Scandinavia during medieval times, for example Danevirke at Hedeby in Denmark,[23] whereas the fort at Eyri (Eyrr) in Arnarfjǫrðr (modern Hrafnseyri), mentioned in *Sturlunga saga*, was evidently made of stone.[24] During recent investigations at Eyri a row of large stones was discovered, similar to the one found at Reykholt (see below). They belong to a stone and turf wall which seems to have been two metres wide.[25] When the study area was enlarged, it was established that the wall belonged to an enclosure rather than a building.[26]

It might have been difficult to lift somebody up onto a high timber-built fortification,[27] and equally difficult to build such a high structure of stones and turf alone. A combination of the two might therefore have been a perfect solution. The row of large stones, marking the eastern boundary of the farm site at Reykholt, which runs into the south-east corner of the turf wall enclosing the cemetery (see fig. 5), may well have served as the foundation for a fortification made in this way. The turf-built cemetery wall seems to continue to the west (446 in fig. 5). The foundation of the north side of the fortification would then have been made of turf alone and that part of the foundation wall would have served

---

20   The following discussion is based on Guðrún Harðardóttir 2006, and Guðrún Sveinbjarnardóttir 2009b.
21   *Sturlunga saga* I, 456.
22   *Sturlunga saga* I, 388.
23   Hellmuth Andersen *et al.* 1976.
24   *Sturlunga saga* I, 221.
25   Margrét H. Hallmundsdóttir and Guðný Zoëga 2013, figs. 4 and 5.
26   Margrét H. Hallmundsdóttir, e-mail 3 December 2015.
27   See *Sturlunga saga* II, 155.

three functions: as the northernmost wall in the farm complex, the south side of the cemetery and as a fortification wall. A narrative from *Sverris saga* (The Saga of King Sverrir Sigurðarson) is of interest in this context for throwing light on how the timber element of the fortification might have been put together: "Kastalarnir váru svá gǫrvir at stafir fjórir stóðu ok syllr upp í milli ok þar á inar neðri hurðir milli stafanna. ...".[28] The upper part of the fortification at Reykholt might have been constructed in a similar way.

Building complex 10/11

This structure consists of a sunken foundation which, although representing a structure slightly less than 10 metres long and 2.3 to 2.85 metres wide, seems to have had two activity areas (see fig. 5). In the smaller and narrower space, Building 10, which takes up about three metres of the total length in the west end of the foundation, there were some fragmentary floor layers and remains of wooden panelling, whereas the larger space, Building 11, had no floor layers. Here there was a fairly broad feature carved into the natural soil along the centre, creating bench-like elevations along the sides, and a paved passageway serving as an entrance in the south-east corner the access to which was sunken. The foundation is that of a cellar on top of which the house proper must have rested. The wall foundations were made of a single row of stones facing into the building, backed with earth and turf. The building was dug into a slope with the depth varying from 0.25 metres in the west to up to a metre in the east end. Lying parallel to the outside of the south wall, at a distance of about 1.5 metres, there were the remains of a single row of stones which marks the outer edge. The internal width of the building, between the inner stone faces, is narrow for any kind of building. It is suggested that this space simply represents a cellar, while the floor of the building would have extended all the way to the outer stone face of the wall.[29] That way the internal width of the building would have been at least 5 metres, or even as much as 6.5 metres if there was originally a similar row of stones on the north side. However, there was no sign of this during the excavation. Interpreting the floor area in that way, the

---

28 "The fortifications were made with four upright posts with staves between them, where the lower doors were placed" (*Sverris saga,* 269).

29 We are grateful to architect Hjörleifur Stefánsson for suggesting this possibility.

Figure 8. Building complex 10/11 under excavation, looking south-east. Photo: Guðrún Sveinbjarnardóttir.

total internal area of Building complex 10/11 would have been 50 or 65 square metres.

The subterranean passageway turns approximately 45 degrees to the east into the corner of the west end of this building complex where it was mounted by stone steps through a circular staircase (fig. 9). The fact that it runs into the south wall rather than directly into the building indicates that either it is not contemporary with that part of the building or it was deliberately run into the wall to hide it. Although it is not possible now to be certain of this, the latter suggestion is preferred since there are no signs of the passageway having run anywhere other than into the sunken foundation of Building 10, and there is every reason to believe that the whole of the south wall of Building complex 10/11 is contemporary.

The sunken stone foundation of Building complex 10/11 has been interpreted as a cellar, most likely for a wooden building. This suggestion is not based on the discovery during the excavation of remains of

Figure 9. The circular staircase. Photo: Guðrún Sveinbjarnardóttir.

structural wood, but rather on the fact that the foundation is a sunken stone construction with comparisons in Norway where timber buildings rested on similar foundations during the medieval period. The timber remains discovered were insignificant and probably only the remains of posts, panelling and perhaps flooring. Any significant structural timbers would have been removed and recycled when the building fell out of use. The narrow sunken area is further support for this interpretation. It is suggested that it represents a cellar in the central part of the building only, while the floor within the building would have been wider, extending all the way to the outer stone edge of the walls, part of which was preserved in the south wall. Such a design is reminiscent of a Norwegian *stafloft*, although that type of building is not sunken. Today most *lofts* are raised above the ground on a wooden frame or stone pillars.[30]

30   See e.g. the figure in Guðrún Harðardóttir 2006, 56.

Interpreting the extent of the floor within the building in this way makes it similar in size to the floor space in *stofur* (sing. *stofa*) of the medieval period in Norway. The best known of these is the thirteenth-century Raulands-stova in Uvdal in Numadalr (Numedal), which is 52 square metres in size internally (58 square metres with the two smaller rooms).[31] Cellars are not common in *stofur* in Norway during this period, but are sometimes found at larger farms, where they generally only extended under part of the building.[32] An exception is the Lagmannsstova in Aga in Harðangr (Hardanger), dated to the late thirteenth century, where the two-roomed cellar extends under the whole of the building.[33]

The foundations of the byre and barn built in 1929 cut right into the outside of the east gable wall of Building 11, obliterating any structural remains that may have been in that area before. There is no evidence of an entrance into another building in that location, but a building of equal size to 10/11 would fit into the space between it and a line marking the eastern extent of the farm mound, in a straight southerly direction from the previously mentioned boundary wall fragment. A row of two buildings placed end to end could thus be created, perhaps similar in layout to the farm complex at Grọf in Ørœfi, for example, which was abandoned during an eruption in Ørœfajökull in 1362,[34] or even the one at Stọng in Þjórsárdalr to some extent, which, according to recent research, may have been occupied until the thirteenth century.[35] It is also possible that there was a building at right angles to Building complex 10/11 in this space, as suggested by Þórhallur Þráinsson in his reconstruction drawing (see fig. 10). Both suggestions will, however, have to remain a hypothesis, since the area has been completely destroyed by the deep foundations of the twentieth-century byre and barn. Whatever the case was, the layout of the buildings at Reykholt during Phase 2 differs from that at the above-mentioned sites and the nature of Building complex 10/11 is unique, with no known parallels in Iceland to date.

31   Ekroll 2017, 225ff.; Berg 1989, 156–157.
32   Berg 1989, 156.
33   Øye 2002, 285.
34   Gísli Gestsson 1959.
35   Roussell 1943; Vilhjálmur Ö. Vilhjálmsson 1989.

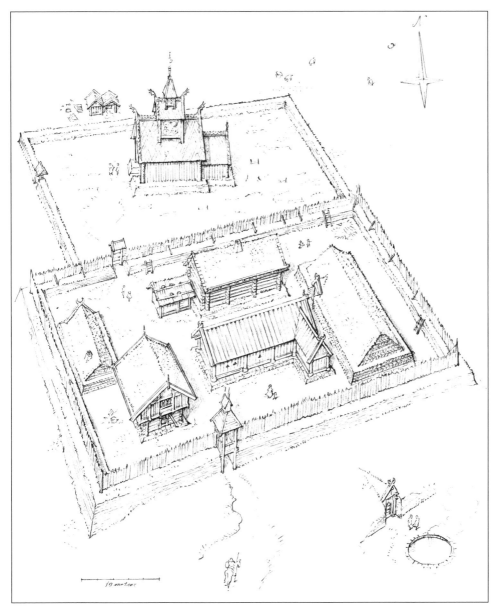

Figure 10. Reconstruction of the Phase 2 buildings at Reykholt, based in part on the excavated remains. The building in the middle at the front is Building complex 10/11 into which corner on the left the subterranean passageway from the pool ran. The complex may have housed the *stofa* and *litlastofa* mentioned in *Sturlunga saga*. Parallel to it at the back is Building 12. The *skáli* would have been to the right, the *litluhús* with loft and *kjallari* to the left, and the *skemma* where Snorri slept, behind them. To the north of the church is the smithy. Drawing: Þórhallur Þráinsson.

Building 12

Just to the north of Building complex 10/11, with the same orientation, the remains of a paved building foundation, Building 12, were encountered. The paved area was about 6.8 metres long and 3.5 metres wide. Adding the unpaved area in the east end makes the building about 8.6 metres long, or a total of around 30 square metres in size internally (see fig. 5). The long walls were made of an inner face of stones, with a maximum of three layers preserved. Three columns built of stone up to a height of about 0.65 metres rested directly on the paved floor up against the south wall, at intervals of about a metre. They were to a large extent built of geyserite stones.[36] On top of all three columns there were large flat stones made of geyserite, close to a metre in diameter. The one on the middle column had a man-made hole about 10 centimetres in diameter in the centre. At the north wall the collapsed remains of only the middle column were found. It is assumed that there were originally also three columns at the north wall, which were torn down when the building ceased being used and the stones re-used elsewhere. The evidence for this are pavements and wall fragments to the north and east of the building made of geyserite, which post-date it. They include a flat stone fragment with a man-made hole in it about 7.5 centimetres in diameter, which may originally have rested on one of the columns in Building 12. The flat stones in the floor of the building, most of which were of geyserite, were rather small, laid tightly together and firmly into gravel. Just to the east of the middle of the paved area there was a circular depression, 1.15 by 1.25 metres in size and a maximum of around 0.6 metres in depth, stone-lined at the base but not on the sides, which seems to be contemporary with the floor (fig. 5). This was the only internal feature in the building. A pile of small stones covered in hot-spring deposit was discovered lying in loose turf in the south-east corner of the building. It is suggested that these stones, which have been exposed to geothermal water or steam, may in some way have been associated with the heating generated in the building.

The conduit, which was excavated from just to the east of the boundary wall marking the eastern extent of the farm site, ran into the building. It was sunk into the ground, the sides were made of stone and it was

36 Geyserite is a brittle, easily carved material formed in geothermal areas. The nearest outcrop is above the farm Úlfsstaðir, c. 2.5 kilometres to the north of Reykholt.

covered with flat stones and turf on top creating a space about 0.17 metres wide and 0.25 metres high through which the hot air or steam will have travelled, presumably from the hot spring Skrifla, which lies about a hundred metres away, although later disruptions in the area meant that it was not possible to establish a connection. Some wood remains were discovered within it suggesting that it may have been lined with wood, but the evidence for this is insubstantial. The conduit seems to have been partly dismantled by the time it was excavated.

The boundary wall underneath which the conduit ran was preserved for a length of around 4.5 metres, at which point it was cut by the foundations of the twentieth-century byre and barn (fig. 5). It was made of large boulders which had been smoothed on the side facing outwards and were placed in a row which ran into the cemetery wall which was built of turf containing the *landnám* tephra (fig. 11). Remains of what seems to be the same cemetery wall appeared in further sections along the northern edge of the excavation area and also running along the length of the foundation of the old church which is still standing, built in 1886/7 (fig. 5). The site of the previous church, which was excavated, lies right in the centre of the cemetery enclosed by this wall.

Attempts to reconstruct Building 12 with the help of architects have not led to any single conclusion, although discussions have been useful. Like Building complex 10/11, Building 12 is unusual, so far with no known parallels. Both gables of the building seem to have been made of an inner and an outer face of stones filled with turf in the middle, with the conduit running through and underneath the entrance in the east gable. The construction of the side walls is less clear. A trench seems to have been dug for a stone wall foundation facing into the building. There were no remains of an outer row of stones like in the gables, and the only remains of turf were found at the south-east corner and as collapse within the building, but these could have come from the roof. The compressive strength of the geyserite stones used in the stone columns on the inside of the side walls was measured showing that the material does not have great strength and the columns would not have been strong enough to carry roof-supports, for example.[37] With a width of 3.5 metres, the roof could just have rested directly on the walls, or on posts placed on the

---

37   Rannsóknarstofnun byggingariðnaðarins, rannsókn nr. H03/622 dated 11.9.2003. A report kept in the Reykholt excavation archives at the National Museum of Iceland.

Figure 11. Boundary wall and conduit, looking west. Photo: Björn Sveinsson.

flagstone floor up against the walls. The stone columns obviously served a very particular function in the building, perhaps as part of some kind of internal fitting the nature of which is, however, uncertain. The use of the building is also uncertain, although the presence of the conduit leading into it, the paved floor and absence of any finds have prompted the suggestion that it may have been used as a bath-house.[38] An alternative suggestion, based on the heat being fed into the building and the discovery of insect remains in the nearby rubbish heap [577] associated with mouldy grain, is that it was possibly used in connection with brewing.[39] Both interpretetions are open to doubt. Attempts to match this building to any

38   Guðrún Sveinbjarnardóttir 2005. But see discussion in Guðrún Sveinbjarnardóttir 2012a.
39   Guðrún Sveinbjarnardóttir 2009.

particular house named in *Sturlunga saga* have produced no convincing conclusion.

The Smithy

The remains of a medieval smithy were discovered underneath the old church built in 1886/87 during its renovation.[40] It contained a cistern 0.8 metres deep and built of stone, dug into the natural substrate and lined on the inside with flat stones of geyserite, and a hearth which contained evidence of metalworking with precious metals. Pieces of slag were found, one of which was identified as smelting slag, i.e. the residue of iron ore extraction. Other ironworking equipment was discovered as well as an area for wood storage. The extent of the floor deposit indicates that the smithy was about 3 by 2 metres in size, and since no signs were found of walls it was suggested that the work was carried out in the open. Post-holes in the wood storage area were interpreted as the remains of some kind of shelter. A sample of charred birch collected from the hearth was radiocarbon dated with calibrated estimates falling between AD 1040 and 1260.[41] No descriptions of a smithy at Reykholt exist which are contemporary with the archaeological remains.

The Church

The Type 2 church made use of the foundations of the earlier building. A chancel has now definitely been added at its eastern end which was sunk to the same depth, marked by large boulders, with small flat stones along the sides, similar to the ones in the earlier building, serving as post-pads. The building was also extended to the west. The walls in the nave had largely been removed as a result of later building activities. What remained were large post-pads at even intervals. Parallel to them, but lying inside the nave, two continuous rows of stones appeared, interpreted as the remains of wall foundations, at the earlier stage only supporting the side walls and a wooden floor.

The sunken space in the nave and chancel could have served as a cellar or crypt area, although no traces of burials were found. There are no other known churches in Iceland with such sunken spaces, but the eleventh-century churches at Varnhem in Västergötland and the Church

---

40 Agnes Stefánsdóttir and Kristinn Magnússon 2005.
41 Guðrún Sveinbjarnardóttir 2012a, table 2.

of the Holy Trinity in Lund, Sweden, had sunken spaces, both under the nave and the chancel, which have been interpreted as burial chambers or for storing valuables.[42] There are references in written sources to churches in Iceland having been used for storage, at least during turbulent times.[43]

The nave and chancel of the earlier phase of this building type were roughly of the same width. During the second phase, the width of the nave was increased considerably with the addition of large circular post-holes (about 1.5 metres in diameter) on both sides, just outside the cut for the church, where the chancel and nave meet, and outside the corners of the west gable (see figs. 5 and 12; the one assumed to be in the north-west corner remains unexcavated). They contained gravel and large stones on which the posts will have rested, forming part of the stave construction. The size of the post-holes clearly indicates how large the posts which rested in them must have been. This is a further indication of the great height of the building. The internal width of the nave would thus have been 5.8 metres, of the chancel 3.5 metres and the total length is estimated to have been around 12 metres, making the internal space a total of about 60 square metres. By way of comparison, the total length of the timber church from 1886 still standing at Reykholt is close to 15 metres. At this stage the internal wall foundations divided the nave into three aisles, making it into a basilica-type church. Although this church is believed to have been made entirely of wood, there were remains of very fragmentary turf walls in two places, on the outside of the south and north walls. Similar protective walls have been suggested for the medieval church at Skálholt.[44] The Type 2 church at Reykholt is dated to between the twelfth and fourteenth centuries on the basis of radiocarbon dates on charred wood and the objects found,[45] and therefore belongs to the period Snorri lived there.

This church was replaced by a somewhat larger building, the Type 3 church, the two phases of which are now dated to between the fourteenth and sixteenth centuries.[46] The sunken foundation was filled with stones, the walls in the nave rested on long slabs of geyserite laid into gravel, serving the same function as dry-stone walls in churches for example in

---

42   Vretemark 2017, 152; Cinthio 1997.
43   See e.g. *Sturlunga saga* I, 392, 421.
44   Hörður Ágústsson 1990, 298, fig. 155.
45   Guðrún Sveinbjarnardóttir 2009, 62; 2016.
46   Guðrún Sveinbjarnardóttir 2016.

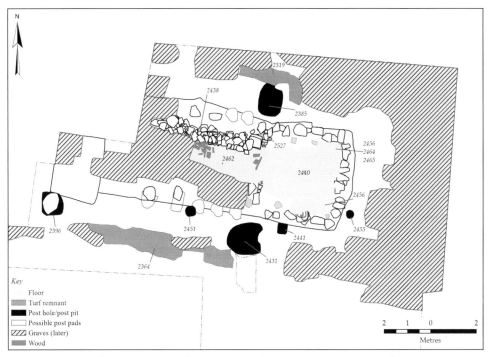

Figure 12. The church during Phase 2ii (fig. 4.2.10 in Guðrún Sveinbjarnardóttir 2016).

Norway, the *aurstokkar*, on which the stave construction rested. During
the second phase of this type an entrance was added in the south wall and
passageways or wings along the side walls. This church was now around
13 metres long and a maximum of around 8 metres wide including the
wings, making it about 95 square metres in area internally. This is the
largest of the medieval churches at Reykholt, coinciding with the height
of its wealth, according to the written sources, in the fifteenth century.[47]

The first church charter, which gives some idea about the building,
dates to 1358.[48] It lists a large number of altar cloths suggesting that at the
time the church had a number of altars. It also lists clothing for eleven
members of the clergy indicating that the church enjoyed the services
of several clerics at that time.[49] After the Reformation the system for

47 Benedikt Eyþórsson 2008, 40–42.
48 *DI* III, 123.
49 Guðrún Harðardóttir 2003, 17. Benedikt Eyþórsson (2005, 112–114) estimates,

keeping an eye on the property of the church was made more rigorous. This manifests itself in the introduction of appraisal records. The oldest of such preserved records for the church date to 1664, and for the farm buildings to 1732. The closer to the present the records get, the more detailed they become.

There is no mention in the written sources of Snorri having had a church built, but his donation of sacred objects mentioned in *Reykja-holtsmáldagi* is of interest. It is somewhat confusing and difficult to determine from the *máldagi* who gave what. But it is clear that Snorri and the priest Magnús, who occupied Reykholt before Snorri, together gave a reliquary to the church: "Skrin þat es stendr a altara meþ helgom domom gefa þeir Magnús oc Snorre at helfninge hvarr þeirra oc es þetta kirkiofe umb fram of þat es aþr es talet".[50] They may have given the reliquary as a symbol of the agreement they made between themselves at the time. Such a reliquary would have been a prestigious gift, both as a piece of artwork and because of the relic itself. For comparison, the importance of a donation of a relic is presented as a grand gesture in *Magnúsarsona saga* (The Saga of the Magnússons) in *Heimskringla*, when King Sigurðr Jórsalafari (Jerusalemfarer) Magnússon presented the relic of the Holy Cross to the church at Konungahella along with other precious objects.[51] The later medieval charters of the Reykholt church indicate that the reliquary Snorri and Magnús gave remained in the churches of Reykholt until 1538, when it is mentioned in an inventory for the last time.[52] It is not revealed by the charter which relic was in the shrine, but we are told in *Reykjaholtsmáldagi* that "Kirkia su er stendr i reykiahollti es helguð með guði Mariv moðvr drottins ok hinum helga petro postula ok envm hælga dionisio biskvpi ok henni helgv Barbare meyio".[53] It has been suggested

based on other inventories in Iceland, that there were four or five clerics at Reykholt at that time, while Gunnar F. Guðmundsson (2016, 169) suggests that there were two priests and a deacon, by comparing it with the church at Laufás in northern Iceland and giving examples of how a church could inherit vestments over a long period of time.

50 "Magnús and Snorri give the shrine with relics that stands on the altar, each giving half, and it is church property in addition to that which has previously been listed" (*DI* I, 351; *Reykjaholtsmáldagi*, 14–15).

51 *Heimskringla* III, 276.

52 *DI* X, 397.

53 "The church that stands at Reykjaholt is dedicated with God to Mary the mother of Our Lord and to the Holy Apostle Peter and to the Holy Bishop Dionysius and to the Holy Virgin Barbara" (*DI* I, 476–477; *Reykjaholtsmáldagi*, 14–15).

that the cult of St Dionysius (St Denis) in Reykholt and Viðey stems from Snorri Sturluson.[54] On that basis, it is quite possible that the donated reliquary indeed held a relic of St Dionysius, athough St Peter is also a strong candidate, being the patron saint of the church.

In addition to the reliquary Snorri also donated some church bells and some vellum to the church of Reykholt. In *Reykjaholtsmáldagi* it is documented that Snorri and his wife Hallveig gave more than one bell to the church, and that Snorri gave six calf hides: "Kirkia a enn um fram klukur þær er þav Snorre ok halveig leggia til staðar... Snorri Sturlus vi kalfascinn".[55] The enrichment of the church was one way for a chieftain to make his status and power visible.

The liturgical development in Iceland has only been investigated to a very limited extent. It is, however, to be expected that the liturgical practices at a place like Reykholt would have carried a great deal of prestige, since the most prominent chieftains at the time would have been ambitious in that respect for their churches.[56] An illustration of this can be found in an example taken from *Sturlunga saga* during the residency of Egill Sǫlmundarson, son of Helga, the sister of Snorri Sturluson, at Reykholt when Þorgils *skarði* (Harelip) paid him a visit:

> Lögðust þeir Þorgils þá til svefns ok allr flokkr nema þeir menn, er vöktu, en Egill bjó til greiða. Ok er Þorgils vaknaði, lét hann syngja sér messu De Sancta Margareta. En er tíðum var lokit, gengu þeir í stofu. Var hún vel tjölduð ok upp settir bjórar. Var þá Egill inn glaðasti ok beini inn bezti ok drukkit nökkut af alþjóð. En er menn váru mettir, lét Egill kalla Þorgils ok Sturlu, ... í litlustofu ok svá margt manna, svá at [litla]stofan var full. Var þá drukkit fast ok veizla in bezta.[57]

---

54 Cormack 1994, 93.

55 "The church owns, in addition to the bells which Snorri and Hallveig donate to the estate ... Snorri Sturluson 6 calfskins" (*DI* I, 467–477; *Reykjaholtsmáldagi*, 14–15).

56 Kristján Valur Ingólfsson 2006, 447.

57 "The group lay down to sleep with Þorgils, except for those who kept watch and Egill provided with refreshments. When Þorgils woke up he arranged for a mass De Sancta Margareta to be sung, after which they went to the *stofa* which was adorned with wall hangings, and with wall hangings on wooden gables. Egill was cheerful and the faire was good and there was some general drinking. When the people were satiated, Egill had Þorgils and Sturla ... called to the *litlastofa* together with many others until the room was full. There was heavy drinking and a good feast" (*Sturlunga saga* II, 172).

This narrative presents itself as a description of an extravagance, of which the liturgical practice is a part, together with the decorations and the refreshments.

Cemeteries, but in particular churches, often served as defences for homes during the Commonwealth period.[58] There are numerous accounts of this in the written sources, such as the one in *Þorgils saga skarða* in *Sturlunga saga*, relating to Reykholt, where the fortification wall surrounding the farm buildings is also mentioned. Egill Sǫlmundarson flees to the church when he sees Þorgils *skarði* with his army approaching. Egill subsequently asks for mercy, which is granted and he can then leave the church safely,[59] and invites Þorgils to the feast quoted above.

Names of buildings in Sturlunga saga

The buildings at Reykholt mentioned in the narratives of *Sturlunga saga* are the following: a hall (*skáli*), which, from the wording, must have been located roughly mid-way between the two entrances in the fort. It could be accessed directly from the outside and seems to have been separate from the *eldahús* (from where fire was fetched).[60] The hall had many beds[61] and windows in the roof.[62] In 1233 a living room (*stofa*) was built of wood fetched from Skagafjǫrðr in the North.[63] Both imported wood and driftwood were used for building houses in Iceland. In this case it is more likely that the wood was imported since Reykholt did not own the rights to driftwood collection in the North, but rather in the West.[64] Further support for this interpretation is that there was a harbour for ocean-going vessels at Kolbeinsáróss (Kolkuóss) in Skagafjǫrðr at that time.[65] This is probably where the wood was fetched from, suggesting that it was imported. The description does not indicate whether the *stofa* was made of stone and turf with internal panelling, as, for example, the one at Stǫng in Þjórsárdalr seems to have been,[66] or exclusively of wood like

---

58   Guðrún Harðardóttir and Þór Hjaltalín 1998.
59   *Sturlunga saga* II, 171–172.
60   *Sturlunga saga* II, 155.
61   *Sturlunga saga* II, 155.
62   *Sturlunga saga* I, 456.
63   *Sturlunga saga* I, 362.
64   *DI* III, 122–123.
65   Archaeological investigations indicate that there was activity at the site from the tenth until the sixteenth century, http://holar.is/holarannsoknin/kolkuos/index.html, accessed 28 September 2011.
66   Hörður Ágústsson 1987, 327.

the Norwegian ones. No remains of log-constructed buildings have been found in Iceland, but a description of the *stofa* built in the fourteenth century by Bishop Auðun rauði (the Red) Þorbergsson at Hólar indicates that it was built in that way (fig. 13).[67] During recent excavations at Hólar the remains of a building, interpreted as a *stofa* built of wood, were discovered. It was 7.7 by 4.5 metres in size (34.65 square metres in area) and stood separate from the other buildings. The outer walls were made of stone and turf, except for the north gable which was made of wood. Several hearths were discovered in the floor. The building has been dated to between the twelfth and thirteenth centuries[68] and would therefore have been contemporary with the *stofa* at Reykholt, but preceeding Bishop Auðun's *stofa* by some thirty years. Timber-built *stofur* of similar dates to the one at Reykholt are also known from Papa Stour in Shetland[69] and Kirkjubœr in the Faroe Islands,[70] areas where building traditions were similar to those in Iceland. These *stofur* were equal in width and length. The description in *Sturlunga saga* does not indicate where the *stofa* at Reykholt was located in relation to the *skáli*. A list of property in a charter of the church from 1392 includes some tables giving some indication of how the *stofa* was furnished.[71]

Also mentioned is a *litlastofa* (*litla* means "small")[72] which, based on the descriptions, seems to have been entered from the *stofa* and used for private functions such as eating and drinking, and for sleeping in. It is suggested that it was the private room of the master of the household and might as such have served as Snorri's scriptorium.[73] *Litluhús* with *loft* above and cellar (*kjallari*) below seem to have been entered from the *litlastofa*. It was in the cellar that Snorri was killed in 1241 after leaving the *skemma* where he was sleeping.[74] Reykholt is the only place where *litluhús* are mentioned in *Sturlunga saga*, suggesting that these were special and unusual buildings in the medieval building tradition in Iceland. The *loft* was used for sleeping in and for holding several prisoners, suggesting that it must have been of reasonable size. It could have been either an attic,

67   *Biskupa sögur* III, 343–346.
68   Ragnheiður Traustadóttir 2009.
69   Crawford 2002, 27–28.
70   Stocklund 1996, 67.
71   *DI* III, 482; Hörður Ágústsson 1989, 283.
72   *Sturlunga saga* I, 395; *Sturlunga saga* II, 155, 172.
73   Guðrún Harðardóttir 2006.
74   *Sturlunga saga* I, 454.

Figure 13. A reconstruction of Auðunarstofa at Hólar. Photo: Guðrún Harðardóttir.

which seems to have been the case at Flugumýri (-mýrr) in Skagafjǫrðr,[75] whereas a *loft* at Hvammr in Dalasýsla, which has its own entrance,[76] sounds more like a Norwegian style *loft*, or in other words an individual and free-standing building. Such a building at Reykholt would have been fitting for Snorri's prestige. The *skemma*, which in later times refers to a storage building, is mentioned a few times in *Sturlunga saga* as a house for sleeping in. There are indications that it was also a free-standing building,[77] where men of high status slept.[78]

A comparison between the descriptions of the buildings in the written sources and the archaeological remains is restricted by several factors. The limited excavation area together with the damage caused by modern buildings at the site means that the excavated remains do not give a complete picture of the farm site as it was during Snorri's time there. In

75 *Sturlunga saga* I, 492.
76 *Sturlunga saga* II, 276.
77 *Sturlunga saga* I, 497.
78 *Sturlunga saga* II, 240–241.

addition, not all the buildings at the site are mentioned in *Sturlunga saga*, but, due to the narrative nature of the saga, only those in which something happened. A major difference between written descriptions of buildings and archaeological remains is also that in most cases the written sources only tell us what function the building had by giving us its name, such as a *stofa* and *eldahús*, without describing it in any detail, whereas the archaeological remains give us information about dimensions and the way a building was constructed without necessarily revealing what it was used for. Building 12 at Reykholt is an example of this.[79]

Despite these difficulties an attempt can be made to match the archaeological remains with the written descriptions in *Sturlunga saga* as follows. The wall fragment made of large stones marking the eastern limit of the farm site and running into the turf-built cemetery wall, could well represent Snorri's fort. The excavated remains suggest that the south wall of the cemetery also served as the north wall of the fortification surrounding the farm-buildings. If so, the lowest part of the fortress, at least in that location, must have been made of turf. Based on the descriptions and on comparative material known from elsewhere, the *skáli* and *eldahús* are likely to have been turfhouses, whereas the *stofa, litlastofa, loft* and *skemma* were probably timber buildings, or at least completely panelled internally. Of these, the *stofa* and *litlastofa* are most likely to have been heated. If the conduit running into Building 12 served for heating purposes, the building could be interpreted as either of these. In size it is similar to *litlustofur* that are known in the seventeenth and eighteenth centuries.[80] Alternative interpretations put forward for this building are that it was either a steam-bath house or a building used in connection with brewing,[81] but these interpretations are open to question. Neither type of building is mentioned in *Sturlunga saga*.

A more plausible candidate for the *litlastofa*, thought to have been the private room of the master, is Building 10, which has the most direct access to the pool that was used by Snorri, as described in *Sturlunga saga*. Snorralaug was the only visible remains at Reykholt that could possibly be linked to Snorri through the written sources before the excavations began in the twentieth century. If the above interpretation of Building 10 is adopted, the *stofa* would then be Building 11, since the *litlastofa* was

79   Guðrún Sveinbjarnardóttir 2009.
80   Guðrún Harðardóttir 2006, 59.
81   Guðrún Sveinbjarnardóttir 2005; 2009.

entered from there. Archaeologically, Building complex 10/11 has been interpreted as a timber building. It is suggested that the *skáli* could have been located in the space between Building complex 10/11 and the farm boundary, where the byre and barn were built in the twentieth century. The *litluhús*, which included the *loft* and *kjallari*, were entered from the *litlastofa* and would therefore, as part of this interpretation, have been to the west of complex 10/11. The archaeological evidence for buildings in that location was meagre, but included a near-circular sunken area, about 2.5 metres in diameter, which may be the remains of a building foundation in that location. The area further to the west was not excavated, but will have contained other farm buildings. Among them may have been the *skemma* in which Snorri slept. The fact that he runs from there into the cellar may indicate that neither of these was connected to the subterranean passageway, since otherwise he might have been expected to try to escape through there.[82] That interpretation fits the suggestion that the *litluhús*, which included the cellar, lay to the west of the *litlastofa*, which is interpreted as having been housed in Building complex 10/11.

Other texts that contain relevant material include *Óláfs saga helga* (The Saga of St. Óláfr (Olav)) in *Heimskringla*: "Óláfr konungr lét húsa konungsgarð í Niðarósi. Þar var gǫr mikil hirðstofa ok dyrr á báðum endum. Hásæti konungs var í miðri stofunni ...". The saga also says: "... Í garðinum var ok mikill skáli er hirðmenn sváfu í. Þar var ok mikil stofa er konungr átti hirðstefnur í".[83] The point here is that King Óláfr serves as the unquestionable model for other chieftains in the medieval period. It is therefore not unlikely that attempts were made to imitate him in building activities at a magnate's farm in Iceland and that the above description may be reflected in the buildings at Reykholt.

In *Sverris saga* we are told that during a stay at Túnsberg (Tønsberg), one of the towns Snorri visited on his travels in Norway, a person "hljóp suðr ór stofunni til heituhúsanna".[84] The *heituhús* here refers to a brewery[85] and may be relevant to the interpretation of Building 12 as a brewery,

---

82   Guðrún Harðardóttir 2006, 59.

83   "King Ólafr had a palace built at Niðaróss. It contained a royal *stofa* with doors at both gables. The king's high seat was in the middle of the *stofa* ... there was also a large *skáli* in the courtyard where the retainers slept. It also contained a large *stofa* where the king held court meetings" (*Heimskringla* II, 72–73).

84   "... ran south from the *stofa* to the brewery" (*Sverris saga*, 209).

85   Cf. *heitumaðr*, interpreted as one who makes ale (*Sturlunga saga* I, 267).

perhaps modelled on the knowledge of such a building abroad. Such an interpretation of Building 12 may also find an illustration in a quote from *Sturlunga saga* (*Þorgils saga skarða*) where brewing activity is described: "Þat höfðust menn at í Stafaholti um nóttina, at húsfreyja var at ölgerð ok með henni Björn Sigurðarson ræðismaðr ok höfðu úti hitueldinn, því at þau vildu eigi gera reyk at mönnum. Ok váru því dyrr allar opnar ...".[86]

The Wider Context – Conclusion

Snorri Sturluson was an aristocrat, brought up at Oddi, one of the most prestigious places in Iceland, and while there he must have observed upper-class living standards and ways of thinking. Snorri also travelled widely abroad. On these travels he, like other Icelandic travelling aristocrats, would have had ample opportunity to see buildings and other constructions, not least those belonging to the elite, and to gather ideas for what must have been appropriate buildings he had erected at Reykholt during his time there, thus identifying himself with the elite. Among his destinations were Norway and Götaland in Sweden, where the places he visited included Túnsberg, Þrándheimr (Trondheim) and Bjǫrgvin (Bergen). Although the influences for the buildings erected at Reykholt during Snorri's time there can therefore have been derived from various places, it is plausible to suggest that they were all built in the North Atlantic tradition, which included timber buildings, stave construction, fortifications and wooden churches. Snorri's trips abroad are referred to in *Sturlunga saga*,[87] and here Christmas drinks are also said to have been served at Reykholt in the Norwegian tradition,[88] suggesting that this was an unusual practice in Iceland. Building complex 10/11 has been interpreted as a wooden building in a style that was common in Norway, and Snorri might have seen conduits of the type discovered at the site on his visit there in 1238/39.[89] The construction of Building 12 has parallels to some extent in Norwegian building types such as *loft*

---

86 "Activities during the night at Stafaholt involved the mistress of the house brewing together with the household manager Björn Sigurðarson, keeping the fires outside so that the smoke would not bother people. The doors were all open ..." (*Sturlunga saga* II, 129).

87 E.g. *Sturlunga saga* I, 444.

88 *Sturlunga saga* I, 315.

89 Hertz 1976, 329; *Sturlunga saga* I, 444.

and *stabbur*, and, for example, the *bud* in Arnegarden, Eikrem in Volda. Here the floors of the buildings are, however, elevated, resting on the columns,[90] whereas the columns in Building 12 form part of the walls on the inside of the building. In Norway, however, this type of building was originally built more like Building 12, with the walls resting on a low stone foundation.[91] The different state of preservation of individual sites means that comparisons are problematic.

Aristocratic residences in Norway were constructed in line with European standards, with key elements being a chapel, a hall and a chamber.[92] The words used in describing Icelandic aristocratic residences appearing in *Sturlunga saga* seem to be in line with this and Reykholt is part of that picture, the *stofa* being the equivalent of a hall and the *litlastofa* being the equivalent of chamber. A *loft* would be of an additional aristocratic value.

The stave-church which stood at Reykholt during Snorri's time has some parallels in Iceland and also in Norway and the whole of the North Atlantic area.[93] Examples in Norway include the churches at Holtålen in Þrændalǫg (Trøndelag), Røldal in Harðangr and Urnes in Sogn.[94]

It is clear that none of the Norwegian examples mentioned above are exactly like the Reykholt buildings, for which there are, so far, no excavated parallels in Iceland either. In *Sturlunga saga*, Snorri is described as being very much in charge of all building activities at Reykholt: "... hafði inar beztu forsagnir á öllu því er gera skyldi".[95] This is in accordance with his position as an elite patron. As such it would be normal to copy ideas from places of a slightly higher, or at least similar, status. In view of Snorri's visits to Norway, places there would be expected to be the main source of inspiration, something that would also apply to other magnates in Iceland during the medieval period.[96] The buildings that have been excavated at Reykholt show signs of both sophistication and high status. They include unusual buildings, so far not encountered elsewhere in Iceland during the same period. The use of geothermal energy by feeding it into buildings through stone-built conduits, which could represent an adaptation of the so-called

---

90   See e.g. fig. in Guðrún Harðardóttir 2006, 59.
91   Ekroll 2017, 218.
92   Ekroll 2006, 178–179.
93   Guðrún Sveinbjarnardóttir 2009; 2016, Chapter 8.
94   Hauglid 1976, 344, 363; Christie 1959, figs. 4–6.
95   *Sturlunga saga* I, 269.
96   See also pp. 92–97 in this volume on possible influences from Western Götland.

hypocaust system, may have been seen by Snorri on his travels abroad, and most probably he saw a circular staircase in the archbishop's palace in Niðaróss (Trondheim). The use of circular staircases in the history of medieval architecture has been confined to the elite, while poorer people made do with ladders and trap-doors. Circular staircases were mainly used for communication between floors.[97] The one excavated at Reykholt leads into the building from the passageway which lies below, and is hidden in the wall of Building 10. Whether it continued up to yet another floor has not been revealed by the archaeological remains.

The excavations at Reykholt show that there was a distinct change in the arrangement and types of buildings at the site in the twelfth century. The original longhouse, built largely of turf and stone, a type of building common elsewhere in Iceland during the earliest period of settlement, seems to have been replaced by individual wooden buildings with specific functions. A similar development is also seen for example in Norway, where it occurs in general somewhat earlier, or in the eleventh century.[98]

Archaeological evidence of twelfth- and thirteenth-century buildings at sites of a similar status to Reykholt are at present thin on the ground for comparison. Other descriptions of such buildings are, on the other hand, available in the written sources. A good example is the description of Flugumýri in Skagafjǫrðr in the North, which was burnt down in 1253 according to the account in *Sturlunga saga*. Its high status is clear from comments made about the farm after it has been burnt down where it says that it was the second most impressive farm in Skagafjǫrðr after the bishop's seat at Hólar. The buildings are said to have been made to a very high standard, with the passageways leading to the *stofa* completely panelled, and the walls in the *skáli* and *stofa* profusely covered with wall hangings.[99] In the account of the burning the following buildings are mentioned: a *skáli*, divided with panelling into separate sections for men and women, a *stofa, litlastofa, búr, eldhús, gestahús, klefi*, southern and northern entrances. Some distance away from the farm complex there is a church, as well as an outdoor pantry and a fold.[100] A fortification is

97   Steane 2001, 111–112.
98   Ekroll 2017, 210.
99   *Sturlunga saga* I, 494.
100 *Sturlunga saga* I, 486–493.

also mentioned at Flugumýri.[101] The description indicates that all the buildings that are mentioned above are within the one complex since the people occupying them were unable to escape the fire. On that basis a plan of how the farm complex at Flugumýri may have looked has been drawn up.[102] It is completely modelled on farm complexes that had, not long before the plan was made, been excavated in Þjórsárdalr in the South, such as at Stǫng. The arrangement of the buildings excavated at Reykholt is somewhat different to that at Stǫng. Whether this is an indication of regional differences or a sign of status remains to be explored further when more comparative material has come to light.

The building remains unearthed during the excavations at Reykholt are certainly impressive and fitting for a chieftain of Snorri's status. A comparison between them and the descriptions of the buildings at Reykholt in *Sturlunga saga* is, however, by no means straightforward. The experiment presented in this article is a reminder of the difficulties that can be encountered when these two types of sources, written descriptions and archaeological remains, are used to support each other. But despite their incompatibility, both types of sources suggest that the buildings at Reykholt are special. This is certainly the case when comparing them with other material excavated in Iceland. It is also clear that both types of sources include definite elite elements in what they have to say about the buildings at Reykholt.

---

101 *Sturlunga saga* I, 508.
102 *Sturlunga saga* I, 486.

Bibliography

Agnes Stefánsdóttir and Kristinn Magnússon 2005. *Fornleifakönnun í grunni Reykholtskirkju í Borgarfirði. Rannsóknarskýrslur Þjóðminjasafns 2001/16.* Reykjavík: Þjóðminjasafn Íslands.

Arnheiður Sigurðardóttir 1966. *Híbýlahættir á miðöldum.* Reykjavík: Bókaútgáfa Menningarsjóðs og Þjóðvinafélagsins.

Benedikt Eyþórsson 2005. "Reykholt and Church Centres". In Helgi Þorláksson (ed.), *Church Centres. Church Centres in Iceland from the 11th to the 13th Century and their Parallels in other Countries.* Snorrastofa, vol. II. Reykholt: Snorrastofa, 105–125.

Benedikt Eyþórsson 2008. *Búskapur og rekstur staðar í Reykholti 1200–1900.* Reykjavík: Sagnfræðistofnun Háskóla Íslands.

Berg, Arne 1989. *Norske tømmerhus frå mellomalderen I. Alment oversyn.* Oslo: Riksantikvaren og Norsk folkemuseum: Landbruksforlaget.

Biskupa sögur III. Ed. Guðrún Ása Grímsdóttir. Íslenzk fornrit XVII. Reykjavík: Hið íslenzka fornritafélag, 1998.

Christie, Håkon 1959. "Urnes stavkirkes forløper belyst ved udgravninger under kirken". *Årbok for Foreningen til norske Fortidsmindesmærkers Bevaring 1958,* 49–74.

Cinthio, Maria 1997. "Trinitatskyrkan i Lund – med engelsk prägel". *Hikuin* 24, 113–134.

Cormack, Margaret 1994. *The Saints in Iceland. Their Veneration from the Conversion to 1400.* Bruxelles: Société des Bollandistes.

Crawford, Barbara E. 2002. "The Background to the Papa Stour Project". *Collegium medievale 2002,* 13–35.

DI = Diplomatarium islandicum, Íslenzkt fornbréfasafn I-XVI. Copenhagen and Reykjavík, 1857–1972.

Ekroll, Øystein 2006. "Ei anna historie". *Norsk mellomalder i arkeologisk lys.* Trondheim: Tapir.

Ekroll, Øystein 2017. "The Residences of Norwegian Magnates in the Middle Ages". In Guðrún Sveinbjarnardóttir and Bergur Þorgeirsson (eds), *The Buildings of Medieval Reykholt. The Wider Context.* Snorrastofa, vol. IX. Reykjavík: Snorrastofa and University of Iceland Press, 209–244.

Gísli Gestsson 1959. "Gröf í Öræfum". *Árbók Hins íslenzka fornleifafélags 1959,* 5–87.

Guðrún Harðardóttir 2003. "Gerðir horfinna Reykholtskirkna". Appendix 1 in Guðrún Sveinbjarnardóttir and Orri Vésteinsson, *Reykholtskirkja. Fornleifarannsókn 2002.* Skýrslur Þjóðminjasafns Íslands 2003:4, 17–23.

Guðrún Harðardóttir 2006. "The Physical Setting of Reykholt According to Sturlunga Saga". In Else Mundal (ed.), *Reykholt som makt- og lærdomssenter i den islandske og nordiske kontekst.* Snorrastofa, vol. III. Reykholt: Snorrastofa, 43–64.

Guðrún Harðardóttir and Þór Hjaltalín 1998. "Varnir heimilis í miðstjórnarlausu samfélagi. Hlutverk virkja og skipulags bæjarhúsa í ljósi Sturlungasögu". In Guðmundur J. Guðmundsson and Eiríkur K. Björnsson (eds), *Íslenska söguþingið 28.–31. maí 1997. Ráðstefnurit* I. Reykjavík: Sagnfræðistofnun Háskóla Íslands and Sagnfræðingafélag Íslands, 95–106.

Guðrún Sveinbjarnardóttir 2005. "The Use of Geothermal Resources at Reykholt in Borgarfjörður in the Medieval Period". In Andras Mortensen and Símun A. Arge (eds), *Viking and Norse in the North Atlantic. Select Papers from the Proceedings of the Fourteenth Viking Congress, Tórshavn, 19–30 July 2001.* Annales Societatis

Scientiarum Færoensis. Supplementum XLIV. Tórshavn: Føroya Fróðskaparfelag, 208–216.

Guðrún Sveinbjarnardóttir 2009a. "Kirkjur Reykholts. Byggingasaga". In Guðmundur Ólafsson and Steinunn Kristjánsdóttir (eds), *Endurfundir. Forleifarannsóknir styrktar af Kristnihátíðarsjóði 2001–2005*. Rit Þjóðminjasafns Íslands 19. Reykjavík: Þjóðminjasafn Íslands, 58–69.

Guðrún Sveinbjarnardóttir 2009b. "Fornleifafræði og sagnfræði. Hugleiðingar um túlkun mannvirkjaleifa í Reykholti í Borgarfirði". In Guðmundur Jónsson, Helgi Skúli Kjartansson and Vésteinn Ólason (eds), *Heimtur. Ritgerðir til heiðurs Gunnari Karlssyni sjötugum*. Reykjavík: Mál og menning, 176–187.

Guðrún Sveinbjarnardóttir 2012a. *Reykholt. Archaeological Excavations at a High Status Farm in Western Iceland*. Publications of the National Museum of Iceland 29. Reykjavík: Snorrastofa and the National Museum of Iceland.

Guðrún Sveinbjarnardóttir 2012b. "The Reykholt Churches: The Archaeological Evidence in a North Atlantic Context". In Helgi Þorláksson and Þóra Björg Sigurðardóttir (eds), *From Nature to Script*. Snorrastofa, vol. VII. Reykholt: Snorrastofa, 141–163.

Guðrún Sveinbjarnardóttir 2016. *Reykholt. The Church Excavations*. Publications of the National Museum of Iceland 41. Reykjavík: The National Museum of Iceland, in collaboration with Snorrastofa and University of Iceland Press.

Guðrún Sveinbjarnardóttir, Egill Erlendsson, Kim Vickers, Tom H. McGovern, Karen B. Milek, Kevin J. Edwards, Ian A. Simpson and Gordon Cook 2007. "The Palaeoecology of a High Status Icelandic Farm". *Environmental Archaeology* 12 (2), 197–216.

Guðrún Sveinbjarnardóttir and Bergur

Þorgeirsson (eds) 2017. *The Buildings of Medieval Reykholt. The Wider Context*. Snorrastofa, vol. IX. Reykjavík: Snorrastofa and University of Iceland Press.

Gunnar F. Guðmundsson 2016. "Liturgical Practices at Reykholt in the Middle Ages". In Guðrún Sveinbjarnardóttir, *Reykholt. The Church Excavations*. Reykjavík: The National Museum of Iceland, in collaboration with Snorrastofa and University of Iceland Press, 167–174.

Gunnar Karlsson 2007. *Inngangur að miðöldum*. Handbók í íslenskri miðaldasögu I. Reykjavík: Háskólaútgáfan.

Hauglid, Roar 1976. *Norske stavkirker, bygningshistorie*. Oslo: Dreyer.

Heimskringla II. Ed. Bjarni Aðalbjarnarson. Íslenzk fornrit XXVII. Reykjavík: Hið íslenzka fornritafélag, 1945.

Heimskringla III. Ed. Bjarni Aðalbjarnarson. Íslenzk fornrit XXVIII. Reykjavík: Hið íslenzka fornritafélag, 1951.

Hellmuth Andersen, H., Hans J. Madsen and Olfert Voss 1976. *Danevirke*. 2 vols. Copenhagen: I Kommission hos Gyldendalske Boghandel, Nordisk Forlag.

Hertz, Johs. 1976. "Värmeledning". *Kulturhistorisk leksikon for nordisk middelalder* XX, 328–330.

Hörður Ágústsson 1987. "Íslenski torfbærinn". In Frosti F. Jóhannsson (ed.), *Íslensk þjóðmenning* I. Reykjavík: Bókaútgáfan Þjóðsaga, 227–344.

Hörður Ágústsson 1989. "Húsagerð á síðmiðöldum". In Sigurður Líndal (ed.), *Saga Íslands* IV. Reykjavík: Hið íslenzka bókmenntafélag, Sögufélag, 261–300.

Hörður Ágústsson 1990. *Skálholt. Kirkjur*. Staðir og kirkjur I. Reykjavík: Hið íslenzka bókmenntafélag.

Íslendingabók. Landnámabók. Ed. Jakob Benedikts-

son. Íslenzk fornrit I. Reykjavík: Hið íslenska
fornritafélag, 1968.

Karl Grönvold, Níels Óskarsson, J. Johnsen,
Henrik B. Clausen, Claus U. Hammer, Gerard
Bond and Edouard Bard 1995. "Ash Layers
from Iceland in the Greenland GRIP Ice Core
Correlated with Oceanic and Land Sediments".
Earth and Planetary Science Letters 135, 149–155.

Kristján Valur Ingólfsson 2006. "Helgihald á
biskupsstólunum í Skálholti og á Hólum". In
Gunnar Kristjánsson (ed.), *Saga biskupsstólanna.
Skálholt 950 ára -Hólar 900 ára.* Akureyri: Hólar,
428–456.

Lísabet Guðmundsdóttir 2008. *Viðargreiningar
á fornum við úr kirkjum Reykholts.* BA thesis.
University of Iceland.

Margrét H. Hallmundsdóttir and Guðný Zoëga
2013. *Fornleifakönnun á Hrafnseyri við Arnarfjörð.
Framvinduskýrsla* 1. Náttúrustofa Vestfjarða, NV
nr. 14–13.

Milek, Karen B. 2012. "The Roles of Pit Houses
and Gendered Spaces on Viking-Age Farmsteads
in Iceland". *Medieval Archaeology* 56, 85–130.

Ólafur Eggertsson 1993. "Origins of Driftwood
on the Coasts of Iceland, a Dendrochronological
Study". *Jökull* 43, 15–32.

Páll Vídalín 1854. *Skýringar yfir fornyrði lögbókar
þeirrar er Jónsbók kallast.* Reykjavík: Hið íslenzka
bókmenntafélag.

Ragnheiður Traustadóttir 2009. "Ekki í kot vísað".
In Guðmundur Ólafsson and Steinunn Kristjánsdóttir (eds), *Endurfundir. Forleifarannsóknir
styrktar af Kristnihátíðarsjóði 2001–2005.* Rit
Þjóðminjasafns Íslands 19. Reykjavík: Þjóðminjasafn Íslands, 16–29.

Reykjaholtsmáldagi. Ed. Guðvarður Már Gunnlaugsson. Reykholt: Reykholtskirkja – Snorrastofa, 2000.

Roberts, Howell M., Mjöll Snæsdóttir, Natascha
Mehler and Orri Vésteinsson 2003. "Skáli frá
víkingaöld í Reykjavík". *Árbók Hins íslenzka
fornleifafélags 2000–2001,* 219–234.

Roussell, Aage 1943. "Stöng, Þjórsárdalur". In
Mårten Stenberger (ed.), *Forntida gårdar i Island.*
Copenhagen: Ejnar Munksgaard, 72–97.

Schmid, Magdalena E., Andrew J. Dugmore,
Orri Vésteinsson and Antony J. Newton 2016.
"Tephra Isochrons and Chronologies of Coloni-
sation". *Quaternary geochronology* 2016, 1–11.

Sigurður Vigfússon 1885. "Reykjaholt". *Árbók
Hins íslenzka fornleifafélags 1884–1885,* 113–124.

Steane, John M. 2001. *The Archaeology of Power.*
England and Northern Europe AD 800–1600.
Stroud: Tempus.

Stenberger, Mårten 1943. *Forntida gårdar.* Copenhagen: Ejnar Munksgaard.

Stocklund, Bjarne 1996. *Det Færøske hus i kulturhistorisk belysning.* Copenhagen.: Ca.A. Reitzel

Sturlunga saga I–II. Ed. Jón Jóhannesson, Magnús
Finnbogason and Kristján Eldjárn. Reykjavík:
Sturlunguútgáfan, 1946.

Sverris saga. Ed. Þorleifur Hauksson. Íslenzk
fornrit XXX. Reykjavík: Hið Íslenzka fornritafélag, 2007.

Úlfar Bragason 2005. "Sagas of Contemporary
History (*Sturlunga saga*): Texts and Research".
In Rory McTurk (ed.), *A Companion to Old
Norse-Icelandic Literature and Culture.* Oxford
and Victoria, Australia: Blackwell Publishing,
427–446.

Vilhjálmur Ö. Vilhjálmsson 1989. "Stöng og
Þjórsárdalur-bosættelsens ophør". *Hikuin* 15,
75–102.

Vretemark, Maria 2017. "Aristocratic Farms and
Private Churches – the Varnhem Case Study".
In Guðrún Sveinbjarnardóttir and Bergur

Þorgeirsson (eds), *The Buildings of Medieval Reykholt. The Wider Context*. Reykjavík: Snorrastofa and University of Iceland Press, 143–158.

Øye, Ingvild 2002. "Landbruk under press 800–1350". In Björn Myhre and Ingvild Øye (eds.), *Norges landbrukshistorie* I. 4000 f.Kr.–1350 e.Kr. Del 2. Oslo: Norske samlaget, 215–414.

¶ GUÐVARÐUR MÁR GUNNLAUGSSON

The Deed of the
Church of Reykholt

Introduction

HE *MÁLDAGI* (DEED) OF THE CHURCH OF REYKHOLT (*Reykjaholtsmáldagi*) is an exceptional document in many ways. It consists of a single vellum leaf containing a list of the entitlements and assets of the church from before the middle of the twelfth century until about the year 1300 (see figs. 1 and 2).[1]

From this document it is possible to learn a great deal about the church's real holdings, furnishings, and rights in others' land, as well as the names of some of the people associated with the church. The *máldagi* also contains a great deal of information about the history of the Icelandic language, including the evolution of spelling and script from the middle of the twelfth century to the late thirteenth. The *máldagi* is therefore a very important historical and linguistic primary source.

The earliest part of it is perhaps the oldest surviving original document written in Old Norse with Latin letters. Only a small handful of Icelandic manuscript fragments are considered by scholars to be from the twelfth century. The first part of the document has traditionally been thought to be from between 1150 and 1200, while other parts date from

---

1   A list of assets and entitlements is called *máldagi* in Icelandic.

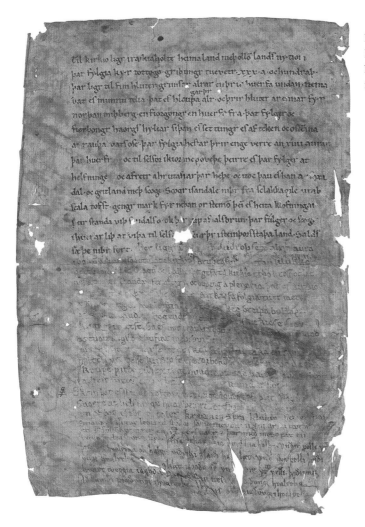

Figure 1.
Reykja-
holtsmáldagi,
f. 1r.

the thirteenth century. The *máldagi* is preserved in Þjóðskjalasafn Íslands (the National Archives of Iceland) in Reykjavík.

It was important for churches to own liturgical books, sermons and homilies, and, if possible, the life of the patron saint. In some early manuscripts the first and last leaves or pages were left blank; they acted as flyleaves and were meant to protect the other pages in the manuscript. Such empty pages were often used to record *máldagar* or other information, as seen in *Helgastaðabók* (Isl. perg. 16 4to and *Skarðsbók postulasagna* (SÁM 1).

Sometime in the twelfth century, someone wrote the *máldagi* of the church at Reykholt on an empty page in a manuscript. The remainder of the manuscript is lost. This is hardly surprising as many ecclesiastical

Figure 2.
Reykja-
holtsmáldagi,
f. 1v.

manuscripts were lost during the Reformation in the middle of the sixteenth century and the following decades. Protestants had little use for Catholic liturgical books, so some manuscripts were thrown away, while others were used for bookbinding or other practical purposes. The ink in other manuscripts was scraped away so that the vellum could be used for more orthodox texts. Even the few manuscripts that survived were damaged by neglect.[2] But the Reformation is not guilty of treating every book poorly, since many manuscripts became worn out through use. It must be remembered that not all manuscript owners did their best

2   Guðvarður Már Gunnlaugsson 2017, 164–169.

to take care of their books, and this applies for the vernacular books as well as the Latin.

The manuscript that *Reykjaholtsmáldagi* originally belonged to suffered the same fate as so many others. However, it is worth noting that the *Reykjaholtsmáldagi* shows signs of having been bound at least twice, since there are holes left over from two different bindings on either side of the leaf, indicating that the leaf was at one time bound with the main text facing up and at another time facing down. This suggests that the original volume to which it belonged may simply have fallen apart from frequent use. Furthermore, it shows that those in charge of the church had reason to preserve the deed itself, which provided a valuable record of the church's property.

The earliest external reference to the *Reykjaholtsmáldagi* occurs in a legal context: in a letter written at the general assmebly *Öxarárþing* at Þingvellir on July 1, 1562, the judges are quoted as saying that they have been presented with a *máldagi* from Reykholt.[3]

Reykjaholtsmáldagi and AM 237 a fol.

Others added more information to the original text of *Reykjaholtsmáldagi*, and the additions were made at six different times. The *máldagi* is now 36 lines long on one side of the leaf, with a few lines in two columns on the reverse side. Except for the interpolation line (R7), the sections are marked in the order they appear on the leaf:[4]

R1: Lines 1–14, traditionally dated to around 1150–1200.
R2: Lines 14–29, from around 1204–1208.
R3: Lines 29–32, from around 1224–1241.
R4: Lines 32–36, dated to around 1300.
R5: The first column on the reverse side (four lines), from the latter part of the thirteenth century.
R6: The second column on the reverse side (five lines), dated to around 1224–1241.
R7: An interpolation between lines 14 and 15, probably from around 1242–1247.

3   *DI* XIII, 751.
4   *ONP*, 494.

Figure 3.
AM 237 a
fol., f. 2r.

In the Árni Magnússon Institute for Icelandic Studies in Reykjavík there are two manuscript leaves (a single bifolium) containing two homilies from around 1150 with the catalogue shelf mark AM 237 a fol. (see fig. 3).[5]

The leaves were originally part of a larger manuscript that doubtless was in the possession of a church, since the second of the homilies is a sermon that would have been delivered on the church's consecration day. It is therefore very likely that someone with clerical training wrote the manuscript.

5   Hreinn Benediktsson 1965, iii; ONP, 436.

The hands in the AM 237 a fol. leaves and in the oldest part of the Reykholt church deed (*Reykjaholtsmáldagi*, R1) seem to be so similar that Stefán Karlsson has suggested that one and the same scribe was responsible for both even though the orthography and the use of abbreviations are not the same in both documents. Ólafur Halldórsson put forward the idea that if this is the case then the deed must have been written on an empty leaf in the same book to which the homily fragment belonged.[6] However, this is not the case: the leaves cannot have belonged to the same manuscript because both their sizes and formats are different. The width of the three leaves is similar, around 205 or 210 millimetres, but the two AM 237 a fol. leaves are taller than the *máldagi*-leaf, being 312 millimetres as opposed to 297.[7] Moreover, the upper margin of the AM 237 a fol. *bifolium* has been trimmed and would originally have been larger than it is now and the trimmer has almost cut into the text in one place in the right margin as can be seen on fol. 2; the *máldagi*-leaf does not seem to have been subjected to the same treatment.[8]

AM 237 a fol. is thought to have been written around 1150, but such precision regarding the date ought to be treated with caution, since it is not possible to date manuscripts more precisely than within a half-century margin on the basis of script and orthography, unless there are other conclusive arguments.[9] Thus, the dating "around 1150" means that the manuscript could be thought to have been written at some point between 1125 and 1175. Given this date range, the same man could have written AM 237 a fol. and R1, which traditionally has been dated to between 1150 and 1200.[10] Actually, the original dating is around 1178 to 1193, or the time Bishop Þorlákr Þórhallsson was in office, because he urged church holders to make lists of assets and entitlements of their church.[11] It is unlikely, however, that the scribe is the same person on palaeographic and orthographic grounds. The orthography is different in AM 237 a fol. and R1, as J. Hoffory has pointed out, and the use of abbreviations differs.[12] In fact, there is a significant difference between

---

6   Ólafur Halldórsson 1989, 67. — Stefán did not write anything on this subject but Ólafur cited him orally in this article.
7   Hreinn Benediktsson 1965, ii–iii.
8   *Reykjaholtsmáldagi*, 18–19, 33–34.
9   Stefán Karlsson 1982a, 185; Stefán Karlsson 1982b, 322.
10 *ONP*, 1989, 494.
11 *Íslendínga sögur* I, xxxvii; *Reykjaholts-máldagi*, 20.
12 *Reykjaholts-máldagi*, 22–23; Ólafur Halldórsson 1989, 67. According to Ólafur Stefán

the two. In R1, only two ligatures appear, <æ> and <a͛> (each once) for /ę́/ and /ey/. In addition to this, the digraph <ao> for /ǫ/ appears once. On the other hand, only on f. 2r in AM 237 a fol. <ǫ> and <ǫ́> appear seventeen times and <ę>, <ę́> and <ǫ́> appear quite often, as does the digraph <eó> which occurs seven times. <ǽ>, <ao> and <aó> can also be seen but only a few times. Accents above vowels are not used in R1 but they are used widely in AM 237 a fol., for example there are six instances of <á> and eleven of <ó>. In certain ways, the scribe of AM 237 a fol. has thus adopted ideas about Icelandic orthography that appear in the work of the First Grammarian (see below) but the scribe of R1 has not.[13] In R1, a macron standing for /m/ after a vowel is found four times above vowels, but other abbreviations are not used. In AM 237 a fol, on the other hand, words are frequently abbreviated. There are eighty abbreviations, for example, on f. 2r. Fifty of these are macrons that appear above vowels but in addition to this there are abbreviations for /ra/, /va/, /ve/ and /er/, and finally, the words *hann* and *hans* are abbreviated twelve times with a bar through the ascender on <h>.

The hands in R1 and AM 237 a fol. are palaeographically similar at first glance, and closer examination of the letter forms reveals that they are almost identical. However, is it possible that a scribe could have changed his orthography as much as the orthographical difference on R1 and 237a shows during his age as a scribe? On the other hand, it is strange that what ought to be a dot over <y> is more like an accent than a dot in AM 237 a fol., but it does not look like this in R1 (see fig. 4, 5 and 6).[14]

The dating of R1

It was mentioned above that the *máldagi* can be divided into seven parts. The second part of the *máldagi* was written when Snorri Sturluson moved to Reykholt, as stated in the *máldagi*:

þeſſe kirk[i]o fe eſ ero i bokoᵐ oc imeſſoſotoᵐ oc i [kirkio] [ſ]
kruþe ɣirðo til ſex togo hvndraþa vaþmala [i][h]en[d]r S[n]or[r]

Karlsson also noticed the orthographical difference and that the use of abbreviations differs.

13   *FGT*, 206–247.

14   The accent in AM 237 a fol. is an oblique stroke — as an accent normally is — but the dot over <y> is more like a tick; in R1 the dot is a dot.

a. þeir Gizo[R oc þor]þr[.oc k]et[ill] her[mu]nd[a]r f.oc [hogne
preftr][15]

It is known from other sources that Snorri moved to Reykholt early in
the thirteenth century but the exact year is not known. It is known that
he still lived at Borg in 1204 but he had definitely moved from Borg to
Reykholt by 1208; most scholars think he moved in 1206. The first part
of the *máldagi* is the first item on the page and is therefore considered to
be older than the second part. Scholars consider it to have been written
in the second half of the twelfth century and some scholars have even
thought it was written when Magnús Pálsson (*c.* 1152 to 1223) took
Reykholt over from his father, Páll Sǫlvason (*c.* 1115 to 1185), in 1185.[16]

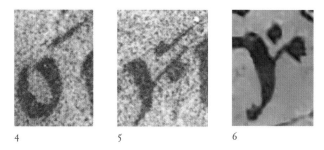

4   5   6

Figure 4. The letter <o> with an accent in AM 237 a fol., f. 2rb, l. 17: ó fýnelegom.
Figure 5. The letter <y> with a tick in AM 237 a fol., f. 2rb, l. 14: fcýlem].
Figure 6. The letter <y> with a dot in Reykjaholtsmáldagi, f. 1r, l. 5: fýlger.

The script of R1 is almost pure Carolingian script. It therefore does not
point to the end of the twelfth century when Gothic influence began
to appear in Icelandic and Norwegian script. The intermediate stage
between Carolingian script and a fully developed Gothic script, has been

15   "Gizurr and Þórðr and Ketill Hermundarson and Hǫgni the priest appraised the
     church property which is in books and vestments and church ornaments at 60
     hundreds of homespun [when the church was handed over] to Snorri" (*Reykja-
     holtsmáldagi*, 10, 18).
16   This thought has led to that conclusion that either Páll or Magnús wrote the first
     part of the *máldagi*. And that conclusion led to the idea that Páll wrote AM 237 a
     fol. and Magnús wrote R1 (see *DI* I, 279–280; *PA*, no. 44–45; Hreinn Benediktsson
     1965; *Reykjaholtsmáldagi*, 26, 54–55).

called Pregothic by Albert Derolez.[17] He mentions many details that he considers significant in the development of Carolingian minuscule into Proto-Gothic script, such as a reduction in the length of ascenders and descenders (the ratio between minims and letters with ascenders increased from about 0.4–0.5 in Carolingian script to 0.6–0.7 in Proto-Gothic script). However, the general aspect of Proto-Gothic script is round, not angular as in Gothic *textualis*.[18]

The only Icelandic manuscripts or manuscript fragments in Old Norse written with Carolingian script are the first two parts of *Reykjaholtsmáldagi*, AM 237 a fol. and AM 674 a 4to. However, there exist other fragments written in Protogothic script which are definitely from the twelfth century, AM 315 d fol. and GKS 1812 IV 4to (along with AM 249 l fol.). These arguments lead to that conclusion that the *máldagi* is older than most of the other fragments and could easily be from the middle of the twelfth century as AM 237 a fol.

The orthography of the first part of the *máldagi* also shows interesting features. It is well known that the author of *Fyrsta málfrœðiritgerðin* (The First Grammatical Treatise, *FGT*) wanted Icelanders to modify the orthography of the language to make it more regular, economical, and efficient; he therefore introduced many new letters. He introduced new letters for sounds which were not common in Latin (<y>, <ø>, <ę>, <ǫ>, though perhaps he had seen these letters in English or German manuscripts). He also suggested that the Anglo Saxon <þ> should be used for *th*-sound (both voiced and unvoiced) and the letter <c> should be used for velar and palatal stop (he rejected <k> and <q>). He also recommended that vowel length should be shown with accents (<í>, <ý>, <ú>, <é>, <ø̄>, <ó>, <ę́ >, <á>, <ǫ́>) and consonant length with small capitals (<B>, <D>, <F>, <G>, <L>, <M>, <N>, <P>, <R>, <S>, <T>) but for a long <c> he introduced the letter <ᴋ> because a small capital <c> (<ᴄ>) is too similar to the minuscule; he also introduced <ŋ> for /ng/.[19]

However, upon closer examination of the twelfth century Icelandic manuscripts, we observe many different interpretations and applications of the First Grammarian's proposed orthography. Small capitals (<N>, <R> and <G>) are used in AM 315 d fol., AM 674 a 4to, GKS 1812 IV 4to,

17 Derolez 2003 56–57. I prefer the term 'Protogothica' to 'Prægothica', which is used by Derolez.

18 Derolez 2003, 58.

19 *FGT*, 206–247. At that time the normal minuscule *s* was <ſ>, not <s>.

R2 (but not R1), and AM 237 a fol., On the other hand, the other letters introduced by the First Grammarian (<ø>, <ę>, <ǫ>, with or without an accent, and <ŋ>) are used in AM 237 a fol. as well as AM 315 d fol. and AM 674 a 4to.[20] The only manuscript which does not show influence from the ideas of the First Grammarian is R1. This fact can be used to argue that R1 was written before *Fyrsta málfrœðiritgerðin*, or at least before its suggestions became known and accepted in every literary environment.

Fyrsta málfrœðiritgerðin was most likely written around or before the middle of the twelfth century, i.e. around 1140 to 1150.[21] Though R1 is perhaps older than the treatise, it is not likely to have been written before about 1130. The reason for this statement is that it was legislated that each man, who was in a charge of a church, should make a written list of all the church's belongings when the Christian laws of *Grágás* were enacted sometime in the years 1122 to 1133.[22] Thus, R1 may have been written sometime in the years between 1130 and 1150.

20   This does not mean that these letters are used everywhere they might be used.
21   *FGT*, 31–33.
22   Hjalti Hugason 2000, 282–285; *Grágás*, 12.

Bibliography

Derolez, Albert 2003. *The Palaeography of Gothic Manuscript Books. From the Twelfth to the Early Sixteenth Century*. Cambridge: Cambridge University Press.

DI = *Diplomatarium islandicum, Íslenzkt fornbréfasafn* I-XVI. Copenhagen and Reykjavík, 1857–1972.

FGT = *The First Grammatical Treatise. Introduction, Text, Notes, Translation, Vocabulary, Facsimiles*. Ed. Hreinn Benediktsson. University of Iceland. Publications in Linguistics 1. Reykjavík: Institute of Nordic Linguistics, 1972.

Grágás. Lagasafn íslenska þjóðveldisins. Ed. Gunnar Karlsson, Kristján Sveinsson and Mörður Árnason. Reykjavík: Mál og menning, 1992.

Guðvarður Már Gunnlaugsson 2013. "Carolingian and Proto-Gothic Script in Norway and Iceland". In Espen Karlsen (ed.), *Latin Manuscripts of Medieval Norway. Studies in Memory of Lilli Gjerløw*. Oslo: Nota Bene, Studies from the National Library of Norway — Novus Press, 199–213.

Guðvarður Már Gunnlaugsson 2017. "Latin Fragments Related to Iceland". In Åslaug Ommundsen and Tuomas Heikkila (eds), *Nordic Latin Manuscript Fragments. The Destruction and Reconstruction of Medieval Books*. London: Routledge, 163–183.

Hjalti Hugason 2000, "Frumkristni og upphaf kirkju". In Hjalti Hugason (ed.), *Kristni á Íslandi* I. Reykjavík: Alþingi.

Hreinn Benediktsson 1965. *Early Icelandic Script. As Illustrated in Vernacular Texts from the Twelfth and Thirteenth Centuries*. Íslenzk handrit. Icelandic Manuscripts. Series in Folio II. Reykjavík: The Manuscript Institute of Iceland.

Íslendínga sögur, udgivne efter gamle Haandskrifter I. Copenhagen: Det kongelige nordiske Oldskrift-Selskab, 1843.

ONP = *Ordbog over det norrøne prosasprog. A Dictionary of Old Norse Prose*. Registre. Indices. Copenhagen: Den arnamagnæanske kommission, 1989.

Ólafur Halldórsson 1989. "Skrifaðar bækur". In Frosti F. Jóhannsson (ed.), *Íslensk þjóðmenning VI. Munnmenntir og bókmenning*. Reykjavík: Bókaútgáfan Þjóðsaga, 57–89.

PA = *Palæografisk atlas. Oldnorsk-islandsk afdeling*. Copenhagen & Oslo: Kommissionen for Det Arnamagnæanske Legat, 1905.

Reykjaholts-máldagi. Det originale pergamentsdokument over Reykjaholt kirkegods og -inventarium i 12. og 13. årh., litografisk gengivet, samt udførlig fortolket og oplyst. Copenhagen: Samfund til udgivelse af gammel nordisk litteratur XIV, 1885.

Reykjaholtsmáldagi. Ed. Guðvarður Már Gunnlaugsson. Reykholt: Reykholtskirkja – Snorrastofa, 2000.

Stefán Karlsson 1982a. "Provenance and History of Helgastaðabók". In Selma Jónsdóttir, Stefán Karlsson and Sverrir Tómasson (eds), Helgastaðabók. Nikulás saga. Perg. 4to nr. 16 Konungsbókhlöðu í Stokkhólmi. *Íslensk miðaldahandrit. Manuscripta Islandica medii aevi* II. Reykjavík: Lögberg bókaforlag, Sverrir Kristinsson, 177–201.

Stefán Karlsson 1982b. "Saltarabrot í Svíþjóð með Stjórnarhendi". *Gripla* V, 320–322.

¶ GÍSLI SIGURÐSSON

Snorri Sturluson and the Best of Both Worlds

Introduction

The wide and varied corpus of Old Norse secular prose narratives written between the twelfth and the fifteenth centuries, overwhelmingly in Iceland but in a few cases in Norway, presents a challenge to received views of the development of European literature. These texts have been classified into a number of discrete literary genres, but they all have much in common and share features that set them apart from literary developments elsewhere in Europe. In many ways the Sagas of Icelanders (*Íslendingasögur*, also called family sagas) seem closer to the historical novel of later times than to any of the popular literary genres found in vernacular languages in other parts of medieval Europe. Of course, many of the models for and ideas found in the Icelandic sagas build on works produced within the continental courts and clerical centres of learning (which themselves built to varying degrees on the Christian book of books, the Bible). Tracing influences in the sagas from learned, secular and religious writings can often be instructive.[1] But the fact remains that the ultimate inspiration for the poetry and storytelling of Scandinavia is

---

1 Literary borrowing and direct written and learned influence, both from continental writings and from other works within Iceland, is a well-trodden area of research among saga scholars and has been for many years: see for instance Bjarni Einarsson 1975; Sverrir Tómasson 1988; 1992a; Baldur Hafstað 1995; Torfi H. Tulinius 2004.

not to be found in pre-existing written literature, the Bible, or cultural exchanges with the more southerly societies that became known in the North with the arrival of Christianity. Its roots lie elsewhere.

The art of storytelling is not the art of writing; narrative art exists in a range of other media. But faced with a written text, people are inclined to imagine that the words they are reading are exactly the same as the words they may have heard in oral performances of similar material. This illusion ignores a fundamental difference between these two manifestations of verbal art, oral verbal performance on the one hand and reading words from a book on the other, either silently or out loud to an audience. Composing and/or structuring a text for the written medium enables those doing it to create something new, something that would not have been possible in oral performance – something that requires writing to exist in the form that it does.

Every medium of storytelling has its own particular strengths and weaknesses. Cinematography, for example, can call on technical resources beyond the scope of individual storytellers or theatre groups to convey its dramatic and narrative intentions. The same holds true for writing: as the people of north-western Europe came to master its potential, they discovered little by little how to adapt its special technical demands to the verbal arts of poetry and storytelling that had previously existed only in oral form and constituted part of their traditional cultural heritage.

With the fall of the Roman Empire, book culture in Europe came under the virtual monopoly of the Church. It was a culture whose primary purpose was to exalt the Lord and spread the holy word of God, often in collaboration with secular leaders who saw the benefits the new religion had to offer them in raising and consolidating their status in society. By aligning themselves with the Church, rulers could justify a power structure with themselves at the top as something ordained by the God the clerics preached about in church. Kings had accounts of their lives written to demonstrate how God's favour had singled them out, thereby establishing their positions within the Christian world-view with its roots in Rome and the lands of the Mediterranean.[2] Here and there in Western Europe, secular material found its way onto parchment, at least partially influenced and inspired by the Christian book culture, for instance the

---

2   Hastrup 2009.

Old Irish sagas, Old English poetry and the French romances, but none of these literatures developed into anything remotely similar to the secular authorial works we know today. The concept of the "author" in its modern sense does not really begin to emerge in Western thinking before the Italian Renaissance, in particular in the figure of Dante Alighieri (1265–1321);[3] Dante explicitly claimed his writings as his own creations, thereby laying the foundations for modern thinking and assumptions about the "author", and these ideas spread outwards through the same channels as Christian culture and Christianity had taken earlier, first on the ideological basis of religion and then later moving gradually into secular spheres.

How easily ideas spread in the Middle Ages, and to a large extent since, owes much to the language they were first expressed in. Florence lay at the heart of the European medieval world, and when men of culture there took up individualistic writing with authorial intent in the fourteenth century their works and ideas were read and emulated, helping to sow the seeds of the Italian Renaissance and the profound intellectual changes it initiated throughout Europe. But they were not the first. It is interesting to compare the position of Dante, Petrarch and Boccaccio with that of Snorri Sturluson (1178/9–1241) in Iceland. The best part of a century before Dante, Snorri had done something similar, something equally exceptional and new, and had he been writing in one of the "central" languages of Europe it is easy to imagine that his innovations would have had widespread and lasting consequences. "Unfortunately" for Western civilization, Snorri's farm lay almost at the final reaches of the European world at the time; beyond Iceland lay only Greenland, once the Vikings had abandoned their attempts in around the year 1000 at pushing their boundaries back to the coast of North America. It was only within his native Iceland that Snorri's innovation had an impact, but it was an innovation so profound that nearly eight hundred years after his death we are still writing books and holding conferences about him.[4]

The works attributed to Snorri (putting aside the genuine and serious doubts we have about medieval authorship in general and exactly what part Snorri may or may not have played in the composition of these

3   Ascoli 2008, 3–64.
4   Vésteinn Ólason 2002.

works) are the *Óláfs saga helga in sérstaka* (The Separate Saga of St Óláfr)[5] the collection of Kings' Sagas known as *Heimskringla*, his manual on traditional poetics in the *Edda*, and *Egils saga Skalla-Grímssonar*. All these works (and particularly when viewed together as the output of a single writer) show such a high level of originality that if Snorri was indeed their author they represent a level and breadth of innovative thinking that it took men and women of letters elsewhere in Europe many centuries to replicate: historical criticism from a secular viewpoint (for instance in the way Snorri evaluates his sources in the Prologue to *Heimskringla*); literary restructuring of traditional oral learning (in the arrangement and systematization of mythological and metrical lore in the *Edda*); and prose narratives that prefigure the historical novel as a literary form (in the portrayal and development of the character of Egill Skalla-Grímsson in the saga that bears his name). And if Snorri is indeed behind all these works, the roots of this originality presumably lie in his experiences as a young man, that is, in the intellectual milieu in which he grew up in preparation for his adult career as poet, storyteller, man of law and politician.[6]

Life

Snorri was born in the winter of 1178/9. His father, Hvamm-Sturla Þórðarson (Sturla of Hvammr, his farm), was a minor chieftain from the west of Iceland, not in any way exceptional on a national level. For instance, Sturla never achieved, or came close to achieving, the highest office of Commonwealth Iceland, that of lawspeaker, nor was he a member of the group of leading chieftains who promoted the growing influence of the Church during the twelfth century. The most powerful chieftain in the country at the time was Jón Loftsson (or Loptsson) of Oddi in the South. As the son of an illegitimate daughter of King Magnús *berfœttr* (Bareleg), Jón seems to have seen himself as a representative of royal power in Iceland, which probably explains the

5   In modern Norwegian the name of the saint is Olav.
6   It should be stressed that Snorri's authorship is highly problematic and by no means undisputed, partly because the scholars addressing the issue do not all apply the same notions of authorship: see Gísli Sigurðsson 2012. See also Jakob Benediktsson 1955; Jonna Louis-Jensen 1997; 2009; Haukur Þorgeirsson 2014.

social expectations of those who grew up under his tutelage at Oddi.[7] In 1181 he happened to act as mediator in a local feud in which Sturla was involved. As part of the settlement Jón offered to foster the infant Snorri. Such an offer must have been regarded as a great honour for Snorri's family, providing their son with the opportunity to grow up at the main centre of learning in the country where young boys received the best Iceland had to offer in the way of education as part of their preparation for holy orders.

We would dearly like to know a lot more about Snorri's upbringing at Oddi and the nature of the education he received there: how much Latin did he have, for example? And how familiar was he with the books that formed part of the education of the aspiring clerics among whom he grew up? Did he, for that matter, ever actually learn to read and write himself? Discussing the background to Snorri's *Edda* (known also as the *Prose Edda* or *Snorra-Edda*), Anthony Faulkes[8] observes that, despite showing some familiarity with scholastic learning and Latin writings on poetics, Snorri shows no clear sign of actually having read them; but it is obvious from the *Edda* that whoever was responsible for writing it was well acquainted with the philosophical and religious ideas of the times.[9] Recently Helgi Þorláksson has argued for a compromise position, suggesting that Snorri may have been ordained into minor holy orders even though the primary focus of his education was on preparing him for a future career in public life.[10]

Snorri's legal and political training is beyond dispute. He acted as advocate in court cases at *þings* (assemblies) and was elected lawspeaker for the first time in the summer of 1215. By this time his family had established their position in the legal and political world: during the entire period between 1181 and 1276 all the lawspeakers/lawmen of Iceland came from one or other of the two dominant families in the country, Snorri's own, the Sturlungar, and the Haukdælir. As lawspeaker, Snorri seems to have worked in close collaboration with Styrmir *fróði* (the Learned) Kárason, and this collaboration is likely to have extended to other fields as well.[11] Unfortunately, we know very little about Styrmir

---

7   Halldór Hermannsson 1932.
8   Faulkes 1993. See also Gísli Sigurðsson 2004, 5–17.
9   Clunies Ross 1987; Sverrir Tómasson 2007.
10 Helgi Þorláksson 2014.
11 Helgi Þorláksson 2006.

other than as a writer; we know he compiled a version of *Landnámabók* (The Book of Settlements) and an earlier saga of St Olav (Óláfr) than Snorri's (both works are now lost but it is possible to deduce something of their contents from later works that may have used them), and played some role, perhaps as editor, in *Sverris saga*, the biography of King Sverrir (in modern Norwegian Sverre) of Norway originally written by Karl Jónsson, abbot of the monastery of Þingeyrar.[12] Styrmir was twice elected lawspeaker, first for 1210 to 1214 (after which he was succeeded by Snorri for the following four summers) and then again in 1232, when Styrmir acted as lawspeaker again for four summers after Snorri had served for ten summers in a row. According to the *Lǫgsǫgumannatal* (The Register of Lawspeakers) in the Uppsala codex of *Snorra-Edda*, Snorri's second term started in the summer of 1222, when he succeeded Teitr Þorvaldsson.[13] Styrmir was priest at Reykholt, Snorri's home farm, from before 1228 until he took charge of the Augustinian monastery on the island of Viðey in the year 1235, where he served until his death in 1245. The monastery of Viðey had been established around 1225 through the joint initiative of Snorri and Þorvaldr Gizurarson, the brother of the Bishop of Skálholt. Sigurður Nordal[14] suggests that Styrmir may have been the son of Kári Runólfsson, abbot of Þingeyrar, who died in 1187 or 1188. Styrmir may thus have been associated with the monastery of Þingeyrar in his early years, and this could explain his contribution to *Sverris saga*. Styrmir and Snorri clearly had shared interests and their entwined careers also strongly suggest a bond of friendship between them.

The power and status of the other clan or family that dominated Icelandic politics in the last hundred years of the Commonwealth (930–1262), the Haukdælir, derived much more from a close alliance with the Church than did the Sturlungar. Snorri made numerous attempts, not all equally successful or lasting, to build links with the Haukdælir, both through marriage alliances and friendships. We are extremely well informed on Snorri as a political figure thanks to the near contemporary records in the *Sturlunga saga* collection and other sources, all assembled critically in Óskar Guðmundsson's fine life of Snorri.[15] What these records make absolutely clear is that Snorri used all means at his disposal

---

12 Þorleifur Hauksson 2007, xxxix–xl.
13 Gísli Sigurðsson 2004, 53–92.
14 Sigurður Nordal 1953, 210.
15 Óskar Guðmundsson 2009.

to extend his power and influence, making and breaking alliances with other chieftains, marrying into their families and manipulating the workings of the law.

Beyond this, Snorri was also a professional poet (*skáld*) and used his craft to gain access to the inner circles of the Norwegian court. In this he clearly saw himself as a representative of a tradition going back to pre-Christian times. Poets were employed to elevate the status of living rulers and keep alive the oral memories of their predecessors, and this function seems to have become a preserve of Icelanders from around the time of the conversion or even earlier. The Uppsala codex of *Snorra-Edda*, immediately before the *Lǫgsǫgumannatal*, contains a *Skáldatal* (The Register of Poets), carefully arranging the court poets chronologically and associating them with the various kings and chieftains under whom they served.[16]

The Literary Milieu

At the time Snorri was born, writing in Europe had the primary functions of spreading the Gospel and elevating the status of kings and nobles through the composition of historiographical works. Earlier, of course, in the classical period, the Greeks and Romans had produced books about gods and heroes, envisaging them as housed in the sky and reflected in the stars in the way people have done throughout the world. This is the picture we find, for instance, in Ovid's *Metamorphoses*, which remained widely known and read throughout the Middle Ages. But Ovid's example had little effect on the cultures that were gradually being brought within the Christian fold and acquiring from it the art of writing; their newly abandoned gods and myths were clearly not felt to be suitable material for scribal endeavours. Nor do we find narratives about people from humbler ranks of society – farmers and chieftains, for example; subjects of this kind did not naturally lend themselves to the values and attitudes that came with the Church and the kind of literature it fostered. Although secular vernacular writing became increasingly common, it tended to remain strongly aristocratic. The impetus for such writing originated mainly in France: from the late eleventh and twelfth centuries we get the

16   Guðrún Nordal 1992; 2001, 50–55; 2006.

chansons de geste, oral heroic poetry transformed into literary book form; and around the same time we find the first written *romances*, probably inspired by the stories and poems of Breton singers of tales. This kind of literary activity opened the way for a variety of other secular narratives in French, both in poetry and prose, probably commissioned by learned laymen (*le chevalier lettré*) of the nobility – that is, by people of a comparable social standing to Snorri in Iceland and around the time that Snorri was coming of age. These written stories have provoked considerable discussion about the role of the author in their creation and the nature of their relationship to any possible oral tradition lying behind them, very much along the same lines as the continuing debate about the origins of the Icelandic sagas.[17]

The literary scene in Iceland that Snorri inherited was very different from the one he bequeathed to others. The writing of extended narratives in Iceland had started with accounts of the kings of Norway written by the monks of Þingeyrar, both in Latin and Icelandic. This work was presumably well known to Styrmir, especially if it is correct that he grew up at Þingeyrar as has been suggested. Snorri's revolution lay in his seeing possibilities in the skills and techniques that the monks possessed to create something entirely different. By a bold leap of the imagination he realized that subjects beyond the lives of saints and kings could also be put into books, first the mythology inherited from pre-Christian times in his *Edda* and later perhaps the lives and feuds of historical figures like Egill Skalla-Grímsson. This required an adaptation of the methods and ideas on literary structure that he had perhaps become acquainted with at Oddi. His own education may not have been focused in this direction but Styrmir certainly possessed the skills and knowledge required. Snorri may therefore have worked with Styrmir and his scribes on a new and novel task, taking the knowledge, scholarship, poetry and stories that he had learned in his younger years from the lips of his learned elders – material that had hitherto been entirely oral and that had prepared him for his adult career in the world of politics, legal disputes, storytelling and court poetry – and converting it into book form.

Secular literature from continental Europe first becomes accessible in the North in 1226 with *Tristrams saga*, Brother Robert's Norwegian version of Thomas of Britain's *Tristran*. Robert's translation reflects a

---

17   Torfi H. Tulinius 2002, 31–43.

new interest in Norway in literary trends from what were perceived to be the more cultured regions of Europe and may well have played a part in inspiring Snorri to think about how writing could be put to use to create something new out of domestic subject matter. *Tristrams saga* was followed by a spate of further translations as well as original works in the same vein. Similarities of style, etc. have led many scholars in recent years to link the writing of the so-called *fornaldarsögur Norðurlanda* (The Legendary Sagas, sagas of ancient times) with this chivalric literature. *Fornaldarsögur Norðurlanda* is a nineteenth century term used to describe a group of Icelandic prose narratives, interspersed with verse, set outside Iceland in Viking and pre-Viking times. While the *fornaldarsögur* contrast with the Sagas of Icelanders proper in several respects – in their purported period, their settings (which range over the wider Viking world of Scandinavia and the lands to the North, East, South and South-west), their fondness for mystery, and their exaggerated heroics – the two genres share many characteristics of style and composition. The similarities to the *fornaldarsögur* are particularly marked in episodes of the Sagas of Icelanders set outside Iceland. Though there are similarities and parallels with the continental literature, the differences are even more striking, e.g. in the sagas' obvious independence in vocabulary and in their treatment of subjects such as love and the emotions, which can hardly be explained unless they were based on a source of inspiration and a system of values from somewhere other than the translated literature.[18] Once again we have a pattern where the Icelanders adopted techniques, themes and structure from continental literature but adapted them to existing stories that came from their own native tradition. It is not beyond the realms of imagination that it was once again Snorri who inspired this new trend, since his *Edda* contains synopses of some of the same heroic legends we find in the *fornaldarsögur*, in particular the story of Sigurðr *Fáfnisbani* (the Dragon-Slayer), the hoard of dragon's gold, and the destruction of the Vǫlsungar/Nibelungs.

It need come as no surprise if the people responsible for writing the Sagas of Icelanders themselves came under the influence of continental secular literature, particularly when this literature had been translated and was thus available to secular Icelandic storytellers. This influence is probably most evident in a group of sagas known as the poets' sagas (*Gunnlaugs*

18 Sävborg 2007, 617–622.

saga ormstungu, Hallfreðar saga, Kormaks saga, Bjarnar saga Hítdælakappa, and Víglundar saga), all of which centre on the theme of thwarted love that forms the mainstay of the continental courtly literature.[19]

Natural Development and Intellectual Breakthrough

In view of his foster-father Jón Loftsson's connection with the royal house of Norway and the precedent already set by the earlier hagiographic kings' lives, it is hardly surprising that Snorri started his writing career with kings. However, Snorri's biographical work is clearly of a far higher quality than that of his predecessors; apart from a superior command of narrative, Snorri manages to incorporate the political motivations of his characters and reflects the contemporary ideas of educated Icelanders on society and the role of the king and the state.[20] In his separate *Óláfs saga helga in sérstaka*, and in *Heimskringla*, Snorri raises the already well established writing of Kings' Sagas to a new artistic level. *Heimskringla* evidences considerable care over form and structure: the collection of sagas is given a mythological framework in its opening saga, *Ynglinga saga*, while the main body of the work is centred in Biblical fashion around the lives of the two missionary kings, Óláfr Tryggvason and Óláfr Haraldsson. In addition, Snorri cites as evidence large numbers of skaldic stanzas not found in earlier written sources.[21] *Heimskringla* can thus be read as a natural but brilliant extension of earlier saga writing, from both Iceland and elsewhere, relating the lives of royal leaders. It is also likely that

---

19 Bjarni Einarsson 1961, 280–299.
20 See Bagge 1991.
21 It is generally accepted that Snorri exploited various written sources, some known, others now lost, in the writing of *Heimskringla*; for an overview of Snorri's sources, see Diana Whaley 1991 and Tommy Danielsson 2002. In particular, it has often been claimed that one of his principal sources was a collection of early Kings' Sagas of which copies survive in the manuscript *Morkinskinna* from the latter half of the thirteenth century; see Ármann Jakobsson 2014 and Gade 2000. This may be true in so far as the material relating directly to the kings is concerned, but there is a problem: *Morkinskinna* also contains much material that Snorri does not appear to have been aware of, or at least did not use, notably the "short stories" describing the adventures of Icelanders in Norway, the so-called Íslendingaþættir. These þættir form an essential part of the narrative aesthetics of *Morkinskinna*, as argued by Sverrir Tómasson 1992b, 383–386, and elaborated further by Ármann Jakobsson 2011.

Snorri intended his royal biographies to raise his own profile among the social elite of Norway, where he had high personal ambitions for himself.

The real breakthrough comes, however, when Snorri sets about writing, or having written, works that do not build directly on familiar literary models, most notably his *Edda* – though this of course is not to say that he learned nothing from ideas and narrative techniques found in earlier works.[22] And from here it may gradually have occurred to him that the secular chieftains of Iceland, like the kings and knights of Europe, could equally raise their "cultural capital"[23] by having the lives of their forefathers set down in writing, and it may be from this that came the germ of the idea for *Egils saga Skalla-Grímssonar*.[24]

If Snorri was indeed behind the idea for the *Edda* that bears his name, he was presumably the first European since classical times to realize the potential of book writing to record a whole system of learning that had hitherto been transmitted entirely orally. Traditional court poetry required a knowledge of the accumulated heritage of poems of ancient heroes, mythological poems and narratives about the world and its place in the greater cosmos, intricate poems of praise to kings and nobles and occasional verse, poetic metres and diction, etc., and all this needed to be arranged within a coherent framework. Oral poetics were presumably studied in a fairly formal way among aspiring oral poets. It was neither folk culture nor folklore in the customary sense of these words, but rather an all-encompassing system of knowledge that only fully trained individuals could ever aspire to master after years of serious and demanding training. The ultimate goal would have been the acquisition of the ability to compose verse in the various skaldic metres using the tropes and poetic language of the trade.

Snorri stood at a cultural crossroads: while in his youth he was being immersed in this world of oral poetry and storytelling as part of his training for a career in poetry and law, he was also a member of one of the first generations to realize the profound changes the introduction of writing was bringing to this society. In particular he must have been aware of how the written codification of the law was changing power structures within Iceland, in particular the status and influence of the orally trained

22   See Baetke 1950; Clunies Ross 1987.
23   Wanner 2008; Torfi H. Tulinius 2009.
24   Sigurður Nordal 1973, 27–30; Hallberg 1962; Vésteinn Ólason 1968; 2002.

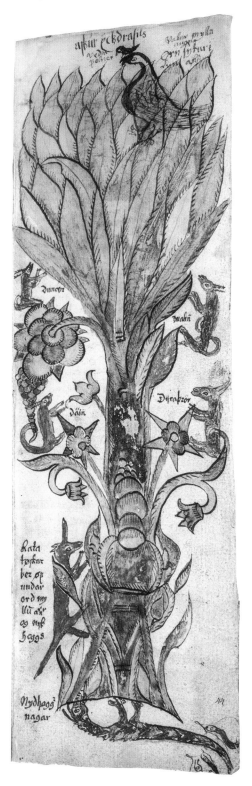

Figure 1. The biggest and best tree in and above the sky, *Askr Yggdrasils* (the ash of Yggdrasill), as it is described by Snorri in his *Edda*, drawn by an unknown seventeenth-century artist in the manuscript Edda oblonga, AM 738 4to 43r. The Árni Magnússon Institute for Icelandic Studies. Photo: Jóhanna Ólafsdóttir.

lawmen and lawspeakers.[25] Snorri may also have observed with some envy the young men around him at Oddi training for priesthood, who could read and review in a systematic fashion all the learning and wisdom they had to acquire – while he in his secular curriculum had to make do with purely oral sources. He would have had every opportunity to observe how useful books could be for structuring clerical learning, and from there to make the leap to

25   I have argued elsewhere (Gísli Sigurðsson 2004, 53–92) that the written codification of the law at the instigation of people with Church affiliations probably created a tension between the old and established power blocs and the new and upcoming clerical class that had command of the skills of reading and writing. The written law became so important that the power of adjudication in legal disputes was eventually transferred from the orally trained lawspeaker and his selected allies to the lawbook – and not just any lawbook, but specifically to the one kept by the bishop at Skálholt.

applying these techniques to the kind of learning he himself had had to acquire.

What makes the works attributed to Snorri so new and important is therefore not just their literary value but, and more importantly, the fact that they reach across the boundary between the oral and the written worlds in a way unprecedented in medieval Europe. If Snorri is the man behind the *Prose Edda*, it must have been his idea to build this bridge between these two worlds, setting his work apart from other medieval writings in which authors utilized oral information and stories in written compositions.[26] Snorri had actually grown up in and was part of the oral culture he sought to turn into writing. Secular literary works had been written earlier using traditional material from oral sources – the *chansons de geste*, for example, and possibly Marie de France's Breton *Lais* – but none attempted the kind of systematic exposition of an entire area of culture in the way Snorri did in the *Edda*. The *Edda* provides us with a rounded view of an entire mythology, written by an insider (with clear authorial intent), from a time when that mythology can be assumed to have still been a living tradition. With Snorri, the writer is his own main informant, and we cannot therefore visualize him as a modern scholar or collector of folk material and see his evidence in any context other than the one in which we find it. We cannot assume, as many scholars have done, that the *Edda* is full of misunderstandings perpetrated by Snorri himself in trying to recreate a system out of disparate fragments of information. Such ideas are liable to lead to the misconception that in some pure and pristine past there was an "authentic" or "original" version of a myth or poem, but that this had been lost or corrupted by Snorri's time, forcing him to create a reconstructed form of dubious validity to pass on to us.[27]

The writing of the *Edda* is a very different matter from the collection, ordering and reconstruction of fragmentary material by outsiders, such as scholars, missionaries and fieldworkers for example. Nowhere else in medieval Europe, at a time when Christianity was spreading from the South and dominated all literary endeavour, do we find someone taking pen to page and compiling a comparable account of their local mythology – even though it may be assumed that all cultures

---

26   For the interplay between the oral and the written in Snorri's work, see for example Meulengracht Sørensen 1992; Lönnroth 1991; Mortensen 2006.
27   Clunies Ross 1992; Weber 1993.

had their own individual or to some extent shared mythologies. The *Edda* therefore represents an extraordinary achievement, a defiance of the accepted categories of writing to produce a work that was secular and both learned and popular, based on traditional oral material, and literary and authorial in a sense we do not find elsewhere in Europe before the Florence of Dante and Boccaccio. Snorri, or whoever it was who composed the *Edda*, was not the only European of his time to think of writing secular literature, and his writings were indisputably influenced by other texts, both Icelandic and foreign, but the work he produced is so unusual that it deserves a very special place in the history of European thought.

Traditional Knowledge and Traditional Science

In an oral society, the accumulated knowledge of a people is kept alive by telling stories, reciting poems and performing certain acts that embody ideas about the past and the moral and ethical values on which society is built. Such a tradition passes on knowledge of all kinds. It is the means by which succeeding generations learn about matters such as law and genealogy, navigation, traditional skills and, not least, astronomy, mankind's oldest systematic stockpile of "scientific" knowledge. A detailed knowledge of the sky and the movements of heavenly bodies is common to all human cultures, however technologically primitive, typically expressed in preliterate societies through mythological narratives and poems.[28]

Such a knowledge must have been part of the traditional training among the Norse oral cultural elite from long before the arrival of book learning and written astronomy from the Mediterranean South[29] – all the more so, perhaps, since the Scandinavians were a mobile and seafaring people who required accurate observations of the heavens for their travels. This traditional knowledge is likely to have been embedded in the mythological conception of the world, which helps us to understand how it survived the Christianization of the religious aspects of life to eventually find its way into *Snorra-Edda*. It remained both essential to the training of aspiring poets in the skaldic tradition and part of the everyday

28 Freidel *et al.* 1993; Selin 2000; Chamberlain *et al.* 2005.
29 Etheridge 2013.

vocabulary used in describing astronomical phenomena. By Snorri's time the myths had presumably lost their religious and ritual functions, but they are likely to have remained current as part of the age-old language used to describe the arch of the heavens and the movements of the sun, moon, planets, fixed stars and other celestial bodies.

In *Gylfaginning*, the first part of the *Edda*, Snorri presents a remarkably lucid and systematic exposition of the inherited cosmological world-view, couched in the context of an illusion (the name means "Gylfi's illusion"). The central feature of the illusion is to envisage deities and mythological phenomena as being located at various points in the sky – *staðir* (places) or *salir* (halls) á *himni* (in the sky). The oldest translated texts on astronomy in Icelandic use equivalents from the Roman pantheon to refer to the planets: Óðinn is identified with Mercury, Freyja with Venus, Týr with Mars, Þórr (Thor) with Jupiter.[30] The naming and describing of celestial phenomena is one of the many roles of myths in all known cultures and there is no reason to suppose that Old Icelandic/Norse culture was any different. Despite the superficial Latin clothing, what we have here is almost certainly traditional Scandinavian star lore. From this perspective *Snorra-Edda* is not a learned synthesis or reconstruction of paganism based on poetic sources, but rather a systematic presentation of a coherent traditional world-view current among the elite of poets in the twelfth and thirteenth centuries, expressed in mythological terms and set down in writing for the benefit of young students in the art and practice of skaldic poetry.[31] The world, and the heavenly dome in particular as it can be observed with the naked eye, is not what it appears to be, but is rather the setting for the myths and adventures related in the stories.

The most likely and straightforward explanation is that Snorri was thoroughly familiar with the concept of applying mythological terminology to real celestial phenomena. In other words, when Snorri speaks of the "sky", that is precisely what he is talking about. This traditional terminology about the "sky" is likely to have been reinforced by the recently acquired access to classical astronomy in written literary representations of mythologies, such as in Ovid's *Metamorphoses*, which may have encouraged Snorri to present his knowledge in a similar or comparable way. And if you want to observe the sky and the stars on

30 *Alfræði íslenzk* II, 63.
31 Gísli Sigurðsson 2014.

dark winter nights, it is very handy to have a hot tub in your back yard to recline in, as owners of them in our own times can confirm, and as Snorri had at Reykholt.

Snorri's career shows every sign of his having been trained in the oral culture in his youth and this lay at the heart of his intellectual development. That is not to say that Snorri was not a man of his times. It is only natural that Snorri's work also evidences contemporary learning and generally accepted ideas, attitudes and knowledge that are now accessible to us only through books. Snorri's special contribution to the world's cultural heritage is not based on any encyclopaedic knowledge or command of the book learning of his contemporaries. Rather it derives from his realization of the potential of book writing as a medium for the scholarship and learning which he and endless generations before him had grown up with only in oral form, passed on by word of mouth.

If we accept, as seems irrefutable, that Snorri was brought up in the oral tradition, his work becomes more important and reliable, i.e. an authentic reflection of the ideas current in his own time about what was regarded as the old mythology – which is quite different from, and should not be confused with, an authentic account of the mythology as it may have been in pre-Christian times. For one thing, all talk of any "renaissance"[32] is highly misleading if we accept a model of continuity rather than revival in the preservation and transmission of traditional knowledge from the oral culture onto vellum. We cannot speak of ancient knowledge gained from written sources or archaeological artefacts being "revived" in Iceland in the twelfth and thirteenth centuries in the way the term "renaissance" is used of Italian culture in the late Middle Ages.

Egils saga Skalla-Grímssonar and the Birth of a New Literature

There are grounds for believing that Snorri's wellspring of literary innovation was not exhausted with his transformation of systematic oral mythological "science" and poetics into the written medium. There are many indications that he may also have been behind the writing of *Egils*

32   Mundal 2007; Hermann 2007; Úlfar Bragason 2007.

saga Skalla-Grímssonar, the biography of his forefather, the poet, chieftain and warrior Egill Skalla-Grímsson, and so instituted the crowning glory of medieval Icelandic literature, the Sagas of Icelanders.[33] Many scholars have been struck by parallels between Egill's and Snorri's own life and fate, giving good reason to think that the stories Snorri inherited about Egill must have struck a particular chord with him. The oldest manuscript fragment we have of any of the Sagas of Icelanders is the so-called *theta* fragment of *Egils saga*, dated to the middle years of the thirteenth century, making it by no means impossible that this particular manuscript was actually written before Snorri's death in 1241. With this manuscript we are on firm ground; all ideas and speculation about other sagas being older than *Egils saga* rely on theories and impressions that are impossible to prove. Most of these theories are based on insecure notions of literary development within the saga genre and putative written connections between them (so-called *rittengsl*[34]); but of other sagas existing earlier in written form there is no hard evidence.

The suggestion that *Egils saga Skalla-Grímssonar* is the work of Snorri Sturluson and that it was the first of the sagas of Icelanders to be written fits in well with the picture outlined here of Snorri's centrality to the development of Icelandic letters, although of course nothing here can be taken as certain. The parallel with his work on the *Edda* is striking: the use of book writing to record and pass on traditionally oral learning (and traditional oral poetry). It should be remembered that, even after Snorri had committed it to parchment, such learning continued to be transmitted by word of mouth as it had been since time immemorial, and that such oral presentation was cheaper, quicker, easier and more natural than writing it down. Snorri's willingness to defy received practice therefore constitutes a major ideological revolution.

Literary histories tend to depict an entirely natural progression in Icelandic literature, from hagiographical literature, to royal historiography interspersed with short narratives about Icelanders at court, to the longer Sagas of Icelanders proper. This is a misconception: the step taken in writing works like the *Edda* and *Egils saga* was far from self-evident or simply the product of a natural development. For this step to take place requires some individual in special circumstances to realize the possibility,

---

33 Jónas Kristjánsson 1990.

34 For a critical discussion of the methodological premises behind these proposed
   rittengsl, see Gísli Sigurðsson 2004, 123–128.

Table 1. The Sagas of Icelanders and the dates of their earliest known manuscripts. The dates given for manuscripts are based on *Ordbog over det norrøne prosasprog. Registre* 1989. The principal setting of the saga is given in brackets. The table omits *Færeyinga saga* and the Vínland sagas, their settings being mainly outside Iceland.

1250	*Egils saga Skalla-Grímssonar* (West)
1250–1300	*Laxdæla saga* (West)
1300	*Heiðarvíga saga* (North-west), *Eyrbyggja saga* (West), *Brennu-Njáls saga* (South)
1302–10	*Fóstbrœðra saga* (West fjords)
1300–1350	*Gunnlaugs saga ormstungu* (West)
1330–70	*Droplaugarsona saga* (East), *Hallfreðar saga* (North-west), *Kormaks saga* (North-west), *Víga-Glúms saga* (North-east), *Bandamanna saga* (North-west), *Finnboga saga ramma* (North-east, North-west)
1350–1400	*Bjarnar saga Hítdœlakappa* (West)
1390–1425	*Vatnsdœla saga* (North-west), *Gísla saga Súrssonar* (West fjords), *Bárðar saga Snæfellsáss* (West), *Flóamanna saga* (South), *Harðar saga* (West), *Þórðar saga hreðu* (North-west), **Hœnsa-Þóris saga* (West), **Kjalnesinga saga* (West), **Króka-Refs saga* (West fjords)
1400	*Ljósvetninga saga* (North-east), *Reykdœla saga* (North-east), *Gull-Þóris saga* (West fjords)
1400–1500	*Hœnsa-Þóris* saga (West)
1420–50	*Vápnfirðinga saga* (East)
1450	*Svarfdœla saga* (North-east)
1450–1500	*Kjalnesinga saga* (West), *Króka-Refs saga* (West, Westfjords)
1475–1500	*Grettis saga Ásmundarsonar* (North-west)
1500	*Víglundar saga* (West)
1500+	*Hrafnkels saga Freysgoða* (East)
1600+	*Valla-Ljóts saga* (North-east), *Fljótsdœla saga* (East), *Gunnars saga Keldugnúpsfífls* (South), *Hávarðar saga Ísfirðings* (Westfjords)
1700	*Þorsteins saga/þáttr Síðu-Hallssonar* (East)

* indicates that the manuscript in question is no longer extant but there is firm evidence for it having existed at the time implied. Consequently, the same saga can be mentioned twice.

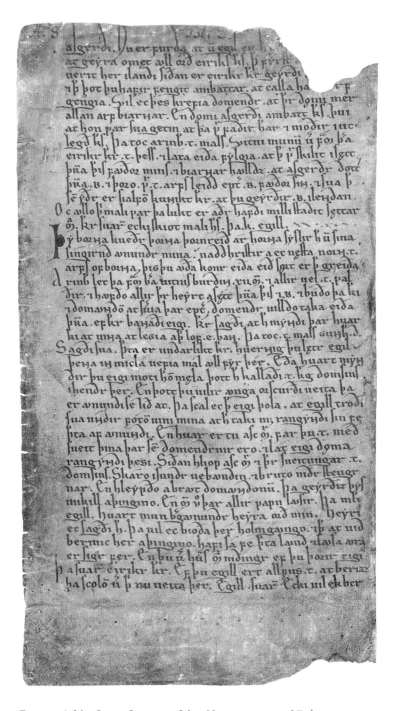

Figure 2. A folio from a fragment of the oldest manuscript of *Egils saga Skalla-Grímssonar* þeta/theta, written in the middle of the thirteenth century: AM 162 A þeta fol. 2v. The Árni Magnússon Institute for Icelandic Studies. Photo: Jóhanna Ólafsdóttir.

to receive a unique flash of inspiration (never forgetting that new ideas do not come out of thin air but are always part of the culture, time, trends, learning and thinking of their times). The individual in question needed to be thoroughly familiar with both media and what each had to offer, and how each was limited – the oral in status and permanence, the written in permitted subject matter and established technique.

If this model of the origins of saga writing is accepted, the Sagas of Icelanders can be seen as the outcome of an original idea in the mind of an individual innovator (in the way that seems indisputable in the case of the *Edda*) rather than as the result of a long development from the primitive to the mature, as the standard model proposes. The age of manuscripts is of course a simplistic way of dating the sagas but it is still a more secure starting point than can be obtained from uncertain and impressionistic methods based on stylistic sophistication and inter-borrowing. This suggests that the innovation found in *Egils saga Skalla-Grímssonar* triggered a gathering avalanche of written sagas which drew on the oral world of storytelling that was clearly spread out throughout the country. Traditions of the settlements clearly preoccupied the minds of later Icelanders; characters were related between stories through bonds of family and friendship; and individual chieftains played a part in several stories, mostly locally but sometimes on a national level. This preoccupation is also manifest in *Landnámabók* which preserves brief records of the settlers in all regions of the country, including many who turn up in the sagas. Often the information found in the sagas corresponds to that in the *Landnámabók*, sometimes it contradicts it, which is only to be expected in a traditional culture whose records were preserved orally, and should not be seen as evidence for highly speculative theories about lost sagas, as has often been the case.[35] The picture that emerges is of a people united by a homogeneous system of values, laws and vision of the past, but with clear regional differences. These were the stories that people now started to transform into the written medium. Remarkably, they also saw that the same methods could be applied equally to their own real-life experiences of closer and contemporary events in the twelfth and thirteenth centuries, therein engendering the sagas compiled as *Sturlunga saga* and preserved in manuscripts from the second half of the fourteenth century. The narrative themes and structures found in the contemporary sagas in

---

35 Jakob Benediktsson 1968, lix–lx.

the *Sturlunga* collection have much in common with those in the Sagas of Icelanders even if the writers clearly stand much closer to the actual events and people they describe.[36]

Once Snorri had set the ball rolling and proved willing to invest the small fortune required to commit to parchment secular stories about individuals of his own social class, others were ready to follow his lead. Monks and clerics could continue to write about saints and evangelizing kings and the life of Christ and his apostles, but Snorri had shown that it was possible to treat other subjects in books and how to go about it. The age of surviving manuscripts suggests that it was Snorri's neighbours (and perhaps relations) in the west of Iceland that were the first to pick up on the new trend, since the next oldest manuscripts contain *Laxdæla saga*, *Eyrbyggja saga* and *Heiðarvíga saga*, all set in the West. After this we get the earliest manuscripts of *Brennu-Njáls saga*, suggesting perhaps a level of ambition on the part of the people of Rangárþing in the southern lowlands where Snorri grew up, a conscious attempt perhaps to outdo their western predecessors by producing something much longer and more complex than had hitherto been attempted.

Once the trend for saga writing had been established, it is only natural to assume that it may have come to play a role in local identity and regional self-esteem. It is possible to imagine something not altogether dissimilar from the competition among different families and power groups in Italy late in the twelfth century to build ever taller and more glorious towers (or at least some tower!) as in the small town of San Gimignano, where the craze generated no fewer than seventy-two towers before it fell out of fashion. In Iceland, the enthusiasm for saga writing spread across the country until eventually every region other than the Reykjanes peninsula in the South-west had written sagas of some kind or another.

The age of known manuscripts is obviously problematic and based on limited evidence. Manuscripts have been lost and sagas may have been written that do not survive in any extant copies. But a comparison of the age of manuscripts and the regional settings of the sagas, good, bad or indifferent, contained in them can be instructive. The picture that emerges is of a trend originating in the central western part of Iceland and spreading out until it comes to cover the whole country, a very different picture from that found in many literary histories of a rather swift chain

36 Tranter 1987; Jónas Kristjánsson 1988; Úlfar Bragason 2010; Andersson 2012, 1–34.

of natural development in the thirteenth and fourteenth centuries from primitive to mature and finally to decadence and decline.

Closing Remarks

From the written works attributed to Snorri it is clear that the person behind them had received a comprehensive education in the secular spheres required by a young man of chieftainly class aspiring to get on in the world as a poet and a politician: law, poetry, genealogy, cosmology, mythology, and the art of storytelling. A feature of Snorri's work is the reduced emphasis he places on miracles and divine intercession, both in his reworking of the *Óláfs saga helga* (King Óláfr Haraldsson) and in his *Edda*. In the *Edda* in particular Snorri goes to great lengths to present a euhemerised interpretation of the Norse gods: these gods, he says, were really mortals whom people in their ignorance started to venerate. Snorri faces up to the fundamental questions of the creation and fate of the universe. In his retelling of the heroic tales and in the Kings' Sagas he contemplates the moral laws and ethics of human society, and in *Heimskringla* he considers the authenticity and reliability of historical sources, in particular the role of poets when they praised chieftains in the hope of financial reward and enhanced prestige (as was no doubt in part his own motivation). Finally, in *Egils saga Skalla-Grímssonar*, he investigates the position of the individual in his struggle with men of power and divine forces. In his portrayal of the poet Egill Skalla-Grímsson, Snorri also gives us a character of remarkable roundness and depth, tracing his life from birth to death at an advanced age and presenting it through the stylistic contrasts between the terse and dispassionate narrative prose and the highly personal and forceful poetry put into the mouth of the central character. The person who created *Egils saga* marks himself out as an author in a sense more modern than medieval, capable of expressing a wide and often conflicting range of personal ideas and emotions.

Once Snorri had completed his account of the received tradition of myths and poetics in the *Edda*, it may in many ways have been the logical next step to broaden the platform and write a saga based on the poems and stories of a family of settlers in the new country – indeed, in the very part of the country Snorri could best identify with, where he was born and where he chose to spend his mature years and exercise his influence.

Snorri, or someone very close to him, put a very personal mark on all the works attributed to him, just as storytellers do every time they perform a piece orally to an audience. But the writing process allowed for new possibilities, in particular a more ordered and systematized presentation of the material than oral tellers or teachers would have wanted, or been able, to achieve. That Snorri seems to have been able to secure the best of both worlds suggests a personal vision and an authorial awareness of a kind we identify with writers of fiction in later centuries. The advent of the modern notion of the author in Western literature may be generally associated with Dante, but in Snorri and the authors who followed his example we can push this back by the best part of a century. The difference is, of course, that Dante wrote in an influential language in an influential region; Snorri wrote on the periphery and his works barely travelled beyond his native land. And if we could show that *Egils saga* was indeed the first saga to be written and that Snorri was indeed its author, perhaps we would be tracing the origins of the modern novel to the creative spark that enabled Snorri Sturluson in the final years of his life to conceive the idea for the book that has come down to us as *Egils saga Skalla-Grímssonar*.

Acknowledgements

I would like to thank my friend Nicholas Jones for his help in translating the parts of my text originally written in Icelandic and copyediting the parts originally written in English.

Bibliography

Alfræði íslenzk II. Eds Kristian Kålund and Natanael Beckman. Copenhagen: Samfund til udgivelse af gammel nordisk litteratur 1914–1916.

Andersson, Theodore M. and Kari Ellen Gade 2000. *Morkinskinna: The Earliest Icelandic Chronicle of the Norwegian Kings (1030–1157)*. Islandica 51. Ithaca and London: Cornell University Press.

Andersson, Theodore M. 2012. *The Partisan Muse in the Early Icelandic Sagas (1200–1250)*. Islandica LV. Ithaca, New York: Cornell University Press.

Ascoli, Albert R. 2008. *Dante and the Making of a Modern Author*. Cambridge: Cambridge University Press.

Ármann Jakobsson 2011. *Morkinskinna* I–II. Ed. Jónas Kristjánsson and Þórður Ingi Guðjónsson. Íslenzk fornrit XXIII. Reykjavík: Hið íslenzka fornritafélag.

Ármann Jakobsson 2014. *A Sense of Belonging: Morkinskinna and Icelandic Identity, c. 1220*. Translated by Fredrik Heinemann. Odense: University Press of Southern Denmark.

Baetke, Walter 1950. "Die Götterlehre der Snorra-Edda". *Berichte über die Verhandlung der Sächs. Akad. d. Wiss. zu Leipzig (Phil.-hist. Kl)* 97: H.3. Reprinted in Walter Baetke, *Kleine Schriften*. Weimar: Hermann Böhlaus Nachfolger 1973, 206–246.

Bagge, Sverre 1991. *Society and Politics in Snorri Sturluson's* Heimskringla. Berkeley, Los Angeles, Oxford: University of California Press.

Baldur Hafstað 1995. *Die Egils saga und ihr Verhältnis zu anderen Werken des nordischen Mittelalters*. Rannsóknarrit. Reykjavík: Rannsóknarstofnun Kennaraháskóla Íslands.

Bjarni Einarsson 1961. *Skáldasögur. Um uppruna og eðli ástaskáldasagnanna fornu*. Reykjavík: Bókaútgáfa Menningarsjóðs.

Bjarni Einarsson 1975. *Litterære forudsætninger for Egils saga*. Rit 8. Reykjavík: Stofnun Árna Magnússonar á Íslandi.

Chamberlain, Von Del, John B. Carlson and M. Jane Young (eds) 2005. *Songs From the Sky: Indigenous Astronomical and Cosmological Traditions of the World*. University of Maryland, College Park. Center for Archaeoastronomy: Ocarina Books.

Clunies Ross, Margaret 1987. *Skáldskaparmál: Snorri Sturluson's* ars poetica *and Medieval Theories of Language*. The Viking Collection, 4. Odense: Odense University Press.

Clunies Ross, Margaret 1992. "The mythological fictions of *Snorra Edda*". In Úlfar Bragason (ed.), *Snorrastefna*. Reykjavík: Stofnun Sigurðar Nordals, 204–216.

Danielsson, Tommy 2002. *Sagorna om Norges kungar: Från Magnús góði till Magnús Erlingsson*. Södertälje: Gidlunds förlag.

Etheridge, Christian 2013. "A possible source for a medieval Icelandic astronomical manuscript on the basis of pictorial evidence". In Karina Lukin, Frog and Sakari Katajamäki (eds), *Limited Sources, Boundless Possibilities: Textual Scholarship and the Challenges of Oral and Written Texts*. Helsinki: University of Helsinki, 69–78.

Faulkes, Anthony 1993. "The sources of Skáldskaparmál: Snorri's intellectual background". In Alois Wold (ed.), *Snorri Sturluson. Colloquium anlässlich der 750. Wiederkehr seines Todestages*. ScriptOralia 51. Tübingen: Gunter Narr Verlag, 59–76.

Freidel, David, Linda Schele and Joy Parker 1993. *Maya Cosmos: Three Thousand Years on the Shaman's Path*. New York: William Morrow and Company, Inc.

Gísli Sigurðsson 2004. *The Medieval Icelandic Saga and Oral Tradition: A Discourse on Method.* Cambridge, MA: Harvard University Press.

Gísli Sigurðsson 2012. "Poet, singer of tales, storyteller, and author". In Slavica Rankovic (ed.), *Modes of Authorship in the Middle Ages.* Toronto: Pontifical Institute of Medieval Studies, 227–235.

Gísli Sigurðsson 2014. "Snorri's Edda: The sky described in mythological terms". In Timothy R. Tangherlini (ed.), *Nordic Mythologies: Interpretations, Intersections, and Institutions.* Berkeley, Los Angeles: North Pinehurst Press, 184–198.

Guðrún Nordal. 1992. "Skáldið Snorri Sturluson". In Úlfar Bragason (ed.), *Snorrastefna 25.–27. júlí 1990.* Reykjavík: Stofnun Sigurðar Nordals, 52–69.

Guðrún Nordal 2001. *Tools of Literacy. The Role of Skaldic Verse in Icelandic Textual Culture of the Twelfth and Thirteenth Century.* Toronto, Buffalo, London: University of Toronto Press.

Guðrún Nordal 2006. "Snorri and Norway". In Else Mundal (ed.), *Reykholt som makt- og lærdomssenter i den islandske og nordiske kontekst.* Snorrastofa, vol. III. Reykholt: Snorrastofa, 77–84.

Halldór Hermannsson 1932. *Sæmund Sigfússon and the Oddaverjar.* Islandica 22. Ithaca, New York: Cornell University Library.

Hastrup, Kirsten 2009. "Northern Barbarians: Icelandic canons of civilisation". *Gripla* 20, 109–136.

Hallberg, Peter 1962. *Snorri Sturluson och Egils saga Skallagrímssonar. Ett försök till språklig författarbestämning.* Studia Islandica 20. Reykjavík: Menningarsjóður.

Haukur Þorgeirsson 2014. "Snorri versus the copyist. An investigation of a stylistic trait in the manuscript traditions of *Egils Saga, Heimskringla* and the *Prose Edda*". *Saga Book* 38, 61–74.

Helgi Þorláksson 2006. "Var Reykholt lærdomssenter på Snorri Sturlusons tid?" In Else Mundal (ed.), *Reykholt som makt- og lærdomssenter i den islandske og nordiske kontekst.* Snorrastofa, vol. III. Reykholt: Snorrastofa, 13–23.

Helgi Þorláksson 2006. "Snorri Sturluson, Reykholt og augustinerordenen". In Else Mundal (ed.), *Reykholt som makt- og lærdomssenter i den islandske og nordiske kontekst.* Snorrastofa, vol. III. Reykholt. Snorrastofa, 65–75.

Helgi Þorláksson 2014. "Snorri í Odda: Um menntun Snorra Sturlusonar, uppeldi og mótun". *Skírnir* 188 (haust), 353–380.

Hermann, Pernille 2007. "Den norrøne renæssance og dens forudsætninger". In Karl G. Johansson (ed.), *Den norröna renässansen. Reykholt, Norden och Europa 1150–1300.* Snorrastofa, vol. IV. Reykholt: Snorrastofa, 41–61.

Jakob Benediktsson 1955, "Hvar er Snorri nefndur höfundur Eddu?" *Skírnir* 129, 118–127.

Jakob Benediktsson 1968. "Formáli". *Íslendingabók, Landnámabók.* Íslenzk fornrit I. Reykjavík: Hið íslenzka fornritafélag, v–cliv.

Jónas Kristjánsson 1988. "Íslendingasögur og Sturlunga: samanburður nokkurra einkenna og efnisatriða". In Guðrún Ása Grímsdóttir and Jónas Kristjánsson (eds), *Sturlustefna. Ráðstefna haldin á sjö alda ártíð Sturlu Þórðarsonar sagnaritara 1984.* Rit 32. Reykjavík: Stofnun Árna Magnússonar á Íslandi, 94–111.

Jónas Kristjánsson 1990. "Var Snorri Sturluson upphafsmaður Íslendingasagna?" *Andvari* 115, 85–105.

Louis-Jensen, Jonna 1997. "Heimskringla – Et værk af Snorri Sturluson?" *Nordica Bergensia* 14, 230–245.

Louis-Jensen, Jonna 2009. "Heimskringla og Egils saga – samme forfatter?" *Studier i Nordisk 2006–2007*, 103–111.

Lönnroth, Lars 1991. "Sponsors, writers, and readers of early Norse literature". In Ross Samson (ed.), *Social Approaches to Viking Studies*. Glasgow: Cruithne Press, 3–10.

Meulengracht Sørensen, Preben 1992. "Snorris frœði". In Úlfar Bragason (ed.), *Snorrastefna*. Reykjavík: Stofnun Sigurðar Nordals, 270–283.

Mortensen, Lars Boje 2006. "Den formative dialog mellem latinsk og folkesproglig litteratur ca. 600–1250. Udkast til en dynamisk model". In Else Mundal (ed.), *Reykholt som makt- og lærdomssenter i den islandske og nordiske kontekst*. Snorrastofa, vol. III. Reykholt: Snorrastofa, 229–271.

Mundal, Else 2007. "Med kva rett kan vi tale om ein norrøn renessanse?" In Karl G. Johansson (ed.), *Den norröna renässansen. Reykholt, Norden och Europa 1150–1300*. Snorrastofa, vol. III. Reykholt: Snorrastofa, 25–39.

Ordbog over det norrøne prosasprog. Registre. 1989. Copenhagen. The Arnamagnean Commission.

Óskar Guðmundsson 2009. *Snorri. Ævisaga Snorra Sturlusonar 1179–1241*. Reykjavík: JPV útgáfa.

Sävborg, Daniel 2007. *Sagan om kärleken. Erotik, känslor och berättarkonst i norrön litteratur*. Acta Universitatis Upsaliensis. Historia litterarum 27. Uppsala: Uppsala Universitet.

Selin, Helaine (ed.) 2000. *Astronomy across Cultures: The History of Non-Western Astronomy*. Dordrecht: Kluwer Academic Publishers.

Sigurður Nordal 1953. *Sagalitteraturen*. Nordisk kultur 8b. Stockholm, Oslo, Copenhagen: Albert Bonniers, H. Aschehough and J. H. Schultz forlag, 180–273.

Sigurður Nordal 1973. *Snorri Sturluson*. Önnur prentun. Reykjavík: Helgafell.

Sverrir Tómasson 1988. *Formálar íslenskra sagnaritara á miðöldum: Rannsókn bókmenntahefðar*. Rit 33. Reykjavík: Stofnun Árna Magnússonar á Íslandi.

Sverrir Tómasson 1992a. "Erlendur vísdómur og forn fræði". In Vésteinn Ólason (ed.), *Íslensk bókmenntasaga 1*. Reykjavík: Mál og menning, 517–571.

Sverrir Tómasson 1992b. "Konungasögur". In Vésteinn Ólason (ed.), *Íslensk bókmenntasaga 1*. Reykjavík: Mál og menning, 358–401.

Sverrir Tómasson 1997. "'Upp í garð til Sæmundar': lærdómssetrið í Odda og Snorri Sturluson". *Goðasteinn 33*, 188–202.

Torfi H. Tulinius 2002. *The Matter of the North: The Rise of Literary Fiction in Thirteenth-Century Iceland*. Translated by Randi C. Eldevik. Odense: Odense University Press.

Torfi H. Tulinius 2014. *The Enigma of Egill: The Saga, the Viking Poet and Snorri Sturluson*. Translation by Victoria Cribb. Ithaca: Cornell University Library.

Torfi H. Tulinius 2009. "Pierre Bourdieu and Snorri Sturluson. Chieftains, sociology and the development of literature in medieval Iceland". In Jon Gunnar Jørgensen (ed.), *Snorres Edda i europeisk og islandsk kultur*. Snorrastofa, vol. V. Reykholt: Snorrastofa, 47–71.

Tranter, Stephen N. 1987. *Sturlunga Saga. The rôle of the Creative Compiler*. Frankfurt am Main, Bern, New York: Peter Lang.

Úlfar Bragason 2007. "Genealogies: A return to the past". In Karl G. Johansson (ed.), *Den norröna renässansen. Reykholt, Norden och Europa 1150–1300*. Snorrastofa, vol. IV. Reykholt: Snorrastofa, 73–81.

Úlfar Bragason 2010. *Ætt og saga. Um*

frásagnarfræði Sturlungu eða Íslendinga sögu hinnar miklu. Reykjavík: Háskólaútgáfan.

Vésteinn Ólason 1968. "Er Snorri höfundur Egils sögu?" *Skírnir* 141, 48–67.

Vésteinn Ólason 2002. "Inngangur". *Snorri Sturluson. Ritsafn* I. Reykjavík: Mál og menning, xi–lxxvi.

Wanner, Kevin J. 2008. *Snorri Sturluson and the Edda. The Conversion of Cultural Capital in Medieval Scandinavia*. Toronto, Buffalo, London: University of Toronto Press.

Weber, Gerd Wolfgang 1993. "Snorri Sturlu-sons Verhältnis zu seinen Quellen und sein Mythos-Begriff". In Alois Wolf (ed.), *Snorri Sturluson. Colloquium anlässlich der 750. Wiederkehr seines Todestages*. ScriptOralia 51. Tübingen: Gunter Narr Verlag, 193–244.

Whaley, Diana 1991. *Heimskringla: An Introduction*. University College London: Viking Society for Northern Research.

Þorleifur Hauksson 2007. "Formáli". *Sverris saga*. Íslenzk fornrit XXX. Reykjavík: Hið íslenzka fornritafélag, v–xc.

Oral Rhetoric and Literary Rhetoric

HE INTERRELATION BETWEEN LATIN LEARNING AND VER-nacular cultures is a multifarious field: the foreign impact is sometimes more or less self-evident, sometimes hardly discernible. In the case of rhetorical education, parts of the tradition are clearly traceable through certain texts, while other parts of the tradition are not documented in the same way. Here, it is useful to distinguish between oral rhetoric and literary rhetoric: in the end, I suggest, this makes us able to understand the origin of the concept *kenning* better.

In forming an idea of what basic education was like in twelfth-century Iceland, we are guided by a number of manuscripts that document the knowledge and use of certain Latin texts. Obviously, these do not give a complete picture: texts have been lost, and books were only a limited part of education as at most the teacher could be expected to own or have access to a book. To a very great extent, medieval teaching will have been based on oral interaction.[1] Where Icelandic sources end, it is however possible to deduce educational structures from the situation in the rest of medieval Europe, as some general aspects of education can be more or less taken for granted. One of these is the strong continuity of classical education and learning.

From antiquity, basic education began with the *trivium*, the three basic arts: grammar, rhetoric and dialectics. Grammar was the basic

---

1   E.g. Orme 2006; Kraus 2009; Fafner 1982, 143.

element in learning to read. As is well known, there are clear traces in Iceland of textbooks covering that field, since the grammatical treatises of the twelfth century are based on Latin grammarians such as Donatus, Priscianus, Eberhard and Alexander de Villa Dei. Donatus starts with the absolute basics and goes on to the figures and tropes, and in his view even the figures of speech (tropes) belong to grammar, not to rhetoric.

These textbooks were widely spread throughout Europe during the Middle Ages and constituted a kind of universal basic learning (but only for those who actually received an education, obviously).[2] It has been pointed out that Donatus was especially central for students of Latin as a second language: he invited careful analysis of this foreign language.[3] Still, in Iceland, these textbooks were soon converted into Icelandic versions, not only written in Icelandic but also substituting the Latin examples with Icelandic ones gathered from the skaldic poetry. As Guðrún Nordal has shown, theoretical texts such as the third and fourth grammatical treatises and *Snorra-Edda* were used together with skaldic diction as a corpus for teaching select Icelanders to compose in a way equal to the Latin masters, at the same time equating the old skalds with the old Roman poets. In that sense, Guðrún points out, skaldic diction became a "crucial link between the study of *grammatica* and the indigenous traditions in Iceland."[4] The political and ideological aspects of this kind of textual culture were, of course, considerable, and resulted in highly skilled authors both in Latin and Icelandic. Here, as elsewhere, *grammatica* formed a social elite.[5]

Grammar thus incorporated parts of what we would usually label as rhetoric, especially figurative language. If one is to judge Icelandic education in the twelfth century from the surviving texts, it would seem that the only aspect of rhetoric to have had any impact was that part dealing with figurative language and adorned discourse. However, this dimension of rhetoric was entirely secondary to what can be labelled "oral" rhetoric.

Traditionally, rhetoric was considered to consist of five parts. In Cicero's *De inventione*, which was the most influential rhetorical treatise in the Middle Ages, followed by the *Rhetorica ad Herennium*, which was

---

2   For a rich collection of examples, see Carruthers and Sluiter (eds) 2009.
3   E.g. Kraus 2009, 70.
4   Guðrún Nordal 2001, 340.
5   Cf. Irvine 1994, 461.

long considered also to be the work of Cicero,[6] the parts of rhetoric are listed thus:

inventio ("finding" topics and arguments)
dispositio (arranging them)
elocutio ("dressing" the topics and arguments in efficient words)
memoria (command of the speech to be presented orally)
pronuntiatio (delivery)

The textbooks of Donatus and others concern *elocutio*, in which the key word is *ornatus*, adornment: precisely that which was demonstrated in the examples from poetry. The different literary techniques described and labelled (metaphor, metonymy etc.) provided concepts both for analysing poetry and for creating poetry.

That these books can be traced to Iceland does not mean that *elocutio* was the only part of rhetoric that was incorporated into Icelandic education. To a great extent, the reason that these kinds of textbooks were so widely used during the Middle Ages was that they were the keys not to rhetoric but to grammar: through them, students learnt to read, analyse and compose. They did not, however, in themselves constitute a training in rhetoric. Rather, *elocutio* concerns what we may call *literary* rhetoric. *Elocutio* was the part of rhetoric that was especially developed by certain authors from the first century AD, when Dionysius of Halicarnassus, Demetrius and Longinus started writing rhetorical treatises devoted to literary composition. This has been spoken of as the "literaturization" of rhetoric: from being a discipline devoted to oral presentation, these authors exemplify its development into a discipline of literary presentation. We may thus see "the adaptation of primary, oral rhetoric into a secondary, literary rhetoric for readers" visible "in the use of topics, in the presentation of ethos and pathos, in patterns of arrangement, in application of progymnasmatic exercises and features of declamation, and especially in the use of tropes, figures, and *sententiae*".[7]

Dionysius, Demetrius and Longinus were not influential during the Middle Ages and their treatises were intended for considerably more sophisticated users than the grammatical treatises of Donatus and

---

6   E.g. Murphy 2005.
7   Kennedy 1999, 129.

Priscianus, but the distinction between oral and literary rhetoric can be applied to them as well: taking up only the aspects of tropes, figures and ornate language, they conveyed the means not for rhetorical invention or delivery in an oral situation, but for deliberate, thorough consideration of the values of each word. In this respect, the grammatical treatises present a literary rhetoric. Invention and disposition are also necessary in literary rhetoric, but in the treatises it is above all *elocutio* that matters, while no interest whatsoever is directed toward mnemonics or techniques of oral delivery. On the other hand, oral rhetoric is much preoccupied with invention and disposition, but less interested in the highly elaborated refinery of *elocutio* – and it substantially focuses on memorizing and delivery.

In the medieval tradition, literary rhetoric, or the basic parts of it, appears quite dominant through the frequent manuscripts of Donatus, Priscianus and others. But there was also a strong interest in *inventio*, which is most obvious in the fact that the most influential rhetorical handbook from antiquity was Cicero's *De inventione.* As Copeland and Carruthers have very effectively demonstrated, invention was in effect the prerequisite of several central activities.[8] Inventing one's store of topics, arguments, examples, images, etc., was the prerequisite not only for written compositions, but also for creating, performing and improvizing in all kinds of endeavours. These practices became increasingly important in the Middle Ages, as they were employed within the religious sphere: Carruthers thus elucidates "monastic" practices. Obviously, disposition became a natural part of invention: the things retrieved must be ordered in an efficient way. In the material preserved, least attention seems to have been devoted to *memoria* and *pronuntiatio,* the two parts that exclusively belong to oral performance.[9]

However, if the prerequisite of learning and communication is invention, the prerequisite for all kinds of invention is memory. As Carruthers emphasizes, all invention, all use of the resources of mind, was dependent on memory. Memory was the storeroom, where practically everything was stored as images – the basic notion being that sense impressions were really impressed, stamped, into the wax tablet of the mind. Memory is thus locational: things could be stored in different places and retrieved

---

8   Copeland 1991, 151–178; Carruthers 1998. On the traces of classical texts in the Middle Ages, see Munk Olsen 1982–2014, especially 2014.

9   Cf. Copeland 1991, 236 n7.

along different routes. Memory was not the ability to reproduce but the "matrix of a reminiscing cogitation, shuffling and collating 'things' stored in a random-access memory scheme, or set of schemes – a memory "architecture" and a library built up during one's lifetime with the express intention that it be used inventively".[10]

For any knowledge to be kept or developed, memory was thus the prerequisite. This was encoded in the rhetorical treatises of antiquity, especially Quintilian's *Institutio oratoria* and the *Rhetorica ad Herennium*, and thus concerned all parts of secular interaction. With Carruthers and the sources she adduces, we can also conclude that memory was the prerequisite for meditation and life in God. It is true that no mnemotechnical advice from antiquity seems to have been very much preserved,[11] but the reason for this is not that memory lost its importance – rather, it appears to have been the foundational presupposition of all education, especially rhetorical. The mnemotechnical systems of antiquity lost their place, and instead a basic insight into the importance and function of memory was generally taken for granted and basic techniques of memory were codified. The works first of Yates and then Carruthers, as well as others, shed light on the medieval art of and view on memory not from elaborate treatises on the subject, but by finding clues in a variety of sources.

What, then, would be the general view on memory during the Middle Ages? Due to the immense time-span and variety of regions, classes etc., the question cannot be answered with any accuracy, but I think that Carruthers' description must be close to giving a general outline:

> Monastic *memoria*, like the Roman art, is a locational memory; it also cultivates the making of mental images for the mind to work with as a fundamental procedure of human thinking. Because crafting memories also involved crafting the images in which those memories were carried and conducted, the artifice of memory was also, necessarily, an art of making various sorts of pictures: pictures in the mind, to be sure, but with close, symbiotic relationships to actual images and actual words that someone had seen or read or heard – or smelled or tasted or touched, for all the

---

10 Carruthers 1998, 4.
11 See Evans 1980.

senses, as we will observe, were cultivated in the monastic craft of remembering.[12]

Carruthers stresses the dynamic aspect of memory, as opposed to Yates who has a more static view on it, but she shares Yates' foundational conclusion: "the great principle of classical artificial memory [is] the appeal to the sense of sight".[13] Memory, then, is a space or storeroom where everything is stored – thus we may want to create the space of a house, or a road along which we mark (*notamus*) images for all the things we wish to remember, with Quintilian's method.[14] It is crucial that the "things" be made into images, as is also stressed in the *Rhetorica ad Herennium*: "Rei totius memoriam saepe una nota et imagine simplici conprehendimus".[15] A *nota* is a sign, but a sign of a particularly visual character. *Nota*, with derivatives such as *notatio*, is a key word to effective memorizing throughout tradition. A little further on it is stated: "Imagines igitur nos in eo genere constituere oportebit quod genus in memoria diutissime potest haerere. Id accidet si quam maxime notatas similitudines constituemus; si non multas nec vagas, sed aliquid agentes imagines ponemus".[16]

In other words, the images are to be strong and memorable, and the word for this is *notatus*. *Notatio* is not only characterizing, but particularly powerful characterizing. In the same work, the term also designates a figure for visualizing a person through remarkable characteristics: "Notatio est cum alicuius natura certis describitur signis, quae, sicuti notae quae, naturae sunt adtributa".[17] In the teaching of mnemonics, the advocation of *notae*, according to Carruthers, was ubiquitous.[18] Although the classical artificial art of memory was not transmitted, the importance and nature of memory were a universal occupation, and regularly codified in the

12 Carruthers 1990,10.
13 Yates 1966, 186–187.
14 *Institutio oratoria* 11.17–21.
15 "Often we encompass the record of an entire matter by one notation, a single image" (*Rhetorica ad Herennium* III.33).
16 "We ought, then, to set up images of a kind that can adhere longest in the memory. And we shall do so if we establish likenesses as striking as possible; if we set up images that are not many or vague, but doing something" (*Rhetorica ad Herennium* III.33).
17 "Notatio [Character Delineation] consists in describing a person's character by the definite signs which, like distinctive marks, are attributes of that character" (*Rhetorica ad Herennium* IV.63).
18 Carruthers 1998, 122 and 313, n. 14; also Carruthers 1990, 107–108.

Figure 1. *Snorra-Edda* is an important –
and complex – source for Norse mythology. The wolf Fenrisúlfr has a prominent
part in this mythology. Here it is drawn
by an unknown seventeenth-century
artist in the manuscript Edda oblonga,
AM 738 4to 43r. The Árni Magnússon
Institute for Icelandic Studies. Photo:
Jóhanna Ólafsdóttir.

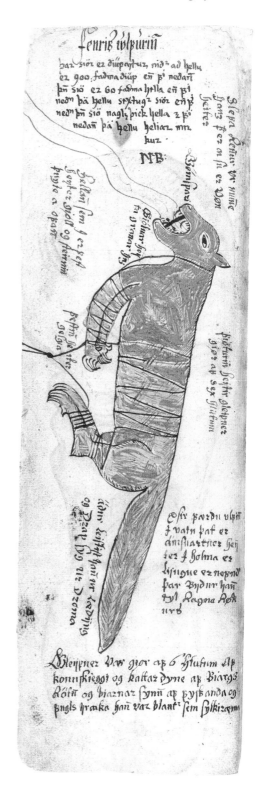

words for *nota*. Even Augustine used
it in his *Confessions*.[19]

In a society such as twelfth-century Iceland, memory was obviously vital as the carrier of the whole
culture before it came into writing.
Even as literacy spread, books and
parchment were rare and precious.
Students needed to exploit memory
not only to preserve knowledge, but
also to be able to use it. The medieval characteristic of a genius was
largely built on memory, as Carruthers demonstrates by comparing
descriptions of Thomas Aquinas
and Albert Einstein.[20] This is an
aspect of twelfth-century education
and learning that does not emerge
from the preserved manuscripts, but
is part of the bigger picture. It also
raises questions about Old Norse
imagery.

19 X.17.26; see Carruthers 1998, 30.
20 Carruthers 1990, 2–4.

The word *kenning* as a term for the poetic device is not known before *Snorra-Edda*. The poetic imagery of *kennings* may very well have been developed without there being a term for them, and at some point in the development of Latin education leading up to *Snorra-Edda* the term *kenning* appears to have been devised, possibly by Snorri himself. Although we cannot know to what extent, we do know that Snorri was influenced by European learning. Even as in the beginning of *Háttatal*, probably the first part of his *Edda* he wrote, he divides poetry into three kinds "in accordance with rule, or licence, or prohibition" ("setning, leyfi ok fyrirboðning"), he adheres to the Latin's traditional *pars praeceptiva*, *pars permissiva* and *pars prohibitiva*.[21] Obviously, Snorri's ambition was to enable contemporary poets to use the old mythology in their poems, thereby saving the old myths and poems from oblivion. The reason for his focus on the *kenning* is in this respect self-evident: it is a spectacular literary device, and in this device, as it were, myth is stored.

According to Snorri, one can take a synonym or circumlocution for the person or thing referred to and characterize (*kenna*) it with a determinator. This determinator places that which is referred to, the signified, in the context where it should be understood, and it does so to a great extent through visualization: the determinator *hanga-* (of the hanged) when added to the word *Týr* visually evokes, in the *kenning* *farmatýr*, Óðinn, who is associated with the hanged. The determinator *sævar* (of the sea) creates an entire space where the word *hestr* (horse) immediately stimulates the inner eye and makes it understand *hestr sævar* as "ship".

The *kenning* Snorri also calls *kennt heiti*: a *heiti* is a name or noun (horse) which is determined, *kennt*, with a determinator: a noun in the genitive (of the sea) as the "classical" *kenning* is made, or an adjective. This leads us to the conclusion that the central feature of the *kenning* is not the base word, but the determinator: the actual *kenning*, characterizer, is not the word meaning "horse" but the word meaning "sea". Throughout the *Edda* Snorri is careful to use the word *kalla* when discussing the *heiti*, the base word that substitutes the signified, and to use the word *kenna* when discussing the determinator which is there to describe the *heiti*.

---

21   *Háttatal* 0/7; see the commentary p. 48. The comprehensive study of Latin learning in *Snorra-Edda* is Clunies Ross 1987.

Hvernig skal kenna mann? Hann skal kenna við verk sín, þat er hann veitir eða þiggr eða gerir. Hann má ok kenna til eignar sinnar þeirar er hann á ok svá ef hann gaf, svá ok við ættir þær er hann kom af, svá þær er frá honum kómu. Hvernig skal hann kenna við þessa hluti? Svá att kalla hann vinnanda eða fremjanda eða til fara sinna eða athafnar, víga eða sæfara eða veiða eða vápna eða skipa.[22]

This should mean that the word *kenning* as a two-part poetic periphrase is a secondary meaning: the primary meaning must have been "characterizer", that is, it was originally a word for the determinator, not the *heiti* and not the periphrase as a whole. It thus corresponds to other meanings of the word *kenning* concerning "knowledge", "insight", and "learning": the poetic device *kenning* adds knowledge about the signified, adds by characterizing. Agency in the image as a whole is important, "calling him the achiever or performer" says Snorri, while *Rhetorica ad Herennium* speaks of images "doing something" (*agentes imagines*). That is, action in the image strengthens its sense of actuality and effect according to both the Latin and the Icelandic author.

The *kenning* then consists in a characterization collected from a sphere proper to the signified, just like the Latin *nota* may also consist in a characterizing image collected from a sphere proper to the signified, as Quintilian formulates it: "Tum quae scripserunt vel cogitatione complectuntur aliquo signo quo moneantur notant, quod esse vel ex re tota potest, ut de navigatione, militia, vel ex verbo aliquo: nam etiam excidentes unius admonitione verbi in memoriam reponuntur".[23]

While *Rhetorica ad Herennium* may have been known in Iceland, it is less probable (but not impossible) that Quintilian's *Institutio oratoria* was known there.[24] The quotation is useful in that it eloquently formulates

---

22   "How shall a man be referred to? He shall be referred to by his actions, what he gives or receives or does. He can also be referred to by his property, what he owns and also if he gives it away; also by the family lines he is descended from, also those that have descended from him. How shall he be referred to by these things? By calling him the achiever or performer of his expeditions or activities, of killings or sea voyages or huntings, or with weapons or ships" (*Skáldskaparmál* 31).

23   "The next stage is to mark what they have written or are mentally preparing with some sign which will jog their memory. This may be based on the subject as a whole (on navigation or warfare, for example) or on a word, because even people who lose the thread of what they are saying can have their memory put back on track by the cue of a single word" (Quintilian, *Institutio oratoria* 11.2.19).

24   But cf. Halldór Halldórsson 1975, 12–13.

what was a general axiom: the *nota* is a striking image, characterizing and/ or evoking associations and context of the signified. The *kenning* is an image – not always but very often striking – characterizing the signified through evoking associations and context (e.g. weapons or ships according to Snorri, e.g. navigation or warfare according to Quintilian). There was probably no direct contact between Quintilian's work and Snorri, but it would be very difficult to think that Latin education in Iceland had not introduced memory and its techniques, conspicuous among them *nota* and *notatio*, as a vital prerequisite of learning.

The *kenning* is only indirectly associated with memory, and the *nota* is not always associated with memory either: it can consist in mere characterization according to the *Rhetorica ad Herennium*. However, the essence of *kenning* is very close to *nota* and *notatio*: the forceful visualization of characteristics. The Latin discussions of memory do not always include the terms *nota* or *notatio*, but the techniques developed within the rhetorical tradition were certainly of a kind that is parallel to the *kenning* in several ways. As we have seen, the very terms *nota* and *notatio* were widespread and constantly used. Grammar, rhetoric and learning were essential to Christian erudition and administration: they naturally followed when the Church was established in Iceland. As natural parts of rhetoric, the techniques for memory will have been introduced. And what would the suitable translation of *notatio*, this knowledge-transmitting characterization with visualizing aspects, be? Obviously, *kenning*. The primary meanings of *kenning* (according to Fritzner) are sense, sensation; knowledge, recognition; doctrine, teaching. The physical aspect of sense is not part of Latin *nota*, but knowledge and recognition are precisely what the term is about. *Nota* is a sign and *notatio* is the use of *nota*: a marking, noting, describing, characterizing, corresponding to the term *kenning*. The verb *notare* is to mark, signify, observe, corresponding to the verb *kenna*. At bottom lies the verb *noscere*: that which is *notum* is that which is *kennt* – known or made known. *Kenning* thus appears to be the appropriate translation of *notatio*. Just as *notatio* in this rhetorical sense furthers knowledge, understanding and clarification by visualizing, so does the *kenning*.[25]

25   For a more extensive discussion of the interpretation of *kennings* see Malm 2007, and for a wider discussion of the memorial and imaginative aspects see Bergsveinn Birgisson 2007.

We know that some of Snorri's terms were developed from the Latin rhetorical and grammatical traditions, but the term *kenning* has not hitherto been explained: it has often been understood as "naming", but this does not connect it to any Latin device, and as we have seen, such a meaning of the word is indeed not primary. Snorri himself made no attempt to explain the *kenning* in the light of Latin tradition, but his nephew Óláfr Þórðarson did so by connecting it to the metaphor and the description, *epitheton*, in the *Þriðja málfrœðiritgerðin* (The Third Grammatical Treatise). This way of discussing the *kenning* as part of rhetoric's *elocutio* has been followed by scholars in our time, with good results, but without a conclusive explanation of the term *kenning*.[26] Instead of trying to explain the *kenning* as a part of *literary* rhetoric, it seems to me more reasonable to understand it as part of *oral* rhetoric, and more particularly memory. The *kenning* as a poetic device was obviously developed without aid from abroad, but the concepts and terminology for discussing it were a contribution from Latin rhetoric. Not, however, from the literary rhetoric of stylistics, but from the basic oral rhetoric of mnemonics.

Acknowledgements

For valuable ideas and suggestions, I would like to thank Margaret Clunies Ross, Andreas Harbsmaier, Pernille Harsting, Henrik Janson, Judith Jesch, Thomas Lindkvist, Else Mundal and Vésteinn Ólason. When I presented this interpretation at a conference in Reykholt in 2005, Bergsveinn Birgisson added that the connection between Icelandic words for "image" and "remember", *mynd* and *muna*, enforces the connection between memory and imagery in Icelandic thought. Bergsveinn has treated the similar functions of the *nota* of classical rhetoric and the Old Norse kenning on a general level.[27]

26 See, primarily, Brodeur 1952; Halldór Halldórsson 1975; Clunies Ross 1987; 2005, 236–245. For a more extensive discussion of the interpretation of *kenning*, see Malm 2007.
27 Bergsveinn Birgisson 2007, 120–122.

Bibliography

Bergsveinn Birgisson 2007. *Inn i skaldens sinn. Kognitive, estetiske og historiske skatter i den norrøne skaldediktningen.* Bergen: Universitetet i Bergen.

Brodeur, Arthur G. 1952. "The meaning of Snorri's categories." *University of California Publications in Modern Philology* 36, 129–147.

Carruthers, Mary J. 1990. *The Book of Memory. A Study of Memory in Medieval Culture.* Cambridge: Cambridge University Press.

Carruthers, Mary J. 1998. *The Craft of Thought. Meditation, Rhetoric, and the Making of Images, 400–1200.* Cambridge: Cambridge University Press.

Clunies Ross, Margaret 1987. *Skáldskaparmál. Snorri Sturluson's Ars Poetica and Medieval Theories of Language.* The Viking Collection. Studies in Northern Civilization 4. Odense: Odense University Press.

Clunies Ross, Margaret 2005. *A History of Old Norse Poetry and Poetics.* Cambridge & New York: D.S. Brewer.

Copeland, Rita 1991. *Rhetoric, Hermeneutics, and Translation in the Middle Ages. Academic Traditions and Vernacular Texts.* Cambridge: Cambridge University Press.

Copeland, Rita and Ineke Sluiter (eds) 2009. *Medieval Grammar and Rhetoric: Language Arts and Literary Theory, 300 AD to 1475.* Oxford: Oxford University Press.

Evans, Gillian R. 1980. "Two aspects of memoria in eleventh and twelfth century writings." *Classica et Mediaevalia* 32, 263–278.

Fafner, Jørgen 1982. *Tanke og tale. Den retoriske tradition i Vesteuropa.* Copenhagen: Reitzels Forlag.

Fritzner, Johan 1883–1896. *Ordbog over det gamle norske Sprog* 1–3, Kristiania: Feilberg & Landmark. Bd. 4. Rettelser og tillegg ved Finn Hødnebø. 1972. Oslo: Universitetsforlaget.

Guðrún Nordal 2001. *Tools of Literacy. The Role of Skaldic Verse in Icelandic Textual Culture of the Twelfth and Thirteenth Centuries.* Toronto, Buffalo, London: University of Toronto Press.

Halldór Halldórsson 1975. *Old Icelandic heiti in Modern Icelandic.* Reykjavík: Institute of Nordic Linguistics.

Irvine, Martin 1994. *The Making of Textual Culture. 'Grammatica' and Literary Theory, 350–1100.* Cambridge: Cambridge University Press.

Kennedy, George A. 1999. *Classical Rhetoric and its Christian and Secular Tradition from Ancient to Modern Times.* 2nd revised and enlarged ed. Chapel Hill and London: University of North Carolina Press.

Kraus, Manfred 2009. "Grammatical and rhetorical exercises in the medieval classroom". In Rita Copeland *et al.* (eds), *New Medieval Literatures* 11. Special Issue. Medieval Grammar and the Literary Arts, Turnhout: Brepols, 63–89.

Lewis, Charlton T. and Charles Short 1980. *A Latin Dictionary, Founded on Andrew's Edition of Freund's Latin Dictionary* [1879]. Oxford: Clarendon.

Malm, Mats 2007. "Varför heter det *kenning?*". In Jon Gunnar Jørgensen (ed.), *Snorres Edda i europeisk og islandsk kultur.* Snorrastofa, vol. V. Reykholt: Snorrastofa, 73–90.

Munk Olsen, Birger 1982–2014. *L'Étude des auteurs classiques latins aux Xi^e et XIIe siècles* I–IV, Paris: CNRS Éditions. I (1982): *Catalogues des manuscrits classiques latins copiés du Ixe au XIIe siècle. Apicius-Juvenal.* II (1985): *Catalogues des* manuscrits classiques latins copiés du Ixe au XIIe siècle. Livius-Vitruvius. Florilèges-Essais de plume. III.1 (1987): Les Classiques dans les bibliothèques médiévales. III.2 (1989): Addenda et Corrigenda. Tables. IV.1 (2009): La réception de la littérature classique. Travaux philologiques. IV.2 (2014): La réception de la littérature classique. Manuscrits et textes.

Murphy, James J. 2005. "Western rhetoric in the Middle Ages". In Latin Rhetoric and Education in the Middle Ages and Renaissance. Aldershot: Ashgate, 1–26.

Murphy, James J. 2005. "The teaching of Latin as a second language in the twelfh century". In Latin Rhetoric and Education in the Middle Ages and Renaissance. Aldershot: Ashgate, 159–174.

Orme, Nicholas 2006. Medieval Schools from Roman Britain to Renaissance England. New Haven and London: Yale University Press.

Óláfr Þórðarson 1927. Málhljóða- og málskrúðsrit. Grammatiskretorisk afhandling udgiven af Finnur Jónsson. Copenhagen: Andr. Fred. Høst & søn.

Quintilian: The Orator's Education. Ed. and translated by Donald A. Russell. I–V. Cambridge, Mass. & London: Harvard University Press, 2001.

Raschellà, Fabrizio D. 2007. "Old Icelandic grammatical literature: The last two decades of research (1983–2005)". In Judy Quinn, Kate Heslop and Tarrin Wills (eds), Learning and Understanding in the Old Norse World. Essays in Honour of Margaret Clunies Ross. Turnhout: Brepols, 341–372.

[Cicero] Rhetorica ad Herennium. With an English translation by Harry Caplan. Cambridge, Mass. & London: Harvard University Press, 1954.

Snorri Sturluson. Edda. Háttatal. Ed. Anthony Faulkes. London: Viking Society for Northern Research, 1999.

Snorri Sturluson. Edda. Skáldskaparmál. 1: Introduction, Text and Notes. 2 Glossary and Index of Names. Ed. Anthony Faulkes. London: Viking Society for Northern Research, 1999.

Snorri Sturluson. Edda. Translated from the Icelandic and introduced by Anthony Faulkes. London and Melbourne: Dent, 1987.

Ward, John O. 1978. "From antiquity to the renaissance: Glosses and commentaries on Cicero's". In James J. Murphy (ed.), Rhetorica, Medieval Eloquence. Studies in the Theory and Practice of Medieval Rhetoric. Berkeley, Los Angeles & London: University of California Press, 25–67.

Yates, Frances A. 1966. The Art of Memory. London: Routledge and Kegan Paul.

℈ KARL G. JOHANSSON

The Learned Sturlungar and the Emergence of Icelandic Literate Culture

Introduction

THE CONCEPT OF "LEARNED STURLUNGAR" SHOULD NOT BE A bone of contention among scholars. The authorship of Snorri Sturluson, Sturla Þórðarson and Óláfr *hvítaskáld* (White Poet) Þórðarson has generally been recognized by most students of Old Norse literature. The general acceptance of the attribution of a wide range of literature to these three men, from grammatical and rhetorical treatises, such as *Þriðja málfræðiritgerðin* (The Third Grammatical Treatise) and *Skáldskaparmál,* through individual lives of kings and chieftains, including *Hákonar saga Hákonarsonar* and the Icelandic *Íslendinga saga,* to the large scale compilation *Heimskringla,* provides us with a vast body of material for understanding their learned view of the world. There have also been suggestions from individual scholars attributing other works to these three, such as *Egils saga Skalla-Grímssonar* and *Þrymskviða* to Snorri or an encyclopaedic compilation to Sturla (*Alfræði Sturlu Þórðarsonar*). The few scholars who have questioned the first mentioned works have not convinced the majority, while the last mentioned attributions have perhaps generally been regarded with some caution by many scholars. If we accept this material as a corpus reflecting a more general intellectual and ideological milieu, however, and do not attribute the individual works to one single author, we have an opportunity to form an outline of the learned manuscript culture of the Sturlungar.

The main focus of this paper concerns the background for the learned Sturlungar, their education, the traditions and new influences they encountered. The Old Norse, and in particular the Icelandic, vernacular literate culture admittedly presents a rather different image from that of the emerging literate culture in the rest of Europe. This does not mean, however, that the indigenous tradition of this region was untouched by Latinate culture or the models of writing and thinking it provided. The focus in scholarly tradition has often been on the indigenous oral traditions at the cost of insights into processes that are similar to and have parallels in contemporary European culture. In order to assess the manuscript culture and stages of literacy of the thirteenth-century Sturlungar, I therefore argue that we need to start in the twelfth century of Latin writing and translations of Latin works, all of them more or less linked to the early monasteries and church schools.

In order to pursue this aim it is necessary first to clearly define various actors and institutions in the field of literacy and literary activities, and secondly to be open to the obvious interplay between these actors and institutions. If we look at the twelfth-century Benedictines, they will present one view of Icelandic literacy during this period, while church institutions such as the episcopal sees at Skálholt and Hólar present a different picture. The major churches at larger farms controlled by the aristocracy may very well provide a different perspective again, while in the late twelfth century the Augustinian canons have other biases in their use and transformation of the tools provided by writing. But then again, there are constant overlaps between these institutions and the actors that we know of from the period. The most obvious is that the church institutions, as well as the monastic orders, all depended on men from the lay elite, i.e. there was always a need for economic support as well as protection, and it would have been important for the existing elite to control the recruitment of new clerics and members of the orders, especially for the higher offices. It is central to our understanding of the conditions for the emerging literate culture that the church provided the first institutions for education and training, also of the priests working at the churches at the major farms.

Here I will therefore approach twelfth- and thirteenth-century literacy, literary activities and manuscript culture by defining the main institutions and some of the actors working within them and at the same time illustrating the overlap between the institutions caused both by personal connections and shared versus conflicting interests. By doing this, the overall view of literacy and manuscript culture in the period is further illuminated as well, I hope, as appearing more heterogeneous.

Some Preliminary Starting Points

Some of the concepts relevant to the following discussion need to be defined or at least it must be made clear what is meant by them in this context. The understanding of "learned" is not always clear-cut in scholarship.[1] If we consider the contemporary use of attributes such as *fróði* for some of the persons mentioned below, it implies that to be learned in the twelfth and thirteenth centuries was, first to be trained in the art of reading and writing (Latin and subsequently the vernacular), and secondly, also to have a knowledge of genealogy, old traditions and indigenous poetics. This could lead us into the debate about oral tradition and its conversion into a written corpus, something that will not, however, be central in the following discussion where the focus is on the European background and its implications for the vernacular literate culture in the thirteenth century. To be learned in this context would be to have access to the literate book culture through linguistic training and reading. It is important to stress that the European understanding of what it meant to be learned, a *litteratus*, implied knowledge of Latin. In the twelfth and thirteenth centuries we could expect that anyone who learned to read and write would do this from a training in Latin, whether the student aimed at a clerical position or was from the secular elite. From a European perspective, education in reading and writing among the aristocracy does not seem to have been the rule until the late Middle Ages. From the above attributions of written works it must, however, be concluded that the Icelandic elite probably preceded most of their European counterparts in this respect to some extent. Snorri Sturluson and many of his contemporaries would at least have been able to read,

---

1   See e.g. Meulengract Sørensen 1992. A recent contribution is Kaplan 2011, e.g. 101–105.

and so they would have learned to read Latin.[2] Anthony Faulkes states in the introduction to his edition of *Skáldskaparmál*:

> The intellectual background to *Skáldskaparmál* thus seems to be the same as that for the Grammatical Treatises; it is a scholarly and didactic milieu, concerned with the techniques of poetical expression. Both the author and the audience must have been fully literate, and there is little reason to connect the work with oral tradition of any kind.[3]

It is plausible that they could also manage to write, perhaps on a more basic level. Whether they could indeed write in manuscript hand is another matter, as this was a craft that would have demanded special training; it is therefore more likely that they employed scribes for that task.

The very idea of a *school* is not clear from a modern perspective. Training in reading and writing was as far as we can see from the sources and from European parallels primarily provided in clerical milieux, whether at the larger churches located at major farms, at the two episcopal sees at Skálholt and Hólar, or in one of the monasteries.[4] The teaching was in the hands of clerics and the main objective would have been to educate clerics. The number of pupils was never large. When the secular elite gets involved in establishing schools, and when their young men, and subsequently women, are introduced to reading and writing at these schools, the training is handled by clerics with a similar education to clerics in any other part of Europe.

---

2   The discussion as to whether Snorri knew Latin would seem to neglect all knowledge of twelfth- and thirteenth-century training in reading and writing. See e.g. Hoff 2012. Clunies Ross 1987, has convincingly argued that Snorri was acquainted with contemporary European learning, and his nephew, Óláfr *hvítaskáld* Þórðarson, definitely shows a knowledge in the grammarians of his time which would have required Latin training.

3   Faulkes 1998, xxxvii.

4   The earliest organized schools could very well have been initiated by the first Benedictine contingent in northern Iceland, i.e. in the second quarter of the twelfth century. The Benedictines had a long tradition of establishing schools, primarily for the education of oblates for the monastery, but especially in smaller communities these schools were also open to members of the local aristocracy. See e.g. Clark 2011, 186.

The Learned Twelfth Century: Episcopal Sees, Monasteries, Church Schools and the Vernacularization of the Written Word

The intellectual background of the learned Sturlungar is obviously also the background for the transformation of literate culture in the thirteenth century more generally. In the twelfth century the Latin book culture is slowly vernacularized, as translations of Latin texts could be expected to also provide models for indigenous written works. All over Europe the vernacular is established in writing in this period, but the transformation of the European Latin book culture in Iceland, apart from what could be expected from a European point of view, leads to works in the vernacular that have no counterparts elsewhere, such as the indigenous saga literature. The origin of saga literature has therefore, not surprisingly, been a topic of great importance in Old Norse studies.[5] The focus on this exclusively Icelandic genre has sometimes, however, led to a tendency to forget that the very medium for transmission is the Roman script and knowledge of Latinate literacy.[6]

To reach a further understanding of the state of literacy and learned studies in Iceland in the thirteenth century we need therefore to start in the twelfth, or even eleventh century when the use of Roman script was first introduced to Iceland and the Scandinavian mainland. The earliest literate scholars in Iceland came from abroad. They are called bishops and were probably missionaries. They worked within the church institutions and had their education from schools and monasteries on the Continent or in England. Ari *fróði* (the Learned) mentions Friðrekr, Bjarnharðr *inn bókvísi* (literally "learned in, or knowledgeable of, books"), Kolr, Hróðólfr, Jóhan *inn írski* (the Irish), another Bjarnharðr and Heinrekr, Ǫrnolfr and Goðiskolkr, as well as three *ermskir* bishops, Petrus, Abrahám and Stephánus (from Ermeland (Warmia) or Armenia, probably Greek orthodox),[7] and some of these men are also mentioned in *Kristni saga* and other sources. In *Hungrvaka*, foreign bishops are also named, such as one Bjarnvarðr, called *inn bókvísi*, who is said to have come with Óláfr *helgi*

---

5   See e.g. Andersson 1964; 2006.
6   See e.g. Andersson 2012, where the written culture is more or less invisible while the focus is on oral tradition.
7   *Íslendingabók. Landnámabók*, 18.

(the Saint) Haraldsson from England to Norway.[8] Another Bjarnvarðr is in *Hungrvaka* called *inn saxlenzki* (the Saxon).[9] It is obvious, however, that the knowledge of these early bishops was already limited by the time of Ari, and perhaps even more so in *Hungrvaka*. There are a few references to the earliest missionaries in the eleventh century, but our knowledge of their learning and activities is scant.

When the first institutional structures of the church are established in the mid-eleventh century, we can expect the local elite to have taken a keen interest in controlling this new institution.[10] It is here, in the second half of the eleventh century, that the first Icelanders seem to have been sent to monastery or church schools abroad to receive a formal education. This is described in later sources such as *Íslendingabók* or *Kristni saga*. In *Hungrvaka* it is told that the first bishop of Skálholt, Ísleifr Gizurarson, went to Herford in Germany "til læringar abbadísi einni" (to learn from an abbess),[11] and about Sæmundr *fróði* (the Learned) Sigfússon, *Íslendingabók* tells that he returned to Iceland after having been to Frakkland (Franken or France), presumably to study.[12]

It is only from the second part of the twelfth century that we find information about literate activities in the Icelandic monasteries (see fig. 1). The first abbot of the new Benedictine monastery Munka-Þverá, Nikulás Bergsson (probably between 1155 and 1159) wrote a guidebook for pilgrims. By the end of the century several Benedictine brothers had produced important works in Latin, and to some extent in the vernacular, e.g. Gunnlaugr Leifsson and Oddr Snorrason at Þingeyrar. A new monastic order appears in Iceland in the second half of the twelfth century, the Augustinian canons, first represented by Þorlákr Þórhallsson, a strong political force, and soon followed by literate men such as Gamli *kanoki*, a canon from Þykkvabær and the poet behind *Leiðarvísan*.

The observation that there are different tendencies at play in the extant saga material is not new. Sigurður Nordal divided the stages of

8   *Biskupa sǫgur* I, 11. King Óláfr Haraldsson became St Olav (Óláfr *helgi*, modern Norwegian Olav *den hellige*).

9   *Biskupa sǫgur* I, 12.

10   For a general introduction to the establishing of Christian institutions see Orri Vésteinsson 2000. A critical view of Orri Vésteinsson's book was presented by Johansson 2004. For a more European understanding of the forming of a Christian Western Europe, see Nyberg 2000.

11   *Biskupa sǫgur* I, 6.

12   *Íslendingabók. Landnámabók*, 20–21. For a discussion of the evidence for Sæmundr's foreign studies see Garðar Gíslason 2001.

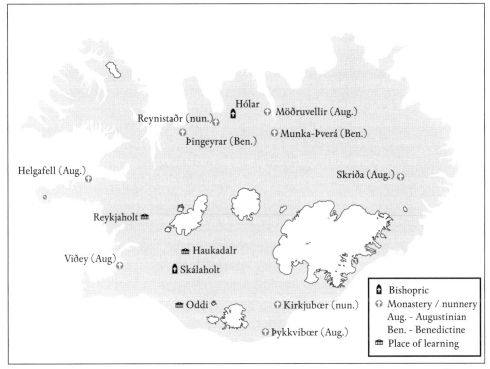

Figure 1 Monasteries in mediaeval Iceland, the bishops' seats and places of learning. Map: Stefán Ólafsson.

saga writing into three literary schools, *sunnlenzki skólinn* (the southern school), *Þingeyraskólinn* (the Þingeyrar school) and *borgfirzki skólinn* (the Borgarfjǫrðr school).[13] His observations were based on the known works thought to have been produced in these areas and the dominant idea of his time of individual authors forming parts of a chronological literary history. He was therefore not interested in the processes of establishing a vernacular script and a literate culture based on the Latin matrix or the processes of textual change of a manuscript culture. Nevertheless, his observations are similar to those being presented here; the conclusions will, however, be rather different.[14]

Sigurður Nordal thinks the first school was established by the chieftains in southern Iceland, more precisely at the two chieftain farms Oddi

13 Sigurður Nordal 1933, lxiii–lxvii. For a recent discussion of Sigurður Nordal's views, see Ásdís Egilsdóttir 2002, xxv–xxvii.
14 Cf. Theodore Anderson's work which I will discuss further in the following.

and Haukadalr.[15] The earliest known authors from this school are Sæmundr *fróði* Sigfússon and Ari *fróði* Þorgilsson, the former considered to
be the first to have written about kings' lives, presumably in Latin, while
the latter was educated in Haukadalr and is the author of *Íslendingabók*.
This earliest vernacular tradition, in Sigurður Nordal's opinion, seems
then to be a lay tradition. The earliest writings known to us were secular
and to some extent formed in the vernacular. There are, however, reasons to be a little cautious about these early works, whether they were
supposedly written in Latin (by Sæmundr) but are now lost, or in the
vernacular (by Ari) and are still partly extant. The lost work of Sæmundr
would have provided an early example of the Latin chronicle genre. In
the case of Ari's work, supposedly originally written in the vernacular
but obviously based on the European chronicle tradition, it is today
extant only in two seventeenth-century manuscripts. This means that
our knowledge of the use of the Roman script during this early period,
whether in Latin or in a vernacular written language, is based on very
little direct evidence. The general conclusions based on international
literacy scholarship would lead us to consider an original work in the
vernacular, such as Ari's, to be an anomaly; it is simply a single example
in a vast body of material suggesting that it would take more than another
half century before chronicles were to be written again in the vernacular.
But the work is there and needs to be explained.[16]

A second school (in Sigurður Nordal's view) was the Þingeyrar
school, formed at the monastery of Þingeyrar in the northern diocese of
Hólar.[17] Sigurður argues that the Hólar diocese was more dominated by
the church, and that Hólar was the centre where the first school of the

15   Sigurður Nordal 1933, lxiii–lxv.
16   Concerning the first written law code Hoff concludes: "Denn als die Gesetze im
     Winter 1117/1118 geschrieben wurden, war die isländische Schriftsprache noch
     nicht besonders weit entwickelt, was die vielen etwas unbeholfen klingenden,
     aber inhaltlich sehr ausdifferenzierten Formulierungen in der *Staðarhólsbók* gut
     erklären mag" (2012, 107–108). Hoff argues that the first generation of ordained
     priests learned in Latin was primarily recruited from the higher echelons of society,
     and that this would indicate that there was a high degree of literacy, Latin and
     subsequently vernacular, in the Icelandic elite already in the first half of the twelfth
     century (see e.g. 2012, 34, 51). This would provide a partial explanation of the early
     literacy, at least in Latin, while the early interest in writing in the vernacular is not
     necessarily explained. It is, however, worth noting that Hoff suggests the Benedic-
     tine monastery at Þingeyrar as a possible provider of scribes for the production of
     the first law code (2012, 47, 51).
17   Sigurður Nordal 1933, lxv–lxvii.

northern areas was formed by Jón Ǫgmundarson. Sigurður concludes concerning the importance of this school: "Þar vitum við ekki um neina skóla á borð við skólana í Haukadal og Odda. Hins vegar varð kirkjan og hinn klerklegi andi þar ríkari. Áhrifin frá Jóni Ögmundssyni og skóla hans á Hólum setti svip á menntalíf fjórðungsins um langt skeið".[18] In Sigurður's view the southern school has had an impact on the works produced at Þingeyrar, but "andinn er annar" (the spirit is different).[19] This is relevant for my further discussion of the institutions involved in the processes of the vernacularization of script and textual culture and the subsequent secularization of the word. The early Benedictines of northern Iceland and the church at Hólar must from this point of view rather represent a more monastic and, at least at the outset, a more Latinate culture than the southern school.[20] There is, however, also reason to modify this observation. There is no question that the brothers of Þingeyrar were highly productive in writing Latin works conformable with works found all over contemporary Europe, but it is also from this milieu that the earliest translations into the vernacular are known, and one of the earliest Kings' Sagas, Karl Jónsson's *Sverris saga* (The Saga of King Sverrir Sigurðarson) must be considered as a part of the Benedictine tradition. This is mentioned in Sigurður Nordal's discussion,[21] but the implications for the vernacularization and secularization of the written word are not examined.

Sigurður mentions the earliest known saga works, the Bishops' Sagas, as examples of two different styles, but also of how influences can be seen between them:

Þegar höfundur Hungurvöku talar um ritaðar sögur, á hann vafalaust einkum við sögur þær úr Þingeyraklaustri, sem þegar er getið. Jóns saga hefur ýtt undir Sunnlendinga að skrásetja sögur

---

18 "We do not know of any school there, similar to the schools in Haukadalr or Oddi. On the other hand the church and clerical spirit was richer there. The impact of Jón Ǫgmundsson and his school at Hólar was considerable on the cultural life of the area for a long time" (Sigurður Nordal 1933, lxv).

19 Sigurður Nordal 1933, lxvi.

20 This would be supported by what we know of the Benedictines in general, see e.g. Clark 2011.

21 Sigurður Nordal 1933, lxv–lxvi.

Skálholtsbiskupa, en þeir rita þær í miklu raunsærra anda og
hófsamara en Gunnlaugur hafði samið sína bók.[22]

Even if we do not accept this secular explanation as to why *Hungrvaka*
and *Þorláks saga* were composed, Sigurður Nordal's observations are
interesting as they point in the direction of various traditions present in
the extant material. There have, as far as the extant material allows us to
conclude, already been different approaches to writing and the use of the
vernacular at this early point. In what follows these observations will be
related to the transformation of vernacular literacy in the twelfth- and
thirteenth-century manuscript culture.[23] The learned Sturlungar did not
appear from thin air. Their use of the written word in the vernacular and
for secular purposes has its precedents in the various interests invested
in this culture.

The link between the northern school and a new school, the *borgfirzki*
skóli, in Sigurður Nordal's view is the priest and later Augustinian canon
Styrmir Kárason, who most probably received his education at Þingeyrar
and later moved to Reykholt to work for Snorri Sturluson. Sigurður
concludes that Snorri merges the tendencies of both previous schools.[24]

Sigurður notices tendencies in the materials which he interprets from
the point of view of his own time, but his approach to texts and writing is
rather different from that found in present scholarship, where the focus
is on the more general questions of literacy and manuscript culture. It
is therefore relevant to place the three more or less chronological stages
in the development of saga literature he suggested under new scrutiny
and relate them to recent scholarship. Any explanation of the processes
of forming a vernacular literacy in Iceland in the twelfth and thirteenth
centuries that takes only one institution, a single order or individual
writers as its starting point must end up with too simplistic an answer.
We must expect there to have been forces moving in different directions

---

22 "When the author of *Hungrvaka* mentions written sagas, he without doubt particu-
    larly means those sagas from the monastery of Þingeyrar that are already mentioned.
    Jóns saga has encouraged the southerners to record the sagas of the bishops of
    Skálholt, but they compose them in a much more realistic and humble spirit than
    Gunnlaugr had done in his book" (Sigurður Nordal 1933, lxvii).

23 The Augustinians, introducing ideas from the monastery of St Victor in Paris, would
    emphasize the importance of *historia* and a literal reading in relation to a more
    spiritual focus found in the Benedictine tradition, see e.g. Clark 2011, 199.

24 Sigurður Nordal 1933 lxvii.

and continuing negotiations as to what was accepted, influences from individuals and groups with their own interests in the written word, and so on. Below I shall tentatively take as a starting point a division between four relatively well defined institutions which all had interests in the use of writing and the traditions established within the twelfth-century manuscript culture.

1. The Church, primarily the schools at the episcopal sees
2. Private schools at church centres and major farms
3. Benedictine monasteries
4. Augustinian canons

These four major institutions will be treated separately here in order to get a clearer view of political, theological and intellectual impulses, but it should again be clear that the borders would never have been absolute. The group of men working with letters in twelfth-century Iceland was most likely of a size that makes it probable they all knew each other and had more or less well established contacts. It will therefore be relevant to discuss these overlaps between the positions here defined as institutions in order to assess the influences and implications of communication and conflict.

Skálholt and the Church Centres and Major Farms

In the earliest phase of what Sigurður Nordal called the southern school, Sæmundr *fróði* Sigfússon of Oddi and Ari *fróði* Þorgilsson of Haukadalr are important representatives. In Sigurður's view, the school at Oddi was the place where a vernacular literature had its roots. Ari *fróði* is better attested in the written sources (see fig. 1). First, there are two paper manuscripts from the middle of the seventeenth century containing *Íslendingabók*,[25] presumably the first historical work produced in the Old Norse vernacular. In a second important work from this early period, *Fyrsta málfræðiritgerðin* (The First Grammatical Treatise) dated to around 1140, but today only extant in the manuscript AM 242 fol

---

25 AM 113 a fol and AM 113 b fol, both attributed to the scribe Jón Erlendsson. For an introduction to the origin and provenance of *Íslendingabók*, see Jakob Benediktsson 1968.

(Codex Wormianus) from between 1340 and 1370,[26] we find interesting information about the use and understanding of the written vernacular language.[27] There is, therefore, no reason to doubt *a priori* that Ari and his contemporaries were already using the Roman script to render the vernacular at this early stage. It is interesting, however, to note that the Old Norse of *Íslendingabók* has been characterized as obviously influenced by Latin syntax.[28] And there are problems related to these early works in the vernacular. Ari *fróði* and the First grammarian in the first half of the twelfth century are difficult to place chronologically in a discussion of the processes of transformation of Latin literacy into vernacular and subsequently secular, lay literacy, as we would rather have expected both to use Latin in this kind of work at this stage.[29] In relation to the lost Latin chronicle by Sæmundr *fróði*, Svend Ellehøj concludes: "Hertil kommer, at Latin er det sprog, som man på forhånd ville vente ad finde anvendt, når tiden og forfatterens uddannelse tages i betragtning".[30] The period and education of Ari and the first grammarian would be the same.

Nevertheless, these two characters, Sæmundr *fróði* of Oddi and Ari *fróði* who is associated with Haukadalr, seem to have been given the role of "founding fathers" of teaching and writing (in Latin and the vernacular) in Iceland in later works, like *Hungrvaka* and *Jóns saga Hólabyskups ens helga*. It is also clear that the farms at Haukadalr and Oddi are central in the early phases of Icelandic church politics; most of the main characters in the contemporary works treating this period are in one way or another connected to these two farms and sites of churches where teaching may have taken place already in the eleventh century.

From a source-critical perspective the value of the historical information provided by the sources for the earliest period of Icelandic history

---

26 For the most recent discussion of the production and provenance of the manuscript AM 242 fol, see Johansson 1997.

27 For a discussion of the origin and provenance of *Fyrsta málfræðiritgerðin*, see Hreinn Benedictsson 1972, introduction.

28 See e.g. Jakob Benediktsson 1968, xxvi.

29 There are contemporary grammatical works in the vernacular from the British Isles but they are related to the learning of Latin and do not discuss the vernacular as a written language in the way the first grammarian does, see Porter 2002. In the Benedictine monastery schools the study of Latin grammar was central, but the vernacular was not of particular interest (Clark 2011, 204). The interest in the vernacular is yet again something specific for Norse literacy.

30 "It follows that Latin is the language one would already expect to be used, taking the period and the education of the author into account" (Ellehøj 1965, 18).

is clearly uncertain, but as far as literacy and the importance of learning and the written word are concerned, even a *topos* provides important information. When the narrative about Sæmundr was written, it was relevant to form an image of him as learned and as a secular chieftain who was active in promoting literary studies. This indicates that learned occupations and a concern for teaching young men classical knowledge had prestige in the society where the narrative was composed a generation or two later. Most probably this was the same society that shaped the image of the learned Sturlungar, rather than the twelfth century itself.

First let us have a brief look at the political importance of the major church farms and their control. The larger church farms and their functions in general have been scrutinized from various perspectives in recent research within the Reykholt Project,[31] but their functions as schools or centres of learning have not been specifically addressed. Our sources suggest that the earliest educational centres in Iceland were located at these large church farms. It is from these centres[32] that we know of the earliest writings in the vernacular, and it is obvious that they played an important role in the transformation of Latin book culture, where the written vernacular expanded its legitimacy, and where oral traditions were formed in and adjusted to writing. In the first phase of establishing church institutions the aristocrats were, as far as we can judge from the sources, highly active and controlled the important positions, most significantly as bishops and abbots. The aristocratic interest therefore in this period coincided with the interests of the church. When we reach the second half of the twelfth century, this situation is changing. As the two episcopal churches at Skálholt and Hólar were established, and along with the Benedictine monasteries in the North of the country provided schools, the need to establish new church centres was no longer as strong. This decrease in establishing new church centres has often been explained as a reaction against Bishop Þorlákr Þórhallsson's demand for church control.[33] A reduced economic interest in such establishments has also been suggested as a primary cause.[34]

---

31   See e.g. pp. 22, 28–29 in this book.

32   Meaning *staðir* and the major *bændakirkjur*. For definitions see pp. 112, 115–116 and 415–415 in this book.

33   See e.g. Benedikt Eyþórsson 2005, 39–40. In relation to Þorlákr's claims for church sovereignty, Orri Vésteinsson (2000, 115) argues that the description in *Þorláks saga* is rather based on events in the late thirteenth century.

34   Orri Vésteinsson 2000, 115–123.

The image of Þorlákr as a reformer in conflict with the aristocracy, however, bears some similarities to contemporary church activities in Scandinavia and the rest of Europe, as evidenced in the descriptions of the conflicts between two successive archbishops of Niðaróss, Eysteinn (modern Norwegian Øystein) Erlendsson and Eiríkr Ívarsson (Eirik Ivarsson) – both Augustinians and in contact with Þorlákr – and King Sverrir (modern Norwegian Sverre). The description should possibly rather be seen as a topic. The political and economic explanation for the decreasing interest in establishing new church centres could therefore be complemented by taking into account the fact that by the end of the twelfth century there was no need for further centres for education and instruction for the priesthood. The church had established itself as the central institution for education in Iceland.

We should now turn to the two aristocrats connected to Oddi and Haukadalr and contemporary with Þorlákr: Jón Loptsson (or Loftsson) and Gizurr Hallsson. Sæmundr Sigfússon is perhaps the best known of the Oddaverjar, while his grandson Jón Loptsson is also often mentioned in the sources. He is known as a powerful chieftain, but also as a learned man and the one who fostered Snorri Sturluson, and definitely represents the old aristocracy. Further, he had close connections with the Norwegian nobility. His mother is mentioned as the daughter of the Norwegian king Magnús *berfœttr* (Bareleg) Óláfsson.

The other example of a powerful chieftain who takes an active role in church politics is Gizurr Hallson, the owner of Haukadalr, the other large farm with a church where we know that education was already being provided early in the twelfth century. Gizurr Hallson had a strong interest in Skálholt and was politically influential there. According to *Páls saga biskups* it was, for example, he who suggested that Jón Loptsson's son Páll should be elected bishop at Skálholt after the death of Þorlákr. This indicates a close relationship between the two aristocrats, Jón Loptsson and Gizurr Hallsson; they represent the highest layer of the Icelandic aristocracy, and they seem to have claimed the rights of the old aristocracy in conflict with new ideals introduced by the church.

As has been pointed out by Guðrún Nordal, the aristocratic culture in Iceland in the twelfth century was partly built on indigenous traditions and partly on European court culture. By the end of the twelfth century the European tendencies were strong. Guðrún Nordal concludes: "Icelandic chieftains began to identify themselves with European aristocrats in the twelfth century, and particularly in the thirteenth century, through the writing of royal histories, genealogies, myths of the settlement and skaldic poetry".[35]

By the end of the twelfth century these chieftains represented an old aristocracy. They still had a strong influence in society, and both Gizurr Hallsson and Jón Loptsson seem to have been involved in controversial issues relating to church politics. Their farms, Haukadalr and Oddi were still important centres where children received an education.

Hólar and the Benedictines

The northern diocese of Hólar seems generally to have been more clearly allied with the European church by the mid-twelfth century than the diocese of Skálholt which was more or less in the hands of the aristocracy. In the North we also find the earliest examples of Benedictine monasteries. There is mention of a monastery at Þingeyrar early in the twelfth century, but it is only officially established in 1133. The second Benedictine monastery was founded at Munka-Þverá in 1155. We know very little about the establishing of the two early Benedictine houses and have even less information about their activity in the twelfth century.[36]

Interesting accounts of how the northern church was founded are provided by *Jóns saga Hólabyskups ens helga*, which is originally supposed to have been written as a Latin *vita* by the Þingeyrar brother Gunnlaugr Leifsson. Of the three extant recensions distinguished by the editor Peter Foote,[37] the L recension, which is attributed by various scholars to either Bergr Sokkason or Árni Lárentíusson (both brothers of the Þingeyrar monastery in the fourteenth century), is considered to be based on Gunnlaugr's Latin *vita*.[38] It is hard to verify, however, if this saga in its earliest form has "ýtt undir Sunnlendinga að skrásetja sögur Skálholtsbiskupa" (encouraged the southern Icelanders to record the sagas of the bishops of Skálholt), as Sigurður Nordal suggested,[39] as it

---

35 Guðrún Nordal 2006, 79. See also pp. 33–78 in this book.
36 See e.g. Orri Vésteinsson 2000; Johansson 2006.
37 Foote 2003.
38 See Foote 2003, 125; Sigurgeir Steingrímsson *et al.* 2003, ccxxx–ccxxxiii.
39 Sigurður Nordal 1933, lxvii and above, 341–342.

was probably written at about the same time as *Hungrvaka* and *Þorláks saga ens helga Skálholtsbyskups*, about or just after 1200.[40]

The first bishop of Hólar, Jón Ǫgmundarson, is presented with a perfect (and aristocratic) background for his role. As a child his mother spent time at the court of Óláfr *helgi* Haraldsson, and when Jón was a child his family stayed with the Danish court of King Sveinn Úlfsson. It is clear that the description of Jón's early years serves to present him as loyal to the king as the highest representative of God. It is told that Jón's mother meets with Óláfr Haraldsson, and the king foresees that she will lay the foundation of "gǫfgastr ættbogi á Íslandi" (a most noble kin in Iceland).[41] When Jón is noticed as a child by the Danish queen Ástríðr, she is filled with "spaleicks anda" (visionary spirit) and predicts that Jón will become a bishop.[42] The royal sanction is definitely in place. In his subsequent education Jón receives his legitimacy from the first Icelandic bishop, Ísleifr Gizurarson, the father of Gizurr, bishop of Skálholt and contemporary of Jón. *Jóns saga ins helga* relates that when Jón had finished his initial schooling, he was placed in "meistara dóm sæls Ísleifs byskups" (a master class with the blessed Bishop Ísleifr).[43]

From *Jóns saga ins helga* it is clear that the first bishop of Hólar was associated with the aristocracy and its importance for the early church institutions. Here we are told how Jón Ǫgmundarson, when he was abroad in order to be consecrated as bishop of Hólar in Lundr (Lund), makes a journey through Europe to bring Sæmundr *fróði* back to Iceland. Sæmundr has studied abroad and has settled with a learned teacher, who is at first unwilling to let him leave. But after a number of mysterious events where the teacher is outsmarted by Sæmundr, they can leave for Iceland. When they arrive, Jón takes up the office of bishop of Hólar where he sets up an important school, which is described in some detail. Sæmundr goes back to his home farm at Oddi and lays the foundations for a centre for learned clerics which is often mentioned in modern scholarship. If the two events are seen together, as they are presented in *Jóns saga biskups*, it appears as if they should be seen as parts of a narrative strategy chosen by the narrator rather than as historical accounts. It was important to establish two founding fathers for schools,

40 See e.g. Sigurgeir Steingrímsson *et al.*, ccxvi.
41 *Biskupa sögur* I, 180; Foote 2003, 60.
42 *Biskupa sögur* I, 179; Foote 2003, 59.
43 *Biskupa sögur* I, 181; Foote 2003, 60.

apart from the one mentioned in Skálholt, founded by Ísleifr Gizurarson The connection between the early church and the aristocracy is stressed, whether the aristocracy is situated in Haukadalr or at Oddi.

The northern milieu seems to have been productive of various types of texts. One of the earliest known works is considered to have already been produced in the vernacular in the period between 1154 and 1159 by the Benedictine abbot at Munka-Þverá, Nikulás Bergsson, after his return from a pilgrimage to Jerusalem.[44] His *Leiðarvísir* is today extant only in later manuscripts, AM 194 8vo, dated to 1387, and the fragment AM 736 II 4to, dated to around 1400, but it has never really been questioned when it was written. It could be argued, however, obviously without any strong empirical support, that at least parts of this text were originally written in Latin and only later translated into Old Norse, as there is a short passage in the description of the St Peter basilica formulated in Latin.[45]

The best-known works from this milieu are perhaps the two, now lost, Latin lives of Óláfr Tryggvason produced by Oddr Snorrason and Gunnlaugr Leifsson at Þingeyrar. The former was subsequently translated into Old Norse, and is preserved in this form to the present day, while the latter in its translated form is extant only as parts of *Óláfs saga Tryggvasonar en mesta* in the Flateyjarbók version. Gunnlaugr Leifsson is, as mentioned, also known to have composed a Latin life of Jón Ǫgmundarson, which is today lost, but is thought to have been used by a later Benedictine brother in the L recension of the extant *Jóns saga Hólabyskups ens helga* (also *Jóns saga ins helga*) mentioned above, which is today found in, for example, Holm perg 5 fol from the second part of the fourteenth century.[46] It is also generally agreed that Gunnlaugr translated the Latin prose text *Prophetia Merlini*, written by Geoffrey of Monmouth as part of his *Historia Regum Britanniæ* (c. 1134), into an Old Norse verse form, the poem we call *Merlínusspá*.[47] Oddr Snorrason is known to have written (apart from the life of Óláfr Tryggvason) a Latin story about the prehistoric hero Yngvarr *víðfǫrli* (the Widely Travelled) characterized by Lars Boje Mortensen as a Latin *fornaldarsaga* (a Legendary Saga).[48] If the

---

44 Nikulás according to *Annales Regii* and the *Gottskálks annáll* arrived back in Iceland in 1154 from his pilgrimage. He is mentioned as abbot at Munka-Þverá, and his death is reported in 1159. For a recent discussion of *Leiðarvísir*, see Johansson 2006.

45 See e.g. Johansson 2006, 166.

46 See e.g. Foote 2003, 125.

47 See e.g. Johansson 2005.

48 Mortensen 2006, 257.

production of known texts from this milieu is gathered together, it does not seem too strong to suggest that the early Benedictines of the North were highly Latinate and in many ways resemble in their interests the general image of the Benedictine tradition at this stage.[49]

There is one work in the vernacular preserved from this early period of the monastic houses of northern Iceland, the *Sverris saga*, at least partly produced by the Benedictine brother Karl Jónsson in the early thirteenth century. The saga is the earliest extant text that treats the life of a Norwegian king in the vernacular, and which is written by someone who must have had personal contact with the king in question; Karl Jónsson was in Norway and in close proximity to the king when he started his work.[50]

The tendency in the northern part of Iceland in the period of reforms and conflicts between the bishop of Skálholt and the chieftains seems to be loyalty to the king and the traditional aristocracy. This is suggested by the narrative of *Sverris saga* as well as by *Jóns saga Hólabyskups*. If this political leaning can be further supported, it could also indicate that the Benedictines of northern Iceland carried on an older tradition of text production, which would point in two directions: England and Germany, the two routes we expect the earliest influences on Icelandic literacy to have taken. Helgi Þorláksson is fully in line with this understanding when he argues that the northern Benedictines formed an alternative to the Augustinians by 1200:

> Karl Jónssons Sverrissaga og Oddurs Ólafs saga var under på-
> virkning av verdslige høvdinger, disse munkene skrev litteratur
> som ikke var i samsvar med det som reformivrige klerker og
> kanniker av augustinerordenen fant mest passende, folk, som
> erkebiskopen Øystein i Nidaros eller biskop Þorlákur på Island.[51]

---

49 Cf. e.g. Clark 2011, 82–84.

50 Karl Jónsson in many ways follows the Benedictine tradition of close collaboration with royal power and writing the history of the king in power, see e.g. Clark 2011, 54, 187. It is his choice of the vernacular language that is a novelty; Karl Jónsson is otherwise just continuing the work initiated by Oddr Snorrason and Gunnlaugr Leifsson, as Clark (2011, 187), formulates it, to settle the royal regime in the provinces.

51 Helgi Þorláksson 2006, 65. "*Sverris saga* of Karl Jónsson and *Óláfs saga* by Oddr were under the influence of lay chieftains; these monks wrote literature that was not in line with what clerics and canons of the Augustinian order, eager for reforms, found most suitable, people such as Archbishop Eysteinn of Nidaros or Bishop Þorlákr in Iceland".

This is central to the present argument, not only concerning the forming and transformation of literacy in the late twelfth and early thirteenth century, but perhaps also in relation to the political activities previously discussed. The literary tendency seems here to interplay with a political tendency; the northern Benedictines were part of the early church establishment in Iceland, which was challenged by the arrival of the Augustinians and their ideas for church reform.

In an article on Benedictine influences on the Sunniva myth in Norway, Stephan Borgehammar describes the Benedictine reform movement in tenth-century England. Borgehammar mentions a number of tendencies that signify the Anglo-Saxon reformation of the Benedictine order as follows:[52]

1. The Anglo-Saxon Benedictines had a close contact with the institutions of power. They were often in liaison with the king.
2. The Anglo-Saxon Benedictines were not only interested in the development of their own order, but also took part in the work of the church. Abbots were often elected bishops.
3. The Anglo-Saxon Benedictines had a great interest in pastoral work: they founded schools, produced and translated texts in the vernacular and wrote handbooks on pastoral subjects.

Borgehammar describes the importance of the Benedictines for the development of a written vernacular culture in Anglo-Saxon England and demonstrates how individual Benedictines played major parts in this development. About Bishop Æthelwold he concludes: "Æthelwold själv skrev och undervisade så pass mycket på folkspråket att man har föreslagit att han borde kallas den standardiserade fornengelskans fader".[53]

The Anglo-Saxon Benedictines are thus clearly diverging from the general line of the Benedictine order. On the role they may have played in the Christianization of the Nordic countries, Borgehammar concludes:

---

52 Borgehammar 1997, 129–130.
53 Borgehammar 1997, 130. "Æthelwold himself wrote and taught so much in the vernacular that it has been suggested that he ought to be called the father of standardized Old English".

När man betraktar de engelska benediktinernas betydelse för Nordens kristnande kan man med fördel börja med deras produktion av litteratur på folkspråket, och främst då den pastorala litteraturen, helgonvitorna och predikningarna. Det är inte bara framställandet av enskilda skrifter som är betydelsefullt, utan ännu mera själva attityden. Utåtriktat, pastoralt arbete har ingen självklar plats i benediktinsk spiritualitet – många skulle säga att det strider mot Benediktusregelns väsen. Men de engelska benediktinerna var en aktiv sort.[54]

It is, I suggest, not difficult to see parallels between the description given by Borgehammar of the Anglo-Saxon Benedictines and some tendencies we can study in the Icelandic material from the twelfth to the fourteenth century. Orri Vésteinsson concluded that very little is known about monastic life in Iceland,[55] and there is, admittedly, limited direct information on social and political activities, and even less on the religious life of the Benedictine monasteries. But from analogies with Anglo-Saxon tradition, new light could be shed on the activity of the order in Iceland.

It is interesting to note in this context that the northern intellectual milieu already shows a divergent tendency when it comes to the production of new works from the twelfth century. Margaret Cormack, fully in line with the Anglo-Saxon parallels mentioned by Borgehammar, has pointed out the focus on hagiographic literature, and the translation of Latin lives of saints in the northern milieu:

There are indications that the diocese of Hólar was especially productive of hagiographic literature. Although most saints' sagas, like secular ones, are anonymous, some translators are known by name; of those whose ecclesiastical affiliations are also known, the

---

54 "When one considers the impact of the English Benedictines for the Christianization of Scandinavia one may benefit from starting with their production of literature in the vernacular, and primarily the clerical literature, *vitae* of saints and sermons. It is not only the production of individual texts that is important, but rather the general attitude. Extrovert, clerical work has no obvious place in Benedictine spirituality – many would say that it is against the idea of the Benedictine Rule. But the English Benedictines were of an active kind" (Borgehammar 1997, 134–135). For a recent support of Borgehammar's general observations about the Benedictines, see Clark, e.g. 2011, 130–131.

55 Orri Vésteinsson 2000.

majority are associated with the northern quarter, in particular with the monasteries at Þingeyrar and Munkaþverá.[56]

From this discussion, we get a fragmentary image of the literary production of the Benedictine brothers in the northern parts of Iceland. We cannot, of course, draw any definite conclusions from this scant material, but there are some tendencies that can be noted. It is obvious that there has been a preference for Latin text production in the milieu. Both Gunnlaugr Leifsson and Oddr Snorrason appear as Latinate scholars with a high degree of learning, and the same could be said about Nikulás Bergsson and Karl Jónsson, who in their works display their knowledge of European Latin culture in various ways. There is also reason to stress the relation between the late twelfth-century Benedictines and the early church as has been argued above. It is now time to move on to the arrival of the Augustinians in the second half of the twelfth century, and the impact and implications of their ideals and world-view on Icelandic intellectual life.

Skálholt and the Augustinians

In the second half of the twelfth and in the thirteenth century there are two important centres of education and European culture in Scandinavia; the archbishop's see in Lundr, where among others Saxo Grammaticus was active, and the archbishop's see in Þrándheimr (Trondheim), or Niðaróss (Nidaros), where a number of archbishops trained in Paris and the Augustinian monastery of St Victor dominated the scene. Periodically these bishops were forced to leave Norway when their demands for the church brought them into open conflict with the king. Archbishop Eysteinn lived in exile in England for a number of years, and his successor, Eiríkr, was forced to leave for Lundr after a dispute with King Sverrir. It is not too far-fetched, therefore, to think that there were strong intellectual links between these archbishops and their learned contemporaries in Paris, Lundr and England. By the late twelfth century, Niðaróss was also an important centre of influence for Iceland. Þorlákr Þórhallsson had

---

56 Cormack 2000, 304.

most likely studied in Paris at about the same time as the contemporary archbishops of Niðaróss, and was in close contact with them.

The Augustinian canons appear in Iceland in the second half of the twelfth century with Þorlákr. He is the first abbot of the first monastery at Þykkvabœr (1168), which was established on what was one of the major farms. In *Þorláks saga* his interest in teaching and education is stressed, but this may, needless to say, just be a *topos*; it appears in most of the Bishops' Sagas. In 1178 Þorlákr became bishop of Skálholt.

The two central characters closely related to the Augustinians who play the role of church reformers are Bishops Þorlákr Þórhallsson and Guðmundr *góði* (the Good) Arason. Þorlákr became Iceland's first saint as has already been mentioned. In the first decades of the thirteenth century, not many years after the death of Þorlákr, Latin *vitae* about him were produced, now largely lost.[57] During the thirteenth century these were, however, transformed into a number of vernacular versions, referred to as *Þorláks saga byskups*.[58] Of Þorlákr's earlier years we know nothing. According to the saga he was educated at the school in Oddi, where he was taught by the son of Sæmundr *fróði*, the priest Eyjólfr.[59] Eyjólfr could immediately see that Þorlákr had special gifts: "Eyjólfr virði Þorlák mest allra sinna lærisveina um þat allt er til kennimannsskapar kom, af því at hann sá af sinni vizku ok hans meðferð, sem síðarr reyndisk".[60]

This is one of the obvious *topoi* found in both indigenous Bishops' Sagas and in the translated Saints' Lives. After studies in Iceland, and having been ordained priest, Þorlákr (according to the saga) went to Paris to continue his studies "svá lengi sem hann þóttisk þurfa" ("for as long as he thought he needed"), before continuing to Lincoln in England. His foreign studies lasted for six years.[61] After his years of education Þorlákr returned to Iceland, where he settled down at Kirkjubœr. After six years there (where a Benedictine nunnery was established in 1186), he was approached by the farmer (and later Augustinian canon)

---

57 See Gottskálk Jensson 2004.

58 For the latest discussion of the manuscripts of *Þorláks saga*, see Ásdís Egilsdóttir 2002, xxxi–lii.

59 *Biskupa sögur* II, 49–50.

60 "Eyjólfr honoured Þorlákr most among his students in everything that concerned erudition, as he saw, in his own wisdom and from Þorlákr's actions, what would later be revealed" (*Biskupa sögur* II, 50).

61 *Biskupa sögur* II, 52.

Þorkell of Þykkvabœr in Ver and asked to establish the first Augustinian monastery on his farm. About the strong foundation of this establishment it says:

> Þá var Þorlákr vel hálffertøgr er hann rézk í Ver ok var þar sjau vetr. Kanokavígslu tók hann fyrst ok var þá í fyrstu príor settr yfir þá kanoka er þar váru, ok samði hann þegar svá fagrliga þeira líf at á því lék þá orð vitra manna at þeir hefði hvergi jafn góða siðu séna, þar er eigi hafði lengr regulu líf saman en þar verit.[62]

This monastery was soon to be famous for its learning and for attracting visitors:

> Menn fóru til kanokasetrs Þorláks ábóta ór ǫðrum munklífum eða reglustǫðum, bæði samlendir ok útlendir, at sjá þar ok nema góða siðu, ok bar þat hverr frá er þaðan fór at hvergi hefði þess komit at þat líf þœtti jafn fagrliga lifat sem þar er Þorlákr hafði fyrir sét.[63]

When Þorlákr was elected bishop at Skálholt, two chieftains are said to have supported him, the previously mentioned Jón Loptsson from Oddi and Gizurr Hallsson from Haukadalr. The general tendency in all narratives about the Skálholt diocese at that time seems to be to focus on these two chieftains and their influence on church politics. In *Þorláks saga* they are mentioned as "byskups vinir" ("friends of the bishop").[64] To be ordained bishop, however, Þorlákr had to travel to Archbishop Eysteinn in Niðaróss.[65]

---

62 "Þorlákr was over thirty five years old when he moved to Ver and stayed there for seven years. He first entered the Augustinian order and in the beginning he was chosen prior for the canon friars that were there, and at once he ruled their life in such a beautiful way that it was said among wise men that they had never seen such good customs in a place where the life under the Rule was so recently established" *Biskupa sögur* II, 58).

63 "People travelled to the canon convent of Abbot Þorlákr from other monasteries or places under the Rule, both from within the land and from outside to see and learn the good customs, and everyone who left there could tell that in no place was that life thought to be more beautifully lived than in the place where Þorlákr had been in charge" (*Biskupa sögur* II, 60).

64 *Biskupa sögur* II, 63.

65 *Biskupa sögur* II, 64–66.

The second important agent in the network of clerics who should be treated briefly here is Guðmundr *góði* Arason, bishop of the diocese of Hólar in northern Iceland. Guðmundr is known for his struggle with chieftains, but also for his good relations with some of them. It is also worth noting that one of the fullest sources on Guðmundr's life is found in *Íslendinga saga*, attributed to Snorri's nephew, Sturla Þórðarson.[66] As he is described in the sources, Guðmundr seems to have had good relations first of all with Þórðr Sturluson, but also with Snorri Sturluson and Hrafn Sveinbjarnarson. There is no information about Guðmundr Arason having studied abroad, but he is still generally described as a learned and well educated man. When he is nearing death, it is described how he was read to in Latin:

> Lǫngum var hann lítt heill, því at hann var eigi bókskygn, þá er hann fór ór Hǫfða, en blindr með ǫllu inn síðasta vetr, er hann lifði. Andlítsmein hafði hann, ok lá verkr í inni hægri kinn ofan frá auganu. Hann sǫng lǫngum, eða lét lesa fyrir sér sǫgur heilagra manna á látínu, þá er hann vakti.[67]

The bishop was also modern in his views on the role of the church, and this was, according to the sources, what caused his conflicts with the aristocracy. It has therefore been suggested by Svanhildur Óskarsdóttir, with reference to Régis Boyer, that Guðmundr appears very much as an Augustinian canon even though there are no indications that he ever entered this order. Svanhildur concludes: "Með því að rekja rætur hugmynda Guðmundar til kanúka má tengja hann trúarlífi á Íslandi, nýbreytni hans reynist þá vera ávöxtur þeirra fræja sem Þorlákur biskup og reglubræður hans sáðu".[68]

---

66 The *cultus* of Guðmundr góði Arason has recently been treated in a study by Skórzewska (2007), where the sources are thoroughly discussed. I refer to this study for further information about the sources for Guðmundr's life.

67 "Often he was in bad health for a long time, because he could not see well enough to read when he left Hǫfði, and he was completely blind during the last winter of his life. He felt an illness in his face, and the pain was situated in the right cheek below the eye. He often sang for a long time or had someone reading to him tales of holy men in Latin whenever he was awake" (*Sturlunga saga* I, 489).

68 "By tracing the roots of Guðmundr's ideas to canons, he can be linked to religious life in Iceland; his innovation then turns out to be the fruit of the seeds sown by Bishop Þorlákr and the members of his order" (Svanhildur Óskarsdóttir 1992, 237).

Figure 2. The Viðey island, close to Reykjavík, with the mountain Esja in the background. The white buildings were erected in the eighteenth century. Based on archaeological investigations, the buildings of the Augustinian monastery stood just behind the white buildings. Snorri Sturluson took an active part in establishing this monastery. Photo: Mats Vibe Lund.

The central issue here concerns Guðmundr's three stays with Snorri Sturluson in 1209, 1227 and 1231, all described in *Íslendinga saga*. During these stays, he would most likely have been involved in the intellectual life at Reykholt, with Snorri himself and with the clerics active at the church. Together with the already mentioned Styrmir *fróði* Kárason, who was a cleric at Reykholt in this period, Guðmundr would form an intellectual link to the Benedictine centres in the North, while at the same time both of them represent the Augustinian ideas; Styrmir soon became the first prior in the Augustinian monastery on Viðey, which was financed by amongst others Snorri Sturluson.

The Augustinians and the Old Norse Renaissance

Icelandic literate culture is obviously a part of European literate culture, the Latin book culture of Europe. As Lars Boje Mortensen has pointed out, this is often stated in studies of Old Norse vernacular literature, but perhaps with few implications. Mortensen states:

> Selv om den latinske lærdom, i Vesteuropa, ofte bliver nævnt som essentiel baggrund for folkesprogslitteraturerne, får den alligevel ikke megen plads som en egentlig aktiv dialogpartner i litter-aturhistorien. Den reduceres nemlig til baggrund: når redegørelsen for den er afviklet, kan den trænges i baggrunden når man skal behandle den egentlige, folkesproglige litteratur.[69]

The interplay between Latin and indigenous traditions, and the individ-uals and institutions representing them, must be the starting point if we are to understand the role of the Augustinians in Iceland and Norway. Their education was primarily within the Latin book culture Mortensen describes, and their use of script was generally in the Latin language; they would not have been the ones to introduce an interest in the vernacular. When they establish themselves in the Scandinavian world of learned clerics their general background is not the vernacular learning, but rather the Latin learning of Europe. It is when they encounter the indigenous culture and use writing to represent it that they become part of the making of a vernacular manuscript culture.

Both of the archbishops from Niðaróss mentioned above had their training in the Parisian milieu of St Victor, and thereby had a direct connection to the twelfth-century renaissance tendencies that appeared there. The named, but otherwise unknown, author of *Historia de antiq-uitate regum Norwagiensium*, Theodoricus monachus, is also mentioned in connection with the monastery in Paris. It has been suggested that he is identical to the Archbishop Þórir (modern Norwegian Tore) who fol-lowed Eiríkr in Niðaróss, or, as an alternative, Bishop Þórir of Hamarr.[70]

---

69   "Even if the Latin erudition, in Western Europe, is often mentioned as an essential background to the literature in the vernaculars, it nevertheless receives little space as a real and active dialogue partner in the literary history. And it is in fact reduced to forming the background: as soon as it is mentioned, it can be placed in the background when one is to deal with the real, vernacular literature" (Mortensen 2006, 229).

70   See e.g. Ellehøj 1965, 176.

In this milieu the Icelandic Bishop Þorlákr had his foreign education, and he was in close contact with his Augustinian brothers in Norway. This has to be taken into account when we try to assess the actions taken by Þorlákr after his return to Iceland, where he was appointed prior and abbot of the first Augustinian house at Þykkvabœr, and subsequently elected bishop of Skálholt. There should be no doubt that he was a well educated man with a level of Latin learning that must have been equal to that of any bishop in Europe at the time.

Latin was the precondition of a vernacular literacy. From the nature of the preserved material from the twelfth century, it could easily be concluded that Iceland and Norway were the exceptions to the rule, but the lack of Latin manuscripts must rather be explained by the destruction of manuscripts in subsequent centuries.[71] A work such as Ari *fróði* Þorgilsson's *Íslendingabók* has already been mentioned as an early example of writing in the vernacular. *Fyrsta málfræðiritgerðin* also provides an example of not only learned writing in the vernacular, but in a field where there are few examples in other contemporary vernaculars, perhaps with the exception of Irish.[72]

Fyrsta málfræðiritgerðin is an early reflection of an interest in language and poetics (with the explicit aim of creating a writing system for the vernacular) which throughout the Middle Ages takes on unique forms in Icelandic literature. Its treatment of the principles for writing the vernacular with Roman script, and its explicit description of the relation between spoken and written Icelandic, demonstrates an interest in *grammatica* applied to the vernacular.[73] Since the 1930s, this interest in language and poetics, often in relation to local or regional history, and with the designation "Old Norse Renaissance", has frequently been associated with the tendencies found in France and the northern parts of Italy in the twelfth century, generally depicted as the twelfth-century renaissance. Both concepts are problematic, and have never been generally

---

71 For Iceland, see e.g. Gottskálk Jensson 2004. For Norway, see the articles in Karlsen 2013.

72 It could be argued that *Fyrsta málfræðiritgerðin* is only preserved in a manuscript from the mid-fourteenth century (AM 242 fol), and that *Íslendingabók* is extant in two paper manuscripts from the seventeenth century and only provides secondary sources to the period under discussion here. There are otherwise only fragments left of a written culture in the vernacular from the twelfth century.

73 See e.g. Guðrún Nordal 2001.

accepted by scholars, however, and recently this has again been the subject of discussion.[74]

The first to suggest a twelfth-century renaissance was H.C. Haskins in 1927. He argued from the perspective of intellectual history that the definition of the Italian Renaissance was too rigid, and that there were good reasons to postulate an earlier renaissance, primarily in the northern parts of Italy and in the region of Paris.[75] In the twelfth century, Paris becomes one of the centres of learning in Europe. The Augustinian monastery of St Victor is a leading institution of higher education in this period, and thus also central in the education of scholars, *magistri*, for the European market. Robert I. Moore provides a description of these educated *magistri* of the twelfth century that is highly relevant for our understanding of the role of Þorlákr and his followers in Iceland, as well as for the archbishops of Norway.

> Their shared culture and common destiny, as well as their use-fulness to princes, enabled the *magistri* of the twelfth century to establish themselves as the custodians and interpreters of the texts by whose authority, transmitted through them, Christendom was to be ordered – the Latin classics and the Holy Scriptures.[76]

The earliest mention of an Old Norse renaissance is found in Jan de Vries *Altnordische Literaturgeschichte* which was published in its first redaction in 1941–1942. Here the European renaissance suggested by Haskins is seen as the spark for the flowering of Old Norse culture in the twelfth and thirteenth centuries, where the European interest in classical literature and art triggers the Norse interest in its own past.[77] Jan de Vries'

---

74 See e.g. Johansson (ed.) 2007.
75 Haskin's suggestion of an early renaissance has been both accepted and challenged by later scholarship (see e.g. Lindkvist 2007). One recent example of a similar approach is Moore 2000, where the lines of change are drawn from the tenth century until the Lateran council in 1215, however without using the *renaissance* concept. Moore's contention is that Europe was not formed in the first millennium, but rather in the second, with a long revolution forming the European unity (see e.g. 2000, 1). The concept *renaissance* should according to some scholars be confined to the Italian renaissance of the fourteenth and fifteenth centuries. This has been challenged by Goody, 2010, who expands the use of the concept to similar periods and phenomena from a global perspective and in relation to our understanding of modernity.
76 Moore 2000, 146.
77 Vries 1941–1942, II, 2.

suggestion of an Old Norse Renaissance has not been generally accepted by later scholars.[78] It has for example been argued that the flowering of Norse culture in the late twelfth century should not at all be set in relation to Haskins' European renaissance, but rather seen as a separate and independent event.[79] As Else Mundal points out, it could also be that the flowering of Old Norse literature should rather be understood as the transition from an oral to a more literate culture, that is, the tradition has been there all the time, but it is only with the new medium that it takes the form that we know.[80] It has been argued, however, that a renaissance for the Eddic or skaldic poetry would imply that this poetry was recovered from a forgotten treasure of literature, and that this would have as a prerequisite a written culture. In an oral culture anything that was forgotten would be lost forever.[81] A renaissance of an oral tradition is not what is suggested by the extant material, but rather a literalization of traditions as part of the processes of transforming Latin literacy and Latin book culture in relation to the vernacular.[82] This process is well under way in the late eleventh or perhaps early twelfth century, but it is obvious that it is in the later twelfth century that the vernacular really begins to conquer new domains of writing. And it is for this period that we would expect Augustinian influence, and therefore the influence of the European Renaissance, to play an important part.

The Augustinians formed strong networks throughout Europe. This is not a controversial contention. This was a tendency of the twelfth century-church and the learned men it housed. Olle Ferm characterizes the twelfth century:

> 1100-talet var de internationella nätverkens genombrottstid. Sam-hällsekonomin expanderade och det feodala samhället tog definitiv gestalt. Kyrkan var visserligen äldre än så, men dess uniformering – organisatoriskt, institutionellt och doktrinmässigt – började på allvar under 1100-talet, då Norden definitivt inlemmades i västkyrkan.[83]

---

78 See e.g. Mundal 2007 for a presentation of this debate.

79 See e.g. Mundal 2007, 28.

80 Mundal 2007, 30.

81 See e.g. Hermann 2007, 43; Thorvaldsen 2007, 83.

82 See e.g. Sverrir Jakobsson 2007, 65 for a similar view.

83 "The twelfth century meant the breakthrough for the international networks. The economy expanded and the feudal society took its definite form. The church was

Above I mentioned the three archbishops of Niðaróss, Eysteinn, Eiríkr and Þórir, who are all thought to have been educated in Paris. It is clear from the sources that these men were in close contact with both England, where Eysteinn spent his years in exile, and the archiepiscopal diocese of Lundr, where Eiríkr stayed when he was in conflict with King Sverrir, and most likely was in contact with both Saxo grammaticus and the Archbishop Absalon.[84] Þorlákr was obviously part of this network. It is also clear that he and his nephew (and successor as bishop at Skálholt) Páll Jónsson, were in England, Páll perhaps also in Lincoln, at one point. This all provides us with indications of a strong Augustinian network between the two archiepiscopal dioceses of Scandinavia, Skálholt in Iceland, and two European centres of learning, Paris and Lincoln. If Þorlákr and Páll were among those who brought what we may call renaissance ideas from Paris to Scandinavia, they were both well equipped to do so, and successful in their mission.

Two important works should be briefly treated here; the already mentioned *Historia de antiquitate regum Norwagiensium* (= *Historia*) and the *Passio et miracula Beati Olavi*. Parts of the latter are attributed to Archbishop Eysteinn, while the first is associated with a Parisian tendency and closely related to the ideas found in contemporary French historical works. Lars Boje Mortensen has pointed out the common tendencies of *Historia* and *Passio Olavi*. He also stresses the contacts with France and the different approach of these works in relation to *Historia Norwegie* (= *HN*):

> The foreign authorities that Theodoricus draws on are all French or Roman (he would almost certainly have used Adam of Bremen had he known of him). Nor are there any positive signs that Theodoricus used written Icelandic sources. The axis of learning between Trondheim and northern France is completely ignored by the author of *HN*: not only is Theodoricus unknown, but also

obviously older than this, but its conformity – in organization, institutions and doctrine – was established for real in the twelfth century when the Nordic realm was definitely included in the Western church" (Ferm 2001, 93).

84 For a recent treatment of the three archbishops and the Scandinavian relations to the St Victor monastery in Paris, see Gunnes 1996, 195–221. I have often had discussions on this topic with Gottskálk Jensson, who treats the literary implications of the network I sketch here in detail in his research. His further work will provide more important insights into the influences of the French Augustinian canons on Norwegian and Icelandic vernacular literature in the late twelfth and early thirteenth century.

Passio Olavi is undetectable; in particular the debate about the place of Olav's baptism could have left traces in *HN* – had it been known to the author. We find it in Theodoricus, *Passio Olavi*, an exchange between Øystein and the Pope, and in a northern French manuscript of *Passio Olavi* copied in the last quarter of the twelfth century from a Norwegian exemplar.[85]

The focus on the saint king, *Olauus perpetuus rex Norwegie*, is common to *Historia* and the *Passio Olavi* and marks a change from *HN* where Óláfr Tryggvason plays the more significant role. This change of focus is generally related to the Augustinian canons and the establishing of the Niðaróss archdiocese in the second half of the twelfth century. In an article on the importance of Niðaróss for the *cultus* of Óláfr Haraldsson, Lars Boje Mortensen and Else Mundal suggest that the earliest, fragmentary literature on Óláfr *helgi* Haraldsson could represent a Norwegian contribution to the twelfth century renaissance.[86] In their discussion about this material on Óláfr *helgi* they conclude:

> Sjølv om nokre av forteljingane kan ha vorte til kort tid etter Olavs død, kan det, som vi har peikt på ovanfor, vere tale om islandske eller ikkje-lokale tradisjonar som kanskje først vart "gesunkenes Kulturgut" i Nidaros etter at vi fekk ei intensivering av Olavsdyrkinga med auka byggjeverksemd i 1130- og 1140-åra og med opprettinga av erkebispestolen i 1152/53. I tilfelle vil det ulike utvalet av mirakel i den latinske Olavslegenda og dei tekstar som går attende på den, på den eine sida og i skaldedikt og sagalitteratur på den andre, reflektere ulike tradisjonar ved ulike institusjonar og i ulike litterære miljø.[87]

---

85 Mortensen (ed.) 2003, 20–21.
86 Mortensen and Mundal 2003, 259.
87 "Even if some of the narratives may have been composed shortly after the death of Olav, it may, as have been noted above, be Icelandic or non-local traditions that perhaps only became 'gesunkenes Kulturgut' in Nidaros after we see an increase in the veneration of Olav contemporary with the increased building activity in the 1130s and 1140s, and the establishing of the episcopal see in 1152/53. If this is the case the difference in choice of miracles between the Latin legend of Olav and those texts that rely on it on the one hand, and in skaldic poetry and saga literature on the other, reflect different traditions in different institutions and in different literate milieux" (Mortensen and Mundal 2003, 364).

This supports the main contention of the present article, that there were not one, but many lines of change and influences in the establishment of a literate culture of the vernacular in the twelfth and thirteenth centuries. And, also important to stress, a significant part of the new influences on Old Norse literate culture is played by the expansive Latin book culture in Niðaróss in the days of Archbishop Eysteinn.[88] In another context Mortensen stresses the French influences further:

> As already noted by Koht and others, it is significant that the Trondheim-based historian Theodoricus (*c.* 1180) and the author of *HN* show no signs of knowing each other. This lack of cross-reference implies another place of composition for *HN*; such an impression is strengthened when we consider that the French learning of Theodoricus and the German *HN* seem to be worlds apart.[89]

There has been a discussion of the function of the versions of *Thomas saga Becket* in three different periods where the church was in conflict with the Icelandic aristocracy concerning the ownership of and power over churches.[90] Stefán Karlsson pointed out that the three versions of the saga could very well be connected to known clerics in three periods of conflict. From the nineteenth century, the oldest translation of the *vita* of Thomas has been attributed to the cleric Bergr Gunnsteinsson.[91] He was, as Stefán Karlsson puts it, "among the travelling companions of the bishop-elect Guðmundr and the chieftain Hrafn Sveinbjarnarson when Guðmundr went to Norway for consecration in 1202".[92] The main textual source for the oldest translation was most probably the now lost work of the Augustinian prior Robert of Cricklade. The translation was dated to around 1200 by Peter Foote.[93] Stefán Karlsson sketches the network of connections of Bergr Gunnsteinsson and his time:

88   Mortensen and Mundal 2003, 360.
89   Mortensen (ed.) 2003, 20.
90   See e.g. Würth 1994.
91   See Stefán Karlsson 2000, 137.
92   Stefán Karlsson 2000, 136.
93   Foote 1961, 444.

Bishop Þorlákr Þórhallsson (1178–93) studied in England a few years before Thomas became archbishop, and his nephew and successor at Skálholt, Bishop Páll Jónsson (1195–1211), also pursued studies there, probably a few years after Robert of Cricklade wrote his *Vita et miracula* of Thomas. Shortly before the turn of the century the pious Icelandic chieftain Hrafn Sveinbjarnarson went to Canterbury and made St Thomas an offering of Walrus ivory, and we know that Hrafn was aquainted with Bergr Gunnsteinsson.[94]

Stefán could perhaps have added that Thomas studied in Paris a few decades before the two later Norwegian archbishops Eysteinn and Eiríkr, and possibly also the Icelandic Bishop Þorlákr. In the 1160s Thomas was in exile in Paris for a while before returning to his martyrdom in 1170; this would have been close to the time of the Scandinavians' stay in the same milieu.

Reykholt and the Sturlungar

In the above, my aim has been to show how different institutions within the church, such as the dioceses of Skálholt and Hólar, and the Benedictine and Augustinian monasteries, as well as the aristocracy and individuals, all played a role in the processes of transforming the Latin book culture into the vernacular culture. This will now be related to the Sturlungar, and I shall point out some important implications for our understanding of the aristocratic appropriation of literate skills in the thirteenth century, especially represented by the Sturlungar family.

It should be obvious that the church institutions played a significant role in the establishing of Latin as well as vernacular literacy in Europe. However, in earlier scholarship on the emerging Old Norse literate culture this has generally been neglected in favour of a focus on the oral traditions. It is therefore necessary here to point to fields where there is need for further studies rather than to formulate strong conclusions. From the survey I have presented above, it should be obvious that there has been a continuous interplay between the various institutions and the individuals within them over time, both on the political scene and

94 Stefán Karlsson 2000, 149–150.

in the transformation of the literate culture. I can therefore only agree partly with Helgi Þorláksson's conclusion about the relevance of the monastic orders:

> Her har jeg prøvd å henlede oppmerksomheten på at det kanskje ikke var klosterordenene som var den viktigste inspirasjonskilden for Snorri som forfatter, men de omtalte kongregasjoner av lærde gejstlige. Det var disse mennene som Snorri mest sannsynlig ga i oppdrag å studere skriftlige kilder og samle stoff for ham. De var viktige for hans forfatterskap, og det spiller mindre rolle om de var mest påvirket av benediktiner- eller augustinerordenen.[95]

Helgi Þorláksson is absolutely right in pointing out the importance of the learned clergy in Snorri's nearest milieu, but in a wider perspective they are – as is also recognized by Helgi Þorláksson in his article – rather one of many agents taking part in this interplay of establishing a vernacular literate culture. If we are to understand more fully the intellectual context of the Sturlungar in the thirteenth century we need to take all the agents, institutional as well as individual, into closer account. And, it goes without saying, this approach is not limited to the Sturlungar, but rather has implications for our general views on the growth and expansion of a vernacular literate culture in the period under scrutiny.

The first relevant group of interest to be considered is the aristocracy, which is the group where the Sturlungar primarily belong. It is clear from the sources that this elite was already active when Church institutions began to be established in Iceland, but it is also clear that the group's position changed in the course of the twelfth and in the first half of the thirteenth century. There is a general consensus that in this period the aristocracy moved from being independent of a central state into being dependent on the emerging state for its status and power. This change can be discerned in the historical events taking place in the civil war known as the *Sturlungaöld*, and the subsequent change in the role played

---

95   "I have here tried to point out that it was perhaps not the monastic orders that provided the most important source of inspiration to Snorri as an author, but rather the mentioned congregations of learned clerics. These men were most probably the ones that Snorri commissioned to study written sources and collect materials for him. They were important for his authorship, and it is of less consequence whether they were influenced more by the Benedictines or the Augustinians" (Helgi Þorláksson 2006, 73).

by members of the Sturlungar family. In the twelfth century, however, the aristocratic families (if the sources are correct) took an active role in establishing schools and in forming a learned elite. The schools at Oddi and Haukadalr have been used as significant examples of this above, and individuals such as Ari Þorgilsson and Sæmundr Sigfússon were seen as representatives of aristocratic involvement. By the end of the twelfth century the two chieftains, Jón Loptsson and Gizurr Hallsson, were significant in relation to schools and education. And here lies the first implication for the education and learned literate activities of the Sturlungar, as Snorri Sturluson was raised and educated at Oddi, the farm owned by Jón Loptsson, and where another important individual in the early thirteenth century, Páll Jónsson, most likely had his initial training as a cleric. This points in the direction of an aristocratic training for Snorri, but it also clearly shows how vague the borders are between the various group interests in this period, as Páll was later trained in England and became bishop of Skálholt, where he is said to have stressed the importance of scholarly training of the clerics.

It is important to stress here that earlier scholarship in many ways seems to have avoided addressing the question of the ideological and intellectual influences on the Icelandic aristocracy in the twelfth century. It is obvious, however, that the court culture which was established in Europe in the age of the Crusades was also introduced into the Scandinavian countries in the twelfth and early thirteenth century, and it most likely also contributed to shaping the world-view of an aristocrat such as Snorri Sturluson. In recent research on European materials this court culture has often been considered as part of the political process, as a means of achieving conformity and discipline in the ruling classes.[96] The growing importance of international contacts and influences within the European aristocracy has been stressed by many scholars.[97] For Iceland this influence seems to have been initiated in the second half of the twelfth century, in the same period as the first flowering of a vernacular literature can be observed. It is obvious that the transformations taking place in Europe play an important role also in Scandinavia. In a discussion of the role of the leading aristocratic families and their relation to Norway and the king's court Guðrún Nordal concludes:

[96] See e.g. Bumke 1986 I–II.
[97] See e.g. Bumke 1986 I, 83–112.

The Oddaverjar, Haukdælir and Sturlungar were the three families most overtly engrossed in their relationship with the Norwegian royal house in the thirteenth century. Haukdælir and Sturlungar were in direct competition for the earldom of Iceland.[98]

Already in the late twelfth century these families were moving towards the new role that they were to occupy fully in the course of the thirteenth century, that of an administrative elite in the close proximity of the king and the emerging state. Guðrún Nordal argues that in his literary works Snorri promoted himself in this role as an aristocrat.

> *Heimskringla* is clearly written from an aristocratic point of view, notwithstanding these Icelandic fingerprints. It is abundantly apparent from the patterns of Snorri's life that he did not regard himself as an ordinary Icelandic farmer. He was an aristocrat and a courtier, not only in Norway but also when in Iceland.[99]

A central interest in the learned aspirations of the Icelandic aristocracy concerned genealogies. Ole Bruhn argues that a transformation of the role played by the aristocracy takes place in the period from Ari fróði's *Íslendingabók* (which Bruhn interprets as part of the integration of Iceland as an independent part of the European world) to the mid-thirteenth century where the genealogies were primarily aimed at legitimizing the demands of the old aristocracy to keep their position and power as servants of the king. Bruhn states:

> I perioden fra Ari skrev Íslendingabók, og frem til Styrmir og Sturla laver deres Landnámabók-redaktioner, er der altså sket nogle sociale og politiske udviklinger, som har gjort Aris historiesyn og hans historiefremstilling uaktuel. Forestillingen om, at det er islændingene selv, der gennem samarbejdet i deres institutioner, Alting og kirke, i fælleskab udvikler deres samfund og skaber deres egen historie, er afløst af en forestilling om, at denne historie er led i en større institutionel sammenhæng, som

---

98 Guðrún Nordal 2006, 80.
99 Guðrún Nordal 2006, 79.

inkluderer det norske kongedømme, og hvor historien ses som en videreudvikling af det, som blev grundlagt i begyndelsen.[100]

Bruhn says that this transformation cannot be considered as an isolated phenomenon in Icelandic history. Rather he claims that this is part of a general change in Europe.[101] Moore comes to a similar conclusion in his discussion of what he considers to be the first European revolution, where he notes an interest within the European aristocracy in establishing genealogies and nourishing the ideas of ancestry. And the importance of stressing an heroic and valiant descent is clear. He concludes:

> The confusion of ancestry which had previously prevailed is marked, and disguised, by the mythical descent from some valiant, even supernaturally favoured adventurer, to whose skill and luck the inauguration of the family fortune is attributed. One such was the 'Siffredus' from whom the descent of the Counts of Guines was traced by Lambert of Ardres, another the 'Guillaume Taillefer' who was supplied as the founder of their line by the anonymous historian of the Counts of Angoulême, both writing late in the twelfth century.[102]

Substitute the names of Egill Skalla-Grímsson or Þorfinnr *karlsefni* and the early aristocratic families of Iceland, and this passage could just as well be written about *Egils saga Skalla-Grímssonar* or *Eiríks saga rauða*. The form is different, but the intent may very well be similar. Moore goes on to discuss the reason for this interest, and his argument strongly resembles the one put forward by Bruhn. Moore says:

> On the contrary, the elevation of the warrior class and knightly values through the language of holy war and the cult of chivalry

---

100 "From the period when Ari wrote *Íslendingabók* and the time when Styrmir and Sturla composed their versions of *Landnámabók*, there have obviously been some social and political changes that have made Ari's view of history and his presentation of history irrelevant. The idea that the Icelanders themselves through the collaboration in their institutions, *Alþingi* and church, together develop their society and create their own history has been replaced with an idea that this history is part of a larger institutional context, including the Norwegian kingdom, where history is seen as a development of what was there in the beginning" (Bruhn 1999, 196).
101 Bruhn 1999, 196.
102 Moore 2000, 70.

was designed to secure, and at the same time to obscure, the marginalization and subordination of the knights themselves.[103]

Sverre Bagge has argued along the same lines as Bruhn and Moore concerning the descriptions of King Sverrir Sigurðarson (*c.* 1150–1202) and King Hákon Hákonarson (modern Norwegian Håkon Håkonsson, Håkon IV, 1204–1263), who have both been described in individual biographies, *Sverris saga* and *Hákonar saga Hákonarsonar*, and their relation to the aristocracy.[104] Bagge writes:

> Sverrir was primarily the leader of a closely knit community of warriors, and the success of his claim to the Norwegian throne depended on his ability to gain the confidence of these men and make them fight for him. Although the idea of the Lord's anointed is also present in *Sverris saga*, it is far more prominent in *Hákonar saga*. That is to say that the royal office plays a more important role in *Hákonar saga* than in *Sverris saga*, while the importance of the individual is correspondingly greater in *Sverris saga*. Thus the two sagas give an example of changing ideas of the individual person as a consequence of the growth of the state.[105]

It is interesting in the present discussion to note again that *Sverris saga* was composed, at least partly, by the Benedictine Karl Jónsson from the Þingeyrar monastery and possibly further edited by Styrmir *fróði* Kárason, who was most likely receiving his initial education in the northern part of Iceland, but later worked at Reykholt as a cleric, while *Hákonar saga Hákonarsonar* was composed by one of the Sturlungar, Snorri's nephew Sturla Þórðarson, a learned man who definitely had close links to the son of King Hákon, King Magnús *lagabœtir* (Lawmender) Hákonarson. In the line of reasoning I am trying to pursue here, the earlier saga would represent the Benedictine tradition, and with Styrmir the link to the Sturlungar, while *Hákonar saga Hákonarsonar* provides direct evidence for the literary achievements of the new kind of aristocracy which emerged with the stronger state. The elite in Iceland, from the generation of Snorri,

103 Moore 2000, 193.
104 Bagge 1996, provides thorough presentations of the two sagas and the state of their preservation.
105 Bagge 1996, 12.

necessarily had to look to Norway for legitimacy and promotion. Guðrún Nordal states: "Snorri Sturluson was preoccupied with Norway all his life, and by Norway I mean the Norwegian aristocratic milieu, the court, the earls and the king himself".[106]

In this concern lay the need to promote oneself, and the Sturlungar seem to have chosen, in the tradition of Ari *fróði* and Sæmundr *fróði*, to take into their possession the relatively new technology of writing in the vernacular to achieve their goals. This intention has been discussed thoroughly by Kevin Wanner in relation to Snorri Sturluson's *Edda*.[107] Wanner claims that Snorri, by taking part in the learned discourse of his time, is manifesting his position as a leader, and that his work is supporting vernacular poetry as a means of cultural capital.

From this it could be concluded that the aristocratic traditions of the Sturlungar, as well as the political transformations leading to a change in the status and role of the aristocracy, played a significant part in the forming of the literate attempts of members of the family. Snorri Sturluson's approach to the history of the Norwegian kings as well as his work on poetics and poetic traditions in the prose *Edda* (*Snorra-Edda*) could partly be explained as a strategy for retaining status. In this strategy he would in many ways resemble his contemporaries on the Continent, in content if not in form.

If *Heimskringla* could be seen as at least partly the result of changes in the status of the aristocracy, it must also be seen as a result of new approaches to history, approaches that are further enhanced in Sturla Þórðarson's *Hákonar saga Hákonarsonar* written about half a century later. Both Snorri and Sturla, however, composed their works within a secular strand of vernacular literacy based on and parallel to the European production of Latin chronicles at the time. If the form and function of these works are more or less parallel to the European contemporary tendencies, the choice of language is not. It remains therefore to assess the various influences on the emerging vernacular literacy.

The importance of the church for the early phases of the introduction of Roman script and book culture in Iceland is obvious. It is also clear that the Icelandic aristocracy immediately took part in the establishment of the church institutions, first in the form of churches and church centres

106 Guðrún Nordal 2006, 77.
107 Wanner 2008.

and the two archiepiscopal dioceses, but soon also in establishing the first Benedictine monasteries in northern Iceland. From the extant material it seems as if the *staðir* or large church farms played a more central role in the growth of literate culture in the southern parts of Iceland, while in the northern parts, the episcopal see at Hólar and the monasteries were of greater importance for the training of a book-learned elite. When we reach the late twelfth century the interests of church and aristocracy were probably coinciding in many ways, and the church centres were controlled by aristocrats such as Jón Loptsson and Gizurr Hallsson.

The establishing of church centres should probably be related to this shared interest of the church and the aristocrats. It could also be seen in relation to the intensive building activity of churches in this period, something which is often characterized as specific to Iceland.[108] It could be argued, however, that this activity did not differ in any significant way from what we see in Norway, or for that matter in the rest of Europe at the time.[109] In his discussion of the first European revolution, Moore stresses the importance of church building for the nobility in contemporary Europe:

> In France alone some eighty cathedrals, five hundred other large churches and several thousand parish churches were built and re-built during the eleventh, twelfth and thirteenth centuries. Church building played very much the same part in the transformation of Europe in this period as did the construction of railways in the industrial revolution of the nineteenth century.[110]

This should, in my opinion, be understood in relation to the interests of the aristocracy in establishing and supporting schools for the education of clerics. For Snorri Sturluson and his generation of Sturlungar, the available early education was to be found in these centres for clerical training. It can be stated as certain that Snorri had his primary education at Oddi where he spent his childhood. It can therefore also be suggested that he received a similar primary education to his contemporary Páll Jónsson, who later studied in England and returned to become bishop of Skálholt.

---

108 See e.g. Orri Vésteinsson 2000. On church centres see in this book pp. 115–116, 415–416.
109 See e.g. Johansson 2004, with references.
110 Moore 2000, 37.

In this generation education in the southern parts was dominated by the collaboration between the aristocracy and the church.

In the northern parts of Iceland, Hólar has been suggested as the earliest centre for the education of clerics. Here the church centres never seem to have played the same important role as in the South. When the first Benedictine monasteries were established these institutions obviously soon become centres of learning and education. In this milieu Latin was initially the first language for the production of indigenous texts, but almost from the outset the vernacular is also introduced, both in the production of new texts and in translations of Latin works.

In a number of recent studies Andersson has discussed the relation between Snorri Sturluson and the Benedictine monastery of Munka-Þverá in Eyjafjǫrðr.[111] Andersson argues that the tradition of writing Kings' Sagas, rather than having Reykholt as a point of departure and Snorri as one of the most important developers, was shaped at Munka-Þverá under the influence of the writings of history created at the other Benedictine monastery in northern Iceland, Þingeyrar. The historical writings of this monastery were, according to Andersson's view, developed further at Munka-Þverá with a tendency to stress the Icelandic perspective, as is apparent for example in *Morkinskinna*.[112] It was, again according to Andersson, from this tradition that Snorri created his *Heimskringla* and perhaps also *Egils saga Skalla-Grímssonar*. Andersson writes:

> In Iceland Snorri was an overwhelmingly dominant figure, both intellectually and politically. In retrospect the historical and political events of the thirteenth century seem to be arranged around him, but that may finally be truer of the political arena, in which Snorri makes a relatively late appearance. What I will argue in the following pages is that he is not the classical or pivotal figure in Icelandic saga writing, but rather the harvester of a tradition that was already fully ripened.[113]

On the relation between Snorri and the monastery at Munka-Þverá, Andersson argues: "Furthermore, Snorri's use of *Morkinskinna* as the foundation for *Heimskringla* III shows, if anything, that the literary

111 Andersson 1993; 1994.
112 For a similar view of *Morkinskinna*, see Ármann Jakobsson 2002.
113 Andersson 1993, 9–10.

impulses went not from Reykholt to Munkaþverá but rather in the opposite direction".[114]

The importance of the Benedictine monasteries for the development of the historical sagas about Norwegian kings has of course also been noted by earlier scholars. Sigurður Nordal, in "Sagalitteraturen" from 1953, pointed to Þingeyrar as the cradle for the Kings' Saga tradition. He concluded that, not only was there a cultural centre at Þingeyrar which had much influence on saga writing, but it was also a centre for a culture that was different from the culture of the major farms of the country.[115]

Andersson discusses the relation between the Sturlungar and the monastery at Munka-Þverá. He argues, on the basis of relations between three important families in Eyjafjǫrðr and known contacts with the monastery, that the saga tradition of Munka-Þverá could have influenced the Sturlungar, and then, of course, primarily Snorri. Instead of seeing Snorri as the pivotal point he states: "[W]e might rather suppose that the Eyjafjǫrðr tradition interacted with the Sturlungar tradition on an equal footing. These traditions were presumably not chronologically sequential but parallel."[116]

Andersson's view of the relation between the Benedictines of northern Iceland and Snorri Sturluson in Reykholt must be taken into account when we assess the intellectual background for the Sturlungar family. It is important to stress that influences from the Benedictines would have interacted with the vernacular culture from the first establishment of monasteries, as the young men (and soon also women) who were educated at the monasteries had this aristocratic culture present in their environment. As soon as a monastery was established, it would recruit from the local community, preferably from the elite. In these processes the Sturlungar must be expected to have taken an active part, and it is against this background that the intellectual works of Snorri Sturluson and his nephews, Óláfr *hvítaskáld* Þórðarson and Sturla Þórðarson should be understood.[117]

114 Andersson 1993, 21.
115 Sigurður Nordal 1953, 199.
116 Andersson 1994, 19.
117 Here it is also relevant to point to the discussion in Andersson (1994) about the role of Sturla Sighvatsson's literary interests. Andersson argues that Sturla would have known the Kings' Saga tradition from his own education in the northern part of Iceland, and that Snorri's work should be seen as secondary to this tradition in which e.g. *Morkinskinna* was produced.

The Benedictine tradition was influenced by European reforms and new trends, but at the same time there are indications that the northern literate culture takes another direction in the thirteenth century from what can be discerned in the works of the Sturlungar and other users of the written medium. In a recent work, Sveinbjörn Rafnsson treats the establishing of a vernacular (and more secular) Kings' Saga tradition in connection with Snorri Sturluson's Reykholt.[118] He reaches the conclusion that the earliest *vitae* of Óláfr Tryggvason were subsequently secularized in compilations such as *Heimskringla* – a conclusion quite similar to the one presented by Andersson – while a more monastic tradition which focused on the saintliness of the two missionary kings was continued within the monasteries. This conclusion obviously also fits well with the observations made by Sigurður Nordal. Again it is important to stress the interplay between the institutions defined above.

The northern milieux discussed here produced the earliest known vernacular work concerning an individual king's life, *Sverris saga*. According to the argument advanced above, this would represent the Benedictine tradition, i.e. the tradition of composing lives of saints transferred to the writing of a king's life, and the change of language from Latin to the vernacular. It is also in these milieux that *Morkinskinna*, which is considered by Andersson as central in the development of the Kings' Saga compilations, is formed. Two named individuals have been mentioned here in relation to the contacts between the northern monastic tradition and Reykholt: Styrmir Kárason and Guðmundr *góði* Arason. Both lived for periods at Reykholt and in direct contact with Snorri Sturluson and the Sturlungar, and represent both the tradition and the transformation of tradition in the period under discussion.

After his stay at Reykholt, Styrmir became an Augustinian canon and the first prior of the Viðey monastery, founded by among others Snorri Sturluson and Þorvaldr Gizurarson, while Guðmundr, as mentioned above, has many of the characteristics of the reformatory Augustinian canons.[119] This means that they not only form a link between the northern milieux and the Sturlungar, but they also relate to the contemporary cultural influences introduced from the Continent, and in many cases associated with the Augustinian canons. The Augustinian order was at

---

118 Sveinbjörn Rafnsson 2005.
119 Svanhildur Óskarsdóttir 1992.

this time influential in the southern diocese of Skálholt, and it seems obvious that the elite recognized their interests in supporting this order. Here, once again, it is necessary to stress the interplay between the church, the Augustinians, and the chieftains. In southern and western Iceland the Benedictines were less influential. It is interesting to note in this context that Snorri's nephew, Óláfr Þórðarson, according to *Sturlunga saga*, composed a poem dedicated to Þorlák which is today lost.

> Óláfr Þórðarson hafði ort drápu um Þorlák biskup um vetrinn næsta fyrir andlát Magnúss biskups. Hann fór um fǫstuna suðr í Skálaholt ok gaf sér þat til erindis at færa drápuna, en hann vildi þó hitta Snorra Sturluson, sem hann gerði, þá er hann fór sunnan.[120]

In the few extant stanzas of Óláfr's work there are also fragments of a poem dedicated to Thomas Becket and one stanza about Hákon Hákonarson. The Augustinian saints Thomas and Þorlákr were central in the first half of the thirteenth century, and the king was, for Óláfr as well as for Snorri, the central authority to whom to relate.

From this, it is not difficult to argue that new influences from the Continent brought by the Augustinian canons also reached Iceland and played a role in the transformation of Icelandic literate culture. Primarily, one would expect the influences to be on church matters, for example in the conflicts between church and aristocracy documented in the sources. This has been discussed only briefly here, but has often been the topic of historical inquiries regarding the importance of Þorlákr's introduction of reformatory ideas. But we could also expect the intellectual influences from the Continent to have been important. Here it is again relevant to point out the education Snorri must have received at Oddi, the aristocratic church centre. Þorlákr is admittedly described by some sources as the opponent of Jón Loptsson, but he is also closely connected to him, and he is the uncle of the next bishop at Skálholt, Páll Jónsson. It is not, therefore, too far-fetched to suggest that new tendencies in literature and historical writing could have had an impact on the training of clerics

120 "Óláfr Þórðarson had composed a *drápa* about Bishop Þorlákr in the winter before the death of Bishop Magnús. During the fast he went south to Skálholt and said his errand was to perform the *drápa*, but in fact he wanted to meet Snorri Sturluson, as he did, when he went back" (*Sturlunga saga* I, 493).

at Oddi in the last decades of the twelfth century; there are no definite borders between the traditions, rather they constantly mix to various degrees.

The Augustinian network I have tentatively sketched out here included the archiepiscopal diocese of Lundr, where Saxo Grammaticus was producing his work on Danish history just a couple of decades before the composition of the two large compilations *Morkinskinna* and *Heimskringla*. Clear evidence for a knowledge of Saxo's work in these compilations has never been put forward. In a recent article I pointed to a similar approach to the ages of the world in *Gesta Danorum* and the first part of Snorri's compilation, *Ynglinga saga*.[121] This suggestion does not, however, necessarily lead to the conclusion that Snorri knew Saxo's work. It may indicate, rather, that the milieu in Reykholt was influenced by similar new ideas of chronicles reaching back to the pre-Christian past of the Scandinavian lands that served as the incentive for Saxo.

The Victorines were deeply involved in the reform movement of the twelfth century. It therefore should come as no surprise that Þorlákr seems to have promoted reformist ideas in Iceland. More interesting in our context, however, is tracing the literate influences that this learned man and his contemporary Augustinians could have brought to Norway and Iceland. Beryl Smalley states about the orderly community of the Victorines:

> Only these activities and this background can explain the strange richness and diversity of the Victorine literature. We remember it best for the religious lyrics, which have all attached themselves to the Breton poet, Adam, and for the mystical theology of Hugh and Richard; it includes history, chronicles, geography, grammar, philosophy, psychology, education, together with the usual sermons, commentaries, and various kinds of manuals.[122]

It could be argued that these types of texts were also produced by others than the Augustinian scholars from St Victor, but it is important to point out the need to focus on an *historical* reading of the Bible before the other levels of understanding the text (allegorical, tropological and anagogical)

121 Johansson 2010.
122 Smalley 1964, 84.

can be applied, and the production of historical and geographical aids to study stressed by Smalley.[123] Victorines such as Hugh of St Victor were clearly noted for their interest in *historia*, the literal understanding of the historical texts. Smalley states:

> Hugh effected a differentiation between the three senses, which enormously increased the dignity of the historical sense. Instead of contrasting the lowly foundation of the 'letter' with the higher spiritual senses, he groups together the letter and allegory, which pertain to knowledge, and contrasts them with tropology! The importance of the letter is constantly stressed.[124]

The Victorines also seem to have played an important role in the development of the encyclopaedic literature which is attested in Old Norse material from the thirteenth century onward.[125] Smalley presents the encyclopaedic plans of Richard of St Victor, where there would be sections on world history and geography.[126] She later concludes that the Victorines played an important role in moving learning out of the monasteries:

> The Victorine programme, which Hugh set forth in his *Didascalicon*, and which Andrew and Richard tried to realize in their teaching, made *lectio divina* acceptable to the Paris scholar. The Victorines, being both *claustrales* and *scholares*, were able to transmit the old religious exercise from the cloister to the school.[127]

To state that the Victorines, primarily represented by Þorlákr, did not influence the Old Norse learned tradition in the thirteenth century would be closing one's eyes to the obvious. A further parallel can be found in Smalley's final remark on English biblical studies in the twelfth and thirteenth centuries:

---

123 Smalley 1964, 85.
124 Smalley 1964, 89.
125 For the Old Norse encyclopedic tradition see e.g. Stefán Karlsson 2000, and Gunnar Harðarson and Stefán Karlsson 1993. For a recent treatment of this tradition in Iceland see Sverrir Jakobsson 2005. A treatment of the encyclopaedic tradition in a European perspective is presented by Brincken 1969.
126 See e.g. Smalley 1964, 87.
127 Smalley 1964, 196.

The special interest that Englishmen seem to have taken in biblical studies derives more probably from the interest in antiquities and in the writing of history which goes back to the Anglo-Saxons. Our biblical scholars fit into place beside the poet of *Exodus* and the piece on the ruins of Bath, the compilers of the Anglo-Saxon Chronicle, the twelfth-century historians and the thirteenth-century Matthew Paris.[128]

This would lead us back to the Anglo-Saxon Benedictines discussed in relation to the northern monasteries above, but now at a later stage in history. It could be suggested that the English twelfth and thirteenth centuries could perhaps provide more parallels to the Icelandic development in this period than what is generally thought.

Elizabeth M. Tyler has recently discussed the relation between Anglo-Saxon, Latin and French in eleventh- and twelfth-century England. She concludes that the special development of written Anglo-Saxon had an impact on the use of Latin in what she characterizes as a *hermeneutic* style:

> Such a style could only become dominant in a context, like Anglo-Saxon England, in which written communication was carried out in the vernacular: in other words, written English enables the practice of hermeneutic Latin in England because English did so much of what Latin did on the Continent – law, poetry, government, history-writing, science and so forth. Paradoxically, hermeneutic Latin encouraged lay access to the 'story-world' of Rome. The Old English translations of Orosius, *Apollonius of Tyre*, *The Letter of Alexander* and Boethius are part of a world in which Latin had retreated from communication.[129]

There are similarities here to what we see in Iceland. Latin seems relatively soon to have become, more or less exclusively, the language of the Church and further education, while the vernacular established itself in many domains, such as the translations of *Antikenromanen*[130] and indigenous works such as Snorri Sturluson's *Edda*, which, despite being

128 Smalley 1964, 369.
129 Tyler 2009, 168.
130 See e.g. Würth 1998.

composed in the vernacular, form part of the European interest in poetics and *grammatica*.[131] Tyler goes on to discuss the role of works like *Beowulf* in the English twelfth century, and concludes:

> The juxtaposition of Scandinavians and Trojans, which *Beowulf* and Gaimar share, points to the way in which the Anglo-Saxon lineage of Gaimar extends beyond his translation of the Chronicle to his participation in the vernacularization of the Roman story-world, which allowed the Anglo-Saxon, and then the Anglo-Norman, lay aristocracy a head start in developing that very European habit of using the Roman past to understand the present. This habit, which would flower in the early *romans d'antiquité*, marked both Gaimar's *Estoire* and *Beowulf*.[132]

It is difficult not to come to a similar conclusion for the intellectual milieu in which Snorri Sturluson and the Sturlungar of the late twelfth and thirteenth century were a part, in relation to genres such as skaldic and Eddic poetry as well as for the emerging saga literature. And the implications for Old Norse literate culture could perhaps be formulated in a way similar to Tyler's final conclusion:

> But Gaimar, with his Danes and Romans, can indeed help us to rescue *Beowulf* from the Germanic mists and to secure this poem a place in European literary history. Reading *Beowulf* through historiography and romance makes the point that it was not a Conquest that brought England into Europe. Anglo-Saxon literary culture, including (rather than in spite of) *Beowulf*, played a key role in shaping European literary culture in the twelfth century: a role the Conquest accelerated rather than pre-empted.[133]

In the late twelfth century, the learned Icelanders were in the same position as their European contemporaries, involved in the forming of a vernacular literate culture, with translations from Latin and Latin models meeting indigenous traditions. In these processes the various European impulses merged with local traditions in works as the prose

131 See e.g. Guðrún Nordal 2001.
132 Tyler 2009, 177–178.
133 Tyler 2009, 178.

Edda or in compilations as the one of Eddic poems found in Codex Regius (GKS 2365 4to). Later on in the thirteenth century works like the *Þriðja málfræðiritgerðin* by Óláfr Þórðarson are more evidently translations of European *grammatica*, adapting it to apply to indigenous poetics.

From the European impulses in the late twelfth century it is interesting to turn to the different choice of languages by Snorri Sturluson and Saxo Grammaticus in their respective works. While Saxo used the universal language of his contemporaries from all over Europe, Snorri followed a partly new path in using the vernacular. His inspiration for doing so must probably, in line with Andersson's reasoning, be found in the Benedictine tradition, which seems to have had close contacts with England, and perhaps more importantly, Benedictine England. This would indicate that a Benedictine tendency to turn to the vernacular language in compiling chronicles is here combined with a more recent tendency in the forming of these chronicles, and this may very well have its origin in the Augustinians returning from a Continental education.

It is obvious that the powerful families in Iceland more or less at once adapted to the European culture and invested their sons in the activities of the church. Already in the eleventh century Icelanders are mentioned in the sources as going abroad to study, and it is in this century that the first priests of Icelandic origin are mentioned who have studied at foreign schools. One of the most often mentioned examples is of course the one about Sæmundr *fróði* Sigfússon. There is, however, one thing that almost all of our sources for this early period have in common: they are written at a late date, often in the thirteenth century or even later. We therefore have to treat these sources with caution, as they are likely to represent contemporary literacy and learning rather than giving an accurate account of the use of script, education and learned activities in the period they allegedly describe.

Snorri Sturluson and his contemporaries did not live in a closed world with no contacts with the rest of Europe. Rather they took active part in the exchange of ideas and learning in the Catholic world. The earliest translations of Latin works as well as the more contemporary translations from French and German were in some cases made in Iceland, and the translations produced in Norway were at least to some extent known to the learned in Iceland, which is obvious from the later manuscript tradition, well attested by the manuscripts from the second half of the thirteenth and the fourteenth century containing versions of these works.

It is, of course, not known with any certainty exactly which works, and in which form, were known to Snorri or any of his contemporaries, but we can with some certainty provide a general view of the knowledge and learning that was accessible in this period.

Conclusion

The intellectual background for the Sturlungar family was multifaceted. There was without doubt a lively oral tradition of poetry and storytelling as well as a practical knowledge of the world in the milieu. The focus in this article, however, has been on the various channels through which European learning and new influences could have reached and played a part in the transformation of local traditions. The relatively early adjustment of the Roman script to the vernacular in Norway and Iceland has long been connected to the English mission in this area, where Anglo-Saxon traditions of writing in the vernacular seem to have been of importance. In the twelfth century the church institutions and the elite obviously collaborated in the establishing of schools where Latin, as in all parts of Europe, was central to the training of young boys for priesthood as well as of the sons of aristocrats. This collaboration between church and elite was particularly strong in the southern and western parts of Iceland.

In the northern parts the Benedictines had a stronghold which also influenced the learned activities at Hólar. The Benedictines, to judge from European parallels, could be expected to have been well versed in Latin and to have had an interest in the production and propagation of Christian works, something which is corroborated by what we can deduce from the fragmentary material from the late twelfth and early thirteenth century.

At the end of the twelfth century, the new order of Augustinians, often with an education from the Parisian monastery of St Victor, is significant for the church reforms in Norway and, arguably, in Iceland. The Augustinians also brought with them new trends in the use of writing, such as new attitudes to the writing of chronicles, which can be expected to have influenced the emerging saga writing tradition in Old Norse.

If we return to Sigurður Nordal's suggestion of three schools in saga writing it could perhaps be elaborated to some degree from the above discussion. The earliest school, or rather the earliest literacy in Latin and the vernacular, is formed within the early church with support from the aristocratic families. The literate achievement of this first period is impressive with works such as Ari's *Íslendingabók*, and it lays the foundation for the future. The Benedictines of the northern school should probably be seen as a transitional link; their main role seems to have been to introduce European genres in Latin, such as *vitae* and translations. The second school is, in this sense, perhaps rather the first, that is to say it is only in the North that a literate tradition prospers. It is not necessary to attribute a new school to the Augustinians. Rather they introduce new ideas of genres and of the use of writing in general.

The Sturlungar are part of the political changes of their time, transforming the role of the aristocracy, but they are also affected by the literate tendencies. From the North they get impulses to write chronicles of kings and aristocrats in the *vitae* tradition, while the Parisian influences change the focus, for example from the king as saint to the king as the ruler of the royal realm and God's anointed. The fragmentary evidence for the early period of literacy in Iceland presents a multitude of lines to be pursued, and it is the very heterogeneity of this emerging literate culture and the conditions for the learned and intellectual discourse of the time that still challenges our curiosity.

Bibliography

Andersson, Theodore M. 1964. *The Problem of Icelandic Saga Origins. A Historical Survey.* New Haven: Yale University Press.

Andersson, Theodore M. 1993. "Snorri Sturluson and the Saga School at Munkaþverá". In Alois Wolf (ed.), *Snorri Sturluson. Kolloquium anlässlich der 750. Widerkehr seines Todesdages.* ScriptOralia 51. Tübingen, 9–25.

Andersson, Theodore M. 1994. "The Literary Prehistory of Eyjafjǫrðr". *Samtíðarsögur. Preprints for the Ninth International Saga Conference.* Akureyri. 16–30.

Andersson, Theodore M. 2006. *The Growth of the Medieval Icelandic Sagas (1180–1280).* Ithaca: Cornell University Press.

Andersson, Theodore M. 2012. *The Partisan Muse in the Early Icelandic Sagas (1200–1250).* Islandica LV. Ithaca: Cornell University Press.

Ármann Jakobsson. 2002. *Staður í nýjum heimi. Konungasagan Morkinskinna.* Reykjavík: Háskólaútgáfan.

Ármann Jakobsson. 2012. "Inventing a Saga Form: The Development of the Kings' Sagas". *La 'Heimskringla' e le Saghe dei Re/ 'Heimskringla' and the Kings' Sagas.* Filologia Germanica/ Germanic Philology 4, 1–22.

Ásdís Egilsdóttir 2002. "Formáli". *Biskupa sögur* II. Ed. Ásdís Egilsdóttir. Íslenzk fornrit XVI. Reykjavík: Hið íslenzka fornritafélag, v–cliv.

Bagge, Sverre. 1996. *From Gang Leader to the Lord's Anointed. Kingship in Sverris saga and Hákonar saga Hákonarsonar.* Viking Collection 8. Odense.

Benedikt Eyþórsson. 2005. "History of the Icelandic Church 1000–1300. Status of Research". In Helgi Þorláksson (ed.), *Church Centres. Church Centres in Iceland from the 11th to the 13th Century and their Parallels in other Countries.* Snorrastofa, vol. II. Reykholt: Snorrastofa, 19–69.

Biskupa sǫgur I = *Biskupa sǫgur*, 1. hefte. Ed. Jón Helgason. Copenhagen: Munksgaards, 1938.

Biskupa sögur I. Ed. Sigurgeir Steingrímsson, Ólafur Halldórsson and Peter Foote. Íslenzk fornrit XV. Reykjavík: Hið íslenzka fornritafélag, 2003.

Biskupa sögur II. Ed. Ásdís Egilsdóttir. Íslenzk fornrit XVI. Reykjavík: Hið íslenzka fornritafélag, 2002.

Borgehammar, Stephan. 1997. "Sunnivalegenden och den benediktinska reformen i England". In Rindal, Magnus (ed.), *Selja – heilag stad i 1000 år.* Oslo, 123–159.

Boyer, Régis. 1967. L'évéque Guðmundr Arason, témoin de son temps. Études Germaniques, 427–444.

Brincken, Anna Dorothee von den. 1969. "Die lateinische Weltchronistik". *Mensch und Weltgeschichte. Zür Geschichte der Universalgeschichtsschreibung.* Forschungsgespräche des internalen Forschungszentrums für Grundfragen der Wissenschaften Salzburg 7, 43–66.

Bruhn, Ole. 1999. *Tekstualisering. Bidrag til en litterær antropologi.* Århus: Aarhus Universitetsforlag.

Bumke, Joachim. 1986. *Höfische Kultur. Literatur und Gesellschaft im hohen Mittelalter I–II.* Munich: Deutscher Taschenbuch Verlag.

Clark, James G. 2011. *The Benedictines in the Middle Ages.* Woodbridge: Boydell Press.

Clunies Ross, Margaret. 1987. *Skáldskaparmál. Snorri Sturluson's Ars Poetica and Medieval Theories of Language.* The Viking Collection 4. Odense: Odense University Press.

Cormack, Margaret. 2000. "Sagas of Saints". In Margaret Clunies Ross (ed.), *Old Icelandic Literature and Society*. Cambridge: Cambridge University Press, 302–325.

Egils saga Skalla-Grímssonar. Ed. Sigurður Nordal. Íslenzk fornrit II. Reykjavík: Hið íslenzka fornritafélag, 1933.

Ellehøj, Svend 1965. *Studier over den ældste norrøne historieskrivning*. Bibliotheca Arnamagnæana vol. XXVI. Copenhagen: Munksgaard.

Faulkes, Anthon (ed.). 1998. *Snorri Sturluson. Edda. Skáldskaparmál*. 1: *Introduction, Text and Notes*. London: Viking Society for Northern Research.

Ferm, Olle. 2001. "Universitet och högskolor". In Per Ingesmann and Thomas Lindkvist (eds), *Norden og Europa i middelalderen*. Skrifter udgivet af Jysk Selskab for Historie nr. 47. Århus, 93–129.

Foote, Peter 1961. "On the Fragmentary Text Concerning St Thomas Becket in Stock. perg. fol. nr. 2". *Saga-Book* XV, 403–450.

Foote, Peter (ed.) 2003. *Jóns saga Hólabyskups ens helga*. Editiones Arnamagnæanæ, Series A, vol. 14. Copenhagen.

Garðar Gíslason 2001. "Hvar nam Sæmundur fróði?" In Garðar Gíslason et al. (eds), *Líndæla. Sigurður Líndal sjötugur 2. júlí 2001*. Reykjavík, 135–153.

Goody, Jack 2010. *Renaissances. The One or the Many?* Cambridge: Cambridge University Press.

Gottskálk Jensson 2004. "The Lost Latin Literature of Medieval Iceland. The Fragments of the Vita Sancti Thorlaci and Other Evidence". *Symbolae Osloenses* 79, 150–170.

Guðrún Nordal 2001. *Tools of Literacy: The Role of Skaldic Verse in Icelandic Textual Culture of the Twelfth and Thirteenth Centuries*. Toronto: University of Toronto Press.

Guðrún Nordal 2006. "Snorri and Norway". In Else Mundal (ed.), *Reykholt som makt- og lærdomssenter i den islandske og nordiske kontekst*. Snorrastofa, vol. III. Reykholt: Snorrastofa, 77–84.

Gunnar Harðarson and Stefán Karlsson 1993. "Hauksbók". In Phillip Pulsiano et al. (eds), *Medieval Scandinavia: An Encyclopedia*. New York: Garland, 271a–272b.

Gunnes, Erik 1996. *Erkebiskop Øystein. Statsmann og kirkebygger*. Oslo: Aschehoug.

Haskins, Charles Homer 1927. *The Renaissance of the 12th century*. Cambridge, Mass.: Harvard University Press.

Helgi Þorláksson 2006. "Snorri Sturluson, Reykholt og augustinerordenen". In Else Mundal (ed.), *Reykholt som makt- og lærdomssenter i den islandske og nordiske kontekst*. Snorrastofa, vol. III. Reykholt: Snorrastofa, 65–75.

Hermann, Pernille 2007. "Den norrøne renæssance og dens forudsætninger". In Karl G. Johansson (ed.), *Den norröna renässansen. Reykholt, Norden och Europa 1150–1300*. Snorrastofa, vol. IV. Reykholt: Snorrastofa, 41–61.

Hoff, Hans Henning 2012. *Hafliði Másson und die Einflüsse des römischen Rechts in der Grágás*. Ergänzungzbände zum Reallexikon der Germanischen Altertumskunde, Band 78. Berlin: De Gruyter.

Hreinn Benediktsson (ed.). 1972. *The First Grammatical Treatise*. Reykjavík: University of Iceland Publications in Linguistics 1.

Íslendingabók, Landnámabók. Ed. Jakob Benediktsson. Íslenzk fornrit I Reykjavík: Hið íslenzka fornritafélag, 1968.

Jakob Benediktsson 1968. "Formáli". *Íslendingabók*,

Landnámabók. Íslenzk fornrit I. Reykjavík: Hið íslenzka fornritafélag, v–cliv.

Johansson, Karl G. 1997. *Studier i Codex Wormianus. Skrifttradition och avskriftsverksamhet vid ett isländskt skriptorium under 1300-talet.* Nordistica Gothoburgensia 20. Göteborg.

Johansson, Karl G. 2004. "Kyrka, kloster och kristnande i det tidigmedeltida Island". [Review of Orri Vésteinsson. *The Christianization of Iceland. Priests, Power, and Social Change 1000–1300.* Oxford 2000.] *Gardar. Årsbok för Samfundet Sverige-Island i Lund-Malmö* XXXIV, 41–45.

Johansson, Karl G. 2005. "Översättning och originalspråkstext i handskriftstraderingens våld" – *Merlínusspá* och *Vǫluspá* i *Hauksbók.* In Susanne Kramarz-Bein (ed.), *Neue Ansätze in der Mittelalterphilologie – Nye veier i middelalderfilologien.* Frankfurt am Main: Peter Lang, 97–113.

Johansson, Karl G. 2006. "Om nordiskt och lärt hos de tidiga benediktinerna på Island. Nikulás Bergssons Leiðarvísir og borgskipan och isländsk litteracitet". In Lars Bisgaard and Tore Nyberg (eds), *Tidlige klostre i Norden.* Odense: University Press of Southern Denmark, 157–175.

Johansson, Karl G. (ed.) 2007. *Den norröna renässansen. Reykholt, Norden och Europa 1150–1300.* Snorrastofa, vol. IV. Reykholt: Snorrastofa.

Johansson, Karl G. 2010. "Snorri, Saxo och medeltidens berättelser om kungarnas historia". In Jon Gunnar Jørgensen *et al.* (eds), *Saxo og Snorre.* Copenhagen: Museum Tusculanums Forlag, 131–166.

Jóns saga ins helga, see *Biskupa sögur* I.

Jóns saga Hólabyskups ens helga, see Foote 2003.

Kaplan, Merrill 2011. *Thou Fearful Guest. Addressing the Past in Four Tales in Flateyjarbók.* Helsinki: FF Communications Vol. CXLVIII, No. 301.

Karlsen, Espen (ed.) 2013. *Latin Manuscripts of Medieval Norway. Studies in Memory of Lilli Gjerløw.* Oslo: Novus.

Lindkvist, Thomas 2007. "1100-tallsrenässans eller den första europeiska revolutionen?" In Karl G. Johansson (ed.), *Den norröna renässansen. Reykholt, Norden och Europa 1150–1300.* Snorrastofa, vol. IV. Reykholt: Snorrastofa, 11–24.

Meulengracht Sørensen, Preben 1992. "Snorri's fræði". In Úlfar Bragason (ed.), *Snorrastefna 25.–27. júlí 1990.* Rit Stofnunar Sigurðar Nordals, vol. 1. Reykjavík, 270–283.

Moore, R.I. 2000. *The First European Revolution c. 970–1215.* Oxford: Blackwell.

Mortensen, Lars Boje and Else Mundal 2003. "Erkebispesetet i Nidaros – arnestad og verkstad for olavslitteraturen". In Steinar Imsen (ed.), *Ecclesia Nidarosiensis 1153–1537. Søkelys på Nidaroskirkens og Nidarosprovinsens historie.* Senter for middelalderstudier, NTNU. Skrifter nr. 15. Trondheim, 353–384.

Mortensen, Lars Boje (ed.) 2003. *Historia Norwegie.* Copenhagen: Museum Tusculanum Press.

Mortensen, Lars Boje 2006. "Den formative dialog mellem latinsk og folkesproglig litteratur ca 600–1250". In Else Mundal (ed.), *Reykholt som makt- og lærdomssenter i den islandske og nordiske kontekst.* Snorrastofa, vol. III. Reykholt: Snorrastofa, 229–271.

Mundal, Else 2007. "Med kva rett kan vi tale om ein norrøn renessanse?". In Karl G. Johansson (ed.), *Den norröna renässansen. Reykholt, Norden och Europa 1150–1300.* Snorrastofa, vol. IV. Reykholt: Snorrastofa, 25–39.

Nyberg, Tore 2000. *Monasticism in North-Western Europe, 800–1200.* Aldershot, Burlington USA, Singapore, Sydney: Ashgate.

Porter, D.W. 2002. *Excerptiones de Prisciano: The*

Source for Ælfric's Latin-Old English Grammar. Anglo Saxon Texts 4. Cambridge.

Orri Vésteinsson 2000. *The Christianization of Iceland. Priests, Power, and Social Change 1000–1300.* Oxford: Oxford University Press.

Sigurður Nordal 1933. "Formáli". *Egils saga Skalla-Grímssonar.* Ed. Sigurður Nordal. Íslenzk fornrit II. Reykjavík: Hið íslenzka fornritafélag, v–cv.

Sigurður Nordal 1953. "Sagalitteraturen". In Sigurður Nordal (ed.), *Litteraturhistorie. B. Norge og Island.* Stockholm: Almqvist & Wiksell, 180–273.

Sigurgeir Steingrímsson *et al.* 2003. "Formáli". *Biskupa sögur* I. Ed. Sigurgeir Steingrímsson, Ólafur Halldórsson and Peter Foote. Íslenzk fornrit XV. Reykjavík: Hið íslenzka fornritafélag, v–ccclv.

Skórzewska, Joanna Agnieszka 2007. *Constructing a Cultus. The Life and Veneration of Guðmundr Arason (1161–1237) in the Icelandic Written Sources.* Unpublished PhD thesis from the University of Oslo. Oslo.

Smalley, Beryl 1964. *The Study of the Bible in the Middle Ages.* Notre Dame, Indiana: Notre Dame University Press.

Stefán Karlsson 2000. "Icelandic Lives of Thomas à Becket: Questions of Authorship". In Guðvarður Már Gunnlaugsson (ed.), *Stafkrókar. Ritgerðir eftir Stefán Karlsson gefnar út í tilefni sjötugsafmælis hans 2. desember 1998.* Reykjavík: Háskólaútgáfan, 135–152. [Originally published in *Proceedings of the First International Saga Conference. University of Edinburgh 1971.* London 1973.]

Stefán Karlsson 2000. "Alfræði Sturlu Þórðarsonar". In Guðvarður Már Gunnlaugsson (ed.), *Stafkrókar. Ritgerðir eftir Stefán Karlsson gefnar út í tilefni sjötugsafmælis hans 2. desember 1998.* Reykjavík: Háskólaútgáfan, 279–302. [Originally

published in *Sturlustefna. Ráðstefna haldin á sjö alda ártíð Sturlu Þórðarsonar sagnaritara 1984.* Reykjavík 1988.]

Sturlunga saga I-II *Sturlunga saga efter membranen Króksfjarðarbók udfyldt efter Reykjarfjarðarbók.* Kristian Kålund (ed.) 1906–11. Copenhagen: Gyldendalske boghandel.

Svanhildur Óskarsdóttir 1992. "Að kenna og rita tíða á millum: Um trúarviðhorf Guðmundar Arasonar". *Skáldskaparmál. Tímarit Um íslenskar bókmenntir fyrri alda,* 229–238.

Sveinbjörn Rafnsson 2005. *Ólafs sögur Tryggvasonar. Um gerðir þeirra, heimildir og höfunda.* Reykjavík: Háskólaútgáfan.

Sverrir Jakobsson 2005. *Við og veröldin. Heimsmynd Íslendinga 1100–1400.* Reykjavík: Háskólaútgáfan.

Sverrir Jakobsson 2007. "Det islandske verdensbillede og dets udvikling fra opblomstring til renæssance". In Karl G. Johansson (ed.), *Den norröna renässansen. Reykholt, Norden och Europa 1150–1300.* Snorrastofa, vol. IV. Reykholt: Snorrastofa, 63–72.

Thorvaldsen, Bernt Øyvind 2007. "Om eddastrofene i samtidssagaenes drømmeskildringer og "den norrøne renessansen". In Karl G. Johansson (ed.), *Den norröna renässansen. Reykholt, Norden och Europa 1150–1300.* Snorrastofa, vol. IV. Reykholt: Snorrastofa, 83–90.

Tyler, Elizabeth M. 2009. "From Old English to Old French". In Jocelyn Wogan-Browne (ed.), *Language and Culture in Medieval Britain. The French of England c. 1100–c. 1500.* York, 164–178.

Vries, Jan de 1941–1942. *Altnordische literaturgeschichte* I–II. Berlin: Walter de Gruyter.

Wanner, Kevin J. 2008. *Snorri Sturluson and the Edda. The Conversion of Cultural Capital in Medieval Scandinavia.* Toronto: University of Toronto Press.

Würth, Stefanie 1994. "Thomas Becket: ein literarisches und politisches Modell für die islandische Kirche im 13. Jahrhundert". *Samtíðarsögur/The Contemporary Sagas. Preprints from the Ninth International Saga Conference, Akureyri 1994*, 878–891.

Würth, Stefanie 1998. *Der "Antikenroman" in der isländischen Literatur des Mittelalters. Eine Untersuchung zur Übersetzung und Rezeption lateinischer Literatur im Norden*. Basel und Frankfurt am Main: Helbing & Lichtenhahn.

¶ TORFI H. TULINIUS

The Social Conditions for Literary Practice in Snorri's Lifetime

S AN ECCLESIASTICAL, POLITICAL AND INTELLECTUAL centre in thirteenth-century Iceland, Reykholt did not exist in a vacuum. It is likely that comparable centres (albeit not quite so productive) existed in other parts of Iceland and that even in the Borgarfjǫrðr region centres such as Stafholt or Bœr may also have had their importance.[1] This is why some reflection on the social conditions of literary practice in Snorri's time is possibly relevant, not only for Reykholt but for Iceland in general. The interest is even greater when focusing on the time between 1210 and 1240, when Snorri Sturluson resided at Reykholt. These first decades of the century are also the period in which many of the most important developments in Old Norse-Icelandic literature are believed to have taken place: the high point of the *konungasǫgur* or Kings' Sagas, the appearance of romance, both translated and autochthonous, and, perhaps most significantly, the rise of the *Íslendingasǫgur* genre or "sagas about early Icelanders".[2] It is likely that these developments took

---

1   Stafholt was one of Snorri's places of residence, and is often mentioned in the contemporary sagas. After Snorri's demise, his nephew, Óláfr *hvítaskáld* (literally, "white poet") Þórðarson, lived there. He was a renowned poet and scholar, and possibly a saga writer. Bœr is mentioned as a place of learning in the early history of Christianity in Iceland.

2   For a discussion of this dating see Jónas Kristjánsson 2007, 157, 217. In a recent

place in secular centres of learning such as Reykholt. By "secular centre of learning", I mean a place where there were a number of clerics, but where their scholastic learning interacted with, and to some extent was subordinated to, the specific cultural practice and needs of laymen.

Snorri's "Library"

What little evidence there is of saga-writing in the contemporary sagas suggests an evolution from oral entertainment based on poetry and stories, either remembered or improvised, to oral entertainment based on written texts. In the period that interests us, however, we must assume a co-existence of both oral story-telling and written literature. It is useful to have an overview of this literature, because it brings to light the richness of this secular culture, which was both Christian and preoccupied with lay concerns, and where clerical learning was interwoven with a sincere interest in the pagan past, legitimized by the widespread interest in pre-Christian culture that existed throughout Western culture in the period.[3]

By the time Snorri moved to Reykholt, scholars have shown that there already existed a considerable amount of written literature in the vernacular. These included:

- Historical works about Iceland, such as *Íslendingabók*, earlier (and now lost) versions of *Landnámabók* and possibly the first sagas about Icelandic bishops (such as *Hungrvaka*, *Þorláks saga*).
- Historical works about Nordic rulers, such as the lost works of Ari and Sæmundr, Oddr Snorrason's *Ólafs saga Tryggvasonar*, hagiographies of St Óláfr and probably a *Skjǫldunga saga*; possibly also an *Orkneyinga saga* as well as sagas about contemporary kings such as *Sverris saga*. Works in Latin were circulating in Iceland at the time, but there may also have existed translations of works of general history, for example *Rómverja saga* and maybe even a translation of *Historia regum Britanniae* (*Breta sögur*).
- Religious literature, such as sermons (*Hómilíubók*), hagiographical

book, Gísli Sigurðsson (2013) has argued for a more decisive innovatory role of Reykholt and Snorri's direct collaborators. See also his contribution in this book.

3   Torfi H. Tulinius 2009, 199–216.

works (translated Saints' Lives) and possibly a *Maríu saga*. There may already have been some translations from the Bible (parts of *Stjórn*).
· Law books.
· Religious and lay poetry may already have been written down by this time and not only composed orally and/or memorized.

At the same time, all kinds of narratives and poetry will have circulated orally, for example:

· Eddic poetry, both mythological and heroic.
· Skaldic poetry, both older poetry about kings of the past, and more recent poetry about later kings and other noteworthy people, among them Icelandic chieftains. It is not unlikely that stanzas or poems ascribed to early Icelanders also circulated in Snorri's time.
· Prosimetrum as indicated by the description of "hverju skemmt var" (the entertainment) at Reykhólar (formerly Reykjahólar) in 1119 (that is, stories of olden days interspersed with stanzas and perhaps containing long narrative poems in the Eddic style).
· Tales of prominent Icelanders of the past and present, their adventures abroad and the conflicts they were involved in at home.
· Myths, legends and stories of strange occurrences.
· Religion was also transmitted orally through sermons; it is likely that there were many stories circulating from the common store of medieval Christian traditions.

We must beware of making too sharp a distinction between oral and written literature at this time. Indeed, there is much to indicate that it was precisely in this period that both Eddic and skaldic poetry were being written down, as well as other material that also circulated orally, and found its way, more or less transformed, into a literary form. Conversely, stories originally taken from books, for example the Bible, may have been disseminated orally, or transmitted in a predominantly oral form, such as in exempla used in sermons. Furthermore, the practice of public reading (i.e. the reading out loud of written texts to a gathering of people) was probably already well-established in Snorri's days.

Culture as Practice

Were there any particular social conditions that favoured the practice of literature in lay centres of power such as Reykholt? It might be argued that an oral tradition, ultimately traceable back to the settlement era, is the main factor that supports this possibility, and this idea should not be discarded. However, rather than focusing on "tradition", this article presents an approach that highlights individual and collective choices within a certain social environment. It is based on French sociologist Pierre Bourdieu's "theory of practice", and its aim is to explain how behaviour is produced by social circumstances, which are in turn shaped by behaviour. Bourdieu's notion of cultural capital is especially useful in the current context, since it allows an understanding of how cultural and intellectual practices such as composing poetry, historical works or narrative entertainment might result in other benefits within society.[4]

As in any other culture, Icelandic society is shaped by geographical realities. People live on individual farms and the physical surroundings create communities, for example a valley or valley complex, a fjord, or a region separated from others by a river. This space is occupied by farmers, some of them freeholders, some working other people's land. There are both horizontal and vertical relationships between these people. The horizontal ones involve cooperation, for example in sheep-herding, match-making or resolving neighbourly conflicts, to name but a few. The vertical ones are the result of some people being more prominent and having more power than others. This hierarchy was presumably there from the beginning of this society, with some individuals holding bigger, more fertile or better situated land than others. Yet this hierarchy also evolved as society developed and changed. Reykholt and its valley is a good example of this, since it gradually became a centre, due to its location at an intersection of many roads and, more decisively, when the church there became a *staðr* receiving tithes from a substantial number of farms.[5]

It can be assumed that centres, big or small, would be places where literary activity (probably oral, at least to begin with) would have had a social function. Households would have been bigger and more composite than elsewhere, and people also gathered there in even greater numbers

---

4   Pierre Bourdieu's theories have recently been applied to Old Norse-Icelandic litera-
     ture by Wanner 2008 and Torfi H. Tulinius 2014, 167–209; 2009; and specifically to
     Saxo Grammaticus by Gottskálk Þ. Jensson 2010, 187–207.
5   Guðrún Sveinbjarnardóttir 2006, 25–27. On *staðr* see in this book 115–116.

for feasts and other social events. There would have been a demand for entertainment on such occasions, as can be seen in the famous account of the wedding feast at Reykhólar in western Iceland, where the host, Ingimundr Einarsson, entertained his guests with poetry and stories.[6] This was probably also true for centres other than those controlled by lay chieftains. It is, for example, quite likely that monasteries and episcopal seats, where we can assume that many people also lived, would have had social events where literary entertainment was appreciated.

As ecclesiastical and secular centres of power grew in size, especially as power and wealth became concentrated in the hands of the new overlords (*stórgoðar*) in the late-twelfth and into the thirteenth century, households would have grown and with them the demand for entertainment. There probably would have been emulation both within and between households that would have enhanced both the quality and quantity of such entertainment. Again the description in *Þorgils saga ok Hafliða* gives us at least an indication that some people put considerable effort into telling stories and composing poetry, and that they gained reputations for it. Ingimundr Einarsson "fór mjǫk með sǫgr ok skemmti vel kvæðum ok orti" ("told a lot of stories and entertained well with poems as well as composing poetry"). His neighbour Hrólfr of Skálmarnes, a prominent landowner living nearby, "var ok sagnamaðr ok orti skipulega" ("was a storyteller and composed poetry in an orderly way").[7] This tells us of a need within society for entertainers such as these, whether it was in the early twelfth century, when these men are said to have lived, or in the mid-thirteenth century, when *Þorgils saga ok Hafliða* is believed to have been composed.[8]

An interesting point is that these "entertainers" were not considered to occupy a subordinate position in society, quite the contrary. Hrólfr owned a rich farm and Ingimundr was a priest and the heir to a chieftaincy (*goðorð*) that he had given to his cousin Þorgils Oddason. This is an important aspect of the social framework for literary activity in Iceland, as many examples show. The dominant classes within society engaged in it, as we can see from other figures such as Sæmundr Sigfússon or Snorri Sturluson and his nephews, Sturla and Óláfr *hvítaskáld*. This might be because dominant classes, being free from manual labour, could indulge

---

6 *Þorgils saga ok Hafliða*, 13–18.
7 *Þorgils saga ok Hafliða*, 17–18.
8 *Þorgils saga ok Hafliða*, xxix.

in such pursuits. It is also likely that such activities were a way to confirm one's social prominence. That would explain why somebody like Hrólfr who was a "lagamaðr mikill ok fór mjǫk með sakir" ("who was well-versed in the law and engaged in many lawsuits"), would also cultivate his literary abilities, and why a priest and aristocrat (gǫfugr) such as Ingimundr would do the same. This might have been an important element of the popularity he cultivated among his contemporaries ("hélt sér mjǫk til vinsælda við alþýðu"). It goes without saying that this situation puts Snorri Sturluson's presumed literary activities in a specific Icelandic social context.[9]

Another interesting point is that Ingimundr and Hrólfr were neighbours. This implies that there was some kind of network of households where literary activities were pursued, with works circulating between them, either orally or in a written form. When thinking of society in spatial terms, it is important to note this circulation of people and cultural artefacts from one place to another. The development of writing in the vernacular would have been encouraged by a demand for entertainment which could circulate in a much easier way through books than through oral performers having to come in person to each household. The public reading of Tómasar saga erkibyskups at Hrafnagil in 1258 is a good example of this. Þorgils skarði (Harelip) Bǫðvarsson spends the night and the offer is made to entertain him with stories. He is allowed to choose between several, but these are not oral stories told by the people at the farm. Indeed, Þorgils is given a choice among the written stories that were available there.[10]

One can assume that literature circulated between most of the centres in Iceland, secular or ecclesiastical, either orally or in the form of manuscripts that were lent, given or copied. This is the case for Snorri Sturluson's nephew, Sturla Sighvatsson, who had the "sögubækr" (books with stories) composed by Snorri copied, presumably to be able to have them read to his own household or during feasts he himself held.[11]

However, the circulation of culture was not only internal to Iceland. Icelanders shared a language with the rest of Scandinavia, especially

9   In a recent article, the historian Árni Daníel Júlíusson (2010) has provided evidence for the existence of "manorial demesnes" in medieval Iceland, i.e. that most of the wealth was in the hands of wealthy aristocrats and landowners. The writing of the Íslendingasǫgur as well as that of the contemporary sagas was the work of this social group and not that of poor farmers.
10   Sturlunga saga II, 218.
11   Sturlunga saga I, 342.

Norway and the other islands of the North Atlantic, and poetry and stories travelled between these places. In this respect, one could say that there was a thriving export and import of both types of literature. Skaldic and Eddic poetry came to Iceland from the rest of Scandinavia, perhaps even Greenland, as might be suggested by the title of the poems of Codex Regius, *Atlamál* and *Atlakviða*. Since they do not tell a story that takes place in Greenland, but of an episode in the Nibelung legend, the title might indicate that they circulated there, though only preserved in an Icelandic manuscript. The same can be said of all the learned or romantic literature that was translated, either in Iceland or elsewhere in Scandinavia, before being imported to Iceland where much of it was preserved.[12]

Exporting "Cultural Capital"

Icelanders also exported both poetry and stories. *Þorgils saga ok Hafliða* and its presentation of the two men who entertained at the wedding feast at Reykhólar is a good example of this, since Ingimundr Einarsson composed "góð kvæði" (good poems) and received "laun fyrir utanlands" (was recompensed for them abroad).[13] We do not know what these poems were or who rewarded Ingimundr for them abroad, but we see here an example of one characteristic of Icelandic culture, probably from the Settlement period and at least until the end of the thirteenth century. Countless sagas tell us of poets of older times who travel abroad and deliver poetry at foreign courts, mostly in Norway and Denmark. Snorri Sturluson himself gives us a very good example since we are told in *Íslendinga saga* that he composed a poem for one of the rulers of Norway, Hákon *galinn* (literally "frantic"). It is possible that the poem was sent in writing, since Snorri did not present the poem to Hákon himself. Nevertheless, he was handsomely rewarded for the poem, receiving a sword, a shield and a mail coat from the *jarl* (earl), who also sent him a letter, asking him to come abroad so he could bestow even greater honours on him.[14]

---

12 For a good overview of these literary exchanges, see the relevant essays in McTurk (ed.) 2005.
13 *Þorgils saga ok Hafliða*, 3.
14 *Sturlunga saga* I, 269.

It seems that Icelanders had a reputation in Denmark and Norway for being knowledgeable about the past. This is attested by Saxo's glowing remarks about the Icelanders' cultivation of their poetic treasures, and his mention of a certain Arnaldus Tylensis, who may have resided at the court of Archbishop Absalon in Lundr.[15] Icelanders are also referred to as sources by Theodoricus, an early historian of Norwegian kings.[16] This indicates that by the late twelfth century, Icelanders had developed a kind of special skill in conveying knowledge about the past to Nordic leaders. They must have reaped some benefits from this, for example the right to stay at court and even the possibility of taking up official positions within it, or else perhaps some compensation, either in money or in kind.

Knowledge of tales and poems about the past of the Nordic countries would then have been a type of *cultural capital*, to use Pierre Bourdieu's concept. This capital allowed some Icelanders to engage in social interaction abroad. Being rooted in the past, the Scandinavian royal families and aristocracy would have treated those who had special knowledge of these matters with respect. The same holds true of the composition of Kings' Sagas, since it would be a way for an Icelandic aristocrat to ingratiate himself with Danish or Norwegian rulers by writing their history. There were already precedents for this in the figures of the abbots Karl Jónsson and Oddr Snorrason, writing respectively about the contemporary King Sverrir Sigurðarson of Norway or his predecessor Óláfr Tryggvason, who reigned two centuries earlier.[17] The book would have played an important role in this, not only for the information it conveyed, but as an object in itself, costly both in material (parchment) and work (scribal manpower). A codex full of stories of kings and heroes from ancient times and adorned with poetry of old would have been an honourable gift from an Icelandic dignitary to a Norwegian ruler. It would have embodied different types of capital: economic because of what it took to produce it, cultural because of the knowledge it contained and finally symbolic, both

---

15 *Saxonis Gesta Danorum* 2000, prologue and book 10.

16 *Monumenta historica Norvegiae*, 3: "... quos horum memoria præcipue viger creditur, quos nos Islendinga vocamus, qui hæc in antiquis carminisbus percelebrata recolunt" ("... those amongst whom it is believed this memory thrives especially, whom we call Icelanders, and who celebrate these deeds in their ancient songs").

17 Discussions about the time of writing and authorship of these two sagas are to be found in the introductions to their editions in the *Íslenzk fornrit* series. The modern Norwegian names of these kings are Sverre Sigurdsson and Olav Tryggvason.

of the recipient's high status but also of that of the donor. Just owning a book might also have symbolic value and not merely cultural, a sign of distinction for whoever had it in his possession. We know that Snorri had books in his possession and that they were considered valuable, since in his dealings with the sons of his second wife after her death, the only part of the inheritance they could agree on dividing were the books and other movable property.[18]

The theories of Pierre Bourdieu have recently been used to understand Snorri and his trajectory in Icelandic and Norwegian society. Using Bourdieu's concepts of *capital*, *habitus*, *field* and *illusio*, Kevin J. Wanner and I both developed separate readings of Snorri's behaviour and the context in which it took place. I focused more on the idea of *virðing* or "respect"; when Snorri's *virðing* is said to be at its highest around 1215, it means that he had accumulated a great deal of the different types of capital – economic, symbolic and cultural – available to an Icelandic chieftain in that period. I also put to use Bourdieu's concept of *field*, i.e. different compartments of social space in which actors compete for the specific types of capital that are relevant in this particular field.[19] It allowed me to understand better Snorri's (and other chieftains') relationships to different types of actors or institutions, for example their friends and supporters among the free landholders or *bœndr*, or the field of religion, i.e. the Church, or the Norwegian court and the institution of monarchy. Like many chieftains, Snorri was active in all these fields, a fact that can help explain his behaviour. I also proposed the idea that a special field had evolved in Iceland, centred on the literary activities of lay persons, which I termed a *literary field*, another concept borrowed from Pierre Bourdieu.[20]

It comes as no surprise that Wanner and I agree on many things, for example that Snorri's success as a courtier in Norway, which his brothers seem not to have striven for, must have had to do with the fact that he had been brought up in Oddi, by a grandson of a Norwegian king. There, Snorri acquired a certain "habitus", i.e. a way of thinking

18 *Sturlunga saga* I, 437. Stefán Karlsson (1979) has done decisive research on the export of books from Iceland to Norway in the latter half of the thirteenth and in the fourteenth century.

19 Bourdieu's basic concepts are usefully presented in Bourdieu and Wacquant 1992.

20 Torfi H. Tulinius 2009, 65–68.

and ascribing value to things, which gave him an advantage over his elder brothers.[21]

However, Wanner pays much more attention than I to Snorri's Norwegian activities. Indeed, Snorri seems to have devoted a considerable amount of his energy to endearing himself to Norwegian rulers by composing court poems, most of which are lost. Though King Sverrir Sigurðarson died in 1202 when Snorri was in his early twenties, he is said to be one of the king's skalds.[22] He is also known to have composed skaldic panegyrics to his successors, King Ingi Bárðarson, and the *jarl* Hákon *galinn*, as has already been mentioned. Later, Snorri came to Norway where he made friends with other important Norwegians by composing poetry to honour them.[23] Though it is not mentioned at this point, it is tempting to interpret in this light the composition of *Háttatal*, a *clavis metrica* that was also a tribute to the regents Earl Skúli Bárðarson (Skule Bårdsson in modern Norwegian) and King Hákon Hákonarson (Håkon Håkonsson in modern Norwegian or Håkon IV).[24]

There is probably a complex and not entirely direct relationship between Snorri's poetic activity and the great honours that were bestowed upon him by the Norwegian rulers. Indeed, he was made a *lendr maðr*, a position of dignity at the royal court no other Icelander had attained before him. His poetic achievements may have been a sort of token of exchange, a kind of ritual of gift and reward, while the real reason the Norwegian rulers were willing to ensure his rise was that they believed he was in a good position to promote the cause of Norwegian sovereignty over Iceland.[25]

Wanner is well aware of this and uses Bourdieu's notion of the "conversion" of one type of capital to another. Snorri's cultural capital, which gave him the skill and talent to compose the skaldic encomia, was converted into symbolic capital, i.e. the favour he received from the rulers.[26] Indeed, Snorri might very well be described as an accumulator of different types of capital, and in some cases as an innovative manipulator of this capital.

---

21   Wanner 2008, 39–40; Torfi H. Tulinius 2014, 185.
22   *Edda Snorra Sturlusonar* vol. 3, 255.
23   *Sturlunga saga* I, 269, 271.
24   *Edda. Háttatal*, ix.
25   *Sturlunga saga* I, 278.
26   Wanner 2008, 10–11.

As a lay aristocrat who produced books about the past, Snorri was, in a way, taking over the cultural capital of the church in order to use it for his own purposes. This is not an isolated phenomenon in medieval Europe, where we see many examples of what have recently been called *chevaliers lettrés*, or lettered aristocrats, i.e. laymen of high social standing who had appropriated for themselves the writing techniques of the Church and devoted much of their time and resources to literature.[27] This appropriation would have been quite easy in ecclesiastical centres such as Reykholt which were under the control of secular chieftains like Snorri Sturluson. Indeed, one of Snorri's motivations for gaining control of Reykholt may have been to have access to the clerics there and put their particular means of cultural production to use to further his own aims.[28]

As the author of the *Edda*, a handbook for practitioners of skaldic poetry, Snorri was, in Wanner's opinion, attempting to maintain or renew the standing of skaldic poetry at the Norwegian court, which was being replaced by other means of literary entertainment, especially the recent translations of French romances ordered by King Hákon. In other words, through the composition of the *Edda*, Snorri was attempting to save or enhance the worth of a particular type of capital in which he had invested a lot and from which he had received considerable gains in the past. It is useful here to use Bourdieu's concept of *field*, a limited area within social space where actors are competing for certain types of capital by following the same rules.[29] Though skaldic poetry continued to be appreciated at home within the sociological field of the Icelandic

---

27 Martin Aurell coined this expression to highlight the literary activities of the lay aristocracy in the late twelfth and thirteenth centuries. He devotes a short section of his book to Snorri Sturluson whom he sees as participating in this development within the culture of the medieval West (Aurell 2011, 191).

28 In recent contributions to a collective volume on church centres in Iceland, Helgi Þorláksson (2005), and Benedikt Eyþórsson (2005) write about the particular nature of the so-called *staðir*, i.e. church centres where the land nominally belonged to the Church but was managed and gave revenue to a layman who controlled it. Snorri is such a layman and in a personal communication, Helgi has suggested that these laymen may have had a special relationship with the Church, different from other secular chieftains. As caretakers of property belonging to saints, they would have needed to be worthy of their trust, both morally and as capable administrators (see in this book, pp. 70–71). The fact that Snorri took over Reykholt because the sons of its previous holder were not considered "fœrir til staðarforráða" ("fit to take over control of the *staðr*", *Sturlunga saga* I, 211) might indicate that particular qualities were required.

29 Torfi H. Tulinius 2009, 62–65.

chieftains, it seems to have been losing ground in Norway, especially in the sphere of the royal court. As an ambitious member of the upper echelons of society intent on climbing even higher in the social hierarchy, Snorri knew how to conduct himself in many fields.[30] In the second half of his life, he was mostly involved in two particular arenas, the Norwegian court and Icelandic internal politics. It is however reductive to attempt to explain the literary activities of someone like Snorri purely from the point of view of his Norwegian ambitions, since their social role was more complex and diverse.

Literary Practice and Distinction

Though the relative absence of Icelandic works having survived in Norway may be explained in other ways, there is little doubt that most of the literature that we still have was composed for local consumption and not for export. It must therefore have been important within Icelandic society itself. What was the significance of poetry and sagas for early-thirteenth-century Icelanders, since they devoted so much time and resources to the production of such cultural artefacts?

Their entertainment value must not be underestimated. During the long winter nights, there would always have been a demand for entertainment, made necessary by the congregation of many people in households, especially large ones, with armed men of diverse origin, if only to keep their minds off fighting. There would also have been competition between the chiefs of households as to who could provide the most brilliant entertainment, as has already been mentioned. Being able to provide it would be a sign of munificence, and increase the respect other members of society felt for the magnate in question. This might explain why Sturla Sighvatsson is said to have been eager to have copies made of the *sögubækr* his uncle composed at Reykholt. This is also true of all other types of poetry or narratives, oral or written, and it would be a sign of distinction for an Icelandic chieftain to encourage such practices in his household. It is likely that the households of chieftains were growing during this period, when chieftains were becoming richer and more powerful. There was probably an increased

---

30   Torfi H. Tulinius 2009, 62–63.

Figure 1. There was a pool and passageway at Reykholt during Snorri's time there. *Sturlunga saga* reports that Snorri sat in the pool with several men one evening in 1228 and discussed politics. He was acclaimed by them as the most powerful chief in Iceland, not least because of his in-laws. Snorri acknowledged this, but, one of his men, on guard at the pool, in a strophe warned Snorri of his in-laws, saying that they were similar to the in-laws of Hrólfr *kraki*, a king in Denmark of ancient times, meaning that they could not be relied on. There are more examples in *Sturlunga saga* of men treating contemporary incidents critically through verse-making with reference to old lore. Photo: Snorrastofa.

demand for entertainment in these households, which also would have encouraged literary activity.

Given the time, care and resources that were devoted to them, it seems likely that the most elaborate poems or stories would have been especially produced for important social gatherings, even when sagas were composed in writing.[31] Sources tell us that chieftains were noted for their ability to hold brilliant banquets, for example when Sturla Þórðarson talks about how the Oddaverjar and Haukdælir held the most beautiful feasts, or when Snorri is said to hold "jóladrykki eftir norrænum sið" (Christmas feasting in the Norwegian style), most likely banquets such as those that were held at royal or aristocratic courts in Norway.[32]

31 Surprisingly, few scholars have associated saga composition with feasting, see Torfi
    H. Tulinius 2014, 263.
32 *Sturlunga saga* I, 483, 315. Viðar Pálsson has recently defended a thesis about feasts

Composing sagas and poetry was therefore a form of practice, in the sense that it was a socially significant activity.[33] Yet its significance was not limited to its entertainment value or as a show of munificence. One must not neglect either the role of orally transmitted poetry and narrative or the different types of literature in transmitting ideology, whether Christian or more related to the ethos of this armed chieftain class. Indeed, their social importance must also have resided in the fact that they transmitted important messages to the community, for example messages about identity, both of Icelanders themselves as well as of significant others such as Norwegian kings. Sagas would also have conveyed information about social transactions of different types, for example matters of law, matrimony, property rights, etc. They would have been important suppliers of collective wisdom about how to behave in society, for example at the Althing (*Alþingi*), or in dealing with one's neighbours, and also at court. Finally, they would have given vivid examples of the disruptiveness of violence and other passions in society.[34]

In this respect, the *Íslendingasǫgur* (or sagas about early Icelanders as they are now often called) would have had special significance as literary communications in households and at feasts and other social gatherings among prominent laymen in Iceland in the first half of the thirteenth century. However, it seems quite unlikely that they would have had any relevance for a Norwegian audience. Indeed, there is no indication that they ever left Iceland.

Conclusion: *Egla*, Distinction and Identity-building

Egils saga Skalla-Grímssonar is a case in point here, since it is believed to have originated in Snorri's milieu, whether or not he composed it himself.[35] The saga can be conceived as a sort of myth of origins of

and gift-giving in medieval Iceland. See Viðar Pálsson 2011, 149 for his presentation of Snorri's activities in this respect. See also Viðar Pálsson 2016.

33 In a recent book on *Sturlunga saga*, Úlfar Bragason (2010, 296) has spoken of the contemporary sagas as "performative utterances", in very much the same spirit as my approach here.

34 There is a long list of authors who have considered this aspect of literary communication in medieval Iceland. Among them I will mention Meulengracht Sørensen 1995; Miller 1990; Torfi H. Tulinius 2002; Ármann Jakobsson 2014.

35 For a recent discussion of Snorri's possible authorship of *Egils saga (Egla)* see Torfi H. Tulinius 2014, 211–217.

the society of the Borgarfjǫrðr region in Snorri's times, describing its settlement by the common ancestor of the major chieftains of the area, Skalla-Grímr, and his distribution of land to others, who presumably were the ancestors of most of the landholders. It also describes a complex and somewhat contradictory relationship with royal power, for on the one hand it shows the fascination that the royal court exerted on young men who saw royal service as a means to social advancement. On the other hand, it could be an excessively dangerous career path to take because of the king's suspicion of all those who might threaten his power. Finally, the saga is an illustration and celebration of skaldic poetry, presenting a unique portrait of a skald of pagan times.

There was much for Snorri and his milieu to identify with in the saga of Egill and his family, for Snorri and many of his followers were Egill's descendants. If the saga was indeed written near the end of Snorri's life, he and his followers would also have been in conflict with King Hákon, just like Egill engaged in a struggle with those who ruled Norway in his days. Snorri took sides with Earl Skúli in his clash with the king that resulted in Skúli's killing in 1239. Finally, Snorri and many of his known followers were practitioners of skaldic poetry, and *Egils saga Skalla-Grímssonar* certainly is a portrait of a wonderful poet.

If we think of a work such as *Egils saga Skalla-Grímssonar* being read aloud for the first time, it would probably have been during a gathering that most of Snorri's followers must have attended. In an earlier study on the saga, I suggested that it might have been on the occasion of a wedding feast given by Snorri at Reykholt in the early months of 1241, when his nephew, Tumi Sighvatsson, married Þuríðr Ormsdóttir of the Oddaverjar family.[36] The wedding was highly significant in the political situation at that particular moment in Icelandic history. Different factions of the Sturlungar family, led by Snorri on one hand and his nephew Sturla Sighvatsson on the other, had been at each other's throats for the better part of the previous fifteen years. However, Sturla was killed in the battle of Ørlygsstaðir in 1238, a major setback for the whole clan. Snorri had been driven from Reykholt by his nephew two years earlier. He now seized the opportunity given to him by Sturla's death to come back to Iceland and reclaim his former domain. From the information we can glean from *Sturlunga saga* about his activities during what turned

36 Torfi H. Tulinius 2014, 264.

out to be the last two years of his life, he seems to have been trying to federate his kinsmen and resolve the different conflicts that had arisen between them over the years. Arranging the wedding between Sturla's surviving younger brother Tumi and Snorri's own sister-in-law, Þuríðr Ormsdóttir, would have been an important milestone, and the wedding feast was designed not only to celebrate the strengthening of the ties between Sturlungar and Oddaverjar, but also the reconciliation of different branches of the former family. The story of a family engaged in a prolonged conflict with certain Norwegian kings, but also suggesting an underlying tragedy of internecine strife within the family, may have had an appeal to this group at that time.

Whether or not this was the particular event for which the saga was composed, the audience present at its first reading would have been fairly socially mixed.[37] The gathering would not only have comprised members of the chieftain class, but also prominent landowners, members of the clergy and of Snorri's household. Within the same audience, there would thus have been different types of social actors with different backgrounds, interests and capacities. Consequently, they would have been more or less capable of understanding different levels of discourse: allegory, symbol, word-play or irony.[38]

Egils saga Skalla-Grímssonar lends itself well to such multifaceted understanding, as I have attempted to show in my book on the saga.[39] Indeed, some of its aspects would have been perceived only by a small group of what might be called 'initiates'. Special practices, such as the cultivation of skaldic poetry, probably created groups of people who had the intellectual skills and knowledge to pursue the practice of skaldic poetry.[40] In this case, literary practice – composing poetry and sagas – would have been a 'distinction' in itself, i.e. a way, in Bourdieu's terms, to show that one belonged to a certain class and not another.

This might also be true of saga writing, especially as it evolved during

37 See Lönnroth 2009, and other works of his referenced there.
38 Bourdieu 2012, 101, refers to practices of speaking on different levels to a mixed audience as characteristic of the public figure, but also of literary communication, both in Kabylian society and ancient Greece.
39 Torfi H. Tulinius 2014, especially in chapters 2 and 3.
40 Lindow 1975, suggests this in a seminal article. Guðrún Nordal 2003, gives an interesting account of the importance of the cultivation of skaldic poetry in the development of aristocratic Icelandic literary culture from the eleventh century onwards, see especially page 15.

Snorri's lifetime. The ability of those who controlled centres such as Reykholt to write entertaining sagas, full of exciting episodes and exquisite poetry, may have been considered as a sign of their distinction. These stories must also have been deeply meaningful to them; after all they were about their ancestors and told of the origins of the social world they lived in. Belonging neither to royalty nor to the clergy, this group of literary-minded secular chieftains and their followers may well have viewed the story of Egill – with all its contradictions, uncertainties and ironies – as a myth with which to identify, given to them by whoever composed it, whether it was Snorri Sturluson himself or an unknown genius.

Bibliography

Aurell, Martin 2011. *Le chevalier lettré: Savoir et conduite de l'aristocratie aux XIIe et XIIIe siècles*. Paris: Fayard.

Ármann Jakobsson 2014. *A Sense of Belonging. Morkinskinna and Icelandic Identity c. 1220*. Odense: University Press of Southern Denmark. Viking Collection 22.

Árni Daníel Júlíusson 2010. "Signs of Power: Manorial Demesnes in Medieval Iceland". *Viking and Medieval Scandinavia* 6, 1–30.

Benedikt Eyþórsson 2005. "History of the Icelandic Church 1000–1300. Status of Research". In Helgi Þorláksson (ed.), *Church Centres. Church Centres in Iceland from the 11th to the 13th Century and their Parallels in Other Countries*. Snorrastofa, vol. II. Reykholt: Snorrastofa, 19–70.

Bourdieu, Pierre 2012. *Sur l'état. Cours au Collège de France 1989–1992*. Paris: Seuil.

Bourdieu, Pierre and Wacquant, Loïc 1992. *An Invitation to Reflexive Sociology*. London: Polity Press.

Færeyinga saga. Ólafs saga Tryggvasonar eptir Odd munk Snorrason. Ed. Ólafur Halldórsson. Íslensk fornrit XXV. Reykjavík: Hið íslenzka fornritafélag, 2006.

Gísli Sigurðsson 2013. *Leiftur á horfinni öld. Hvað er merkilegt við íslenskar fornbókmenntir?* Reykjavík: Mál og menning.

Gottskálk Þór Jensson 2010. "Tylensium thesauri. Den islandske kulturkapital i *Gesta Danorum* og *Heimskringla*". In Jon Gunnar Jørgensen, Karsten Friis-Jensen and Else Mundal (eds), *Saxo og Snorre*. Copenhagen: Museum Tusculanums Forlag, 187–207.

Guðrún Nordal 2003. *Skaldic Versification and Social Discrimination in Medieval Iceland*. London: Viking Society for Northern Research.

Guðrún Sveinbjarnardóttir 2006. "Reykholt, a Center of Power. The Archaeological Evidence". In Else Mundal (ed.), *Reykholt som makt- og lærdomssenter i den islandske og nordiske kontekst*. Snorrastofa, vol. III. Reykholt: Snorrastofa, 25–42.

Helgi Þorláksson 2005. "Why Were the 12th Century Staðir Established?". In Helgi Þorláksson (ed.), *Church Centres. Church Centres in Iceland from the 11th to the 13th Century and their Parallels in Other Countries*. Snorrastofa, vol. II. Reykholt: Snorrastofa, 127–156.

Jónas Kristjánsson 2007 (1988). *Eddas and Sagas. Iceland's Medieval Literature*. Translated by Peter Foote. Reykjavík: Hið íslenska bókmenntafélag.

Lindow, John 1975. "Riddles, Kennings, and the Complexity of Skaldic Poetry". *Scandinavian Studies* 47–3, 311–327.

Lönnroth, Lars 2009. "Old Norse Text as Performance". *Scripta Islandica* 60, 49–60.

McTurk, Rory (ed.) 2005. *A Companion to Old Norse-Icelandic Literature and Culture*, London: Blackwell.

Meulengracht Sørensen, Preben 1995. *Fortælling og ære: Studier i islændingesagaerne*. Odense: Universitetsforlaget.

Miller, William Ian 1990. *Bloodtaking and Peacemaking: Feud, Law, and Society in Saga Iceland*. Chicago: University of Chicago Press.

Monumenta historica Norvegiae. Ed. Gustav Storm. Kristiania 1880.

Saxonis Gesta Danorum. Saxos Danmarks Historie 2000. Ed. and transl. Peter Zeeberg. Copenhagen: Danske Sprog og litteraturselskab.

Stefán Karlsson 1979 (2000). "Islandsk bogeksport til Norge i middelalderen". *Maal og minne* 1–2, 1–17. Reprinted in Guðvarður Már Gunnlaugsson (ed.), *Stafkrókar*. Reykjavík: Stofnun Árna Magnússonar, 188–205.

Sturlunga saga I–II 1946. Eds Jón Jóhannesson, Magnús Finnbogason and Kristján Eldjárn. Reykjavík: Sturlunguútgáfan.

Sverris saga. Ed. Þorleifur Hauksson. Íslensk fornrit XXX. Reykjavík: Hið íslenzka fornritafélag, 2007.

Torfi H. Tulinius 2002. *The Matter of the North: The Rise of Literary Fiction in Thirteenth Century Iceland*. Odense: Odense University Press. Viking Collection 13.

Torfi H. Tulinius 2009. "The Self as Other. Iceland and the Culture of Southern Europe in the Middle Ages". *Gripla* XX, 199–216.

Torfi H. Tulinius 2009. "Pierre Bourdieu and Snorri Sturluson: Chieftains, Sociology and the Development of Literature in Medieval Iceland". In Jon Gunnar Jørgensen (ed.), *Snorres Edda i europeisk og islandsk kultur*. Snorrastofa, vol. V. Reykholt: Snorrastofa, 47–71.

Torfi H. Tulinius 2014. *The Enigma of Egill. The Saga, The Viking Poet, and Snorri Sturluson*. Translated by Victoria Cribb. Ithaca NY: Cornell University Library. Islandica 57. (Originally published as *Skáldið í skriftinni: Snorri Sturluson og Egils saga*. Reykjavík: Hið íslenska bókmenntafélag, 2004).

Úlfar Bragason 2010. *Ætt og saga: Um frásagnarfræði Sturlungu eða Íslendinga sögu hinnar miklu*. Reykjavík: Háskólaútgáfan.

Viðar Pálsson 2011. *Power and Political Communication. Feasting and Gift Giving in Medieval Iceland*. Unpublished PhD dissertation in History, University of California, Berkeley.

Viðar Pálsson 2016. *Language of Power: Feasting and Gift-Giving in Medieval Iceland and Its Sagas. Islandica*. Cornell: Cornell University Library.

Wanner, Kevin J. 2008. *Snorri Sturluson and the Edda. The Conversion of Cultural Capital in Medieval Scandinavia*. Toronto: University of Toronto Press.

Þorgils saga ok Hafliða. Ed. Ursula Brown. London: Oxford University Press, 1952.

Reykholt and its Literary Environment in the First Half of the Thirteenth Century

Reykholt and the Growth of Written Culture

I N *ÍSLENDINGA SAGA*, WRITTEN BY STURLA ÞÓRÐARSON, WE find the oft-quoted paragraph:

> Nú tók at batna með þeim Snorra ok Sturlu [Sighvatssyni] ok var
> Sturla löngum þá í Reykjaholti ok lagði mikinn hug á at láta rita
> sögubœkr eftir bókum þeim, er Snorri setti saman.[1]

The first decades of the thirteenth century in Iceland are known as a period during which the medieval literary life of Iceland flourished. Snorri Sturluson's farm at Reykholt – where Snorri lived most of the time after he moved there from Borg, probably in 1206, until his death in 1241 – is supposed to have been one of the great literary centres in Iceland at this time. We have good historical sources for this period in

---

1 "Things now began to go better between Snorri and Sturla [Sighvatsson], and Sturla spent much time at Reykholt and was very keen to have copies made of the saga books which Snorri was composing" (*Sturlunga saga* I (1946), 342; *Sturlunga saga* I (1988) 329). Translations from Old Norse here and throughout the article are my own.

the form of *Sturlunga saga*, and the picture of life at Reykholt and other farms in the area owned by members of the Sturlungar family is fuller and more detailed than that for most other districts of Iceland. This is partly because of the political and social dominance of the Sturlungar family during this period and partly because the saga that fills nearly half of the *Sturlunga* cycle, *Íslendinga saga*, was written by a member of this family, Snorri's nephew Sturla Þórðarson.

Taking into account the comprehensive nature of the source, it is remarkable that *Sturlunga saga* has so little to say about the composition of sagas and other types of writing. The brief comment about Snorri composing books and Sturla Sighvatsson letting them be copied, quoted above, is all that is said directly about writing and literary activity at Reykholt. In fact, Sturla Þórðarson and the other authors behind the other sagas included in the *Sturlunga* cycle did not spend time and vellum on describing literary activity. In *Haukdœla þáttr* it is mentioned in passing about Gizurr Hallsson: "Oft fór hann af landi brott ok var betr metinn í Róma en nökkurr íslenzkr maðr fyrr honum af mennt sinni ok framkvæmð. Honum varð víða kunnigt um suðrlöndin ok þar af gerði hann bók þá er heitir Flos peregrinationis".[2]

Bishop Guðmundr Arason's literary interest and his copying of books is mentioned;[3] it is also mentioned that Kygri-Bjǫrn and the deacon Lambkárr took care of the writing (*ritagerðir* and *bréfagerðir*) for Kolbeinn Tumason during the winter when Kolbeinn occupied the episcopal see at Hólar.[4] However, in the whole of *Sturlunga saga* only a few lines are devoted to writing activity. Writing of sagas was obviously not *sǫguligt*. By comparison, the composition and performance of skaldic poetry is mentioned quite often, and a large number of skaldic stanzas are quoted in *Sturlunga saga*. Judging from the literature describing life in and around Reykholt, it is easy to get the impression that skaldic poetry was still the type of literature that really mattered.[5]

However, despite the scarcity of the sources on writing activities, *Sturlunga saga* paints a picture of the development from a society in the

2   "He often made journeys abroad and was more highly regarded in Rome than any previous Icelander for his skill and prowess. He had a wide knowledge of the countries in the South and he wrote a book about them which is called Flos peregrinacionis" (*Sturlunga saga* I (1946), 60; *Sturlunga saga* I (1988), 193).
3   *Sturlunga saga* I (1988), 118.
4   *Sturlunga saga* I (1988), 203.
5   See pp. 445–451 in this book.

early twelfth century where entertainment (*sagnaskemmtan*) meant oral storytelling to a society some generations later in which oral storytelling could be replaced by reading aloud from books, meaning that both books and their use had spread. The frequently mentioned description in *Þorgils saga ok Hafliða* of the entertainment at the wedding at Reykjahólar in 1119 provides us with an insight into the oral culture of the time:

> Hrólfr frá Skálmarnesi sagði sögu frá Hröngviði víkingi ok frá Óláfi Liðsmannakonungi ok haugbroti Þráins berserks ok Hrómundi Gripssyni ok margar vísur með. En þessari sögu var skemmt Sverri konungi, ok kallaði hann slíkar lygisögur skemmtiligstar. Ok þó kunna menn at telja ættir sínar til Hrómundar Gripssonar. Þessa sögu hafði Hrólfr sjálfr saman setta. Ingimundr prestr sagði sögu Orms Barreyjarskálds ok vísur margar ok flokk góðan við enda sögunnar, er Ingimundr hafði ortan, ok hafa þó margir fróðir menn þessa sögu fyrir satt.[6]

Whether the details of this story are historically true or not is difficult to say, but the story tells us that when this saga was written, probably relatively early in the thirteenth century, people took it for granted that early in the twelfth century *sagnaskemmtan* was an oral performance of stories from memory.

In the first decades after Christianization, the books needed by the Church were imported, and late in the eleventh century such books were also copied in the North.[7] The great majority of the books that existed were liturgical books, and books could be expected to be found almost

---

6   "Hrólfr from Skálmarnes told a saga about Hrǫngviðr the Viking and about Óláfr, king of the *liðsmenn*, and about Þráinn breaking into the grave mound, and Hrómundr Gripsson – together with many strophes. King Sverrir was entertained by this saga, and he said that such fables were enjoyable. Still, men can trace their lineage back to Hrómundr Gripsson. Hrólfr himself had compiled this saga. Ingimundr the priest told the saga of Ormr Barreyjarskáld with many stanzas, and towards the end of the saga a good *flokkr* which Ingimundr himself had composed, and many wise men believe this saga to be true" (*Sturlunga saga* I (1946), 27; *Sturlunga saga* I (1988) 22; the latter leaves out "berserks" and has "skemmtiligar" for "skemmtiligstar", both followed here.)

7   The development from a phase when books were only imported to one in which books were also copied late in the eleventh century can easily be seen in the preserved fragments of Latin texts in Norway. See Pettersen and Karlsen 2004, especially part II written by Karlsen. We must assume that this change took place more or less at the same time both in Norway and Iceland.

exclusively in connection with churches and ecclesiastical institutions. Early in the twelfth century, the period described in *Þorgils saga ok Hafliða*, books were still rare, but in Iceland we now get the earliest original Icelandic works that we know of, Sæmundr's work about Norwegian kings in Latin and Ari's *Íslendingabók*; and the laws were written down during the winter of 1117/18. Written texts were no longer only those texts needed by the Church. Around 1150, the anonymous author of the so-called *Fyrsta málfræðiritgerðin* (First Grammatical Treatise) mentions the different types of written texts that existed in Icelandic society at the time: law, genealogies, religious literature ("þýðingar helgar")[8] and Ari's works. At this time, literature and literary production still seem to be limited, and literature needed by the Church probably made up the greatest part of what existed, but other types of texts, such as historical works and practical literature (law and genealogies), were also produced. In the last part of the twelfth century, literary production increased. From the sources we get the impression that some people (clerics) now owned private collections of books that clearly exceeded the minimum required in their work. *Prestssaga Guðmundar Arasonar* mentions an episode that took place in 1181. Ingimundr *prestr* (priest) lost his book chest at sea in a storm. Ingimundr was very sad when he found that his books were gone, and the author comments that "... þar var ynði hans sem bækrnar váru ...".[9] His book chest was later found, and Ingimundr was able to dry his books out. Some years later the same Ingimundr gave all his best books to Guðmundr Arason, who later became bishop.[10]

In an episode mentioned in *Þorgils saga skarða*, which is supposed to have taken place in the year 1258, we find a description of *sagnaskemmtan*, as in *Þorgils saga ok Hafliða*, but now, some 140 years later, the *sagnaskemmtan* is no longer described as oral storytelling. Written books to be read out can now replace the oral stories:

Þorgils reið til Hrafnagils. Var honum þar vel fagnat. Skipaði hann mönnum sínum þar á bœi. Honum var kostr á boðinn hvat til gamans skyldi hafa, sögur eða dans, um kveldit. Hann spurði

8   It is uncertain whether "þýðingar helgar" means "learned religious literature" or "translated religious literature". In this early context it could probably mean both.
9   "...his delight was where his books were" (*Sturlunga saga* I (1946), 128; *Sturlunga saga* I (1988), 112).
10   *Sturlunga saga* I (1988) 117.

hverjar sögur í vali væri. Honum var sagt, at til væri saga Tómass erkibiskups ok kaus hann hana, því at hann elskaði hann framar en aðra helga menn. Var þá lesin sagan ok allt þar til er unnit var á erkibiskupi í kirkjunni ok höggvin af honum krúnan. Segja menn, at Þorgils hætti þá ok mælti: "Þat myndi vera allfagr dauði."[11]

The sagas that were offered to Þorgils "til gamans" could in principle be oral or written, but in this text it is taken for granted that they were written, and Þorgils is reading – or is being read to – from a book.[12] In this case it is obvious that there are a number of books at the farm ("hverjar sögur í vali væri") from which the guest is invited to choose one, and among the written texts to choose from there are sagas suitable for entertainment. The written culture has finally conquered the field of *sagnaskemmtan* previously dominated by the oral culture.

Reykholt as a Centre of Literary Activity

The literary activity at Reykholt in Snorri's time must be seen in connection with the development from an oral to a written culture, and at the same time the literary centre that Snorri built up at Reykholt most likely contributed greatly to this development.

The short note about Sturla Sighvatsson copying books at Reykholt, with which this article opened, is not very detailed, yet provides us with a great deal of information, as well as grounds for further

---

11 "Þorgils rode to Hrafnagil. He was warmly received there, and he arranged for places for his men at neighbouring farms. He was offered to choose what entertainment they should have for the evening, sagas or dances. He asked what sagas there were to choose from, and was told that there was the saga of Archbishop Thomas, and he chose this for he loved him above all other saints. The saga was then read aloud right up to the point when the archbishop was assaulted in the church and his crown struck off. Men say that Þorgils then stopped and said: 'That would be a very fine death'" (*Sturlunga saga* II (1946), 218; *Sturlunga saga* II (1988), 734).

12 This does not mean that reading in all cases replaced oral storytelling. The two types of performance, oral storytelling and reading from books, probably existed side by side throughout the Middle Ages and even longer. A performance in between the oral and the written, oral telling with the book at hand, also became a possibility. This type of performance is recorded in *Sturlu þáttr*. There Sturla is described as having a book at hand, but he is telling the story ("sagði mikinn hluta dags sögu"), rather than reading it (*Sturlunga saga* II (1946), 233; *Sturlunga saga* II (1988), 766).

speculation. It has been a matter of discussion whether Snorri wrote *Heimskringla*, and if he did, how much of it.[13] His nephew, Sturla Þórðarson, who should have known better than anyone else, says that he "setti saman" (composed) "bœkr" (books). This has been taken as a reference to Snorri's sagas of kings, and if so, it most likely means that he composed sagas about more than one king, although that cannot be proven by the plural form *bœkr*. If Sturla Sighvatsson copied books only for his own use, it seems that Snorri must have written quite a number. Sturla Sighvatsson spent much time at Reykholt, and Sturla Þórðarson's wording, "láta rita sögubœkr", indicates that he not only wrote himself,[14] but also had copyists working for him. If Sturla copied for his own use, it is likely that other people could do the same, and Reykholt would then function as a centre for writing, where people could come and make copies from what was in the library. Another possibility is that Sturla Sighvatsson took care of the copying of Snorri's books intended for distribution, both as gifts and books for sale, or even for export. In any case, the level of activity in the *scriptorium* of Reykholt in 1230 – the summer Snorri, the lawspeaker, did not ride to the *Alþingi* but sent Styrmir *prestr* (Styrmir *fróði* (the Learned) to act for him[15] – seems to have been considerable.

Despite the scarce information in the sources about libraries and book production at Reykholt, there is one little piece of information in *Sturlunga saga* that tells us that the collection of books at Reykholt during Snorri's last days must have been both large and valuable. In *Íslendinga saga*, Sturla tells us that after the death of Hallveig, Snorri's wife, in the summer of 1241 Snorri quarrelled with Hallveig's sons, Klængr and Ormr, about Hallveig's inheritance. They were unable to agree on how to divide the land between themselves, but they divided movables and books ("þeir skiptu gripum ok bókum").[16] The fact that books are mentioned separately indicates that the library belonging to Snorri and Hallveig must have been extensive.

13 The comment about Sturla confirms that Snorri wrote *sögubœkr*, which scholars agree must mean, or include, sagas of kings, but whether *sögubœkr* refers to all the sagas of kings that have later been attributed to Snorri is impossible to know. On this problem see Jonna Louis-Jensen 1997, 230–245. See also the article by Guðrún Nordal and Jon Gunnar Jørgensen, pp. 442–445 in this book.
14 The wording does not prove that Sturla himself copied at all, but that is the most logical interpretation since he stayed at Reykholt when the work was carried out.
15 *Sturlunga saga* I (1988), 328–329.
16 *Sturlunga saga* I (1946), 452; *Sturlunga saga* I (1988), 437.

Figure 1. Stafholt (Stafaholt). The church was built in 1875–1877. The medieval *staðr* of St Nicholas at Stafholt was quite rich. In the background is the mountain Skarðsheiði (-heiðr), at the front the banks of the river Norðurá (Norðrá) are prominent. Photo: Guðlaugur Óskarsson.

However, the literary activity at Reykholt should not be seen in isolation. Reykholt is better characterized as a centre in a literary network. In
the closest circles of this network were other big farms in the Borgarfjǫrðr
area. On many farms there were churches. Some were annex churches
and others were chapels, where priests had no permanent residence, but
on many of the church farms there lived a priest, or two priests, or even
more and several other clerics. Some of the churches owned the whole of
the farm land and these were called *staðir*. Others owned only a part of it
and shared the land with the farmer. These were called farmers' churches
(*bændakirkjur*). The most important of the churches in both categories
have been defined as *church centres*, and in these places there lived several
clergymen, at least one priest but sometimes even two or more.[17]

17   *Staðir* (sg. *staðr*) were institutions that owned themselves, meaning that the church
     owned the farm on which it was built. See chapter 11 in Magnús Stefánsson 2000.
     On *staðir* see also in this book, pp. 115–116. A *church centre* has been defined as: 1)

The priests needed books containing liturgical texts of different types. It is probable that most priests were able to copy books for the church themselves, or else they would be the ones responsible for having the necessary books copied or bought. The farmers who had churches on their farms and kept priests were not necessarily interested in literature and written culture. However, where there existed priests who were trained in reading and writing, there was at least a possibility that members of the farmer's household would learn how to read and write, and as written literature started to spread – as well as types of literature other than those texts needed for the church – the church farms might have developed into small literary milieux in the sense that books were owned and read. Yet in actual fact, the church farms – particularly those with several priests, of the type that can be defined as *church centres* – had the potential for developing into literary centres where books were not only owned and read but also copied, and where the actual production of new texts might even have taken place if conditions were favourable.

Reykholt is a good example of a *staðr* that developed into a centre of writing and learning. One of the favourable conditions that promoted this development may have been Snorri Sturluson taking over Reykholt, probably in 1206. This was around the time when he also took over Stafholt, another *staðr* close to Reykholt, and therefore acquired a number of clerics who were now at his disposal. As a literary centre it is in fact difficult to distinguish Stafholt from Reykholt, especially since Snorri lived there for some years (1221–1224/25), which may have been among the most productive in his literary career. In the local literary network in the Borgarfjǫrðr area, of which Reykholt – or Reykholt and Stafholt – eventually became the centre, other large farms were probably the beneficiaries of the copying and purchasing.

Outside the Borgarfjǫrðr area, Reykholt can be seen as one point in a literary network that also included centres of writing throughout the rest of Iceland. These include ecclesiastical centres such as the two Icelandic episcopal sees in Skálholt and Hólar, Icelandic monasteries,[18]

a place with a larger church building than usual; 2) the area from where tithe was collected, consisting of at least twenty farms; 3) a place where at least three clergy-men – and at least one of them a priest – were working at the church; 4) a church that had at least two annex churches; 5) a church with a good and central location (Benedikt Eyþórsson 2005).

18   Snorri Sturluson was one of the founders of the Augustinian monastery in Viðey

secular centres of learning such as Oddi where Snorri grew up, important *staðir*, and of course bigger farms all over Iceland with owners or other inhabitants who had family relationships (or other types of relationships) with Reykholt.

It is hard to say whether it is likely that the literary centre at Reykholt was of sufficient size and importance to have direct lines of contact with literary centres abroad, which would then place Reykholt in the context of an international literary network. The question is whether books from abroad, including books that were meant to be translated, were imported directly to Reykholt, or whether such texts came to Reykholt via other Icelandic centres such as monasteries, the episcopal sees, or established centres of learning such as Oddi. There are strong indications that Snorri Sturluson had direct contact with centres of literary production abroad, at least partly because of his literary skills, although admittedly in his capacity as a *skáld* and not as a prose author. Additionally, there are good reasons for believing that Snorri's prose works were written with a foreign (particularly Norwegian) audience in mind. If books were exported – for instance from Reykholt to Norway – then they could also have been imported to Reykholt.

Foreign Literary Influence at Reykholt

In *Skáldatal* (The Register of Skalds) Snorri Sturluson is mentioned as one of the court poets of both King Sverrir and King Ingi, and he also composed a poem in honour of the Norwegian Earl Hákon *galinn* (literally, "frantic").[19] Since these poems were composed before Snorri's first journey to Norway, he must have sent them to Norway in written form. Of course, the fact that Snorri sent skaldic poems to the Norwegian court does not prove that he was regarded as a great skald and an authority with whom the circles around the court wanted to develop contacts. Nevertheless, we know from *Íslendinga saga* that Earl Hákon *galinn*, who died in 1214, had commissioned Snorri to compose a poem in honour of his wife Kristín,[20] which is a good indication that Snorri was well

(1223–1226), and the connection between Reykholt and this monastery must therefore have been strong.

19   *Sturlunga saga* I (1988), 254.
20   *Sturlunga saga* I (1988), 256.

known and appreciated in Norway at the time. Close and direct lines of communication thus seem to have been established between Snorri and the Norwegian royal house and persons closely connected with it around 1214 at the latest, but probably even before Snorri settled at Reykholt since the kings and the earl must have expressed their thanks to Snorri in some way.

According to the sources, one of Snorri's motivations for going to Norway in the late summer or autumn of 1218 seems to have been to perform the poem before Kristín, who by that time had moved to Sweden and married the Swedish nobleman Áskell (modern Eskil) Magnússon. Before this time, however, Snorri had sent poems to the two Norwegian kings and the earl without going there to perform them himself. When he chose to travel to Norway in 1218, it is tempting to think that performing a poem to an earl's widow was not the main reason for his journey. Could it be, perhaps, that he had been given reason to understand that the Norwegian court wanted his services as an author in other capacities?

In Snorri's time, the Norwegian court developed into a literary centre, not only for the composition and performance of skaldic poetry as it had been from ancient times, but also for the writing of prose literature and, not least, a centre for the translation of foreign literature. King Sverrir had engaged Karl Jónsson to write his biography in the 1180s. The writing of the saga started at the Norwegian court, and when Karl Jónsson left for Iceland in 1188 to become abbot at the monastery of Þingeyrar, direct contact was established between the Norwegian court and this Icelandic monastery. The writing of two sagas about the Norwegian King Óláfr Tryggvason by the monks Oddr Snorrason and Gunnlaugr Leifsson in this same monastery in the following decade must of course be seen in connection with the special status that this particular Norwegian king had in Iceland, as the king who christianized their country. However, the monastery's interest in the sagas of Norwegian kings should probably also be seen in connection with the direct links established by their abbot between this monastery and the Norwegian court.

We do not know from the sources whether Snorri was engaged by the court to write about Norwegian kings in the same way as Karl Jónsson was engaged by King Sverrir, but we know that contact had been established before his arrival and we know that he was engaged as a skald, and that several of his poems were known in Norway in written form. That indicates that Reykholt should probably be seen as a literary centre then, with direct lines of communications to literary centres abroad (in this case to the Norwegian court). Further, there is little doubt that Snorri's *konungasǫgur* (Kings' Sagas)[21] must have been written with Norwegian audiences in mind. The *konungasǫgur* focus on the Norwegian kings and so include descriptions of life in Norway; therefore, they must have been at least as interesting to a Norwegian audience as to an Icelandic one.[22] Furthermore, in *Snorra-Edda* there are some details in *Gylfaginning* that might indicate that Snorri wrote that work with a Norwegian audience in mind as well. In the Prologue of *Snorra-Edda* names are sometimes given in forms that probably are meant to form associations with the languages and cultures of lands beyond Scandinavia and Iceland, through which the gods, according to Snorri, travelled on their journey to the North.[23] At the beginning of *Gylfaginning*, there are several occasions where names are given in two variants, one beginning with an initial consonant *h* and the other without, such as in the enumeration of Óðinn's names in chapter 3: "þriðja [name] er Nikarr eða Hnikarr, fjórða er Nikuz eða Hnikuðr".[24] The alternatives seem to be an Icelandic form and a Norwegian/Scandinavian form (which at the time was probably also an Orcadian form), and may very well have been put there at the beginning of the work to catch the foreign audience's attention and to signal that the author was writing for two audiences with slightly different languages.

If Snorri's first visit to Norway opened direct channels of communication with the literary milieu connected to the Norwegian court of King Hákon Hákonarson (modern Norwegian Håkon Håkonsson, Håkon IV), there is also the possibility that Reykholt became one of the key Icelandic literary centres through which knowledge of chivalric literature spread. As far as we know, *Tristrams saga ok Ísǫndar* was translated by a certain Brother Robert at the request of King Hákon in the year 1226 – a few years after Snorri's first visit to Norway – and in the following years

---

21 We do not know exactly what proportion of what is now known as *Heimskringla* Snorri wrote or composed himself (see Louis-Jensen 1997, with references). There is no doubt, however, that he did write certain Kings' Sagas, and manuscripts containing Kings' Sagas were exported to Norway in the Middle Ages.

22 See Guðrún Nordal 2006, 77–84.

23 By using a name like Loricus the author probably meant to call forth associations with the Latin language, while Frioðigar is probably meant to be connected to an old form of a Germanic language. See Faulkes (ed.) 1988, 4–5.

24 "... the third [name] is Nikarr or Hnikarr, the fourth Nikuz or Hnikuðr" (Faulkes (ed.) 1988, 8).

more sagas followed. We know that this type of literature became very popular in Iceland. Chivalric literature may have been imported directly to Iceland rather than via Norway, and no doubt the Norwegian court had contacts with literary centres in Iceland other than Reykholt. Members of the Sturlungar family, first Snorri Sturluson and later Sturla Sighvatsson, were, however, the men on whom the Norwegian king relied in his struggle for power in Iceland in the 1220s and 1230s.[25] This fact makes it very likely that literary impulses from the Norwegian court reached Reykholt very early on, although this can hardly be proved on the basis of the sources.

The Ecclesiastical Impact at Reykholt, Clerics and Library

It is, of course, difficult to say why Reykholt developed into such an important literary centre. One very important consideration is that Reykholt was a so-called *staðr* with a high number of clerics. Furthermore, the fact that both Reykholt and another neighbouring *staðr*, Stafholt, were run by the same man, Snorri Sturluson, from around 1206 meant that a considerable number of clerics were at his disposal.[26] Another factor worth mentioning is that in the Borgarfjǫrðr area and its immediate surroundings, none of the monasteries, prior to 1220, developed into literary centres. According to *Landnámabók* (the *Hauksbók* redaction), only three monks were left behind at the monastery at Bœr – established by the English missionary Bishop Rudolf (Rúðólfr, Hróðólfr) as early as in the 1030s – when their founding abbot returned to England in 1049.[27] A very small number of monks may have continued to live at Bœr for some time, but we do not know for how long. In Hítardalr, there was a monastery from around 1166 to 1201. Not much is known about this

---

25 *Sturlunga saga* I (1988) 263; *Hákonar saga Hákonarsonar*, 480.

26 According to the *máldagi* (the deed) for the church (*DI* I, 180) there should be three priests, a deacon (*messudjákn*) and a cleric of lesser order who could read matins in Stafholt. The number of priests at Reykholt is not mentioned anywhere, but Benedikt Eyþórsson has argued that there probably were four, perhaps even five, clerics at the place (2003, 20–26). Gunnar F. Guðmundsson (2016), on the other hand, argues that the number was as a rule two priests and a deacon.

27 *Íslendingabók, Landnámabók*, 65. In England Rudolf became abbot at a Benedictine monastery in Abingdon, which may suggest that the monastery at Bœr belonged to the same order.

site except the names of two abbots, and this monastery too must have been very small. The bishop's see at Skálholt was quite distant, and the absence of flourishing monasteries in the area around 1200 may have made it easier for a secular centre of writing to develop. Why Reykholt and no other local *staðr* developed into a centre of writing has probably something to do with the personality and the background of the man who took over the *staðr* at Reykholt – and Stafholt – in around 1206, Snorri Sturluson. Nothing is known of the literary interests of Snorri's father, Hvamm-Sturla. However, Snorri came to live at Oddi in the household of his foster-father, Jón Loptsson (or Loftsson), when he was only two years old, and he stayed there until he moved to Borg as a married man in 1202. At that time, Oddi was a centre of learning and writing with a recognized school.[28] There is an Old Norse saying "fjórðungi bregðr til fóstrs".[29] In Snorri's case his upbringing in the learned milieu at Oddi can hardly be overestimated when looking for factors to explain why Snorri came to love books and learning.

Snorri's artistic skill is of course a very important factor in explaining his success in life, but also his learning, his ambition and desire to better himself socially – which he probably had inherited from his own family – not least through his marriages to rich women.[30] Snorri's learning would have made him a good cleric or copyist, his artistic skill and knowledge would have made it possible for him to work as an

---

28 The word "school" is here used in a broad sense. The relationship between Snorri and Jón Loptsson is in the sources spoken of as a foster-son/foster-father relationship, and teachers are often called foster-fathers in Old Norse sources. However, in the cases where a foster-father, or place of fostering, was chosen mainly because a young boy could be educated there, it is reasonable to regard such a milieu as a "school". It seems that in the cases where young boys were sent away to be educated, the social rank of the foster-father was normally at least as high as that of the child's father. These foster-son/foster-father relationships are therefore slightly different from those most commonly described in the Sagas of Icelanders where we often get the impression that men of lower rank than the child's father offered to foster a child, probably to get the friendship, help and protection from a mightier family.

29 "One fourth [of a person's character] comes from the fosterage".

30 Snorri married Herdís, the daughter of Bersi *auðgi* (the Wealthy) in 1199. When he died in 1202, Snorri [as the husband of his daughter] received the inheritance (*Sturlunga saga* I (1988), 210). *Sturlunga saga* does not mention other children of Bersi *auðgi* than Herdís, and she may have been the only child. In that case, Herdís inherited all of her father's wealth. Snorri and Herdís moved to Borg after Bersi's death. In 1206 Snorri left Herdís behind at Borg and moved on to Reykholt, although they were probably still formally married. In 1224 Snorri took up with the rich widow Hallveig Ormsdóttir, the daughter of his foster-brother Ormr Jónsson.

author in a literary institution or in the service of a rich chieftain, while his ambitions and wealth made it possible for him to use his skill and learning to fulfil both the roles of author and chieftain at the same time.

From *Reykjaholtsmáldagi* we learn that Snorri took over some books together with the *staðr* in Reykholt.[31] Otherwise we have no exact knowledge of how the collection of books that Snorri finally had to divide between himself and Hallveig's sons had come to Reykholt. It is, however, possible to point to some events in Snorri's life that might have been favourable for a collector of books. Snorri would hardly have left Oddi without books amongst his possessions. His father-in-law Bersi *auðgi* (the Wealthy) had been a priest at Borg, and since he was a rich man he may have possessed more books than the minimum needed for his work. When Snorri left Borg and his wife Herdís Bersadóttir behind, it is hard to say what would have been Snorri's share of books, either of those originally belonging to Bersi or of those Snorri might have acquired while at Borg. If, as Óskar Guðmundsson has argued, Herdís and Snorri were on friendly terms after they had separated,[32] it is likely that Snorri – who was probably more interested in books than Herdís – got more than his fair share of the library. If Snorri was commissioned to write about Norwegian kings, it is likely that he collected – or received as gifts – source material, even written sagas about kings while in Norway. Hallveig, who moved to Reykholt to live with Snorri in 1224, was the granddaughter of Jón Loptsson in Oddi, and a rich widow. Thus, she would probably also have brought additional books with her to Reykholt.[33]

Priests and clerics working at the *staðr* at Reykholt may also have brought books there, and even though they did not belong to Snorri's personal library, they would be available at Reykholt. Priests and clerics at a *staðr* like Reykholt would of course use the books belonging to the *staðr*

---

31 It is impossible to say how many books Snorri took over, since the value of the books that he received is mentioned together with vestments and church ornaments, which together are estimated as being worth 60 hundreds of homespun. Besides the books belonging to the church mentioned in the *máldagi*, there could have been books belonging to the *staðr*.

32 Óskar Guðmundsson 2009, 104–105.

33 The fact that after her death in the summer of 1241 Snorri and Hallveig's sons divided books between themselves may indicate that Hallveig had her share in the library. Books were precious objects, and Hallveig had of course the right to her share of the books that Snorri had acquired after they had established joint ownership of their property, but among the books they shared there may also have been books that Hallveig brought to Reykholt.

in their work, but it is reasonable to assume that some clerics, especially those with literary interests, owned some books themselves. One of the priests working at Reykholt was a well-known author himself: Styrmir Kárason *fróði* came to Reykholt in around 1220 and stayed for many years. He is known as the author of a saga about King Óláfr the saint as well as one version of *Landnámabók*. In the prologue of *Sverris saga* in *Flateyjarbók* Styrmir's name is connected to that saga, probably as a copyist or possibly as the author who finished the saga. Styrmir has also been mentioned as a possible author of one of the Sagas of Icelanders, the older, lost version of *Harðar saga*.[34] We do not know whether Styrmir wrote any of these works at Reykholt; he had most likely written the saga about King Óláfr before he moved there. However, it is likely that when he moved to Reykholt he would have brought with him not only what he had composed himself, but also some books that he had copied or bought for his own library. Vellum manuscripts were of course very costly for ordinary priests and clerics, but were affordable if they could do the work themselves. Being an author, Styrmir would most likely have possessed more books than an ordinary priest. If Snorri had anything to do with Styrmir's arrival in Reykholt, this might indicate that he was looking for clerics with literary interests, and if Styrmir himself had chosen Reykholt he might have done so because at that time Reykholt had become a very interesting place for clerics with literary interests to stay at.

A clergyman who might have contributed to the establishment of a literary milieu at Reykholt was Bishop Guðmundr Arason, Guðmundr *góði* (the Good). According to *Íslendinga saga*, Bishop Guðmundr stayed the whole winter of 1209/10 at Reykholt. The background for this was the struggle between the bishop and some of the chieftains in northern Iceland.[35] Snorri first supported the chieftains against the bishop, and he was to be found among the men who had met up at Hólar to force the bishop to leave his see and who had planned to attack some outlawed men who were under the bishop's protection. However, in order to resolve the conflict without using physical force against the bishop, Snorri eventually invited him to stay at Reykholt. There may be several reasons why it was Snorri in particular who invited the bishop to stay with him. The relationship between the bishop and Snorri's family had

34 See Þórhallur Vilmundarson 1991, xlivf.
35 *Sturlunga saga* I (1988) 214–227.

earlier been good, and the bishop had attended Snorri's wedding some ten years before. Another reason might have been that only three years after Snorri's take-over of the *staðr*, Reykholt was regarded as the most suitable place for a bishop to stay.

Bishop Guðmundr is known for his bibliophily, and even though the description of his love of books is found in his *vita* in order to present a positive picture of him, it cannot be disregarded. He was the foster-son of Ingimundr *prestr* (the one with the book chest mentioned above), and when he was ordained in 1185, Ingimundr gave him his best books.[36] Later, probably in the year 1200, it is reported that he received a very precious book, which had belonged to Bishop Páll, as a gift from the priest Jón Brandsson.[37] It is said of the young priest Guðmundr Arason that he invited young men to his home to educate them, and every day between the services his main occupations were teaching and writing. What he was writing, the text does not say, but most likely he copied religious texts. It is also said that wherever he went he examined people's books and collected such items that he did not already have, which means that he copied the texts or had them copied for him.[38]

At the time he was forced to leave his see to stay at Reykholt, Bishop Guðmundr had in all likelihood managed to build up a large collection of books. The circumstances surrounding his departure from Hólar were such that it cannot be taken for granted that he was allowed to take his library with him, and he departed together with Snorri in a hurry on the same day that Snorri invited him to Reykholt.[39] We must assume, however, that the bibliophile wanted to bring his books with him; we must also believe that Snorri – for selfish reasons – would have supported the bishop's wishes. It is, therefore, reasonable to assume that the bishop brought at least some books with him to Reykholt, and he certainly brought his interest in books with him. Bishop Guðmundr's stay at Reykholt may thus have been of great importance for the development of Reykholt as a centre of writing. It would be strange if Snorri did not take the opportunity to have however many books the bishop probably brought with him copied during his stay, and we must assume that Bishop

---

36 *Sturlunga saga* I (1988) 117.
37 *Sturlunga saga* I (1988), 179.
38 *Sturlunga saga* I (1988), 118.
39 *Sturlunga saga* I (1988), 223.

Guðmundr himself also continued collecting and copying books while at Reykholt.

Works by Snorri and his Contemporaries

It is impossible to get a clear picture of both the size and the content of the library at Reykholt in Snorri's later years, but the works attributed to Snorri leave us with the impression that they were written in a milieu of learning with books available to consult. As Sverrir Tómasson argues, *Snorra-Edda* cannot have been written without a considerable knowledge of European learned literature.[40] In this case, however, it is difficult to say whether Snorri was building on his school learning acquired at Oddi or whether he also had some of his "school books" in his library. Kings' Sagas that have been attributed to Snorri clearly show that the author must have had quite a number of books at his disposal since he often quotes from other sagas, frequently word for word. Snorri seems to have had access to almost everything that had been written about Norwegian kings before his time – both in Iceland and in Norway – except the Norwegian chronicles written in Latin, which were probably not among the sources he made direct use of. However, it cannot be ruled out that he may have known one or more of them. This might indicate that Snorri's library was extensive in other fields as well. Some of the books Snorri used might of course have been borrowed from other places in the literary network of which Reykholt was a part, but Snorri's wealth and the many men at his disposal with the ability to read and write at his two *staðir* make it reasonable to suppose that most books that were borrowed would have been copied before they were sent back.

There are not many books about which we can say with certainty that they were written at Reykholt (or, indeed, Stafholt). We are almost certain that Snorri Sturluson is the author of *Edda*. His authorship is considered to be proven by the wording at the start of the text in the Codex Upsaliensis manuscript: "Bók þessi heitir Edda. Hana hefir saman setta Snorri Sturluson ...".[41] If Snorri wrote *Edda* shortly after his first journey to Norway (the view held by most scholars), it is more

---

40   *Íslensk bókmenntasaga* I, 534–542.
41   "This book is called Edda. It is composed by Snorri Sturluson ..." Faulkes (ed.) 1988, xiii

likely that *Edda* was written at Stafholt than at Reykholt since Snorri stayed at Stafholt most of these years. It is attested by Sturla Þórðarson that Snorri had written *sǫgubækr* before the summer of 1230. In the preserved manuscripts containing Kings' Sagas that have been attributed to Snorri, his name is not mentioned. However, in the learned milieu of sixteenth-century Norway, Snorri seems to have been known as an author of Kings' Sagas. His name appears in Laurents Hanssøn's Norwegian translation of Kings' Sagas from 1551 (printed by Gustav Storm 1898) and in the printed edition of Peder Claussøn Friis' Norwegian translation from 1599 (printed by Ole Worm in 1633).[42] From Laurents Hanssøn's translation it is difficult to see which periods of time were covered in Snorri's Kings' Sagas, since his translation ends with a story about Earl Hákon Sigurðarson at Hlaðir (Lade). Peder Claussøn Friis' translation with the title *Snorre Sturlesøns Norske Kongers Chronica* ends with the saga about Hákon Hákonarson, but it is clear from Ole Worm's preface to the 1633 edition that the saga about King Magnús Erlingsson was regarded as the last one written by Snorri.

It cannot be proven that Styrmir *fróði* wrote any of the works attributed to him at Reykholt, but the possibility cannot be excluded either, and other clerics working at Reykholt or Stafholt may have worked as authors as well, although this too cannot be proved. It is an old theory, supported by many scholars, that Snorri Sturluson was the author of *Egils saga Skalla-Grímssonar*. This theory is also impossible to prove. We can, however, be fairly sure that *Egils saga Skalla-Grímssonar* was written in the Borgarfjǫrðr area in Snorri's time, and that the author, whoever he was, would have benefited from the literary milieu that Snorri had built up at Reykholt. The rise and the growth of the written genre of the *Íslendingasǫgur* (Sagas of Icelanders) seem to be more or less concurrent with the rise of the literary centre at Reykholt. This may be a coincidence, for Sagas of Icelanders were written in other places in Iceland as well, and perhaps also before the first Saga of Icelanders was written in the Borgarfjǫrðr area. It is, however, interesting that some sagas from the Borgarfjǫrðr area are counted among the oldest within the genre.

---

42 How Laurents Hanssøn and Peder Claussøn Friis were able to connect Snorri's name with the sagas they translated is discussed in detail by Jon Gunnar Jørgensen. See Jon Gunnar Jørgensen 1995, and the article by Guðrún Nordal and Jon Gunnar Jørgensen, pp. 458–466 in this book.

Few scholars doubt that *Heiðarvíga saga* is old.[43] The age of *Bjarnar saga Hítdœlakappa* is disputed; some scholars consider this to be a young saga,[44] while others think that it is among the oldest.[45] *Egils saga Skalla-Grímssonar* must also be counted among the older sagas of the genre if it was written in the 1230s, as most scholars think, and the saga is no doubt the oldest among the long Sagas of Icelanders. *Gunnlaugs saga ormstungu* has been regarded traditionally as younger than the other so-called *skáldasǫgur* (Skald Sagas). However, Theodore M. Andersson has recently argued that this saga is also old, and written in the same period as the other Skald Sagas.[46] This seems to indicate that quite a number of Sagas of Icelanders were written in the Borgarfjǫrðr area in the same period during which there was a flourishing literary centre at Reykholt. We are not able to connect any of these sagas to Reykholt with certainty or to a named author living there, but it is hardly too much to assume that these anonymous authors knew the milieu at Reykholt very well and might have benefited from it when writing their sagas.

The number of books written at Reykholt or Stafholt may have been considerably higher than the very few we are able to connect to these places with any certainty. Snorri's *Edda* and his Kings' Sagas are of course extremely important books, but the main activity in the literary centre at Reykholt may not have been the composition of new books. The collection of old poetry – both Eddic and skaldic – may have been seen as a necessary foundation for Snorri's writing. We do not know, however, how much Snorri or his clerics collected, whether he could build on collections made by others, or whether he mostly collected Eddic and skaldic poems and stanzas from the oral tradition. Nevertheless, it is very likely that the collection of such traditional material was one of the activities that can be connected to Reykholt.

As mentioned earlier, Sturla Þórðarson states that Sturla Sighvatsson copied books at Reykholt in the summer of 1230. This is probably a type of activity that we can assume took place continuously at Reykholt. Snorri's main goal as an intellectual leader was not necessarily to be remembered as an author, but to build up a learned centre with a col-

---

43   Bjarni Guðnason 1993 has argued that *Heiðarvíga saga* is not old. He dates it to around 1260.
44   Bjarni Guðnason 1994.
45   See Mundal 2000.
46   Andersson 2009.

lection of books that would bring honour and prestige both to himself and to Reykholt.

The Death of Snorri and the Fate of the Library

We do not know what happened to the library at Reykholt after Snorri's death. As mentioned in *Sturlunga saga*, the library had begun to fall apart even before Snorri was killed. After Hallveig's death, Snorri and Hallveig's sons divided the books between themselves. Since books are mentioned as a separate item, it is likely that the share of Hallveig's sons would have been much more than just a few books. After Snorri's death there was a bitter struggle over his property, which is described in *Sturlunga saga*, but what happened to his remaining books is not mentioned. Snorri went to Norway for the second time in the summer of 1237, and after he had returned from Norway in the summer of 1239 without the permission of King Hákon Hákonarson, the latter's reaction was very severe. The king now turned to Gizurr Þorvaldsson – who turned to Kolbeinn *ungi* (the Young) Arnórsson for help – to carry out his will in Iceland. Both these men were Snorri's former sons-in-law. In a letter from the king – which Gizurr, according to *Íslendinga saga*, carried with him on his journey to Reykholt to kill Snorri – the king accused Snorri of being a *landráðamaðr* (traitor).[47] We do not know the exact basis for this severe accusation, but it is likely that the king considered Snorri to be guilty of a more serious crime than having left Norway without his permission. Earl Skúli (modern Norwegian Skule Bårdsson), King Hákon's father-in-law, revolted against the king in the late autumn of 1239, and after Skúli's revolt, the king might have suspected Snorri of being in league with Skúli. Something of this nature is in fact hinted at by Sturla Þórðarson. In *Íslendinga saga* he mentions that Skúli might have appointed Snorri as his earl in Iceland before he left Norway, and that Styrmir *fróði* had called Snorri *fólgsnarjarl* (earl-in-secret) in writing.[48] The truth of these accusations will not be discussed here, but if the king really regarded Snorri as a traitor, it would also be the king's opinion that Snorri had forfeited all his property, including his books.

---

47   *Sturlunga saga* II (1988), 439.
48   *Sturlunga saga* I (1988), 430.

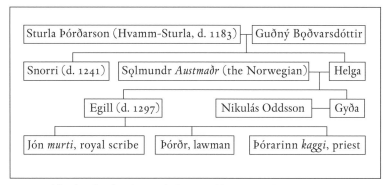

Figure 2. The family of Helga Sturludóttir and her son Egill.

According to *Þorgils saga skarða* the king "kallaði arf Snorra Sturlusonar hafa fallit undir sik, slíkt it sama lendur þær, er Snorri hafði átt á deyjanda degi, útan stað í Reykjaholti".[49] To mention that Reykholt was excepted should not have been necessary as Snorri was not the owner of Reykholt, only its rightful keeper. However, despite the fact that the king and his men in Iceland recognized that Reykholt could not be confiscated, the way they acted shows that they wanted to take control over the *staðr* and place men loyal to the king in Reykholt. When Gizurr and Kolbeinn *ungi* decided who should run Reykholt, they at least gave the impression that they acted on the king's behalf, and later Þórðr *kakali*[50] and Þorgils *skarði* (Harelip) both took possession of Reykholt as the men of the king. The reasoning behind this may have been that while they recognized that the *staðr* at Reykholt was not part of the inheritance left by Snorri, the right to run the farm was.[51] Snorri's family, on the other hand, held the opinion that the king had no right to confiscate Snorri's property – and

49 "... claimed that the inheritance left by Snorri had fallen under him, as well as all the land that Snorri had owned on the day of his death except the *staðr* in Reykholt" (*Sturlunga saga* II (1946), 118; *Sturlunga saga* II (1988) 585).
50 On this nickname, *kakali*, see in this book, pp. 149–150.
51 In *Íslendinga saga* (*Sturlunga saga* I (1988), 211) the circumstances around Snorri's taking over of Reykholt in 1206 is explained in detail, and from this account we can see that the right to run a *staðr* was inherited according to the normal rules of inheritance. The right to rule Reykholt was therefore an "inheritance" that the king – as he and his men saw it – could confiscate and hand over to one of the king's men.

this seems to have been the common opinion in Iceland – but had to give way to a superior force.[52]

Whether or not Snorri's property, including his books, was moved away from Reykholt after his death is important for how the *staðr* at Reykholt developed in the period after 1241. However, it is difficult to answer this question based on the sources available to us. Snorri had two children who survived him, his son Órœkja and his daughter Þórdís. They were, however, both illegitimate, and therefore Snorri's closest heir was his legitimate sister Helga, who was married to a Norwegian, Sǫlmundr (fig. 2).

After Snorri's death on September 23, Gizurr and Kolbeinn decided that Klængr, son of Hallveig, should settle at Reykholt. However, before this could happen he was killed by Órœkja's men on the second day of Christmas in the same year. Shortly after Snorri's death, Gizurr also sent for Snorri's sister Helga and her husband, and they came to Reykholt to meet Gizurr. Egill, Helga's son, was rather generously favoured with a large sum from the inheritance left by Snorri (two hundred hundreds[53]) and it was also decided that his sister, Gyða, should have as much as was needed for her dowry.[54] However, Sturla also reveals that Gizurr put pressure on Helga and Sǫlmundr to authorise him to be the executor

52 *Sturlunga saga* II (1988), 588.
53 See p. 246, in this book, note 8, for a definition of 'hundred'.
54 It seems that some of the men of the king – Gizurr and later Þórðr *kakali* – to some degree tried to be considerate towards Snorri's closest family and heirs. The reasons for this may have been that they were afraid to provoke Snorri's family and friends too much since many people did not recognize the king's right to confiscate the inheritance left by Snorri, and they were, of course, aware that they acted in a grey area between Icelandic and Norwegian laws. It may also be questioned as to what degree Gizurr (and Kolbeinn) acted on the king's behalf or followed their own impulses, and felt that they were on unsafe ground when they killed Snorri. According to *Hákonar saga Hákonarsonar*, 583, the king said to Snorri's son Órœkja when he arrived in Norway in 1243 that his father would not have been killed if he had come to him. The king might have anticipated that Snorri would return to Norway. According to the letter from the king mentioned by Sturla in *Íslendinga saga* (*Sturlunga saga* I (1988), 439), Snorri was to come to Norway, or if he refused, he was to be killed. However, according to Sturla, Gizurr said that he knew that Snorri would not go to Norway voluntarily, and he was killed without being given the opportunity to save his life. When Þorgils *skarði*, who was less considerate towards Snorri's closest family, came to Iceland with authority from the king, the followers of Þórðr *kakali* were very unhappy (*Sturlunga saga*, 585, 592). Þórðr had earlier "skipat eignir Snorra Sturlusonar vinum sínum" ("handed Snorri Sturluson's landed property over to his friends") (*Sturlunga saga* II (1946), 119; *Sturlunga saga* II (1988), 585). Snorri's closest relatives, such as Egill, were obviously counted among Þórðr's friends.

of the estate left by Snorri. They did so, but they had earlier given this power to Sturla Sveinsson, the son of Snorri's half-brother, Sveinn Sturluson.[55] Early in 1242, Helga and her husband gave control of Snorri's inheritance to his son Órœkja; according to Sturla this was now given to Órœkja for the second time,[56] and later in the year, on the July 29, Órœkja, not Gizurr, was awarded the right to be the executor of Snorri's estate as part of a settlement between Órœkja on the one side and Gizurr and Ormr (the brother of Klœngr) on the other.[57] During this struggle over Snorri's property it is likely that some of the library – perhaps the majority of it – was moved away from Reykholt. However, the question of what proportion of Snorri's library remained in Reykholt may be dependent on several factors. One crucial issue is whether some of the books were regarded as the property of the church rather than Snorri's personal property. Another question is whether there were people at Reykholt who ensured the continuity of the learned milieu that had existed before Snorri's death.

The clerics working at Reykholt may have represented such a continuity in several ways. They would probably have held the view that some books should follow the church, i.e. *staðr*, and it is also likely that the clerics at Reykholt owned more books themselves than an average cleric at an average church or *staðr* since they no doubt had the opportunity to copy many interesting books for their own use. One cleric was Egill Sǫlmundarson, mentioned above, the son of Snorri's sister Helga. He is of special interest as a possible link between the learned environment at Reykholt during Snorri's time and the more modest conditions that existed there after his death. Egill Sǫlmundarson was ordained subdean (*súbdjákn*),[58] although it is uncertain when, and he lived at Reykholt for a long time. We do not know exactly when he settled at Reykholt, but we know that he returned from Norway together with Snorri in 1239.[59] It is not known how long he had been in Norway or what he had been doing there. If he was born around 1215, as is commonly believed, he would have been around twenty-five when he returned to Iceland in 1239, and one possibility is that Egill, who was half Norwegian, had studied in

55 *Sturlunga saga* I (1988), 440.
56 *Sturlunga saga* I (1988), 450.
57 *Sturlunga saga* I (1988), 455–456.
58 *Sturlunga saga* II (1988), 787.
59 *Sturlunga saga* I (1988), 430.

Norway. The next time Egill is mentioned in the sources is shortly after Snorri's death when Gizurr secured him the rather generous portion of the inheritance left by Snorri. Whether this inheritance included books is of course impossible to say, but since Egill, being a cleric, was of all Snorri's heirs the one who was probably most interested in books, this is a reasonable guess. It would probably also have been less problematic for Gizurr to give him movables rather than land. In 1243 and 1244 Egill is mentioned among the followers of his relative Þórðr *kakali*, but it is not said where he lived. *Þórðar saga kakala* mentions that Þórðr returned to Iceland from Norway in the summer of 1247, after having spent one year at the king's court, with extensive authority from the king. He decided to stay the following winter at Reykholt, and "er hann kom í Borgarfjörð tók hann undir sik sveitir allar ok allt fé Snorra Sturlusonar ok svá heraðit í Borgarfirði".[60] "All the property of Snorri Sturluson" probably refers to the landed property that constituted the foundation of his political power, which was what the king was interested in.

In the winter of 1248 Nikulás Oddsson celebrated his wedding at Reykholt.[61] His bride was Gyða, the daughter of Helga and Sǫlmundr, and this indicates that Snorri's sister and her family had now moved to Reykholt. Whether Helga and her family already lived at Reykholt when Þórðr *kakali* arrived and he moved in with them, cannot be told from the sources. Neither can it be told whether Egill also lived at Reykholt at the time. However, in *Þorgils saga skarða* it is mentioned that Þorgils *skarði* Bǫðvarsson, also of the Sturlungar family, came from Norway in 1252 with a letter from the king that appointed Þorgils as the king's representative in all legal matters concerning the inheritance left by Snorri: "Skyldi Þorgils vera heimtandi ok sækjandi allra þessa mála er löglig mætti á standa meðferð þessa fjár".[62] According to this saga, Egill, now spoken of as *Egill í Reykjaholti* (Egill at Reykholt), and a priest called Þórarinn Vandráðsson, seem to have been running the place at the time. They were more or less forced to hand over the estate to Þorgils *skarði*.[63] It is, however, clear from *Þorgils saga skarða* that both the priest Þórarinn

60   "...when he came to Borgarfjǫrðr he subjugated all troops, and all the property of Snorri, and also the whole Borgarfjǫrðr area" (*Sturlunga saga* II (1946), 84; *Sturlunga saga* II (1988), 547).
61   *Sturlunga saga* II (1988), 548.
62   *Sturlunga saga* II (1946), 118, *Sturlunga saga* II (1988), 585.
63   *Sturlunga saga* II (1988), 587–589.

Figure 3. A glass goblet of French origin, dated to the late thirteenth or fourteenth century, found during excavations at the church site. It could have belonged to Snorri's nephew, Egill Sǫlmundarson, who died at Reykholt in 1297. Photo and reconstruction: Reykholt excavations.

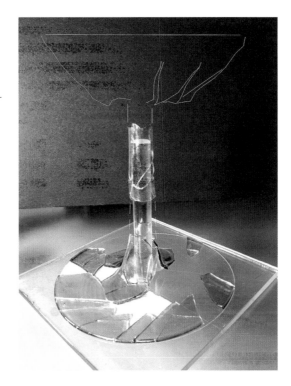

and Egill stayed on at Reykholt after Þorgils had taken over, even though it is unclear from the source what the function of the three men at the *staðr* might have been.

The fact that the *fylgikona* (mistress) of the priest Þórarinn continued as *ráðskona* (housekeeper) at Reykholt may indicate that Þórarinn lived on the farm belonging to the church. It is clear from the sources that Þorgils collected the income that in Snorri's time would have fallen to him, while Egill nonetheless seems to have been *kirkjubóndi*[64] at Reykholt and liable for the financial aspects of running the *staðr*. The relationship between Egill and Þorgils *skarði* was not a good one. One of the reasons for conflict seems to have been that Þorgils was in debt to the *staðr*.[65] Þorgils' stay at Reykholt turned out, however, to be a short one, he was very unpopular in the region, and chose to move to Staðr in Snæfellsnes the following

64 A *kirkjubóndi* was a farmer who ran a farm with a church.
65 Þorgils' debt to the *staðr* at Reykholt was later (1255) paid by Egill after Þorgils had made an attack on Reykholt and Egill had to ask for *grið* (peace) (*Sturlunga saga* II (1988), 684–685).

spring,[66] while Egill continued to live at Reykholt. His death in 1297 is mentioned in *Skálholtsannáll* and here too he is called *Egill í Reykjaholti*, which shows that he continued to live at Reykholt until his death in his old age.[67] In the sources he is also called *Egill bóndi* (the Farmer), indicating that he most likely ran the farm as *kirkjubóndi*.[68]

Egill may have come to Reykholt together with his relative Þórðr *kakali* in 1247. If Egill, his mother Helga and her family moved to Reykholt together with Þórðr *kakali*, the interests of Snorri's heirs and the king would come together. Alternatively, if Snorri's heirs had established themselves at Reykholt at an earlier date, the interests of the king and the family would not have come into conflict had Þórðr moved in with them and they were on good terms.

There is also a possibility that Egill could have moved to Reykholt as early as 1239 when he returned from Norway with Snorri, living and working as a cleric there from that time on, and at some point rising to *kirkjubóndi*. If Egill had settled at Reykholt as early as Snorri's time and remained there, subsequently receiving parts of Snorri's library as his inheritance, he would have secured a sort of continuity between the learned centre as it was in Snorri's time and the more modest literary centre that it subsequently became. Also, if he moved to Reykholt later, but carried some of Snorri's books with him, this would have also ensured continuity.

Óláfr Þórðarson at Stafholt

The potential importance of Stafholt as a scene of literary activities and learning has perhaps been somewhat neglected, since Snorri's name has been so closely connected with Reykholt. However, the two *staðir* were united during the period when Snorri controlled them both, and Stafholt continued to be an important place after Snorri's time. *Þorgils saga skarða* tells us that Snorri's nephew Óláfr Þórðarson *hvítaskáld* (literally, "white poet") had settled at Stafholt by 1252. It is hard to tell how much earlier he was there, but he was certainly back in Iceland no later than 1248, for that year he was chosen as a lawspeaker. He had spent some considerable

---

66 *Sturlunga saga* II (1988), 615–616.
67 *Islandske Annaler indtil 1578*, 198.
68 *Sturlunga saga* II (1988), 608, 611.

time abroad, both in Norway and in Denmark, and was highly regarded as a very learned man. He was the author of the *Þriðja málfræðiritgerðin* (Third Grammatical Treatise), dated to around 1250, and this learned book may have been written at Stafholt. Additionally, he has been frequently mentioned as a possible author of *Knýtlinga saga*,[69] and if he were, then *Knýtlinga saga* was in all likelihood written at Stafholt. Many scholars are, however, inclined to think that *Knýtlinga saga* was written some years after the death of Ólafr *hvítaskáld* in 1259.[70] Ólafr is, in fact, mentioned in the saga as a person who had many interesting stories to tell, and these he had learned from King Valdimarr the Victorious.[71] Scholars who have seen Ólafr Þórðarson as the author of *Knýtlinga saga*, have understood the passage about Ólafr being with King Valdimarr and learning stories from him as a reference to the author, but it could as well be a reference to Ólafr as a source. However, if Ólafr is referred to as a source, the author, whoever he was, must have spent time with Ólafr Þórðarson *hvítaskáld* somewhere, and Stafholt would be a good guess. Jonna Louis-Jensen has argued that it was Ólafr *hvítaskáld* who first combined the three parts of *Heimskringla* to create the work that we have today.[72] If that is true, then Stafholt would probably be the place where this reworking of earlier sagas of kings had taken place, and at the same time we can argue that Ólafr *hvítaskáld* is taking up the legacy of his uncle and taking it further in Snorri's secondary centre of writing. *Þorgils saga skarða* mentions a priest – in connection with events that took place in the year 1255 – who "hafði verit til kennslu í Stafaholti með Ólafi Þórðarsyni".[73] This shows that Ólafr Þórðarson had established a school at Stafholt after he returned to Iceland from abroad, most likely in the middle of the 1240s. Compared to Reykholt it is probable that Stafholt gained ground during the years when it was controlled by Ólafr Þórðarson *hvítaskáld*.

---

69 Bjarni Guðnason argues in favour of Ólafr being the author (1982, lxxi–clxxxvii, see especially clxxix–clxxxiv).

70 An overview of scholars holding this view is found in Bjarni Guðnason 1982, clxxix–clxxx.

71 *Knýtlinga saga*, 315.

72 Louis-Jensen 1997, 230–245.

73 "... had been studying at Stafholt under Ólafr Þórðarson" (*Sturlunga saga* II (1946), 184; *Sturlunga saga* II (1988), 697).

Conclusion

The killing of Snorri Sturluson must have been a serious blow to the centre of writing and learning that he had built up at Reykholt. As we have seen, the sons of Hallveig Ormsdóttir had already reduced the size of Snorri's library before his death. The circumstances surrounding Snorri's death as well as his family relations make it very uncertain what happened to Snorri's books and other valuables. As has been argued here, Egill Sǫlmundarson may have represented a link between the literary milieu at Reykholt before Snorri's death and the community as it was afterwards, for since he was granted a considerable proportion of Snorri's inheritance it is in fact likely that parts of Snorri's library became Egill's property. The *staðr* at Reykholt never regained the same level as a centre of power and learning that it had had in Snorri's time, but even after the days of Snorri the *staðr* did foster learned men. Of Egill Sǫlmundarson's many children, one son became priest, another lawman (*lǫgmaðr*),[74] and the third was a royal scribe, something that might indicate that they grew up in a learned milieu.

At Stafholt, Snorri's nephew Óláfr Þórðarson *hvítaskáld* may have been able to re-establish Snorri's secondary literary centre a few years after his death. Óláfr Þórðarson would not have received any inheritance from Snorri, but as a close family member it is not unthinkable that he received some books as gifts and was able to buy books as well. However, the main reason for suggesting that Óláfr represented a link going back to Snorri's learned world is that being close relatives both he and his father and brother (Sturla Þórðarson) would have been able to copy books – or have them copied – from Snorri's library before Snorri's death. It is also possible that there remained some books at Stafholt from Snorri's time that were regarded as the property of the *staðr*.

However, the circumstances surrounding Snorri's death make it reasonable that parts of Snorri's library, or what was left after Hallveig's sons had taken their share away, were "taken care of" by the executors of Snorri's property, perhaps sold and disseminated to other parts of the country. This would of course have been a loss for the literary and learned centre at Reykholt, but such a scattering of the books may have enabled literary impulses to spread from the centre at Reykholt to other areas with a greater strength than ever before.

---

74   *Sturlunga saga* II (1988), 788.

Acknowledgements

In writing this article I received many useful comments from the editor, Helgi Þorláksson, for which I am most grateful.

Bibliography

Andersson, Theodore M. 2009. "The Native Romance of Gunnlaugr and Helga the Fair". In Kirsten Wolf and Johanna Denzin (eds), *Romance and Love in Late Medieval and Early Modern Iceland: Essays in Honor of Marianne Kalinke*, Islandica 54. Ithaca: Cornell University Library, 33–63.

Benedikt Eyþórsson 2003. "Í þjónustu Snorra. Staðurinn í Reykholti og klerkar þar í tíð Snorra Sturlusonar". *Sagnir* 23, 20–26.

Benedikt Eyþórsson 2005. "History of the Icelandic Church 1000–1300. Status of Research." In Helgi Þorláksson (ed.), *Church Centres. Church Centres in Iceland from the 11th to the 13th Century and their Parallels in other Countries*. Snorrastofa, vol. II. Reykholt: Snorrastofa, 19–69.

Bjarni Guðnason 1982. "Formáli". *Knýtlinga saga. Dana konunga sögur*. Ed. Bjarni Guðnason. Íslenzk fornrit XXXV. Reykjavík: Hið íslenzka fornritafélag.

Bjarni Guðnason 1993. *Túlkun Heiðarvígasögu*. Studia Islandica 50. Reykjavík: Bókmenntafræðistofnun Háskóla Íslands.

Bjarni Guðnason 1994. "Aldur og einkenni Bjarnarsögu Hítdœlakappa". In Gísli Sigurðsson, Guðrún Kvaran and Sigurgeir Steingrímsson (eds), *Sagnaþing helgað Jónasi Kristjánssyni sjötugum 10. apríl 1994*. Reykjavík: Hið íslenzka bókmenntafélag, 69–85.

DI = *Diplomatarium islandicum. Íslenzkt fornbréfasafn* I. Kaupmannahöfn: Hið íslenzka bókmentafélag, 1857–1876.

Faulkes, Anthony (ed.) 1988. *Snorri Sturluson. Edda, Prologue and Gylfaginning*. London: Viking Society for Northern Research/Viking Collection.

Guðrún Nordal 2006. "Snorri and Norway".

In Else Mundal (ed.), *Reykholt som makt- og lærdomssenter i den islandske og nordiske kontekst*. Snorrastofa, vol. III. Reykholt: Snorrastofa, 77–84.

Gunnar F. Guðmundsson 2016. "Liturgical Practices at Reykholt in the Middle Ages". In Guðrún Sveinbjarnardóttir, *Reykholt. The Church Excavations*. Publications of the National Museum of Iceland 41. Reykjavík: The National Museum of Iceland, in collaboration with Snorrastofa and University of Iceland Press, 167–174.

Harðar saga. Eds Þórhallur Vilmundarson and Bjarni Vilhjálmsson. Íslenzk fornrit XIII. Reykjavík: Hið íslenzka fornritafélag, 1991.

Hákonar saga Hákonarsonar. Eds Þorleifur Hauksson, Sverrir Jakobsson and Tor Ulset. Íslenzk fornrit XXXI, Reykjavík: Hið íslenzka fornritafélag, 2013.

Islandske Annaler indtil 1578. Ed. Gustav Storm. Christiania: Grøndal & Søns Bogtrykkeri, Christiania, 1888.

Íslendingabók, Landnámabók. Ed. Jakob Benediktsson. Íslenzk fornrit I. Reykjavík: Hið íslenzka fornritafélag, 1968.

Íslensk bókmenntasaga. Eds Guðrún Nordal, Sverrir Tómasson and Vésteinn Ólason, Reykjavík: Mál og menning, 1992.

Jørgensen, Jon Gunnar 1995. "Snorre Sturlesøns fortale paa sin chrønicke". *Gripla* 9, 45–62.

Kjær, A. (ed.) 1985–1987/1852–1941. *Det Arnamagnæanske Haandskrift 81 a Fol. (Skálholtsbók yngsta). Sverris saga. Bǫglunga sǫgur, Hákonar saga Hákonarsonar*. Oslo: Kjeldeskriftfondet.

Knýtlinga saga. Dana konunga sǫgur. Ed. Bjarni Guðnason. Íslenzk fornrit XXXV. Reykjavík: Hið íslenzka fornritafélag, 1982.

Louis-Jensen, Jonna 1997. "Heimskringla – Et værk af Snorri Sturluson?" *Nordica Bergensia* 14. Nordisk institutt, Universitetet i Bergen, 230–245.

Magnús Stefánsson 2000. *Staðir og staðamál. Studier i islandske egenkirkelige og beneficialrettslige forhold i middelalderen.* Historisk institutt, Universitetet i Bergen. Skrifter 4.

Mundal, Else 2000. "Bjarnar saga hítdœlakappa. Svak soge med interessante sider". *Nordica Bergensia* 23. Nordisk institutt, Universitetet i Bergen, 187–203.

Óskar Guðmundsson 2009. *Snorri. Ævisaga Snorra Sturlusonar.* Reykjavík: JPV útgáfa.

Pettersen, Gunnar and Espen Karlsen 2004.

"Katalogisering av latinske membranfragmenter som Forskningsprosjekt". *Riksantikvaren. Rapporter og retningslinjer* 16. Oslo: Arkivverkets forskningsseminar, Gardermoen 2003, 43–58 and 58–88.

Sturlunga saga I–II. Eds Jón Jóhannesson, Magnús Finnbogason and Kristján Eldjárn. Reykjavík: Sturlunguútgáfan, 1946.

Sturlunga saga. Ed. Örnólfur Thorsson. Reykjavík: Svart á hvítu, 1988.

Þórhallur Vilmundarson 1991. "Formáli". *Harðar saga.* Ed. Þórhallur Vilmundarson and Bjarni Vilhjálmsson. Íslenzk fornrit XIII. Reykjavík: Hið íslenzka fornritafélag.

9   GUÐRÚN NORDAL AND JON GUNNAR JØRGENSEN

The Literary Legacy of Snorri Sturluson

Introduction

THE PICTURE OF SNORRI STURLUSON'S LITERARY MILIEU AT Reykholt from around 1206 to 1241 must be pieced together through scattered references in *Sturlunga saga*, *Snorra-Edda*, *Skáldatal* (The Register of Poets) and the Kings' Sagas. There are many allusions to Snorri's writings, of relevance not only to the prose works commonly associated with his name, but also to our understanding of the way his own skaldic verse-making and literary compositions underpinned his social climbing at the royal court in Norway in the first decades of the thirteenth century. None of the works attributed to Snorri Sturluson (*Snorra-Edda*, *Heimskringla* or *Egils saga Skalla-Grímssonar*) are preserved in their original versions, and neither are those of the other writers and poets known to have resided in or had proven contact with Reykholt in the first half of the thirteenth century, e.g. Styrmir *fróði* (the Knowledgeable) Kárason, Óláfr Þórðarson *hvítaskáld* (literally, "the white poet") and Sturla Þórðarson. *Reykjaholtsmáldagi* (The Deed of the Church of Reykholt), the inventory of the church at Reykholt, is the only extant document that can be proven to have been written during Snorri's time at Reykholt.

*   The first four sections are by Guðrún Nordal, the section on *Heimskringla* is by Jon Gunnar Jørgensen.

The deed lists the property of the church at Reykholt in the late twelfth and thirteenth century, including lands, livestock and moveable assets such as books belonging to the church.[1] Snorri Sturluson acquired the Reykholt estate in around 1206 and lived there until his sudden death in 1241. Hallveig Ormsdóttir, a woman of considerable means, entered a partnership (helmingarfélag) with Snorri in 1224 and died there in 1240. Snorri and Hallveig are noted together in the deed as the donors of bells to the church. Upon Hallveig's death, her sons, Ormr and Klængr, from her first marriage to Bjǫrn Þorvaldsson (Gizurr Þorvaldsson's brother), received their share of objects and books ("skiptu gripum ok bókum")[2] from the estate, indicating that Hallveig and Snorri owned a substantial collection of manuscripts. The existence of a *scriptorium* at Reykholt is alluded to by the unique account of Sturla Sighvatsson's long stays at Reykholt in 1230 where he planned to "láta rita sögubækr eftir bókum þeim, er Snorri setti saman".[3] This is the only direct reference to the writing of sagas at Reykholt, or indeed at other seats of learning in the country, in the whole of *Sturlunga saga* whereas allusions to Snorri's skaldic versifying are numerous.

The archaeological excavations of one third of the Reykholt farm site from the first half of the thirteenth century (Phase 2) have not exposed the location of Snorri's *scriptorium* with any certainty, but they reveal that the owners of the estate in this period made substantial changes to the earlier farm. Snorri and Hallveig clearly sought to elevate themselves by erecting buildings which emulated the lodgings at aristocratic milieux in Norway; as both "buildings, and associated conduit and passageway, are a sign of sophistication and luxury, and are fitting monuments for a chieftain of Snorri Sturluson's calibre".[4] To date, no other comparable structures have been found in Iceland from this time. The unique buildings and the ground-breaking literary productions of the Reykholt literary milieu in the thirteenth century combine to express Snorri's political, cultural and social aspirations which aimed at enhancing and expressing his status as an aristocrat at the Norwegian court.

It is not to be expected that the excavations at Reykholt would unearth

1   *Reykjaholtsmáldagi*, 14.
2   *Sturlunga saga* (1946) I, 452; *Sturlunga saga* (1988) I, 437.
3   "to write books of sagas after the books which Snorri put together" (*Sturlunga saga* I (1946), 342; *Sturlunga saga* I (1988), 329).
4   Guðrún Sveinbjarnardóttir 2012, 96.

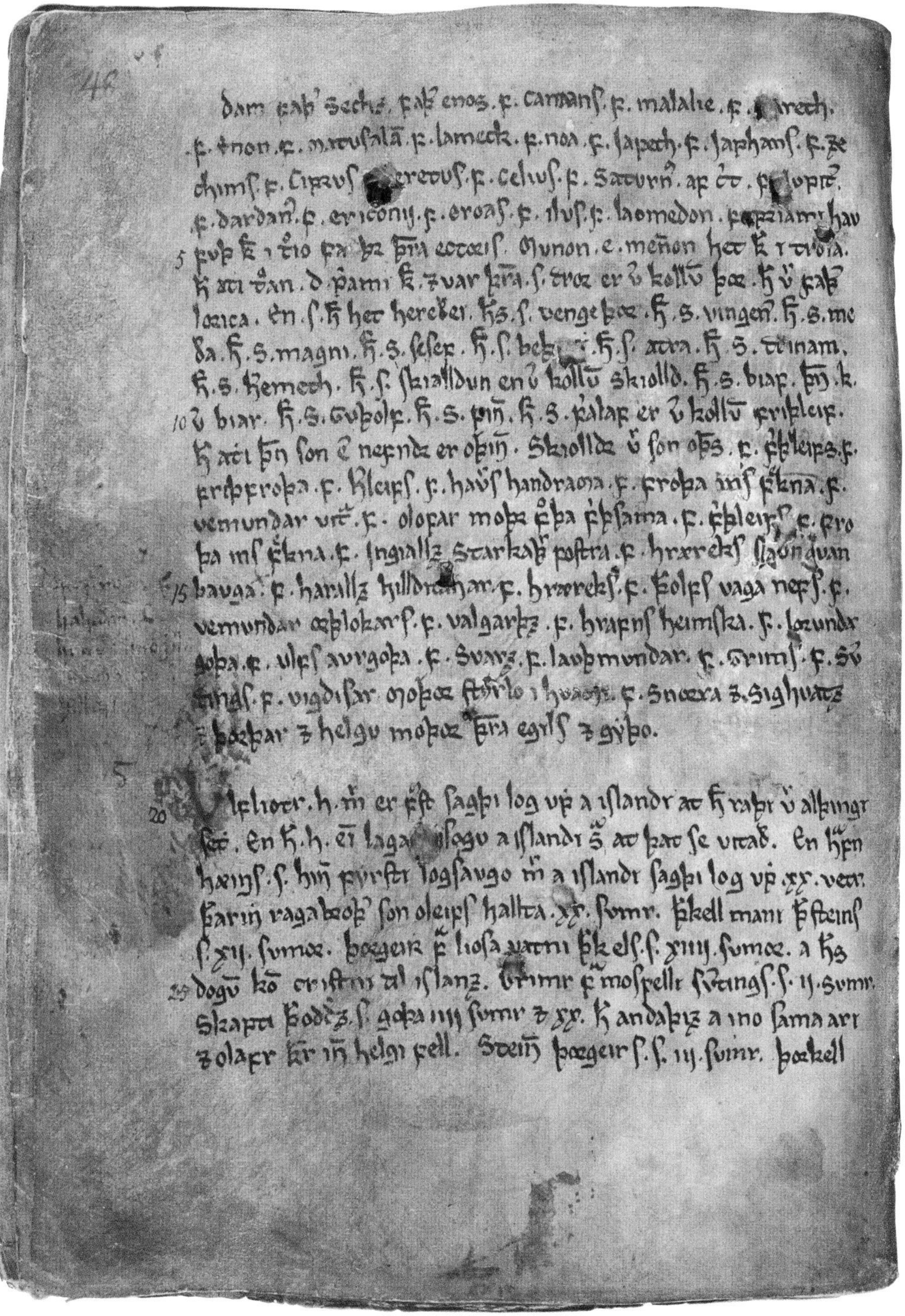

Figure 1. A folio from *Snorra-Edda* in Uppsala, Sweden (Uppsala-Edda), UUB MS DG 11, fol. 48 (25v), containing the genealogy of the Sturlungar (top of the page) and the beginning of the *Lǫgsǫgumannatal* (List of lawspeakers). Uppsala University Library. Photo: Uppsala universitetsbibliotek.

artefacts of the kind noted at Hallveig's death, and it is indeed impossible to give a clear account of how and which books were produced and enjoyed at Reykholt in the first half of the thirteenth century. The attributions of *Snorra-Edda*, *Heimskringla* and *Egils saga Skalla-Grímssonar* to Snorri depend on criteria of different value. Snorri's authorship of *Snorra-Edda* is most reliable, as he is noted as the compiler of the work in two manuscripts from around 1300, Codex Upsaliensis and AM 748 I b4to which contains *Skáldskaparmál* in association with Óláfr Þórðarson's *Þriðja málfræðiritgerðin* (Third Grammatical Treatise).[5] Snorri is not referred to as the author of *Heimskringla* in any of the manuscripts of the work, but in *Óláfs saga Tryggvasonar in mesta* it is noted five times that he wrote kings' sagas.[6] His authorship of *Egils saga Skalla-Grímssonar* is inconclusive and not based on any medieval sources, even though it is likely that the saga originated in a milieu equally preoccupied with skaldic poetry and the history of the Mýramenn who were among the forefathers of Snorri's family, the Sturlungar.[7]

The manuscript history of Snorri's works, such as *Snorra-Edda* and *Heimskringla*, does not bring us closer to Snorri's milieu or the *scriptorium* at Reykholt in the four first decades of the thirteenth century, but rather to the time when the manuscripts were written and read. The oldest manuscripts of the *Edda* date from around 1300 and the complete text of *Heimskringla* has come down to us in sixteenth- and seventeenth-century copies of the two known medieval manuscripts, Jǫfraskinna (*c.* 1300) and the Kringla manuscript (*c.* 1260) which perished except for one leaf of Kringla in the fire of Copenhagen in 1728. Parts of the text of *Heimskringla* are in Frísbók (Codex Frisianus) Eirspennill and AM 39 fol (see the section entitled *Heimskringla* below). The writers and editors of these manuscripts disclose their social and cultural disposition by editing and rewriting the text of *Snorra-Edda* and *Heimskringla*. This is also true of other works written by Snorri's immediate literary circle, during and after his lifetime, such as Sturla Þórðarson's version of *Landnámabók* (The Book of Settlements) and his *Hákonar saga Hákonarsonar* (The Saga of King Hákon Hákonarson) and Óláfr *hvítaskáld* Þórðarson's *Þriðja málfræðiritgerðin*. The earliest complete manuscripts of these seminal works differ among themselves

5   Also called *Málskrúðsfræði Óláfs hvítaskálds Þórðarsonar*. Guðrún Nordal 2001, 42–72.
6   Ólafur Halldórsson 1979, 123–127.
7   Sigurður Nordal 1933, lxx–xcv.

in their rendering of the texts, and each manuscript preserves *de facto* a new edition of the respective works. The originals of Snorri's works may be lost, but the manuscript transmission indicates an active and continuous interest in the works he is thought to have left behind. The vitality and importance of the works attributed to him for the following generations are also revealed by a readiness of the audience in the thirteenth and fourteenth centuries to reinterpret and rewrite his works in light of shifting social, political and cultural requirements. It is this vibrant legacy that will be explored in this article.

Skaldic Poetry

Snorri Sturluson's literary activity is anchored in skaldic verse-making, the study of skaldic poetics and the application of the verse in saga writing. He was not only an accomplished poet but had at his command the corpus of court poetry from the ninth century to his own day. Snorri and his learned community are responsible for transmitting about one sixth of the preserved skaldic corpus, which is the greater part of the respected skaldic canon of the Kings' Sagas and *Snorra-Edda*.[8] The mapping of the corpus in *Snorra-Edda* and *Heimskringla* was achieved in the first half of the thirteenth century and was for the most part reproduced unchanged in the ensuing tradition of royal historiography and skaldic poetics until the end of the fourteenth century.

The impetus for writing *Heimskringla* and *Snorra-Edda* must have lain in the turbulent political environment in Norway in the first decades of the thirteenth century. The writing of *Heimskringla* coincides with a time of violent internal strife between the contenders for the Norwegian throne resulting in the accession of Hákon Hákonarson to the throne in 1217 at the tender age of 13 (modern Norwegian Håkon Håkonsson, Håkon IV). After more than twenty years of sharing his power with his father-in-law Earl (later Duke) Skúli Bárðarson (modern Norwegian Skule Bårdsson), Hákon consolidated his sole rule of the country on Skúli's death in 1240, taking his royal splendour to its greatest height with his coronation by the Pope's cardinal in 1247. The prologue to *Heimskringla* does not state that the work was written for the king or Earl Skúli, even

8   See the website on skaldic poetry: http://www.abdn.ac.uk/skaldic/db.php.

though a royal or noble patronage of either the king or the earl is highly
likely for a work of such political significance. Snorri's *Háttatal*, preserved
as the third part of *Snorra-Edda*, may be of assistance here. The 102-stanza
long *clavis metrica*, accompanied by a learned commentary, is clearly
composed in honour of both Hákon and Skúli, indeed favouring Skúli.[9]

Theodoricus monachus in his *Historia de Antiquitate Regum Norwagiensium* (The History of the Kings of Norway, 1177–1188) and Saxo
Grammaticus in *Gesta Danorum* (The Deeds of the Danes, *c.* 1200) both
noted that the Icelanders preserved a wealth of knowledge of the past,
which could be used to inform their Latin chronicles, but these oral riches
were without value in a historical context unless they could be converted
into transferable goods in the new textual culture. Snorri Sturluson and
his contemporaries succeeded in transferring the five-hundred-year
long oral indigenous skaldic tradition into a highly charged political and
literary vehicle in the kings' sagas. This was achieved by using skaldic
verse as the bridge between the oral traditions of the past and classical
learning in the schools, between oral storytelling and royal chronicle
writing. The authorization of skaldic verse through royal chronology and
the classical grammatical method seems to have been accepted by writers
and audience alike throughout the thirteenth century.

The encoding of skaldic verse in the Kings' Sagas in the first half of
the thirteenth century served at least three ends:

(1) To solidify the Icelanders' position, of men like Snorri and his milieu,
    as the carriers of the unique skaldic tradition and the collective
    memory of the Scandinavian past.
(2) To authenticate the verse, of pagan and Christian origin, as a foun-
    dation for the writing of royal vernacular historiography, according
    to the classical model of chronicle writing elsewhere in Europe (e.g.
    Geoffrey of Monmouth's *Historia Regum Britanniae* (History of the
    Kings of Britain).
(3) To serve as a prerequisite for the authorization of Hákon's family's
    claim to the throne and the mythologization of his royal lineage.

All these goals were as important for the Norwegian courts as for the
upwardly mobile Icelandic chieftaincy in the early thirteenth century. The

9   Guðrún Nordal 1992, 58–62.

interlacing of the verse by Icelandic poets in the sagas of the Norwegian kings, with whom a number of Icelandic chieftains at the time claimed kinship, was furthermore a highly political act. The translation of the verse from oral transmission to written texts coincided with the first visible attempts of the Icelandic aristocracy at cutting out a niche for themselves at the court in Norway and it was skaldic poetry that gave them the most significant advantage at the political and literary level in Norway. It was no coincidence that political recognition followed on the heels of a significant cultural breakthrough.[10]

Snorri Sturluson forcefully made this claim at the Norwegian court and he did not merely use the court poetry of his fellow countrymen as the key to opening doors at the court, but sent his own poems to Norway as a young man to further his own reputation. Icelandic court poets had not belonged to the highest strata of Icelandic society in the preceding centuries, but Snorri, at his most prolific as a poet and a writer, was one of the most powerful chieftains in Iceland. His poetic and literary skills were the weapons with which he fought his way to the top. Snorri was preoccupied with Norway all his life, and by Norway we mean the Norwegian aristocratic milieu, the court, the earls and the king himself. Long before his first journey abroad in 1218, probably in his formative years at Oddi before 1200 where he was fostered by Jón Loftsson (also Loptsson), a man who claimed direct kinship with the Norwegian royal house, he sent a now-lost poem to King Sverrir Sigurðarson (modern Norwegian Sverre Sigurdsson). Some argue that this was a memorial poem sent after Sverrir's death in 1202, but it could just as likely have been sent to Norway during Sverrir's reign. Some years later he bequeathed a poem, also lost, to Earl Hákon *galinn* (literally, "frantic") Sverrir's nephew and a contender to the throne, and received precious gifts from Norway in return: a shield, a sword and armour, a complete knightly outfit, as well as a laudatory stanza by the court poet Máni, known from *Sverris saga*. The icing on the cake was a generous invitation to stay with Hákon *galinn*. In 1217, Snorri marched into the terrain at *Alþingi* with six hundred (or seven hundred and twenty) men, and among those were eighty Norwegians carrying shields.[11] Where

---

10 On the poetry of the aristocratic elite in Iceland in the thirteenth century, see Guðrún Nordal 2001, 138–141.

11 *Sturlunga saga* I (1946), 269; *Sturlunga saga* I (1988), 254. The number of men depends on whether the author is using "hundred" as large hundreds, 10 x 12 (where 120 equals hundred), or 10 x 10 (where 100 equals hundred). See also pp. 41–42 in this book.

did they and their costly armour come from? Why did Snorri maintain such a large Norwegian following in Iceland in the period before his first known journey to Norway? On this same occasion, it is noted that he called his booth *Grýla*, the same name that is associated with a part of The Saga of King Sverrir Sigurðarson, *Sverris saga*.[12] These glimpses into Snorri's life are important clues to his disposition towards the court and courtly life before he arrived in Norway in 1218. The young Snorri was already eagerly imitating foreign aristocratic models in Iceland, and thirsty for the royal recognition he enjoyed as a mature man.

Skáldatal is one of the most valuable sources for the social aspirations of Snorri and his literary milieu in Norway. In this list we find poets from the ninth century to the end of the thirteenth listed alongside their royal and aristocratic patrons. It is not merely a catalogue of poets, but primarily a list of successive kings and earls of Scandinavia, and therefore a sign of the context in which skaldic verse was placed at this time. It is a list of poets who composed for kings and earls, exactly those poets whom Snorri Sturluson regarded as the most trustworthy sources in his prologue to *Heimskringla*. There are even clear textual echoes between the prologue of *Heimskringla* and sections in *Skáldatal*.[13]

The transmission of *Skáldatal* furthermore underscores its cultural significance and centrality in the transmission history of Snorri's works. The list is preserved in, or in conjunction with, two of Snorri's key texts, in Codex Upsaliensis of *Snorra-Edda* and in the Kringla manuscript of *Heimskringla* (now only preserved in seventeenth-century copies, except for one leaf). These two manuscripts merit our special attention, and will be discussed below. The list notes that Snorri not only composed poetry for King Sverrir, Earl Hákon *galinn*, King Hákon and Earl Skúli (later Duke), but also for King Ingi Bárðarson (Inge Bårdsson). Snorri is blatantly using skaldic poetry for his own political ends in Norway. He is composing eulogies for all of the main contenders for the throne among the Birkibeinar at the beginning of the thirteenth century, and sending them with carriers to Norway since he did not travel abroad until 1218, a year after King Hákon came to the throne.

Sturlunga saga furthermore notes the poem *Andvaka* composed for

---

12   The name Grýla for the first part of *Sverris saga*, seems to mean that which frightens people without good reason, see Þorleifur Hauksson 2007, lvi. See also p. 42 in this book.

13   Guðrún Nordal 2001, 123–124.

Kristín, Earl Hákon *galinn*'s wife. Snorri delivered the poem in person in the summer of 1219, when he travelled to see her and her then husband Áskell (modern Eskil), lawman in Western Götland in Sweden.[14] Kristín gave him a remarkable gift in return, which may indicate that he was not rewarded solely for his poetry, but that Snorri's accomplishments in relation to historical writing were well known to her at this early time: "Hon gaf honum merki þat, er átt hafði Eiríkr Svíakonungr Knútsson. Þat hafði hann þá er hann felldi Sörkvi konung á Gestilsreini".[15] Why would she give him such a symbolic gift? Perhaps she was encouraging him not only to write sagas of the kings of Norway, but also to write the history of the Swedish royal line up to then?

Sturla Þórðarson cites Snorri's occasional stanzas in *Sturlunga saga*, and four further references are made to his verse in the grammatical treatises and a fourteenth-century version of *Skáldskaparmál* which are fragments of religious verse and love stanzas. Snorri clearly composed his verse for different audiences: for the royal courts in Norway as well as for his personal and political ends in Iceland. The same is true of his nephews, Óláfr *hvítaskáld* and Sturla, and his son-in-law Gizurr Þorvalds-son. These three men from Snorri's close circle followed in his footsteps in Norway, embracing the indigenous tradition of skaldic verse-making and thereby emulating Snorri's striking success at the courts of Hákon and Skúli. Gizurr Þorvaldsson's first wife was Ingibjǫrg, the daughter of Snorri, and he was therefore in Snorri's inner circle for at least eight years (1224–*c*.1232), during a very creative period at Reykholt. Gizurr and Ingibjǫrg parted in or just after 1232, and it is not known whether she married again or when she died. Ingibjǫrg is the only one of Snorri's children to be noted in the *Reykjaholtsmáldagi* as the donor of some calf skins.[16] Gizurr is listed as a poet of King Hákon Hákonarson in *Skáldatal*, even though his verse is ignored in *Hákonar saga Hákonarsonar* by Sturla Þórðarson, except for one casual stanza.

Óláfr *hvítaskáld*, the slightly elder brother of Sturla, both sons of Þórðr Sturluson, Snorri's brother, is cited in *Skáldatal* in association with King

---

14 See a map in this book, p. 93.

15 "She gave him the emblem which Eiríkr Knútsson, the king of Swedes, had owned. He had it when he killed King Sørkvir at Gestilsrein" (*Sturlunga saga* I (1946), 272; *Sturlunga saga* I (1988), 257, has Gestilsreyni). Translated by GN. See also pp. 93–94 in this book.

16 *Reykjaholtsmáldagi*, 14.

Hákon Hákonarson, Duke Skúli Bárðarson, the young Hákon Hákonarson
and Earl Knútr Hákonarson in Norway. Óláfr is, however, the only man
in Snorri's close circle who sought royal recognition for his poetry outside
Norway. He is noted as the poet of King Eiríkr of Sweden and King
Valdimarr of Denmark, and it is known that he spent a winter at the court
of Valdimarr in 1240/41. Valdimarr's court had close ties with European
aristocracy in the early part of the thirteenth century, as is clear from his
marriages to two European princesses, Margarethe of Bohemia (known
as Queen Dagmar) and Berengária of Portugal. Óláfr Þórðarson may have
been inspired to adapt Donat's *Ars maior* to the Icelandic skaldic tradition
when he was in Denmark, and it is of some significance that he refers to
the Danish king by name in *Þriðja málfræðiritgerðin*. The reference to the
king in the treatise suggests that Óláfr took part in a learned debate at the
court about issues of writing with runes. Moreover, Óláfr is noted as an
important source in the section on King Valdimarr's death in *Knýtlinga
saga*, the saga of the Danish kings, before the author lists Valdimarr's own
children. Óláfr's authorship of *Knýtlinga saga* has been strongly argued by
Bjarni Guðnason; he clearly had a hand in its creation.[17]

King Hákon's court in Norway not only focused on patronizing the
writing of Kings' Sagas and the composition of indigenous skaldic poetry
in the first decades of the thirteenth century. The king actively sought to
extend its literary boundaries and fostered the translation of courtly romances, starting in the 1220s with the translation of *Tristan* from French.
The coronation in 1247 reveals that he was building a strong European
monarchy. He actively enlarged his kingdom and sought a husband for
his daughter Kristín in Spain. New literary impulses from Europe were
therefore at play when Óláfr was in Norway.[18] It is obviously impossible
to speculate about the literary influences on Óláfr during his time in
Scandinavia, except to evaluate the characteristics of his textual output.
His works belong to the same categories as Snorri's and Sturla's, yet they
are strikingly different. He writes a saga about the Danish kings, adapts
a popular Latin textbook into Icelandic, and composes not only court
poetry, but a poem about St Þorlákr and Aron Hjǫrleifsson, an adversary
of his nephew, Sturla Sighvatsson; Aron made a famous pilgrimage to
Jerusalem.

17   Bjarni Guðnason 1982, clxxix–clxxxiv.
18   Larrington 2009.

In Óláfr's hands, Snorri's legacy, the poetic skills used for the benefit of kings and clergy alike, the writing of a saga for the kings of Denmark and the scholastic study of Norse poetics, blossomed and was furthermore brought into new contexts. He was the finest poet of the three kinsmen (the others Snorri and Sturla), his adaptation of Donat's textbook in the *Þriðja málfræðiritgerðin* reveals an imaginative scholar in command of the scholastic and indigenous tradition and the reference to him in the epilogue of *Knýtlinga saga* shows that he was not only in command of historical knowledge of the western Nordic region, but also of Danish history. Óláfr established a school upon his return to Iceland and the choice of Stafholt, where Snorri had lived for three years, or so, reveals Óláfr's strong relationship with Snorri.

Sturla Þórðarson's career abroad, on the other hand, was more inward looking and focused on Norway and the Norwegian court. Sturla is not known to have travelled to Norway until 1263, when the Sturlungar had lost their powerbase in the west of Iceland. He travelled to Norway to seek a royal hearing after the Sturlungars' defeat. Sturla never met King Hákon or Duke Skúli, but was commissioned by King Magnús to write *Hákonar saga Hákonarsonar* and the now lost *Magnúss saga lagabœtis* (The Saga of King Magnús Lawmender). He composed poems about King Hákon, as is amply manifest in his saga of the king, but also for King Magnús and Duke Skúli even though those poems are now lost.

Snorri's nephews enjoyed considerable success as court poets, and it is of interest that both brothers, like Snorri, wrote or are associated with writing chronicles for royal patrons in Scandinavia. They furthermore modelled themselves on their uncle in their proficiency in legal matters; both held the position of lawspeaker in Iceland (Óláfr from 1248 to 1250, and 1252; Sturla in 1251), and Sturla, served as a lawman from 1272 to 1282. These men clearly moved in the highest political circles in Scandinavia, and their social eminence was generated by their poetic, literary and legal skills, which they used strategically in the service of royal patrons in Scandinavia.

Prose

Snorri moved to Reykholt in Reykholtsdalr from Borg, at the beginning of the thirteenth century and lived there until his violent death on

September 23 1241, with the exception of the time he lived at Stafholt
(1221–1224/5). The Reykholt estate remained in the hands of his family
for most of the thirteenth century. His only surviving legitimate sibling,
his sister Helga Sturludóttir, was his primary heir as his living children
were illegitimate (see fig. 2). She, however, transferred the farm over to
Snorri's illegitimate son Órækja shortly after Snorri's death. Órækja died
in 1245, and Egill, the son of Helga, and Helga's husband Sǫlmundr, a
Norwegian of unknown descent, later held the estate.

Snorri Sturluson was perhaps imitating his royal friends in Norway
by creating a cultural and learned centre at Reykholt. Even though there
is no evidence that Snorri ran a formal school at Reykholt, the possibility
cannot be excluded that he emulated the school at Oddi, run by his
foster-father Jón Loftsson, by setting up a teaching milieu at Reykholt.
Styrmir *fróði* Kárason, the Augustinian prior and writer, was clearly
known for his learning, as were Snorri's two nephews, Sturla and Óláfr
hvítaskáld. It is unlikely that it is merely a chance of transmission that
the two most famous textbooks of the thirteenth century, *Snorra-Edda*
and *Þriðja málfræðiritgerðin* are linked to Snorri at Reykholt and Óláfr
at Stafholt.

Snorri's prose and poetic productions, as well as those of his learned
collaborators, reveal their efforts in creating and presenting the history
of Iceland as a prolongation of or a parallel to the history of Norway
and the history of the Scandinavian kings. The list of known works
attributed to Snorri and other writers in his cultural milieu is impressive:
Landnámabók (Styrmir Kárason and Sturla Þórðarson), *Íslendinga saga*
(Sturla Þórðarson), and possibly *Kristni saga* (Sturla Þórðarson), *Sturlu
saga* (sometimes attributed to Snorri), and most likely some of the early
sagas of Icelanders (such as *Egils saga Skalla-Grímssonar*, *Eyrbyggja saga* and
Laxdæla saga), *Heimskringla* (Snorri Sturluson), the now lost *Lífssaga Óláfs
helga* (The Life of St Óláfr (Styrmir Kárason),[19] *Sverris saga* (possibly
linked to Styrmir in *Flateyjarbók*), *Hákonar saga Hákonarsonar* (Sturla
Þórðarson), *Magnúss saga lagabœtis* (Sturla Þórðarson) and *Knýtlinga saga*
(Óláfr Þórðarson). These sagas were not all written during Snorri's
lifetime, but were inspired by the cultural manifesto set by this strong
literary community.

19 St Óláfr is King Óláfr Haraldsson, later Óláfr *helgi* (the Saint), modern Norwegian
    Olav *den hellige*, also called Óláfr *digri* (the Stout).

Styrmir was respected for his learning, but none of his works have survived. The writer of *Flateyjarbók* refers to Styrmir's Saga of St Óláfr, but only a handful of lines, the so-called *Articuli*, have been preserved.[20] Styrmir's name is noted in a manuscript of *Sverris saga* though it is not clear if he was directly involved in writing it. Styrmir is best known for his now lost version of *Landnámabók*, the so-called *Styrmisbók*, which could have been written at Reykholt under the patronage of Snorri Sturluson. In the view of the known writers of *Landnámabók*, it is highly likely that Snorri, a politician eager for recognition in Norway, would have had an invested interest in the documentation of the Norwegian origin of the settlers of Iceland. Styrmir's codex clearly remained in the possession of members of the Sturlungar family. Haukr Erlendsson notes that Sturla Þórðarson relied on *Styrmisbók* in his version of *Landnámabók*, which in turn was the source for Haukr's redaction of *Landnámabók*.

Interest in the settlement, a strong legal career in Norway and writing skills went hand in hand in the ensuing generations. It is of note that all three preserved medieval versions of *Landnámabók*, *Sturlubók*, *Melabók* and *Hauksbók*, are attributed to three Icelandic men in the post-Commonwealth period who have a similar profile to Snorri. They are lawmen who therefore had a strong relationship with Norway: Sturla Þórðarson, Snorri Markússon at Melar (who was a lawman and died in 1313) and Haukr Erlendsson (d. 1334). Only *Hauksbók* is preserved in its original manuscript from the beginning of the fourteenth century. A fragment is all that remains of a late fourteenth-century manuscript of *Melabók*; the text is otherwise preserved in seventeenth-century paper copies. *Sturlubók*, the version by Sturla Þórðarson, is only preserved in a seventeenth-century copy of a manuscript from around 1400. The writing of *Landnámabók* at this late time clearly reflects an interest of members of the Icelandic aristocratic elite in the late thirteenth and the fourteenth centuries in arguing for close ties between Iceland and Norway, the old homeland for many of the settlers, now the seat of the king when Iceland became a part of the Norwegian kingdom (from 1262 to 1264). The oldest sagas of Icelanders, some of which have been linked to the Sturlungar milieu such as the Skalds' Sagas and possibly *Laxdæla saga* and *Eyrbyggja saga*, also reflect a strong interest in telling the classical tale of the settlement of Iceland from Norway.[21]

Literary Heritage

The cultural artefacts left to us by the inhabitants of Reykholt in the thirteenth and early fourteenth centuries are scarce, as is clear from the recent excavations at the medieval estate, but perhaps we may tentatively add Codex Upsaliensis to the list, one of the main manuscripts of *Snorra-Edda*, written somewhere between 1300 and 1325. We cannot name its first owner, nor do we know its patron, but the manuscript is associated with the descendants of Snorri's legitimate sister, Helga Sturludóttir (see fig. 2).

The dimensions of Codex Upsaliensis are small, roughly fourteen centimetres by twenty centimetres. The layout is straightforward, one main text neatly written throughout. The scribe concludes his work in the middle of Snorri Sturluson's *Háttatal* on fol. 56r, and thus breaks off the poem even though he has enough vellum at his disposal. There is room for figurative drawings in the margins or on blank parts of vellum pages; of a knight, women and men dancing, some in contrived positions. These images are thought to originate in the fourteenth century, later than the original hand, although this is by no means certain.[22] Rubrics are used in headings, as is customary in *Snorra-Edda* manuscripts, particularly in *Skáldskaparmál*.

The manuscript evidence is the strongest indicator of the way texts were contextualized in the thirteenth and fourteenth centuries, and the manuscripts of *Snorra-Edda* highlight the relationship between *Snorra-Edda*, skaldic verse and grammatical treatises in Icelandic textual culture in a society that otherwise did not leave behind much evidence about its educational system. *Snorra-Edda* is found in Codex Upsaliensis as a compilation of its four principal components, *Prologus*, *Gylfaginning*, *Skáldskaparmál*, *Háttatal*, and in conjunction with *Ǫnnur málfræðiritgerðin* (The Second Grammatical Treatise). The text of *Skáldskaparmál* is

---

21   Guðrún Nordal 2001, 50–55. Guðrún Nordal 2013, 203–207.
22   Aðalheiður Guðmundsdóttir 2012.

furthermore interlaced with three lists: the *Skáldatal*, *Lǫgsǫgumannatal* and the genealogy of the Sturlungar.

Codex Upsaliensis is exceptional as being the only manuscript to refer to Snorri Sturluson as the person who put the whole of *Snorra-Edda* together: "Hana hefir saman setta Snorri Sturluson eptir þeim hætti sem hér er skipað".[23] The heading at the beginning of the manuscript not only mentions Snorri's name but alludes to the tripartite structure of the *Edda* – while not mentioning the other additional material:

1. The stories of the æsir and Ymir.
2. The explanation of the "skáldskapar mál ok heiti margra hluta" ("the poetic diction and the names for many things") in *Skáldskaparmál*.
3. Snorri's *Háttatal*.

The phrase used for Snorri's authorship is to "setja saman" (put together) i.e., this is a compilation. This is the same phrase used in *Sturlunga saga* of Snorri's saga writing.[24] A similar reference is found in the A manuscript of *Snorra-Edda*, which only contains a redaction of *Skáldskaparmál*: "[sem] Snorri hefir síðan samanfœra látit".[25] The clause in Codex Upsaliensis may indicate that there existed an earlier version of the *Edda*, before Snorri's time.

The components of *Snorra-Edda* are entered in the traditional order, that of *Prologus*, *Gylfaginning*, *Skáldskaparmál* and *Háttatal*.[26] The two school book parts, *Skáldskaparmál* and *Háttatal*, however, are placed in a different context from that of the most widely used manuscript of *Snorra-Edda*, Codex Regius. The edition of *Skáldskaparmál* fits a particular chronological, social and cultural framework, infiltrated by three highly political and socially charged lists which place *Skáldskaparmál* in a new context, partly emphasizing status in Icelandic society and partly looking for cultural associations in Norway in particular. Snorri Sturluson's *Háttatal* is also placed in a wider learned European context of the school book, by linking it to *Ǫnnur málfrœðiritgerðin*. The most persuasive evidence for the interrelationship between the study of skaldic poetics

---

23 "Snorri Sturluson has put it together in the way in which it is presented here" (*Uppsala-Edda*, 152). See Jan de Vries 1967, 215–216.

24 *Sturlunga saga* I (1946), 342; *Sturlunga saga* I (1988), 329.

25 "[which] Snorri later had collected together" (*Edda Snorra Sturlusonar*, 427–428).

26 See a discussion of the manuscript in Heimir Pálsson 2012.

and *grammatica* in Iceland are the manuscripts that place *Snorra-Edda* alongside the grammatical treatises. Through a codicological analysis of the manuscripts it is possible to substantiate the claim that these texts operated within the same ideological framework, at least around 1300, and that the study of skaldic verse-making was continuously being adapted to the needs of new audiences. The auxiliary material is clearly indicative of the purpose of the book and of its patrons. Let us look at the three lists more closely, the genealogy of the Sturlungar, the *Skáldatal* and the list of lawspeakers.

The Sturlungar genealogy and the list of lawspeakers in the manuscript link the Sturlungar family to the writing of *Snorra-Edda*.[27] There are striking textual similarities between the prologue to *Snorra-Edda* and the genealogy.

Prologue to *Snorra-Edda*	Sturlungar genealogy
Konungr hét Menon. Hann átti dóttur Priamuss konungs Trójam. Sonur þeirra hét Trór, er vér köllum Þór (*Uppsala-Edda*, 153).[28]	Múnon eða Mennon hét konungur í Trója, hann átti Tróan, dóttur Priami konungs, og var þeirra son Trór, er vér köllum Þór (*Uppsala-Edda,* 220).[29]

These sentences in the genealogy of the Sturlungar are probably taken from the prologue, or from a common source. The writing of genealogy was a political undertaking of the aristocracy generally in the Middle Ages, done to establish a noble mythic background for their families.[30] This genealogy moves along popular lines. The prologue begins with a reference to Adam as the forefather of all men, and then moves on to the Trojans, Priam's daughter, and Óðinn the founder of Scandinavia. By presenting their own genealogy in the middle of *Skáldskaparmál*, the Sturlungar emphatically underlined their claim to share their genealogical background with the kings of Scandinavia among others, which therefore linked them to Norway. Their genealogy in *Sturlunga saga* traces their

---

27 Finnur Jónsson 1931, xi.
28 "The King's name was Menon. He was married to Troia, the daughter of King Priamus. Their son was Trór, whom we call Þórr".
29 "The King of Troya was called Múnon or Mennon. He was married to Tróan, the daughter of King Priamus and their son was Trór, whom we call Þórr".
30 Bloch 1983, 79–83.

ancestry to Snorri *goði*, the grandson of the settler Þórólfr *Mostrarskegg* (the Inhabitant of Mostr (Moster).[31]

The story of Úlfr *inn óargi* (the Courageous), a forefather of the Sturlungar, is only found in *Skáldatal* in Codex Upsaliensis. This clause provides further substance to the genealogy and aristocratic background of this family, which is most firmly associated with the composition of skaldic poetry and writing of kings' sagas in the thirteenth century:

Úlfr inn óargi var hessir [sic] ágætur í Noregi í Naumudali, faðir Hallbjarnar hálftrölls, faðir Ketils hængs. Úlfr orti drápu á einni nótt ok sagði frá þrekvirkjum sínum. Hann var dauður fyrir dag (*Uppsala-Edda*, 219).	Úlfr the Courageous was a famous *hersir* in Norway in Naumudalr, the father of Hallbjǫrn *hálftroll*,[32] who was the father of Ketill *hœingr* (the Salmon). Úlfr composed a *drápa* overnight and recounted his deeds in it. He was dead before daybreak.

This story is not known elsewhere. Úlfr is the forefather of the Hrafn-istumenn, the Mýramenn, and therefore of the Sturlungar. This prose section relates directly to the genealogy of the Sturlungar. The reference to Úlfr is inserted before the list of the Norwegian chieftains, starting with Þorleifr *spaki* (literally, "calm" or "wise") and thus the Sturlungar family are associated with the noble chieftains in Norway.

The genealogy of Helga Sturludóttir, the sister of Snorri, concludes with her children. She was married to the Norwegian, Sǫlmundr *Aust-maðr* (the Norwayman), which adds another dimension to this side of the family. Their son Egill Sǫlmundarson (probably named after Egill Skalla-Grímsson), lived at Snorri Sturluson's former residence at Reykholt in Borgarfjǫrðr.[33] He had three sons, Jón *murti* (Small Trout) Egilsson, who is one of the court poets mentioned in *Skáldatal*, in Codex Upsaliensis (not in *Skáldatal* in the Kringla version), Þórðr *lǫgmaðr* (lawman) and the learned Þórarinn *kaggi* (the Keg), who is discussed in the section entitled *Heimskringla* below.

31 Úlfar Bragason (2010) has written on the significance of genealogy for the writing of contemporary history in *Sturlunga saga*.

32 There are several suggestions for the meaning of this nickname, such as unfriendly, dwarf, half a Sami.

33 On the arrangements after Snorri's death, his inheritance and the disposition of Reykholt see pp. 428–434 in this book.

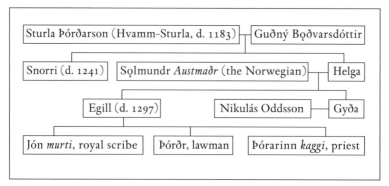

Figure 2. The family of Helga Sturludóttir and her son Egill.

The most important poets of the Sturlungar family, Snorri Sturlu-son, Sturla Þórðarson and Óláfr Þórðarson, were also lawspeakers and therefore the third list, *Lǫgsǫgumannatal* (The Register of Lawspeakers) completes the tripartite documentation of the achievements of these kinsmen.[34] On the basis of these three lists the manuscript throws into relief the three pillars on which the social status of a chieftain was based: the aristocratic lineage, closely linked to the mythic background of the Norwegian royal house, a cultural status which is exemplified in the poet's relationship with the courtly milieu abroad and Norway in particular, and a political base in the local milieu, represented by the prestigious position of the *lǫgsǫgumaðr*. Their legacy is carried forward in the careers of Helga's two grandsons, Jón *murti* and Þórðr.

Heimskringla

Of the works attributed to Snorri, *Heimskringla* is probably the one that has had the most significance in Scandinavia through the ages. The work came to the attention of scholars as early as the sixteenth century and quickly became a major source for historians both in Denmark and Sweden. The version of *Heimskringla* that can be said to have established

---

34 Krömmelbein 1992, 123, made a case for the association of these three aspects of the aristocrat's identity (the lineage, poet and lawspeaker) with Snorri Sturluson only, but I think they relate more likely to his descendants who may have instigated the writing of Codex Upsaliensis.

the work is Kringla. All textual restorations, complete editions and translations are based on this manuscript. Moreover, Stefán Karlsson has presented a reasoned hypothesis that links Kringla with Reykholt. There is therefore good reason to draw particular attention to this manuscript here.

Traditionally, *Heimskringla* has been firmly linked with Snorri Sturluson. Both in editions of the work and in literary histories, Snorri is unequivocally presented as the author of *Heimskringla*. This attribution of authorship may be correct, at least to an extent, although there is no certain evidence for it. The claim should at least be qualified somewhat. In this connection, the redaction of *Heimskringla* also deserves discussion. The work was not originally written as a continuous whole, as we know it today. Thus, it cannot be taken for granted that it was all written by the same author. Let us first establish that *Heimskringla* was passed down to posterity as anonymous literature, just like all Old Norse saga literature dealing with a distant past. Latin chronicles are often attributed to an author, as with *Historia Norwegiae* or Oddr Snorrason's *Óláfs saga Tryggvasonar*. *Sverris saga* or *Hákonar saga Hákonarsonar* deal with the author's own time and recent past, and that is perhaps why they have been regarded as works of personal authorship. When the subject matter is in the distant past, the author must rely on the accounts of others, on poetry and oral tradition. Then it seems that there is no tradition in Old Norse literature for linking the work to an author, even though the creative effort involved in creating the text could be considerable.

It is therefore just as one would expect that no clear attribution of authorship has been passed down in any *Heimskringla* manuscript. Nevertheless, Snorri's name was linked to the work at an early date. It occurred first in Laurents Hanssøn's saga translation (1551),[35] and then in the published edition of Peder Claussøn's saga translation (1633). Laurents Hanssøn's translation was only published much later (in 1899 by Gustav Storm) and has therefore no significant history of influence. In the 1633 edition, the attribution of authorship was added by the editor, Ole Worm. It is unlikely that this was found in the original, but rather that Worm has taken the information from another Peder Claussøn manuscript, *Norrigis Bescriffuelse* (Description of Norway), that Worm had published a year

35 AM 93 fol.

earlier (1632).[36] Thus, both Peder Claussøn and Laurents Hanssøn knew about the attribution of authorship, without there being any indication that Peder was familiar with Laurents's translation. These two facts must be seen as the strongest arguments for attributing authorship to Snorri.

Finnur Jónsson and Gustav Storm were convinced that Laurents Hanssøn had found details of authorship in the prologue of the Kringla manuscript, a prologue that had supposedly then been lost shortly afterwards. However, we have no evidence of the existence of such a prologue. In an article in *Skírnir* in 1955, Jakob Benediktsson[37] showed that Laurents Hanssøn probably did not use Kringla at all for his translation. Furthermore, the independence of the two instances of attribution has been questioned. According to Jørgensen it seems unlikely that any of the *Heimskringla* manuscripts was the source of the information, but that it has come from references to Snorri in other works,[38] and that it became known in Bergen circles in Laurents Hanssøn's time. Peder Claussøn may have found the information in papers he acquired from his mentor Jon Simonssøn. Jon Simonssøn was active in humanist circles in Bergen before becoming a magistrate (*lagmann*) in Agder, Peder's home county.

Although there is no conclusive evidence for attributing *Heimskringla* to Snorri, there are some good reasons. The question was first examined systematically by Gustav Storm and his arguments were judiciously supplemented and reviewed by Ólafur Halldórsson.[39] In *Sturlunga saga* a brief mention is made of Snorri putting together historical works,[40] while other sagas (*Óláfs saga Tryggvasonar en mesta* (The Great Saga of Óláfr Tryggvason), *Orkneyinga saga*) refer to a work of saga literature that Snorri is considered the author of, and that matches *Heimskringla*. We can sum up this overview by saying that *Heimskringla* is in principle anonymous literature and that no direct attribution of authorship has been preserved. However, we know that Snorri wrote such literature – or had it written for him – and there is good reason to believe that it is *Heimskringla* that is referred to.

Heimskringla is familiar to us as a work of Kings' Sagas that starts with *Ynglinga saga* and then deals with the kings of Norway in chronological

---

36 *Norriges oc omliggende Øers sandfærdige Bescriffuelse.*
37 Jakob Benediktsson 1955, 123–124.
38 Jørgensen 1995, 54–59.
39 Storm 1873; Ólafur Halldórsson 1979.
40 *Sturlunga saga* I (1946), 342.

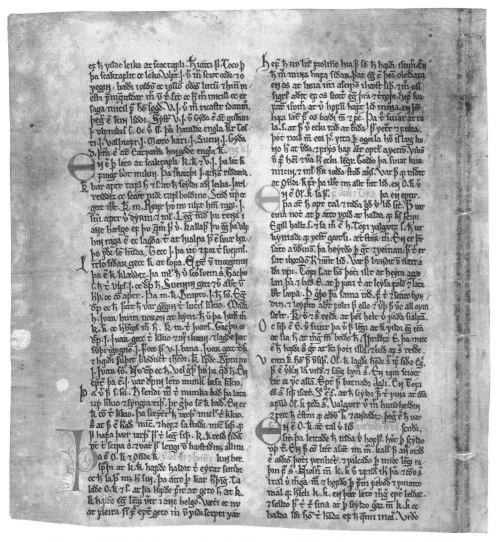

Figure 3. The Kringla leaf. Lbs frg 82 1v. The only folio preserved from the manuscript Kringla. The text is from *Óláfs saga helga* (the Saga of St Óláfr Haraldsson). National and University Library of Iceland. Photo: Helgi Bragason.

order, from Halfdan *svarti* (the Black) up to and including Magnús Erlingsson. The account of Magnús's life, incidentally, does not continue up to his death. It ends after the Battle of Re in 1177, where *Sverris saga* begins. At the core of *Heimskringla* is *Óláfs saga helga*, which comprises about a third of the whole work. The sagas before this saga of St Óláfr constitute the first third, and the sagas after him the last third. This tripartite division is clearly reflected in the transmission of the work. Among the manuscripts containing parts of *Heimskringla* there are few (if any) that share the same redaction. Kringla and Jǫfraskinna contain all three parts. The same goes for Peder Claussøn's translation, but this may be based on different text sources. These three versions all have differing redactions of *Óláfs saga helga*. Frísbók (Codex Frisianus) and the fragmentarily preserved AM 39 folio contain the first and the last third, while Eirspennill and Gullinskinna only contain the last. The three main parts of *Heimskringla* turn out to have separate histories of transmission. On this basis Jonna Louis-Jensen has questioned whether the various redactions come from a single, common original.[41] She cogently argues against the existence of such a common original, suggesting that the parts were edited together in various ways at a later date.

A simple observation that clearly confirms Louis-Jensen's conclusion is the way St Óláfr's (Olav's) miracles are edited into *Heimskringla* III. At the end of *Óláfs saga helga in sérstaka* (The Separate Saga of St Óláfr) there is a collection of miracles. These are said to have taken place at various points in time after the saint king's death. When Saint Óláfr's Saga was edited into a new whole and followed by *Heimskringla* III, the editor was obliged by chronology to do something about these miracles. He either had to delete them or distribute them in *Heimskringla* III where they belong chronologically. This editing was done differently in the various manuscripts that contain *Heimskringla* III. Kringla is the only manuscript to include all the miracles.[42] Thus, there are good reasons to believe that *Heimskringla* as we know it today did not see the light of day in Snorri's *scriptorium*, but was redacted together from three main parts later. Snorri may still be the author of one, two or all the parts, but there are also other possibilities.

As mentioned, two medieval manuscripts contain all three of the main parts of *Heimskringla*. They are the Kringla manuscript (from the 1260s) and Jǫfraskinna (*c.* 1300). Both belonged to the University Library in Copenhagen and were lost in the fire of 1728. But fortunately there were good and reliable transcriptions, so the content of both codices is well known to us. Kringla has been linked to Reykholt and is in many respects the most important of all the *Heimskringla* manuscripts and is

---

41 Louis-Jensen 1997.
42 Jørgensen 2000; 2007, 94–97.

also the basis for nearly all editions of the work. For that reason we will give this manuscript particular attention here.

Kringla contains a coherent version of the work we today call *Heimskringla*. Of the main text only two leaves were missing from the first third when the book was transcribed in 1680/81 by Jón Eggertsson (Holm papp. fol. 18). When it was transcribed a few years later by Ásgeir Jónsson (AM 35, 36 and 63 fol), a leaf from *Óláfs saga helga* was also missing. But this has since been recovered (the Kringla leaf: see fig. 3 and below).

Two well-known *Heimskringla* manuscripts have included a prologue to the work: Jǫfraskinna and Frísbók. The *Heimskringla* prologue is closely related to the prologue to the great *Óláfs saga helga*, which is preserved in several manuscripts. During the time it has been known to exist, Kringla has not included a prologue. We cannot be certain if it once did. In addition to *Heimskringla*, Kringla also contained *Skáldatal*; this is included in Jón Eggertsson's transcription and also copied separately by Árni Magnússon in AM 761 a-b 4to.

In connection with his extensive editorial work on *Heimskringla* at the end of the nineteenth century, Finnur Jónsson left no stone unturned in his search for textual corroboration of *Heimskringla*. In the Royal Library in Stockholm a package was found containing five parchment leaves with text from *Óláfs saga helga*. Finnur managed to determine that four of the leaves had belonged to the Jǫfraskinna manuscript, while the fifth came from Kringla. Since the vellum books had been lost in 1728, these leaves were of enormous value as "samples". We can be certain of where the leaves belong, because they fit exactly where the transcriptions indicate lacunae in the codices. All five leaves have been described and rendered in facsimile by Finnur Jónsson.[43]

The Kringla leaf measures 23.3 to 23.5 centimetres in width and approximately 25.6 to 26.6 centimetres in height. It has been extensively trimmed at the bottom, but most likely without any text being lost. The text is beautifully written in two columns with fine, illuminated initials. Although only one leaf, it actually contains a considerable amount of text, corresponding to eight pages in the Íslenzk fornrit edition.[44] This amount of text corresponds well with the amount of text missing in the lacunae

43   Finnur Jónsson 1895.
44   *Heimskringla* II, from page 280, line 16, to page 288, line 8.

in the beginning, and it implies homogeneity. The leaf also provides valuable information concerning palaeography and orthography and gives an impression of what a magnificent manuscript this was. The amount of text on the leaf and in the lacunae provide a basis for estimating the size of the codex at between 140 and 150 leaves.[45]

The manner of the Kringla leaf's arrival in Sweden is highly suspicious. When Jón Eggertsson transcribed the text for his Swedish employers in 1681/82, it was still in place in the codex, but was probably missing in the autumn of 1682 when Tormod Torfæus took Kringla to Karmøy (Kǫrmt), for it was not in place when Ásgeir Jónsson transcribed the book for Torfæus there. In recent times the suspicion has been that Jón Eggertsson removed the leaf and sent it to Sweden as a sample of the codex. It is easy to suspect Jón, since he challenged the limitations of the law on several other occasions in his dramatic life. However, there are other suspects. One is the Swede J.G. Sparfwenfeldt who got his hands on Kringla in the spring of 1682 when he used it and Jǫfraskinna to make a transcription of *Ynglinga saga*. Whoever the thief was, we should not only forgive him, but thank him, for if the leaf had not come to Sweden it would have burned in Copenhagen. Now it is safely stored in Reykjavík in its original homeland. In 1975 the Kringla leaf was transferred to Iceland in connection with a royal visit. It is now to be found in the National and University Library of Iceland with the signature Lbs frg 82. In this connection Stefán Karlsson wrote a comprehensive essay about Kringla in which he addresses the origins and age of the vellum manuscript.[46]

The text of Kringla gives a fairly certain *terminus post quem* for the manuscript when it mentions that Emperor Frederick "nú var keisari i Rúmaborg" (now was emperor in Rome), where "var" (was) is a variant of the more authentic *er* (is). This implies that Kringla must have been written after Frederick's death in 1250.[47] In addition, Gizurr Þorvaldsson is referred to as "earl", a title he first gained in 1258. An indication of a *terminus ante quem* is to be found in *Skáldatal*. Here Sturla Þórðarson is not included among King Magnús Hákonarson's skalds, despite the fact that he wrote a poem about Magnús in 1263. He is, however, mentioned among King Hákon Hákonarson's skalds. Stefán Karlsson thus concludes with a fairly precise dating of 1263/64, believing that Sturla's poem

---

45   Jørgensen 2007, 39–40.
46   Stefán Karlsson 1977.
47   Storm 1873, 203.

about Hákon was composed no earlier than spring 1263. He supposes that Kringla must have been written shortly before Sturla's poem about Magnús became known in Iceland.[48]

Stefán Karlsson went one step further in his shrewd description of Kringla. By suggesting a possible scribe he links the manuscript directly to Reykholt. His hypothesis cannot be said to have been confirmed. It presupposes a number of uncertain conclusions, but as conjecture it is perfectly plausible. Stefán confirms the earlier assumption that the Kringla scribe is identical with the scribe of the main part of the law manuscript *Staðarhólsbók* (AM 334 fol). Furthermore, he links *Staðarhólsbók* to the Sturlungar through a bill dating from between 1330 and 1340,[49] which is entered in the book. Here the name Benedikt is mentioned, identified (tentatively) as Benedikt Kolbeinsson (d. 1379). One of his forefathers was Þórarinn *kaggi* (d. 1283), who in *Laurentius' saga* is referred to as "klerkr góðr ok hinn mesti nytsemðamaðr til letrs ok bókagjörða sem enn mega auðsýnaz margar bækr sem hann hefir skrifat Hólakirkju ok svá Vallastað".[50] Þórarinn was the illegitimate son of Egill Sǫlmundarson, Snorri's nephew and heir, who lived at Reykholt (see fig. 2). Stefán Karlsson's bold but interesting conjecture is that Þórarinn wrote Kringla at home at Reykholt in his youth, before travelling North and writing books for the churches at Hólar and Vallastaðr.

As mentioned earlier, Jonna Louis-Jensen discussed the redactional history of *Heimskringla*. As the oldest manuscript containing all three parts, Kringla has a significant role here too. She also links the redaction with the Sturlungar. On the basis of similarities of detail, Louis-Jensen links Kringla with *Knýtlinga saga*, which is attributed to another of Snorri's more famous nephews, Óláfr Þórðarson *hvítaskáld*. If Óláfr wrote Kringla himself, it must have been one of the last things he did, and it must be dated to the year 1258/59. One possibility is that Óláfr may have edited a manuscript that *Kringla* is a transcription of.

Although the details surrounding the origins of *Heimskringla* and Kringla are difficult to determine with any certainty, there is no doubt

48 Stefán Karlsson 1977, 17–19.
49 *DI* V, 1.
50 "A good clerk [scholar] and a man of great skills in writing and book production, which still shows in many books that he has written for the church at Hólar and also the *staðr* of Vellir" (*Lárentíus saga biskups*, 217. Quoted by Stefán Karlsson 1977, 24) (Jørgensen's translation).

that the work is entirely in keeping with the business of power politics
and scholarship associated with Reykholt. Snorri had his works on the
Norwegian kings written at Reykholt, and what is more natural than
that his descendants should have developed this work further? The
manuscript history of *Heimskringla* provides strong evidence that the work
was put together after the individual parts were in circulation, as Jonna
Louis-Jensen has shown. This gives Kringla an even more significant
position in *Heimskringla*'s history than earlier research has accorded it.
Through Kringla, or its (unknown) original, the work *Heimskringla* was
established about twenty years after Snorri's death.

Conclusion

Snorri Sturluson was at all stages in his life, and in all his works, in-
defatigably interested in his Norwegian audience. His literary output,
Heimskringla, that is the Kings' Sagas, *Snorra-Edda*, the great testament
to the art of the court poets and to their eminence in the written culture, and possibly *Egils saga Skalla-Grímssonar*, focuses on kingship, the
court and the adoration of royal power. Even though Snorri may have
become disillusioned with royal autonomy in the last two years of his
life we have no difficulty in deciding that his verse is a product of court
sentimentality, and functions in a courtly milieu; we can therefore ask,
why not his prose works?

If we regard Snorri Sturluson merely as an Icelandic chieftain,
certainly influential and wealthy, but nevertheless rooted in his distinct
Icelandic social milieu and family context, we miss an opportunity to
appreciate the hidden agenda behind his literary output, which was to
facilitate an interaction with Norwegian royalty and aristocracy, and to
reflect the distinct courtly values of the Norwegian court, be it at the
command of King Hákon or Earl (later Duke) Skúli. These ambitions
are also evident in the activities of his learned colleagues, Styrmir
fróði, Óláfr *hvítaskáld* and Sturla Þórðarson – and in the reception of
their works in the fourteenth century. These values were not limited
to Norway, but common to courtly life in Europe and were probably
imitated in one way or another at Snorri's court at his uniquely structured estate Reykholt.

Bibliography

Aðalheiður Guðmundsdóttir 2012. "The Dancers of La Gardie 11". *Medieval Studies* 74, 307–330.

Bjarni Guðnason 1982. "Formáli". *Danakonunga sǫgur*. Ed. Bjarni Guðnason. Íslenzk fornrit XXXV. Reykjavík: Hið íslenzka fornritafélag.

Bloch, Howard R. 1983. *Etymologies and Genealogies: A Literary Anthropology of the French Middle Ages*. Chicago: University of Chicago Press.

De Vries, Jan 1967. *Altnordische Literaturgeschichte* II. Berlin.

DI = *Diplomatarium islandicum, Íslenzkt fornbréfa-safn*, V. Copenhagen and Reykjavík, 1899–1902

Edda Snorra Sturlusonar II. Copenhagen: Legatus Arnamagnæani, 1848–1887.

Finnur Jónsson 1895. *De bevarede brudstykker af skindbøgerne Kringla og Jöfraskinna*, STUAGNL 24. Copenhagen: S.L. Möllers Bogtrykkeri.

Finnur Jónsson 1931, "Indledning". *Edda Snorra Sturlusonar udgivet efter haandskrifterne*. Copenhagen.

Flateyjarbók I–III. Ed. Guðbrandur Vigfússon and C. R. Unger. Christiania, 1860–1868.

Frank, Roberta 1985. "Skaldic Poetry". In Carol J. Clover and John Lindow (eds), *Old Norse-Icelandic Literature. A Critical Guide*. Islandica XLV. Ithaca/London: Cornell University Press, 157–196.

Guðrún Nordal 1992. "Skáldið Snorri Sturluson". In Úlfar Bragason (ed.), *Snorrastefna 25.–27. júlí 1990*. Rit Stofnunar Sigurðar Nordals 1. Reykjavík, 113–129.

Guðrún Nordal 2001. *Tools of Literacy. The Role of Skaldic Verse in Icelandic Textual Culture of the 12th and 13th Centuries*. Toronto: University of Toronto Press.

Guðrún Sveinbjarnardóttir 2012, *Reykholt. Archaeological Investigations at a High Status Farm in Western Iceland*. Publications of the National Museum of Iceland 29. Reykjavík: Snorrastofa and Þjóðminjasafn Íslands.

Heimir Pálsson 2012. "Introduction". *Snorri Sturluson. The Uppsala Edda. DG 11 4to*. London: Viking Society for Northern Research.

Heimskringla II. Ed. Bjarni Aðalbjarnarson, Íslenzk fornrit XXVII. Reykjavík: Hið íslenzka fornritafélag. 1945.

Islandske Annaler indtil 1578. Ed. Gustav Storm. Christiania: Det norske historiske kildeskrift-fond, Grændahl & Søns Bogtrykkeri, 1888.

Jakob Benediktsson 1955. "Hvar var Snorri nefndur höfundur Heimskringlu?". *Skírnir* 129, 118–127.

Jørgensen, Jon Gunnar 1995. "Snorre Sturlesøns fortale paa sin chrønicke". *Gripla* IX, 45–62.

Jørgensen, Jon Gunnar 2000. "Passio Olavi og Snorre". In Inger Ekrem *et al.* (eds), *Olavs-legenden og den latinske historieskrivning i 1100-tallets Norge*. Copenhagen: Museum Tusculanum Press, 167–169.

Jørgensen, Jon Gunnar 2007. The Lost Vellum *Kringla*. Bibliotheca Arnamagnæana 45.

Krömmelbein, Thomas 1992. "Creative Compilers. Observations on the Manuscript Tradition of Snorri's Edda". In Úlfar Bragason (ed.), *Snorrastefna 25.–27. júlí 1990*. Rit Stofnunar Sigurðar Nordals 1. Reykjavík, 113–129.

Larrington, Carolyne 2009. "Queens and Bodies: The Norwegian Translated *lais* and Hákon IV's Kinswomen". *Journal of English and Germanic Philology* 108, 506–527.

Lárentíus saga biskups. *Biskupa sögur* III. Ed. Guðrún Ása Grímsdóttir. Íslenzk fornrit XVII. Reykjavík: Hið íslenzka fornritafélag, 1998.

Louis-Jensen, Jonna 1997. "Heimskringla – et

værk af Snorri Sturluson". *Nordica Bergensia* 14, 230–245.

Maurer, Konrad 1867. *Ueber die Ausdrücke: altnordische, altnorwegische & islandische Sprache.* Munich: Königlich-bayerische Akademie der Wissenschaften.

Norriges oc omliggende Øers sandfærdige Bescriffuelse. Copenhagen, 1632.

Ólafur Halldórsson 1979. "Sagnaritun Snorra Sturlusonar". In Gunnar Kalsson and Helgi Þorláksson (eds), *Snorri, átta alda minning.* Reykjavík: Sögufélag, 113–138.

Reykjaholtsmáldagi. Ed. Guðvarður Már Gunnlaugsson. Reykholt: Reykholtskirkja/ Snorrastofa, 2000.

Sigurður Nordal 1933. "Formáli". *Egils saga Skalla-Grímssonar.* Ed. Sigurður Nordal. Íslenzk fornrit II. Reykjavík: Hið íslenzka fornritafélag.

Sigurður Nordal 1952. *Sagalitteraturen* (Nordisk kultur VIIIB).

Skáldatal. In *Heimskringla. Lykilbók.* Eds Bergljót S. Kristjánsdóttir, Bragi Halldórsson, Jón Torfason and Örnólfur Thorsson. Reykjavík: Mál og menning, 1991.

Stefán Karlsson 1977. "Kringum Kringlu". *Árbók Landsbókasafns 1976,* 5–25. Reykjavik.

Storm, Gustav 1873. *Snorre Sturlassøns historieskrivning.* Copenhagen.

STUAGNL = Samfund til udgivelse av gammel nordisk litteratur.

Sturlunga saga I–II. Eds Jón Jóhannesson, Magnús Finnbogason and Kristján Eldjárn. Reykjavík: Sturlunguútgáfan, 1946.

Sturlunga saga I–II. Eds Örnólfur Thorsson *et al.* Reykjavík: Svart á hvítu, 1988.

Uppsala-Edda. Uppsalahandritið DG 11 4to. Snorri Sturluson. Ed. Heimir Pálsson. Bókaútgáfan Opna/Snorrastofa í Reykholti, 2013.

Úlfar Bragason. 2010. *Ætt og saga. Um frásagnarfræði Sturlungu eða Íslendinga sögu hinnar miklu.* Reykjavík: Háskólaútgáfan.

Þorleifur Hauksson 2007. "Formáli". *Sverris saga.* Íslenzk fornrit XXX. Reykjavík: Hið íslenzka fornritafélag.

List of Contributors

Benedikt Eyþórsson (b. 1976), MA (Reykjavík, Medieval History), Archivist, National Archives of Iceland, Laugavegur 162, 105 Reykjavík.

Kevin J. Edwards (b. 1949), PhD (Aberdeen, Physical Geography), Professor of Physical Geography and Adjunct Professor of Archaeology, Department of Geography and Environment, School of Geosciences, University of Aberdeen, St Mary's, Elphinstone Road, Aberdeen AB24 3UF.

Egill Erlendsson (b. 1971), PhD (Aberdeen, Physical Geography), Associate Professor, Faculty of Life and Environmental Sciences, University of Iceland, Sturlugata 7, 101 Reykjavík.

Gísli Sigurðsson (b. 1959), Dr. Phil. (Reykjavík, Medieval Literature), Research Professor, The Árni Magnússon Institute for Icelandic Studies, Árnagarður v./Suðurgata, 101 Reykjavík.

Guðrún Gísladóttir (b. 1956), PhD (Stockholm, Physical Geography), Professor of Geography, Faculty of Life and Environmental Sciences and Institute of Earth Sciences, University of Iceland, Sturlugata 7, 101 Reykjavík.

Guðrún Harðardóttir (b. 1966), MA (Reykjavík, Medieval History), Expert, Historic Buildings' Collection, National Museum of Iceland, Setberg, Suðurgata 43, 101 Reykjavík.

Guðrún Nordal (b.1960), Dr. Phil. (Oxford, Medieval Literature), Professor of Medieval Icelandic Literature, Director of The Árni Magnússon Institute for Icelandic Studies, Árnagarður v./Suðurgata, 101 Reykjavík.

Guðrún Sveinbjarnardóttir (b. 1947), PhD (Birmingham, Archaeology). Project Manager, Reykholt Excavations. Honorary Research Associate, Department of Scandinavian Studies, University College London, Gower Street, London WC1 E6BT.

Guðvarður Már Gunnlaugsson (b. 1956), cand. mag. (Reykjavík, Icelandic Linguistics), Senior Research Lecturer, The Árni Magnússon Institute for Icelandic Studies, Árnagarður v./Suðurgata, 101 Reykjavík.

Helgi Þorláksson (b. 1945), Dr. Phil. (Reykjavík, Medieval History), Professor Emeritus (History), University of Iceland. Seljavegur 10, 101 Reykjavík.

Karl G. Johansson (b. 1959), PhD (Gothenburg, Scandinavian Languages), Professor of Old Norse Philology, Department of Linguistics and Scandinavian Studies, Faculty of Humanities, University of Oslo. Henrik Wergelands hus, Blindern, 0317 Oslo. PO Box 1102 Blindern, 0317 Oslo.

Jon Gunnar Jørgensen (b. 1953), Dr. Philos. (Oslo, Scandinavian Languages), Professor of Old Norse Philology, Department of Linguistics and Scandinavian Studies, Faculty of Humanities, University of Oslo. Henrik Wergelands hus, Blindern, 0317 Oslo. PO Box 1102 Blindern, 0317 Oslo.

Mats Malm (b. 1964), PhD (Gothenburg, Comparative Literature) Professor of Comparative Literature, Department of Literature, History of Ideas and Religion, University of Gothenburg. PO Box 200, SE405 30 Göteborg.

Else Mundal (b. 1944), cand. philol. (Oslo, Old Norse Philology), Professor Emerita, Department of Linguistics, Literary and Aesthetic Studies, University of Bergen. PO Box 7805, 5020 Bergen.

Sverrir Jakobsson (b. 1970), Dr. Phil. (Reykjavík, Medieval History), Professor of Medieval History, University of Iceland, Árnagarður v./Suðurgata, 101 Reykjavík.

Torfi H. Tulinius (b. 1958), Dr. (Paris IV-Sorbonne, Medieval Literature), Professor of Medieval Icelandic Studies, University of Iceland, Árnagarður v./Suðurgata, 101 Reykjavík.

Kim Vickers (b. 1978), PhD (Sheffield, Archaeology), Honorary Research Fellow, Department of Archaeology, University of Sheffield, Northgate House, West Street, Sheffield, S1 4ET.

Viðar Pálsson (b. 1978), PhD (Berkeley, Medieval History), Assistant Professor of History, University of Iceland, Árnagarður v./Suðurgata, 101 Reykjavík

Indexes

General Index

Entries too common to be included are among others arch-bishop, author, bishop, book, church, farm, house, king, Latin, Old Norse, poet, write, writing. Sagas included are Sagas of Icelanders for the Borgarfjǫrðr area, sagas of Heimskringla *and sagas of* Sturlunga saga *and two sagas of Snorri's contemporary bishops at Skálholt.*

abbot 46, 122, 140, 147, 296, 338, 345, 349, 351, 354–355, 359, 396, 418, 420, 421
administration 45–46, 72, 111–112, 152, 328
administrator 44–45, 47, 53–54, 61, 63–64, 72, 399
agriculture 132, 164–165, 172, 191, 194
Alþingi (Althing) 7, 34, 41–42, 54, 56, 61, 146, 238, 402, 414, 447
animals (domestic) 23–25; see also livestock
appraisal record 242, 244, 264; see also *úttekt*
armour 36, 51, 447; see also weaponry
aristocrat, aristocratic, aristocracy 7, 20, 22, 33, 37–38, 40–50, 53–59, 62–64, 68, 70, 72, 81, 90–91, 94, 99, 101, 110–111, 113, 123–125, 137, 152, 271–272, 297, 334–336, 345–350, 356, 364–374, 376, 380, 382–383, 394, 396, 399, 401, 404, 442, 447–448, 450, 453, 456–458, 466
Art of War by Vegetius 51, 67
assembly (*þing*) 7, 34, 41, 118, 120, 130, 134–135, 144, 146, 295, 369; see also *Alþingi*
audience 21, 206, 292, 313, 336, 402, 404, 417, 419, 445–446, 449, 456, 466
Augustinian 21, 92, 296, 334, 338–339, 342–343, 346, 350–351, 353–365, 375–377, 381–383, 416, 452
Ásbirningar family 117, 119

Baglar (in Norway) 36, 79–81, 85, 91–92, 94–95, 103
banquet 41, 44, 47, 52, 69, 99, 401; see also feast, feasting, *veizla*
bathhouse 22
Benedictine 21, 42, 334, 336, 338–345, 347, 349–354, 357, 365–366, 370, 372–376, 379, 381–383, 420
Bible 291–292, 377, 391
birch 128, 165–166, 172, 175–176, 179–181, 183–187, 191, 195, 214–215, 217, 223, 247
    charred 178, 183, 216, 220, 243, 261–262
Birkibeinar (in Norway) 36, 40, 50–51, 61, 64, 79–82, 85–86, 91–92, 94–97, 103, 152, 448
Bishops' Sagas 341, 354
Bjarnar saga Hítdœlakappa 300, 427

book culture 292, 335, 337, 345, 358, 361, 364–365, 371
book production 109, 123, 414, 465
brewing 22, 24, 260, 269, 271
building, wooden building, 238, 246, 254, 271, 273; see also bathhouse, cellar, longhouse, *litlastofa, litluhús, loft, skáli, stafloft, stofa*

calf skin / hide 22, 265, 449,
canon law 62–64
capital
    cultural 116, 121, 301, 371, 392, 395–399,
    symbolic 116, 397–398
castle, see *kastali*
cellar 87, 99, 102, 242, 247, 253–256, 261, 267, 270; see also *kjallari*
centrality 109, 111–112, 119–120, 125, 133, 135, 137–138, 152, 307, 448
centralization of power 20, 26; see also consolidation of power
centre of learning / writing 22, 120, 295, 390, 416, 421, 424, 435–436; see also learned centre, literary centre
centre of power 20–23, 26, 29, 109, 112, 116, 121, 123, 125–126, 129, 133, 137–138, 151–152, 231, 436; see also *valdamiðstöð*
cereal (growing) 23–24, 101, 165, 170, 206
charcoal making / production 186, 195–196, 209, 214, 217, 223, 230
charter 22, 136, 193, 207–210, 218, 220, 222, 224–227, 229, 244, 263–264, 267; see also deed and *máldagi*
chieftain (leader, lord, magnate) 17, 21, 24, 34, 36–37, 42–43, 50, 52–55, 61–62, 71, 81, 84, 92, 116–117, 125–128, 130, 132, 134, 136–138, 143, 145–148, 151, 169, 175, 190, 206, 250, 265, 270, 274, 294, 297, 301, 307, 310, 312, 333, 339, 345–347, 350, 355–356, 364–365, 367, 376, 391, 393, 397, 399, 400–405, 422–423, 442, 447, 457–458, 466; see also magnate
chieftain farm, farming 25, 175, 190, 339
chivalry 44, 124, 369
chronicle 340, 344, 371, 377, 379–383, 425, 446, 451, 459
clergy 52–53, 59, 263, 366, 404–405, 451
cleric 7, 43, 46, 53–54, 63, 111, 116, 121–122, 136,

140, 263–264, 292, 295, 311, 334, 336, 348, 350, 356–358, 364, 366–367, 370, 372–373, 376, 390, 399, 412, 415–416, 420–423, 426–427, 431–432, 434

clerical gentry 43, 53–54, 137, see also *kirkjugoði*

climate (weather) 162, 165, 168–170, 180, 183, 187

code of conduct (behaviour) 41, 45–47, 54, 59, 68, 70

Commonwealth period in Iceland 26, 138, 266, 453

communications 83, 118, 127, 135, 402, 419

conduit 18, 20, 225, 248, 258–259–260, 269, 271, 272, 442

consolidation of power 117, 138, 149, 152

Contemporary Sagas, see *samtíðarsǫgur*

court (law) 34, 43, 54, 60, 295, 402

court (*hirð*) 7, 20, 22, 34, 36–42, 44–49, 53–54, 56, 59, 61, 70, 73, 79, 90, 96–97, 100, 270, 291, 297, 298, 307, 348, 367, 371, 395–397, 397–401, 403, 417–420, 432, 441–442, 446–451, 466; see also *hirð*

court culture 346, 367

courteous, courtier, courtly values 22, 33–34, 36–41, 43–44, 46–48, 50, 53–61, 64, 69–70, 72, 79–80, 83, 86, 88, 97, 100–101, 125, 300, 368, 448, 450, 458, 466

court poet / poetry 40, 70, 297–298, 301, 398, 417, 445, 447, 450–451, 457, 466

cultus 356, 363

cultural artefact 394, 400, 454

deed 22–24, 69, 207–208, 210, 279, 282, 284, 420, 441–442; see also charter and *máldagi*

Dei gratia 90–91, 96

driftwood 136, 205, 206, 227–228, 231, 246, 248, 266

drink, drinking (ale, beer, mead) 39, 47–48, 69, 150, 265, 267, 271

dróttkvæði / skaldic poetry 7, 96–97, 305, 320, 347, 361, 363, 391, 399, 403–404, 410, 418, 427, 444–445, 447–448, 450, 455, 457

duke 35, 102, 445, 448, 450–451, 466

earl 7, 21, 33–36, 38, 40–41, 47, 54, 56–58, 60–61, 64–68, 70, 73, 80–85, 87, 89–103, 151, 371, 395, 398, 403, 417–418, 426, 428, 445–450, 464, 466

Edda, see *Snorra-Edda*

Eddic poetry 380, 391, 395, 427

education 21, 37, 46, 59–60, 72, 295, 298, 312, 319–321, 323, 325–326, 328, 334, 338, 342, 344–348, 353–354, 358–360, 367, 370, 372–374, 376–377, 379, 381–382

Egils saga Skalla-Grímssonar 21, 133, 140, 142, 164, 205, 294, 301, 306–310, 312–313, 333, 369, 373, 402–404, 426–427, 441, 444, 452, 466,

eldahús 266, 269

elite 21, 36, 101, 113–115, 120, 124, 142, 271–274, 301, 304–305, 320, 334–336, 338, 340, 366–368, 370, 372, 374, 376, 382, 447, 453,

entertainment 390–394, 399–402, 411, 413

erosion 21, 165, 168, 170, 174, 181–182, 184, 188–189, 217, 223

Family Sagas 140–141, 291; see also *Íslendingasǫgur*

feast, feasting 7, 69, 109, 118–119, 124, 132, 190, 265–266, 393–395, 401–404; see also banquet, *veizla*

feud 152, 295, 298, 361

fish / fishing 23–25, 71, 136, 164, 168, 193–194, 206–208, 225–231

fjórðungr, see Quarter

Flateyjarbók 4, 35, 82, 349, 423, 452

fornaldarsǫgur (Legendary Sagas) 299

friendship 83, 90, 103, 296, 310, 421

food 24–25, 39, 48, 166, 190

fort, fortress, fortification 7, 18, 20, 69, 117, 124–125, 242, 252–253, 266, 269, 271, 273; see also *virki*

forskáli 18, 242, 252; see also passageway (subterranean)

genealogy 59, 304, 312, 335, 443, 455–457

generosity 47, 52, 90, 103

geothermal 19, 24, 224–225, 258, 272

goði (ar), 24, 34, 42–43, 45, 50, 52–56, 126, 135–137, 151, 457; see also *kirkjugoði*, *stórgoði*

goðorð 43, 60, 121, 131, 133, 151, 393

grammatica 320, 359, 380–381, 456

Grágás 24

Gunnlaugs saga ormstungu 140, 143, 299–300, 427

Gylfaginning 60, 305, 419, 454–455

habitus 37, 44–47, 54, 72, 397

Harðar saga 133, 135, 423

Hákonar saga Hákonarsonar 35, 65, 333, 370–371, 444, 449, 451–452, 459

Háttalykill 58

Háttatal 39, 47, 56, 58, 60, 61, 65–66, 326, 398, 446, 454–455

Haukdælir family 44, 62, 117–119, 295–296, 368, 401

haymaking 128, 174, 180, 185, 195, 209, 222,

heathland 168, 218–219, 222, 229

Heiðarvíga saga 140, 143, 210, 311, 427

heilagramannasǫgur 354

Heimskringla, 7, 17, 47, 49, 70–71, 79, 81, 87–91, 96, 103, 264, 270, 294, 300, 312, 333, 368, 371, 373, 375, 377, 414, 419, 435, 441, 444–445, 448, 452, 457–463, 465–466

héraðsríki (domain) 17, 20, 29, 43, 117, 137, 139, 144, 149, 152, 403 hero, heroic 48–49, 297–299, 301, 312, 349, 369, 391, 396

hersir 39, 457

hierarchy (social) 90, 392, 400

hirð, hirðlog, hirðstjóri 34, 38–39, 72

Hirðskrá 34, 39

historiography 307, 380, 445–446

hof 118–119, 125, 132

holy orders 54, 57, 295

honour 29, 34, 36, 41, 51, 53, 55, 58, 70, 116, 137, 295, 395, 398, 417, 428, 446; see also respect

hot spring 18–19, 127, 134, 224–225, 238, 248, 258–259

Hrafns saga Sveinbjarnarsonar 55, 57, 84

Hœnsa-Þóris saga 130, 133, 140, 143

höfðingjasetur (residence of a leader) 109, 125–126

illusio (Bourdieu) 397

imagery 325–326, 329

immunity 118, 122, 137

infield 23, 128, 190, 196, 209

iron production / extraction 162, 186, 214, 223

Íslendingabók 111, 130, 133, 338, 340, 343, 344, 359, 368, 383, 390, 412

Íslendinga saga 36, 53, 58, 244, 252, 333, 356, 395, 409, 410, 414, 417, 423, 428–430, 452

Íslendingasǫgur, 291, 389, 394, 402, 426; see also Family Sagas, Sagas of Icelanders

kastali 51, 124

kenning 21, 319, 326–329

Kings' Sagas 294, 300, 312, 341, 373, 389, 396, 419, 425–427, 441, 444–446, 450, 457, 460, 466; see also *konungasǫgur*

kirkjubóndi 433–434

kirkjugoði, 55, 137; see also clerical gentry, *goði*

kjallari 242, 257, 267, 270; see also cellar

knight 33, 39, 44–45, 49, 55, 124, 301, 369–370, 454

konungasǫgur, 389, 419; see also Kings' Sagas

Konungs skuggsjá (The King's Mirror) 34, 41, 46

Kringla 444, 448, 457, 459–466

kurteiss 40, 46

landnám, landnám tephra 28, 162–163, 172–174, 177, 180–181, 183–184, 193–194, 196, 214, 246, 259

Landnámabók (The Book of Settlements) 18, 23, 40, 122, 126–127, 131, 133, 140–144, 185, 191, 196, 248, 296, 310, 368–369, 390, 420, 423, 444, 452–453

landscape 164–165, 168, 171, 175, 184, 187–190, 193, 223, 238

    cultural 21, 26, 28, 161–162, 167, 190, 192, 195, 208, 161–162

    natural 28, 161–162

Landscapes Circum landnám Project 28, 162–163

Latinate culture 334, 341

Latin learning 21, 42–43, 59–60, 319, 326, 358–359

law 34, 43, 49, 57, 60, 62–64, 288, 297, 301–302, 304, 310, 312, 340, 379, 391, 394, 402, 412, 430, 464–465

lawman 15, 62, 64, 69, 72–73, 80, 82, 87, 93–100, 103, 294–295, 302, 429, 436, 449, 451, 453, 457–458; see also *logmaðr*

lawspeaker (*logsogumaðr*) 7, 56, 59, 62–64, 68, 87, 122, 294–296, 302, 414, 434, 443, 451, 456, 458

learned centre 427, 434, 436, 452

lendr maðr 20, 33, 34, 37–39, 48, 50, 61, 64–68, 71–73, 79, 86–87, 89, 96–97, 100, 152, 389

Legendary Sagas, see *fornaldarsǫgur*

library 21, 323, 390, 414, 420, 422–425, 428, 431, 434, 436

Leiðarvísir Nikuláss Bergssonar ábóta á Þverá 46, 349

libertas ecclesiæ 63, 79–80, 92

lifestyle 25, 33, 37, 40–44, 47, 54–55, 68, 72, 91, 124, 137, 190

literacy 29, 64, 120, 325, 334–335, 337, 340, 342, 344, 345, 350–351, 359, 361, 365, 371, 381–383

literary activity 298, 292, 393, 401, 410, 413, 415, 445

literary centre 21, 409, 413, 416–420, 426–427, 434, 436; see also centre of learning

literary culture (*bókmenning*) 29–30, 43, 120, 380, 404

literary rhetoric 21, 319, 321–322, 329

literate culture 21, 333–335, 337, 339, 358, 361, 363–366, 372, 375–376, 380, 383

literature 26, 47, 64, 117, 164, 184, 291–293, 297–300, 304, 306–307, 313, 333, 337, 342–343, 350, 352, 358–363, 367, 376–378, 380, 389–392, 394–395, 399–400, 402, 410, 412, 416, 418–420, 425, 459–460

litlastofa 257, 265, 267, 269–270, 272–273

litluhús 257, 267, 270

liturgical book / text 280–281, 411, 416

livestock 164–166, 182, 193, 205–207, 209, 223, 229, 442

loft 68, 255, 257, 267–272; see also *stafloft*

longhouse 20, 68, 132–133, 196, 220, 246–247, 273

lore (old lore) 58–61, 64, 67, 294, 305, 401

lowland 128, 166, 168, 170–171, 183–184, 188, 190–191, 194–195, 210, 218, 223–224, 311

logmaðr (lawman) 436, 457

logsogumaðr (lawspeaker)

Logsogumannatal (Register/list of Lawspeakers), 296–297, 443, 455, 458

macrofossils 162–164, 170, 186

magnate 7, 24, 55, 68, 83, 87–88, 90, 139, 142–143,

145, 148, 151–152, 237, 270, 272, 400; see also chieftain

Magnúsarsona saga (Magnússona saga) 264

máldagi 264, 279–280, 282, 284–287, 420, 422; see also charter and deed

manuscript 22, 39, 121, 226, 279–284, 287–288, 300, 302, 307–311, 319, 322, 325, 334–336, 339–340, 343–344, 349, 354, 358–359, 363, 381, 394–395, 419, 423, 425–426, 442, 444–445, 448, 453–456, 458–466

memory 57, 322–325, 327–329, 396, 411, 446

merchant 36, 41–42, 62, 64, 67, 70, 80–81, 83, 89, 101

metre, poetic, 60, 301

monastery 92, 122, 147, 296, 336, 338–340, 342, 344, 347, 353–355, 357–358, 360, 362, 370, 373–375, 382, 416–418, 420–421

monk 54, 298, 311, 350, 418, 420

Morkinskinna 40, 48, 68, 88–89, 300, 373–375, 377

myth, mythology 7, 59–61, 67, 294, 297–298, 300–301, 303–306, 312, 325–326, 347, 351, 369, 391, 402, 405, 446, 456, 458

narrative art, see storytelling

network 30, 111–112, 356, 361–362, 364, 377, 394, 415–417, 425

nobility 33, 37–38, 44, 298, 346, 372

nobleman 37, 44, 58, 418

Noregskonungatal 42, 58

Oddaverjar (the Oddi family) 33, 36, 44, 59–60, 62, 72, 81, 88–89, 92, 103, 120, 346, 368, 401, 403–404

Orkneyinga saga 56, 81–85, 98, 99, 390, 460

Óláfs saga helga 47, 60, 71, 81, 96, 270, 294, 300, 312, 461–463

Óláfs saga Tryggvasonar 349, 390, 444, 459, 460

oral, orality 21, 57, 64, 284, 292, 294, 297–298, 301–304, 306–307, 310, 313, 319–322, 329, 334–337, 345, 361, 365, 382, 390–392, 394, 400, 402, 411–413, 427, 446–447, 459

oral rhetoric 21, 319–322, 329

orthography 9, 284–285, 287, 464

palaeoecology 21, 161–162, 169, 185

palaeoenvironment 161–163, 181, 183–184, 191

Páls saga byskups (Páls saga biskups) 54, 58, 346

palynology 164–165

parchment 22, 292, 307, 311, 325, 396, 463

passageway (subterranean) 7, 18, 20, 236, 238–240, 242, 248, 250–252, 254, 257, 270, 273, 401, 442; see also forskáli

peasant 91, 98–99, 128

poem 36, 40, 42, 47, 51, 56, 58–59, 93, 96, 298, 301, 303–304, 312, 326, 349, 376, 380–381, 391, 393,

395–396, 398, 401, 417–418, 427, 447–451, 454, 464–465; see also *dróttkvæði*, strophe, verse

poetry 7, 60–61, 64, 291–293, 298, 301, 307, 312, 321, 326, 361, 371, 379, 382, 390–391, 393, 395–396, 398, 400, 402, 404–405, 447–450, 459; see also court poetry, skaldic poetry, Eddic poetry/poetics

politician 21, 63, 79, 87, 312, 453

pollen, analysis 24, 161, 163, 164–165, 171–177, 179–188, 214, 217

pool 7, 18, 19–20, 69, 109, 125–128, 130, 133–135, 224–225, 236–238, 242, 248, 250, 252, 257, 269, 401

Prestssaga Guðmundar góða 412

preudomme 37, 44–45, 48–49, 51, 54

priest 17, 24, 43, 50, 53–54, 59, 69, 70, 111, 122, 126, 131–132, 136–137, 143, 145, 147–148, 151, 264, 286, 296, 334, 340, 342, 354, 381, 393–394, 411–412, 415–416, 420, 422–424, 429, 432–433, 435–436, 458

prior 122, 355, 357, 359, 364, 375, 452

Quarter (of Iceland, *fjórðungr*) 130, 138, 141–144, 150–151, 353

radiocarbon dating 178, 182, 190, 196, 214–216, 241, 243, 246–247, 261–262

Raulandsstova 68, 243

reading 48, 88, 292, 297, 302, 335–336, 342, 356, 377, 380, 391, 394, 397, 404, 411, 413, 416

renaissance 60, 293, 306, 358–363

respect (*virðing*) 25, 29, 45, 49, 53, 57–58, 72, 121, 396, 397, 400, 453; see also honour

Reykholt Project 7, 20, 22, 25–29, 33, 41–42, 137, 161, 163, 345

Reykholt Shieling Project 27, 28, 162

riddari, see knight

ritmenning, see literary culture

rittengsl (inter-borrowing) 307

ríki (proto-state) 39, 62, 65, 138

romance 293, 298, 380, 389, 399, 450

royal power 64, 80, 82, 88, 90–91, 94–96, 103, 294, 350, 403, 466

royalist, Snorri as 79, 88, 91

royalty 22, 405, 466

rune, runes 56, 450

Sagas of Icelanders, 133, 244, 291, 299, 307–308, 310–311, 421, 423, 426–427, 452–453; see also *Íslendingasögur*

sagnaskemmtan 411–413; see also entertainment

saint 71, 84, 115, 136, 230, 265, 280, 294, 298, 311, 338, 352, 354, 363, 375–376, 383, 391, 399, 413, 423, 452, 462

Saints' Lives, see *heilagramannasǫgur*

samtíðarsǫgur 310, 389, 390, 394, 402

scholars (*magistri*) 360

school 334, 336–345, 348, 351, 354, 367, 372, 378, 381–383, 421, 425, 435, 446, 451–452, 455

scribe 79, 140, 284–285, 298, 336, 340, 343, 429, 436, 454, 458, 465

script 279, 284, 286–287, 337, 339–341, 344, 358–359, 371, 381–382

scriptorium 109, 120, 414, 442, 444, 462

sel 21–23, 26–28, 136, 163–165, 178–179, 181–182, 185, 187, 193, 207–211, 213–220, 224–227, 229–230

settlement, see *landnám*

sheriff, see *sýslumaðr*

shieling, see *sel*

skaldic poetry / poet, see *dróttkvæði*

skáld, skald 297, 320, 398, 403, 417–418, 464

skáldasǫgur (Skald Sagas) 427, 453

Skáldatal (Register of Poets) 297, 417, 441, 448–449, 455–457, 463–464

Skáldskaparmál 60, 333, 336, 444, 449, 454–456

skáli 244, 246, 257, 266–267, 269–270, 273

skutilsveinn 33–34, 36–39, 41, 51, 61, 65, 72, 97

Snorra-Edda 7, 17, 21, 39, 59–60, 294–299, 301–305, 307, 310, 312, 320, 325–326, 371, 379, 381, 399, 419, 425–427, 441, 443–446, 448, 452, 454–457, 466

Snorrastofa at Reykholt 7–8, 16, 18–19, 25–26, 29

Snorralaug (Snorri's pool) 7, 18–19, 224, 237–238, 240, 248, 250, 269

sport 48, 56–57

staðr (estate church) 17, 23–25, 29, 109, 114–115, 121–123, 125–126, 127, 131–133, 136–138, 148–149, 209–210, 392, 399, 415–416, 420–422, 424, 429–431, 433, 436, 465

stafloft 255

stallari (spokesman of a king) 38, 48–49, 54, 63, 70

stofa / stofur 68, 243–244, 246, 256–257, 265–267, 269–270, 272–273

stórgoði 40, 52, 67, 71–72, 87, 152; see also *goði*

strophe, see also poem, verse 39, 56, 66, 401, 411

storytelling, storyteller 291–292, 294, 298–299, 301, 310, 312–313, 382, 393, 411–413, 446

Sturlu saga 145, 452

Sturlunga saga 9, 18, 65, 66, 68, 102, 138, 140–141, 144, 237, 241–244, 250, 252, 257, 261, 265–269, 271–274, 296, 310, 376, 401–403, 410, 414, 428, 441–442, 448–449, 455–457, 460

Sturlungar family 21, 62, 70, 139, 147, 150, 295–296, 333–334, 337, 342, 345, 365–368, 370–372, 374–375, 380, 382–383, 403–404, 410, 420, 432, 443–444, 451, 453, 455–458, 465

subdeacon 54, 60, 150

Sverris saga 42, 253, 341, 448

sýslumaðr 98–100, 102, 144, 151

textual culture 26, 29, 120, 320, 341, 446, 454

tephra, see *landnám*

tithe 110–116, 392, 416

topos 345, 354

úttekt 242, 244; see also appraisal record

vaðmál (homespun) 67, 101

valdamiðstöð 43, 109, 125, 152; see also centre of power

veizla (feast, banquet) 265

veizla (benefice) 38, 66

verse 56, 60, 299, 301, 349, 401, 441, 445–449, 454, 456, 466; see also see poem, strophe

Viking Age, period, Vikings 7, 162, 207, 247, 293, 299, 411

violence 51–52, 55, 124, 147, 402

virðing, see honour, respect

virki 69, 242, 252; see also fort, fortress, fortification

vita 347, 352, 354, 364–365, 375, 383, 424,

wax tablet 22, 322

weaponry 124

wetland 128–129, 166, 168, 171–173, 175–176, 179, 183–184, 188–192, 195, 214, 224

wooden building, see building

woodland 21, 165–168, 172–176, 178, 180–181, 183–188, 191, 193, 195–196, 208, 213–214, 221, 223–224, 229–230

world-view 292, 305, 353, 367

writing culture, written culture 22, 337, 359, 361, 409, 413, 416, 466; see also literary culture

written texts 292, 390–391, 412–413

Ynglinga saga 300, 377, 460, 464

þingvald 87

Þorgils saga ok Hafliða 393, 395, 411, 412

Þorgils saga skarða 266, 271, 412, 429, 432, 434, 435

Þorláks saga byskups 83, 137, 342, 345, 348, 354, 355, 390

Þórðar saga kakala 432

þættir (*þáttr*) 40, 300

Index of Place Names

Prepared by Bergur Þorgeirsson

The entries Borgarfjǫrðr, Iceland and Norway are too numerous and have been excluded

Abingdon 420
Aðalstræti in Reykjavík 247
Aga in Harðangr (Hardanger) 256
Agder 460
Akranes 115, 143, 145, 146
Akurey 24
Álftafjǫrðr 135
Álptanes (Álftanes) 205, 206
Andakíll 195
Armenia 337
Arnarfjǫrðr 126, 252
Arnegarden in Volda 272
Árnesþing 119
Asia Minor 60
Áss 117, 119, 192, 208, 223
Auðsstaðir 192
Augastaðir 192

Bakki in Øxnadalr 116, 118
Ballará 131
Bari 63
Bath 379
Bessastaðir 25, 65
Biskupstungur 115, 117
Bjǫrgvin (Bjǫrgyn, Bergen) 64, 68, 81, 89, 99, 100, 271, 460
Bolastaðir 192
Bólstaðr in Álftafjǫrðr 135
Borg at Mýrar 81, 118, 137, 141–144, 147–149, 151, 152, 164, 205, 286, 409, 421, 422, 451
Breiðabólstaðr 121, 123, 126–134, 142–144, 187, 190–195, 209, 210, 248
Breiðafjǫrðr 126, 132, 147, 150
Breiðaflói 129
Breiðavatn 129, 163, 164, 169, 170, 175–177, 185, 187, 191, 223, 229
Brennistaðir 195
Britain 28, 298
British Isles 164, 344
Brœðratunga in Biskupstungur 117
Búrfell 192
Bœr in Bœjarsveit 115, 128, 143, 144, 147, 148, 151, 208, 218, 389, 420
Bœjarsveit 115, 195

Caithness (Katanes) 80, 82, 84, 85, 98–100, 103
Canterbury 365

Copenhagen 444, 462, 464

Dalasýsla 268
Dalir 116–118, 132
Danevirke at Hedeby 252
Deildartunga 25, 192, 194
Denmark 25, 58, 59, 215, 252, 395, 396, 401, 435, 450, 451, 458
Djúp 24

Eastern Quarter of Iceland 150
Effersey 24
Egge (Egg) in Trøndelag 87
Eikrem 272
Eiríksjǫkull 122
Elliðavatn 129, 130, 134, 135
England 17, 39, 44, 45, 54, 337, 338, 350, 351, 353, 354, 362, 365, 367, 372, 379–381, 420
Ermeland (see Warmia)
Esja 357
Europe 47, 124, 237, 291–294, 297–299, 301, 303, 304, 319, 320, 334, 336, 337, 341, 346, 348, 358–361, 365, 367, 369, 372, 381, 382, 399, 446, 450, 466
Eyjafjǫll 161, 196
Eyjafjǫrðr 115, 117, 120, 373, 374
Eyrar 67
Eyrr (Eyri) in Arnarfjǫrðr 55, 118, 126, 252
Eyvindarstaðir 65

Faroe Islands 91, 188, 267
Faxadalr 163, 193, 207, 208, 218, 219, 229
Ferjubakki 120, 140, 151
Ferstikla on Hvalfjarðarstrǫnd 142
Finland 175
Firðafylki (Fjordane) 66
Fljótsdalr 117
Flói 117
Flókadalr 195, 218
Florence 293, 304
Flugumýri 117, 120, 268, 273, 274
Fólgsn (see Fosen)
Forest of St Peter (Pétursskógr) 224
Fosen 66
France (Frakkland) 44, 45, 124, 297, 338, 359, 362, 372
Franken (see France)
Frioðigar 419

Garðar on Akranes 115, 145, 147, 148, 151, 152, 208
Gautland (see Västergötland)

Geitá 220

Geitland 23, 131, 132, 163, 193, 196, 197, 207, 208, 220, 221, 224, 229, 230

Germany 46, 338, 350

Gestilsrein (Gestilren) 93, 94

Giljar 192

Gilsbakki 137, 143, 144, 146, 151, 152, 179, 208

Glóðafeykir 119, 120

Greece 60, 404

Greenland 293, 395

Grímsá 193, 207, 225, 226, 230

Grímsstaðir 192, 209, 210

Grund in Eyjafjǫrðr 117, 127

Grǫf in Ørœfi 256

Gullberastaðir in Lundarreykjadalr 142

Götland 271

Hallkelsstaðir in Hvítársíða 142

Háfr 192, 193, 209, 210, 222

Háls 162, 163, 176, 186, 194, 196

Hálsar, see also Háls 192

Hálsasveit 115, 164, 168, 176, 191, 224

Hamraendar 221

Hamrar 192

Harðangr (Hardanger) 256, 272

Haukadalr in Biskupstungur 115, 118, 119, 340, 341, 343, 344, 346, 347, 349, 355, 367

Hedeby in Denmark 252

Hegranes 119

Helgafell 135, 140, 147

Herford in Germany 338

Hestr 226

Hítardalr 115, 143, 146, 148, 208, 226, 420

Hítarnes on Mýrar 115

Hnappadalr 142

Hof in Vopnafjǫrðr 117

Hofstaðir in Mývatnssveit 119, 135, 161

Hofstaðir in Hálsasveit 132, 192

Hólakot 163, 164, 175, 176, 178, 181, 183, 188

Hólar 92, 115, 267, 268, 273, 334, 336, 340, 345, 347, 348, 352, 356, 365, 372, 373, 382, 410, 416, 423, 424, 465

Hólmr in Akranes 146

Holtålen in Trøndelag 272

Hrafnagil in Eyjafjǫrðr 115, 128, 394, 412, 413

Hrafnseyri (see Eyri (Eyrr) in Arnarfjǫrðr)

Hraun in Keldudalr 125

Hraunsáss 192, 209, 224, 230

Hrísar 184, 218

Hrísbrú 133–135

Hrunamannahreppr 117

Hruni in Hrunamannahreppr 117, 128

Hrútafjarðarheiði 193, 207, 208, 220, 222, 229

Húnaþing 20, 137, 149, 152

Hurðarbak 192

Húsafell 115, 168, 208, 220

Hvalfjarðarstrǫnd 142, 143

Hvammr in Dalir 118, 145, 208, 268

Hvanneyri 192, 196, 208, 226

Hvítá 102, 126, 130, 142–144, 168, 191, 192, 196, 222, 223, 225

Hvítárbakki 238

Hvítársíða 142, 143, 169, 176, 210, 211, 226

Hœgindi 123, 192, 193, 209, 210, 222, 228, 229

Hǫfði 356

Hǫrðaland 66

Innri-Hólmr on Akranes 143, 208

Ísafjarðardjúp 115

Jerusalem 349, 450

Jutland 93

Kaldaðarnes 117

Kaldakvísl 135

Kallaðarnes in Flói (Kaldaðarnes) 117, 119

Kalmanstunga 146, 147, 220

Katla 196

Keldudalr 125

Ketilsstaðir 188

Kirkjubœr 354

Kirkjubœr in the Faroe Islands 267

Kjalarnes 134, 135

Kjalarnesþing 130, 134, 135

Kjalvararstaðir 192

Kjarará 179, 185, 193, 211, 225–227, 230

Kjarardalr 164, 168, 178, 180, 181, 185, 187, 189, 193, 209, 210, 216, 224–227, 229, 230

Kjarrá (see Kjarará)

Kjarradalr (see Kjarardalr)

Kjǫr 207, 208

Kleppjárnsreykir 143, 192

Klif 185

Kolbeinsáróss (Kolkuóss) in Skagafjǫrðr 266

Kollafjǫrðr 134, 135

Kollslœkur 192

Konungahella 264

Kópareykir 192

Kot 221

Kvitingsøy 92

Langjǫkull 168

Laufás 264

Laugar in Sælingsdalr 127

Leiðhamrar 135

Leiðvǫllur 135

Leiruvágr 134

Lincoln 354, 362

Loricus 419

Lund (Lundr) in Sweden 262, 348, 353, 362, 377, 396

Lundarreykjadalr 142, 147, 184

Lundarreykjadalshreppr 222

Lundr 151, 184

Melar 145, 146, 148, 208

Melhus (Meðalhús) 87

Mosfell 129, 133–135

Mosfellssveit 24

Mostr 457

Munka-Þverá 338, 347, 349, 353, 373, 374

Mýrar 115, 142, 205, 206

Mývatnssveit 119, 135, 161, 167, 193–195, 197

Mæri (see Nordmøre)

Mǫðruvellir in Eyjafjǫrðr 115

Naumudalr (see Numadalr)

Niðaróss (Þrándheimr) 100, 147, 270–272, 346, 350, 353–355, 358, 362, 363

Nikulásarker 71

Nordmøre 66

Norðrreykir 123, 192, 193, 209, 210

Norðrland 209, 222, 228, 229

Norðrá 102, 120, 168, 415

Norðrárdalr 143, 168, 224

Norðtunga 143, 211

Norðtungusel 163, 178, 185, 189, 211–214, 229, 230

North America 293

North Atlantic region 206, 272, 395

Northern Iceland 341, 350, 356, 373

Numadalr (Numedal) 256, 457

Oddi in Rangárvellir 17, 20, 33, 42, 50, 58–60, 62, 64, 65, 67, 68, 81, 83–86, 101, 109, 110, 117, 120, 136, 146, 152, 271, 294, 295, 298, 302, 339, 341, 343, 344, 346–349, 354, 355, 367, 372, 376, 377, 397, 417, 421, 422, 425, 447, 452

Orkney 21, 56, 57, 58, 80–85, 91, 97–103

Oslo 81

Oxford 62

Papa Stour in Shetland 267

Paris 342, 353, 354, 358, 360, 362, 365, 378

Pétursskógr (Peter's Forest) 71, 136

Rangárvellir 20

Rangárþing 117, 311

Rauðamelr in Hnappadalr 142

Rauðavatn (see Reyðarvatn)

Rauðavatnsós 207, 208

Rauðsgil 192

Re 461

Refsstaðir 192

Reyðarvatn 193, 208, 222, 225, 227

Reyðarvatnsóss 227, 230

Reykhólar (Reykjahólar) 24, 391, 393, 395, 411

Reykholt (Reykjaholt) 7, 8, 16–30, 33, 43, 52, 53, 68–71, 80, 92, 101, 102, 109, 110, 117–138, 140, 141, 143–145, 147–152, 161–164, 168–172, 174, 178, 179, 184, 186–194, 196, 197, 207, 208–211, 218–231, 236–244, 248, 249, 252, 253, 256–259, 261–274, 279, 280, 282, 284–286, 296, 306, 342, 357, 365, 370, 373–375, 377, 389, 390, 392, 399–401, 403, 405, 409, 410, 413–436, 441, 442, 444, 449, 451–454, 457, 459, 462, 465, 466

Reykholtsdalr 122, 126, 129, 130, 134, 142, 143, 162–164, 168–170, 174–176, 183, 186, 189–197, 209, 210, 221, 223, 224, 451

Reykholtsdalr valley (see Reykholtsdalr)

Reykholtsdalshreppr 168

Reykholtssel 163, 164, 178–183, 185, 187, 188, 211, 216, 217, 229

Reykir in Borgarfjǫrðr (see Norðrreykir)

Reykir in Mosfellssveit 24

Reykir in Ǫlfus 117

Reykjaá (Suðurá) 134, 135

Reykjadalr (see Reykholtsdalr)

Reykjadalr nyrðri (see Reykholtsdalr)

Reykjadalr syðri (see Lundarreykjadalr)

Reykjadalr valley (see Reykholtsdalr)

Reykjadalsá 122, 126, 164, 168, 170, 171, 191, 194, 195, 222, 225

Reykjanes by Djúp 24

Reykjanes in the South (see Reykjanes peninsula)

Reykjanes peninsula 20, 137, 149, 152, 311

Reykjavík 24, 247, 283, 357, 464

Reynines 119

Reynistaðr (Staðr í Reyninesi) 119

Roman Empire 292

Rome 55, 60, 63, 292, 379, 410, 464

Røldal in Harðangr 272

Sauðafell in Dalir 116–118, 127

Saurbœr 208

San Gimignano 311

Sanddalr 136, 207, 208, 224, 229, 230

Saxony (Saxland) 39, 46

Scandinavia 25, 26, 63, 164, 252, 291, 299, 346, 352, 353, 362, 367, 394, 395, 419, 448, 450, 451, 456, 458

Scotland 80, 86

Selárdalr 125

Seljaeyri 102
Shetland 81, 83, 267
Síðumúli 169, 179, 226
Sigmundarstaðir 192
Signýjarstaðir 192
Skagafjǫrðr 68, 117, 119, 127, 266, 268, 273
Skálholt (Skálaholt) 115, 121, 187, 262, 296, 302, 334, 336, 338, 342, 343, 345–350, 353–355, 359, 362, 365, 367, 372, 376, 416, 421
Skammadalr 135
Skáney 192, 194
Skáneyjarbunga 171, 176
Skara (Skarar) in Västergötland
Skarðsheiði 168, 415
Skarðsströnd 115
Skjaldmeyjargil 178, 187
Skógar 184
Skorradalr 168
Slakkagil 207, 208
Snæfellsnes 117
Snœldubeinsstaðir 192
Sogn 272
South Iceland 188, 195, 224
Southern Quarter of Iceland 130, 141–144
St Peter basilica 349
St Victor in Paris, monastery 342, 353, 358, 360, 362, 377, 382
Staðarhraun (Staðr undir Hrauni) by Hítardalr 115
Staðarstaðr in Snæfellsnes 117, 433
Staðr í Reyninesi (see Reynistaðr) 119
Staðr á Ǫlduhrygg (see Staðarstaðr in Snæfellsnes)
Stafholt (Stafaholt) 17, 25, 68, 70, 71, 101, 102, 115, 120, 122, 130, 149–152, 192, 208, 271, 389, 415, 416, 420, 421, 425–427, 434–436, 451, 452
Stafholtsey 130, 169
Steindórsstaðir 192, 208, 210, 224, 229
Steinþórsstaðir (see Steindórsstaðir)
Steinþórsstaðaland 207
Stóra-Mǫrk 196
Stockholm 463
Storfosna (see Fosen)
Stóri-Áss (see Áss)
Stórikroppr 192
Strandir 227, 231
Sturlureykir 189, 192, 194
Stǫng in Þjórsárdalr 256, 266, 274
Sunnmæri 66
Svartá 220
Svignaskarð 25, 143, 151, 208
Svínafell in Ǿræfi 117
Svínaskarð 134

Svínatóft 24
Sweden 68, 80, 87, 95, 262, 271, 418, 443, 449, 458, 464
Sælingsdalr 127

Thurso (Þórsá) in Caithness 99
Torfajǫkull 177
Trékyllisvík 246
Trondheim (see Niðaróss)
Troy 60
Trøndelag 87, 91, 272
Túnsberg 270, 271
Tønsberg (see Túnsberg)

Úlfsstaðir 192, 258
Uppsala 443
Uppsalir in Hálsasveit 192
Urnes in Sogn 272
Uvdal in Numadalr (Numedal) 256

Vallalaug in Skagafjǫrðr 127
Vallastaðr 465
Valþjófsstaðr in Fljótsdalr 117
Varnhem in Västergötland 261
Vatnaǫldur 177
Vatnsfjǫrðr by Ísafjarðardjúp 115, 117, 118
Vatnskot 192
Vatnsskarð 119, 120
Ver 355
Vestfirðir 117, 118, 308
Viðey 92, 122, 265, 296, 357, 375, 416
Víðimýri 117, 120
Vilmundarstaðir 192
Volda 272
Vopnafjǫrðr 117
Västergötland (Western Götland) 64, 80, 92–94, 96, 97, 103, 261, 272, 449

Warmia in Polland 337
West Fjords (see Vestfirðir)
Western Europe 26, 37, 38, 60, 292, 338, 358
Western Iceland 164, 376, 393
Western Norway 86, 165
Western Quarter of Iceland 130, 138, 141–144, 150, 151
Wick in Caithness 98
Wyre (Vigr) 101

Þingey 130, 144
Þingeyraklaustrur 341
Þingeyrar 122, 296, 298, 338–342, 347, 349, 353, 370, 373, 374, 418
Þinghóll 130
Þingnes in Borgarfjǫrðr 130

Þingnes at Elliðavatn 129, 130, 134, 135
Þingvellir 41, 282
Þjórsárdalr 20, 187, 195, 247, 256, 266, 274
Þórsmǫrk 167, 196, 197
Þrándheimr (see Niðaróss)
Þrændalǫg (see Trøndelag)
Þverá 130, 144, 185
Þverárhlíð 143, 168, 207, 208
Þykkvabær 338, 354, 359

Æsustaðir 134, 135

Ǫlduhryggr 117
Ǫlfus 117
Ørje (Yrjar) 87
Ørlygsstaðir 403
Ǫrnólfsdalr 178, 187
Ǫrnólfsdalsskógr 163, 178, 185
Øræfajökull 256
Øræfi 117, 256
Øxnadalr 116

Index of Personal names

Prepared by Bergur Þorgeirsson

Abrahám, bishop 337
Absalon, archbishop 362, 396
Adam, Breton poet 377
Adam of Bremen 362
Adam of Melrose, bishop 82, 98
Aldred, Oscar 26
Alexander de Villa Dei 320
Andersson, Theodore M. 88, 89, 373–375, 381, 427
Andréas Gunnason 82, 99–101
Andréas Hrafnsson 82, 99–101
Andrew of St Victor 378
Ari Þorgeirsson 41
Ari *fróði* Þorgilsson 53, 111, 130, 337–339, 343, 344, 359, 367, 368, 369, 371, 383, 390, 412
Ari *sterki* Þorgilsson 146, 147
Arnaldus Tylensis 396
Arngrímr Helgason at Norðtunga 143
Árni Borgnýjarson 146
Árni Daníel Júlíusson 394
Árni Lárentíusson 347
Árni Magnússon 134, 209, 463
Árni *óreiða* Magnússon 53, 54, 61, 70
Arninbjǫrn Þórisson, *hersir* 39
Arnkell Þórólfsson, *goði* 135
Arnórr Tumason, *goði* 45
Aron Hjǫrleifsson 450
Ásbjǫrn at Melhus 87
Ásgeir Jónsson 463, 464
Áskell (Eskil) Magnússon, lawman 64, 80, 93–97, 103, 418, 449
Ástríðr, Danish queen 348
Auðun *rauði* Þorbergsson, bishop 267
Augustine 325
Aurell, Martin 399

Bagge, Sverre 47–49, 63, 87, 88, 90, 370
Barbara, holy virgin 264
Bárðr *ungi* 69
Becket, Thomas (see Thomas Becket)
Benedikt Eyþórsson 420
Benedikt Kolbeinsson 465
Berengária of Portugal 450
Bergr Gunnsteinsson 364, 365
Bergr Sokkason 347
Bergsveinn Birgisson 329
Bergur Þorgeirsson 8, 25, 26
Bersi *hinn auðgi* Vermundsson 50, 147, 148, 421, 422

Bertelsen, Reidar 25
Birgir (Birger) *brosa* 94
Bjarnharðr, bishop 337
Bjarnharðr *inn bókvísi*, bishop 337
Bjarni Einarsson 96
Bjarni Guðmundsson 25
Bjarni Guðnason 427, 435, 450
Bjarni Kolbeinsson, bishop 57, 58, 81, 83, 84, 86
Bjarni Pálsson 226
Bjarnvarðr *inn bókvísi*, bishop 337
Bjarnvarðr *inn saxlenzki* 338
Björn *gullberi* 142
Bjǫrn *austræni* Ketilsson 131
Björn Sigurðarson 271
Björn Þorsteinsson 113, 114
Bjǫrn Þorvaldsson 442
Bloch, Howard R. 44
Blund-Ketill 185
Boccaccio 293, 304
Boethius 379
Borgehammar, Stephan 351, 352
Bourdieu, Pierre 21, 37, 44, 392, 396–399, 404
Boyer, Régis 356
Bruhn, Ole 368–370
Brynjólfur Sveinsson, bishop 209
Byock, Jesse 134
Bǫðvarr Þórðarson 145, 148, 149
Bǫðvarr Þórðarson at Bœr 148

Carruthers, Mary 322–325
Church, Mike 197
Cicero 320–322
Clark, James G. 350
Claussøn Friis, Peder 426, 459, 460, 462
Clunies Ross, Margaret 329, 336
Cobbie Roo of Wyre (Vigr) (see Kolbeinn *hrúga*)
Copeland, Rita 322
Cormack, Margaret 352
Crouch, David 38, 44, 45, 48, 51, 52

Dagfinnr *bóndi*, lawman 64, 69, 80, 95, 96, 103
Dagmar, queen (see Margarethe of Bohemia)
Dagr 69
Dansa-Bergr 70
Dante Alighieri 293, 304, 313
Demetrius 321
Derolez, Albert 287
Dionysius, holy bishop 264, 265
Dionysius of Halicarnassus 321
Donatus 320–322, 450, 451

Eberhard 320

Eggert Ólafsson 226
Egill Erlendsson 172
Egill Skalla-Grímsson 99, 134, 142, 143, 294, 298, 307, 312, 369, 403, 405, 457
Egill Sǫlmundarson 149, 150, 265, 266, 429–434, 436, 452, 457, 458, 465
Einar þambarskelfir Indriðason 87, 88
Einar Eyjólfsson Þveræingr 89, 103
Einar Ól. Sveinsson 42, 84, 120
Einstein, Albert 325
Eiríkr Ívarsson, archbishop 60, 346, 353, 358, 362, 365
Eiríkr Eiríksson, king 450
Eiríkr Knútsson, king 93, 94, 449
Ellehøj, Svend 344
Erlendr Ólafsson 151
Erlingr skakki Ormsson 41
Eyjólfr Sæmundsson 354
Eyjólfr Þorgeirsson 149
Eysteinn Erlendsson, archbishop 346, 350, 353, 355, 362–365
Eysteinn Magnússon, king of Norway 48, 49, 56–58, 89, 90
Eyvindr (Øyvind) Eyvindsson brattr 70

Faulkes, Anthony 295, 336
Ferm, Olle 361
Finnbogi Guðmundsson 83, 84
Finnur Jónsson 460, 463
First Grammarian 285, 287, 288, 344
Foote, Peter 43, 90, 137, 347, 364
Frederick, emperor 464
Freyja 305
Friðrekr 337
Fritzner, Johan 328

Gaimar, Geoffrey 380
Gamli kanoki 338
Gathorne-Hardy, Freddy G. 197
Geir Waage 25
Geoffrey of Monmouth 349, 446
Gísli Sigurðsson 390
Gizurr Hallsson 54, 62, 63, 286, 346, 347, 355, 367, 372, 410
Gizurr Ísleifsson, bishop 136, 348
Gizurr Þorvaldsson 35, 53, 54, 61, 62, 91, 102, 119, 150, 151, 428–432, 442, 449, 464
Goody, Jack 360
Gottskálk Jensson 362
Guðmundr góði Arason, bishop 52, 92, 354, 356, 357, 364, 375, 410, 412, 423–425
Guðmundur H. Jónsson 25
Guðmundur Þorvaldsson dýri 116

Guðný Bǫðvarsdóttir 131, 145, 147, 150
Guðrún Gísladóttir 26
Guðrún Harðardóttir 243
Guðrún Nordal 41, 42, 70, 320, 346, 367, 368, 371, 404
Guðrún Sveinbjarnardóttir 25, 26, 126
Guillaume Taillefer 369
Gunnar F. Guðmundsson 114, 122, 264, 420
Gunnar Karlsson 114, 117
Gunnarr konungsfrændi 67
Gunnlaugr Leifsson 338, 342, 347, 349, 350, 353, 418
Gyða Sǫlmundardóttir 150, 430, 432

Haki Antonsson 104
Hákon galinn, earl 36, 40, 41, 58, 61, 64, 70, 93, 94, 96, 97, 395, 398, 417, 447, 448, 449
Hákon Bótólfsson 70
Hákon gamli Hákonarson, king 33, 35, 46–50, 56, 61, 64, 66, 70, 71, 80, 87, 92, 95, 96, 99–102, 124, 125, 150, 370, 376, 398, 399, 403, 419, 426, 428, 445, 446, 448–451, 464–466
Hákon Hákonarson hinn ungi (the young) 450
Hákon Pálsson, earl 84
Hákon Sigurðarson at Hlaðir, earl 426
Hákon Sverrisson, king 92
Halfdan svarti 461
Hallan, Nils 66
Hallbjǫrn hálftroll 457
Halldór Jónsson 226
Halldórr Egilsson 143, 151
Halldórr Snorrason 48, 49
Hallr Þórarinsson 58
Hallveig Ormsdóttir 68, 265, 414, 421, 422, 428, 430, 436, 442, 444
Hámundr Gilsson 147
Hánefr, sheriff 99, 100
Hanssøn, Laurents 426, 459, 460
Haraldr Eiríksson ungi 84, 97–100
Haraldr Maddaðarson, earl 81–85, 97–101
Haraldr Sigurðsson harðráði, king of Norway 48
Harbsmaier, Andreas 329
Harsting, Pernille 329
Haskins, H.C. 360, 361
Haukr Erlendsson 140, 453
Haukur Jóhannesson 26
Heinrekr, bishop 337
Helga Aradóttir 147
Helga Sturludóttir 150, 265, 429–432, 434, 452, 454, 457, 458
Helga Þórðardóttir 131
Helgi Þorláksson 25, 26, 114, 118, 119, 295, 350, 366, 399, 437

Helle, Knut 25
Herburt 40
Herdís Bersadóttir 50, 147, 421, 422
Hermundr Koðránsson at Kalmanstunga 146, 147
Hjörleifur Stefánsson 25, 253
Hnikarr 419
Hnikuðr 419
Hoff, Hans Henning 340
Hoffory, J. 284
Hrafn (Rafn), lawman in Caithness 82, 98–100, 103
Hrafn Oddsson 139, 150, 151,
Hrafn Sveinbjarnarson, *goði* 42, 53–58, 71, 84, 118, 126, 356, 364, 365
Hreinn Hermundarson 147
Hróaldr Úlfsson 131
Hróðólfr, bishop 337
Hrólfr *kraki*, king 401
Hrólfr of Skálmarnes 393, 394, 411
Hrólfr Hróaldsson 131
Hrólfr Kjallaksson at Ballará 131, 132
Hrómundr Gripsson 411
Hrosskell at Hallkelsstaðir 142–144
Hröngviðr *víkingr* 411
Hugh of St Victor 377, 378
Hvamm-Sturla (see Sturla Þórðarson í Hvammi)
Hǫgni *auðgi* Þormóðsson, priest 147, 286

Illugi *rauði* at Innri-Hólmr 143
Illugi *svarti* Hallkelsson at Gilsbakki 143, 146
Ingi Bárðarson, king 40, 58, 398, 417, 448
Ingibjǫrg Snorradóttir 22, 449
Ingimundr *prestr* 412, 424
Ingimundr Einarsson 393–395, 411
Ísleifr Gizurarson, bishop 338, 348, 349
Ívar *nef* 67

Jaeger, C. Stephen 63
Jakob Benediktsson 132, 460
Janson, Henrik 329
Járn-Skeggi at Ørje 87
Jesch, Judith 329
Jóhan *inn írski*, bishop 337
Johansson, Karl Gunnar 26, 41–43
John, a Scottish bishop of Caithness 98
Jón *stál* 67
Jón Brandsson 424
Jón Eggertsson 463, 464
Jón *murti* Egilsson 457, 458
Jón Erlendsson 140
Jón Erlendsson, scribe 343
Jón Halldórsson 226

Jón (John) Haraldsson, earl 98–101
Jón Jóhannesson 65, 113, 132
Jón Loftsson at Oddi 33, 42, 43, 53, 58–60, 83, 84, 136, 146, 148, 294, 295, 300, 346, 347, 355, 367, 372, 376, 421, 422, 447, 452
Jón Viðar Sigurðsson 116
Jon Simonssøn 460
Jón *murtr* Snorrason 61, 62, 67
Jón Ǫgmundarson (Ǫgmundsson), bishop 341, 348, 349
Jones, Nicholas 313
Jørgensen, Jon Gunnar 426, 460
Jupiter 305

Kári Runólfsson 296
Karl Jónsson 296, 341, 350, 353, 370, 396, 418
Ketill *hœingr* 457
Ketill Hermundarson 147, 286
Ketill Þorsteinsson, bishop 122
Kjallakr Bjarnarson 131, 132
Kleppjárn at Kleppjárnsreykir 143
Klængr Bjarnarson 414, 430, 431, 442
Knútr Hákonarson, earl 96, 97, 450
Koht, H. 364
Kolbeinn *hrúga* 101
Kolbeinn *ungi* Arnórsson 61, 117, 119, 428–430
Kolbeinn Tumason 410
Kolgrímr *enn gamli* 142
Kolr, bishop 337
Kristín in Spain 450
Kristín Nikulásdóttir 93, 95–97, 417, 418, 449
Krömmelbein, Thomas 458
Krǫmu-Oddr 126, 142
Kygri-Bjǫrn 410

Lambert of Ardres 369
Lambkárr, deacon 410
Lawson, Ian 197
Lindkvist, Thomas 329
Loftr Pálsson 53, 54, 58, 70, 84
Loftr Sæmundsson 33
Longinus 321
Louis-Jensen, Jonna 435, 462, 465, 466
Lucas, Gavin 119
Lúðvík Ingvarsson 121, 131

Magnús *berfœttr* Óláfsson, king 33, 59, 68, 83, 294, 346
Magnús Erlendsson, earl 84, 100
Magnús Erlingsson, king 33, 41, 50, 80, 81, 97, 426, 460
Magnús Fjalldal 91
Magnús Gizurarson, bishop 376

Magnús *lagabœtir* Hákonarson, king 370, 451, 464, 465

Magnús Már Lárusson 95

Magnús Ólafsson, king 136

Magnús Pálsson 121, 126, 131, 137, 147–149, 264, 286

Magnús Stefánsson 116

Magnús Þórðarson 121, 131, 136, 143, 151

Magnús Þorláksson 145, 146

Máni, court poet 447

Margarethe of Bohemia 450

Marie de France 303

Mars 305

Mary the mother of Our Lord 264

Margrét Hallgrímsdóttir 26

Markús Þórðarson 148

Matthew Paris 379

Menon, king 456

Mercury 305

Moore, Robert I. 63, 360, 369, 370, 372

Mortensen, Lars Boje 349, 358, 362, 363, 364

Mundal, Else 8, 73, 329, 361, 363

Nikarr (see Hnikarr)

Nikolaus Árnason, bishop 81

Nikulás Bergsson, abbot 46, 338, 349, 353

Nikulás Oddsson 150, 432

Nikuz (see Hnikuðr)

Oddr Snorrason 338, 349, 350, 353, 390, 396, 418, 459

Óðinn 42, 49, 60, 305, 326, 419, 456

Ólafur Gilsson 226

Ólafur Lárusson 113

Óláfr *digri* (see Óláfr *helgi* Haraldsson, king)

Óláfr *Liðsmannakonungr* 411

Óláfr *helgi* Haraldsson, king 58, 81, 89, 90, 122, 270, 294, 296, 300, 312, 337, 338, 348, 363, 390, 423, 452, 453, 461, 462

Óláfr Ragnfríðarson from Steinn 70

Óláfr Tryggvason, king 300, 349, 363, 375, 396, 418

Óláfr *hvítaskáld* Þórðarson 150, 329, 333, 336, 374, 376, 381, 389, 393, 434–436, 441, 444, 449–452, 458, 465, 466

Ólafur Halldórsson 284, 460

Ormr *Barreyjarskáld* 411

Ormr Bjarnarson 414, 431, 442

Ormr Jónsson 53, 421

Orosius 379

Orri Vésteinsson 118, 119, 166, 195, 338, 345, 352

Órœkja Snorrason 101, 430, 431, 452

Óskar Guðmundsson 296, 422

Ovid 297, 305

Páll Guðmundsson 19

Páll Jónsson, bishop 53, 54, 58, 84, 346, 362, 365, 367, 372, 376, 424

Páll Sǫlvason 24, 43, 53, 123, 126, 131, 136, 137, 145–149, 286

Páll Vídalín 209

Peter, holy apostle (see St Peter)

Petrarch 293

Petrus, bishop 337

Philip Augustus 51

Priamuss, king of Trója 456

Priscianus 320, 322

Quintilian 323, 324, 327, 328

Rehren, Thilo 214

Richard of St Victor 377, 378

Richard Lionheart 51

Robert, brother 298, 419

Robert of Cricklade 364, 365

Roger of Howden 98

Rudolf, bishop (see Hróðólfr, bishop)

Rúðólfr (see Hróðólfr, bishop)

Rǫgnvaldr Kali, earl 56–58, 84, 97–100

Sandvik, Gudmund 87, 88, 90

Sawyer, Birgit 90

Saxo Grammaticus 353, 362, 377, 381, 392, 396, 446

Sel-Þórir at Rauðamelr 142

Siffredus 369

Sighvatr Sturluson 146, 147

Sighvatr Bǫðvarsson 150

Sighvatr Þórðarson 49

Sigurðr Erlingsson 81

Sigurðr *Fáfnisbani* 299

Sigurðr Jórsalafari Magnússon 48, 89, 264

Sigurðr *vegglágr* 70

Sigurður Nordal 47, 52, 82, 113, 296, 338–343, 347, 374, 375, 382

Sigurður Vigfússon 242

Símon Jǫrundarson at Bœr 143, 151

Skalla-Grímr Kveldúlfsson 142, 144, 164, 165, 205, 206, 403

Skórzewska, Joanna Agnieszka 356

Skúli Bárðarson, earl 7, 33, 35, 36, 47, 48, 60, 65, 66, 71, 80, 87, 89–92, 94–97, 100–103, 398, 403, 428, 445, 446, 448–451, 466

Skúli Egilsson 143, 151

Smalley, Beryl 377, 378

Smith, Kevin 186

Snorri Markússon 140, 453

Snorri Sturluson 7, 8, 16, 18–26, 29, 33, 34, 36, 37, 39–44, 46–73, 79–82, 85–92, 94–97, 99–103, 118–121, 123–126, 131, 137–142, 144–152, 190, 237–239, 241–243, 248–250, 252, 257, 262, 264, 265, 267–274, 285, 286, 291, 293–307, 311–313, 326–329, 333, 335, 336, 346, 356, 357, 366–368, 370–377, 379–382, 389–391, 393–395, 397–405, 409, 410, 413, 414, 416–436, 441, 442, 444–455, 457–460, 462, 465, 466

Snorri Þorgrímsson, *goði* 135, 457

Snækollr Gunnason 99–102

Sparfwenfeldt, J.G. 464

St Dionysius (St Denis) (see Dionysius, holy bishop)

St Magnús (see Magnús Erlendsson, earl)

St Nicholas 70, 71, 415

St Óláfr (see Óláfr Haraldsson, king)

St Peter 70, 71, 136, 264, 265

St Rǫgnvaldr (see Rǫgnvaldr Kali, earl)

St Sunniva 351

St Þorlákr (see Þorlákr Þórhallsson, bishop)

Stefán Karlsson 284, 364, 365, 397, 459, 464, 465

Stephánus, bishop 337

Storm, Gustav 426, 459, 460

Stummann Hansen, Steffen 25

Sturla Sighvatsson 34, 36, 61, 102, 139, 394, 400, 403, 404, 409, 410, 413, 414, 420, 427, 442, 450

Sturla Sveinsson 431

Sturla Þórðarson 36, 57, 66, 94, 102, 139–141, 150, 151, 265, 333, 356, 368–371, 374, 393, 401, 409, 410, 413, 414, 426, 427, 428, 430, 431, 436, 441, 444, 449–453, 458, 464–466

Sturla Þórðarson í Hvammi 121, 145, 146, 150, 294, 295, 421

Styrmir Hreinsson at Gilsbakki 143, 146, 151

Styrmir Kárason *fróði* 22, 70, 122, 140, 295, 296, 298, 342, 357, 368–370, 375, 414, 423, 426, 428, 441, 452, 453, 466

Sunniva (see St Sunniva)

Svavar Sigmundsson 26

Svanhildur Óskarsdóttir 356

Sveinbjörn Rafnsson 375

Sveinn Ásleifarson 99, 101

Sveinn Sturluson 431

Sveinn Úlfsson 348

Sverrir Jakobsson 71, 137

Sverrir Sigurðsson, king of Norway 40, 49–51, 79–81, 85, 94, 95, 97, 98, 122, 296, 346, 353, 362, 370, 396, 398, 411, 417, 418, 447, 448

Sverrir Tómasson 425

Sæmundr Jónsson 53, 60, 84

Sæmundr *fróði* Sigfússon at Oddi 33, 59, 338, 339, 343–346, 348, 354, 367, 371, 381, 390, 393, 412

Sǫlmundr *Austmaðr*, Snorri's brother-in-law 70, 430, 432, 452, 457

Sǫlvi Hrólfsson 131, 133

Sǫlvi Magnússon 131

Sǫlvi Þórðarson 131

Sörkvir [Sørkvir], king 93, 94, 449

Tafl-Bergr 56, 70

Teitr Þorvaldsson 296

Theodoricus monachus 358, 362–364, 396, 446

Thomas, archbishop (see Tómas erkibiskup)

Thomas of Britain 298

Thomas Aquinas 325

Thomas Becket 46, 364, 365, 376

Thor (see Þórr)

Tómas erkibiskup 413

Tore, archbishop (see Theodoricus Monachus)

Torfi Valbrandsson 133

Tormod Torfæus 464

Trór (see Þórr)

Tumi Sighvatsson 403, 404

Tungu-Oddr Ǫnundarson 121, 126, 127, 130–133, 141–143

Tyler, Elizabeth M. 379, 380

Týr 305, 326

Úlfar Bragason 402, 457

Úlfr *inn óargi* 457

Úlfr Grímsson in Geitland 131, 196

Úlfr Óspaksson 48, 49

Valdimarr the Victorious, king 435, 450

Vegetius 51

Venus 305

Vésteinn Ólason 329

Viðar Pálsson 401

Vries, Jan de 360

Wanner, Kevin J. 66, 371, 397–399

Worm, Ole 426, 459

Yates, Frances A. 323, 324

Yngvarr *víðfǫrli* 349

Þór Magnússon 25

Þóra Magnúsdóttir 33

Þórarinn *kaggi* 457, 465

Þórarinn Vandráðsson 432, 433

Þórdís Snorradóttir 430

Þórðr *gellir* 143
Þórðr *lǫgmaðr* 457, 458
Þórðr Bǫðvarsson 145, 147, 148
Þórðr Magnússon 131, 148
Þórðr Narfason 140
Þórðr *kakali* Sighvatsson 36, 149, 150, 429, 430, 432, 434
Þórðr Sturluson 146–148, 286, 356, 449
Þórðr Sǫlvason 121, 126, 131–133
Þórðr the younger Sǫlvason 131, 136
Þorfinnr *karlsefni* 369
Þorgils *skarði* Bǫðvarsson 139, 149, 150, 265, 266, 394, 412, 413, 429, 430, 432, 433
Þorgils Oddason 393
Þorgnýr, lawman in Sweden 87
Þórhallur Þráinsson 256
Þórir, archbishop (see Theodoricus Monachus)
Þórir, bishop of Hamarr 358
Þorkell of Þykkvabær 355
Þorkell *rostungr* 81, 86
Þorkell *trefill* Rauða-Bjarnarson at Svignarskarð 143
Þorlákr Ketilsson 148
Þorlákr Þórhallsson, bishop 83, 137, 284, 338, 345, 346, 350, 353–356, 359, 360, 362, 365, 376–378, 450

Þorleifr *beiskaldi* 146
Þorleifr *spaki* 457
Þorleifr Þórðarson 148–150
Þórólfr *Mostrarskegg* 457
Þórr 305, 456
Þorsteinn Egilsson 143
Þorsteinn Gíslason at Bær 143
Þorsteinn Snorrason 140
Þorvaldr Gizurarson 53, 54, 296, 375
Þorvaldr Snorrason *Vatnsfirðingr, goði* 53, 55
Þorvarðr at Stafholt 151
Þorvarðr Þórarinsson 150
Þorvarðr Þorgeirsson, *goði* 54
Þráinn *berserkr* 411
Þuríðr Ormsdóttir 403, 404

Æthelwold, bishop 351

Qlvir at Egge 87
Qnundr *breiðskeggr* 126, 142
Qrnolfr 337
Øye, Ingvild 25
Øystein Erlendsson (see Eysteinn Erlendsson, archbishop)